GW01314842

A Functional Biology
of Sea Anemones

Functional Biology Series
General Editor: Peter Calow, Department of Zoology,
University of Sheffield

The titles listed below were all published under the Croom Helm imprint.
Croom Helm science books are now part of Chapman and Hall.

A Functional Biology of Free-living Protozoa★
Johanna Laybourn-Parry
A Functional Biology of Sticklebacks★
R.J. Wootton
A Functional Biology of Marine Gastropods[†]
Roger N. Hughes
A Functional Biology of Nematodes[†]
David A. Wharton
A Functional Biology of Crop Plants[#]
Vincent P. Gutshick
A Functional Biology of Echinoderms[†]
John M. Lawrence
A Functional Biology of Clonal Animals
Roger N. Hughes
A Functional Biology of Sea Anemones
J. Malcolm Shick

Available in the USA from
★ University of California Press
[†] The Johns Hopkins University Press
[#] Timber Press

A Functional Biology of Sea Anemones

J. Malcolm Shick

Professor of Zoology and Oceanography
University of Maine
Orono, USA

SPRINGER-SCIENCE+BUSINESS MEDIA, B.V.

First edition 1991

© 1991 Springer Science+Business Media Dordrecht
Originally published by Chapman & Hall in 1991
Softcover reprint of the hardcover 1st edition 1991
Typeset in Plantin 10/12 pt by Excel Typesetters Ltd, Hong Kong

Apart from any fair dealing for the purposes of research or private study, or criticism or review, as permitted under the UK Copyright Designs and Patents Act, 1988, this publication may not be reproduced, stored, or transmitted, in any form or by any means, without the prior permission in writing of the publishers, or in the case of reprographic reproduction only in accordance with the terms of the licences issued by the Copyright Licensing Agency in the UK, or in accordance with the terms of licences issued by the appropriate Reproduction Rights Organization outside the UK. Enquiries concerning reproduction outside the terms stated here should be sent to the publishers at the UK address printed on this page.

The publisher makes no representation, express or implied, with regard to the accuracy of the information contained in this book and cannot accept any legal responsibility or liability for any errors or omissions that may be made.

British Library Cataloguing in Publication Data
Shick, J. Malcolm
  A functional biology of sea anemones.
  1. Sea anemones
  I. Title   II. Series
  593.6

ISBN 978-94-010-5365-5   ISBN 978-94-011-3080-6 (eBook)
DOI 10.1007/978-94-011-3080-6

Library of Congress Cataloging-in-Publication Data
Shick, J. Malcolm, 1947–
  A functional biology of sea anemones / J. Malcolm Shick.
      p.   cm.
  Includes bibliographical references and index.

  1. Sea anemones.   I. Title.
QL377.C7S33   1990
593.6 — dc20   90-40757
                                                        CIP

To my family

Serge Brignoni, *Les Aquatiques* (1954). Courtesy of the artist.

For elegance and grace, for delicacy of form and quiet beauty of colour, the sea anemones of the Barrier Reef have a charm unrivalled by any other form of life to be found there. They are the flowers of the reef . . .

— T.C. Roughley, *Wonders of the Great Barrier Reef*, 13th edition (1954) Angus and Robertson, Sydney.

Contents

Acknowledgments

I thank the many friends and collegues who have provided advice, information, photographs, preprints (many of which have by now become reprints) and permission to use data and illustrations from their own work. Major portions of the manuscript have been critically read by C.H. Bigger, S.H. Bishop, M.A. Carter, W.R. Ellington, D.G. Fautin, C. Hand, D. Hedgecock, R.J. Hoffmann, C.P. Mangum, R.N. Mariscal, V.B. Pearse, K.P. Sebens, M. Van-Praët and W.E. Zamer. Also, D.J. Chapman, E. Gnaiger, J.M. Pandolfi and J.E.N. Veron clarified several critical points. I particularly thank E.A. Robson for her many helpful suggestions throughout the manuscript. All of these friends provided helpful comments and especially tried to rein in my speculations; to all I am grateful. K.C. Edwards' assistance with photographic printing and layout is much appreciated, as is M. Fisher's drawing of several of the biological illustrations. S. Tyler, B. McCleave, and W. Krall helped with translations from the German, and T. Haines and R.E. Robbins provided translations from the Russian. A portion of the book was prepared at the Australian Institute of Marine Science, where I thank the librarians for their assistance, and A. Dartnall for his artistic expertise and for making the facilities of the Science Communications Studio available to me. I thank P. Calow for his comments on the entire manuscript, and with T. Hardwick and C. Baxter at Chapman and Hall, for remarkable patience as many of my self-imposed deadlines for delivering the manuscript came and went. My research on sea anemones has been supported by the US National Science Foundation, the National Geographic Society, the University of Maine, the Australian Institute of Marine Science, the Bermuda Biological Station and the Plymouth Marine Laboratory. To my past and present graduate students go my thanks for their stimulation, ideas, help and

xii *Acknowledgements*

friendship, together with my apologies to the most recent of them for the amount of my attention this project has diverted from their needs. The advice, encouragement, example and friendship of J.H. Dearborn contributed greatly to the completion of this book; he has served as my sounding-board and as my model of the broadly-interested reader to whom the book is addressed. Finally, my wife Jean and daughter Laura have tolerated and understood my frequent neglect of family activities during the past several years, and have given the love, support, companionship and pleasant home environment without which the book would never have been finished.

Functional Biology Series:
Foreword

General Editor: Peter Calow, Department of Zoology,
University of Sheffield, England

The main aim of this series will be to illustrate and to explain the way organisms 'make a living' in nature. At the heart of this — their *functional biology* — is the way organisms acquire and then make use of resources in metabolism, movement, growth, reproduction, and so on. These processes will form the fundamental framework of all the books in the series. Each book will concentrate on a particular taxon (species, family, class or even phylum) and will bring together information on the form, physiology, ecology and evolutionary biology of the group. The aim will be not only to describe *how* organisms work, but also to consider *why* they have come to work in that way. By concentrating on taxa which are well known, it is hoped that the series will not only illustrate the success of selection, but also show the constraints imposed upon it by the physiological, morphological and developmental limitations of the groups.

Another important feature of the series will be its *organismic orientation*. Each book will emphasize the importance of functional *integration* in the day-to-day lives and the evolution of organisms. This is crucial since, though it may be true that organisms can be considered as collections of gene-determined traits, they nevertheless interact with their environment as integrated wholes and it is in this context that individual traits have been subjected to natural selection and have evolved.

The key features of the series are, therefore:

1. Its emphasis on whole organisms as integrated, resource-using systems.
2. Its interest in the way selection and constraints have moulded the evolution of adaptations in particular taxonomic groups.
3. Its bringing together of physiological, morphological, ecological and evolutionary information.

P. Calow

Preface

When I began writing this book in 1983, a resurgence of experimental investigation of sea anemones was evident, particularly on aspects of their environmental and population biology. Most of the literature for the previous several decades reflected the fascination that these animals have held for students of behavioural and neuromuscular physiology, and of symbiosis. It was also evident that, apart from a section in Hyman's (1940) monograph, Friese's (1972) book and the original (1981) impression of Manuel's (1988) synopsis of the British Anthozoa, there had been no general treatment of the biology of sea anemones since Stephenson's volumes in 1928 and 1935, although anemones figured prominently in review volumes such as that edited by Muscatine and Lenhoff (1974). The literature seemed both diffuse yet sufficiently compact that a comprehensive review and synthesis of its modern references would be useful and feasible.

Since 1983 there has been a proliferation of papers whose titles explicitly mention sea anemones (more than 150 of these are cited in the References here), and reviews of their nutrition (Van-Praët, 1985), energetics (Sebens, 1987a; Steen, 1988), general biology (Doumenc and Van-Praët, 1987) and clonal nature (Hughes, 1989) have appeared. My vision of the comprehensive modern treatise quickly vanished, although the bibliography, while not exhaustive, will probably yield something new to even the most jaded admirer of sea anemones. The older literature is far from completely cited, but is represented by a personal selection of papers, some of which have been chosen for their historical interest as well as for their scientific content. I have tried to keep to the primary literature, although particularly useful reviews are cited. To hold the bibliography within some bounds, the references cited are predominantly those dealing explicitly with sea anemones, but this has meant omitting germane articles on other cnidarians. Lapses in applying this rule were sometimes necessary to document a relevant point for which no paper on sea anemones exists, and they also manifest a frustration over the lack of a current general text to cite on the adaptational physiological ecology of marine organisms: in places, this book is as much about the physiological ecology of sea anemones as about sea anemone physiological ecology.

The diversity of graphic styles throughout the book reflects their long evolutionary history; punctuated events include the advent of Apple's® Macintosh™ computer and laser printers, and my reading of E.R. Tufte's 1983 book *The Visual Display of Quantitative Information*.

Anatomy and morphology are not extensively dealt with, although structural terms are defined when they arise in a functional context. For modern treatments of microanatomy and ultrastructure, the reader is referred to reviews by D.M. Chapman (1974), Doumenc and Van-Praët (1987) and Fautin and Mariscal (1990), as well as to more specialized papers in the References. As noted by Manuel (1988), the classification within the order Actiniaria is in a state of flux, and I have tried to keep myself and the reader abreast of these changes. Unlike Manuel, I have adopted (with some reservations) the classification used by Schmidt (1974), largely for the reasons given but not followed by the former author. The nomenclature here generally follows that in Manuel's synopsis for European species, itself distilling the fruits of R.B. Williams' scholarship. The use of the monotype '*Anemonia viridis*' for European specimens as in Manuel is with some misgivings, for *A.rosea*, *A.rustica*, *A.sulcata*, and *A.viridis* may represent a species complex (K.P. Sauer, personal communication). The nomenclature for other Atlantic species follows that in Cairns, den Hartog and Arneson (1986) and in Sebens (in press). Dunn (1981) has provided a thorough revision of the nomenclature of the clownfish sea anemones (largely Stichodactylidae), which is used here. A worldwide key to the genera of actiniarians is in Doumenc and Foubert (1984).

Non-specialist readers may be dismayed not to find a glossary of anatomical and morphological terms here; I refer them to the excellent examples in Carlgren (1949), Manuel (1988) and Sebens (in press). Glossaries relating to reproduction, population biology and evolution can be found in Jackson, Buss and Cook (1985) and in Hughes (1989). Still, ecologists may lament the lack of a lexicon on physiology, and vice versa, and the general reader may covet a comprehensive glossary between two covers. Accordingly, specialized terms are defined in the text, and the pages on which definitions occur are given in boldface in the index. An annotated list of frequently-used abbreviations and symbols is included, as is a taxonomic and zoogeographical appendix. The synopses placed at the beginnings of Chapters 2–7 are intended to serve as both previews and reviews.

As is the case in other volumes in this series, chapters are organized according to the various functions of an animal or components of its energy budget. My own approach to biology is an integrative one. This is facilitated in writing about sea anemones by their relative simplicity of organization, so that responses to one environmental variable may have diverse physiological consequences; by their very nature sea anemones exemplify the concepts of morphological constraint, compromise and trade-off. In trying to produce a synthesis rather than a synopsis of their biology, I have at times committed blatantly adaptationist speculations. These are not intended as dogma, rather, as an aid in thinking about the functional biology of sea anemones.

J. Malcolm Shick

Symbols and abbreviations

Symbol or abbreviation	Description
A	surface area (cm^2); in a different context, absorbed ration
atm	atmosphere (1 standard atmosphere pressure = 101.325 kPa = 760 mm Hg; 1 atm O_2 = 0.2095 × 101.325 kPa = 21.23 kPa = 159.2 mm Hg)
C_{O_2}	concentration of O_2 (μmol $O_2 \cdot l^{-1}$)
CHN	elemental carbon, hydrogen, and nitrogen content (of a tissue or compound)
CZAR	contribution of zooxanthella-fixed carbon to the host animal's respiratory requirement
D	diameter of basal disc (occasionally, column); D_t diameter at time t in von Bertalanffy growth model; D_{t+1} diameter at time t + 1 year in von Bertalanffy model; D_∞ asymptotic or theoretical maximum diameter
Da	dalton, the unit of molecular weight, 1 Da being the mass of one hydrogen atom
DCMU	3-3,4-dichlorophenyl-1,1-dimethylurea (an inhibitor of electron transport in photosystem II in photosynthesis)
DOM	dissolved organic matter
E_a	Arrhenius 'activation energy'
μE$\cdot$m$^{-2}\cdot$s^{-1}	units of photosynthetic photon flux density (irra-

	diance), where 1 Einstein = 1 mol photons in the range $400-700$ nm (photosynthetically active radiation, PAR)
FAA	free amino acids (dissolved in seawater or body fluids)
G_o, $G_e{}^*$	observed and expected genotypic frequencies in a population
$\Delta G^{\ddagger}$	free energy of activation for a chemical conversion
GDH	glutamate dehydrogenase
GSH	reduced glutathione, a tripeptide (glutamate–cysteine–glycine)
$\Delta H^{\ddagger}$	activation enthalpy in a chemical conversion
$\Delta_c h$	specific enthalpy of combustion of a substance $(kJ \cdot g^{-1})$
$\Delta_k H_{\infty ATP}$	energetic equivalent of dissipative ATP turnover, in $kJ \cdot (mol\ ATP)^{-1}$
$\Delta_k H_{O2}$	oxycaloric equivalent (energetic equivalent of dissipative O_2 consumption), in $kJ \cdot (mol\ O_2)^{-1}$
I	ingested ration; energy intake
I_k	the intersection of tangents to the initial slope (α) and to P_{max} in a photosynthesis-irradiance (P-I) curve, representing the lowest irradiance at which light-saturated rates of photosynthesis are achieved
J	joule, the SI unit of heat (1 thermodynamic calorie $= 4.1868$ J; 1 thermochemical calorie $= 4.184$ J)
$\mathcal{J}^i_{max}$	maximum rate of influx of a substance (e.g., an amino acid), influx of which increases hyperbolically with external concentration
$\mathcal{J}_{O_2}$	diffusive flux of O_2 at the respiratory surface (as $cm^3 \cdot min^{-1}$ in the Fick equation)
K_1	gross growth efficiency (efficiency with which ingested foodstuffs are converted into consumer tissue)
K_2	net growth efficiency (efficiency with which foodstuffs absorbed from the diet are converted into consumer tissue)
K_m	Michaelis constant, the substrate concentration at half-maximal velocity (V_{max}) of an enzyme-catalyzed reaction
K_{O_2}	Krogh's diffusion constant for O_2 $(cm^2 \cdot atm^{-1} \cdot min^{-1})$
K_t	transport constant for a substance (e.g., an amino acid) absorbed from the external medium at rates

	that increase hyperbolically with external concentration; K_t is the concentration at which the rate of influx is half-maximal ($0.5\,\mathcal{J}^i_{max}$)
LD_{50}, LD_{100}	lethal dose$_{50}$ and lethal dose$_{100}$, the levels of a toxin or stressor required to kill 50% and 100% of the individuals exposed to it
LT_{50}	lethal time$_{50}$, the time required to kill 50% of the individuals exposed to a particular level of a stressor
$\dot{M}_{O_2}$	gravimetric rate of oxygen consumption ($\mu g\ O_2 \cdot h^{-1}$)
$\dot{m}_{O_2}$	specific gravimetric rate of oxygen consumption ($\mu g\ O_2 \cdot g^{-1} \cdot h^{-1}$)
mm Hg	millimeters of mercury, a unit of pressure (1 mm Hg = 0.13332 kPa)
MAA	mycosporine-like amino acids (e.g. mycosporine-taurine), UV-absorbing compounds that may be a cellular defense against UV radiation
$\dot{n}_{NH_4^+}$	specific molar rate of ammonium excretion ($\mu mol\ NH_{4^+} \cdot g^{-1} \cdot h^{-1}$)
$\dot{N}_{O_2}$	molar rate of oxygen consumption ($\mu mol\ O_2 \cdot h^{-1}$)
$\dot{n}_{O_2}$	specific molar rate of oxygen consumption ($\mu mol\ O_2 \cdot g^{-1} \cdot h^{-1}$)
NQ	nitrogen quotient (molar ratio of N excreted to O_2 consumed)
nm	nanometer (10^{-9} m)
mOsm	milliosmoles; millimolar concentration of osmotically-active substances
P	production or growth
P-I curve	photosynthesis versus irradiance curve relating changes in the rate of photosynthesis to changes in irradiance (photosynthetic photon flux density)
P_{max}	maximum (light-saturated) rate of photosynthesis seen in a P-I curve
$P_z$net	net daily photosynthetic carbon fixation in zooxanthellae
P_{O_2}	partial pressure of O_2 in a gas or liquid (kPa, mm Hg, or atm)
ΔP_{O_2}	O_2 partial pressure gradient across the respiratory exchange surface (units of atm in the Fick equation)
Pa	pascal, the SI unit of pressure (newton$\cdot m^{-2}$)
PCSA	prey capture surface area (total surface area of tentacles and oral disc, cm^2)
PGI	phosphoglucose isomerase (synonymous with

	glucose phosphate isomerase, GPI)
PQ	photosynthetic quotient (molar ratio of O_2 produced to CO_2 fixed)
PSU	photosynthetic unit, consisting of a P700 chlorophyll reaction centre, additional chlorophyll 'antennas,' accessory pigments (e.g. carotenoids), and electron carriers
$_tQ$	rate of heat dissipation ($mW = mJ \cdot s^{-1}$)
$_tq$	specific rate of heat dissipation ($mW \cdot g^{-1}$)
$\Delta_t Q_{O_2}$	experimentally determined calorespirometric ratio ($_tQ/N_{O_2}$, $kJ \cdot mol^{-1}$); when $\Delta_t Q_{O_2}$ exceeds the maximum theoretical $\Delta_k H_{O_2}$ of $-480\,kJ \cdot (mol\,O_2)^{-1}$ for dissipative aerobic metabolism, the operation of anaerobic energy metabolism is indicated; values of $\Delta_t Q_{O_2}$ significantly below the minimum theoretical value of $-440\,kJ \cdot (mol\,O_2)^{-1}$ indicate non-metabolic utilization of O_2 (e.g. repletion of coelenteric or tissue O_2 stores) or the operation of conservative, endothermic processes (e.g. gluconeogenesis)
Q_{10}	temperature coefficient describing the effect of a 10°C change in temperature on a rate process
R	respiration, expressed in units of energy or carbon
R_a	daily respiration (in carbon equivalents) in the animal moiety of an algal–animal symbiosis
$r.h.$	relative humidity
RQ	respiratory quotient (molar ratio of CO_2 produced to O_2 consumed)
RT curve	rate versus temperature curve relating changes in the rate of a biological process to changes in temperature
$\Delta S^{\ddagger}$	activation entropy in a chemical conversion
‰S	salinity, in parts per thousand, i.e. g salt·(kg seawater)$^{-1}$
S_m	'map surface', the projected surface area of the tentacles and oral disc (cm^2)
S_t	surface area of tentacles (cm^2)
SDE	specific dynamic effect of feeding (also called specific dynamic action) involving increases in O_2 consumption and heat dissipation
SEM	scanning electron micro(scopy) or (graph)
SFG	scope for growth, the difference between the energetic value of ingested food and all uses and losses of it except for growth, under a given set of conditions
SOD	superoxide dismutase

SS1	slow-conducting system 1, an ectodermal sensory nerve net
SS2	slow-conducting system 2, an endodermal inhibitory nerve net
T	percentage of daily net photosynthate translocated from endosymbiotic algae to the host animal's tissues
TCNN	through-conducting nerve net of large bipolar cells in which conduction velocity is high (>10 times that in SS1 and SS2)
TMS	transmesogleal system of neuronal connections between ectodermal sensory receptors and endodermal effectors
UV	ultraviolet radiation having wavelengths of 280–320 nm (UV-B) and 320–400 nm (UV-A)
V_{max}	maximum rate of an enzyme-catalysed reaction at saturating concentrations of substrate
$\dot{V}_{O_2}$	volumetric rate of oxygen consumption (μl or $ml\,O_2\cdot h^{-1}$)
$\dot{v}_{O_2}$	specific volumetric rate of oxygen consumption ($\mu l\,O_2\cdot g^{-1}\cdot h^{-1}$)
W	watt, unit of the rate of heat dissipation (1 W = $1\,J\cdot s^{-1}$)
W	weight or mass; $_aW_p$ weight of prey absorbed; $_{af}W$ ash-free (organic) weight; $_dW$ dry weight; $_rW$ reduced weight (weight in seawater); $_wW$ wet or fresh weight; W_C mass (content) of carbon; W_N mass (content) of nitrogen; W_P mass (content) of protein; W_p weight of prey captured; W_{max} maximum possible individual size, determined by the balance between energy intake and cost; W_{opt} optimal individual size at which energy beyond that used in respiration (and so available for somatic growth and reproduction) is maximal
x	diffusion path length (cm, in Fick equation)
α	initial slope of the *P-I* curve; photosynthetic efficiency
δ	boundary layer thickness
μ	daily specific growth rate of zooxanthellae (doublings$\cdot$day^{-1})

1 Overview of sea anemones

Epigraphs should be avoided . . . To preface your text with an epigraph from a superior author in the same genre is to remind the reader that he might better spend his time with that author than with you.
— John Barth, 'Epigraphs', in *The Friday Book* (1984), Putnam, New York.

1.1 RELATIONSHIPS AND BODY PLAN

To romantics they are Gosse's 'blossomed beauties' and Roughley's 'flowers of the reef', but despite their botanical common name, sea anemones are voracious animals — Dalyell's 'fell devourers of whatever they can overpower'. They belong to the Anthozoa, one of four extant classes (Figure 1.1) within the phylum Cnidaria (tentacle-bearing Radiata having intrinsic nematocysts [cnidae]: Hyman, 1940), the simplest animals among the Eumetazoa. All classes of Cnidaria are evolutionarily derived from a sessile polyp. The strictly marine Anthozoa (including 'anemones', and hard and soft corals) are distinguished from other Cnidaria by their lack of a medusoid stage, being exclusively polypoid in body form. Also, the anthozoan polyp's coelenteron (body cavity) is partially divided into chambers by radially arranged mesenteries (*not* septa) projecting inward from the column wall, and a laterally compressed, tubular actinopharynx extends into the centre of the coelenteron (Figure 1.2). The Anthozoa are viewed by Werner (1973) as having diverged from the other classes and their tetramerous stem form quite early in the evolution of the Cnidaria. Alternatively, Grasshoff (1984) argues that the Anthozoa are the stem of the Cnidaria, the tetraradial construction of the other classes being a secondary simplification related to the production of medusae.

Sea anemones belong to the subclass Hexacorallia, which is distinguished from the other anthozoan subclass, Octocorallia, and from all other cnidarians by its possessing spirocysts, which are glutinant, non-penetrating cni-

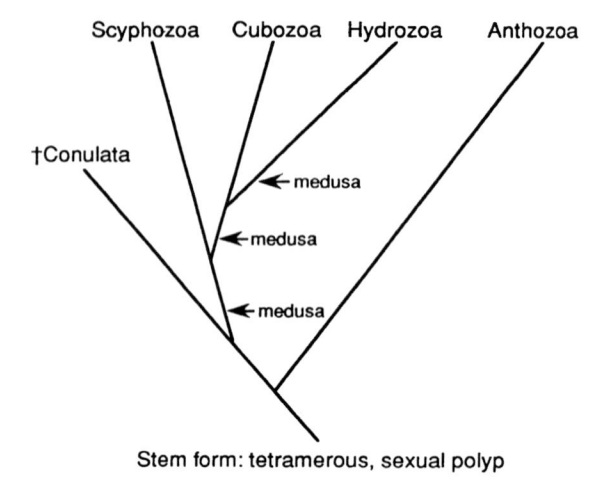

Scyphozoa   Cubozoa   Hydrozoa   Anthozoa

†Conulata

←medusa

←medusa

←medusa

Stem form: tetramerous, sexual polyp

Figure 1.1 Interrelationships among the classes of the phylum Cnidaria. Among the extant classes, only the primitive Anthozoa lacks a medusa, and diverged from the other Cnidaria not far from their common ancestor. Coloniality is present in the polypoid generation of all classes except the Cubozoa (sea wasps or box jellyfish). In the Anthozoa, only sea anemones and ceriantharians lack colonial representatives. See text for discussion. Source: after Werner (1973).

dae. Moreover, Hexacorallia never have just eight unpaired mesenteries or pinnate tentacles, which are characteristic of Octocorallia. The term 'anemone' is sometimes applied to uncalcified, unitary (i.e. non-colonial) polyps such as cerianthids and corallimorpharians, and even to weakly colonial zoanthids, but all of these belong to different hexacorallian orders, themselves distinct from the true *sea anemones* of the order Actiniaria (see Appendix). Here, 'sea anemone', 'anemone', 'actiniarian' and 'actinian' are used synonymously. Alone among the Anthozoa, the Actiniaria and the Ceriantharia have no colonial representatives, although many actiniarians have great powers of vegetative duplication of polyps. This exceptional lack of coloniality demands consideration and seems related to their lack of skeletonization, but first we must know more of the anthozoan body plan.

The position of cnidarians as the simplest eumetazoans is tied to their having fewer types of cells than other animals (Robson, 1985). Indeed, cnidarians contain fewer cell types than does a single organ in most other metazoans. Following Hyman (1940), cnidarians are characterized as having a 'tissue grade of construction'. That is, their cells are organized into discernible tissues having specialized functions, but the tissues are not further grouped into organs having multiple tissue types (see Fautin and Mariscal, 1990). Thus 'the simplicity of a Coelenterate is the simplicity of the tissues of which it is composed' (Pantin, 1960). Often referred to as 'diploblastic', sea anemones to some are triploblastic, as their mesoglea contains distinctive cells most often found in that tissue. Moreover, their three body layers (outer ectoderm, inner endoderm, and connective mesoglea sandwiched between these two epithelia) are formed by the same embryogenic processes as in other metazoans (Fautin, Spaulding and Chia, 1989).

The large size of some anemones belies their delicate nature, and the foregoing descriptions tell us little about their organic architecture. Essentially laminar in construction, their two-dimensional epithelia are folded to yield three-dimensional organisms. Sea anemones, then, are at the 'origami' level of construction. Their simplicity is inescapably linked to such an organization, and its implications for the metabolism and growth of such organisms are discussed in Chapters 3 and 5. Pantin (1965) and Robson (1985) in particular have reiterated the behavioural and physiological consequences of the epithelial construction of the neuromuscular system (see below).

Extant cnidarians have been thought to have their antecedents among the medusoid and pennatulacean-like creatures of the Ediacaran fauna from the late Precambrian (Glaessner, 1984). Although this view has been questioned (Seilacher, 1989), the fact remains that cnidarians have followed one of two known routes to achieving a large body size, by adopting an epithelial construction so that no internal tissue is far from external sources of oxygen and nutrients. A similar but exotic *bauplan*, as Seilacher put it, was tried by the Ediacarans, described as being quilted 'pneu' structures comparable to water-filled air mattresses reinforced by internal struts. There are decided mechanical advantages to inflating the body with water rather than air (see below), and this description seems apt for cnidarians as well, whose maximum individual size of a meter or so in diameter (achieved in some scyphomedusae and stichodactylid sea anemones) approximates to that of the largest Ediacarans. This maximum presumably represents the onset of diffusion limitation or of structural collapse in a laminar architecture without hard supporting parts.

Just as the Ediacarans were a highly diverse group despite the limitations of epithelial construction, so too are the Cnidaria. Within the Anthozoa, the Actiniaria in particular show the greatest morphological diversity (Schmidt, 1974). In tropical environments, the evolution of their diversity may have been driven by their symbiosis with photosynthetic dinoflagellates (zooxanthellae) and with anemonefishes (Fautin, 1987; Fautin and Mariscal, 1990). Some tropical anemones, for example, concentrate zooxanthellae in their unique pseudotentacles or columnar vesicles, which are extended during the day and are unresponsive to prey but instead capture sunlight; the feeding tentacles extend at night (section 2.7.2, page 111). In tropical stichodactylids, their very large size seems enabled by phototrophic symbiosis with zooxanthellae and a morphological arrangement (flattening of the body and presence of tentacles on the oral disc) to maximize their illumination. How-

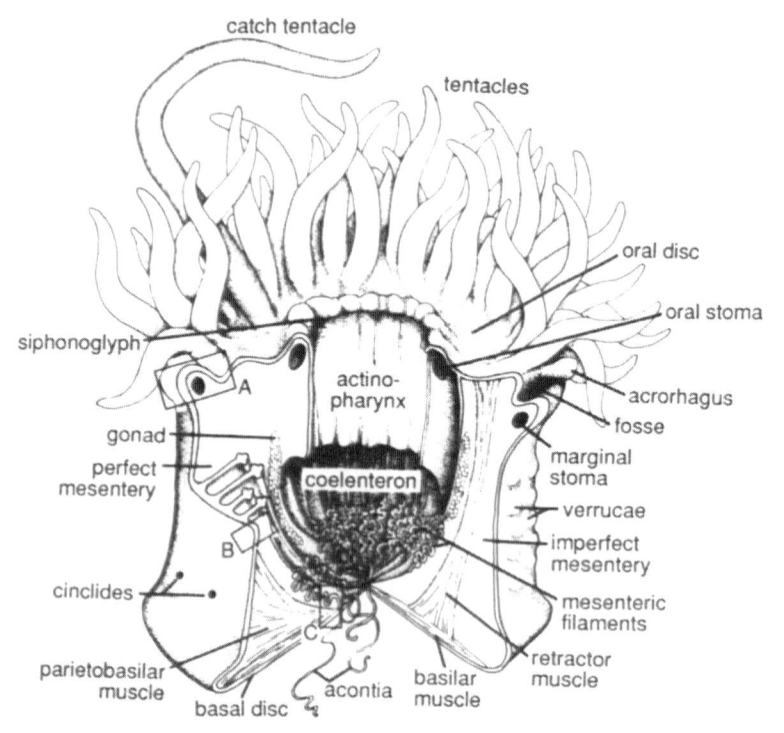

Figure 1.2 General morphology of a sea anemone. In this chimeric representation, an endomyarian anemone such as an actiniid is shown to the right of the cut sector, and a mesomyarian anemone to the left. **A**, **B**, and **C** indicate planes of section, details of which are shown on the facing page. Source: after concepts in Storer *et al.* (1979), and Doumenc and Van-Praët (1987). Original drawing by Marianne Fisher.

ever, this arrangement precludes full contraction of the oral disc, rendering the anemones susceptible to predators. Most such anemones also harbour symbiotic clownfishes, which protect them from predatory fishes (section 7.3.2, page 300). As in other Anthozoa, the incidence of symbiosis between sea anemones and zooxanthellae decreases with increasing distance from the tropics, possibly because zooxanthellae are less thermally adaptable than are their animal hosts (section 2.6.6, page 106).

The radial symmetry that characterizes Cnidaria is a consequence of the polyp's sessile lifestyle, facing the environment on all sides. Although wildly elaborate forms (including colonies) and a wide range of sizes are possible, radial symmetry apparently has a limited 'design potential' (Robson, 1985), for the Cnidaria are an evolutionary dead-end, having given rise to no other taxa. The limitations of radial symmetry are recalled in the Echinodermata, likewise a phylum of fantastically diverse metazoans that has radiated exten-

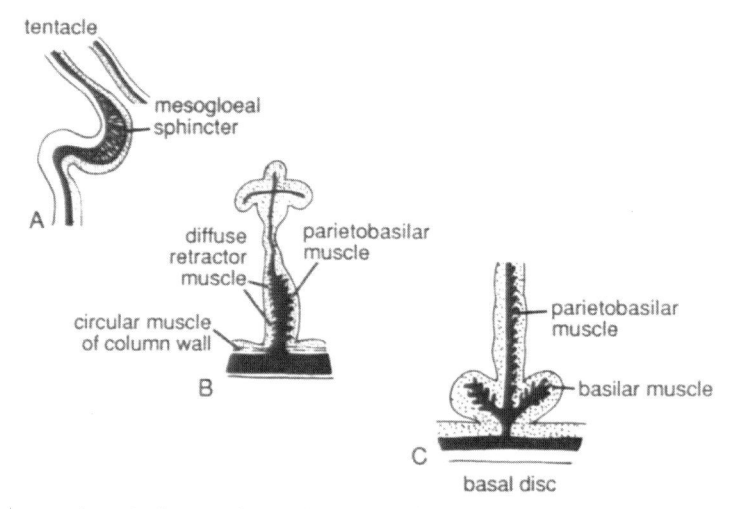

Figure 1.2, continued. Insets show: **A.** longitudinal section through distal portion of column, illustrating mesogleal sphincter muscle; **B.** transverse section through imperfect mesentery, showing diffuse retractor muscle and parietobasilar muscle on opposite faces of mesentery, and circular muscle of column; **C.** vertical section through insertion of a mesentery into the basal disc, showing basilar muscles and parietobasilar muscle. Endoderm stippled, mesoglea solid black, ectoderm unshaded. Source: after Manuel (1988).

sively within itself but not sent forth any new lineages. Radial symmetry is retained in motile, burrowing anemones, as it is in soft-bodied, burrowing holothuroid echinoderms, whose epibenthic relatives are secondarily bilaterally symmetrical to meet the demands of a different way of life (Lawrence, 1987).

Anthozoa are actually biradially symmetrical. Their mesenteries occur as mirror-image couples on opposite sides of the directive axis, itself defined by a plane that bisects the mouth, actinopharynx, siphonoglyph(s) and directive pairs of mesenteries longitudinally (Figure 1.3). In sea anemones this bilateral component to anthozoan symmetry is pronounced. It is related to their hydrostatics (Pantin, 1960), and to their large size and the attendant need to ventilate the coelenteron (Hyman, 1940). The sleeve-like actinopharynx acts as a valve to retain seawater in the coelenteron, and since the actinopharynx collapses laterally under pressure, it imposes bilaterality on the radial symmetry (Pantin, 1960). The presence of siphonoglyphs heightens the bilateral aspect of actiniarian radial symmetry. Siphonoglyphs (Figures 1.2 and 1.3) are longitudinal grooves at the end(s) of the actinopharynx whose ciliation carries water into the coelenteron. They have the dual role of maintaining the volume of the coelenteric fluid (see below) and of supplying oxygenated

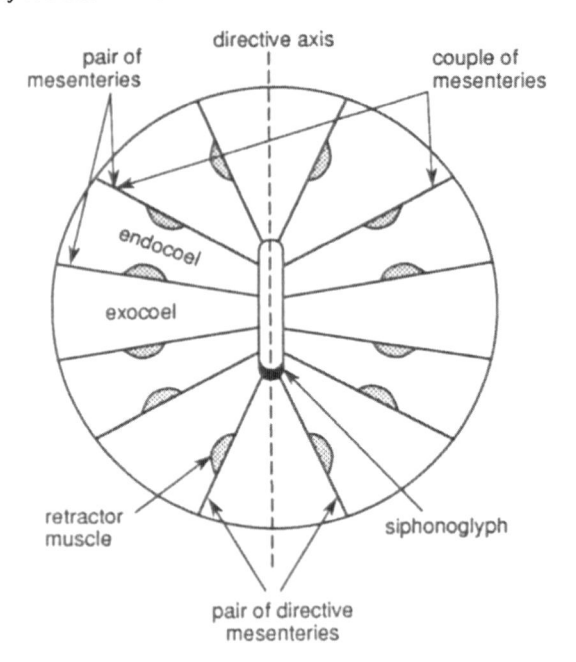

directive axis

pair of
mesenteries

couple of
mesenteries

endocoel

exocoel

retractor
muscle

siphonoglyph

pair of directive
mesenteries

Figure 1.3 Diagrammatic transverse section at the level of the actinopharynx through a young sea anemone having six pairs of perfect mesenteries in the first cycle. Note endocoelic location of retractor muscles on non-directive mesenteries. Additional terminology relevant to biradial symmetry is shown.

water to the mesenteries, especially in large individuals where diffusional gas exchange becomes limiting (see Chapter 3).

The mesenteries are the sites of digestion and absorption, and gamete development. They bear the major longitudinally oriented musculature so important in defensive reactions (see below). Thus they are central to the biology of these cnidarians, and usually are added throughout the life of an individual as it grows, so that there is a positive relationship between individual size and the number of mesenteries (Stephenson, 1928; Hand, 1966). This probably has a mechanical as well as a nutritional and energetic basis, the mesenteric insertions on the inner column wall perhaps acting as battens to reinforce the column. So-called perfect mesenteries have insertions on the actinopharynx as well as on the oral and basal discs, whereas imperfect mesenteries do not reach the actinopharynx (Figure 1.2). Mesenteric insertions on the oral disc often are visible externally as thin lines or stripes.

Mesenteries arise as pairs, each pair enclosing an endocoelic chamber and being flanked by adjacent exocoels (Figure 1.3). Coelenteric fluid may circulate between adjacent chambers via stomata in the mesentery near its oral and marginal insertions (Figure 1.2).

In the Actiniaria, typically one tentacle arises in each endocoel and exocoel. As is the case with mesenteric pairs, tentacles are added in sequential cycles, each member of a cycle being at a similar stage of development. Some anemones of the tribe Mesomyaria have so-called catch tentacles in addition to feeding tentacles (Figure 1.2). The former may develop from feeding tentacles, and are recognizable by their larger size, relative opacity and distinctive cnidome (complement of cnidae: Weill, 1934) consisting especially of large, penetrating holotrichous nematocysts. Rather than catching prey, as their name implies, catch tentacles are used in intraspecific agonistic behaviour (section 7.2.1, page 280). Some members of the tribe Endomyaria (notably in the family Actiniidae) instead have acrorhagi, which are analogous in function to catch tentacles and likewise contain holotrichs, as well as atrichs. Acrorhagi, which Bigger (1982) views as homologues of tentacles, lie in the fosse at the base of the tentacles on the parapet of the upper (distal) portion of the column (Figure 1.2). Many mesomyarian anemones also possess acontia, which are threadlike extensions of the mesenteries below the level of the filaments (Figure 1.2). Heavily loaded with nematocysts, but with a cnidome often more restricted than in the tentacles, acontia function in defence against predators (section 7.4.1, page 311). They become exposed when an anemone is damaged, and may be extruded through the cinclides (perforations of the column in the endocoelic chambers; Figure 1.2) when a disturbed anemone contracts rapidly. Acontia may also be used to subdue ingested prey.

The proximal end of the polyp forms the basal ($\equiv$ pedal) disc, which attaches firmly but reversibly to the substrate, apparently by a protein-chitin cement (Shelton, 1982). Quick release of the basal disc is effected by various cells in the ectoderm during shell-climbing behaviour in species associated with gastropods and hermit crabs and during escape from predators (Chapter 7), and during locomotion using the basal disc (Robson, 1976). In burrowing anemones, however, the base is modified to form a conical physa, which alternately penetrates and anchors the anemone in the substrate via hydrostatic action (Ansell and Trueman, 1968).

1.2 THE HYDROSTATIC SKELETON, MUSCLES AND MESOGLEA

An anemone is an elastic, muscular cylinder open at the oral end and full of seawater, which may account for over 80% of its live weight: at least in terms of biomass, there is less to an expanded anemone than meets the eye. If it contracts its muscles while the mouth is open, it may lose its voluminous

Figure 1.4 Silhouettes of a specimen of *Metridium senile* during different extents of inflation of the hydrostatic skeleton and degrees of expansion and contraction. The coelenteric fluid may comprise over 80% of the live weight of the anemone, yet may be completely expelled when the anemone contracts fully. Source: after Batham and Pantin (1950c).

coelenteric fluid. By keeping its mouth shut and so trapping an incompressible fluid within the confines of the coelenteron, an anemone can transmit the force generated by muscular contraction via the hydraulic fluid to the walls of the cylinder, which responds by deforming. Such a hydrostatic skeleton is a cardinal feature of cnidarians and is exemplified by the anemones, which are famous for their dramatic changes of shape and volume (Figure 1.4). Like the circular muscles that ring the column, discussion of this system has no obvious starting or ending point as the functional components of the system — the hydraulic fluid, the mesoglea, and the muscles — are closely interdependent.

1.2.1 Muscles

The mesoglea provides an anchorage for the elongated, contractile myonemes of the uniquely cnidarian myoepithelial ($\equiv$ epitheliomuscular) cells, which change reversibly from a pavement to a columnar configuration when the myonemes contract (Figure 1.5). The immediate portion of the mesoglea to which the myonemes are anchored buckles and is thrown into folds during

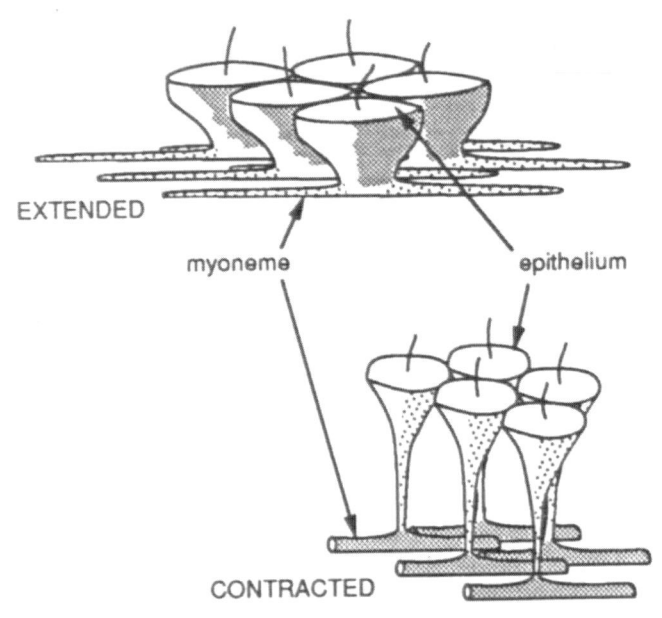

Figure 1.5 Diagram of myoepithelial cells showing reversible changes in cell shape when myonemes are extended (relaxed) or contracted. See text for discussion. Source: after Robson (1957).

such contraction, while the greater part of the mesoglea thickens (Batham and Pantin, 1951). A second type of contractile cell is limited to the endoderm, particularly in the circular muscles of the column and tentacles. The myonemes of these cells are not as elongated as those in myoepithelial cells, and in symbiotic species the cytoplasm characteristically contains zooxanthellae (Doumenc and Van-Praët, 1987).

In actiniarians the major musculature is endodermal, with a diffuse ectodermal component being limited to the tentacles and oral disc, as illustrated in members of the primitive suborder Protantheae and of the tribe Boloceroidaria within the suborder Nyantheae, some of which swim by tentacular flexions (Robson, 1966). The musculature of the tentacles and oral disc is particularly oriented to effect capture, retention and ingestion of prey (Holley and Shelton, 1984), and it is capable of highly localized actions independent of the endodermal musculature that controls body form (Batham and Pantin, 1951). Cerianthids, however, have a powerful, ectodermal longitudinal musculature in the column, associated with their alarm response of withdrawal into their surrounding tube.

Muscle cells are organized into laminar muscle fields, which are defined by the orientation of their major axis and direction of their contraction (Figure

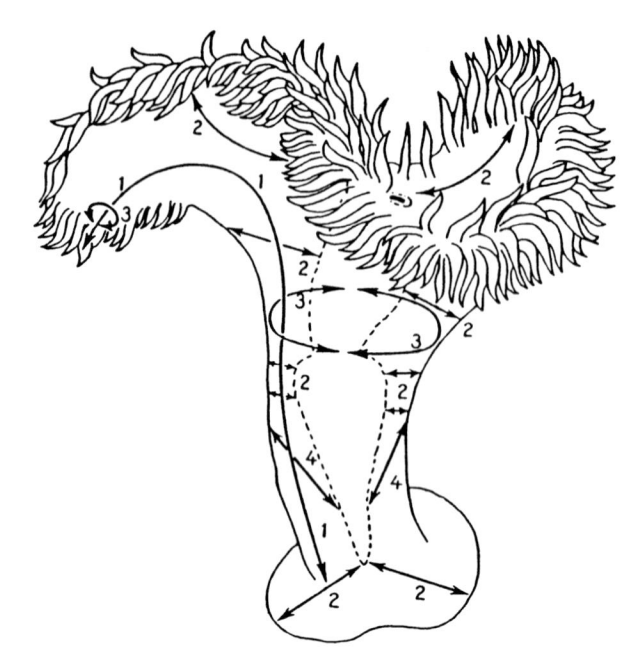

Figure 1.6 Principal muscle fields in *Cereus pedunculatus*, as defined by their major axis and direction of contraction. Longitudinal muscle fields (1) include the powerful retractors located on the mesenteries (as well as the mesenteric parietal muscles in some species), and the ectodermal longitudinal muscles of the tentacles. Radial muscle fields (2) include the endodermal basilar muscles and diffuse transverse muscles of the mesenteries, as well as the ectodermal radial muscles of the oral disc. Circular muscle fields (3) include the endodermal (sometimes mesogleal) marginal sphincter and endodermal circular muscles of the column and of the tentacles. Oblique muscle fields (4) are comprised of the mesenteric parietobasilar muscles. Source: with permission from Doumenc and Van-Praët (1987) after Doumenc (1979).

1.6). The circular muscle field of the column comprises a single diffuse sheet, contraction of which elongates the anemone. In microphagous suspension feeders such as *Metridium senile*, this elongation is important in maintaining the feeding apparatus above the substrate and in the current mainstream. Peristaltic contractions of the circular muscles are also used in burrowing by anemones such as *Peachia hastata* (Ansell and Trueman, 1968), and more generally by most species in flushing the coelenteron and ejecting solid waste and gametes through the mouth. The degree of mouth opening is controlled by the diffuse transverse muscles of the mesenteries.

Amerongen and Peteya (1976) described two ultrastructurally distinct muscle fibres in *Stomphia coccinea* that differ in the dimensions of their un-striated myofilaments. Although the different types of fibre predominate in different muscles, the distribution of the fibres is quite variable in other muscles within an individual. Noting that even in distinct muscle fields capable of different rates of contraction the entire muscle field is involved in the contraction, these authors concluded that there was no evidence for separate fast and slow fibres. Rather, the different dimensions of the myofilaments were interpreted to reflect different degrees of contraction when fixation took place. In the absence of evidence of distinct fibre types associated with physiological and mechanical diversity, then, it appears that muscular specialization in sea anemones is at the morphological, rather than the ultrastructural, level. Because the force that a muscle can develop is proportional to its cross-sectional area, contractions of the laminar, diffuse circular and transverse muscle fields are relatively weak and slow. Greater force and more rapid contraction during deformation can be produced by circumscript muscles having an anchorage raised above the plane of the mesogleal sheet by an arborescent mesogleal process; this produces extensive folding of the muscle sheet and in effect enables a block, rather than a sheet, of muscle to develop.

This anatomical feature is seen in the powerful, longitudinally oriented retractor muscles on the endocoelic faces of non-directive mesenteries, and in some species in the oblique parietobasilar muscles on the exocoelic surfaces of mesenteries (Figure 1.2). Alternating contractions of radially opposed parietobasilars enable some actinostolid anemones to swim and escape predation by sea stars (Sund, 1958). The retractors, however, effect rapid symmetrical withdrawal or depression of the oral disc. Together with contraction of the sphincter muscle of the upper column's margin (Figure 1.2) that acts as a drawstring and covers the retracted oral disc and tentacles, retraction provides an important defence against predation and in intertidal species reduces desiccation (see below). The sphincter muscle when endodermal may also be circumscript and capable of strong, localized contraction, particularly in intertidal species (Stotz, 1979; Zamponi, 1981). In some anemones the sphincter consists of muscle cells embedded within the mesoglea. Sphincters in individuals of *Phymactis clematis* from exposed, wave-swept habitats are more highly developed and generate about 25% greater force than those in conspecifics from sheltered areas (Patronelli *et al.*, 1987). Circumscript, radial basilar muscles (Figure 1.2) facilitate release of the basal disc during locomotion (Batham and Pantin, 1951).

Because of the incomplete partitioning of the coelenteron, all coelenteric fluid compartments are interconnected, so that in addition to its local effect, a contracting muscle will affect more distal areas by displacing some of this fluid. Thus, Batham and Pantin (1950a) pointed out that 'the movement of any muscle affects the mechanical conditions under which operates every other muscle of the body. A local contraction causes a rise in coelenteric pressure, and every muscle must now do more work if it is to shorten than was necessary before'. Therefore it is important that the basal coelenteric pressure be as low as possible — just enough to sustain inflation of the body and to keep it from collapsing under its own weight. This is indeed the case, and the ciliary currents on the siphonoglyph provide the 'trickle charge' to maintain this basal pressure of less than $10 \, mm \, H_2O$ (Batham and Pantin, 1950a).

1.2.2 Mesoglea

Such economy of function is likewise seen in economy of construction. The epithelial organization of cnidarians seemingly necessitates that the support system for their epithelia also be laminar. This framework is the mesoglea, a visco-elastic composite material of collagenous fibres in a liquid matrix of glycoprotein polymers. Elucidation of the molecular and microstructural bases of mechanical differences among mesogleas from anemones subject to diverse internal and external stresses was an early triumph in the burgeoning field of biomechanics. Chapman (1953) showed that the mechanical properties of the body wall of sea anemones can be attributed to the mesoglea alone and not to the muscles attached to it. Because at least its collagen component seems to have a surprisingly rapid turnover (Gosline and Lenhoff, 1968), the synthesis of mesoglea may represent a considerable expense to an anemone. Therefore, if structures are built to meet maximal demand with a 'reasonable' safety margin and little waste, in accord with principles of optimal design (Schmidt-Nielsen, 1984), then the large interspecific differences in the amount and organization of mesoglea in anemones probably have a functional, adaptive basis. This design principle is seen also within an individual. Because at a given coelenteric pressure the tension on the wall of a cylinder is proportional to its radius, it follows that the wall of a tentacle experiences lower tension than does that of the column. Thus it is not surprising that the tentacles have proportionally less reinforcing mesoglea (Batham and Pantin, 1951).

Like many advances in comparative biology, understanding of the role of the actiniarian mesoglea was facilitated by an informed choice of experimental material, an approach taken early by Chapman (1949, 1953). *Calliactis parasitica* is an ectosymbiont on gastropods and on their shells inhabited by hermit crabs (section 7.3.1, page 297). The anemone performs elaborate shell climbing behaviours during which muscular action may be comparatively rapid and finely controlled. During muscular contraction, the coelenteric pressure in this anemone reaches $150 \, mm \, H_2O$ (Chapman, 1949). Most behaviours in *Metridium senile* are slower and the maximum pressure achieved is $100 \, mm \, H_2O$ (Batham and Pantin, 1950a). These differences are manifested in the amounts of mesoglea, their compositions, microstructures and resultant mechanical properties.

In *Calliactis*, the mesoglea in an expanded specimen is up to $1\,500 \, \mu m$

thick at the level of the marginal sphincter, and 200 μm thick even at the edge of the basal disc (Passano and Pantin, 1955). Actively swimming actinostolid anemones likewise have relatively thick mesogleas (Siebert, 1973). In an expanded specimen of *Metridium* of similar size to *Calliactis*, the columnar mesoglea is only 10 μm thick, increasing to 62 μm during contraction (Batham and Pantin, 1951). The greater mesogleal thickness in *Calliactis* compared with *Metridium* is related in part to the higher coelenteric pressures the former's body wall must withstand without rupturing. In both species, cinclides provide safety valves to release excess pressure during extremely rapid contraction. Because both anemones also undergo pronounced changes in shape, the molecular architecture of the collagen fibres in their mesogleas shows regional compromises. In the peripheral areas of the columnar mesoglea, the fibres form a cross-lattice or feltwork pattern suited to changes in shape, whereas the central area consists of parallel fibres arranged circumferentially or radially to reinforce the body wall (Chapman, 1953; Gosline, 1971). The greater stiffness of the mesoglea in *Calliactis*, providing a flexible solid skeleton against which the muscles may act directly (Batham and Pantin, 1951) in localized portions of shell climbing behaviour, is also due to its lower water content and hence higher concentration of polymers in the interfibrillar matrix (cf. Gosline, 1971; Brafield and Chapman, 1983).

Neither the rigidity nor the elasticity of mesoglea is due to direct interconnections among collagen fibres or to their bending or stretching. Rather, the collagen chains form entanglements with polymeric components of the matrix (Gosline, 1971). The importance of this interaction, as well as the foregoing factors, can be appreciated by extending the discussion to a third case, *Anthopleura xanthogrammica*. This anemone is subjected to prolonged wave action on exposed coasts yet undergoes little deformation, remaining upright and expanded to capture prey dislodged by crashing waves (Koehl, 1977a; section 2.2.2, page 39). Nor does it exhibit the extreme postural changes so characteristic of *Metridium* or the somersaulting behaviour of *Calliactis*. Koehl (1977b) has shown that the mesoglea of *A. xanthogrammica* remains rigid accordingly, even after being stressed for several hours, and it stores for elastic recoil a greater percentage of the energy used to stretch it than does that of *Metridium giganteum* (the large, aclonal species of *Metridium* from the northeastern Pacific sublittoral: Fautin, Bucklin and Hand, 1990). These characteristics are due to a greater density of collagen fibres as well as a higher concentration of polymers in the interfibrillar matrix, which together will prolong the entanglement phase (Koehl, 1977a). Finally, the mesoglea of *A. xanthogrammica* has a more homogeneous microstructure than the other species, most of its collagen fibres being arranged in parallel and oriented to reinforce the body wall. Its lack of a lattice or feltwork microstructure emphasizes the role of such regions in the anemones that show radical changes in posture. This principle is seen also in *Actinia equina* and

Cereus pedunculatus, where the cross-lattice pattern is particularly evident in the mesoglea of the mesenteries (Doumenc and Van-Praët, 1987), which undergo extreme compression during contraction of their muscles.

It must be noted also that owing to its relatively low water content and dense packing of collagen fibres, mesoglea may represent a particular barrier to the diffusion of oxygen. The regional distribution, thickness and particular composition of mesoglea within an individual and among species will therefore affect the pathway that oxygen takes to respiring tissues. Also, in studies of biochemical composition and physiological energetics, large amounts of mesoglea, especially its collagen and glycoproteins, present analytical difficulties. These matters are considered in Chapters 3 and 5.

1.2.3 Ultrastructural Adaptation to Cellular Deformation

The drastic deformations of cells accompanying postural changes (e.g. Figures 1.4 and 1.5) necessitate ultrastructural adaptations to maintain cellular functions. Some of these have been demonstrated by Holley in his studies of the basal apparatus of cilia, which anchor the cilia in epithelial cells and orient and coordinate their beat. In the myoepithelial cells of the mesenteries in *Metridium senile*, cilia have novel structures associated with their basal apparatus — flexible arched rootlets that can increase or decrease their span in the cell apex as the cell changes diameter (Holley, 1985). Oriented in the same plane as the movement of the cilium during its effective stroke, the arched rootlet apparently keeps the base of the cilium perpendicular to the cell surface (the most effective orientation for propulsion of water) and in register with the other cilia on the epithelium. This suggested function of arched rootlets is consistent with their absence from ciliated epidermal cells lining the actinopharynx, as these cells primarily propel mucus, which does not require as great a coordination of cilia as does water propulsion (Holley, 1984; Sleigh, 1989). Arched rootlets also are absent from the water-propelling ciliated cells of the siphonoglyph in *M. senile*. But as these cells do not deform nearly as much as mesenteric myoepithelial cells, the absence of arched rootlets again accords with Holley's suggested stabilizing and orienting function for them. It is of interest that the reversal of ciliary flow in the actinopharynx of *Calliactis* during feeding is controlled locally, a rare case in which ciliary beating is not coordinated by an electrical conduction system (Holley and Shelton, 1984).

1.3 NERVOUS SYSTEM

Cnidarians are the simplest metazoans to possess a nervous system, viewed classically as a diffuse, non-directional nerve net (Hertwig and Hertwig,

1879–80). Sea anemones have been favourite subjects in the investigation of this system, beginning with the work of Parker (1919) and greatly extended by the pioneering studies of its functional organization and conduction properties by Pantin (1935a, b). Later, the slow, spontaneous, phasic behaviours so characteristic of sea anemones seemed to Batham and Pantin (1950c, 1954) a fundamental property of the simplest nervous systems, whereas fast reflex responses represented secondary modifications to meet specific purposes. Sea anemones emerged as the paradigm of the 'elementary nervous system' owing in part to the highly stereotyped behaviours in certain species (Parker, 1919; Pantin, 1952; Ross, 1965). As is usually the case, however, the more a system is studied, the more obvious its complications become, and there is now an increasing dissatisfaction with actinians as model neurophysiological preparations (Anderson and Schwab, 1982). This derives in part from the very small size of nerve cells in anemones, which are not conducive to intracellular recordings, and from the presence of anatomically ill-defined, multiple conduction systems.

Using vital staining and silver impregnation, various workers since the Hertwigs have visualized interconnecting bipolar and multipolar neurons in the endoderm and ectoderm and distributed among various body regions. But there is as yet no complete system map for any one species, much of our picture of the actinian nervous system being a collage composed of pieces of the system from several species. As recently as 1984(a) McFarlane noted that ectodermal nervous structure, for example, was poorly understood.

In tentacles, however, there is a readily observable subectodermal plexus around the mesoglea, with connecting fibres to peripheral receptors and to ectodermal myoepithelial cells; possible contacts with cnidocytes and gland cells occur only within the plexus (Van Marle, 1977; also see the previously unpublished electron micrographs by L.L. Minasian in Fautin and Mariscal, 1990). Quaglia and Grasso (1986) described similar subepidermal plexuses at the bases of both the ectoderm and endoderm, each having both bipolar interneurons and multipolar motor neurons, as well as connections to ectodermal and endodermal sensory receptors. Neuronal connections between the ectoderm and endoderm have been seen microscopically in the oral disc (Batham, 1965), and seemingly provide a pathway from the rich sensory fields of the oral disc and tentacles to the mesenteric retractors (Figure 1.7). Neuroethological evidence indicates that in some active species the pathways from ectodermal receptors in the column to endodermal effectors in the mesenteries must be more extensive (the transmesogleal system, TMS, proposed by Lawn, 1980), and anatomical studies at least hint that this is so (Robson, 1963, 1965). Sphincter muscles embedded in the mesoglea are innervated by trans-mesogleal connections from the endoderm (Robson, 1965; Figure 1.8A).

Microscopic studies have also shown that fast-contracting muscles such as

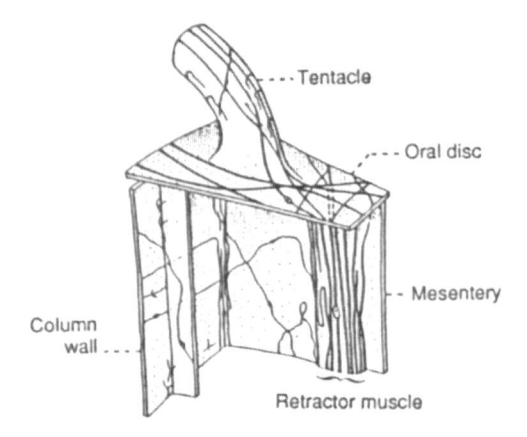

Figure 1.7 Diagram of nerve net in *Mimetridium cryptum*. Note individual neurons running from column wall to mesenteries, from mesenteries through to oral disc ectoderm, and from oral disc to tentacle. Fast-contracting retractor muscle is overlain by dense net of thick, bipolar fibres. Source: with permission from Doumenc and Van-Praët (1987) after Batham (1965).

the retractors are densely overlaid with relatively thick, bipolar nerve fibres, whereas slow muscles such as the circular muscles of the column and diffuse radial muscles of the mesenteries are more sparsely supplied with relatively slender, multipolar nerve cells (Robson, 1961a, 1963; Figure 1.7). These appear to be the anatomical bases for the separate through-conducting and multipolar nerve nets postulated on the basis of electrophysiological data (McFarlane, 1984a; see below). An interspecific comparison provides insight concerning functioning of the latter: a progression of increasing size and abundance of multipolar nerve cells (TMS?), and of increasing conduction velocity and SS1 pulse frequency, is seen in *Metridium senile, Calliactis parasitica* and *Stomphia coccinea* (Robson, 1961a, 1963; Lawn, 1976), a series that also manifests an increasing complexity and speed of behaviours (McFarlane, 1982).

Interaction between cells of the nerve net probably occurs wherever the cells cross each other, which can be at multiple points along the fibre or body of a given cell. Westfall's (1970) studies of *Metridium senile* provided the first ultrastructural evidence that the synapses in the actinian nerve net are chemical, and that they may be unpolarized ($\equiv$ symmetrical) and transmit in both directions, having vesicles of neurotransmitter on both sides of the synapse (Figure 1.8B; see also Quaglia and Grasso, 1986). Westfall's electron micrographs also show chemical myoneural junctions between nerve cells and myoepithelial cells (Figure 1.8C).

In sea anemones there is cytochemical evidence for the presence of adre-

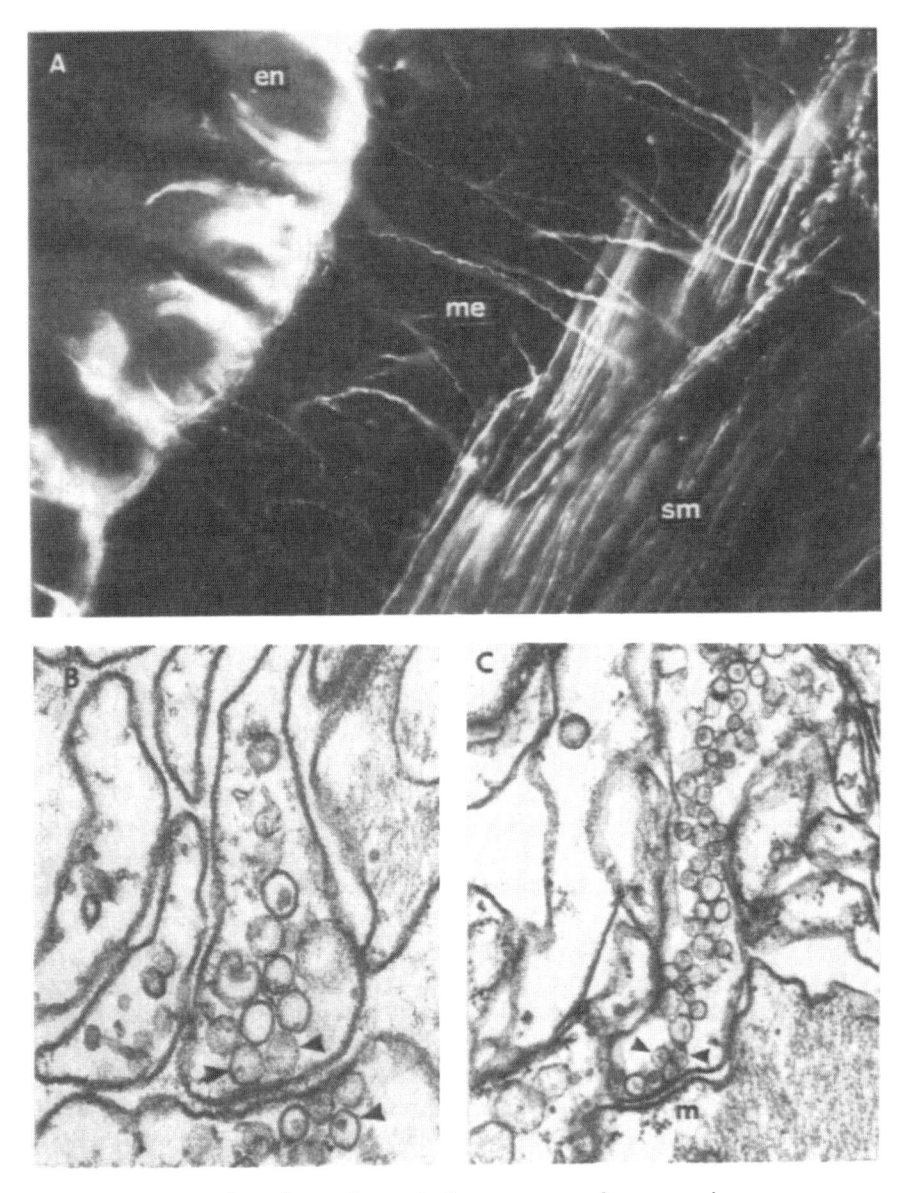

Figure 1.8 Innervation of muscles and ultrastructure of synapses in sea anemones. **A.** Innervation of the mesogleal sphincter muscle (sm) in *Calliactis parasitica* by fibres running across the mesoglea (me) from the endoderm (en). Nervous elements are immunochemically visualized by their reaction with an antiserum against the sequence Arginine-Tryptophan-NH$_2$ present in the sea anemone neuropeptides Antho-RWamide I and II. 270 ×. **B.** Unpolarized (bidirectional) chemical synapse in *Metridium senile*. Note dense-cored vesicles (arrows) in cells on both sides of synapse. 64 800 ×. **C.** Myoneural junction between a nerve cell terminus containing synaptic vesicles (arrows) and a myoepithelial cell (m) containing myofilaments. 36 500 ×. Source: **A.** with permission from Graff and Grimmelikhuijzen (1988); **B.** and **C.** with permission from Westfall (1970).

nergic (Dahl *et al.*, 1963) and catecholaminergic (Van Marle, 1977) neurons, but the results of early pharmacological experiments seeking to identify the exact transmitters involved were negative or equivocal (Ross, 1960a, b; Carlyle, 1969a, b). Several neuropeptides have now been identified in *Anthopleura elegantissima*. Each consists of either four or five basic or neutral amino acids, and is synthesized within a precursor protein, which subsequently yields multiple copies of the peptide (Grimmelikhuijzen, Graff and McFarlane, 1989). The cellular location of these compounds may be the dense-cored, peptidergic vesicles of multipolar, subepidermal nerve cells (Quaglia and Grasso, 1986). The peptides have the general structure <Glu . . . Arg-X-NH_2, where X is an aromatic amino acid (phenylalanine or tryptophan) (Grimmelikhuijzen *et al.*, 1989). The neuropeptide Antho-RFamide (originally isolated from *A. elegantissima*) has proved to be an excitatory neurotransmitter or neuromodulator in ectodermal and endodermal conduction systems in *Calliactis parasitica* (McFarlane, Graff and Grimmelikhuijzen, 1987). A similar but distinct peptide first isolated from *A. elegantissima*, Antho-RWamide I, has been shown by immunocytochemistry to be particularly abundant in neurons innervating the mesogleal sphincter in *C. parasitica* (Graff and Grimmelikhuijzen, 1988; Figure 1.8A). Antho-RWamide I causes slow contractions of all endodermal muscles, and as it has no effect on several electrophysiologically identified, neuronal conducting systems (see below), it appears to be a transmitter at myoneural junctions (McFarlane, in Grimmelikhuijzen *et al.*, 1989). Ewer (1960) demonstrated that the nerve net of *Calliactis* also has inhibitory actions, but inhibitory neurotransmitters remain to be identified. Glutamate released from the contracting sphincter muscle in *Actinia equina* has a subsequent inhibitory effect on contraction via an unknown route (Carlyle, 1974).

The cytological vision of a single, diffuse nerve net was clouded by extra-cellular electrical recordings of nervous activity, which indicated the existence of at least three, and perhaps four, distinct but interconnected conducting systems. Much of the original research on these systems has been done by McFarlane and his colleagues, and was reviewed by that author in 1982. More recently he has provided a model (Figure 1.9) that attempts to integrate the anatomical, behavioural, and physiological data (McFarlane, 1984a), and much of the following is drawn from his reviews.

The portion of the nerve net called the through-conducting system by Pantin (1935a) and in which impulses travel non-decrementally in large, bipolar cells is referred to as the through-conducting nerve net or TCNN (McFarlane, 1982). Its activity is normally evoked by mechanical stimuli and can be recorded in the mesenteries, oral disc, and tentacles. When stimulated electrically, the TCNN has the lowest threshold and fastest conduction velocity ($10-120\,\text{cm}\cdot\text{s}^{-1}$) of the several conduction systems. The TCNN has both excitatory and inhibitory effects on muscles and it may act indirectly via

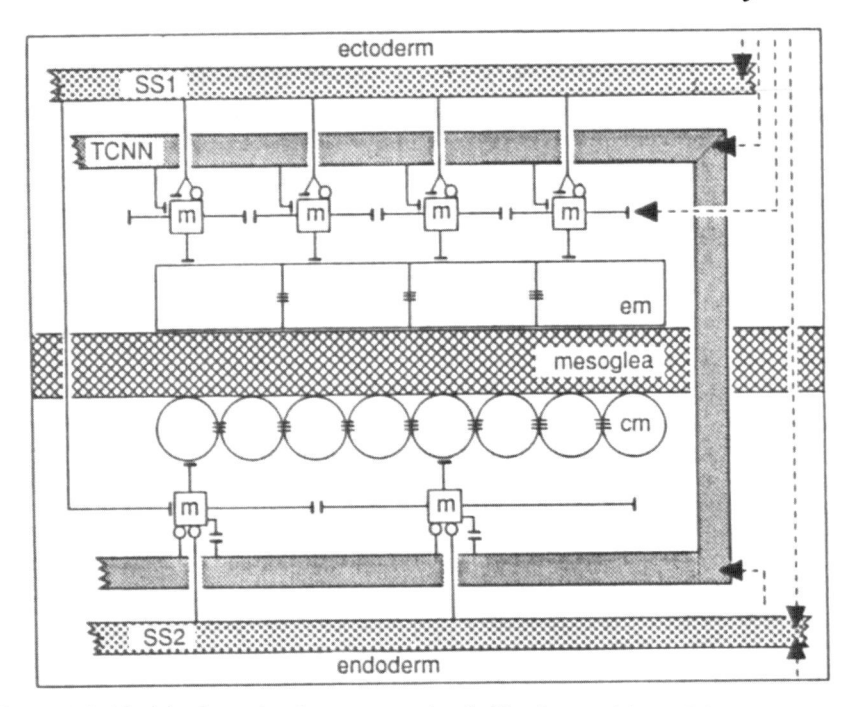

Figure 1.9 Model of conducting systems in *Calliactis parasitica*. Major conduction systems (TCNN, SS1 and SS2) may act indirectly on ectodermal longitudinal and radial muscles (em) of tentacles and oral disc, and on endodermal circular muscles (cm) of column via multipolar nerve cells (m). Excitation may also spread locally by direct conduction between linked muscle cells. See text for discussion. Symbols: ---▸, sensory input; ——⊣, excitatory junction; ——o, inhibitory junction; ⊣ ⊢, unpolarized excitatory junction. Source: with permission from McFarlane (1984a).

a separate, multipolar nerve net, particularly in the tentacles and in the circular muscles of the column, or directly in the marginal sphincter and retractors, which it appears to innervate. It was the relationship of the TCNN to these fast-acting muscles that prompted Josephson (1966) to make the first electrophysiological recordings in *Calliactis polypus*. Some elements of the TCNN are spontaneously active — an example of the pacemakers long popular with cnidariophilic neuroethologists (see Bullock and Horridge, 1965). These pacemakers may be the basis of the slow muscular activity (probably mediated via the endodermal multipolar nerve net) that period-ically flushes the coelenteron, manifested as 'respiratory rhythms' (see below, and section 3.7, page 138).

The small potentials ($<5\,\mu V$) recorded extracellularly from the TCNN can be obliterated by much larger impulses from additional conduction systems, the Slow-conducting Systems in the ectoderm (SS1) and in the endoderm (SS2). These are so named because of their slow conduction velocities relative to the TCNN ($5-12\,\mathrm{cm\cdot s}^{-1}$ in the SS1 and $3-5\,\mathrm{cm\cdot s}^{-1}$ in the SS2). Owing to their slow speed and very large signals, it has been suggested that the SS1 and SS2 represent not nervous elements, but electrically-coupled epithelial cells. This idea was also based on the seeming paucity of nervous elements in the ectoderm, a paradigm that is changing (see above). The abolition of SS1 and SS2 activity by high concentrations of Mg^{2+} (McFarlane, 1973) is more in accord with chemical synaptic transmission than with the propagation of action potentials between electrically-coupled epithelial cells (Anderson, 1980; McFarlane, 1984a; McFarlane et al., 1987). Also, in systems having bona fide epithelial conduction, notably in the Hydrozoa, the cytoplasms of electrically-coupled cells invariably are connected by gap junctions, which are absent from sea anemones (Mackie, Anderson and Singla, 1984). The SS1 and SS2, then, probably are nerve nets, although their exact anatomical substrate remains elusive.

Elements of the SS1 respond to chemical and to mechanical stimulation. Extracts of prey applied to the ectoderm elicit expansion of the oral disc and extension of the tentacles (McFarlane and Lawn, 1972). Oral disc expansion results from SS1 inhibition (presumably via the multipolar nerve net: Figure 1.9) of the ectodermal radial muscles that contract the disc, so that antagonized by a positive coelenteric pressure, the thin disc expands. Extension of the column, another component of feeding behaviour, occurs during prolonged stimulation of the ectodermal SS1. Since this involves contraction of the endodermal circular muscles, a transmesogleal connection is implied. Such is also the case in the escape swimming behaviour by *Stomphia coccinea*, where ectodermal contact with a predatory sea star evokes SS1 activity resulting in contractions of the endodermal circular and parietobasilar muscles (page 11, and section 7.4.2, page 315). The SS1 is also involved in aspects of shell-climbing behaviour in *Calliactis parasitica* (section 7.3.1, page 297), notably in causing detachment of the basal disc, and perhaps in lowering the threshold for discharge of glutinant spirocysts.

The endodermal SS2 is entirely inhibitory. In *Calliactis* this is seen particularly in shell-climbing behaviour, where SS2 inhibits contractions of several sets of endodermal muscles (probably by inhibiting their associated pacemakers in the TCNN and multipolar nerve net) while allowing the SS1 and TCNN to coordinate their actions. Conversely, a reduction in SS2 activity might release the TCNN pacemakers from inhibition and be manifested in a respiratory rhythm of coelenteric flushing (see Jones, Pickthall and Nesbitt, 1977). Chemical stimulation of the SS2 (the location of the receptors is unknown) causes opening of the mouth and protrusion of the actinopharynx by inhibiting contraction of their circular muscles. Stimulation of the SS2 by endodermal mechano- (stretch) and chemoreceptors may be involved in satiation after a meal, and via an undescribed connection with the SS1, may effect the post-prandial increase in threshold for nematocyst discharge (see Shelton, 1982; section 2.2.10, page 68).

In conjunction with his schematic model, McFarlane (1984a) has provided a conceptual overview of the functioning of the actiniarian neuromuscular system, at least in *Calliactis parasitica*. Multipolar nerve cells are viewed as pattern-generating motor neurons that drive particular behaviours directly. Presumably these neurons contain Antho-RWamide I (see above). The behavioural programs may be modified by input from extero- and enteroceptors via the TCNN, SS1 and SS2. Although the SS1 and SS2 have some immediate effects, they are viewed more as switching the output of pacemakers from one phase of spontaneous activity to another. There exist variations on this scenario, particularly in anemones having different morphologies and lifestyles. *Protanthea simplex*, which has longitudinal muscle in its column ectoderm, coordinates this entirely by a local conduction system that does not involve the TCNN, which instead stimulates contraction of the endodermal muscles in the column (McFarlane, 1984b). *Anemonia viridis* (≡ *A. sulcata*), apparently lacking a through-conducting system, does not exhibit symmetrical behaviour but instead shows localized responses to stimulation (Bullock and Horridge, 1965). In the solitary coral *Caryophyllia*, local conduction systems distinct from the TCNN, SS1 and SS2 have been characterized electrophysiologically and are postulated to occur in anemones (Shelton and Holley, 1984). The nature of the mechano- and chemoreceptors involved and their links to the muscles are unknown, but once the muscle field is stimulated, excitation spreads from cell to cell.

Although capable of a surprising variety of complicated and seemingly purposive actions, the sea anemone 'behaviour machine' is limited by two central features of the phylum: the two-dimensional organization of the nervous system, and the relative paucity of cell types within it. Pantin (1965) in particular discussed the topological constraints of a nervous system in which interconnections are limited in number by their general restriction to two dimensions. Such an arrangement, however, does not preclude long-term, adaptive changes in behaviour, including habituation (as distinct from sensory adaptation and fatigue: Logan, 1975; Logan and Beck, 1978) and facilitation (Wilson, 1959). The last author speculated that the site of facilitation is the myoneural junction, but nothing is known of the anatomical basis of long-term retention of facilitation.

Lacking great diversity, nervous elements in sea anemones must be polyfunctional, if only to account for the diversity of observed behaviours. This is illustrated by the dual function of the SS1 in *Calliactis parasitica*. In response to chemical stimuli, low frequency pulses in this system evoke pre-feeding behaviour (section 2.2.9, page 59), whereas contact with a suitable molluscan shell stimulates high frequency SS1 activity culminating in detachment of the basal disc during shell-climbing behaviour (section 7.3.1, page

297). These two functions of the system are not always clearly separated: a hungry anemone sometimes detaches when fed (McFarlane, 1983). Such dual functionality is seen at the microscopical level: ultrastructurally, multipolar neurons in *Actinia equina* appear to act in both neurosecretion and synaptic transmission (Quaglia and Grasso, 1986). Grimmelikhuijzen *et al.* (1989) note that 'sensory cells' immunoreactive with identified neuropeptides also have processes associated with muscle fibres, and so may have both sensory and motor functions. Pantin (1965) comments further on the paucity of sensory structures in cnidarians; it may not be coincidental that some of their receptors ultrastructurally appear to be capable of detecting multiple sensory modalities.

1.4 SENSORY RECEPTORS

Most of the microscopical sensory structures in anemones incorporate a cilium or several cilia. As the sensory modalities to which they respond are not known with certainty, their putative functions are inferred by structural analogy with known mechano- and chemoreceptors in the vertebrates. Cnidarian sensory structures may be limited to single cells, or several adjacent cells may contribute to a complex receptor, which may or may not be associated with a nematocyte. A presumed sensory structure not bearing cilia is the ring of microvilli on the surface of a spirocyte which, by analogy with vertebrate taste buds, appears to be a contact chemoreceptor; there is some physiological evidence for this (section 2.2.10, page 65).

Nematocytes frequently bear a ciliary cone, described early by Pantin (1942) and examined in ultrastructural detail by Mariscal and his colleagues. These studies have revealed that the ciliary cone is a multicellular structure consisting of the central cnidocyte and its cilium surrounded by several additional cells that contribute stereocilia or microvilli to the complex. Their association with nematocysts known to discharge in response to mechanical stimuli suggests a mechanoreceptive function, although the presence of microvilli may also indicate a role in chemoreception (see section 2.2.10). In the ectoderm of *Ceriantheopsis americanus*, ciliary cones not in association with cnidocytes may be mechanoreceptors responsive to water currents (Peteya, 1973), or alternatively they may propel sheets of mucus across the ectoderm (Fautin and Mariscal, 1990). The foregoing sensory structures are illustrated and discussed extensively in Fautin and Mariscal (1990). In the present work, they are considered in their functional contexts in Chapters 2 and 7.

Ironically, no photoreceptor structure or pigment has been identified in any sea anemone, despite the long-standing knowledge of the importance of light in their biology and their responsiveness to it. This is not surprising, for as anemones are some $10^4 - 10^5$ times less sensitive to light in the 500 nm range than are humans or even flatworms (North and Pantin, 1958), their photosensitive pigments and structures must be either correspondingly diffuse or exceedingly small and highly localized. It is no accident that early observations on the behaviour of undisturbed anemones were made by candlelight (Gosse, 1860).

Early clues concerning the nature of actiniarian photoreception came from the work of Bohn (1906a), Fleure and Walton (1907) and Parker (1916), who showed that local illumination of the column of *Metridium senile* caused contraction of the parietal muscles in the illuminated area. Subsequently North and Pantin (1958) demonstrated that local contractions of illuminated parietal muscles occur even if the mesentery is anaesthetized with Mg^{2+}, which eliminates chemical synaptic transmission between neurons and at the myoneural junction. Finally, Marks (1976) found that *Calamactis praelongus* shows local contractions of the column unaccompanied by electrical activity in the nerve net (although it also shows more extensive responses coordinated by the nerve net). Thus it seems likely that the myoepithelial cells themselves are photosensitive. The localization of this sensitivity among the various membrane systems of these cells, including the cilia, remains to be established. Detecting the location of photosensitive pigment will be exceedingly difficult, judging from North's (1957) interesting calculation that *M.senile* may have only $10^6 - 10^7$ photopigment molecules per cm^2 of body surface!

The photoreceptors in anemones show several characteristics common to such systems in general. Dark adaptation (increase in sensitivity during maintenance in the dark) is evident in *Metridium senile* (North and Pantin, 1958) and *Anthopleura xanthogrammica* (Clark and Kimeldorf, 1971). Based on the spectral sensitivities of particular behaviours and isolated muscles, at least two photoreceptors seem to exist: one having a maximum sensitivity at approximately 500 nm (*M.senile* and *A.xanthogrammica*), and a second having a maximum at 350–360 nm (*A.xanthogrammica*). Clark and Kimeldorf (1971) suggest that the retraction of the tentacles of the latter species to far ultraviolet (UV) radiation (peak at 280 nm) is due to absorption by proteins or nucleic acids, although they do not suggest transduction or transmission mechanisms. The marked flexions of the tentacles and oral disc of *A.xanthogrammica* in response to near-UV (350–360 nm) is suggestive of a protective reaction (section 2.7.3, page 111), as is the flexion of the disc and retraction of the tentacles seen in the bright simulated sunlight of a xenon arc lamp. Excitation of the tentacles in *A.xanthogrammica* by UV may spread beyond those irradiated. The high sensitivity of both species to light having a wavelength of 500 nm is similar to that of photoreceptors in general. Slight variations in spectral sensitivity among variously coloured morphs of *M.senile* seem due to the ectodermal melanin and carotenoid pigments filtering the light before it reaches endodermal receptors, rather than to the presence of additional photosensitive pigments (North and Pantin, 1958).

Although few controlled studies are available, both light and oxygen have separate and interacting effects on sea anemone behaviour, particularly in species symbiotic with zooxanthellae (sections 2.7.1, 2.7.2, and 2.7.3). Although the foregoing behaviours in the *Anthopleura xanthogrammica* have optimum wavelengths that do not correspond to chlorophyll action spectra and so are not mediated by intracellular oxygen production in its zooxanthellae, experiments by Fredericks (1976) and Shick and Brown (1977) nevertheless indicate the presence of oxygen receptors in zooxanthellate anemones. Also, behavioural responses to variations in dissolved oxygen by anemones that do not harbour zooxanthellae have long been known (Bohn, 1908; sections 3.8.2, 3.8.3 and 3.8.4). Nothing is known of the cellular location of oxygen receptors in anemones.

1.5 CNIDAE

Cnidae, including spirocysts, ptychocysts and nematocysts proper, have had their classification reiterated and their structures and functions discussed in every multi-chapter review of cnidarians that has appeared, as well as in several specialized reviews and monographs (a sample of these includes Weill, 1934; Picken and Skaer, 1966; Schmidt, 1969, 1972a; Mariscal, 1984; Hessinger and Lenhoff, 1988). The intense interest that cnidae have stimulated derives from their being the most complex intracellular secretion known, from the unique ability of cnidarians to secrete them, from their microstructural beauty, and increasingly from their biomedical importance. Cnidocytes (cnida-secreting cells) and their receptors are providing important insights into the processes of exo- and endocytosis.

Only anthozoans produce all three varieties of cnidae, and just as the Actiniaria are morphologically the most diverse order among the Anthozoa, so too is their cnidome (complement of cnidae) the most varied (Schmidt, 1974). Within an individual, a particular region or structure (e.g. feeding tentacle, catch tentacle, acontium) may have its own characteristic cnidome or size distribution of cnidae. Cnidae are taxonomically important characters within the sea anemones (Doumenc and Foubert, 1984; Fautin, 1988), both in defining higher taxa (Schmidt, 1974) and in identifying species within a difficult group (Manuel, 1988).

1.5.1 Terminology and Classification

For the general explorer of these pages, the terminology associated with cnidae may present an impenetrable thicket as dense as that of everted pty-

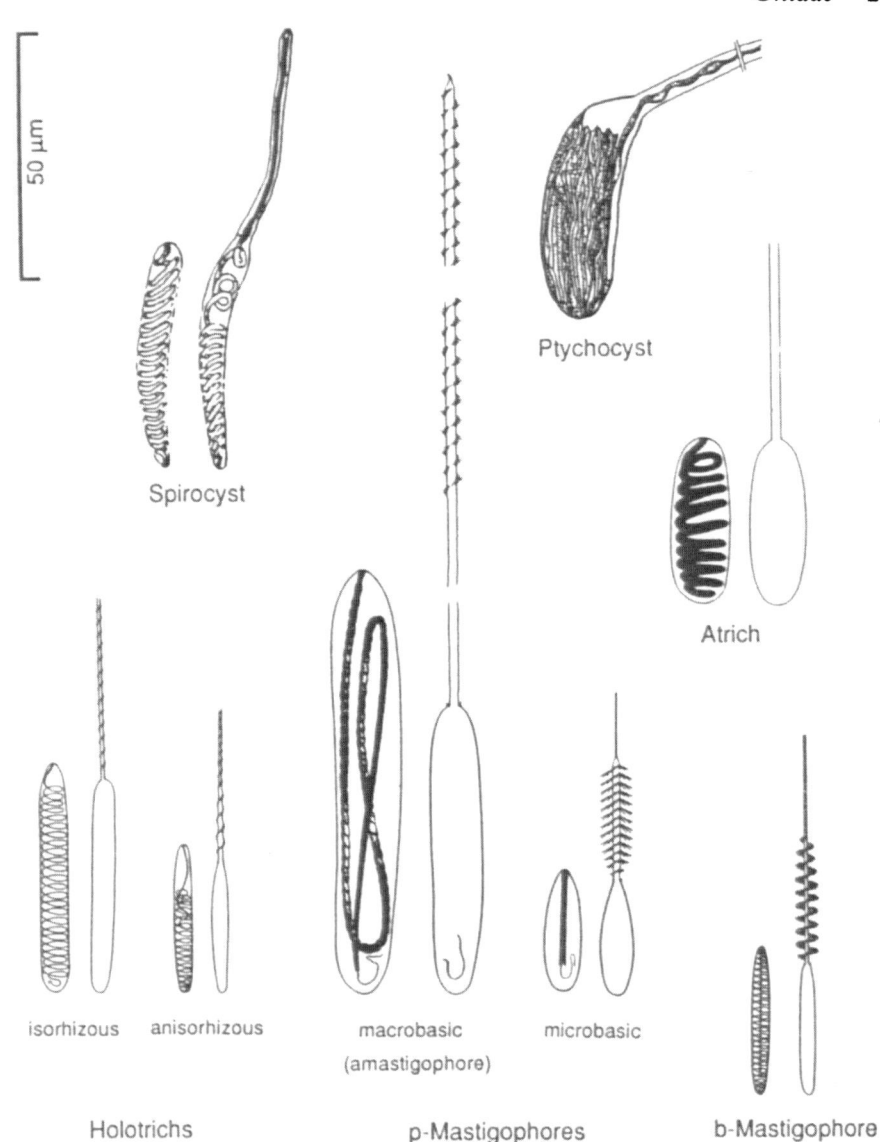

Spirocyst

Ptychocyst

Atrich

Holotrichs

isorhizous   anisorhizous

p-Mastigophores

macrobasic
(amastigophore)

microbasic

b-Mastigophore

Figure 1.10 Representative cnidae from sea anemones, showing undischarged and discharged condition. See text for descriptions. Spirocyst (unique to hexacorallian cnidarians). Ptychocyst (unique to ceriantharians). Atrich (from column of *Bolocera tuediae*). Isorhizous holotrich (acrorhagus of *Actinia equina*). Anisorhizous holotrich (column of *Anthopleura rubripunctata*). Macrobasic p-mastigophore (amastigophore; columnar vesicles of *Alicia mirabilis*). Microbasic p-mastigophore (pharynx of *Cereus pedunculatus*). b-mastigophore (pharynx of *Actinia equina*). Source: spirocyst with permission from Mariscal (1974c); ptychocyst with permission from Mariscal, Conklin and Bigger (1977); all nematocysts with permission from Schmidt (1974).

chocysts comprising the tube of a cerianthid, as clinging as the spirocysts of a shell-climbing *Calliactis*, and as nettling as the nematocysts of an aliciid anemone. Only the essentials are given here and in Figure 1.10. The terminology is modified after Weill (1934) and Schmidt (1974).

Cnidae, produced by cells called cnidocytes, are capsular organelles ranging from about 10 to 100 µm in length and containing a thin, eversible tube (Figure 1.10). The Golgi apparatus secretes the capsule and tube, and after the tube is inverted into the capsule by an unknown mechanism, ultrastructural and chemical changes continue (Watson and Mariscal, 1984a, b). ATP is involved in the maturation and maintenance of cnidae, perhaps in the operation of ion-translocating pumps on the membrane of the organelle (Greenwood, Johnson and Mariscal, 1989).

Spirocysts occur only in the Hexacorallia, primarily on the tentacles, where they are the numerically dominant cnida. They form a fairly homogeneous group characterized by a tube of diameter constant throughout its length that lacks spines but which contains small, helically arranged tubules. When everted these form a fine network of microfibrillae adhering to but not penetrating prey, and gastropod shells and other substrata (the 'sticky friendliness' written of by a Great Barrier Reef poet). Ptychocysts are restricted to the Ceriantharia, especially in the columnar ectoderm and, when everted, mesh together to form the tube inhabited by the polyp (Mariscal, Conklin and Bigger, 1977). Uniquely among cnidae, the uneverted ptychocyst tube is not folded helically within the capsule, being pleated in circumference but not in length.

It is the penetrating nematocysts that inject the venoms used to subdue prey or discourage predators, and the tube of all anthozoan nematocysts is open at the tip. Weill (1934) discerned two broad categories of nematocysts: haplonemes and heteronemes. In haplonemes, neither the tube nor its spiny armature (if present) is divided into distinct regions. Within the haplonemes, atrichs (of only sporadic occurrence among the sea anemones) lack spines, whereas holotrichs have spines, usually along the full length of the tube. Holotrichs may be isorhizous or anisorhizous, the tube in the latter showing a gradual but obvious change in diameter or spination along its length.

In heteronemes, which always have spines, the tube has a distinct basal shaft, differentiated from the distal tube ($\equiv$ thread) by its greater diameter, larger spines or both. There are two sorts of heteronemes: p-mastigophores and b-mastigophores. In p-mastigophores ($\equiv$ p-rhabdoids: Schmidt, 1974) the shaft is always thicker than the thread, and the two meet at a characteristic funnel-shaped junction. In macrobasic p-mastigophores, the undischarged shaft is longer than the capsule and so is folded inside it. Microbasic p-mastigophores have a shaft that is shorter than the capsule and which is unfolded. The thread of p-mastigophores may or may not have spines. Included in this category are amastigophores, whose small terminal thread may break off and remain inside the capsule after discharge. In b-mastigo-phores ($\equiv$ basitrichs; b-rhabdoids), the uneverted shaft lies straight within the capsule and tapers into the thread, which always bears spines and usually coils evenly around the shaft.

1.5.2 Functions

The adhesive functions of spirocysts and the tube-building role of ptycho-cysts have already been mentioned. Nematocysts of sea anemones function in capture and envenomation of prey, and in defence against conspecific competitors and against predators. Certain categories of nematocysts may be polyfunctional. For example, microbasic p-mastigophores act both as pene-trants of prey, and glutinants attaching *Stomphia coccinea* to the substrate after a bout of swimming (Ellis, Ross and Sutton, 1969). Although details of nematocyst microstructure have rarely been linked to particular functions, the spiral arrangement of the spines on everted tubes of nematocysts suggests that they may drill into tissue as the tube spins out of the capsule.

Our best indication concerning the function of particular nematocysts comes not just from their structure but also from their anatomical location and their use in special situations. The atrichs so abundant in the catch tentacles and acrorhagi thus have roles in territorial (most often clonal) defence, as these structures are employed only against conspecific anemones of different genotype (section 7.2.1). Several species of anemones extrude acontia when attacked by predatory nudibranchs. Rather than discharging spiny nematocysts that would anchor them to the predator and render escape behaviours useless, these anemones employ detachable darts (formed when the spines of certain microbasic p-mastigophores are stripped from the everted tube) (section 7.4.1, page 312). The usually large size of acontial nematocysts may also be associated with their defensive role.

Certain aliciid anemones have stalked, branching outgrowths of the column. These 'pseudotentacles' concentrate zooxanthellae, which are sparse in the feeding tentacles. In *Lebrunia* spp., the pseudotentacles and feeding tentacles show complementary diurnal rhythms of extension and contraction, the former expanding during the day to capture photons and the latter expanding at night to capture prey. The cnidome of the pseudotentacles, which do not adhere to potential prey, is distinct from that of the tentacles, and the pseudotentacular cnidae (extremely large macro- and microbasic amastigophores) are restricted to subspherical vesicles scattered on the branches. The failure of the pseudotentacles to capture prey, and the intense nettling of their vesicles to human skin, suggest that their large amastigo-phores have a special role in defence against potential predators. This is particularly the case in large individuals of *Phyllodiscus semoni*, whose seem-ingly vulnerable pseudotentacles are not readily retracted, and which moreover remain extended day and night; the amastigophores in the vesicles of this species are much more painful and damaging to human skin than are the nematocysts (b-mastigophores and microbasic p-mastigophores) in the tentacles (personal observation). By leaving the detached thread in the capsule and everting only the much thicker and heavily spined shaft, it may be that the already-large amastigophores increase both their penetrating ability and the dosage of venom injected.

It is not known whether the structure of the spines in particular types of nematocysts bears any relation to the toxicity of their venom, nor whether different toxins are associated with particular nematocysts. Interestingly, Schmidt and Béress (1971) found that toxicity of actiniarians (assayed by injection of crude toxin into crabs) showed no correspondence with the ability of the anemones to nettle human skin. For example, although *Alicia mirabilis* was far more nettling than the actiniid *Cribrinopsis crassa*, the actiniid was ten times more toxic to crabs. We now know that the neurotoxic and nettling (cytolytic) actions of nematocysts are caused by different molecules, which in some cases are probably contained in different nematocysts (see below). However, these authors found that nettling intensity was not necessarily associated with the possession of, for example, 'p-rhabdoids' (i.e. p-mastigophores, which include amastigophores). Although the highly nettling *A.mirabilis* has large amastigophores in its columnar vesicles (Carlgren, 1949), the notorious nettler *Actinodendron plumosum* (Saville-Kent, 1893, p. 146) lacks p-mastigophores altogether (Carlgren, 1949; Schmidt, 1974). Schmidt also speculates that the evolutionary reduction in distribution, size and structural complexity of nematocysts in the Actiniaria is compensated by their generally higher toxicity, especially in the endomyarian anemones.

1.5.3 Toxins

All of the toxins characterized from whole anemones or their isolated nematocysts are peptides or proteins (Béress, 1982; Kem, 1988a, b). Various of these compounds act as neurotoxins, as painful cytolysins, and as antiproteinases that interfere with vertebrate blood coagulation. The action of the first two in prey capture and predator deterrence are obvious, but the biological relevance of the last is uncertain (see Bikfalvi *et al.*, 1988).

Early work (Béress, Béress and Wunderer, 1975) on *Anemonia viridis* revealed two sorts of peptide neurotoxins, a short toxin having 27 amino acids and a molecular weight of about 3 kDa, and several long toxins having chain lengths of 46 or 47 amino acids and molecular weights of about 5 kDa (Schweitz *et al.*, 1981). Similar long toxins have been found in other actiniid anemones, including *Condylactis gigantea* and *Anthopleura xanthogrammica*, and these 'type 1' toxins are immunologically distinct from the long 'type 2'

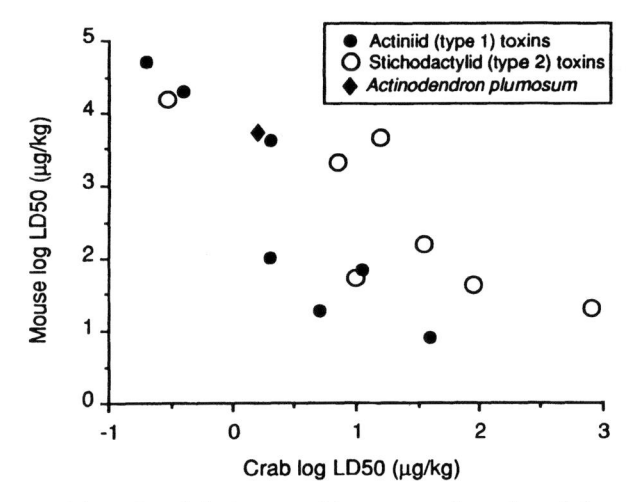

Figure 1.11 Toxicity of actiniarian peptide neurotoxins when injected into body cavities of mice and crabs. See text for discussion. Source: data for actiniid and stichodactylid toxins compiled by Kem (1988a, b); data on mouse LD_{50} and crab LD_{100} for actinodendrid toxin from Schweitz *et al.* (1981).

toxins in stichodactylid anemones, although they share about 30% sequence homology (Schweitz *et al.*, 1985; Kem, 1988a). There exists further a number of cytolytic toxins ranging from 10 to 135 kDa in a taxonomic potpourri of anemones (Béress, 1982; Kem, 1988a, b).

The sea anemone neurotoxins are of particular interest because they all act by slowing the rate of Na^+ channel inactivation and thus prolong the repolarization phase in excitable membranes. This causes massive release of neurotransmitter leading to convulsions and paralysis of prey. There is an interesting inverse relationship between the toxicity of an individual type 1 or type 2 toxin to crabs and to mice (Figure 1.11). This occurs despite the seemingly small structural differences between some toxins: the toxins representing the extreme points at either end of the regression for type 2 toxins in Figure 1.11 differ in only ten amino acids (Kem, 1988a). It is too soon to speculate whether the data in this figure represent specializations for subduing crustacean or other prey. It would be useful to know their comparative toxicities to vertebrates such as fish, more likely than mice as prey for these anemones. In this context it is also interesting that isolated neurons of a crustacean are highly sensitive to toxin AS-II from *A. viridis*, whereas neurons of a cephalopod are insensitive to it (Romey *et al.*, 1976).

Sea anemone peptide toxins are being used to analyse the molecular topography of the sodium channel, especially as proteinaceous binding sites that are resistant to puffer fish toxin (tetrodotoxin, TTX) are extremely sensitive to anemone toxins (Frelin *et al.*, 1984). Because anemone type 1 toxins have the same binding sites as scorpion α toxins yet show no sequence homology with them (El Ayeb *et al.*, 1986), their similarity may lie in their convergent evolution of secondary structures that place hydrophobic residues in a position to interact with the binding site (Gooley and Norton, 1986). The effect of anemone neurotoxins on the Na^+ channel, transient but without altering the cell's resting potential, also gives them potential as therapeutic alternatives to digitalis glycosides (which inhibit the sodium pump and so reduce the resting membrane potential) in treating congestive heart failure (Kem, 1988a, b). By delaying closure of the sodium channel, anemone toxins temporarily enhance influx of sodium into cardiac cells, which in turn may promote Ca^{2+} release from the sarcoplasmic reticulum and so increase the strength of ventricular contraction (i.e. they have a positive inotropic effect).

The cytolysins are a heterogeneous group of proteins that do not appear to bind to protein receptor sites on the cell membrane. Rather, they have affinities for certain membrane lipids such as sphingomyelin (Bernheimer and Avigad, 1976). One class of cytolysins (10–20 kDa) found in actiniid and stichodactylid anemones produces a pore in the cell membrane through which ions may leak, leading Kem (1988b) to call them 'actinoporins'. The complex of cytolytic proteins in *Aiptasia pallida* includes phospholipase A activity that is Ca^{2+} dependent (Hessinger, Lenhoff and Kahan, 1973; Hessinger and Lenhoff, 1976). It is possible that the Ca^{2+} is provided by the discharging nematocyst itself (section 1.5.4 below).

The localization of a cytolysin in the mesenteric filaments of *Metridium senile* suggests a role in the fragmentation of prey prior to its digestion. The function of some cytolysins may be only secondarily lytic, their primary effect being the production of pain, inflammation and neuromuscular paralysis (Kem, 1988a). The localization of several known cytolysins in acontial nematocysts is in keeping with such defensive actions against potential predators. Purely defensive structures such as the vesicles on the pseudotentacles of particularly nettling aliciid anemones would be good candidates to yield high concentrations of cytolysins, and owing to their simple cnidomes (see above), for discerning the association of particular toxins with particular types of nematocysts.

1.5.4 Discharge

Classically considered to be effectors independent of distal control (e.g. Parker, 1919), cnidae are now recognized to be affected by factors beyond the cnidocyte. At the organismal level, this is evident from the threshold for discharge of tentacular cnidae in *Calliactis parasitica* being lower when the anemone's base is not attached to a hermit crab's shell than when it is attached (McFarlane and Shelton, 1975). Thresholds are lower in starved as compared with satiated specimens of *Calliactis tricolor* (Sandberg, 1972), and in *Pseudactinia melanaster* ($\equiv$ *Anemonia sargassensis*) following mechanical stimulation of the column (Conklin and Mariscal, 1976).

Working with *Anthopleura elegantissima*, McKay and Anderson (1988a) showed that isolated but otherwise structurally and functionally intact cnidocytes were less likely to discharge in response to chemical and mechanical stimulation than were cnidocytes *in situ*, suggesting that in their natural condition their discharge is affected by adjacent supporting cells and neurons. This suggestion is particularly apt in view of ultrastructural and cytochemical studies showing that putative receptors in anemones are actually multicellular structures (see Fautin and Mariscal, 1990), and that the binding sites of at least one type of chemoreceptor are on supporting cells and not the cnidocyte itself (Watson and Hessinger, 1987). McKay and Anderson's (1988a) electrophysiological recordings from isolated, voltage-clamped cnidocytes revealed that cnidae do not discharge in response to changes in membrane potential. This result led them to conclude (1988b) that an alternative transduction mechanism, perhaps an intracellular second messenger, exists.

The actual mechanism of cnida discharge is not yet understood. The osmotic hypothesis holds that the intracapsular pressure rises by the uptake of water, perhaps owing to the removal of stabilizing Ca^{2+} from aggregated proteins, allowing them to dissociate and so increase the internal osmotic pressure (Blanquet, 1970; Lubbock, Gupta and Hall, 1981). In the 'stopper' hypothesis, internal osmotic pressure is constant, and cnida discharge occurs when the appropriate stimulus somehow opens the tripartite flaps on the capsule's apex. Neither of the prevailing hypotheses can universally account for the data on different cnidae, especially as some cnidae contain not calcium but large amounts of phosphorus (Mariscal, 1984, 1988), and since opening of the flaps is not necessarily followed immediately by discharge of the shaft (Godknecht and Tardent, 1988). Aspects of both hypotheses may be involved (see Salleo, La Spada and Denaro, 1988). Furthermore, dimensional changes occurring during discharge of the shaft are consistent with an osmotically generated increase in the volume of the nematocyst, whereas the evagination of the tube is driven by the release of tension stored in its twists and coils during nematogenesis (Godknecht and Tardent, 1988). Additional complications include the structural diversity of cnidae, which might imply different discharge mechanisms (Fautin and Mariscal, 1990), and the effects of different isolation procedures on the discharge characteristics of nematocysts (Hidaka and Mariscal, 1988).

1.6 WHY AREN'T THERE ANY COLONIAL SEA ANEMONES?

Based on analysis of their nematocysts and other microanatomical features, Schmidt (1974) has proposed that the order Madreporaria (including scleractinian corals) shares a common ancestor with the stem form of the order

Actiniaria, and that the Zoantharia (≡ Zoanthidea) are descended from a common ancestor with advanced endomyarian actiniarians (see Figure 1.1 and Appendix). These relationships may also bear on the distribution of coloniality (functional and continuous connection of modular units) in the Hexacorallia. Although individual modules can be linked to produce colonial forms, sea anemones lack this innovation, despite the prolific asexual duplication of individuals in some species. Epithelial construction does not preclude colony formation, which is common among the Hydrozoa and Scyphozoa, and indeed among most other Anthozoa. The absence of coloniality from actiniarians and ceriantharians alone among the Anthozoa demands consideration. An explanation may lie in their evolutionary backgrounds, ecologies and life histories.

The oldest Anthozoa have been thought to be the Octocorallia. Typically colonial, they have been so since the late Precambrian (Scrutton, 1979), if Ediacaran sea pens are indeed octocorals. If Ediacaran sea pens are disallowed as Octocorallia (Ford, 1979; Seilacher, 1989; and page 3 above), then the earliest representative of this subclass (a gorgonian) is of middle Cambrian age (Scrutton, 1979), younger than the first possible actinian body fossil from the lower Cambrian (Seilacher, 1983). It is not known whether the Octocorallia and Hexacorallia had a common (Actinula-like?) ancestor (Schmidt, 1974); if so, it must have been very early and prior to the development of coloniality, given the great antiquity of both Ediacaran colonial 'octocorals' and solitary anemones, or even lower to middle Cambrian representatives of these groups.

The Cambrian radiation of life was a time of increased predation and cropping of epifauna. In infaunal cerianthids, from which the other Hexacorallia diverged quite early, the stereotyped response to epibenthic predators is rapid withdrawal into the tube. The antecedents of burrowing actiniarians such as *Peachia* also date back to the lower Cambrian as trace fossils (Scrutton, 1979; Runnegar, 1982); anemones apparently lived epifaunally on sandy bottoms then as well (Seilacher, 1983). Epifaunal anthozoans avoided predatory croppers by growing large, by becoming skeletonized (Brasier, 1979), or sometimes by swimming. It is presumed that a line of small anemones swam by flexing longitudinal muscles in their tentacular ectoderm, a feature still seen in the primitive Protantheae among the Actiniaria and in the swimming arachnanthid larvae of Ceriantharia, and paralleled in the rhythmic pulsations of the tentacles in some octocorals (Robson, 1966; Schmidt, 1974). Ancestral actiniarian anemones opted for large individual size, whereas an offshoot from their common ancestor with the corals opted for skeletonization.

The large size of sea anemones is related to the multiplicity of their 'meristematic zones' (Grebel'nyi, 1981), where new pairs of mesenteries arise both in endocoels and exocoels around the full circumference of the polyp. As predators became larger, many anemones may have been chased into inter-tidal refuges, where asexual binary fission produced extensive clonal aggre-gations of moderately large individuals that monopolized space in the face of intraspecific competition (section 7.2, page 279). Those epifaunal ane-mones that remained sublittoral emphasized large individual size and re-mained aclonal (also see Francis, 1988), which precluded coloniality. Scler-actinians, however, by becoming colonial added the benefits of increased skeletal strength and stability (i.e. reef building), and a mechanism of com-peting for space. Despite the presence of multiple, radially arranged mer-istematic zones, however, coloniality seems to constrain the size of individual single-mouthed coral polyps, perhaps owing to mechanical properties of the skeleton.

The lack of coloniality in clonal intertidal anemones may relate to the mechanical difficulty in closely conjoined members of a sheet-like colony of symmetrical retraction of the tentacles and retention of the coelenteric fluid as defences against desiccation. In a stoloniferous colony, thin inter-polyp connections presumably would be susceptible to dehydration. In both cases, the lack of coloniality in anemones seems related further to their lack of an extraorganismal covering. This is also indicated by corallimorpharians (which superficially resemble anemones but are more closely related to scleractinians: Schmidt, 1974), some of which maintain tenuous connections between clonemates, but are not truly colonial in physiological integration. Sublittoral and without a protective exoskeleton, corallimorpharians survive predation and interference competition by being large (e.g. *Amplexidiscus*: Dunn and Hamner, 1980) or by having particularly large and noxious nema-tocysts (e.g. *Corynactis*: Annett and Pierotti, 1984, and Chadwick, 1987).

In the Zoantharia, where polyp size seems to be constrained by restriction of new mesenteries to the ventro-lateral exocoels (Hyman, 1940; Grebel'nyi, 1981) so that older mesenteries are increasingly crowded together, avoidance of predation has involved development of especially high toxicity (Moore and Scheuer, 1971; Schmidt, 1974) and a rudimentary form of coloniality (so far as physiological integration is concerned: Horridge, 1957). Lacking an exoskeleton and even the axial rod and calcareous spicules found in colonial Octocorallia, zoanthid colonies form simple runners and sheets (Jackson, 1979). However, the ectoderm and mesoglea are impregnated with sand grains, foraminiferan tests etc., which provide support and toughness be-yond that of tissue alone. Colonial zoanthids thus have a periderm and common coenenchyme into which the small polyps can withdraw, affording some protection from predation and desiccation. The latter is important because, owing perhaps to their secondary loss of radial symmetry of the mesenteries, zoantharian polyps seem less efficient than sea anemones in retaining water in the coelenteron when contracted.

Still, it is not clear whether the small polyp size in zoanthids necessitated coloniality (to increase effective size and reduce the free surface area in the face of predation and desiccation), or whether coloniality and encrustation of the coenenchyme restricted the size of polyps. Modules of large-polyped species (e.g. *Palythoa variabilis*) are less closely packed and their columns are connected along less of their length (i.e. they form less integrated colonies) than are those of small-polyped species (e.g. *P.caribaeorum*). These differences may represent mechanical compensations for the different water flow regimes inhabited by the two species (Koehl, 1977d), and the question of which came first in zoanthids, small polyp size or coloniality, remains unanswered. In some tropical habitats the weakly colonial zoanthids seem to be the ecological replacement of intertidal and shallow sublittoral, clonally aggregating sea anemones capable of monopolizing large expanses of substrate. Such replacement may be related also to protection of the tissues by the encrusted coenenchyme from the damaging effects of the tropical sun (also see section 2.7.3, page 112). The protective roles of the zoantharian coenenchyme are presaged in littoral actiniid anemones that attach debris to their columns.

It seems that 'anemones' (including but not limited to the Actiniaria) are an ancient group that adopted early the strategy of large individual size and unitary lifestyle in response to sublittoral predators; when released from predation in intertidal refuges, they emphasized clonal replication of aggregated but anatomically discrete units during intraspecific spatial competition. While not themselves colonial, one line of early 'anemones' gave rise to the scleractinians and another to the older rugose corals (Wells, 1956; Oliver, 1980), which skeletonized groups independently may show evolutionary trends from solitary to colonial forms (Hill, 1956; Wells, 1956). Zoantharians are viewed as reduced forms derived from a common ancestor with the advanced endomyarian anemones (Schmidt, 1974). The weak coloniality in zoantharians seems enabled by the rudiments of an exoskeleton, at least in the context of its protective function.

Conversely, if the Actiniaria are descended from the Scleractinia, as Hand (1966) has argued, one must explain the *loss* of a calcareous exoskeleton in the Actiniaria. Given the centrality of such exoskeletons to the persistence of other metazoan taxa (e.g. barnacles, molluscs and polychaetes) in the intertidal zone, the loss of skeletonization in anemones, which are particularly successful intertidally, might seem unlikely. However, the phenomenon of polyp 'bail-out', in which individual scleractinian polyps may detach from their neighbours and the corallite during times of stress and subsequently settle elsewhere (Sammarco, 1982), provides a potential mechanism whereby a colonial, skeletonized coral could give rise to a solitary, unskeletonized 'anemone'.

This does not address Hand's central argument that mesenteric pairing has possible adaptive significance in the Scleractinia by allowing complete retraction of the polyp into the exoskeleton and around its internal calcareous septa without trapping stagnant pockets of coelenteric fluid. Finding no similar adaptive advantage of pairing for askeletal anemones, he therefore concludes that scleractinians came first, with mesenteric pairing being retained but having no functional significance in their actiniarian descendants.

A potential advantage for paired mesenteries in the Actiniaria, however, is that they might allow a more symmetrical and finely controlled retraction of the oral disc and upper column, by virtue of the symmetrical distribution of retractor muscles on the opposing endocoelic faces of mesenteric pairs. Such controlled contraction seems particularly important in intertidal anemones, where the sub-globoid shape retains coelenteric fluid during aerial exposure (Stotz, 1979). Contraction of retractor muscles on opposing faces of paired mesenteries presumably collapses those mesenteries into the endocoelic space, displacing a corresponding volume of liquid into the exocoelic space (Figure 1.3). Contraction of unpaired retractors located on the same face of every mesentery might result in a more complete collapse of the body and loss of most of the coelenteric fluid, the contracted mesenteries overlapping like fallen dominoes and occupying most of the volume of the coelenteron. Thorough retraction of the oral disc and tentacles without totally collapsing the column and losing the coelenteric fluid is potentially advantageous even to subtidal anemones. It would protect them from predation (both by shielding the vulnerable tentacles — section 7.4.1, page 311 — and by maintaining a large body size), as well as reduce the energetic cost of pumping in water to reinflate the anemone. This, then, is the converse of Hand's argument, which emphasized the importance of *expulsion* of the coelenteric fluid from contracting corals.

If these speculations are accepted, then Hand's postulated evolution of the Actiniaria from the Scleractinia is unnecessary, and the more traditional view of corals arising as calcified anemones is reinforced (Wells, 1956; Oliver, 1980). Still, the phenomenon of polyp bail-out (see above), and the existence of self/non-self recognition abilities in anemones (discussed in the context of the 'somatic cell parasitism hypothesis' and fusion avoidance in corals: see section 7.2.1, page 285) might argue for Hand's phylogeny. The matter is far from being settled.

Because of their familiarity to most visitors to temperate seashores, sea anemones are often used as a skeletonless model in describing less familiar corals (Yonge, 1930; Hyman, 1940). Although this provides a reasonable description of common aspects of their polypoid architecture and perhaps of their biochemistry (Grasshoff, 1981; Kellogg and Patton, 1983), it is also an oversimplification that masks fundamental differences in their growth form and population structure. The latter topics are discussed in Chapters 5 and 6.

2 Nutrition

2.1 SYNOPSIS

Sea anemones have been characterized as predatory behaviour machines and their feeding biology has interested generations of biologists. The cnidocytes and their contained cnidae play a central role in prey capture, responding to mechanical and chemical stimuli from animal prey. The epitome of sit-and-wait predators, sea anemones minimize the energetic cost of obtaining food and so may have relatively high growth efficiencies. Rather than being strict carnivores, however, they emerge as polyphagous opportunists, and like many marine invertebrates include dissolved organic matter and particulate organic detritus in their diets. Their digestive capability is correspondingly broad, and includes enzymes that act extracellularly to fragment large prey, as well as intracellular digestive enzymes that act on small particles taken up by phagocytes. Their polytrophic nature extends even to the level of primary producer in individuals harbouring intracellular algal symbionts. The influence of such endosymbiosis has ramifications not only in energy transfer but also in the recycling of nutrients and nitrogenous wastes, in photobiology and behaviour, and in respiratory gas exchange.

2.2 FEEDING

Sea anemones are sessile feeders that rely on water motion or prey loco-motion to transport food to their capture surfaces. Three basic methods are involved in prey capture: planktonic prey are intercepted by the tentacles and transferred to the mouth by muscular or occasionally ciliary action;

sessile prey dislodged by foraging predators or wave action fall or are washed onto the tentacles or oral disc; and motile prey may blunder into the tentacles. Some specialized tropical corallimorpharians (*Actinodiscus and Discosoma*) capture large and small prey by enveloping them with the entire oral disc (Hamner and Dunn, 1980; Elliott and Cook, 1989).

2.2.1 The Prey Capture Surface

Anemones having numerous fine tentacles or long filamentous tentacles are primarily planktivorous, whereas anemones having large thick tentacles prey on other macrofauna. In the planktivorous, rheophilic species *Metridium senile*, small particles captured on the numerous tentacles by cnidae or mucus are transported to the mouth by ciliary currents. The delicate *Protanthea simplex* inhabits areas of minimal water movement (Manuel, 1988) and, hence, low frequency of prey encounters. Its ubiquitous ectodermal ciliation directed toward ingestion (Carlgren, 1905) probably entrains particles contacting any portion of its body surface. Macrophagous species such as *Urticina felina* ($\equiv$ *Tealia coriacea*), *Actinostola callosa* and *Bolocera tuediae* ($\equiv$ *B.longicornis*) have tentacles heavily armed with cnidae and show a great reduction in ectodermal ciliation (Carlgren, 1905).

Few morphometric data on the prey capture surface of sea anemones are available. As Sebens (1981a) has shown, the frequency of prey contact depends on the projected area of the tentacle crown normal to the direction of current flow, or in turbulent flow on the total surface area available to intercept items, which in *Anthopleura elegantissima* includes the surface area of the tentacles plus that of the oral disc (Zamer, 1986). In *Anthopleura xanthogrammica*, which feeds on dislodged mussels falling onto its tentacles and oral disc, projected surface area (S_m) of this 'target' is the more relevant measure. In the planktivorous *Metridium senile*, prey may be captured by direct interception (Rubenstein and Koehl, 1977) in the eddies within its bushy tentacle crown, as well as by deposition of motile plankton or of sinking negatively buoyant particles onto the tentacles. In this case total tentacle surface area (S_t) may be more informative, especially since the size of prey captured is less than the distance between adjacent tentacles (Sebens and Koehl, 1984).

All of the above surface measures increase approximately isometrically with anemone body size, i.e. at about the 0.67 power of dry body mass ($_dW$) or as approximately the square of basal disc diameter (D). In *A.elegantissima* $S_m = 15.6\,_dW^{0.43}$ and $S_t = 58\,_dW^{0.54}$; in *A.xanthogrammica* $S_m = 13.9\,_dW^{0.74}$ and $S_t = 41\,_dW^{0.87}$; in *M.senile* $S_m = 119\,_dW^{0.72}$ and $S_t = 353\,_dW^{0.84}$ (Sebens, 1981a). In *A.elegantissima*, total area of the prey capture surface (PCSA) = $8.74\,D^{1.74}$ in high-shore anemones, and PCSA = $5.87\,D^{1.93}$ in low-shore specimens (Zamer, 1986). Unlike *Anthopleura* spp., *M.senile* continually adds tentacles as it grows. Although this does not increase the volume of

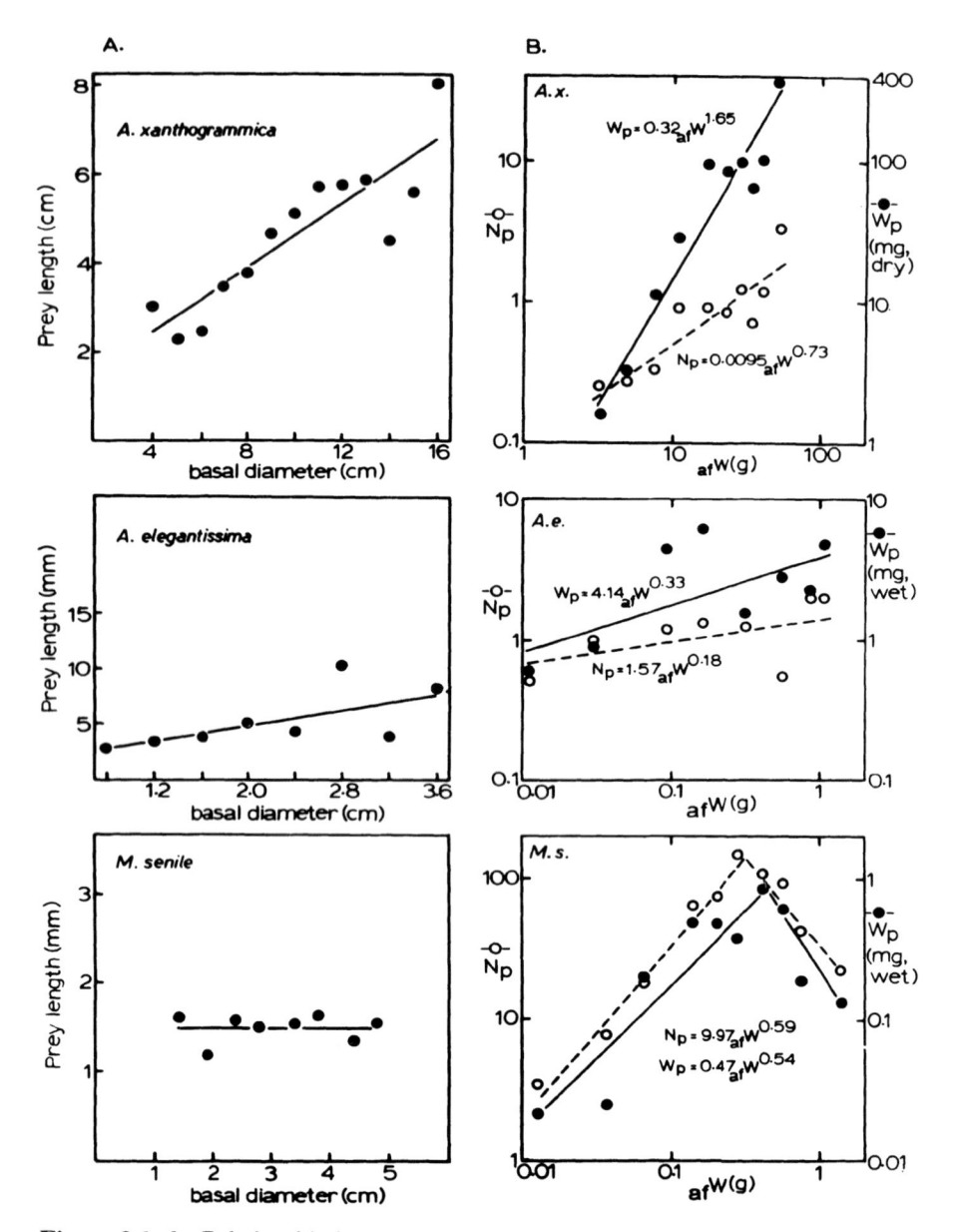

Figure 2.1 A. Relationship between mean length of prey captured and sea anemone basal diameter. **B.** Numbers (N_p) and wet weight (W_p) of natural prey in the coelenterons of freshly-collected sea anemones related to individual anemone ash-free dry weight ($_{af}W$). The relationship of prey capture to anemone body size apparently changes in larger specimens of *M. senile*; the equation given is for the entire data set. See text for further discussion. Source: modified from Sebens (1981a).

water crossing the tentacle crown, it does increase the surface area of tentacles per unit volume flow, which may be necessary for efficient capture of its very small prey, especially in the low flow velocity of its habitat (see below).

The number of natural prey captured by the above three species is approximately related to feeding surface area (0.18 to 0.73 power of weight) (Figure 2.1B). Because neither *M.senile* nor *A.elegantissima* significantly increases the size of prey taken as the anemone grows larger (Figure 2.1A), the weight exponents for prey biomass and prey numbers captured are similar (Figure 2.1B). *A.xanthogrammica*, a large anemone in which the diameter of the oral disc may reach 20 cm, takes larger prey as it grows, so the exponent of prey biomass is much greater than that of prey numbers. Sebens has used these allometric data on prey (energy) intake in conjunction with those on metabolic rate (energy utilization) to formulate an optimal size model for these sea anemones (see sections 5.8, page 219, and 6.4.2, page 258). The rather different prey captured by these anemones (see Figure 2.1A and Table 2.1) is related to differences among them in morphology and habitat, especially the current regime experienced.

2.2.2 Relationships to Water Currents

Anthopleura xanthogrammica on the Pacific shores of temperate North America inhabits the wave-swept open coast, often carpeting surge channels where the maximum speed of the current mainstream may be as great as $3-5 \text{ m·s}^{-1}$. Logs and other floating debris carried by such currents, and foraging sea stars, dislodge mussels which are washed onto the anemones' oral discs (Dayton, 1973). The flow experienced by the anemones is less than that of the mainstream, however, as they do not extend their columns, and by remaining short (a specimen having an oral disc diameter of 10 cm may stand only 2.5 cm tall) effectively hide in the slow-moving boundary layer (Figure 2.2) where the surge velocity is only about 0.2 m·s^{-1} (Koehl, 1977a). Perhaps as an adaptation to the short period between shoreward and seaward flows in the surge channels, the mesoglea of *A.xanthogrammica* is relatively inextensible and recoils elastically between wave impacts, a mechanical property owing to the close packing of collagen fibrils and high concentration of interfibrillar polymers in the mesoglea (Koehl, 1977b; section 1.2.2, page 13).

Anthopleura elegantissima, which also occupies surge channels and exposed intertidal sites, likewise avoids the current mainstream and experiences even lower velocities than *A.xanthogrammica* by virtue of its smaller size. Current-induced drag on *A.elegantissima* individuals is further reduced by their living in densely-packed clonal aggregations (produced asexually by longitudinal fission), which reduces the free surface area of their columns. Both its smaller

Table 2.1 Naturally occurring prey in sea anemones, as percent of total items captured by all anemones sampled, or percent of sampled anemones in which the item occurred

Species of anemone	Coelenteron contents	% of items	Frequency of occurrence (%)	Source
Actinia equina	Crustaceans			Van-Praët
(78 specimens)	Crustacean fragments		23.1	(personal communication)
	Small decapods		11.5	
	Carcinus appendages		3.8	
	Amphipods		2.6	
	Gnathia		1.3	
	Polychaete fragments		12.8	
	Insects		7.7	
	Algal detritus		6.4	
	Fish eggs		2.6	
	Medusa		1.3	
	Mussels (*Mytilus edulis*)		Common[a]	Van-Praët (1983a)
Actinia tenebrosa	Foraminiferans	47.1	1.0	Ayre (1984a)
(3 189 specimens)	Insects	39.7	0.8	
	Gastropods	10.3	0.2	
	Decapod crustaceans	2.9	<0.1	
	Scyphozoans	2.9	<0.1	
Anemonia viridis	Crustaceans		61.9	Möller (1978)
(≡ *A. sulcata*)	Copepods		16.2	
(160 specimens)	Barnacle remains		11.9	
	Amphipods		10.0	
	Decapods (adult)		8.1	
	Euphausids		3.1	
	Isopods		2.5	
	Decapods (larval)		1.9	
	Ostracods		1.2	

	Molluscs		28.1
	Gastropods		26.8
	Lamellibranchs		3.1
	Chitons		0.6
	Insects		16.2
	Polychaetes		15.6
	Algal remains		15.0
	Fish		3.1
	Hydroids		2.5
	Nematodes		2.5
	Bryozoans		2.5
Anthopleura elegantissima	Molluscs			Sebens (1981a)
(112 specimens)	Bivalves	15.8	
	Gastropods	9.6	
	Chitons	5.3	
	Crustaceans		
	Barnacles, barnacle molts	7.9	
	Barnacle cyprids	1.8	
	Amphipods	3.5	
	Isopods	6.3	
	Copepods	2.7	
	Decapods	2.7	
	Decapod fragments	5.3	
	Crustacean fragments	7.1	
	Bryozoan colony fragments	7.9	
	Hydroid colony fragments	7.1	
	Polychaetes	7.1	
	Echinoid spines	1.8	
	Foraminiferans	1.8	
	Eggs	2.7	
	Flatworm	0.9	
	Insect fragment	0.9	
	Mite	0.9	

Table 2.1 Continued

Species of anemone	Coelenteron contents	% of items	Frequency of occurrence (%)	Source
	Plant material (algae, eelgrass, terrestrial plant fragments)	34.7[b]		
Anthopleura xanthogrammica (481 specimens)	Molluscs			Sebens (1981a)
	Bivalves (*Mytilus*)	68.9		
	Gastropods	3.4		
	Crustaceans			
	Barnacles, barnacle molts	23.7		
	Decapods	2.3		
	Colonial ascidians	1.1		
	Echinoid	0.6		
A.xanthogrammica (226 specimens)	Molluscs			Dayton (1973)
	Bivalves (mostly *Mytilus*)	70.7		
	Gastropods	0.4		
	Crustaceans			
	Barnacles	18.1		
	Decapods	7.0		
	Echinoids	2.7		
	Fish	0.8		
Haliplanella lineata (≡ *H.luciae*) (55 specimens)	Copepods	76.4	57.4	Williams (1972b)
	Corophium volutator	9.0	14.9	
	Ostracods	7.9	14.9	
	Idotea sp(p).	5.6	10.6	
	Gammarids	1.1	2.1	
Heteractis malu (90 specimens)	Gastropods			Peterson and Black (1986)
	Swimming opistobranch	25		
	Others	25		

	Crustaceans		
	Amphipods	16.7	
	Decapod	8.3	
	Mysid	8.3	
	Mussel (*Mytilus edulis*)	8.3	
	Seagrass blade	8.3	
Metridium senile[c]	Crustaceans		Purcell (1977a)
(approx. 300 specimens)	Copepods	30	
	Nauplii (copepod, barnacle)	5	
	Cypris larvae	10	
	Decapod larvae, small crabs (2 mm), barnacle molts, amphipods, ostracods, crustacean fecal pellets	Present	
	Molluscs		
	Bivalve larvae	34	
	Gastropod larvae	6	
	Polychaetes		
	Larvae	10	
	Adults	5	
	Sponge spicules, fecal pellets, nematodes, flesh scraps, echinoderm larvae, cyphonautes larvae, opistobranchs, sipunculids, flatworms, detritus	Present	
Metridium giganteum	Crustaceans		Purcell (1977a)
(50 specimens)	Copepods	42	
	Cypris larvae	15	
	Decapod larvae, amphipods	Present	

Table 2.1 Continued

Species of anemone	Coelenteron contents	% of items	Frequency of occurrence (%)	Source
	Molluscs			
	Bivalve larvae	30		
	Gastropod larvae	2		
	Polychaetes			
	Larvae	10		
	Adults	Present		
	Cyphonautes larvae	1		
	Sponge spicules, fecal pellets, nematodes, flesh scraps, echinoderm larvae, cyphonautes larvae, opistobranchs, sipunculids, flatworms, detritus	Present		
Metridium 'senile'[c,d] (107 specimens)	Crustaceans			Sebens (1981a)
	Barnacle cyprids and nauplii	76.1		
	Copepods	11.1		
	Decapod larvae	3.9		
	Molluscs			
	Bivalve veligers	1.3		
	Gastropod veligers	0.9		
	Bryozoan fragments	1.3		
	Polychaetes	0.5		
	Asteroid bipennariae	0.5		
	Eggs	4.4		
Nematostella vectensis (555 specimens)	Crustaceans			Frank and Bleakney (1978)
	Copepods	26.0		
	Ostracods	7.9		

	Gastropods (*Hydrobia*)	27.7	
	Insects	13.0	
	'Worms' (mostly nematodes)	6.8	
	Rotifer	1.0	
	Egg masses	9.0	
	Unidentified (mostly crustaceans)	9.0	
Urticina (≡ *Tealia*) *piscivora* (10 specimens)	Crustaceans		Sebens and Laakso (1978)
	Cumaceans	35	
	Amphipods	10.5	
	Decapod parts	5.8	
	Barnacle parts	2.3	
	Decapod (juvenile)	1.2	
	Fish		
	Scales	35	
	Entire pholids (15–150 mm)	5.8	
	Gastropod	1.2	
	Insect	1.2	
	Sponge	1.2	
	Hydroid	1.2	

Notes: a. Not quantified but very common, comprising most of the biomass in the coelenterons;
     b. Considered by Sebens to be indigestible and excluded from his percentages;
     c. *Metridium senile* (L.), the clonal species on the North American Pacific coast;
     d. *Metridium giganteum*, the large aclonal species from the North American Pacific sublittoral

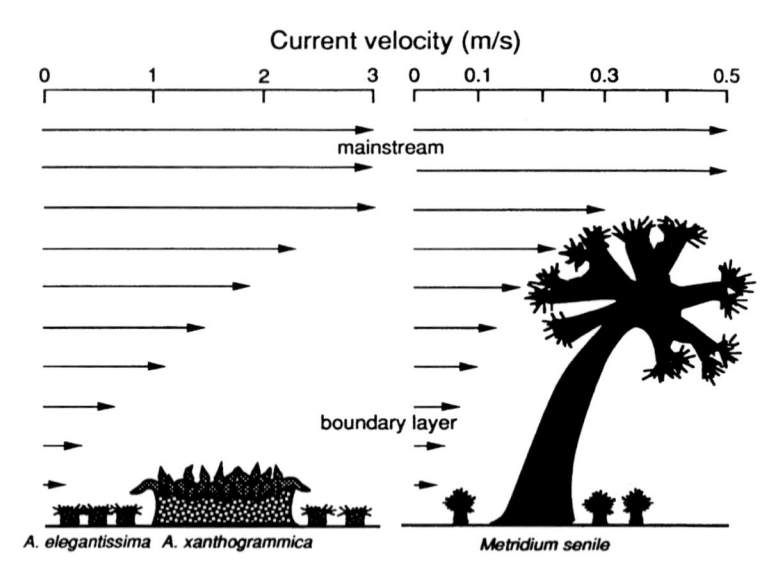

Figure 2.2 Flow regimes experienced in nature by *Anthopleura xanthogrammica* (≈10–15 cm diameter), *A.elegantissima* (≈1–5 cm diameter) and *Metridium senile* (≈0.5–8 cm diameter). See text for discussion.

size and a gentler current regime account for *A.elegantissima's* utilization of predominantly small planktonic prey, although large items such as scyphomedusae may be captured collectively by many clonemates.

Metridium senile (and the larger, aclonal, sublittoral *Metridium* on the North American Pacific coast now described as a separate species, *M.giganteum*: Fautin *et al.*, 1990) is a classic example of a passive suspension feeder on small zooplankton. Large individuals normally occupy habitats where maximum currents rarely exceed 0.5 m·s^{-1} (Koehl, 1977a; Shick, Hoffmann and Lamb, 1979b; Robbins and Shick, 1980; Sebens and Koehl, 1984). This anemone typically assumes a tall columnar shape, its column extending at least 1.5 to 2 times its basal diameter, holding the frilly tentacle crown into the current mainstream (Figure 2.2). At velocities above 0.5 m·s^{-1} the tentacle crown tends to collapse and the anemone may shorten its column, which places the prey capture apparatus in the slower flow nearer the substrate. The slower flow may increase the number of particles retained on the tentacles, for loss of captured particles owing to shear stresses on them increases with current speed (J. Miles, personal communication in Patterson, 1984).

Although the flow experienced by *M.senile* may be less than that on *A.xanthogrammica*, the tall slender shape of the former maximizes tensile stresses on it (Koehl, 1977c). The low flexural stiffness of the upper column of *M.senile* and the greater extensibility of its mesoglea cause it to bend and hold the tentacle crown normal to the current. The greater body wall thickness in *M.senile* than in *A.elegantissima* of the same body mass may be related to the former's need to remain in the erect feeding posture without the column buckling (Shick *et al.*, 1979a).

Very small individuals of *M.senile* produced asexually by basal laceration may be at a particular disadvantage feeding in the slow flow of the boundary layer (Figure 2.2), especially if they are overtopped by other suspension feeders and adult anemones, although some compensation is afforded by their proportionally larger tentacle surface area (Shick *et al.*, 1979a). The need to remain large (tall) and in the current mainstream may select against asexual proliferation by this anemone in very low flow habitats (section 6.4.2, page 262), and the large West Coast *Metridium giganteum* which lives in especially low velocity areas (Koehl, 1977a) does not reproduce asexually. Conversely, very high current constrains individual body size of *M.senile* (Shick *et al.*, 1979b; Shick and Hoffmann, 1980), as very tall anemones would get bent and be unable to feed effectively. Also, because more food is available per unit time in high flow areas (Robbins and Shick, 1980; Shick and Hoffmann, 1980), asexual proliferation is favoured there and thus total biomass of the clone is greater, despite the smaller size of individual anemones (Shick *et al.*, 1979b) (section 5.8, page 223, and 6.4.2). *Metridium senile* on the North American Atlantic coast appears to be an especially plastic species in terms of habitat occupied, growth form and body size, which differences are paralleled in three *Metridium* species on the North American Pacific coast (Bucklin and Hedgecock, 1982).

For the particle sizes and flow velocities routinely encountered by *M. senile*, direct interception is the usual mode of particle capture (Sebens and Koehl, 1984). Sieving does not appear to be a major mechanism, as most of the prey captured by this species are smaller than the gaps between the tentacles. At peak velocities $(0.5 \, \text{m} \cdot \text{s}^{-1})$, inertial impaction (where the momentum of dense particles causes them to leave the flow streamlines and collide with the tentacles) is involved in the capture of large particles. In very slow flow, both gravitational deposition of negatively buoyant particles and direct deposition of motile prey are involved.

2.2.3 Expansion and Contraction Behaviour

The observation of diurnal and tidal rhythms of expansion and contraction of the oral disc and extension and retraction of the tentacles in sea anemones is an old one. In species having intracellular algal symbionts, expansion in daylight promotes photosynthesis by the algae (section 2.7.2, page 111), while in tropical reef anemones expansion at night is related to zooplankton availability (Sebens and DeRiemer, 1977). The persistence of daily and tidal rhythms of expansion and contraction in the laboratory in anemones lacking algal symbionts led to their designation as being 'spontaneous' (Bohn, 1906a) but modifiable by exogenous stimuli (Batham and Pantin, 1950a, b; 1954).

In *Metridium senile*, a major stimulus causing expansion is water movement (Parker, 1919), and even a fully contracted specimen is highly responsive to currents, probably owing to its detection of current-induced deformation of the body wall, the entire hydrostatically supported system acting as a giant Pacinian corpuscle (a pressure-sensitive, capsular mechanoreceptor in vertebrates). The mechanoreceptors in *Metridium* may include sensory cells in the parietal region of the mesenteries (Batham, Pantin and Robson, 1960), which acting through the slow conduction system of the endoderm (SS2), inhibit contraction of the parietal muscles (McFarlane, 1974). Ectodermal 'ciliary cone' mechanoreceptors not associated with nematocysts (section 2.2.10, page 65) may act via the SS1 to inhibit contraction of the ectodermal radial muscles of the oral disc (McFarlane and Lawn, 1972) and via trans-mesogleal connections to stimulate contraction of

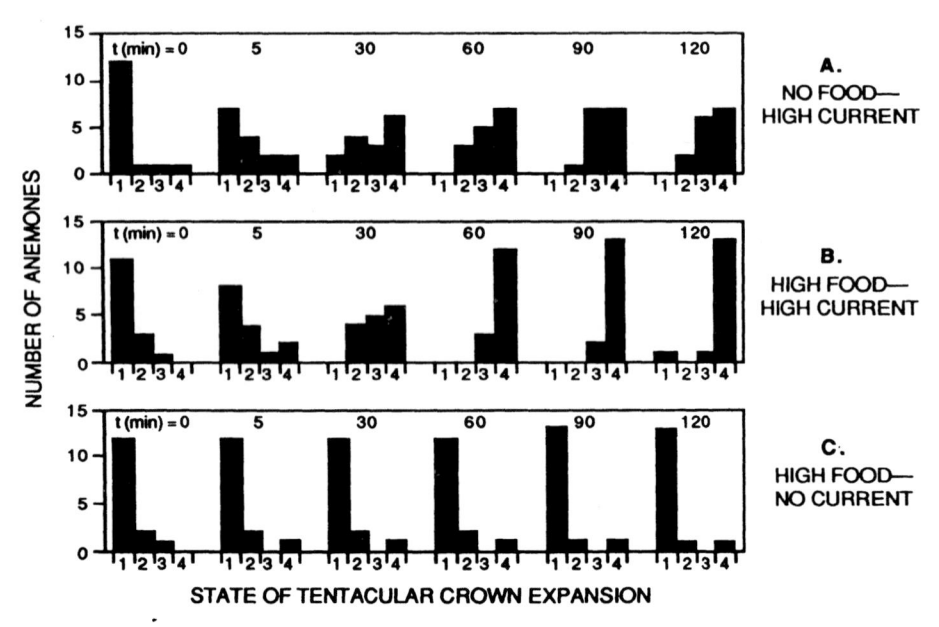

Figure 2.3 Time course of tentacle crown expansion in *Metridium senile* in a flow tank. Numbers on the abscissa indicate expansion states ranging from 1 (fully contracted) to 4 (fully expanded). **A.** Current $30 \, cm \cdot s^{-1}$, no prey available. **B.** Current $30 \, cm \cdot s^{-1}$, 460 *Artemia salina* nauplii/litre available. **C.** No current, 460 *A.salina* nauplii/litre available. Current is the major stimulus eliciting expansion, but prey must be present for a maximum sustained response. Planktonic prey are apparently not detected by contracted specimens of this species in the absence of water currents. See text for further discussion. Source: modified from Robbins and Shick (1980).

endodermal circular muscles (McFarlane, 1976). The net result would be an anemone with an elongated column and expanded oral disc.

Metridium senile inhabits areas having pronounced but gentle tidal currents, and is heavily dependent on them to carry small particles to its tentacles. In such habitats, periodic increases in current speed are good predictors of increasing food availability (Robbins and Shick, 1980). An anemone expanding initially in response to current ('clamouring under the tide', as D.H. Lawrence expressed it) will expose the receptors on its tentacles to available prey, which must be present along with current to effect sustained expansion (Figure 2.3). Considering the apparently few types of differentiated sensory receptors in sea anemones (sections 1.4, 2.2.9 and 2.2.10), it follows that those present will be attuned to the critical features of the environment; in a specialized passive suspension feeder, water flow is an effective stimulus. Contraction at slack water conserves energy by reducing the rate of aerobic metabolism (section 3.8.2, page 149) when few prey are available. The partial expansion seen in many individuals at slack water in habitats rich in suspended particulate detritus probably allows capture of detritus by gravitational deposition.

Unlike the sublittoral *M. senile*, the intertidal *A. elegantissima* spends most of its time expanded, except in very bright sunlight or when exposed to air at low tide. Its greater time expanded is related to illumination of its symbiotic algae in daylight, as well as its greater ability to take larger motile prey and lesser reliance on food brought by tidal currents.

2.2.4 Diet of Sea Anemones

It is clear that differences among species of sea anemones with respect to their morphology and habitats are associated with a wide variety of foods. From anecdotal accounts dating back at least to Aristotle, sea anemones emerge not only as classic sit-and-wait predators, but also as supreme opportunists (e.g. Ayre, 1984a). Despite the fascination their feeding biology has held for biologists, however, there are few quantitative studies of the relative frequencies of prey captured by anemones in nature, and even fewer data on the ration size (biomass) that they ingest.

Table 2.1 summarizes quantitative studies on the natural prey eaten by sea anemones. 'Crustaceans' emerge as the prey most frequently taken by planktivorous and macrophagous anemones, almost certainly because of the great diversity and high abundance of crustaceans in the marine environment. The specialized suspension feeder *Metridium senile* captures holo- and meroplanktonic, as well as demersal crustaceans (Sebens and Koehl, 1984), while the macrophagous *Anthopleura xanthogrammica* and *Urticina* ($\equiv$ *Tealia*) *piscivora* capture large, motile benthic decapods and dislodged barnacles. *Anthopleura elegantissima* and *Actinia equina* occupy similar habitats and are morphologically similar, and can capture both motile and dislodged sessile

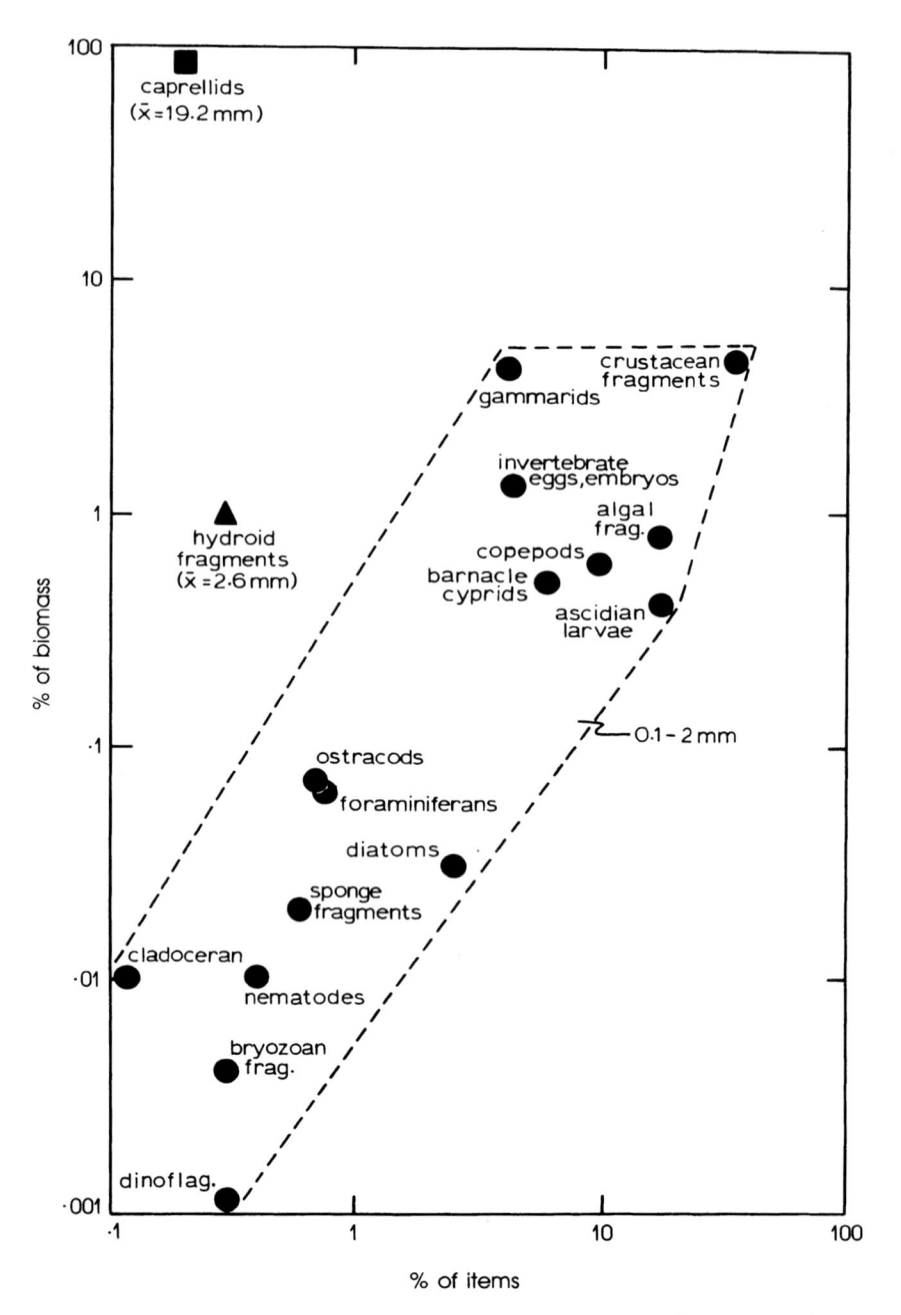

Figure 2.4 Natural prey ingested by sublittoral *Metridium senile* in Massachusetts, USA during a 20-h period. Small items (0.1–2 mm) contribute to total biomass ingested in direct proportion to their frequency in the diet. Large items are rare in the diet but comprise nearly 90% of the biomass ingested when available. Source: drawn from data in Sebens and Koehl (1984).

prey; this is reflected in the wider range of crustacean types in their diets. The very long tentacles of the 'snakelocks anemone' *Anemonia viridis* likewise enable it to capture both planktonic and benthic crustaceans. Gastropod molluscs, rare in the diet of most anemones, are a major prey of *A. viridis*, which may sweep the substratum with its tentacles, and of *Heteractis malu* and *Nematostella vectensis*, which live infaunally.

Macroalgal fragments and detritus are common in the coelenteron contents of *Actinia equina* and *Anthopleura elegantissima*, as well as in *M. senile* (Figure 2.4). Whether these anemones have the enzymic machinery to digest this material remains uncertain (section 2.4, page 78), but algal and other particulate detritus usually is coated with bacteria and diatoms, which are absorbed by digestive phagocytes in *A. equina* and *M. senile* (Van-Praët, 1981, 1983a, and personal communication). Specimens of *Sagartia troglodytes* living in silty mud contain particulate organic detritus, sand, diatoms and unicellular green algae as well as animal remains (Riemann-Zürneck, 1969), and phagocytes in *A. equina* absorb cyanobacteria (Van-Praët, 1981, 1985). Several species of anemones have enzymes which may digest cell walls and storage products of microalgae (see section 2.4). Organic detritus, as well as zooplankton, was suggested as a dietary source of the ovarian carotenoid astaxanthin in *Metridium* sp. (Fox, Wilkie and Haxo, 1978). The nutritional importance to sea anemones of detritus may be enhanced in food-poor deep-sea environments (George, 1981, p. 295; Van-Praët, 1981, 1983b). Bacteria in the coelenterons of *Anemonia viridis* ($\equiv$ *A. sulcata*) and '*Stoichactis giganteum*' ($\equiv$ *Stichodactyla* sp.) may be an order of magnitude more concentrated than in the surrounding seawater, perhaps owing to richer nutritive conditions in the coelenteron following the digestion of macrofauna (Herndl, Velimirov and Krauss, 1985; Herndl and Velimirov, 1985). Although a factor in the coelenteric fluid causes bacterial lysis, it is unknown whether this represents defence against pathogens or extracellular digestion. The very low biomass of bacteria suggests that they form a minor part of the energy intake by *A. viridis* and '*S. giganteum*'. However, bacteria may be very important foods in microbially rich hydrothermal vent habitats (Van-Praët, 1983b, 1985). Rather than being strict carnivores as has long been assumed, many sea anemones may thus be omnivores, especially those species that feed on fine particulates. Also, macrocarnivorous anemones such as *Urticina eques* abound at natural gas seeps, presumably feeding on zoo-plankton attracted to these microbially rich areas (Hovland and Thomsen, 1989).

2.2.5 Are Sea Anemones Selective Predators?

The occurrence of sand, macroalgal detritus and terrestrial plant debris in their coelenteron contents may indicate that sea anemones are rather unselective about what they ingest. Considering the relative scarcity of zoo-plankton per unit volume of seawater and the fact that anemones do not generate currents for suspension feeding, it may be suggested that zoo-planktivorous anemones experience chronically low prey availability and therefore are not subject to pressure selecting for a feeding strategy that maximizes energy gain by rejecting less digestible items (see Townsend and Hughes, 1981).

Since microphagous species such as *Metridium senile* have no obvious mechanism for rejecting the detrital and other refractory particles from among the complex mixture impacting with their mucus-covered tentacles, the selection pressure more likely would be to adopt a numbers-maximizing feeding strategy (Griffiths, 1975) in which all particles are ingested. This in turn would select for the retention of enzymes capable of digesting a diet of detritus. In this respect it is interesting that colonial alcyonaceans (subclass Octocorallia) have a higher fraction of very small particles in their diets (Sebens and Koehl, 1984) and, unlike macrophagous sea anemones, they possess the enzymes to digest some plant materials (section 2.4, page 79).

Conversely, macrophagous carnivores (*Anthopleura xanthogrammica* and *Urticina piscivora*) ingest large prey individually and rarely contain refractory items, so such anemones are energy-maximizers to the extent that they ex-clude indigestible items from their diet. The frequency of availability of large prey, however, is sufficiently low (e.g. *A.xanthogrammica* on average captures a mussel every 3 to 5 days: Sebens, 1982a) that this anemone prob-ably does not discriminate among prey items (mussels, crabs, echinoids, fish) but captures and eats whatever macrofauna it encounters. The same probably applies to *Urticinopsis antarcticus*, which eats adult sea stars (Dayton *et al.*, 1974), and to the tropical anemones *Condylactis gigantea* and *Sticho-dactyla* (≡ *Stoichactis*) *helianthus*, which eat adult sea urchins (Sebens, 1976).

Testing for true selectivity by planktivorous anemones by comparing the available plankton and the prey eaten has been done only in *M.senile* (Pur-cell, 1977a; Sebens and Koehl, 1984). Although zooplankton are captured more or less in proportion to their availability, the anemones show positive selectivity for barnacle cyprids, and ascidian and bivalve larvae, and negative selectivity for invertebrate eggs, copepods and ostracods. It is not known whether the negative selectivities reflect lack of preference by the predator or escape abilities of the prey. Invertebrate eggs and embryos were among the smallest prey captured, and their size may approach the minimum for efficient capture. The efficiency of retention of small phytoplankton has not been assessed. Although the preferentially ingested barnacle and ascidian larvae represent only a small fraction of the total biomass eaten by *M.senile* (Figure 2.4), their elimination may also be viewed as the removal of poten-tial competitors for space, as adult barnacles and tunicates may dominate spatially in the subtidal habitat of this anemone (Sebens and Koehl, 1984).

2.2.6 Ingested Ration

Individual sea anemones tend to capture prey of a relatively narrow size range (Figure 2.1), and so the biomass of prey captured will be linearly related to the frequency of items captured. Since *Metridium senile*, however, may occasionally take large prey (Purcell, 1977a; Sebens and Koehl, 1984), and because prey mass increases as the cube of its linear dimensions, infrequent large prey items may account for a disproportionally large fraction of the biomass ingested (Figure 2.4). This again emphasizes the opportunistic nature of predatory anemones.

The few available data show that anemones ingest about the same daily ration (as percent of their body mass) as other marine invertebrate carnivores of similar body size (the latter summarized by Conover, 1978). When *Actinia equina* was fed *ad libitum* on mussel gonads in the laboratory, the ration ingested by this anemone was inversely proportional to its body mass and ranged from about 2% to 18% per day (Figure 2.5). Ingestion by *A.equina*

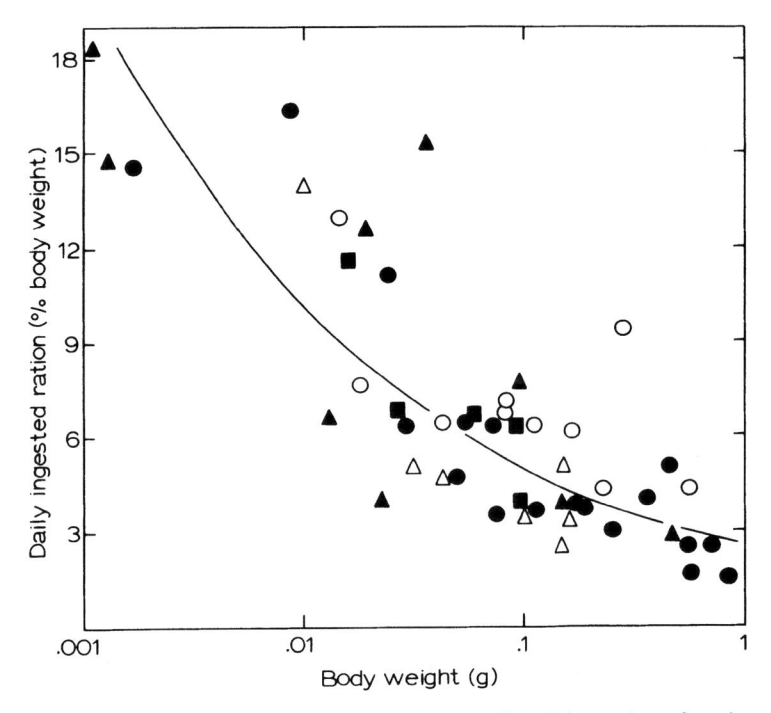

Figure 2.5 Relative rations ingested by specimens of *Actinia equina* of various sizes (dry weight) fed *ad libitum* on tissues of *Mytilus edulis* at 13.8°C (■), 15.7°C (△), 18.7–19.9°C (○), 20–20.5°C (▲) and 21–22.7°C (●). Source: drawn from data in Ivleva (1964).

Table 2.2   Average daily ingested ration (percent of anemone dry body weight), assimilation efficiency (estimated as described in text), and average daily assimilated ration (mg) in *Actinia equina* of 0.2 g dry weight fed *ad libitum* on mussel gonads. Values have been obtained from logarithmic regressions of ingested ration on anemone body weight, and assimilation efficiency on ingested ration, for data at each temperature

Temperature (°C)	Average daily ingested ration (%)	Assimilation efficiency (%)	Average daily assimilated ration (mg)
13.8	3.59	97.1	6.97
15.7	2.85	79.2	4.51
18.7–19.9	5.91	67.1	7.93
20–20.5	4.52	66.0	5.97
21–22.7	3.61	69.0	4.76

Source: calculated from data in Ivleva (1964)

was maximal at 18.7°–19.9°C, where a 0.2 g $_dW$ anemone consumed about 6% of its body weight per day (Table 2.2). The much larger percentage rations ingested by hydroids (Stiven, 1965; Paffenhöfer, 1968) reflects the smaller individual size and higher rates of energy turnover and large investment in asexual proliferation in these short-lived (compared with sea anemones) cnidarians.

Sea anemones in nature rarely experience a saturating food supply. From coelenteron contents, Sebens (1981a) showed that the wet weight of prey (mg $_wW_p$) ingested by *Metridium senile* was related to anemone dry weight (g $_dW$), as $_wW_p = 9.47\,_dW^{0.54}$ (Figure 2.1). Assuming that the prey had been captured within 2 h prior to sampling (which allows for the maximum digestion rate observed) and that the anemone fed continuously, and converting prey wet weight to dry weight, it appears that a 0.2 g specimen in that study would have a daily (24 h) ration of 0.3% of its body weight, which is much less than this anemone will eat when given unlimited food. Extrapolating from coelenteron contents sampled every 4 h for 20 h (Sebens and Koehl, 1984), *M. senile* of 6 cm basal diameter (about 1 g $_dW$) ingested 2.9% of its body weight in 24 h. This calculation includes all prey captured; if two exceptional caprellids (Figure 2.4) are omitted, the daily ration drops to 0.4%, so that the ration ingested by sea anemones is highly stochastic. Detritus and algal fragments comprise only about 1% of the biomass eaten by *M. senile* (Figure 2.4), although this increases to nearly 10% in a high-flow habitat adjacent to kelp beds (R.E. Robbins and J.M. Shick, unpublished).

In *Anthopleura elegantissima*, $_wWp = 4.14\,_dW^{0.33}$ (Figure 2.1B), and the daily ration of 0.2 g $_dW$ anemone would be 3.6%. This larger ration relative to that in *M. senile* of the same size is due to the larger size of prey captured by *A.elegantissima* (Figure 2.1A), as the number of prey captured by *M.senile* is greater (Figure 2.1B). A 3.6% ration is only about half that for a $0.2 g_d W$ *Actinia equina* fed *ad lib.*, and it assumes continuous feeding, which cannot be the case due to intertidal exposure of *A. elegantissima*. The ration size of high shore relative to low shore specimens appears not to decline in direct proportion to exposure time (Zamer, 1986), perhaps because the former are continually 'starved' and more responsive to and able to capture and retain prey more efficiently (sections 2.2.10, page 68, and 2.3.2, page 73).

2.2.7 Feeding by Larvae

Feeding has been examined in some planktotrophic actiniarian larvae. Various ectodermal receptors in the planula, but perhaps not the apical tuft (cf. Widersten, 1968, and Chia and Koss, 1979; section 6.3.4, page 241), may be involved in feeding. The planulae of *Metridium senile* ingest chaetognaths, calanoid copepods and the larvae of other cnidarians, but dinoflagellates comprise most of the food (Widersten, 1968). Likewise, the planulae of *Anthopleura xanthogrammica* ingest a wide variety of unicellular algae (Siebert, 1974). Such ingestion may be the route by which symbiotic dinoflagellates (zooxanthellae) initially establish their symbiosis with certain actinians (see section 2.6.3, page 92).

2.2.8 Uptake of Dissolved Organic Matter

In view of their small ingested rations and the relatively great abundance of dissolved organic matter (DOM) in seawater, sea anemones might derive much of their energy and nutrients by direct absorption of DOM. This was originally suggested by Pütter (1911), who calculated that *Actinia equina* meets 30–40% of its energy needs in this manner. This topic has been reviewed in cnidarians by Schlichter (1980) and Schlichter *et al.* (1987).

The large prey capture surface of sea anemones also presents a surface for the absorption of DOM, and is amplified tenfold by the abundant microvilli (characteristic of absorptive epithelia) on the ectodermal cells (Schlichter, 1980). This mode of nutrition may be particularly important to the ectoderm, which is continually bathed in seawater, and which is partially isolated from the nutritive endoderm by the mesoglea, which itself presents a barrier to the free diffusion of glucose and amino acids (Schlichter, 1973; Chapman and Pardy, 1972; Brafield and Chapman, 1983; see also section 1.2.2, page 14).

The uptake of free amino acids (FAA) from seawater by soft-bodied invertebrates, including sea anemones, generally follows Michaelis–Menten kinetics (Figure 2.6). J^i_{max} is the maximum rate of influx and K_t is the sub-

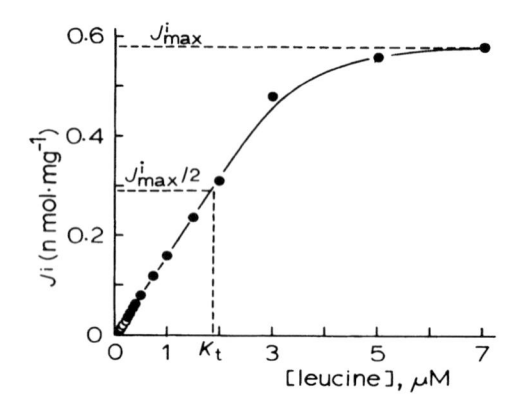

Figure 2.6 Uptake of L-leucine (n mol·mg^{-1} tissue) by isolated tentacle tissue of *Anemonia viridis* in relation to the concentration of leucine in the medium during 10-s incubations. Open circles represent uptake of leucine from natural environmental concentrations. Source: redrawn from Schlichter (1980).

strate concentration at which influx is one-half J^i_{max}. K_t is a measure of the affinity of the uptake system and typically falls at the upper end of the environmental range of substrate concentrations experienced by the animal. For example, whereas the K_t values for amino acid transport by mammalian intestine are about 10^{-2} to $10^{-3} M$, the K_ts for leucine and lysine of 1.9 and $2.6 \times 10^{-6} M$, respectively, in *Anemonia viridis* ($\equiv$ *A.sulcata*) (Bajorat, 1979, cited by Schlichter, 1980), reflect the normally low concentrations of these amino acids in coastal seawater (ca. $10^{-7} M$). These transport parameters have not been measured in burrowing anemones such as *Edwardsia* and *Haloclava*, which may experience FAA concentrations two orders of magnitude greater than do epifaunal species.

The uptake systems for various amino acids are highly specific, i.e. uptake of amino acids in a particular category (neutral, acidic, basic, aromatic) is competitively inhibited by other amino acids in the same category but not by other classes of amino acids (Schlichter, 1978a). This implies the presence of specific carriers for different classes of amino acids, perhaps represented by the amino acid binding proteins isolated by Schlichter (1978b) and Schlichter *et al.* (1987). Although no direct evidence was presented, such a transport function was speculated for the γ-glutamyl transpeptidase in the ectoderm of the tentacles and column of *Metridium senile* (Bennett and Stroud, 1981), both of which locations absorb dissolved glycine (Robbins and Shick, 1980).

Sea anemones, like other marine invertebrates, have high intracellular concentrations of FAA (ca. $10^{-1} M$; see Table 4.2), so that uptake of FAA from an environmental concentration of about $10^{-6} M$ must proceed against a concentration gradient of 10^5. Therefore, any net uptake of FAA must be an active (energy-requiring) process. In addition, the uphill transport of amino acids into membrane vesicles prepared from tentacular ectoderm of *A.viridis* is coupled with the downhill movement of a 'driver' ion, Na^+ (Buck and Schlichter, 1987; Schlichter *et al.*, 1987). Because the intracellular concentration of Na^+ is lower than that in seawater (see Herrera *et al.*, 1989), the energy required for the uphill transport of FAA may come from the electrochemical gradient provided by the coupled downhill transport of Na^+, rather than directly from ATP. The concentration gradient for Na^+ is probably maintained by ATP-requiring transport of Na^+ out of the cell, so that the uptake of FAA ultimately requires ATP. Although anoxia does not diminish amino acid uptake in *A.viridis* (Schlichter, 1974), the energy necessary for active transport could come from anaerobic metabolism; glycolytic blockade by iodoacetate greatly diminishes uptake of phenylalanine, confirming that amino acid uptake requires energy.

Another function of amino acid uptake systems located on the apical membrane may be recovery of endogenous amino acids diffusing out of cells down the large concentration gradient (Gomme, 1982). Schlichter (1980) has suggested that the ectodermal DOM transport systems of anemones reduce the loss of digested materials during ventilation of the coelenteron, as well as taking up the products of food digested by ectodermal hydrolases (see section 2.3.3, page 75). The presumably higher concentrations of DOM in the coelenteric fluid may be a major source of nourishment for embryonic and juvenile anemones brooded by viviparous species (Chia, 1972).

If the high intracellular concentrations of FAA do result in their diffusional leakage to the environment, then the net influx of FAA into sea anemones will be less than that indicated by the uptake of radiolabelled substrates. Although the net uptake of FAA from seawater by various marine invertebrates has been quantified by fluorimetry and high performance liquid chromatography, the net flux in sea anemones exposed to environmentally realistic concentrations of FAA has not yet been studied using these techniques, so the quantitative importance of FAA and other DOM to the nutrition of sea anemones cannot presently be calculated. Schlichter (1975a) calculated that the unidirectional flux of labelled glucose from an environmental concentration of $90\,\mu g \cdot l^{-1}$ could support about 50% of the 'basal' metabolic rate in *A.viridis*.

Experiments with other sessile cnidarians suggest that DOM assumes a major supplementary role during the absence of solid food (Shick, 1975), when the metabolic rate declines to maintenance levels. DOM uptake may be particularly important to small anemones, which have proportionally large tentacle surface areas (Robbins and Shick, 1980), and to burrowing anemones, which may experience higher concentrations of DOM. Nitrogen rather than energy requirements may have selected for the large capacity of a diverse array of marine invertebrates to take up dissolved FAA.

2.2.9 Control of Feeding Behaviour

Whether or not chemoreception is the most primitive sense phylogenetically, chemical stimuli are certainly the major cause of sea anemone feeding behaviours. Purely mechanical stimuli do not elicit a complete sequence of feeding behaviour, except perhaps in extremely starved anemones (Pantin and Pantin, 1943). Tactile stimuli may be more important in some sea anemones such as *Urticina felina* that eat large prey (McFarlane and Lawn, 1990, and personal communication), and in corallimorpharians that envelop large prey in their oral discs (Elliott and Cook, 1989).

Water soluble extracts of prey and various organic compounds act as attractants (*sensu* Lindstedt, 1971b) causing pre-feeding responses such as expansion of the oral disc, opening of the mouth and protrusion of the actinopharynx ('the inquiring mouths of blunt anemones' written of by

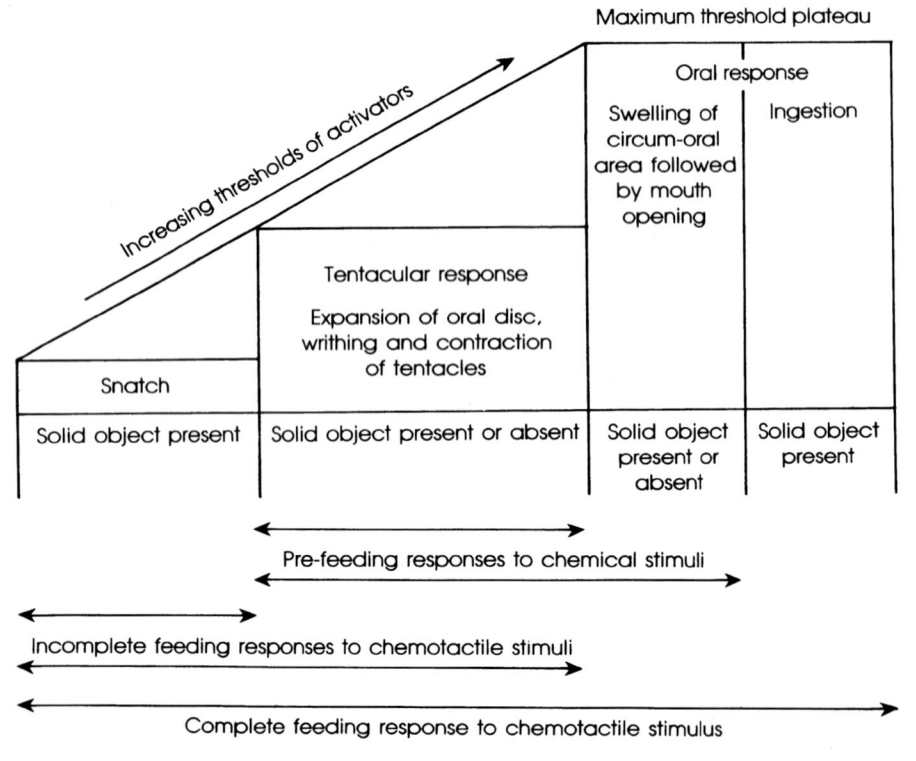

Figure 2.7 The relationships between mechanical and chemical stimuli eliciting particular components of feeding behaviour in macrophagous sea anemones. The 'snatch' refers to the immediate response of one or more tentacles to contact with prey, in which they adhere to it and retract sharply. Source: modified from Williams (1972a).

Patrick White) and extension, writhing, or twitching of the tentacles, and as incitants and stimulants that initiate feeding and ingestion of prey. Although the terms 'pre-feeding response' and 'preparatory activity' have been used interchangeably, it seems useful to apply the former to any overt behaviour evoked by purely chemical stimuli (Williams, 1973) and to reserve the latter specifically for expansion of the oral disc and extension of the tentacles associated with chemically stimulated ectodermal SS1 activity (Lawn, 1975). Following Williams (1972a, 1973), components of the 'feeding response' (tentacular and oral components) are those elicited by chemotactile stimuli (Figure 2.7). The ingestion of prey is effected via ciliary currents on the actinopharynx, which reverse their normal outward beating in response primarily to chemical stimuli (Parker, 1905; Windt-Preuss, 1959; Holley and Shelton, 1984). A complete sequence of these behaviours, from the perception of food to its ingestion, involves a spatially separate array of mechano- and chemoreceptors which may differ in their thresholds and specificities, as well as effectors which are (muscles) or may not be (pharyngeal cilia) coordinated by electrical conduction systems. The morphological changes during this sequence are represented in Figure 2.8.

Chemosensory structures have not been identified electrophysiologically, but by analogy with known gustatory and olfactory receptors in vertebrates, they may be supposed to include the dense ectodermal microvilli (Leghissa, 1965) (often in association with cilia) and perhaps the ciliary cone apparatus (Mariscal, 1974a; Bigger, 1982) of the tentacles and oral disc. Chemosensory

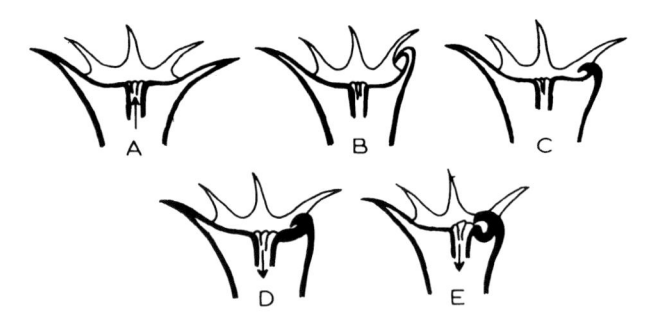

Figure 2.8 The sequence of behaviours involved in the capture and ingestion of a single prey item. Prior to interception of prey, the tentacles are extended and the pharyngeal ciliary currents are directed out of the coelenteron (arrow) (**A**). After the prey contacts the tentacle and is held by discharged tubes of nematocysts and spirocysts, the tentacle folds toward the mouth (**B**) and shortens (**C**), movements caused by contraction of longitudinal muscles of the tentacle. Local contraction of the oral disc radial muscles (**D**) and retractor muscles in the mesenteries (**E**) cause the mouth to protrude toward the prey, placing the latter in contact with the top of the actinopharynx. Chemicals emanating from the prey elicit circum-oral swelling, mouth opening and reversal of the pharyngeal ciliary current (arrows), causing the prey to be ingested. Source: modified from Holley and Shelton (1984).

information may be conducted by the SS1 (Lawn, 1975) and multipolar nerve cells of the ectoderm, to effectors and to the endodermal SS2, which is active during mouth opening and actinopharynx protrusion (McFarlane, 1975). Pharyngeal ciliary reversal is a local phenomenon apparently not coordinated by an electrical conduction system (Holley and Shelton, 1984), which implies the presence of chemoreceptors (perhaps the cilia themselves) on the pharyngeal cells.

Behavioural experiments have indicated that the chemoreceptors involved in various feeding behaviours are located on the tentacles, oral disc, peristome and actinopharynx. As already mentioned, individuals of *Metridium senile* for example must be at least partially expanded when a chemical stimulus is applied for full expansion to result (Batham and Pantin, 1950b), so it appears that the chemoreceptors involved in preparatory activity in this species are located not in the column but on the tentacles or oral disc, a supposition supported by SEM studies (Mariscal, 1974a). In *Urticina felina*, however, behavioural and electrophysiological experiments indicate that the chemoreceptors involved in pre-feeding and preparatory activity are located not on the tentacles, oral disc, or actinopharynx but on the column ectoderm (McFarlane, 1970; Lawn, 1975; Boothby and McFarlane, 1986). This macrophagous anemone can probably detect nearby macrofaunal prey or carrion even when contracted. Robbins and Shick (1980) interpreted the different locations of receptors in these two species in terms of their different modes of feeding, noting especially the heavy reliance of *M.senile* on water movement (sections 2.2.2 and 2.2.3).

Attempts to identify the chemicals eliciting various pre-feeding and feeding behaviours have had mixed success. The behavioural criteria for a positive response have been varied and often vague, and the nutritional status of the anemones prior to the bioassays has not always been stated or has varied among experiments. Test substances have occasionally been found to be impure, and other contamination has not always been controlled. Accordingly, the results summarized in Table 2.3 must be viewed with caution. It is clear nevertheless that a variety of amino acids, the tripeptide reduced glutathione (GSH), betaine, and several B-vitamins evoke responses in different species.

Lenhoff, Heagy and Danner (1976) have suggested that the receptor sites for chemicals that coordinate these behaviours evolved from receptor sites inducing pinocytosis or phagocytosis in single cells, and that a broad specificity of such receptors assured the anemone sufficient food to survive. Implicit in this argument is that the receptors involved were associated with the uptake of particulate food, including fragments of animal prey. It is not surprising that diffusable substances present in natural prey are especially effective, but in studies of sea anemones the correlation between identified chemical feeding activators and prey composition has received only passing attention.

Table 2.3 Chemical activators of feeding behaviour in sea anemones and a ceriantharian, where in most cases the material ingested was filter paper soaked in a solution of the individual compound and concentration indicated

Species	Behaviour	Active Compounds	Concentration (M)	Source
Actinia equina	Tentacular response and ingestion	Ala, Arg, Glu★, Gly, Ser	10^{-7} to 10^{-6} mol/cm^2 filter paper	Steiner (1957)
Anthopleura elegantissima	Tentacle bending and contraction	Asparagine Asp	10^{-5} to 10^{-3} 10^{-3}	Lindstedt (1971a)
A. elegantissima	Preparatory activity[a] Ingestion	Pro GSH	5×10^{-9} 10^{-5} to 10^{-3}	Howe (1976b)
Anthopleura midorii	Retention on tentacles Mouth opening Ingestion	Ala, Cys, Gly, His, Pro Pro Cys, GSH	10^{-1} 10^{-1} 10^{-1}	Nagai and Nagai (1973)
Boloceroides sp.	Tentacle writhing and ingestion Ingestion	Val Ile	10^{-6} to 10^{-3} ?	Lindstedt *et al.* (1968)
Calliactis parasitica	Mouth opening, pharynx protrusion, SS2 activity	Arg, Pro★, Ser, Val GSH	10^{-3} 10^{-5}	McFarlane (1975)
Calliactis polypus	Tentacle writhing Mouth opening, pharynx swelling, ingestion Ingestion (>50% response)	GSH Leu; Pro Gly, Pro, Trp	10^{-8} to 10^{-4} 10^{-4}; 10^{-7} to 10^{-3} 10^{-1}	Reimer (1973)
Condylactis gigantea	Tentacle writhing	15 individual amino acids	10^{-1}	Bursey and Guanciale (1977)

Table 2.3 Continued

Species	Behaviour	Active Compounds	Concentration (M)	Source
	Ingestion and retention (>50% response)	Glu, PentaGly, Met, Pro, Trp	10^{-1}	
Haliplanella lineata ($\equiv$ *H.luciae*)	'Feeding'	Leu	10^{-1}	Lindstedt (1971b)
H.lineata ($\equiv$ *Diadumene luciae*)	Complete feeding response: Snatch, tentacular response, oral response, ingestion (>50% response)	Glutamine, His, Ser GSH	5×10^{-3} to 3×10^{-2} 5×10^{-4}	Williams (1972a)
		Nicotinic acid Pyridoxine	2.5×10^{-2} 5×10^{-2}	
H.lineata ($\equiv$ *D.luciae*)	Snatch and tentacular response only (>50% response)	Asp, Cys, Glu, Glutamine, His, Pro	3×10^{-2} to 10^{-1}	Williams (1973)
		Nicotinamide Pyridoxine	10^{-1} 10^{-1}	
	Complete feeding response (>50% response)	Ser GSH Nicotinic acid Thiamine	2.5×10^{-2} 7.4×10^{-4} 3.2×10^{-2} 4×10^{-2}	
Metridium senile	Pharyngeal ciliary reversal (32% response)	Leu	?	Windt-Preuss (1959)
Pachycerianthus fimbriatus	Ingestion	Arg	10^{-1}	Arai and Walder (1973)
Urticina eques	Columnar SS1 activity	Betaine	10^{-2}	Boothby and McFarlane (1986)
Urticina felina	Columnar SS1 activity	Betaine	10^{-2}	Boothby and McFarlane (1986)

Notes: ★Denotes especially strong but unquantified response;

GSH and proline are especially potent feeding activators in corals and zoanthids (reviewed by Lenhoff *et al.*, 1976), and these compounds also are the most widespread effective substances among sea anemones (Table 2.3). Proline is the predominant free amino acid in the tissues of a variety of decapod crustaceans (Gilles, 1975) as well as in copepods (Burton and Feldman, 1982) and barnacles (Cook, Gabbott and Youngson, 1972), which comprise most of the prey of many sea anemones (Table 2.1), but it is without exception a minor component of the free amino acid pools of the anemones themselves (Table 4.2, page 188). The latter may be important because if, as suggested previously (section 2.2.8), endogenous amino acids diffuse out of cells of the anemones and onto their ectoderms, chemoreceptors there would be saturated continuously with amino acids emanating from the sea anemones themselves. It may be significant in this respect that proline (at a concentration of $5 \times 10^{-9}M$) is the only identified compound eliciting true preparatory activity in a sea anemone (Howe, 1976a). Accordingly, additional free amino acids which would be perceived by anemones to indicate the presence of prey would be those which were high in concentration in the prey but low in the anemone.

The additional data available support this suggestion: alanine and glycine concentrations are high in crustaceans, bivalve molluscs and annelids (Gilles, 1975) but low in most sea anemones (Table 4.2), and these amino acids are effective feeding activators in several anemone species. Likewise, arginine concentrations are high in crustaceans but low in anemones, with the same apparent behavioural manifestation. Conversely, taurine, a major component of the FAA pools both of some sea anemones (including *Anthopleura xanthogrammica*) and their bivalve and crustacean prey, failed to produce a response in *Anthopleura midorii* (Nagai and Nagai, 1973) and in *Urticina eques* and *U.felina* (Boothby and McFarlane, 1986), apparently the only anemones in which it has been tested. In general, the effective concentrations of the amino acids are biologically relevant, i.e. in the same range as that which would be released from prey cells punctured by nematocysts, although the effective concentration appears to vary between tentacular and oral chemoreceptors, which may also differ in their specificities for various chemicals.

Unfortunately, the FAA composition of the particular anemone species tested for chemosensory responses is rarely known. In *Haliplanella lineata* the amino acids eliciting the 'snatch' and tentacular responses involved in prey capture (aspartate, glutamate, glutamine, histidine and proline) are without exception less concentrated in the anemone than in a variety of potential invertebrate prey. This anemone contains rather high concentrations of glycine, which does not elicit feeding behaviour.

The question arises therefore whether some of the inter- and intraspecific variability among sea anemones in their responses to various amino acids is due to individual differences in their endogenous FAA pools. For example, glycine comprises from 1% to 61% of the FAA pool in different species of sea anemones and evokes feeding behaviour in some anemones but not in others. Further, glycine concentration in the actiniid *Bunodosoma cavernata* shows a large variation with reproductive condition (Kasschau and McCommas, 1982), so that reproductive state conceivably could influence receptivity to glycine. Likewise glutamate and glutamine differ interspecifically in their effectiveness in causing feeding behaviour, and comprise from less than 1% up to 26% of the FAA pools in anemones. The one exception to the proposed generalization that effective feeding activators are more concentrated in prey than in predator is glutamate in *Actinia equina* (cf. Tables 2.3 and 4.2); however, the high concentration of glutamate in *A. equina* is in isolated marginal sphincter muscle only (where it may function as a transmitter substance), not necessarily in the entire anemone.

Because sea anemones studied in the laboratory generally do not capture and ingest chemically inert particles and can reject non-prey items, what are the chemical stimuli for feeding on the macroalgal fragments and sand so common in the coelenteron contents of freshly collected specimens? Although marine algae contain FAA, the concentrations are lower than in sea anemone tissues, and non-nitrogenous compounds abundant in algae generally do not evoke feeding responses. It may be that anemones such as *Actinia equina* and *Anthopleura elegantissima* are responding to attached epifauna rather than to the algal fragments themselves, although considering the small ration sizes ingested in the field, anemones there may be more or less continually starved and thus less discriminating in their intake of particulates (see Pantin and Pantin, 1943). As already mentioned, *Metridium senile* has no apparent mechanism for physically separating inert materials from the microcosm of living and non-living particles impinging on its tentacles. The ingestion of particulate organic detritus, bacteria, etc. may thus be largely fortuitous, although there is increasing evidence that anemones can use such foods (sections 2.3.4, page 77, and 2.4, page 77).

2.2.10 Discharge of Cnidae

The cnidocytes and their contained cnidae (nematocysts proper, and spirocysts; also ptychocysts in ceriantharians) have been studied at many levels, and their morphology, classification, chemistry, functions and usefulness in taxonomy have been reviewed by H. Schmidt (1972a, 1974), Mariscal (1974c, 1984, 1988), and Fautin (1988) (section 1.5, page 24). Despite the great diversity of cnidae, in over 60% of the genera of sea anemones examined the cnidome consists of three types only: spirocysts (which act as glutinants to hold prey), microbasic p-mastigophores (penetrants used in prey capture), and b-mastigophores (penetrants employed in defence and in prey capture) (Mariscal, 1974b). In *Anemonia viridis* ($\equiv$ *A. sulcata*) the ratio of spirocysts to nematocysts in the tentacles is 2:1 (G.H. Schmidt, 1982), and the absence of spirocysts but not nematocysts from the endoderm (Van-Praët, 1982a) supports the idea that spirocysts act primarily to hold struggling prey. In other actiniids the ratio of spirocysts:b-mastigophores in the tentacles ranges from 0.96:1 to 3.3:1, and is generally greater than 1:1 (Bigger, 1982).

Mechanical and chemical stimuli effect the discharge of cnidae directly through receptors whose sensitivity may be modified by the nervous system. Anthozoan nematocysts lack the cnidocil apparatus that apparently triggers discharge of nematocysts in Hydrozoa and Scyphozoa. Scanning and transmission electron micrographs have elucidated details of the ciliary cone complex (originally described over 100 years ago), a putative mechanoreceptor involved in nematocyst discharge (Mariscal, 1974b, c; Mariscal, Conklin and Bigger, 1978). This structure consists of a central nematocyte containing a kinocilium, stereocilia and microvilli, surrounded by additional cells which contribute only non-motile stereocilia and microvilli to the complex (Figure 2.9A, B). Ultrastructural studies utilizing colloidal gold coated with mucin suggest that the apical membranes of supporting cells adjacent to the cnidocyte, and not the stereocilia nor the cnidocyte itself, are the receptor sites for N-acetylated sugars commonly found in glycoproteins and mucopolysaccharides (Watson and Hessinger, 1987, 1988). Receptor sites for the second class of chemicals known to sensitize cnida discharge (amino acids, imino acids and histamine: Thorington and Hessinger, 1988) have not been identified. Spirocytes appear not to have ciliary cones, but, instead, a dense circlet of microvilli (Figure 2.9A). In the marginal tentacles of *Ceriantheopsis americanus* an apparatus similar to the ciliary cone but apparently not associated with a nematocyte presumably functions as a proprioceptor (Peteya, 1975). This species is very sensitive to localized water movements.

If ultrastructural analogy indicates functional similarity, then the ciliary cone complex, which bears a remarkable resemblance to the 'hair cells' in vertebrate acoustico-lateralis, vestibular and auditory organs (Mariscal, 1974 b, c; Peteya, 1975), may well respond primarily to mechanical stimuli from prey. The dense microvilli associated with spirocytes are reminiscent of the structure of vertebrate taste buds, and may thus act as contact chemoreceptors.

There is some behavioural and physiological evidence for these suggestions. Gentle mechanical stimulation of the tentacles of *Haliplanella lineata* (≡ *Diadumene luciae*) leads primarily to the discharge of p-mastigophores; when soluble prey extract is presented with mechanical stimulation there is an increase in the number of spirocysts discharged (Williams, 1968). In *Calliactis tricolor*, prey extract in conjunction with mechanical stimulation is more effective in discharging spirocysts than b-mastigophore nematocysts (Sandberg, 1972). Williams suggests that the initial tactile stimulus would discharge the nematocysts, which would penetrate the prey and release its

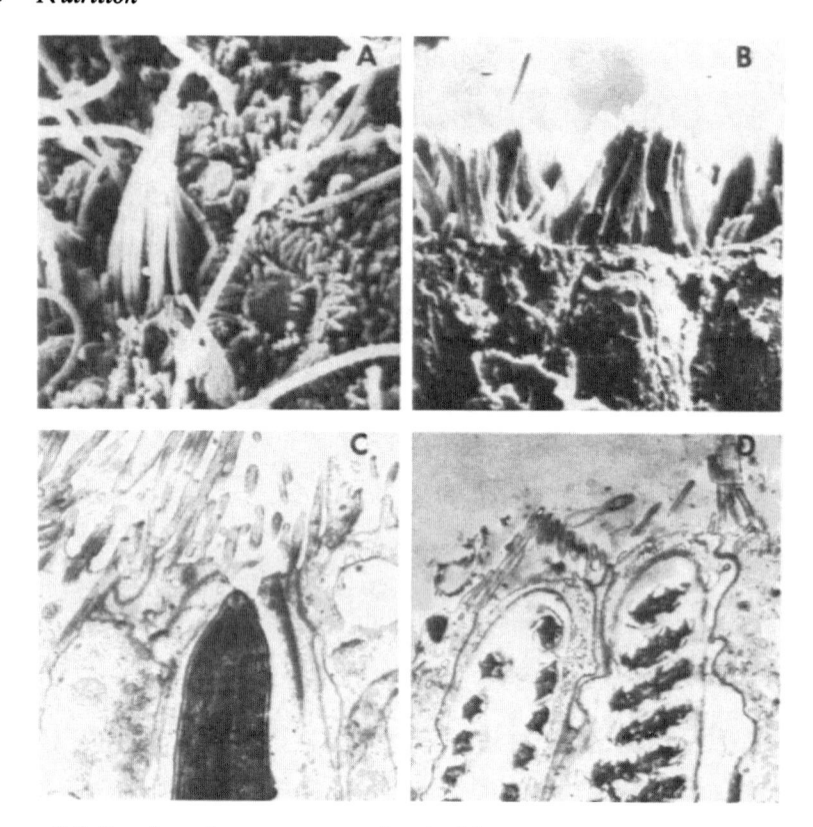

Figure 2.9 Ectodermal receptors associated with nematocysts and spirocysts in sea anemones and a corallimorpharian. **A**. Tentacle surface of the corallimorpharian *Corynactis californica* showing a ciliary cone consisting of a central kinocilium surrounded by stereocilia, adjacent to a spirocyte possessing only a circlet of microvilli. **B**. Fractured acrorhagus of *Anthopleura krebsi* showing a ciliary cone on a nematocyte containing a holotrich nematocyst. **C**. Tentacle surface of *Haliplanella lineata* showing microvilli and stereocilia; note ciliary rootlet in proximity of b-mastigophore nematocyst. **D**. Tentacle surface of *Calliactis tricolor* showing two spirocysts, short microvilli on surface of spirocyte and longer microvilli contributed by adjoining cell(s). Source: **A**. Mariscal (1974a); **B**. Bigger (1982); **C**. Courtesy L. Minasian; **D**. Mariscal *et al.* (1976).

body fluids onto the amino acid chemoreceptors on the spirocytes, which would then discharge and help to hold the prey (Thorington and Hessinger, 1988). Such a two-stage recognition system may also be involved in rejecting non-prey items and thus in conserving cnidae. Spirocysts would presumably also discharge in response to N-acetylated sugars (e.g. surface mucins and chitin) in contact with their chemoreceptors (Thorington and Hessinger, 1988).

Watson and Hessinger (1989) elegantly demonstrated the interaction between chemoreceptors and mechanoreceptors in effecting discharge of microbasic p-mastigophores in *Haliplanella lineata* ($\equiv$ *H.luciae*). Although some cnidocytes would discharge in response to mechanical stimulation alone, after exposing anemones to N-acetylated sugars or mucin, the frequency of mechanical stimulation to which cnidae preferentially discharged decreased from 30–75 hertz to 5–40 hertz, the latter frequencies matching those of the movements of swimming prey. This tuning of the mechanoreceptor by the chemoreceptor apparently involves a lengthening of stereocilia on the supporting cells, and by analogy with vertebrate hair cells, lowering the frequency to which they respond.

As the ciliary cone complex contains microvilli as well as a kinocilium (Bigger, 1982), it may detect both mechanical and chemical stimuli, especially on the acrorhagi (which have few spirocysts) used in agonistic behaviour (section 7.2.1, page 284). In *Anthopleura elegantissima* purely mechanical stimuli fail to discharge acrorhagial nematocysts (Lubbock and Shelton, 1981), suggesting that the ciliary cones there may require chemical sensitization before the combined chemical and mechanical stimuli cause discharge. Possible sites of chemoreception are the microvilli in pits at the bases of cilia, which are increasingly exposed as the acrorhagus expands (Figure 2.10) during agonistic behaviour.

Although formerly regarded as independent effectors responsive only to proximal stimulation, cnidae are subject to distal influence. For example, in shell-climbing behaviour of *Calliactis parasitica* (which attaches to gastropod shells inhabited by hermit crabs), differences in adhesiveness of the tentacles appear to reflect variability in the threshold for discharge of spirocysts according to the particular substrate occupied by the anemone (Davenport,

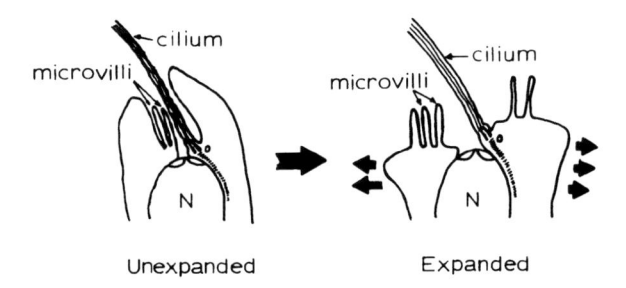

Unexpanded   Expanded

Figure 2.10 Diagrammatic representation of the shape changes in the apical region of an acrorhagial nematocyte as the acrorhagus expands. The increasing exposure of the microvilli in the pit at the base of the kinocilium may reduce the apparent threshold for response to chemical stimuli, and a similar mechanism may apply to tentacular nematocytes. **N** = nematocyst. See text for further discussion. Source: modified from Bigger (1982).

Ross and Sutton, 1961); this threshold may be altered also by ectodermal SS1 stimulation (McFarlane and Shelton, 1975).

It is well known that well-fed anemones are less responsive to food than are starved individuals. Sandberg (1972) and Mariscal (1973) quantified this observation by showing that discharge of cnidae decreases progressively with the increasing amount of food eaten. In *C.tricolor* the greatest decline in discharge of cnidae occurs after the anemone has ingested 6–10% of its body weight (Sandberg, 1972); in *Epiactis prolifera* the corresponding ration is about 10–25% (Mariscal, 1973), perhaps because the individuals of *E.prolifera* tested were smaller and so would tend to consume proportionally larger rations (see Figure 2.5). Mariscal suggested that the ability of an anemone to inhibit the discharge of cnidae after feeding avoids wasting cnidae in capturing food that it cannot ingest or utilize, and indeed the range of ration size at which this occurs yields the minimum assimilation efficiency (see Figure 2.12, page 72). These ration sizes are much larger than those ingested by anemones in the field, so the role of satiation and inhibition of discharge of cnidae in nature is unknown.

Noting the possibility of communication between the ectodermal SS1 and endodermal SS2 conduction systems, Shelton (1982) suggests that distension of the body column by food may be detected by SS2 stretch receptors and result in an increased threshold for discharge of cnidae mediated by the SS1. In this change in threshold he also postulates a role for endodermal chemoreceptors for products of digestion. The latter is supported by Sandberg's (1972) observation that filling the coelenteron with glass beads is less effective than prey intake in decreasing nematocyst discharge.

The relatively retracted and flaccid nature of the tentacles in well-fed anemones (mediated by the SS2) may place the microvilli of the ciliary cones there in the unexposed condition analogous to that in an unexpanded acrorhagus (Figure 2.10), and so raise the threshold for nematocyst discharge (Bigger, 1982). Conversely, the greater sensitivity of the cnidae in starved anemones may be due to the greater extension of their tentacles, which would increase the exposure of microvilli. The neurons associated with some cnidocytes have not yet been shown to affect their probability of discharge. Experiments with isolated cnidocytes, however, suggest that input from other cells is important (McKay and Anderson, 1988a).

2.3 EXTRACELLULAR DIGESTION

Extracellular digestion is a prerequisite for other than microphagous modes of feeding and probably occurred first in the Cnidaria. Extracellular digestion was at first thought to be of little importance to sea anemones, as digestive enzymes were not detected in the coelenteric fluid. Although they did not explain how large prey could be absorbed, the classic studies of Metschnikoff (1880) and Mesnil (1901) on nutritive phagocytosis and intracellular digestion partially resolved the logical discrepancies among ingestion of prey, the seeming lack of hydrolytic enzymes, and the egestion of waste.

2.3.1 Mechanism of Extracellular Digestion

Metschnikoff's demonstration of phagocytosis of carmine particles as a means of utilizing large prey had obvious shortcomings. Krukenberg (1880) provided early evidence that in *Sagartia troglodytes* digestion of prey occurs at the surface of the mesenteric filaments. Bodansky (1923) allowed that in homogenates of mesenteric filaments of *Metridium senile* ($\equiv$ *M.marginatum*) the presence of trypsin and amylase did not preclude a role in extracellular digestion. Ishida (1936) found that protease activity appeared in the coelenteric fluid of *Actinia equina* ($\equiv$ *A.mesembryanthemum*) 3 h after feeding, and he suggested that extracellular digestion was aided by 'slime'. Krijgsman and Talbot (1953) suggested subsequently that a mucous coat served to concentrate extracellular protease and lipase on the surface of the prey ingested by *Pseudactinia flagellifera*.

The most direct and graphic demonstration of the role of the mesenteric filaments in extracellular digestion was provided by Nicol (1959) in *Calliactis parasitica*. The filaments had a strong protease activity that was increased by incubating them with various proteins and peptones, which indicated like Ishida's results, that components of the food caused the release of extracellular digestive enzymes. *In vivo* the mesenteric filaments closely invested the prey, thus concentrating the enzymes in a small volume immediately adjacent to the food mass, which was digested at the interface (Figure 2.11).

Pre-oral digestion of prey occurs on the labial tentacles of *Cerianthus lloydi* and *C. membranaceus* (Tiffon, 1975) and in the reef anemone *Heteractis magnifica* ($\equiv$ *Radianthus ritteri*) (Schlichter, 1980). The products of such digestion are taken up via pinocytosis (Tiffon and Daireux, 1974) or through absorption by microvilli on the ectodermal cells (Schlichter, 1980). Tiffon (1975) postulated a bacteriostatic role for the very strong trypsin present in the columnar ectoderm of *Metridium senile*.

2.3.2 Food Retention, Digestive Efficiency and Absorption Efficiency

Envelopment by the mesenteric filaments provides a mechanism to sequester and digest small meals ingested over a period of time, e.g. during a tidal cycle. This is a necessary adaptation in large metazoans lacking a through-flow alimentary system. Egestion of indigestible remains via ciliary currents (Carlgren, 1905) or by peristalsis of the column circular muscles (Batham and Pantin, 1950b) need not eliminate material still being digested in contact

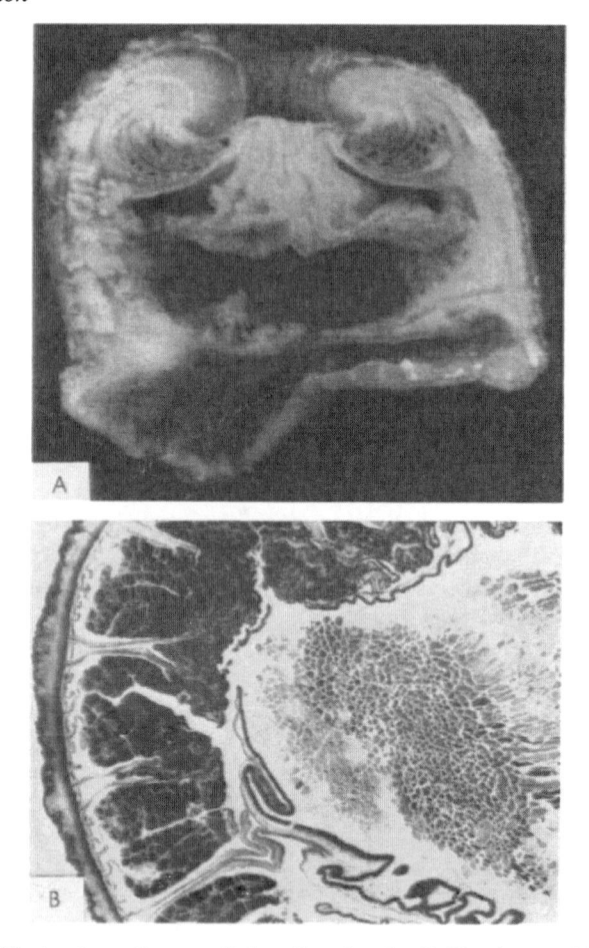

Figure 2.11 Mechanism of extracellular digestion in *Calliactis parasitica*. **A**. Vertical section through a frozen anemone, showing close investiture of ingested food (gelatin pellet) by mesenteric filaments (× 5). **B**. Horizontal section through an anemone digesting a piece of plaice muscle. Note the apposition of the mesenteric filaments to the food mass, and the change in staining density at its margin, owing to partial digestion (× 10). Source: with permission from Nicol (1959), courtesy Marine Biological Association.

with the filaments. The functioning of the actiniarian coelenteron thus seems to combine aspects of the batch reactor and of the continuous-flow, stirred-tank reactor models for animal guts (Penry and Jumars, 1987).

Unlike the situation in higher metazoans having a plug-flow gut, where a single meal is followed after a lag period by a single defecation, in sea anemones egestion may be multiple and discontinuous following a single meal. The mucus-wrapped bolus egested within several hours after feeding (Van-Praët, 1982a; Sebens and Koehl, 1984) contains recognizable indigestible material (sand grains, polychaete setae, larval bivalve shells) and probably represents material not taken up by digestive phagocytes in the endoderm (section 2.3.4). Amorphous material egested 24–48 h after feeding may be the residue of intracellular digestion.

Retention time within the coelenteron varies according to ration size and digestibility of prey. Microphagous *Metridium senile* fed natural zooplankton egested a mucus-wrapped bolus within 4 h after feeding (Sebens and Koehl, 1984); the coelenteron contained recognizable prey fragments (mostly crustaceans) up to 2 h after feeding, but no recognizable items by 4–6 h. Purcell (1977a) noted that this species egested 'waste pellets' 24–48 h after collection. Together, these results indicate a relatively short period of extracellular fragmentation followed by a more prolonged hydrolysis of materials intracellularly.

Tiffon and Bouillon (1975) found similarly that *Cerianthus lloydi* fed pieces of shrimp abdomen had no trace of food left in the coelenteron by 12 h after feeding. Zamer (1986) reported that *Anthopleura elegantissima* given varying rations of adult brine shrimp produced egesta from 3.5 to 8 h after feeding. Prey remains were detected within the phagocytes of *Actinia equina* up to 48 h after a meal of crustaceans (Van-Praët, 1981). The continous output of indigestible remains from 12 to 30 h after feeding in *Sagartia troglodytes* (Riemann-Zürneck, 1969) may reflect the heterogeneous and refractory diet of this detritivore. As a consequence both of their large mass and protective shell valves, mussels (*Mytilus edulis*) were retained in the coelenteron for 40–60 h by *Actinia equina* (Dicquemare, 1773).

There have been few direct studies of absorption efficiency, i.e. [(ingestion − egestion)/ingestion] × 100%, in sea anemones. This is perhaps due to their gradual output of undigested material (measurement of which requires repeated collections of egesta), as well as to the packaging of egesta in mucus (which must be tediously removed or allowed to account for an unknown and variable amount of energy content of the egesta). Ivleva (1964) gave values of prey 'assimilability' in *Actinia equina* ranging from 30.9% to 96.6%, although these values were obtained indirectly from energetic equivalents of [(respiration + growth)/ingestion] × 100% measured over 9 to 23 day periods at several temperatures. Despite the uncertainty of this indirect method, Ivleva's data show a clear inverse relationship between relative ration size and absorption efficiency (or in this case, *assimilation efficiency*, since food was not only absorbed but also used in respiration and biosynthesis) (Figure 2.12). Relative ration size itself was inversely related to anemone body weight in specimens fed *ad lib.* (see Figure 2.5), so that the effects of ration size and body weight are not clearly separable in these data.

Like its capture, the absorption of prey is a surface-related function, and

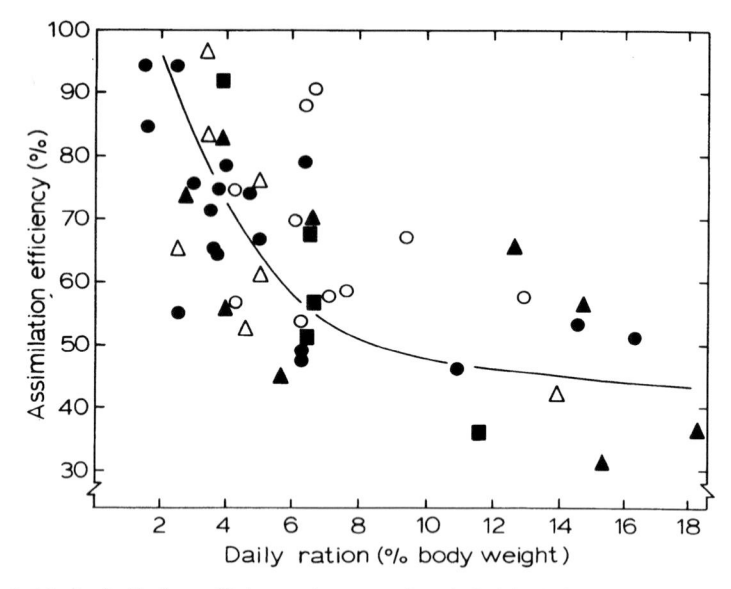

Figure 2.12 Assimilation efficiency (see text for definition) for different ration sizes of mussel gonad ingested by *Actinia equina*. Symbols as in Figure 2.5. Source: drawn from data in Ivleva (1964).

in *A.equina* the weight (mg) of prey absorbed, $_aW_p$, $= 24.55\,_dW^{0.69}$ (calculated from data in Ivleva, 1964). It is also influenced by temperature. In a standard $0.2\,\text{g}\,_dW$ anemone, the daily assimilated ration (the product of ingested ration $\times$ assimilation efficiency) was maximal at $18.7°–19.9°C$, and decreases in assimilated ration above and below these temperatures were due to decreased ingestion (Table 2.2). In a $0.2\,\text{g}\,_dW$ specimen of *A.equina* ingesting a daily ration of 3.6% of its body weight, assimilation efficiency declined from 97.1% at 13.8°C to 69.0% at 21–22.7°C (Table 2.2). The increased assimilation efficiency at the lowest temperature was probably due to increased food retention time, which may partially offset the slower rate of digestive enzyme activity, lower food availability, and ameliorate the loss of body mass which occurs in winter (see Sebens, 1982b).

In *Aiptasia pulchella* fed relatively large rations (25–85% of estimated anemone $_dW$) of brine shrimp, directly measured organic and energetic absorption efficiencies were 70% ($\pm 15\%\,\text{S.D.}$) and 63% ($\pm 15\%\,\text{S.D.}$), respectively (Hunter, 1984). The weights of individual anemones were not given (range $9–14\,\text{mg}\,_dW$), so some of the variability in absorption efficiency probably resulted from the different relative sizes of the fixed ration in anemones of various body sizes. In *Anthopleura elegantissima* of similar body size receiving different ration sizes, directly measured absorption efficiencies for carbon and nitrogen confirm that absorption efficiency is inversely related to ration size (Zamer, 1986). This is the case in many metazoans (reviewed by Calow, 1977a). Sea anemones in nature have very small ingested rations (see section 2.2.6), and absorption efficiency in the field probably exceeds 90%, especially since (unlike laboratory feedings), small amounts of prey are ingested continuously (Sebens and Koehl, 1984) rather than in a single large meal (except in large, macrophagous species such as *A.xanthogrammica* and *U.piscivora*).

In *Anthopleura elegantissima* freshly-collected specimens from high on the shore have consistently greater absorption efficiencies compared with low-shore specimens, which Zamer (1986) interprets as a compensation for reduced feeding time in the intertidal zone. In this species, absorption efficiencies for protein and lipid exceed 95%, whereas only 10–60% of carbohydrate is absorbed from experimental prey (brine shrimp), which is in keeping with the relative availability of these substrates in the prey (Zamer and Shick, 1989). High-shore specimens apparently have a particular ability to absorb lipid more efficiently than do low-shore individuals.

The difference between high and low shore individuals of *A.elegantissima* in their respective absorption efficiencies was due to behavioural adjustments to intertidal exposure and to persistent differences between clones. The latter were not erased by cross-acclimatization to the opposite exposure and feeding regime (Table 2.4). When subtidally-acclimatized individuals were transferred to intertidal conditions they were unable to retain prey in the coelenteron during emersion and showed low absorption efficiency. Ability to retain prey, and absorption efficiency, both increased with acclimatization to intertidal conditions. Modified behaviour thus accompanies physiological adaptation to existence in the food-limited upper shore. Under the same maintenance conditions anemones originating on the upper shore consistently had a significantly greater absorption efficiency than did low shore conspecifics (Table 2.4), so that adaptation to periodic (tidal) feeding may have resulted in greater digestive efficiency (Zamer, 1986).

2.3.3 Extracellular Digestive Enzymes

Most studies of digestive enzymology in sea anemones have centred on proteases, which is understandable given the traditional view of anemones as strict carnivores. What is surprising is that there are so few studies on chitinases, considering the frequency of arthropod prey in the diet of sea anemones. The chitins in marine fungi and diatoms are also possible substrates.

Jeuniaux (1962) demonstrated a strong hydrolysis of native chitin by gastrodermal homogenates of *Adamsia carciniopados* ($\equiv$ *A.palliata*), *Anemonia viridis* ($\equiv$ *A.sulcata*), *Anthopleura ballii* and *Edwardsia claparedii* ($\equiv$ *E.callimorpha*). Likewise, *Metridium senile fimbriatum* had the highest

Table 2.4 Absorption efficiencies in *Anthopleura elegantissima* acclimatized to different shore heights and daily rations in nature and in a laboratory tidal simulator. Freshly-collected high shore (H) and low shore (L) anemones were fed daily rations of adult *Artemia* sp. amounting to 1% of their body weight. Anemones originally collected from high (H) or low (L) intertidal positions and subsequently acclimatized to intertidal (I, two 6-h emersions daily) and subtidal (S, continuous emersion) were fed 4% and 5.4% daily rations during intertidal and subtidal acclimatization, respectively

Treatment	Ration (% body weight)	Gravimetric	Absorption efficiency (%)			
			Organic	C	N	Energetic
Freshly collected						
H	1	85.5	92.5	94.8	94.2	95.5
L	1	81.9	90.0	91.8	91.4	92.1
Acclimatized						
HI	4.0	81.0	84.7	85.9	88.0	85.6
HS	5.6	63.5	72.8	73.7	80.0	72.6
LI	4.0	76.1	79.7	80.4	84.4	79.8
LS	5.6	58.0	66.4	67.9	75.2	67.1

Source: Zamer (1986)

chitinase activity among 37 species in eight phyla of invertebrates tested by Elyakova (1972), explaining in part the very rapid and complete digestion of crustacean zooplankton by this species (see preceding section). However, since the egesta of many sea anemones frequently contain recognizable, incompletely digested fragments of arthropods, it may be that the chitinase is more important in opening energy and nutrient filled packages than in completely digesting their wrappings, although the latter may occur to some extent. Jeuniaux (1962) and Molodtsov and Vafina (1972) also found very high chitobiase activity in anemones, which indicates that they can complete the hydrolysis of the β-1, 4 linkage within the disaccharide chitobiose cleaved from chitin, but the absorption and utilization of the resulting free aminosugar N-acetylhexosamine has not been shown.

Whether sea anemone 'chitinase' activity is restricted to the glycosidic bonds in that homopolymer or whether it can attack a variety of β-1, 4 linkages has not been studied. Two additional speculative roles for 'chitinase' or 'mucopolysaccharidase' are the hydrolysis of such linkages in the N-acetylhexosamine-containing peptidoglycans of bacterial cell walls, and the digestive recycling of the abundantly secreted mucus in microphages such as *Metridium* spp., via cleavage of β-1, 4 linkages in the glycoproteins of the mucus (Bunde, Dearlove and Bishop, 1978). Either of these is a possible role for the 'chitinase' present also in the ectoderm of *Anemonia viridis* (Jeuniaux, 1962).

Once its outer chitinous defences have been cracked, extracellular digestion of prey proceeds through the action of at least two proteases. These have been demonstrated in all studies of anemones where modern enzymic techniques have been used, and from their alkaline pH optima, they appear to be mammalian-type trypsin and chymotrypsin (Gibson and Dixon, 1969; Tiffon and Bouillon, 1975; Van-Praët, 1982b). These enzymes are localized in the lower (digestive) portions of the mesenteric filaments and adjacent mesenteric tissue (Figure 2.13), probably within the zymogen cells abundant there, which ultrastructurally and histochemically resemble mammalian pancreatic zymogen cells (Tiffon and Bouillon, 1975; Van-Praët, 1978). Anemone trypsin and chymotrypsin show a characteristic zymogen activation, with the activity in tissue homogenates reaching a maximum in 1 to 2 h at 20°–25°C (Gibson and Dixon, 1969; Tiffon and Bouillon, 1975). It is probably these proteases whose release is stimulated by protein components of food.

The difficulty of using absolute levels of protease activity as an indicator of the nutritional status of sea anemones has been shown by Van-Praët (1982a, b), who measured trypsin and chymotrypsin activity in *Actinia equina* during the course of starvation, feeding and digestion. The insignificant increase in activity (but great increase in variability of results) between 5 and 96h after feeding was attributed to the involvement in digestion of

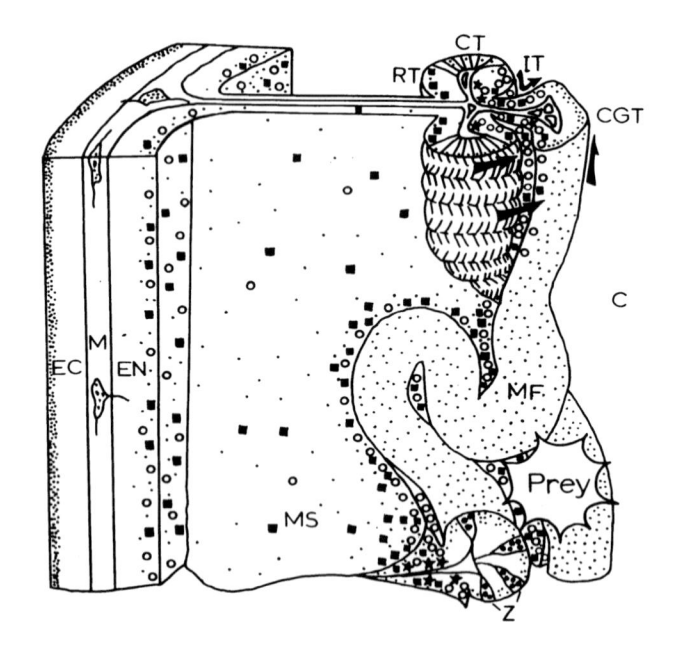

Figure 2.13 Diagram of a portion of an actinian showing the principal regions of digestion and absorption. **C**, coelenteron; **CGT**, cnidoglandular tract; **CT**, ciliary tract; **EC**, ectoderm; **EN**, endoderm; **IT**, intermediate tract; **M**, mesoglea; **MF**, mesenteric filament; MS, mesentery; **RT**, reticular tract; **Z**, zymogen cells; stippling, zone of absorption of dissolved molecules; ■, zone of absorption of macromolecules; ○, zone of absorption of particles up to a few μm in size; ♦, water currents leaving the coelenteron; ★, zone of lipid storage. Prey fragments up to several mm in size are phagocytosed at the lower (digestive) portion of the mesenteric filaments. Source: after Van-Praët (1982a).

only a small amount of the total enzyme present. This idea was supported by histological examination, which revealed no reduction in the number of zymogen cells. During seven days of starvation the activities of both enzymes in homogenates increased, presumably through the accumulation of zymogens. Not surprisingly, three months of starvation led to a decrease in both enzymes. Seasonal variation of enzyme activity in freshly collected *A.equina* also occurred (Van-Praët, 1981, 1982b). In *Anthopleura elegantissima* the greater absorption efficiency in high-shore as compared with low-shore anemones is not associated with significant differences in their chymotrypsin-like protease activity (Zamer, Robbins and Shick, 1987).

Phospholipids, mucus and chymotrypsin of sea anemones contain 2-aminoethylphosphonic acid (AEP) (Quin, 1965; Stevenson, Gibson and Dixon, 1974; Bunde *et al.*, 1978), which includes an unusual carbon-phosphorus bond. Because the C-P bond is resistant to hydrolysis, Kittredge and Roberts (1969) suggested that its presence in endodermal membranes and in chymotrypsin itself may protect these structures against the action of other hydrolases. Likewise, juveniles of *Actinia tenebrosa* which are brooded in the adult's coelenteron (see section 6.4.1) are resistant to digestive enzymes, a protection provided by the juveniles' mucus (Ottaway, 1974). Treatment with hyaluronidase failed to eliminate this protection (Ottaway, 1974), probably because, unlike those in higher animals, the glycoproteins and acid mucopolysaccharide-like components of anemone mucus lack uronic and sialic acids and sulfated sugars, the acidic functional groups of which are apparently replaced by AEP (Bunde *et al.*, 1978).

2.3.4 Absorption

The absorption of sugars, and of free amino acids produced by the extracellular proteases, occurs in cells throughout the mesenteric filaments (Figure 2.13), and especially in the cnidoglandular tract (Van-Praët, 1980). Although there may be some extracellular digestion of triglycerides (Krijgsman and Talbot, 1953), the completion of digestion of lipid droplets, colloidal proteins and prey fragments occurs intracellularly following their phagocytosis by cells in the lower portion of the mesenteric filaments and in the intermediate tract of the trifid upper portion of the filaments (Figure 2.13), the latter being in position to remove particles from the ciliary current leaving the coelenteron.

Fragments of crustacean prey were observed inside phagocytic endodermal cells of *Cerianthus lloydi* (Tiffon and Daireaux, 1974) and *Actinia equina* (Van-Praët, 1982a) within several hours after feeding. The phagocytosis of bacteria and cyanobacteria has been noted in *A.equina* (Van-Praët, 1981, 1982a) and *Metridium senile* (Van-Praët, personal communication), providing further evidence that these anemones are not strict carnivores.

Pinocytosis of macromolecules (ferritin and colloidal carbon) occurs on the hypostome and labial tentacles of ceriantharians and in the intermediate tract of the mesenteric filaments of actiniarians (Tiffon and Daireaux, 1974; Van-Praët, 1982a). Following their emulsification in the coelenteron, lipid droplets accumulate in vesicles of phagocytes, where they induce esterase activity (Van-Praët, 1982a).

2.4 INTRACELLULAR DIGESTION

Following the early investigations by Metschnikoff and by Mesnil, the mechanisms of intracellular digestion in the lower Metazoa have been clarified, especially the role of lysosomes abundant in phagocytes (Tiffon *et al.*, 1973). Characteristic lysosomal enzymes that have been detected in sea anemones include acid phosphatase, β-glucuronidase, β-glycerophosphatase, cathepsin, ribonuclease, and various esterases and hydrolases having acidic pH optima (Corner *et al.*, 1960; Tiffon, 1973, 1975; Tiffon and Hugon, 1977; O'Brien, 1980; Tiffon and Franc, 1982; Van-Praët, 1982a; Zamer *et al.*, 1987).

Amylase has been found in homogenates of mesenteric filaments of *Pseudactinia flagellifera* (Krijgsman and Talbot, 1953), the corallimorpharian *Rhodactis* sp. (Elyakova *et al.*, 1981), and *Actinia equina* and several deep-sea anemones (Van-Praët, 1981, 1982b). Its location has not been pinpointed, but it is not concentrated in the region of the mesenteric filaments that secretes extracellular proteases, and its acidic pH optimum suggests also that it acts intracellularly.

Van-Praët (1982b) correlated seasonal changes in amylase activity in *A.equina* with those of microalgae in the environment, and proposed that phytoplankton are important in the diet of this omnivore. He found similarly high amylase activities also in deep-sea *Paracalliactis stephensoni* and *Phellactis robusta* collected at a depth of about 2 000 m, and proposed that these anemones feed on particles settling out of the water column or collected from the sediment surface (Van-Praët, 1981). Much lower amylase activities were noted in *Actinauge* sp. and *Amphianthus radiatus* collected at 4 000 to 5 000 m, perhaps because the phytoplankton sinking to the greatest depths are diatoms (Bacillariophyceae), which store β-1, 3 linked chrysolaminarins rather than α-1, 4 linked starch and which would therefore not induce amylase activity (Van-Praët, 1983a). The chymotrypsin levels in these anemones are similar to that in *A.equina*, so that generally lower rates of enzymic catalysis and metabolism in food-limited deep-sea animals (Somero, Siebenaller and Hochachka, 1983) may not extend to digestive hydrolases.

Evidence for the ability of anemones to digest plant polysaccharides is a mosaic from which more pieces are missing than are present. Although *Metridium senile fimbriatum* lacks cellulase (Elyakova, 1972), the cell walls of marine algae are generally composed of polysaccharides other than cellulose. β-glucuronidase has been associated with the ingestion of algae in *Cerianthus lloydi* (Tiffon, 1973), and in *M.senile* it was induced by some component of natural particulate organic detritus from which recognizable animal remains had been removed (Zamer *et al.*, 1987). Polysaccharides in the cell walls of brown macrophytes (Phaeophyceae), unicellular and macrophytic green algae (Chlorophyceae), and diatoms (Bacillariophyceae) (all of which groups have been identified in the coelenteron contents of various species of anemones) all contain large amounts of glucuronic acid (Percival and McDowell, 1967) and so are potential substrates for β-glucuronidase. However, the Phaeophyceae (*Ascophyllum*, *Fucus*, *Laminaria*, etc.) and Bacillariophyceae (e.g. *Phaeodactylum tricornutum*) store a variety of laminarins (Percival, 1968), which the few anemones studied lack the enzymes to hydrolyse (Elyakova, Shevchenko and Avaeva, 1981), so that an anemone having β-glucuronidase but no laminarinases could digest the wrapping but not the contents of the package. The Chlorophyceae (*Ulva*, as well as a variety of phytoplankters) store starch, so that an anemone possessing both β-glucuronidase and amylase presumably could digest these plants' cell walls and their storage products. The macrophagous '*Stoichactis*' (*Stichodactyla?*) sp. and the corallimorpharian *Rhodactis* sp. lack laminarinases, but these enzymes are present in several alcyonaceans (Elyakova *et al.*, 1981), which may be more microphagous (see Sebens and Koehl, 1984). Piavaux (1977) found laminarinase in mesenteric filaments of *Anemonia viridis* but not in those of *Calliactis parasitica*. Unfortunately there has been no coordinated study of diet and activities of β-glucuronidase, amylase and laminarinases in a single species of sea anemone. Considering the rather catholic diet and inducibility of β-glucuronidase in *Metridium senile*, such a study could be informative.

Avoidance of digestion by the intracellular algal symbionts of sea anemones is discussed in section 2.6.3. The presence of lysozyme, which lyses bacterial cell walls, has not been tested for in anemones.

The course of events during intracellular digestion is not entirely clear, and some results appear contradictory. Van-Praët (1976) noted an increase in acid phosphatase reaction product in endodermal cells of *Actinia equina* during ten days of starvation but a decrease at about 20 h after feeding, and interpreted this as a utilization of the stock of acid phosphatase during digestion. Conversely, in *Pachycerianthus fimbriatus* Tiffon and Hugon (1977) found that the acid phosphatase reaction was stronger in fed specimens than in individuals starved for eight days. The differences may be resolved by Van-Praët's (1976) observation in minimally-fed *A.equina* that absorptive cells rich in acid phosphatase alternate with such cells devoid of the enzyme, i.e. the simultaneous existence of cells in various stages of the digestive process is indicated, so that a quantitative, statistical study such as those conducted on cells of the digestive diverticula of bivalve molluscs might be useful albeit more difficult. The situation is complicated by the role of lysosomes and autophagosomes in tissue autolysis during prolonged starvation (Tiffon and Franc, 1982), in tissue dedifferentiation prior to regeneration (Van-Praët, 1976) and during tissue replacement (Watson and Mariscal, 1983a).

2.5 TRANSLOCATION AND STORAGE

It is usually assumed that products of digestion in endodermal cells reach the ectoderm by diffusing across the mesoglea (Chapman and Pardy, 1972; Schlichter, 1974). Nutrition of the ectodermal cells also may occur via direct uptake of dissolved organic matter from the environment (section 2.2.8). Present in the mesoglea of anemones are mobile cells rich in glycogen and lipid, especially numerous in the digestive region of the mesenteric filaments. A transport role for these cells is indicated by their greater abundance in anemones, which have relatively thick mesogleas, than in corals, which have thin mesogleas (Van-Praët, 1982a). Mobile cells especially rich in glycogen (termed 'glycocytes' by Boury-Esnault and Doumenc, 1979) traverse the mesoglea and migrate to sites of energy demand during gametogenesis, regeneration and asexual reproduction. There may be a direct transfer of stored materials from such cells to developing oocytes in the mesoglea of *Anemonia viridis* ($\equiv$ *A.sulcata*) (Van-Praët, 1982a).

Endodermal phagocytes appear both to store temporarily the products of intracellular digestion and to synthesize glycogen (Van-Praët, 1982a). Numerous other cell types in the endoderm and ectoderm store glycogen (which has usually been detected histochemically) in amounts comparable with that in equivalent cells in other invertebrates and vertebrates, and which increase during gametogenesis and regeneration (Boury-Esnault and Doumenc, 1979). In the longitudinal musculature of the column, glycogen is stored both as rosettes (in higher animals, typically a long-term storage form: Hochachka, 1980) and as particles (the reserve fuel for rapid contraction), although whether similar roles apply in sea anemones is unknown.

Histochemical studies notwithstanding, glycogen does not appear as the major storage product in *Actinia equina*, where it ranges seasonally from 1.4% to 3.6% of $_dW$ (Ortega, Lopez and Navarro, 1988), or in *Metridium senile* or *Anthopleura xanthogrammica*, where it accounts for 1% and 4% of body dry weight, respectively (Giese, 1966). A coordinated seasonal study of glycogen storage and mobilization during the annual reproductive cycle is necessary before the quantitative importance of this storage product can be stated with certainty. Likewise, glyconeogenesis *per se* has not been studied in any sea anemone.

In *A.elegantissima* Fitt and Pardy (1981) reported higher levels of 'carbohydrate' (up to 7.6% of dry weight), which did not decline during one month of starvation, leading them to suggest that the carbohydrates consisted of mucopolysaccharides rather than glycogen. Using similar biochemical methods, Zamer, Shick and Tapley (1989) found 6.6% of $_dW$ in *A.elegantissima* to be carbohydrate. Mucus and structural protein (especially collagen), however, contain much glycoprotein, which may not be accurately quantified in routine biochemical analysis. When calculated stoichiometrically from CHN content, 'carbohydrate' increased to 16.9% of ash-free dry weight ($_{af}W$) in *A.elegantissima*, and also accounted for 44.4% of $_{af}W$ of mucus from *Metridium senile* (see section 5.3, page 202). In *A.elegantissima*, the variation in total carbohydrate was much greater than that of carbohydrate not associated with protein, perhaps reflecting variable amounts of mucus production (Zamer *et al.*, 1989).

Lipids are the major energy store in most sea anemones, and may account

Table 2.5 Lipid level (percentage of dry body weight) and composition (percentage of total lipid) in sea anemones and a ceriantharian. DG = diglycerides; FS = free sterols (largely cholesterol); N = neutral lipid; P = polar lipid; PL = phospholipid; TG = triglycerides; WE = wax esters

Species	Lipid level (%)	Composition (% total lipid)	Source
Actinia equina	5.1–8.7[a,b]	FS + DG: 12.2–25.2; PL: 52.1–77.3; TG: 5.9–25.2	Ortega and Navarro (1988)
Actinostola callosa	28		Bergmann *et al.* (1956)
Anemonia viridis (≡ *A. sulcata*)	6.7[c]	N:82.4; PL: 16.1	Voogt *et al.* (1974)
A. viridis (≡ *A. sulcata*)	22.1		Janssen and Möller (1981)
Anthopleura elegantissima	6.6[d]		Simon and Rouser (1967)
A. elegantissima	12.9	P: 81.7; TG: 9.3; WE: 9.0	Blanquet *et al.* (1979)
A. elegantissima	7–18[a]		Jennison (1979a)
A. elegantissima	10.3		Fitt and Pardy (1981)
A. elegantissima	7.3[e]–9.4[f]		Zamer and Shick (1987)
A. xanthogrammica	10.1		Giese (1966)
Bolocera tuediae	30.3		Bergmann *et al.* (1956)
Cerianthus membranaceus	12.2[g]	N: 86.5; PL: 11.2	Voogt *et al.* (1974)
Condylactis gigantea	31.1		Bergmann *et al.* (1956)
C. gigantea			
(whole anemone)	43.2		Kellogg and Patton (1983)
(tentacles)		FS: 9.0; PL: 67.8; TG: 15.8; WE: 7.9	
(column)		FS: 1.9; PL: 11.4; TG: 20.4; WE: 65.7	
Epiactis (≡ *Cnidopus*) *japonica*	14[c]		Isay and Busarova (1984)
Gyrostoma sp.			Rajagopal and Sohonie (1957)
(whole anemone)	5.6[h]		
(tentacles)	1.9		
(mesenteries)	5.3		
(gonads)	8.7		
Metridium sp.	8.0		Giese (1966)

Table 2.5 Continued

Species	Lipid level (%)	Composition (% total lipid)	Source
M.senile (≡ *M.dianthus*)	1.9–8.1[i]	FS: 15–20; P: 50–60; TG: 10–18; WE: 10–18	Hooper and Ackman (1971)
M.senile	7.0[i]	N: 60.4; P: 39.6	Voogt *et al.* (1974)
M.senile	6.6–24.2[a,i]	FS: 5.8–25.3; P: 57.2–83.5; TG: 4.1–11.2; WE: 2.3–10.0	Hill-Manning and Blanquet (1979)
M.senile fimbriatum	8.1		Isay and Busarova (1984)
Phymactis clematis	7.0		Orlando Munoz *et al.* (1976)
Phymactis clematis	10.0–12.4[j,k]	N: 68.5–89.2; P: 10.8–31.5	Pollero (1983)

Notes: a. Annual range;
   b. Calculated from fresh weight and a tissue water content of 80%;
   c. Calculated from fresh weight and a tissue water content of 85%;
   d. Calculated from fresh weight and a tissue water content of 77%;
   e. High intertidal specimens;
   f. Low intertidal specimens;
   g. Calculated from fresh weight and a tissue water content of 88%;
   h. Total of PL, cholesterol and cerebroside;
   i. Calculated from fresh weight and a tissue water content of 84%;
   j. Autumn-Spring values;
   k. Calculated from fresh weight and an assumed tissue water content of 81% (see Orlando Munoz *et al.*, 1976)

for over 40% of the anemone's dry weight (Table 2.5). Lipid is preferentially utilized during starvation (Fitt and Pardy, 1981; Janssen and Möller, 1981), which induces esterase activity adjacent to lipid stores in the endoderm (Van-Praët, 1980). The advantages of lipids as storage molecules have been repeatedly emphasized (Kleiber, 1961; Pond, 1981; Brafield and Llewellyn, 1982), especially their high energy content per unit mass ($\Delta_c h$ is $-39.5\,\mathrm{kJ\cdot g^{-1}}$ for lipids versus $-17.5\,\mathrm{kJ\cdot g^{-1}}$ for glycogen). Because the energetic efficiency of synthesis of lipids and glycogen (i.e. the energy incorporated into ester and glycosidic linkages per mol ATP utilized in forming the bonds) are similar (Lehninger, 1973), the greater energetic density of lipid also means that more total energy can be stored in lipid than in glycogen per mol ATP invested in accumulating the store, especially if storage lipids incorporate pre-existing (dietary) fatty acids rather than synthesizing them *de novo*.

Although in mobile terrestrial animals the ability to maximize stored energy while minimizing its mass is important, this is presumably less of a factor in sedentary marine animals having the buoyant support of water. In sea anemones the tissue level of organization precludes specialized storage organs, and anemones moreover lack a circulatory system for the distribution of stored materials to sites of demand (the quantitative significance of the mobile cells discussed earlier has not been established). In anemones most reserve materials may hence be stored within the cells where they ultimately are utilized, so that minimization of volume, rather than of mass, may be a major factor selecting for lipid storage. Such volume constraints may be exacerbated in small specimens of *Metridium senile*, which have less massive columns and mesenteries (the major site of lipid deposition: see also Féral *et al.*, 1979) and which store proportionally more lipid than do large individuals (Hooper and Ackman, 1971), except when the latter are reproductively ripe (Hill-Manning and Blanquet, 1979).

With the possible exception of actively swimming anemones (e.g. *Stomphia coccinea* and *Boloceroides mcmurrichi*), there has been no selective pressure for a storage molecule capable of especially rapid mobilization and catabolism (glycolytic flare-up) during intense activity, one of the few advantages of glycogen. Although lipid has the major disadvantage of being unable to be catabolized anaerobically, the necessity of long-term anaerobiosis is not a factor for most sea anemones. Possible exceptions to this are intertidal species such as *Actinia equina*, *Anthopleura elegantissima* and *Bunodosoma cavernata*, which sometimes are subject to prolonged burial in storm-shifted sand and which all show excellent survival during anoxia, and European populations of *Metridium senile* living in periodically anoxic fjords (Wahl, 1984). Giese's (1966) data (see page 80) suggest that *Anthopleura* has larger glycogen reserves than do North American specimens of *Metridium*, which do not survive prolonged anoxia (Sassaman and Mangum, 1972). As mentioned, *Actinia equina* appears histochemically also to have larger glycogen stores

(Boury-Esnault and Doumenc, 1979) of up to 3.6% of $_dW$ (Ortega *et al.*, 1988) and it survives long-term anoxia. A quantitative comparison of glycogen reserves in euryoxic actiniids with those in less anoxia-tolerant species would be useful. Finally, there is some evidence that proteins (amino acids) may be important substrates for anaerobic energy metabolism in sea anemones (see section 3.4, page ###).

The pathways of biosynthesis have scarcely been studied in sea anemones, but it is unlikely that they differ from those in other metazoans. The relatively high and equal activities of glucose-6-phosphate dehydrogenase (G6PDH) and 6-phosphogluconate dehydrogenase (6PGDH) (two enzymes of the pentose shunt, which is important in generating the NADPH used in lipid biosynthesis) in sea anemones (Powers, Lenhoff and Leone, 1968) may help explain their high lipid levels. In well-fed *Metridium senile* at 5°C, the pentose shunt accounts for $\approx 4-7\%$ of total flow of carbon from glucose, a moderately high percentage (Zamer and Hoffmann, 1989). Hydroids, which lack 6PGDH activity, tend to have higher glycogen than lipid levels (Cook and Kelty, 1982).

Protein- and lipid-rich zooplankton account for the bulk of the diet of many sea anemones (section 2.2.4 and Table 2.1). Although lipid comprises roughly one-third of $_dW$ of the natural and experimental prey of *Anthopleura elegantissima*, it constitutes only 2% of the substrates used in aerobic respiration (Zamer and Shick, 1987; Table 3.2, page 133). Given the absorption efficiency above 90% for lipid, this means that most lipid derived from prey is stored in well-fed *A.elegantissima*, the tissues of which increase in lipid content during laboratory maintenance (Zamer and Shick, 1987). The constituent fatty acids, and perhaps the β-monoglycerides derived from the partial breakdown of prey triglycerides, presumably are available for direct incorporation into sea anemone lipids, so that the high lipid content of anemones in general may in part reflect the rich lipid content of their food. Such direct incorporation will also reduce the cost and increase the efficiency of their lipid synthesis (Parry, 1983). It has been argued (Sargent, 1976, 1978) that the conversion of dietary glucose and amino acids into fatty acids yields a net production of reduced pyridine nucleotides, which may in turn yield ATP; thus, fatty acid synthesis from amino acid precursors is actually an energy-yielding pathway, an advantage to sea anemones on a small ration rich in protein. The deamination of amino acids derived from prey and the incorporation of their carbon skeletons into lipid has been shown in hard corals (Szmant-Froelich, 1981), phylogenetically the closest relatives of sea anemones. Also, the excess NADPH generated in this scheme could be used in the synthesis of wax esters, which are quantitatively very important among the storage lipids of sea anemones (see below and Table 2.5).

The lipid content and composition of sea anemones varies seasonally (although not strictly with temperature: Figure 2.14) and with reproductive

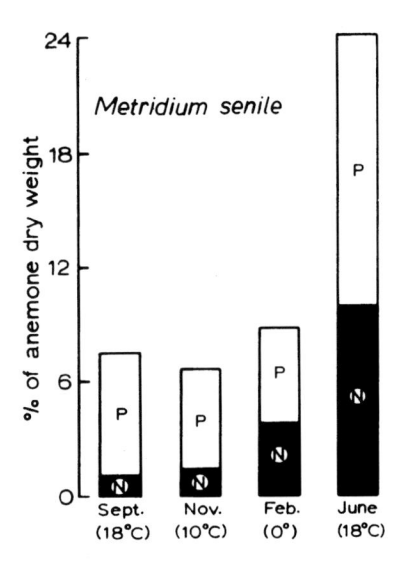

Figure 2.14 Seasonal changes in the lipid level and composition in *Metridium senile* at Massachusetts, USA. N, neutral lipid; P, polar lipid. Seawater temperatures at the times of collection are shown. The temperature-independent accumulation of lipid, especially neutral (storage) lipid, may be due to gamete maturation. Source: drawn from data in Hill-Manning and Blanquet (1979).

state (Hill-Manning and Blanquet, 1979; Jennison, 1979a), but most studies have been restricted to a single season. It is therefore hard to generalize from the data in Table 2.5. As pointed out by the former authors, interpretation of temporal changes in the individual components of total lipid is difficult because any one of them may be influenced by dietary intake, *de novo* synthesis and catabolism. Concentrations of neutral lipids, primarily the storage forms triglyceride and wax ester, usually exceed those of polar or phospholipids, especially when total lipid levels are high. The threefold increase in total lipid content of *Metridium senile* between September and June includes a disproportional increase in neutral lipid (Figure 2.14), probably associated with gametogenesis and maturation. The column, mesenteries and especially the gonads are generally richer in storage lipids than the tentacles. Spawning results in a large decrease in total lipid (Figure 2.15). There is no difference between the sexes in their lipid content in *Anthopleura elegantissima* (Jennison, 1979a). The relatively small annual fluctuation in lipid content (5.1% to 8.7% of $_dW$) in *Actinia equina* may reflect the less pronounced seasonality of reproduction in some populations of this species, although the maximum level of total lipid and especially triglycerides occurs in the spring at the time of reproductive maturity for most individuals (Ortega and Navarro, 1988).

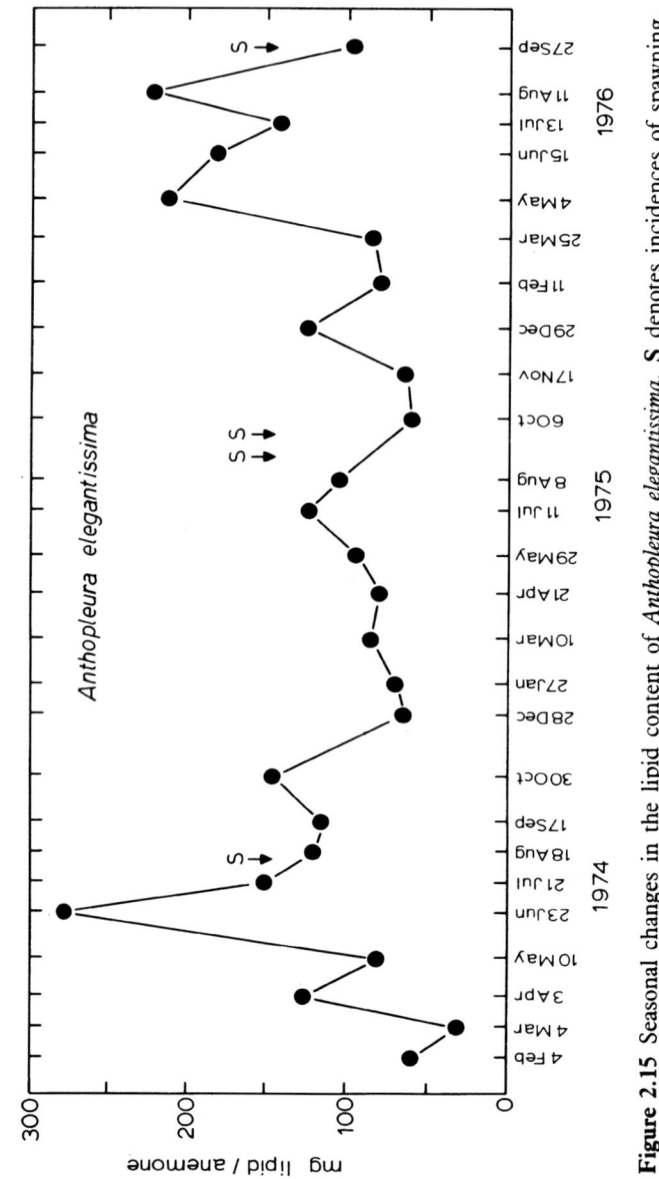

Figure 2.15 Seasonal changes in the lipid content of *Anthopleura elegantissima*. **S** denotes incidences of spawning, detected histologically. See text for additional discussion. Source: after Jennison (1979a).

Although the cold water anemones *Actinostola callosa* and *Bolocera tuediae* are approximately 30% lipid by weight, values as high or higher are found in the tropical *Condylactis gigantea* (Table 2.5). Thus, like other marine ectotherms (Clarke, 1983), there is no tendency for cold water anemones to accumulate more lipid than do warm water species.

The lipids of anemones living in cold water are more unsaturated (i.e. have more double bonds in the hydrocarbon chains of their constituent fatty acids) than those in warm water forms, which probably represents a homeoviscous adaptation to maintain membrane fluidity at low temperature (see Clarke, 1983). It may also be important in maintaining storage lipids in a liquid state for ready mobilization (Kellogg and Patton, 1983). Bergmann, Creighton and Stokes (1956) found predominantly saturated fats in the tropical *C.gigantea* but much unsaturated lipid, including long-chain fatty acids and alcohols, in the arctic species *Actinostola callosa* and in the boreal *Bolocera tuediae*, where the lipids were described as 'viscous oils'. Similarly, Hooper and Ackman (1971) noted high levels of unsaturated fats in the boreal *Metridium senile*. The reported predominance of long-chain saturated fatty acids in '*Metridium senile*' collected in subtropical Florida, USA (Mason, 1972) surely reflects misidentification of the anemone, as *M.senile* does not occur so far south on the Atlantic Coast of North America; the saturated fatty acid composition of the anemone that was analysed, however, is in keeping with its warm-water habitat. Long-chain polyunsaturated fatty acids are virtually absent from the tropical *C.gigantea* (Kellogg and Patton, 1983), whereas the $20:4$, $20:5$ and $22:6$ unsaturated fatty acids (i.e. those having hydrocarbon chains containing 20 or 22 carbon atoms and four, five or six double bonds) comprise about 30% of the total lipid in the temperate zone *Anthopleura elegantissima* (Blanquet, Nevenzel and Benson, 1979). Although oleic acid ($18:1$) comprises only about 2% of the neutral lipids in *C.gigantea*, it accounts for over 20% of the lipid in *A.elegantissima*, where the symbiotic dinoflagellates (zooxanthellae) may contribute the O_2 necessary for the desaturation process (Blanquet *et al.*, 1979). This difference is not simply due to algal endosymbionts, which are present also in *C.gigantea*, so the prevalence of saturated fatty acids, which are resistant to oxidation, may be important to this shallow water actiniarian exposed to bright tropical sun (Kellogg and Patton, 1983) and its photooxidative effects (see also section 2.7.3).

Wax esters (composed of simple esters of C_{14} to C_{22} fatty acids and fatty alcohols) are a major storage product in many marine animals, including sea anemones (Sargent, 1978; and Table 2.5). They are especially abundant in zooplankton that experience short periods of plentiful food followed by long periods of starvation (Lee, Hirota and Barnett, 1971). This condition may also apply to temperate zone anemones such as *A.elegantissima*, which experiences seasonal variation in food availability (Sebens, 1982b). It is important for this anemone to be able to deposit its lipid stores during a relatively short period (Figure 2.15). As noted above, wax ester biosynthesis may provide a mechanism for rapidly elaborating lipid stores from amino acid precursors (Sargent, 1978). The very high levels of wax esters that occur in *C.gigantea* are products of the host animal's metabolism, as the zooxanthellae do not synthesize them (Kellogg and Patton, 1983), although they may provide the precursors. Because wax ester biosynthesis is scarcely affected by hypoxia (Sargent and McIntosh, 1974), it may be of particular importance in enabling lipid deposition to continue in the hypoxic tissues of anemones when they contract during intertidal exposure and non-feeding periods (sections 3.8.2, page 148, and 3.8.5, page 158).

2.6 SYMBIOSIS WITH UNICELLULAR ALGAE

'Certain animals . . . possess chlorophyll, but there is no evidence to show what part it plays in their economy', wrote T.H. Huxley in an 1877 essay. Early investigators identified unicellular algae as the source of the chlorophyll and suggested that they rid the anemone host of carbon dioxide and nitrogenous waste, provided the host with starch, and perhaps were digested by the host. The production of molecular oxygen by symbiotic sea anemones under illumination showed that the algae were functional, and lacking evidence of their digestion, it was assumed that any nutritional contribution was via transfer of soluble photoassimilates. The finding of algal cells in the mesenteric filaments led to the persistent idea that algae were cultivated, harvested and digested by the host. More recent studies have elucidated the translocation of photosynthate to the host, as well as the recycling of nitrogen, phosphorus, and sulphur between animal and algae, so confirming the mutualistic nature of the relationship.

Incorporation of an autotrophic partner by a heterotrophic anemone greatly increases the latter's already considerable trophic flexibility. In addition, the inherent efficiency of a polytrophic system that includes primary producers and consumer in the same functional unit affords great selective advantage (Schlichter, 1973), especially in nutrient-poor environments (Muscatine and Porter, 1977). Such associations offer many possibilities for investigation ranging from cell–cell recognition and control by one genome of another's expression, to coevolution and community development.

2.6.1 Localization of Algal Symbionts

In sea anemones, endosymbiotic algae are invariably localized within the endodermal cells (Figure 2.16). They occur singly in membrane-bounded vacuoles. The intracellular location has implications in the control by the host

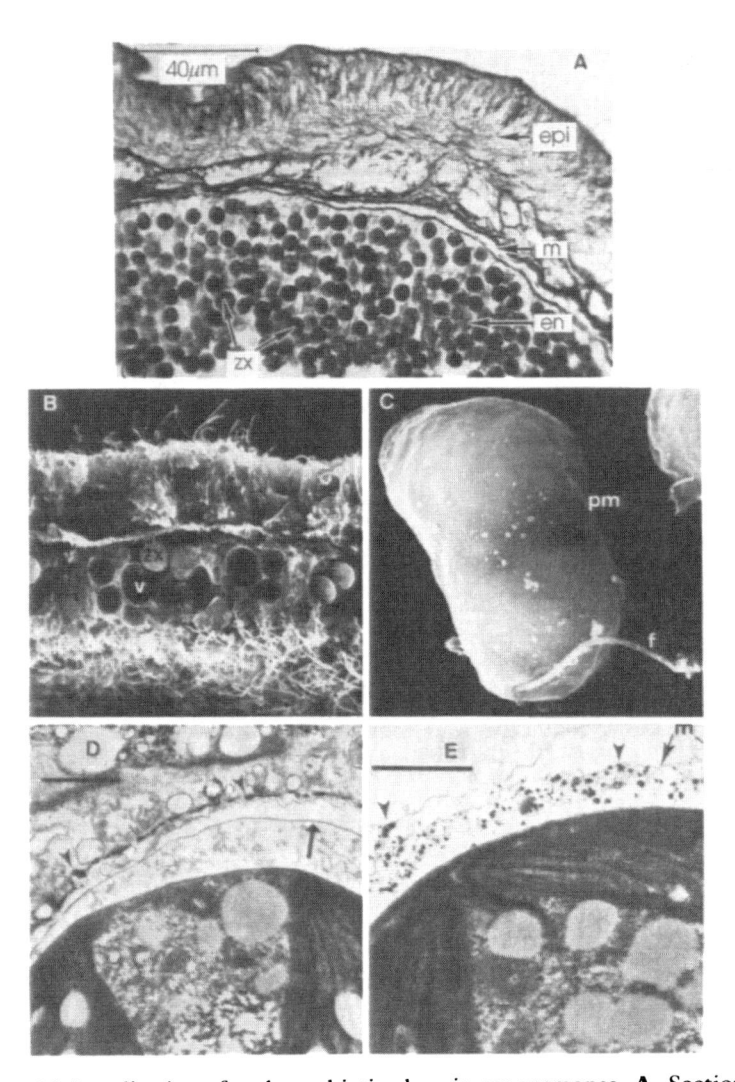

Figure 2.16 Localization of endosymbiotic algae in sea anemones. **A**. Section of the oral disc of *Anthopleura elegantissima* showing confinement of the zooxanthellae (**zx**) to the endoderm (**en**) and their absence from the mesoglea (**m**) and ectoderm (**epi**). **B**. Fractured edge of a tentacle of *Aiptasia pallida* showing zooxanthellae (**zx**) within vacuoles (**v**) of flagellated endodermal cells. Scale bar = 10 μm. **C**. Endodermal cell from enzymatic maceration of *A.pallida* tentacle, showing apical flagellum (**f**) and two zooxanthellae enclosed within the cell's plasma membrane (**pm**). Scale bar = 3 μm. **D**. A zoochlorella and cellular debris (including algal parental cell wall, large arrow) within a host cell vacuole adjacent to the coelenteron in *Anthopleura xanthogrammica*. Note that the acid phosphatase reaction products (black lead deposits indicated by arrowheads) are restricted to areas outside the vacuolar membrane and are absent from cellular debris within the vacuole. Scale bar = 1 μm. **E**. A zoochlorella free within the coelenteron of *A.xanthogrammica*. Acid phosphatase reaction products (arrowheads) are restricted to cellular debris expelled along with the alga. Remnants of the vacuolar membrane (**m**) are present. Scale bar = 1 μm. Source: with permission from **A**. Trench (1971a); **B**. and **C**. Glider *et al*. (1980); **D**. and **E**. O'Brien (1980).

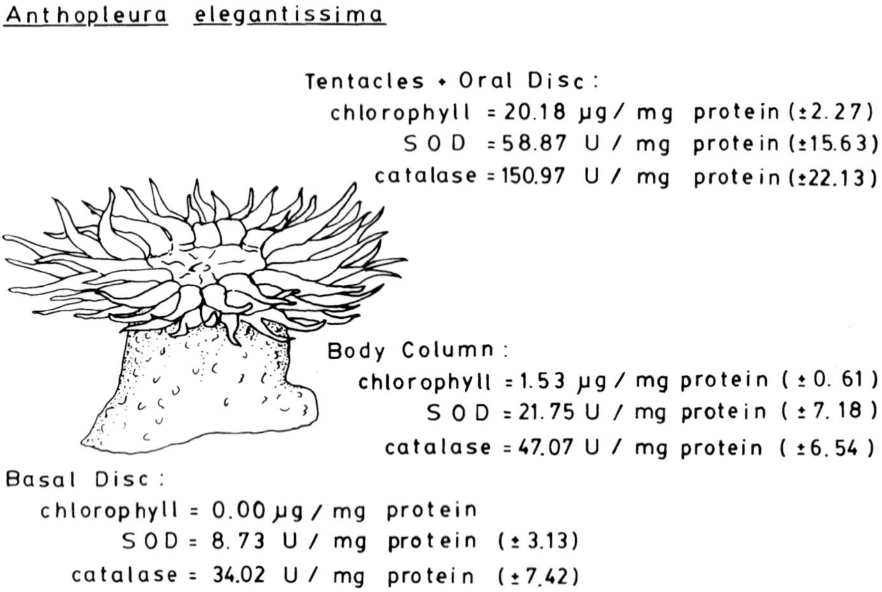

Anthopleura elegantissima

Tentacles + Oral Disc:
chlorophyll = 20.18 μg / mg protein (±2.27)
SOD = 58.87 U / mg protein (±15.63)
catalase = 150.97 U / mg protein (±22.13)

Body Column:
chlorophyll = 1.53 μg / mg protein (± 0.61)
SOD = 21.75 U / mg protein (± 7.18)
catalase = 47.07 U / mg protein (± 6.54)

Basal Disc:
chlorophyll = 0.00 μg / mg protein
SOD = 8.73 U / mg protein (± 3.13)
catalase = 34.02 U / mg protein (± 7.42)

Figure 2.17 Chlorophyll content and superoxide dismutase (SOD) and catalase activities in different regions of *Anthopleura elegantissima*. See text for discussion. Source: drawn from data in Dykens and Shick (1984).

both of the algal population and of the release of algal photosynthate. The algae are concentrated in the tentacles and oral disc (Figure 2.17), a location that provides the most direct exposure to sunlight, a large surface area, little shading by the thin animal tissue, and behavioural control of their illumination by expansion and contraction of the host (see section 2.7.2).

2.6.2 Identity of the Endosymbiotic Algae

The most frequently occurring unicellular algae in sea anemones are dinoflagellates (Dinophyceae) of the genus *Symbiodinium* (≡ *Gymnodinium*), commonly called zooxanthellae (Figure 2.16A–C). The anemones *Anthopleura xanthogrammica* and *A.elegantissima* may also harbour unicellular green algae (Chlorophyceae) called zoochlorellae (Muscatine, 1971; O'Brien, 1978), either alone or with zooxanthellae (Figure 2.16D, E). The ratio of these algae is apparently temperature dependent, with zoochlorellae predominating in cooler water (O'Brien and Wyttenbach, 1980).

Species or individual specimens of anemones that harbour symbiotic dinoflagellates may be termed 'zooxanthellate', whereas those that do not form such symbiotic associations are 'azooxanthellate'. 'Zooxanthellate' is used rather than the more general term 'symbiotic' because the latter can also refer to anemones that form associations with hermit crabs, clownfishes, etc. (section 7.3, page 295). Individuals of a normally zooxanthellate (or zoochlorellate) species which lack algal symbionts, owing either to natural circumstances or to experimental elimination of algae, are termed 'aposymbiotic'.

The worldwide distribution and occurrence of zooxanthellae in a wide variety of radiolarian, cnidarian and molluscan hosts suggests that more than one species of zooxanthella exists, and Schoenberg and Trench (1980a, b, c) found persistent, presumably genetic differences in morphology, ultrastructure, soluble protein and enzyme electromorphs, and infectivity of strains isolated from various hosts. The lack of an identified sexual phase of *Symbiodinium* sp. and scant knowledge of its genetics make such variation hard to interpret. Schoenberg and Trench did not state that the various strains represent distinct species, but the genetic distances they calculated from protein electrophoretic data are consistent with species or sibling species differences in other organisms. The situation is almost certainly not one species of alga to one species of host, however.

More recently, Trench and Blank (1987) used differences in the morphology, ultrastructure, number and size of chromosomes, and nature of the peridinin-chlorophyll *a*-protein (PCP) complexes to describe four species of *Symbiodinium* from four cnidarian hosts. The only anemone in this study is *Capnea* ($\equiv$ *Ragactis*) *lucida* and its symbiont is *S.goreauii*. From marked differences in chromosome number and PCP (Blank and Trench, 1985; Trench and Blank, 1987), the zooxanthella in *A.elegantissima* does not appear to be the same species as in *C.lucida*. Given the uncertain taxonomic status of most zooxanthellae, it is prudent to follow the recommendation of Blank and Trench (1986) and refer to them as *Symbiodinium* sp. until the taxonomic decisions have been made.

2.6.3 Establishment and Persistence of the Symbiosis

Maternal inheritance of algal symbionts occurs in some but not all species of host sea anemone (see also Table 6.1, page 232). Schmidt (1972b) reported that the ova of Mediterranean specimens of *Anemonia viridis* ($\equiv$ *A.sulcata*) and *Cribrinopsis crassa* contain zooxanthellae. Similar results were found in British populations of *A.viridis* and *Anthopleura ballii* (Turner, 1989, and personal communication). It is unknown whether the zooxanthellae found in the larvae brooded by an unnamed species of *Anthopleura* (Atoda, 1954) are initially present in the ova or whether the larvae ingest zooxanthellae that might be present in the parent's coelenteron. Planulae containing zooxanthellae are released by adult *Lebrunia coralligens* (Lewis, 1984) and *Cereus pedunculatus* (Turner, 1989, and personal communication), but whether zooxanthellae are initially present in the eggs is also not known. Conversely,

Siebert (1974) explicitly stated that he found no symbiotic algae in the gametes or planulae of *Anthopleura elegantissima* or *A.xanthogrammica*. Sections of fully-grown oocytes in the zooxanthellate species *Condylactis gigantea* and *Epicystis crucifer* show no evidence of zooxanthellae (photographs in Jennison, 1981). Eggs and planulae of zooxanthellate *Aiptasia pulchella* do not contain zooxanthellae (Muller-Parker, 1984a). Why there is maternal inheritance of zooxanthellae in some species of anemones but not in others (even within the same genus, e.g. *Anthopleura*) is not obvious.

Thus, some species of anemones represent 'open systems' in which each generation must be infected *de novo*, which may be important in the host's securing the particular algal symbiont ecologically suited to the site of settlement (Kinzie, 1974). Infection probably occurs via ingestion and phagocytosis of viable algae, which although not found in the plankton, are available in the egesta of other anemones (Smith, 1939; Steele, 1977) and in the faeces of predators on anemones (Muller-Parker, 1984a). Fitt (1984) showed that motile zooxanthellae are attracted by aposymbiotic potential hosts, and suggested that ammonia and free amino acids from the host elicit their chemosensory behaviour.

The recognition process leading to phagocytosis is probably a cell surface phenomenon involving an antigen–antibody response or lectin–carbohydrate binding (Trench, 1979). The specificity is not absolute, since several strains/ species of zooxanthellae may initially be phagocytosed by a single host individual. Once phagocytosed, the zooxanthella is a foreign entity within the host's cell; to establish a symbiosis it must be recognized by the host as 'self', or prevent the host from digesting or eliminating it. Some strains are recognized as compatible, others not. Axenically cultured strains of zooxanthellae isolated from various cnidarian and mollucan hosts differed in their ability to infect and repopulate aposymbiotic specimens of *Aiptasia pallida* ($\equiv$ *A.tagetes*) (Schoenberg and Trench, 1980c). The greatest success was shown by strains originally from *A.pallida*; the variable success shown by other strains was in general positively related to their electrophoretic similarity to algae from *A.pallida*. Residence within *A.pallida* of less infective algae modified neither their subsequent infectivity nor their electrophoretic pattern.

The finding of a single electrophoretic strain (or clone) within a given host individual does not necessarily indicate that only that strain could infect the host, as the strain present could be the survivor of competition among several strains colonizing the same host, winning by virtue of its greater efficiency, faster growth rate or higher stabilized population density (Schoenberg and Trench, 1980c). Persistence of the algae in a stable symbiosis may be a complex phenomenon involving initial recognition by the host, competition by different algal strains, and perhaps host recognition of potentially advantageous, productive strains via the quantity or quality of translocated metabolites. Recognition and acceptance phenomena might also involve the membrane of the vacuole containing the zooxanthella. Direct evidence for host recognition of strains that enhance fitness is scarce. Kinzie and Chee (1979) demonstrated different growth patterns in formerly apo-symbiotic *Aiptasia pulchella* infected with zooxanthellae from different sources, and anemones infected with homologous algae attained a larger size than did those infected with zooxanthellae from a scyphozoan.

The regular occurrence of (sometimes degenerating) algae in endodermal digestive tissues is responsible for the persistent idea that healthy algae are digested by the host (Boschma, 1925; Steele and Goreau, 1977). There is no unequivocal evidence for this. Although algae in various stages of degener-ation occur in endodermal tissues, this probably represents normal senescence and autolysis of algal cells, which may subsequently be digested. Micro-graphs of such algae almost always reveal a degeneration of their intracellular organelles while the outer cell membranes remain intact.

In general, then, to persist within the host's cells healthy algae must avoid digestion. O'Brien (1980) showed that acid phosphatase reaction product is absent from intracellular vacuoles containing healthy zoochlorellae and cel-lular debris, and that acid phosphatase attacks the debris but not the algae once they have been expelled into the coelenteron of *A.xanthogrammica* (Figure 2.16). This indicates first that algae within vacuoles interfere with the host's intracellular digestive process, probably by inhibiting fusion of lysosomes with the vacuoles, as is the case in symbiotic hydra and scyphozoan polyps, and second, that when outside the host cell, the algal cell wall affords resistance to hydrolytic enzymes.

2.6.4 Control of Algal Numbers

Little is known about the proximal control of the number of algal endo-symbionts under steady-state conditions. Such regulation certainly occurs, for if unchecked, the growth rates of algal populations would allow them to overrun the host's tissues. Both the regulation of algal cell division, and controlled digestion (or more commonly, exocytosis and expulsion) of algae *in hospite* (i.e. 'within the host'), are probably involved. Pellets containing viable zooxanthellae are normally egested by a variety of sea anemones (Steele, 1976, 1977), and as mentioned these pellets may be a source of infection for newly settled young anemones.

In *Anthopleura elegantissima* the doubling time of zooxanthellae *in hospite* ranges from 6.9 to 11.2 days (Wilkerson, Muller-Parker and Muscatine, 1983), that in *Anemonia viridis* ($\equiv$ *A.sulcata*) is 23.5 days (Stambler and Dubinsky, 1987), and that in *Aiptasia pulchella* is 28–42 days (Wilkerson *et al.*, 1983; Muller-Parker, 1984b). All of these rates are far slower than those of zooxanthellae cultured *in vitro* (Chang, Prézelin and Trench, 1983), and indicate some control by the animal host (Palincsar, Jones and Palincsar, 1988), perhaps by its restricting the supply of light or nutrients. Shading of the zooxanthellae densely packed in the anemone tissues (Chang *et al.*, 1983) may contribute to the slower growth rates of zooxanthellae *in hospite*. Growth rates of cultured zooxanthellae isolated from *Aiptasia pallida* decreased with acclimation irradiance experienced by the cultures (Lesser and Shick, 1989a). The faster doubling time for zooxanthellae in the temperate zone *A.elegantissima* than for those in the subtropical *A.pallida* and in a warm-temperate population of *A.viridis* is associated with a higher mitotic index and daily specific growth rate (μ, doublings·day^{-1}) in *A.elegantissima*, and may be due to its exposure to higher levels of nutrients in its environment. In *Aiptasia pallida*, while the mitotic index of zooxanthellae declines if the host is unfed, it increases when inorganic nitrogen or especially phosphorus is added to the oligotrophic seawater in which the anemones are cultured (Cook, D'Elia and Muller-Parker, 1988).

Within a species, and among morphologically similar species, even under

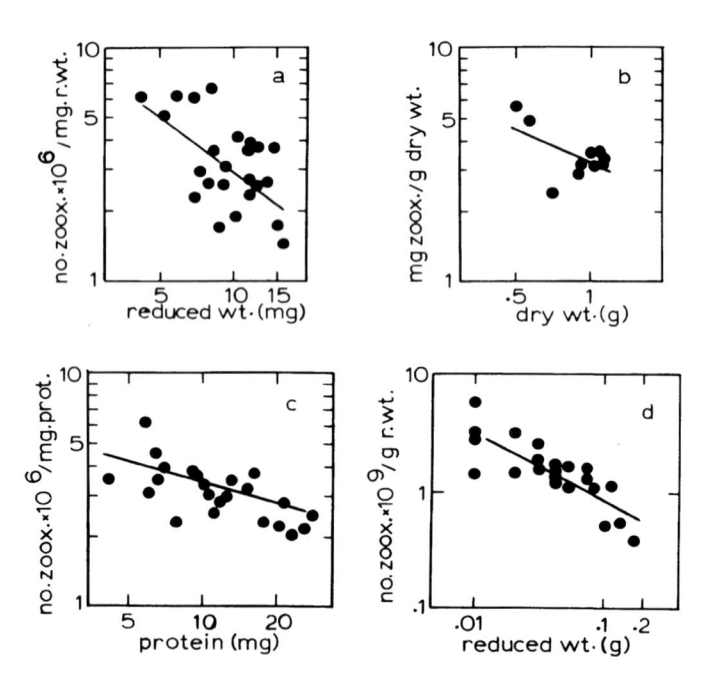

Figure 2.18 Relationship between density of zooxanthellae (numbers or mass per unit anemone mass) and anemone body weight. (**a**) *Aiptasia tagetes*; (**b**) *Anemonia viridis*; (**c**) *Aiptasia diaphana*; (**d**) *Anthopleura elegantissima*. 'Reduced weight' is the apparent weight in seawater. Source: (**a**) and (**b**) drawn from data in Steele (1976) and Taylor (1969a), respectively; (**c**) and (**d**) redrawn from Svoboda and Porrmann (1980) and Fitt *et al.* (1982), respectively.

a variety of environmental, nutritional and seasonal conditions there is a relatively narrow range of algal standing crop (Figure 2.18; Sebens and De-Riemer, 1977; Dykens and Shick, 1984; Muller-Parker, 1985). In *Aiptasia pallida* zooxanthellae reach maximum densities of 4 to 6 per endodermal cell (Glider, Phipps and Pardy, 1980), and in *A.pulchella* they occupy 15–30% of the volume of the animal cell in which they occur (J.P.S. Smith, III, personal communication) and account for 17.7% of the total biomass of the symbiosis (Muller-Parker, 1984b). In the specialized pseudotentacles of *Phyllodiscus semoni*, the concentration of zooxanthellae is higher ($>10^7$ cells/mg protein; cf. values in Figure 2.18), with zooxanthellae accounting for nearly 50% of the total protein biomass (Shick, Lesser and Stochaj, 1990). Intraspecifically there appears to be an inverse relationship between zooxanthella numbers or their mass per unit anemone mass and total anemone mass (Figure 2.18), arising in part from differences in rates of algal photosynthesis and growth. In *Aulactinia stelloides*, for example, these rates in juveniles are about twice those in adult anemones (Smith, 1986). Otherwise, ontogenetic effects on host–zooxanthella interactions have scarcely been studied.

Exposure to stressful conditions (prolonged starvation, continuous darkness, extremely bright light, high temperature, abruptly altered salinity) results in the mass expulsion of symbiotic algae, and is often used as a method for producing aposymbiotic specimens experimentally. The causes of expulsion in these situations are probably varied. The cell shrinkage and self-digestion that occur during starvation may reduce the habitat available for the algae and thus result in their expulsion. In continuous darkness the algae no longer photosynthesize and if they are facultatively heterotrophic as suggested by Steen (1986, 1987), they may represent a drain on the animal cell's energy stores. Also, respiration by the algae in the dark may contribute to tissue hypoxia and so be a factor in their expulsion. Extremely bright light increases photosensitized oxidations associated with chlorophyll, as well as the production of superoxide radicals, singlet oxygen and hydrogen peroxide, the toxicity of which may cause elimination of the algae (section 2.7.3). Toxic effects of active oxygen are exacerbated by high fluxes of ultraviolet radiation and elevated temperatures, and may be a contributing cause of geographically widespread 'bleaching' of coral reef anthozoans (Lesser *et al.*, 1990). Increased temperature may raise algal respiration more than photosynthesis; also, zooxanthellae translocate less photosynthate to the anemone as temperature and energy utilization increase (section 2.6.6). In short, massive expulsion of the algae occurs when their presence in the host's cells is more of a detriment than an asset.

The mechanism of exocytosis of algae has only recently been studied. Brief cold-shock (4°C) and subsequent rewarming to 25°C evokes exocytosis of zooxanthellae from *Aiptasia pulchella* (Steen and Muscatine, 1987). It is hypothesized that low temperature causes a phase change in membrane lipids in the host, which leads to passive ion fluxes and intracellular signal transduction that initiates migration of the algae toward the apical end of the endodermal cells; rewarming restores membrane fluidity necessary for exocytosis (Muscatine, Weissman and Doino, 1989).

2.6.5 Algal Photoadaptation

There have been few quantitative studies of the effects of naturally varying levels of irradiance on sea anemone–algal symbioses. Although Steele (1976) showed that the number of zooxanthellae in *Aiptasia tagetes* increased directly with light intensity during laboratory maintenance, the irradiances were far below the levels that the anemones would experience in nature. The increase in steady-state numbers of zooxanthellae was primarily due to increased rates of algal cell division with increasing light intensity. Conversely, Svoboda and Porrmann (1980) found no differences in numbers of zooxanthellae in light- and shade-maintained *Aiptasia diaphana*, but again the light levels were less than 5% of noon intensities. Muller-Parker (1987) observed that freshly collected *Aiptasia pulchella* from shaded habitats have higher concentrations of zooxanthellae than specimens from brightly lit habitats. The zooxanthellae in the 'shade' anemones are larger and have more thylakoids (photosynthetic membranes) in their chloroplasts than those in 'sun' specimens. There are no consistent differences, however, in growth rates of zooxanthellae from 'shade' and 'sun' anemones.

Studies of photoadaptation in zooxanthellate anemones and their isolated algae involve measuring not only changes in the numbers of zooxanthellae per unit area or mass of host tissue, but also calculating changes in the number, size, or organization of the photosynthetic units (PSU, a composite of P700 reaction centres, chlorophyll 'antennas', accessory pigments such as peridinin, and electron carriers such as ferredoxin) in the algal cell. These changes are not mutually exclusive, and all occur in various coral species. They have only recently begun to be studied in sea anemones.

Changes in PSUs in dinoflagellates are seldom measured directly, but are estimated from parameters in photosynthesis versus irradiance (P-I) curves expressed per unit of chlorophyll a (Figure 2.19). For example, a reorganization of the PSU (involving increasing amounts of accessory pigments such as chlorophyll c_2 and peridinin relative to chlorophyll a under diminished illumination) will increase the slope (α, a measure of photosynthetic efficiency) and decrease the I_k (the intersection of tangents to α and P_{max}, approximating the breakpoint in the P-I curve, which indicates the onset of the maximum rate of photosynthesis, P_{max}), thus enhancing the efficiency of light harvesting and utilization at low irradiances. Conversely, increasing the number of PSUs under low light conditions will not affect α but will initially increase P_{max} (photosynthetic capacity) per unit chlorophyll a, as-

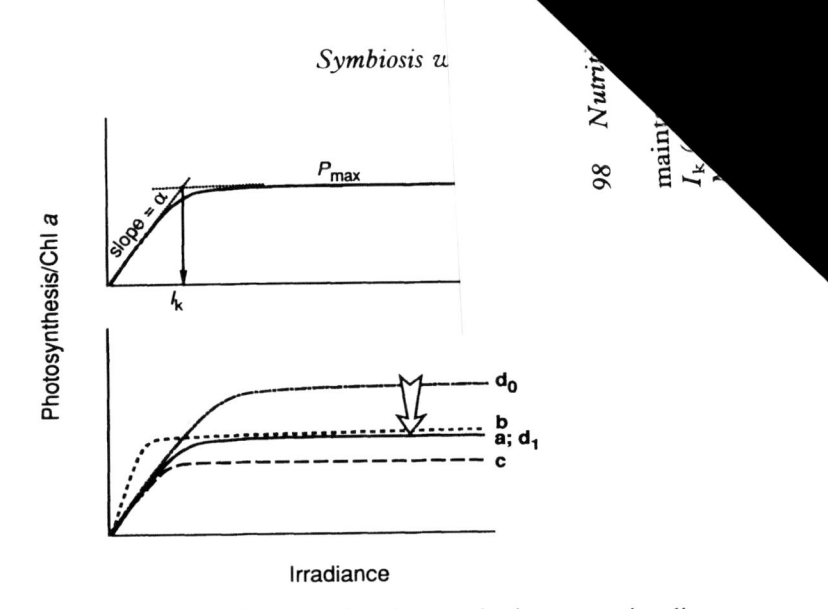

Irradiance

Figure 2.19 Generalized chlorophyll *a*-specific photosynthesis versus irradiance (*P-I*) curves illustrating different mechanisms of shade acclimation in zooxanthellae. (**a**) light acclimated; (**b**) reorganization of the photosynthetic units (PSUs) by increasing the concentration of accessory pigments relative to chlorophyll *a* increases the efficiency of light capture at low irradiances; (**c**) increasing the size of existing PSUs by increasing the amount of chlorophyll *a* decreases photosynthesis per chl *a* (but increases total photosynthesis/cell at a given irradiance); (**d**) increasing the number of PSUs (curve d_0 assumes P700 reaction centres are added first, and bulk chlorophyll is gradually filled in; when acclimation is complete, curve d_1 will be identical with curve **a**). P_{max}, maximum rate of photosynthesis; I_k, minimum irradiance for light-saturated P_{max}; α, photosynthetic efficiency (light-limited slope). For further discussion, see text, Chang *et al.* (1983), Richardson, Beardall and Raven (1983) and Prézelin (1987).

suming that functional reaction centres are added rapidly and bulk chlorophyll is filled in more gradually. When acclimation is complete, P_{max}/Chl *a* will be the same at any irradiance as in zooxanthellae acclimated to bright conditions.

Based on analyses of *P-I* curves and of chlorophyll *a* : peridinin and chlorophyll *a* : chlorophyll c_2 ratios, both a reorganization of PSUs and an increase in PSU number (curves **b** and **d** in Figure 2.19) appear to be involved in shade acclimation during culture of zooxanthellae isolated from *Aiptasia pulchella*. ('Acclimation' rather than 'adaptation' is used here, since a single factor, irradiance, was varied in the controlled experiments by Chang *et al.*, 1983.) Such flexibility may be related to the variable photic regimes that this anemone experiences in nature (Chang *et al.*, 1983). I_k declined with the irradiance at which the algae were grown, and the I_k (128–135 μEinsteins·m^{-2}·s^{-1}) in shade-acclimated algae agrees well with that measured *in hospite* ('within the host') for symbiotic *A. pulchella* (118 μE·m^{-2}·s^{-1})

...ained at similar irradiances (Hunter, 1984). Somewhat higher values of I_k (up to $\approx 300\,\mu E \cdot m^{-2} \cdot s^{-1}$) were found in freshly-collected *A.pulchella* by Muller-Parker (1987), who also showed that in the intact symbiosis, as in the isolated zooxanthellae, I_k generally declined with growth irradiance. Again, the decrease in I_k with acclimatization irradiance indicates that zooxanthellae acclimatized to low-irradiance conditions require less light to saturate photosynthesis. A similar relationship between I_k and irradiance was seen for isolated zooxanthellae of the congeneric *A.pallida* acclimated *in vitro* and *in hospite* (Lesser and Shick, 1989a). At both high ($375\,\mu E \cdot m^{-2} \cdot s^{-1}$) and low ($35\,\mu E \cdot m^{-2} \cdot s^{-1}$) acclimation irradiances, I_k was higher in cultured zooxanthellae than in those acclimated *in hospite*, suggesting an additional shading effect by the host. Values of I_k ranged from $33\,\mu E \cdot m^{-2} \cdot s^{-1}$ in zooxanthellae acclimated *in hospite* at $35\,\mu E \cdot m^{-2} \cdot s^{-1}$ up to $121\,\mu E \cdot m^{-2} \cdot s^{-1}$ in zooxanthellae cultured at $375\,\mu E \cdot m^{-2} \cdot s^{-1}$.

If shade acclimation occurs through an increase in PSU size (and especially if chlorophyll *a* increases disproportionally to other pigments), under saturating irradiance P_{max} per chlorophyll *a* will decrease relative to light-acclimated individuals (curve **c** in Figure 2.19), although total photosynthesis per zooxanthella will of course increase at any given experimental irradiance. Finally, photoacclimation may also involve compensatory changes in the activity of CO_2-fixing enzymes or in photosynthetic electron transport, with or without changes in PSUs (Chang *et al.*, 1983).

Svoboda and Porrmann (1980) did not construct *P-I* curves for the *A.diaphana* symbiosis and so did not calculate α or P_{max}. They found enhanced rates of photosynthesis per unit chlorophyll *a* at both low and high levels of irradiance, however, in shade-acclimated compared with light-acclimated individuals of *Aiptasia diaphana*, despite identical numbers of zooxanthellae and chlorophyll *a* and c_2 contents in the two groups. This suggests an increase in other accessory pigments, or compensatory increases in CO_2-fixing enzymes, during five months of shade acclimation in the laboratory. In cultured zooxanthellae of *A.pulchella*, the peridinin : chlorophyll *a* ratio increases during shade acclimation (Chang *et al.*, 1983).

In contrast to the results of Chang *et al.* (1983) on cultured zooxanthellae from *A.pulchella*, which suggest that shade acclimation involves an increase in PSU number, Muller-Parker's (1985, 1987) *P-I* data indicate that shade acclimation of the intact symbiosis in the laboratory and in nature proceeds by an increase in PSU size, since P_{max}/Chl *a* is directly related to habitat or maintenance irradiance (cf. curves **a** and **c** in Figure 2.19). The basis for the apparent difference between the acclimation mechanism of zooxanthellae *in vitro* and *in hospite* is unexplained (see Prézelin, 1987). Together with the greater number of thylakoid membranes in freshly isolated, 'shade' zooxanthellae, consistent with an increase in PSU number (which seems to occur in culture but not *in hospite*), this points out the difficulty in interpreting *P-I* data for the intact symbiosis. As in the cultured zooxanthellae, those in the anemone also show a higher photosynthetic efficiency (increase in α) at lower habitat irradiance (Muller-Parker, 1987).

Pigment analyses of zooxanthellae from *A.pallida* grown in culture (CZ) and *in hospite* (freshly isolated zooxanthellae, FIZ) suggest that photoacclimation occurs via an increase in PSU size: both CZ and FIZ show an inverse relationship between chlorophyll content and acclimation irradiance (Lesser and Shick, 1989a). *P-I* curves for these groups further indicate a mixed photoacclimatory response involving changes in CO_2-fixing enzymes or in photosynthetic electron transport. Photosynthetic efficiency (α) increases at low irradiance in CZ and in FIZ. In the field, zooxanthellae in *A.pallida* collected from a brightly-lit habitat tend to have lower concentrations of chlorophylls than those in anemones from dim habitats (Lesser and Shick, 1989b). Reciprocal transplants of anemones between the two habitats result in changes in chlorophyll concentrations that are consistent with algal photo-acclimatization: total chlorophyll decreases after ten days in anemones transplanted from dim to bright conditions, whereas it (especially chlorophyll c_2) increases significantly in bright-to-dim transplants.

The higher pigment concentration in zooxanthellae of *A.pulchella* and *A.pallida* when freshly isolated from the host than when grown in culture probably indicates that the algae *in hospite* are shade acclimated, through either self-shading or light attenuation by host tissues (Chang *et al.*, 1983). Similarly, freshly isolated zooxanthellae from the column of *A.pulchella* have greater chlorophyll concentrations than those in the oral disc and tentacles (Muller-Parker, 1987). The host's tissues apparently afford some photo-protection or exert some influence on algal photosynthesis, as high irradiances cause photoinhibition in freshly-isolated zooxanthellae but not in the the the intact symbiosis (Muller-Parker, 1984b; Lesser and Shick, 1989a).

The I_k is $120\,\mu E \cdot m^{-2} \cdot s^{-1}$ measured for zooxanthellae *in hospite* in freshly collected *Anthopleura elegantissima* (Fitt, Pardy and Littler, 1982), which suggests that the algae are relatively shade-adapted. Such shading may arise from the turbidity of the water in its inshore habitat, as well as from the anemone's contraction at low tide (Shick and Dykens, 1984). The seasonal changes in total chlorophyll (*a* plus c_2) in *A.elegantissima* (Figure 2.20) are not due to changes in the numbers of zooxanthellae but to the amount of pigment per alga, and the higher values in winter presumably compensate for the lower solar flux then (Figure 2.20). The disproportional winter increase in chlorophyll c_2 may be a further adaptation to reduced light availability (Dykens and Shick, 1984), analogous to the situation in *Aiptaisia pallida* transplanted from bright to dim habitats. *Aiptasia pulchella* acclimates to declining ambient irradiances in the autumn by increasing photosynthetic capacity (P_{max}) and efficiency (α), however, without a change in chl $a : c_2$ (Muller-Parker, 1987).

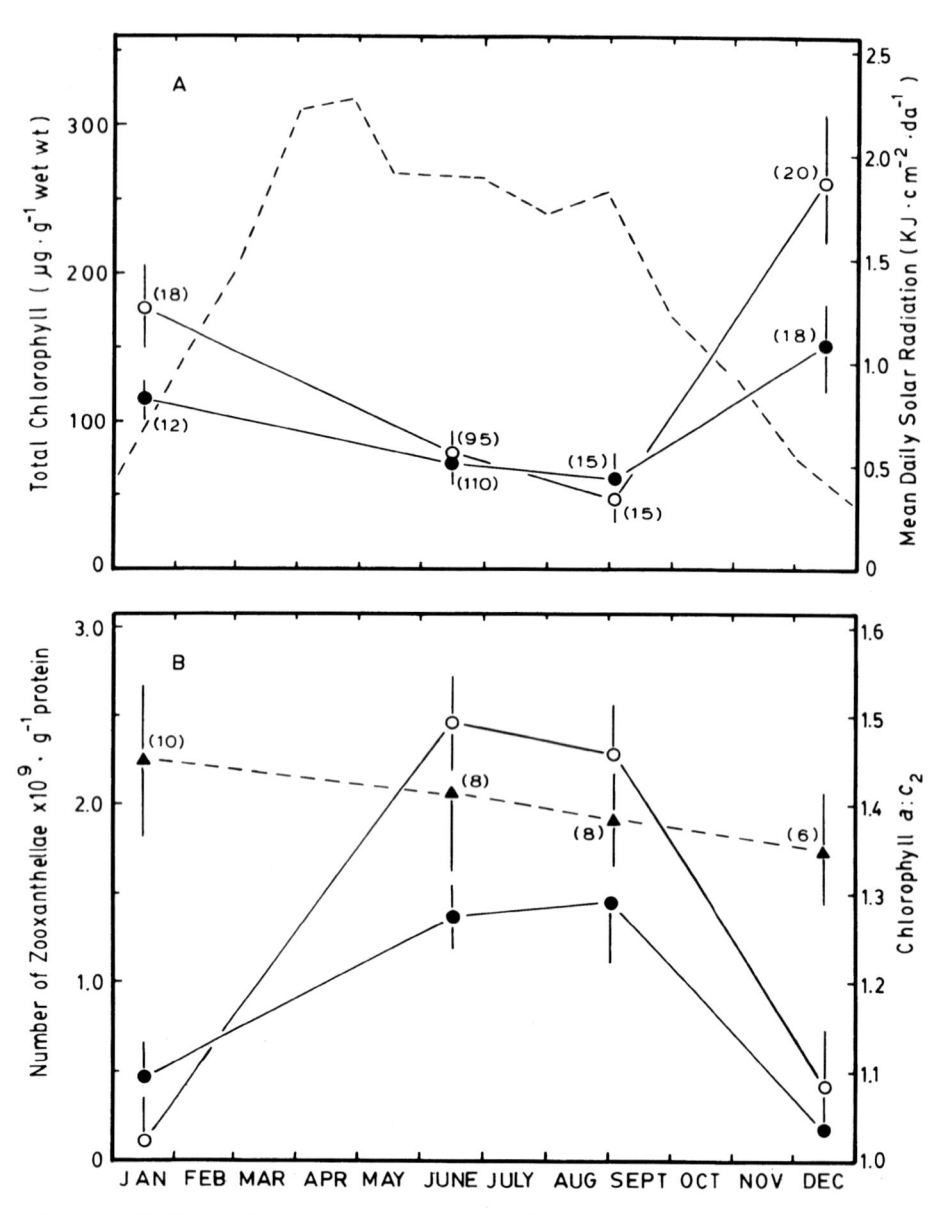

Figure 2.20 Seasonal values of solar radiation (broken line) and numbers of zooxanthellae (▲) in low intertidal specimens of *Anthopleura elgegantissima* at Bodega Bay, California, USA. Also shown are values for total chlorophyll $(a + c_2)$ and chl $a : c_2$ ratio in low intertidal (○) and high intertidal (●) specimens. Numbers of anemones in parentheses. See text for discussion. Source: with permission from Dykens and Shick (1984).

Lesser (1989) and Lesser and Shick (1989a) have also investigated the effect of ultraviolet (UV) light on photoacclimation of zooxanthellae in culture and *in hospite*. As already mentioned, specific growth rate (doublings·d^{-1}) in cultured zooxanthellae decreased with increasing irradiance; this effect was enhanced when cultures were exposed to UV (280–380 nm) in a solar simulator (Lesser and Shick, 1989a). The photosynthetic capacity (P_{max}/cell) in zooxanthellae acclimated *in hospite* was depressed by nearly 50% in those receiving UV as compared with those anemones shielded from UV during two weeks of acclimation in the solar simulator. This depression was evident even when the *P-I* curve for the freshly-isolated zooxanthellae was generated using light without a UV component. Part of this decrease in photosynthetic capacity was due to a reduction in the amount of chlorophyll per zooxanthella in UV-exposed anemones (see also Lesser, 1989), perhaps involving enhanced photooxidation of chlorophyll *a*, but the enhancement by UV of photoinhibition in isolated zooxanthellae at high irradiances suggests an effect of UV other than on chlorophyll (Lesser and Shick, 1989a). Paradoxically, no decrease in P_{max} occurred in cultures of zooxanthellae exposed directly to UV compared with the same clonal culture shielded from UV. Cultured zooxanthellae have a thicker cell wall than those *in hospite* (Palincsar *et al.*, 1988), but it is not known whether the thicker wall can screen out any of the UV spectrum. The possible involvement of active oxygen species, especially in conjunction with UV, and defences against these factors, will be considered in section 2.7.

2.6.6 Metabolic Interchange between Symbiont and Host

This topic has been reviewed by Trench (1979), Cook (1983) and Steen (1988). A nutritional contribution from symbiotic algae to host anemone is suggested by the smaller size of naturally aposymbiotic *Anthopleura xanthogrammica* (O'Brien, 1980) and *A.elegantissima* (personal observations) compared with zooxanthellate individuals in the same populations at the same tidal height, and indeed aposymbiotic *A.elegantissima* loses weight more rapidly than zooxanthellate specimens when both are starved under illumination (Figure 2.21). Zooxanthellate anemones lose weight more rapidly when starved in the dark than when in the light, and gain weight more rapidly when fed in the light than in the dark (Figure 2.21; Tytler and Davies, 1986). Zooxanthellate *A.elegantissima* starved in the dark deplete their lipid reserves more rapidly than those starved in the light (Fitt and Pardy, 1981). Conversely, Muller-Parker (1985) finds that changes in protein biomass in fed hosts are not related to photosynthesis by their zooxanthellae, nor is there a difference in host protein biomass when the anemones (*Aiptasia pulchella*) are starved at different irradiances. Steen (1986) reports that aposymbiotic specimens of *A.pulchella* reinfected with zooxanthellae have less

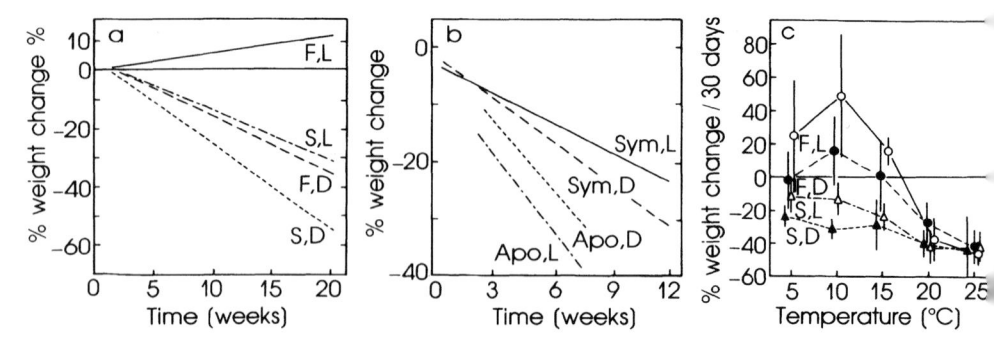

Figure 2.21 Weight change (Δ % of original weight) in zooxanthellate and aposymbiotic sea anemones under various conditions of feeding, illumination and temperature. (a) symbiotic *Anemonia viridis* at 15°C; (b) *Anthopleura elegantissima* starved at 14°C; (c) symbiotic *A.elegantissima* at several temperatures. Apo, aposymbiotic anemones; Sym, symbiotic (= zooxanthellate) anemones; F, fed; S, starved; L, light; D, dark. Source: redrawn from (a) Taylor (1969a); (b) Muscatine (1961); (c) Sebens (1980).

protein biomass and lower survivorship than control aposymbionts, suggesting that the zooxanthellae actually are a drain on the host's resources. The basis for the differences between the effects of the zooxanthellae on the host's well-being in the actiniids and in *A.pulchella* is not known.

Early autoradiographic studies indicated that the algal contribution was in the form of unspecific metabolites incorporated into the animal tissue (Muscatine and Hand, 1958; Taylor, 1969b). Chromatographic studies showed that the metabolites released by zooxanthellae from *Anthopleura elegantissima* and *Aiptasia pulchella* were predominantly glycerol and fumarate/succinate, with lesser amounts of malate, citrate, glycolate and alanine; free glucose was only a minor component (Trench, 1971b). Most of the photosynthate translocated from the zooxanthellae in *Aulactinia stelloides* is in the form of water soluble, low molecular weight compounds (Smith, 1986). The rapid incorporation of acetate (which *in hospite* may be derived both from CO_2 fixation in the dark reactions of photosynthesis as well as from the host's metabolism) into lipid has been shown in zooxanthellae of *A.elegantissima* (Blanquet *et al.*, 1979) and *Condylactis gigantea* (Kellogg and Patton, 1983). The finding in *Condylactis* of large-scale translocation from zooxanthellae of lipid droplets 3–4 μm in diameter consisting of triglycerides and wax esters casts some doubt on the early suggestions of the relative importance of free glycerol, unless it indicates simply a taxonomic difference.

The situation in *Condylactis* is further complicated by the possibility of fixation into lipid by zooxanthellae of CO_2 derived from translocated glycerol oxidized by the host (Battey and Patton, 1984). These workers hypothesized that whatever glycerol algae release to the host is used immediately in supporting its standard metabolism whereas the lipid droplets provide a mechanism for controlled transfer via the coelenteron to generate long-term lipid stores in host tissues lacking zooxanthellae. Subsequent work has confirmed a high concentration of glycerol in the zooxanthellae, its translocation to the host, and rapid conversion to carbon dioxide in the host's aerobic respiration (Battey and Patton, 1987). The high levels of wax esters (83% of total lipid) in the droplets are synthesized from triglycerides or perhaps free fatty acids after release of the droplets from the zooxanthellae, as the algae do not synthesize wax esters (Battey and Patton, 1984). The droplets are transferred from the algae in the tentacles via the circulating coelenteric fluid to the endoderm of the column, which contains 97% of the anemone's total lipid, 66% of which is wax ester (Kellogg and Patton, 1983). Growing juveniles of *Aulactinia stelloides* use equal proportions of translocated photosynthate for synthesis of lipids and of macromolecules, whereas adults put more into storage lipids (Smith, 1986).

Fitt and Pardy (1981) used the respiratory quotient (RQ, the molar ratio of CO_2 produced to O_2 consumed), which varies between 0.72 and 1.0 depending on whether lipid, protein or carbohydrate is being oxidized, to infer what foodstuffs were oxidized by zooxanthellate and aposymbiotic *A.elegantissima*. Whereas during starvation in the light or in the dark the RQ in aposymbiotic anemones declined to about 0.7, as did the RQ in zooxanthellate anemones starved in the dark, indicating lipid oxidation, RQ in starved zooxanthellate anemones in the light ranged from 0.9 to 1.0, interpreted as showing purely carbohydrate oxidation. This finding is consistent with the release of glycerol (a carbohydrate) from zooxanthellae in *A.elegantissima* shown by Trench (1971b).

The organic acids succinate and fumarate were translocation products quantitatively almost as important as glycerol (Trench, 1971b), however, and the complete oxidation of these four-carbon molecules would give an RQ of 1.14, so that if lipid were simultaneously being catabolized, an intermediate RQ between 0.9 and 1.0 would result. Further, since anemones excrete their waste nitrogen as ammonia (section 4.2, page 175), deamination and oxidation of the translocated amino acid alanine would yield an RQ of ≈ 1 (section 3.6, page 133). In short, as the ratios of particular products of zooxanthella photosynthesis actually translocated by the zooxanthellate and used by the animal host in its respiration cannot be stated with certainty, RQ measurements alone cannot be used to infer what classes of foodstuffs are being oxidized.

The amount of algal photosynthate actually translocated to the host is also difficult to quantify. From autoradiographic analysis of insoluble radioactivity in the tissues following long incubation periods, Taylor (1969b) concluded that more than 60% of the carbon fixed photosynthetically by its zooxanthellae was transferred to the host tissue in *Anemonia viridis* ($\equiv$ *A.sulcata*). Using radioisotope techniques, Stambler and Dubinsky (1987) estimated that 45–48% of the photosynthate is translocated to the host in freshly-collected *A.viridis*. Isolated zooxanthellae released about 13% of the total soluble radioactive carbon to the incubation medium; this value increased to 49% when the algae were incubated in a homogenate of host tissues (Taylor, 1969b). Similar results were obtained for *Anthopleura elegantissima* and *Aiptasia pulchella* by Trench (1971c), who also showed that the factor (probably a protein) stimulating release of algal photosynthate was absent from aposymbiotic anemones but could be induced by their infection with zooxanthellae.

Blanquet, Emanuel and Murphy (1988) have shown that host tissues of symbiotic *Aiptasia pallida* and *Condylactis gigantea* contain a factor (molecular weight 2–10 kDa) that inhibits uptake of alanine by zooxanthellae isolated from them and from a scyphozoan. Extracts of aposymbiotic *A.pallida* did not suppress uptake of alanine by zooxanthellae in these experiments, so that the inhibitory factor seems to be symbiosis-specific. It is unknown whether the presence of algae in the anemone's tissues induces the production of inhibitory factors by gene activation or their release from presynthesized stores.

All of these important experiments have implications not only in nutritional aspects of the symbiosis but also in the control of the algal population through a regulated removal of their metabolites by the host (Trench, 1979; section 2.6.4) or active control of their heterotrophic potential. As already mentioned (page 101), specimens of *Aiptasia pulchella* that had been aposymbiotic for several years, when reinfected with zooxanthellae, suffered a loss of weight while their algae had faster growth rates than those in control zooxanthellate anemones (Steen, 1986), perhaps because long-term aposymbiotic anemones had a lesser ability to regulate the zooxanthellae.

Muscatine, Falkowski and Dubinsky (1983) concluded that *in vivo* experiments greatly underestimate the percentage of photosynthate that is translocated from algae to host, perhaps by 50% or more. This has several causes, including a large disequilibrium between ^{14}C and ^{12}C compounds in brief incubations. Knowing the total amount of carbon per algal cell, the total algal population and the carbon-specific growth rate of the algae (estimated from the daily specific growth rate, μ), the fraction of net carbon fixed photosynthetically that is then available for translocation (T) can be calculated. Applying this method to a reef coral having a low value of μ indicated that 98.6% of net fixed carbon must be translocated. Smith (1986) similarly calculated T to be 87% in adult and 89% in juvenile specimens of the tropical anemone, *Aulactinia stelloides*. Calculations have not been made for *Aiptasia pulchella*, but the very low μ value in this species suggests a comparably high value of T; the much greater rate of turnover of zooxanthellae in non-tropical *Anthopleura elegantissima* (Wilkerson et al., 1983) implies a lower value of T in that species.

The feeding regime (0 to 3 times per week) does not significantly alter T in *Aiptasia pulchella*, where T ranges from 40% to 46% as measured by ^{14}C techniques (Clayton and Lasker, 1984). However, total photosynthate translocated declines in starved individuals, for as in other species, starvation results in a decline in the number of zooxanthellae per anemone. Starvation for 16 days led to an increase in translocation from ≈50% to ≈70% in *Anemonia viridis*, perhaps because the zooxanthellae became nutrient-limited and stopped growing, and so translocated photosynthate devoid of nitrogen and phosphorus to the host (Stambler and Dubinsky, 1987; see below). In fed, growing juveniles of *Aulactinia stelloides*, rates of zooxanthella growth and photosynthesis are greater than in adult anemones (as noted on page 95), and although the percentage T values are similar, zooxanthellae in juveniles translocate more photosynthate per day owing to their higher daily photosynthesis (Smith, 1986).

Transfer to algae of materials derived from food ingested by the host has received less attention, but the finding of ^{35}S label in the zooxanthellae of anemones fed labelled protein (Cook, 1971; Steen, 1986) probably indicates translocation of the sulphur-containing amino acids cystine and methionine, and the peptide cystathione (Trench, 1979). Feeding regime does not affect P_{max} expressed per zooxanthella or per µg chlorophyll *a*, nor does it affect the shape of the *P-I* curve (Clayton and Lasker, 1984). Because larger rations increase O_2 consumption (and so CO_2 production) in these anemones, and also increase ammonia production (see section 4.2), it would appear that photosynthesis by zooxanthellae in *Aiptasia pallida* fed once per week is not limited by the availability of CO_2 or ammonia. The potential for CO_2 limitation, however, seems to exist. Much higher activities of carbonic anhydrase (CA) in zooxanthellate than in azooxanthellate species of anemones suggest that the enzyme enhances CO_2 delivery to the zooxanthellae from bicarbonate in seawater (Weis, Smith and Muscatine, 1989). This is supported by the higher activity of CA in zooxanthella-containing tentacular tissues of *Condylactis gigantea* than in columnar tissues lacking zooxanthellae, and by the higher CA activity in zooxanthellate specimens of *Aiptasia pulchella* compared with aposymbiotic clonemates (which increase their CA activity when reinfected with zooxanthellae) (Weis, 1989).

Prolonged lack of feeding of the host leads to nutrient limitation in its zooxanthellae. In *Aiptasia pallida*, anemones not fed for 1.5–2 months consistently have higher rates of inorganic phosphate and ammonium uptake than recently fed specimens (Muller-Parker, D'Elia, and Cook, 1988). In the case of ammonia, this may be because lack of feeding leads to a decrease in deamination of protein and a depletion of host ammonia pools, which results in enhanced diffusional uptake from seawater (D'Elia and Cook, 1988). In anemones unfed for ≈1 month, zooxanthella cell division decreases, chlorophyll *a* content per cell declines and C : N ratio increases (Cook *et al.*, 1988). The mitotic index in zooxanthellae increases when inorganic N or P is added to the oligotrophic seawater in which the anemones are cultured. All of these results indicate that zooxanthellae *in hospite* may become nutrient limited when their hosts are unfed. Field-collected specimens of *A.pallida* have rates of phosphate uptake and times of total phosphorus turnover closer to those in laboratory specimens starved for 0.5–1 month than to those in fed specimens (Muller-Parker, Cook and D'Elia, 1990). This indicates that feeding may be relatively infrequent in the field, and since the phosphorus turnover time in the zooxanthellae *in hospite* was similar to the turnover time for the algal population, the uptake of inorganic phosphate from seawater may provide a major fraction of the phosphorus required by the zooxanthellae under natural conditions (Muller-Parker *et al.*, 1990).

Thermal effects on host-zooxanthella nutritional relationships have scarcely been examined. In the subtropical *Aiptasia pallida*, total photosynthetic carbon fixation increases between 12° and 32°C, although T declines with increasing temperature (Clark and Jensen, 1982). This indicates that as temperature increases more of the gross primary production is required for algal maintenance. Photosynthetic carbon fixation in *A.pallida* shows inverse temperature acclimation (higher rates in warm-acclimated than in cold-acclimated individuals when measured at the same temperature; see section 3.8.7, page 164), and the zooxanthellae appear to be less thermally adaptable than the anemone host. Temperature rather than photic regime may thus be the major determinant of the decreasing frequency of zooxanthella–anemone symbioses with increasing latitude (Clark and Jensen, 1982).

In zoochlorellae from *Anthopleura xanthogrammica*, decreasing mitotic index with increasing temperature may be accounted for by an increased maintenance requirement, and may explain the geographic and intertidal restriction of this symbiosis to cooler areas (O'Brien and Wyttenbach, 1980). It would be very interesting to know the thermal effects on photosynthesis and translocation in this symbiosis. In *A.elegantissima* similar decreases in net photosynthesis and translocated carbon, coupled with a higher metabolic rate of the host, may be involved in the interacting effects of illumination and temperature on weight loss (Figure 2.21). These results suggest also that the expulsion of the zooxanthellae at higher temperatures occurs because their presence begins to subtract from, rather than add to, the host's energy budget (Sebens, 1980).

2.6.7 CZAR

A complete accounting of the contribution of the algae to the host's energy budget has not been made in any symbiosis, owing to the practical difficulties and sometimes tenuous assumptions discussed above. Respiration is the largest fraction of energy utilization, and Muscatine, McCloskey and

Marian (1981) provided a useful approach to determining the percentage contribution of translocated zooxanthella carbon to the daily respiratory carbon requirements of the host animal (CZAR).

Briefly, CZAR $= [(P_{znet} \times T)/R_a] \times 100\%$, where P_{znet} is net daily carbon fixation by the zooxanthellae, T is the fraction of P_{znet} translocated to the host (estimated as discussed in the previous section), and R_a is the daily respiration by the animal, in carbon equivalents. P and R are usually estimated by measuring O_2 changes in the intact symbiosis (Figure 2.22), which includes both algal and animal tissue. Oxygen uptake in the dark can be partitioned into its algal and animal components by subsequently isolating the zooxanthellae and measuring their fractional contribution to the biomass of the association, and assuming that oxygen uptake by each component is directly proportional to its (protein) biomass. Deducting zooxanthella respiration from gross photosynthesis and from total anemone respiration gives $P_z$net and R_a, respectively.

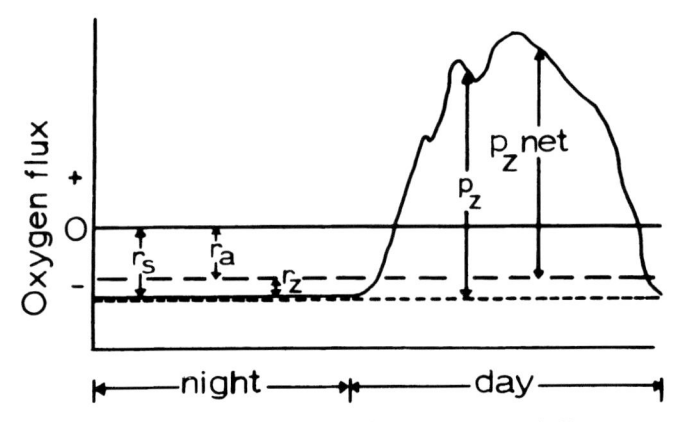

Figure 2.22 Diel curve showing net O_2 flux in a zooxanthellate sea anemone, partitioned among respiration by the entire symbiosis (animal plus zooxanthellae r_s), the animal component (r_a), and the zooxanthella component (r_z); and gross (p_z) and net ($p_z$net) photosynthesis by zooxanthellae. Lower-case r and p indicate hourly rates; upper-case R and P used in text refer to daily totals. See text for further discussion. Source: after Muscatine *et al.* (1981).

Conversion of oxygen production or consumption into carbon units of photosynthesis or respiration involves assumptions regarding the photosynthetic quotient (PQ, mol O_2 produced/mol CO_2 fixed) and the respiratory quotient (RQ), both of which vary according to the particular carbon compounds synthesized or respired (see also page 103 and section 3.6, page 133). Fitt *et al.* (1982) reported PQ values of 0.95 to 1.15 at saturating irradiance. The interconversion of O_2, CO_2 and carbon units may be done as follows:

$$mg\ C = 0.5355 \times ml\ O_2\ [\div PQ\ or\ \times RQ]$$
(for derivation, see McCloskey *et al.*, 1978).

Freshly-collected specimens of *Anthopleura elegantissima* have CZAR values between 34% and 47% at 15° and 20°C (Fitt *et al.*, 1982; Shick and Dykens, 1984). Both studies used the conservative T value of 40%, so CZAR may actually be greater. However, since symbiotic *A.elegantissima* starved in the light lose weight only about half as fast as when starved in the dark (Figure 2.21), a CZAR of about 40% may be correct. The anemone is not wholly photoautotrophic even with respect to carbon and so requires solid prey (Zamer and Shick, 1989). Nevertheless, gross photosynthesis in *A.elegantissima* is similar to that of sympatric macroalgae, and together with its monopolization of available substrates, makes this anemone a major primary producer as well as a spatial dominant in its intertidal community (Fitt *et al.*, 1982; Taylor and Littler, 1982). CZAR is 110% in freshly-collected specimens of *Anemonia viridis*, assuming 10 h of light-saturated photosynthesis per day (Stambler and Dubinsky, 1987).

CZAR is diminished by short-term reductions in P_z that occur due to shading of the algae when the anemone contracts during intertidal exposure (Shick and Dykens, 1984) and when immersed but in full sunlight (Figure 2.23). Although contraction lowers R_a (see section 3.8.2), its shading of the zooxanthellae reduces P_z far more, and CZAR falls to 18% when anemones are exposed to air during daylight low tides (Shick and Dykens, 1984). With increasing shore height the photoautotrophic input to the animal, as well as its time available for heterotrophic prey capture, thus decrease.

Any factors that increase or decrease respiration without affecting photosynthesis will decrease or increase CZAR. Feeding increases respiration in *A.elegantissima* at least twofold compared with starved anemones, and values of CZAR in these groups are 13% and 43%, respectively (Fitt *et al.*, 1982). CZAR in freshly collected *A.elegantissima* is similar to that in starved specimens, confirming the relatively small ingested ration suggested by coelenteron content analyses (see section 2.2.6) and emphasizing the flexibility of the polytrophic nutrition of this symbiotic sea anemone. Finally, it must be remembered that most of the photosynthate provided by the zooxanthellae is rich in energy but low in nitrogen and phosphorus (so-called 'junk food'), so that the capture of prey by the host is necessary to provide these nutrients to both partners.

2.7 PHOTOBIOLOGY

Photobiology includes the biochemical, physiological, and behavioural responses and adaptations to light, which may or may not be mediated through algal endosymbionts.

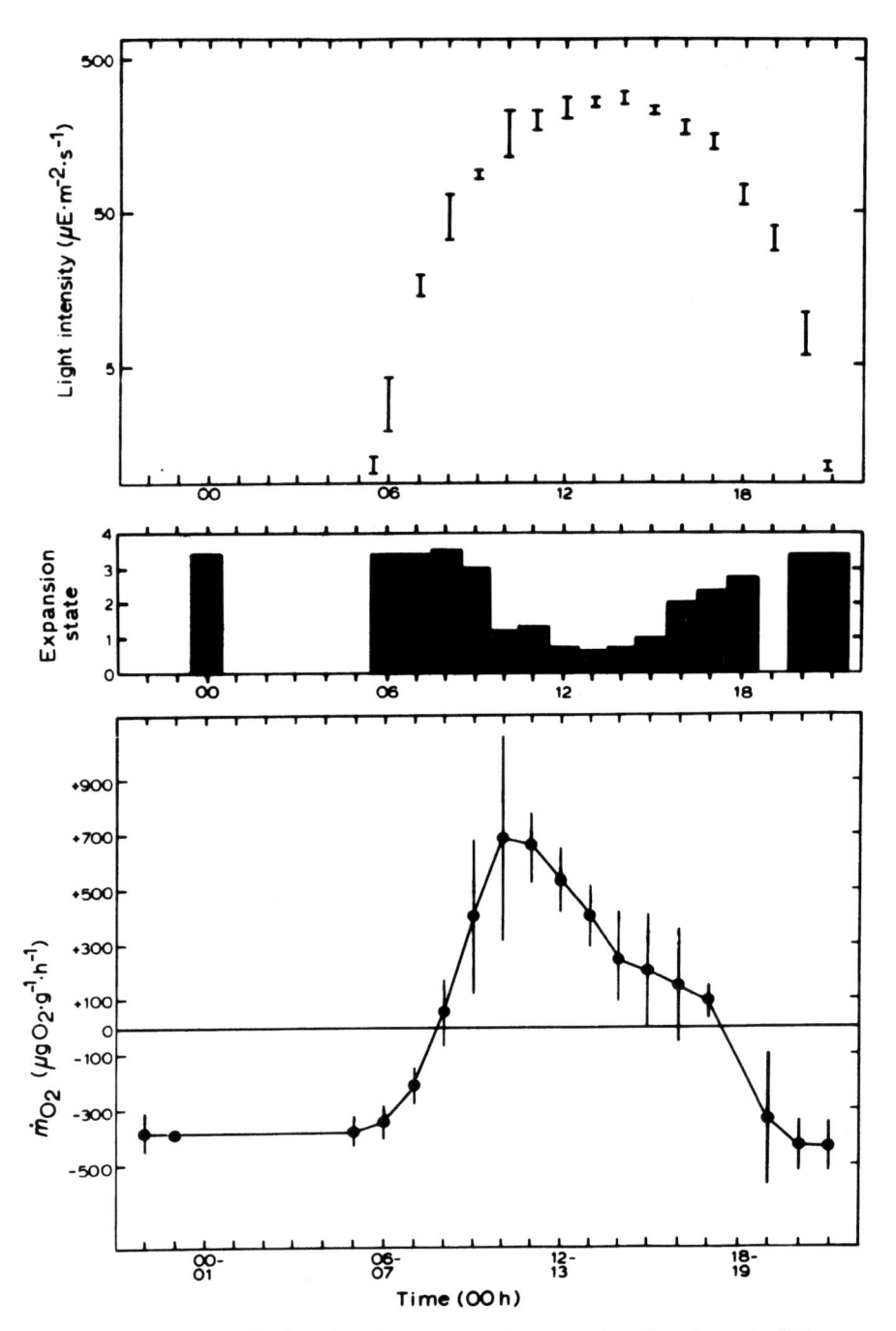

Figure 2.23 Diel net O_2 flux (m_{O_2}) and expansion state (ranging from 0: fully contracted, to 4: fully expanded) in low intertidal *Anthopleura elegantissima* measured under ambient sunlight at Bodega Bay, California, USA. Note the decline in O_2 production associated with anemone contraction under peak irradiance, and the plateau in O_2 production as the anemones re-expand in the late afternoon. CZAR in these anemones is 34%, assuming T = 40%. Source: modified from Shick and Dykens (1984).

2.7.1 Phototaxis

Condylactis gigantea and *Anthopleura elegantissima* show locomotory photo-tactic or photokinetic behaviour that is wholly dependent on the presence of zooxanthellae, which suggests that a chemical either consumed or produced during photosynthesis regulates this behaviour (Zahl and McLaughlin, 1959; Pearse, 1974a). By imposing different dissolved oxygen regimes on the anemones during phototaxis experiments, Fredericks (1976) showed that *A. elegantissima* could detect oxygen differences as small as those produced by unequal illumination of its zooxanthellae, and that photosynthetic oxygen was the proximal cause of the 'phototactic' behaviour. Laboratory experiments supported field observations that zooxanthellate clonemates were more closely packed than aposymbiotic clonemates, perhaps because of the greater availability of oxygen in the former. The (neural) basis for the detection and evaluation of oxygen levels has not been investigated; the actual motile response involving pedal locomotion is probably controlled by the SS1, SS2, and TCNN (section 1.3, page 20).

The direction of phototaxis (the initial movements in the process occur under uniform illumination and may therefore better be termed 'photokinesis'), positive or negative, depends on the intensity of illumination. Zooxanthellate tropical sea anemones and corallimorpharians show negative phototaxis to full sunlight, choosing partly shaded microhabitats (McClendon, 1911; Zahl and McLaughlin, 1959; Sebens and DeRiemer, 1977), although their degree of exposure to bright light may be varied by expansion or contraction of the body (section 2.7.2). The phototactic response also depends on the previous history of the anemones: specimens of non-tropical *A. elegantissima* from sunny habitats show a positive response to illumination of 700 foot candles (approximately $56 \mu \text{Einsteins·m}^{-2}\text{·s}^{-1}$ at 555 nm) but conspecifics from shaded habitats avoid this level of irradiance; when irradiance is reduced to 250 f.c. ($\approx 20 \mu \text{E·m}^{-2}\text{·s}^{-1}$) the shade-acclimatized individuals show positive phototaxis (Pearse, 1974a). Phototactic behaviour may optimize the photic regime experienced on a long-term basis, but the expulsion of zooxanthellae by shade-acclimatized *A. elegantissima* when abruptly exposed to full sunlight indicates the need for short-term defences against high irradiance.

2.7.2 Expansion and Contraction Behaviour

Sea anemones in nature exhibit diurnal and tide-related cycles of expansion and contraction of the oral disc and extension and retraction of the tentacles (see also sections 2.2.3 and 3.8.2, page 146). This aspect of their behaviour has been a topic of fascination at least since P.H. Gosse's poetic description of these animals as 'blossomed beauties'. Light has long been implicated as a determinant of this behaviour, which in zooxanthellate anemones may modulate the illumination of the algae without the need for locomotion. While studies on azooxanthellate species often yield conflicting results, zooxanthellate anemones are quite consistent in their response to illumination, implicating the endosymbiotic algae as mediators of the behaviour.

In the first controlled, quantitative study of expansion and contraction behaviour in a zooxanthellate sea anemone, *Anthopleura elegantissima*, Pearse (1974b) demonstrated that aposymbiotic individuals were indifferent to ambient light while zooxanthellate specimens invariably expanded under moderate illumination. The role of the zooxanthellae in the response to illumination is clearly seen in tropical species that concentrate the zooxanthellae in specialized non-feeding structures such as pseudotentacles (Mc-Clendon, 1911; Gladfelter, 1975; Sebens and DeRiemer, 1977; Steele and Goreau, 1977; Lewis, 1984). These structures are always extended in daylight and in most species are retracted at night; the reverse is true of the tentacles, which have far fewer zooxanthellae and which are used to capture the zooplankton abundant at night (Sebens and DeRiemer, 1977). Extension of the feeding tentacles is more variable than that of the pseudotentacles in *Lebrunia coralligens* (Lewis, 1984). Zooxanthellate anemones without these specialized structures concentrate algae in their tentacles, which remain extended day and night.

Expansion of *A.elegantissima* in moderate light appears to be initiated by light *per se* and reinforced by photosynthetically-produced O_2 (Shick and Brown, 1977). When maintained under anoxia, all specimens contract in the dark but expand fully in moderate light; chemical inhibition of photosynthesis by DCMU results in a relaxation of the marginal sphincter but not in the expansion of the oral disc or extension of the tentacles (Figure 2.24). Apparently relaxation of the sphincter muscle in contracted specimens is a direct response to light (see next section), and it subsequently increases photosynthesis by the zooxanthellae in the partially-exposed oral disc; the oxygen thus produced may be the stimulus for full expansion of the oral disc and extension of the tentacles. The neuromuscular pathways involved could be studied using electrophysiological techniques.

2.7.3 The Dual Menace of High Irradiance (Especially Ultraviolet) and Hyperoxia

Both direct and alga-mediated effects of light are involved in the contraction of sea anemones under intense illumination. Although Pearse (1974b) suggested that contraction by *A.elegantissima* in very bright light may be related to an inhibition of photosynthesis, photoinhibition of zooxanthellae *in hospite* does not occur even under very high irradiances (Fitt *et al.*, 1982; Muller-Parker, 1984b), at least in experiments of short duration. Instead, since such

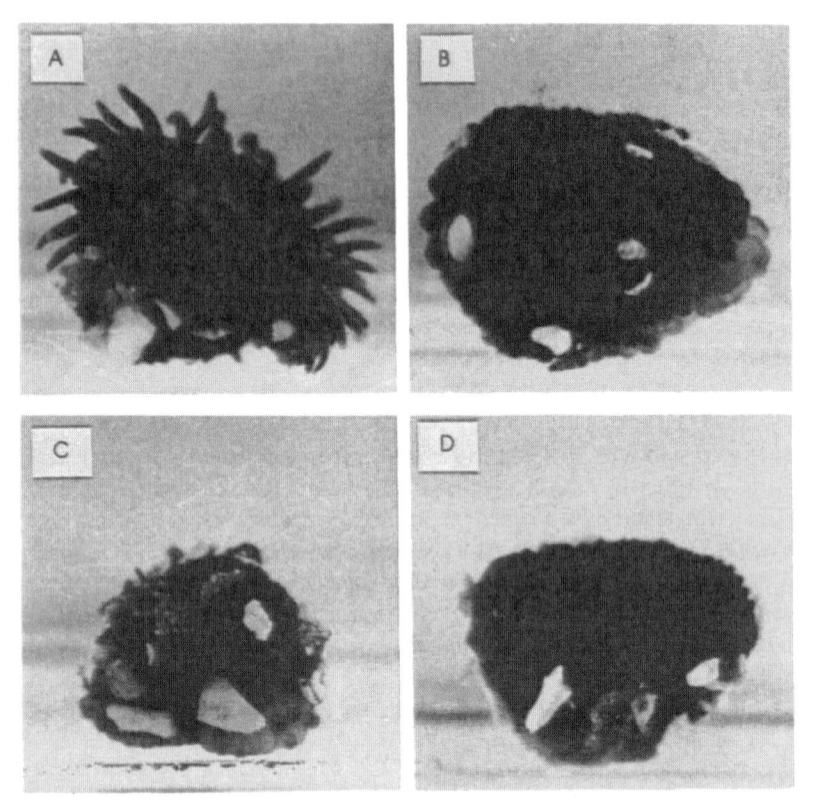

Figure 2.24 Expansion and contraction of *Anthopleura elegantissima* maintained in the laboratory under anoxia and various conditions of dim artificial light, darkness, and chemical inhibition of photosynthesis. (**A**) In light; (**B**) in darkness; (**C**) in light, but with photosynthesis inhibited by DCMU (note relaxation of marginal sphincter but lack of extension of tentacles); (**D**) in darkness plus DCMU (control). Note pieces of gravel and calcareous debris attached to verrucae. Source: with permission from Shick and Brown (1977).

contraction can be diminished by the photosynthesis inhibitor DCMU (Shick and Dykens, 1984), it is more probably a response by the anemones to high levels of photosynthetically-generated O_2 in their tissues, particularly in bright light, which exacerbates oxygen toxicity.

Molecular oxygen itself is relatively unreactive but is potentially toxic because it undergoes univalent reduction to form the superoxide radical, O_2^-, which in turn can give rise to hydrogen peroxide, H_2O_2, and to the highly reactive hydroxyl radical, $HO\cdot$. Photosynthetically produced molecular oxygen and sunlight, particularly its energetic UV wavelengths, act synergistically in the presence of photosensitizing agents such as chlorophyll and flavins to produce superoxide radical and singlet oxygen ($^1O_2$) (Asada and Takahashi, 1987). Superoxide radicals also are generated during the auto-oxidation of ferredoxin, flavins, heme proteins, and quinones in mitochondria and chloroplasts. These active forms of oxygen have a variety of pathological effects (Halliwell and Gutteridge, 1985).

Zooxanthellate specimens of *Anthopleura elegantissima* maintain enzymic defences against such toxicity in the host tissues in direct proportion to their algal complement (Dykens and Shick, 1982; Dykens, 1984). One such defence is superoxide dismutase (SOD), which by catalysing the reaction

$$2O_2^- + 2H^+ \rightarrow H_2O_2 + O_2,$$

keeps cellular levels of superoxide radical, and hence of hydroxyl radical, low. In so doing, however, it generates H_2O_2, which is in turn removed by catalase or peroxidase, which catalyse the reaction

$$2H_2O_2 \rightarrow 2H_2O + O_2,$$

or its equivalent. Not only do the activities of these enzymes in the host vary among individuals according to their chlorophyll concentrations (a measure of the capacity for O_2 production within the host's tissues), but the activities of the enzymes in the host are also directly related to chlorophyll concentration in different regions of the same individual (Figure 2.17). This relationship is not universal among anemones, however, and *Aiptasia* spp. appear to rely on biochemical antioxidants such as uric acid more than on enzymic defences (Tapley, Shick and Smith, 1988). Also, catalase activities in anemones vary less predictably with presumed intracellular oxygen levels (Tytler and Trench, 1988; Tapley *et al.*, 1988). The lower activities of animal catalase in zooxanthellate than in dark-maintained aposymbiotic specimens of *Aiptasia* spp. (see also Tytler and Trench, 1988) moreover seems due to irreversible photoinactivation of catalase in the zooxanthellate individuals (Tapley *et al.*, 1988; Tapley, 1989).

The zooxanthellae themselves show even higher levels of SOD activity, much of which surprisingly appears to arise from the Cu^{2+}-Zn^{2+} form of the enzyme not otherwise reported in unicellular eukaryotic algae (Dykens, 1984). In *Aiptasia pallida* the enzyme in the zooxanthellae is electrophoretically distinct from the Cu^{2+}-Zn^{2+} SOD in the host anemone's cytosol, and from that in the free-living dinoflagellate *Gonyaulax* (Lesser and Shick, 1989a). Zooxanthellae in *A.pulchella* also contain catalase in conjunction with other enzymes of the photorespiratory pathway (Tytler and Trench, 1986), as do those in *A.pallida*, which moreover contain ascorbate peroxidase (Lesser and Shick, 1989a, b).

Peak levels of irradiance may overwhelm these defences, and the anemone's response becomes one of contraction and avoidance by shading the algae. Within a single, partially illuminated specimen of *Anthopleura xanthogrammica* or *A.elegantissima* the response can be highly localized (Dykens and Shick, 1984). Additional shading is provided by the attachment of debris by the verrucae of the column, a response which varies directly with the levels of irradiation and photosynthesis (Dykens and Shick, 1984). Removal of this debris and exposure of the anemone to bright sunlight leads to expulsion of the algae.

Photosynthetic input by the endosymbiotic algae in sea anemones may thus be optimized not only by physiological characteristics of the algae (e.g. variations in chlorophyll *a* and accessory pigment concentrations), which are functions of day length, microhabitat and local weather conditions, but also by the anemone's behaviour, including long-term phototactic selection of microhabitat and short-term modulation of the amount of light reaching the algae. The tentacles and oral disc of *Anthopleura xanthogrammica* show separate and interacting responses to ultraviolet radiation (Clark and Kimeldorf, 1971) that apparently serve to reduce the anemone's exposure to UV (Shick and Dykens, 1984; Dykens and Shick, 1984; and below).

Azooxanthellate sea anemones also are responsive to light, despite their lack of identified, discrete photoreceptors. Early experiments by Bohn (1906a), Fleure and Walton (1907) and others (reviewed by Parker, 1919) demonstrated contraction and local bending of the column in response to local illumination. More recent studies by North and Pantin (1958) suggest that this behaviour arises from the direct effects of light on the circular and parietal muscles (which is facilitated by the occurrence of muscles as sheets a single cell thick), and that the response is subject to dark adaptation (i.e. an increase in sensitivity occurs during maintenance in the dark). The more variable and complex response of the oral disc to illumination may arise from a greater involvement of the nerve net and pacemakers there (Marks, 1976).

The role of various pigments in the differential spectral sensitivities of *Metridium senile* is thought to arise from the role of the pigments as filters rather than as specific photosensitive substances (North and Pantin, 1958). In addition, the role of ectodermal pigments as screens against harmful wavelengths of solar radiation has long been suspected. Elmhirst and Sharpe (1923) associated the pronounced contraction in intense light by specimens of *Urticina felina* (≡ *Tealia crassicornis*) from shaded habitats (first noted by Fleure and Walton, 1907) with the lesser degree of pigmentation in such individuals compared with those from brightly lit areas. The former authors also discerned a series of decreasing pigmentation in this azooxanthellate species ranging from exposed intertidal habitats, through shaded sublittoral areas, to deep water.

Actinia tenebrosa shows no clear preference for a particular level of irradiance in laboratory experiments (Ottaway, 1973) despite its great vagility under conditions of intertidal exposure (Ottaway and Thomas, 1971), but in nature the anemone nevertheless occurs most often in shaded positions. Like *Actinia equina* (Elmhirst and Sharpe, 1920; Stephenson, 1935; Quicke, Donoghue, and Brace, 1983), *A.tenebrosa* tends to be more heavily pigmented in brightly lit habitats (Ottaway, 1973).

The reduced pigmentation in anemones kept in the dark or largely shielded from ultraviolet radiation in glass aquaria has long been known, but the particular pigments in question have not been identified. The marked absorption of violet, blue, and green wavelengths by ether-alcohol extracts of *A.equina*, which was greater in more darkly pigmented individuals (Elmhirst and Sharpe, 1920), is consistent with the absorption spectra of the carotenoids actinioerythrin, astaxanthin, and violerythrin (Figure 2.25) more recently demonstrated in actiniids (Hertzberg *et al.*, 1969; LeBoeuf *et al.*, 1981). Carotenoids account for 0.12% of $_dW$ in exposed intertidal *A.equina* (Hertzberg *et al.*, 1969) and only one-tenth that concentration in sand-covered individuals of another actiniid, *Bunodosoma granulifera* (McCommas and LeBoeuf, 1981). Among the populations of *Metridium* spp. that have been examined, only the large, white *Metridium giganteum*, which is restricted to subtidal habitats, lacks somatic carotenoids. This anemone incorporates astaxanthin into its planktonic eggs (Fox *et al.*, 1978), which probably experience higher irradiances (although sequestration of carotenoids into ova may be a general feature among Animalia, not necessarily a specific photoadaptation).

In azooxanthellate actiniarians the apparent relationship between level of irradiation and carotenoid concentration suggests a role in photoprotection. The role of carotenoids in protecting against photosensitized oxidations via highly reactive singlet oxygen ($^1O_2$) and quenching activated state intermediates in plants and microorganisms is well known (Clayton, 1977; Krinsky, 1978, 1982). Although this is of obvious importance in photosynthetic organisms, where carotenoids are involved in quenching excited chlorophyll in

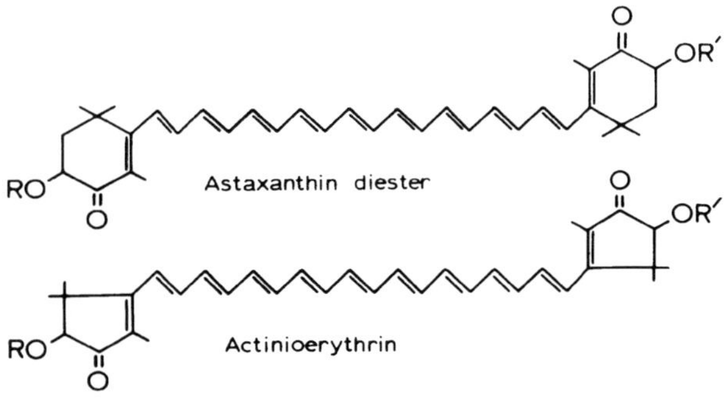

Figure 2.25 The major carotenoids in actiniid sea anemones. See text for discussion.

chloroplast membranes, the scavenging of photochemically-generated $^1O_2$ in non-photosynthetic organisms has also been demonstrated. Only those carotenoids whose polyene chains contain nine or more conjugated double bonds are effective quenchers of $^1O_2$, a criterion met by the major carotenoids in anemones (Figure 2.25).

Investigation of the possibility of carotenoid photoprotection in sea anemones might include the study of carotenoid levels in genotypically identical individuals (clonemates; section 6.5, page 277) fed a defined diet (like other metazoans, anemones cannot synthesize carotenoids *de novo* but can metabolically alter dietary carotenoids: Abeloos-Parize and Abeloos-Parize, 1926) but exposed to different photon fluxes and wavelengths of radiation. Also of interest is whether anemones routinely exposed to high irradiance are more efficient in retaining dietary carotenoids.

SOD activity in aposymbiotic specimens of *Anthopleura elegantissima* transplanted into full sunlight increases by 590% over shaded aposymbiotic individuals (Dykens and Shick, 1984). Both visible and UV light are involved in causing this elevation, which may be due to the direct photochemical generation of oxygen radicals that necessitate higher levels of enzymic defences. In *Aiptasia pallida*, zooxanthellae from anemones living in brightly illuminated habitats had significantly higher activities of SOD and of ascorbate peroxidase than zooxanthellae from hosts living in dim habitats; the difference in SOD activity was reversed by ten days after reciprocal transplantation of bright and dim anemones (Lesser and Shick, 1989b). Zooxanthellae exposed to environmentally realistic levels of UV in culture and *in hospite* showed 30 to 40% increases in SOD activity compared with zooxanthellae experiencing similar irradiances without UV (Lesser and Shick, 1989a). Activities of SOD, catalase, and ascorbate peroxidase were twice as great in zooxanthellae exposed in culture relative to those exposed *in hospite*, which suggests a protective or modulating effect of the host.

Other biochemical defences against components of natural sunlight include the melanins in *M.senile* (Fox and Pantin, 1941; Fox, 1953). Melanins might also act as scavengers of oxygen radicals.

Like other marine invertebrates, sea anemones contain compounds having absorption maxima (310–360 nm) in the ultraviolet. One class of substances, initially called 'S-320 compounds', has since been shown to comprise a family of mycosporine-like amino acids (MAA; Dunlap and Chalker, 1986) consisting of a central mycosporine base structure substituted by various amino acids (Figure 2.26). Owing to the bathymetric decline in the concentration of such compounds in scleractinian corals (Dunlap, Chalker and Oliver, 1986), the rapid increase in their concentration when corals were transplanted from deep to shallow water, and their increase in corals acclimatized to UV compared with specimens shielded from UV (Scelfo, 1986), the assumption has been that MAA protect the corals from UV radiation.

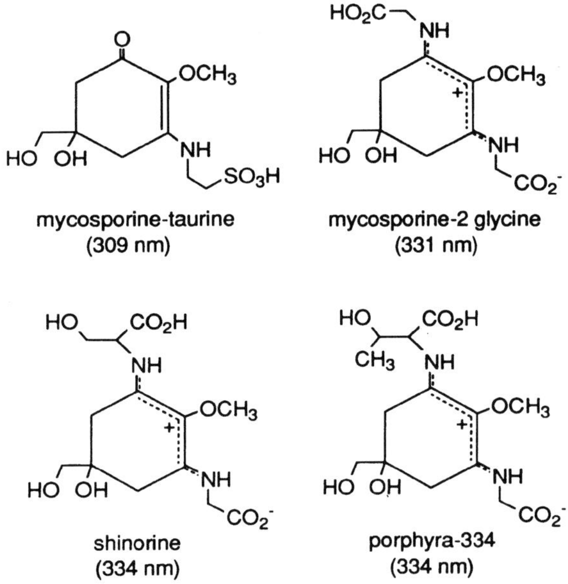

Figure 2.26 The major mycosporine-like amino acids and their absorption maxima in *Anthopleura elegantissima*. Mycosporine-taurine and mycosporine-2 glycine were originally identified from *A.elegantissima*; shinorine and porphyra-334 were originally identified from the red algae *Chondrus yendori* and *Porphyra tenera*, respectively. Source: Stochaj, Dunlap and Shick (unpublished).

In *Anthopleura elegantissima* the concentration of S-320 compounds was greater in zooxanthellae specimens on a sunny shore in California than in aposymbiotic conspecifics from nearby shaded habitats (Shick and Dykens, 1984), but no such difference was found by Scelfo (1988). In *Aiptasia pallida* no significant differences in the concentrations of identified MAA occurred between zooxanthellate specimens from bright and dim habitats in Bermuda (W.R. Stochaj, unpublished data). Moreover, in *A.elegantissima* the concentration of the UV-absorbing compounds did not change during six months of cross-acclimatization to bright and shaded conditions (Scelfo, 1988), nor in *A.pallida* did the concentrations of individual MAA change by ten days after reciprocal transplantation of bright and dim specimens (Stochaj, 1989). Finally, acclimation of monoclonal specimens of *Aiptasia pallida* and of *Anthopleura elegantissima* for two and four weeks, respectively, in the presence and absence of UV at the same irradiance of visible light in a solar simulator did not result in changes in the concentrations of MAA (Stochaj, 1988; Stochaj, Dunlap and Shick, unpublished). Thus, in sea anemones the seeming lack of responsiveness of the concentrations of UV- absorbing compounds to changes in UV flux is unlike the rapid changes in some scleractinian corals, and the importance of these compounds in protection from ultraviolet radiation remains to be established.

However, five months of acclimatization of zooxanthellate *Phyllodiscus semoni* to natural levels of solar UV resulted in a two-fold higher concentration of MAA in its zooxanthellae compared with the algae in conspecific specimens shielded from UV for that time (Shick, Lesser and Stochaj, 1990). This increase in algal MAA was associated with a higher rate of photosynthesis and lack of photoinhibition by UV in freshly isolated zooxanthellae from UV-acclimatized anemones compared with the impaired photosynthetic performance during acute UV exposure of zooxanthellae from the anemones that had been shielded from UV.

Nor is the source of the MAA in marine animals known. The presence of S-320 compounds (probably MAA) and of identified MAA in aposymbiotic *A.elegantissima*, in azooxanthellate species such as *Actinia bermudensis* (Stochaj, 1988), and in other taxa of non-symbiotic invertebrates and vertebrates indicates that MAA are not necessarily provided by zooxanthellae. But it is unknown whether metazoans can synthesize MAA *de novo*, whether MAA are obtained from the diet, or whether in sea anemones MAA or their precursors are translocated from bacteria present in the coelenteron (e.g. Herndl and Velimirov, 1985) or within the epidermal cells (e.g. Palincsar *et al.*, 1989).

As mentioned above (page 114), in *Anthopleura* spp. behavioural defences against UV radiation include retraction of the tentacles and contraction of the marginal sphincter (Clark and Kimeldorf, 1971; Shick and Dykens, 1984), and in *Aiptasia pallida* negative phototaxis includes a direct response to UV (Stochaj, 1989). *A.elegantissima* attaches debris to its column, which serves as a sunscreen (Dykens and Shick, 1984). Such attachment, also noted by Elmhirst and Sharpe (1923) to be more prevalent in exposed than in shaded individuals of *Urticina felina*, occurs both in response to UV and to photosynthetically produced O_2 in zooxanthellate *A.elegantissima* (Dykens and Shick, 1984).

The foregoing behaviours, and the maintenance of enzymic and biochemical defences against photooxidative stress, represent costs the animal must pay to reap the benefits afforded by the algae. Such benefits may include not only the provision of reduced carbon substrates for use in energy metabolism, but also a supplemental respiratory role of photosynthetically-produced O_2; these matters are treated in the next chapter.

3 Energy metabolism and respiratory gas exchange

3.1 SYNOPSIS

'Respiration' in the energy budget classically includes both aerobic and anaerobic processes, but in the strict sense only the former is respiration, whereas the latter is fermentation. During environmental hypoxia and activity, anemones employ fermentative pathways of energy metabolism similar to those found in other euryoxic invertebrates. Both aerobic and anaerobic energy metabolism draw heavily on amino acid catabolism, probably owing to the protein-rich diet of sea anemones. Lacking O_2-carrying respiratory pigments and capable of only limited convection of the ambient seawater, sea anemones seem particularly at the mercy of the Fick equations for diffusive O_2 exchange. Their compensation for decreased O_2 availability involves morphological, cytological, and compositional features that change parameters in Fick's first equation to enhance delivery of O_2 to respiring tissues. Morphological adaptations include the predominantly two-dimensional, laminar body plan, which minimizes diffusion distances and results in O_2 consumption being more nearly directly proportional to body mass than in most Metazoa. In consequence of their variable-volume hydrostatic skeleton and distensible body wall, sea anemones also have a system of gas exchange utilizing variable surface-area and diffusion-distance. These parameters are altered behaviourally in response to changing O_2 availability and demand. The slow nature of their muscular contractions is reflected in a more modest scope for activity in sea anemones than in other metazoans.

Occupation of the intertidal zone exposes anemones both to desiccation and to reduced availability of food; contraction during exposure conserves energy as well as water, in the first case by causing tissue hypoxia that lowers the rate of aerobic respiration. Although sea anemones derive nutritional and occasional respiratory benefits from their zooxanthellae, photosynthesis by the symbionts exposes the host's tissues to O_2 levels well above atmospheric and requires enzymic and biochemical defences against potential oxygen toxicity. In species from thermally extreme or variable environments, including the intertidal zone, both genetically-determined and environmentally-induced biochemical and physiological adaptations to temperature are pronounced.

3.2 SOME DEFINITIONS

Once absorbed, foodstuffs are partitioned among the processes of biosynthesis production (P), excretion (U), and energy metabolism (R). Aerobic respiration is that portion of R in which electrons derived from the oxidation of reduced carbon substrates in the Krebs (tricarboxylic acid or TCA) cycle are passed to molecular oxygen (O_2), the terminal electron acceptor in the electron transfer system (respiratory chain) of mitochondria. Associated with these processes are the production of CO_2 and the utilization of O_2, fluxes of which are termed gas exchange at both the cellular and organismal levels.

In aerobic respiration some of the chemical energy in the respiratory substrates is conserved in ATP, which is formed both via substrate-level phosphorylation of ADP in glycolysis in the cytosol, and especially via oxidative phosphorylation in the mitochondrial respiratory chain. Energy metabolism in the absence of O_2 (anaerobiosis, or more strictly, anoxibiosis) involves ATP formation in a variety of cytosolic and mitochondrial pathways generally termed fermentations. The net energy yield in aerobic respiration is 36 ATP per glucosyl unit; in fermentations the yield is as low as 2 ATP (lactate and 'opines' as endproducts: see below) or as high as approximately 6–7 ATP (propionate as end product) per glucosyl unit (see stoichiometric equations for various fermentations in Gnaiger, 1977, and de Zwaan, 1983). Thus even the biochemically most efficient fermentations show a six-fold reduction in ATP yield compared with aerobic respiration.

Rates of O_2 consumption and CO_2 production are reported in volumetric, gravimetric, or molar terms, and the former are symbolized as $\dot{V}_{O_2}$, $\dot{M}_{O_2}$, and $\dot{N}_{O_2}$, respectively. Molar units are preferred (being necessary to calculate certain metabolic quotients: see below) and will be used here. Units in the literature will be converted to molar terms only where it is necessary and convenient to do so; useful conversion tables can be found in Gnaiger (1983a). Rates of total and of mass-specific oxygen consumption ($\mu mol\,O_2 \cdot h^{-1}$ and $\mu mol\,O_2 \cdot g^{-1} \cdot h^{-1}$) are symbolized as $\dot{N}_{O_2}$ and $\dot{n}_{O_2}$, respectively; 'oxygen consumption' (no rate implied) omits the 'dot' over the N. The mass of anemones is reported as wet $(_wW)$, dry $(_dW)$, and ash-free or organic $(_{af}W)$

weight, reduced or submerged weight (apparent weight in seawater, $_rW$), and occasionally as the mass of their total contents of protein (W_P) or nitrogen (W_N). Authors sometimes provide conversion factors (tabulated in Sebens 1987a).

The availability of O_2 is usually given as a concentration (C_{O_2}, amount of O_2 per unit volume of water), as a partial pressure (P_{O_2}, in mm Hg or kPa), or occasionally as a fraction of an atmosphere (atm). Partial pressure is most commonly expressed in mm Hg, which by reason of familiarity will be retained here, and can be related to preferred SI units (kPa) as:

$$1 \, atm = 101.325 \, kPa = 760 \, mm \, Hg.$$

In dry air, P_{O_2} is the total atmospheric pressure $\times$ the volume fraction of O_2 (0.2095), or about 159 mm Hg. The P_{O_2} in air-saturated seawater is the same as in the atmosphere with which it is equilibrated. The C_{O_2} in air-saturated seawater further depends on temperature and salinity, and decreases as either of these increases. If dissolved O_2 is consumed faster than it is replenished, both P_{O_2} and C_{O_2} decline.

3.3 CELLULAR BASIS OF GLYCOLYSIS AND AEROBIC RESPIRATION

Details of glycolysis, Krebs cycle oxidations and respiratory chain oxido-reductions have been elucidated largely in taxa other than the Cnidaria, but there is no reason to suspect that the latter differ fundamentally from other eumetazoans. The inhibition of oxygen consumption by iodoacetate, malonate and cyanide (CN^-), and its stimulation by succinate, indicates the operation of the above processes in tissues of *Diadumene leucolena* (Beattie, 1971).

In basilar and sphincter muscles of *Metridium senile*, the rather low activities of hexokinase, phosphorylase, and phosphofructokinase suggest a low rate of carbohydrate utilization (Zammit and Newsholme, 1976). Other enzymes of glycolysis have been detected electrophoretically in various species of sea anemones.

The presence of both glucose-6-phosphate dehydrogenase and 6-phosphogluconate dehydrogenase in sea anemones indicates a functional pentose ($\equiv$ hexose monophosphate) shunt (Powers *et al.*, 1968), although in *D. leucolena* as in many other invertebrates it seems of little quantitative importance in glucose oxidation at moderate temperatures (Beattie, 1971). Based on the greater inhibition by 6-phosphogluconate of the electrophoretically slow allozyme of phosphoglucose isomerase (PGI, a mainstream glycolytic enzyme at the branchpoint with the pentose shunt), and an increasing frequency of this allele in more northern populations of *M.senile* (section 3.8.7, page 171), Hoffmann (1983) suggested that the slow allozyme may be favoured in cold water because it increases the contribution of the pentose shunt to glucose oxidation, known to occur in other metazoans in the cold. There is now direct evidence for this hypothesis concerning the slow allozyme of PGI in *M.senile* (section 3.8.7).

Radioactivity derived from ^{14}C-glucose has been detected in most intermediates of the Krebs cycle in *D.leucolena* (Ellington, 1977) and *Actinia equina* (Navarro and Ortega, 1984). In both species the production of $^{14}CO_2$ is much greater under oxygenated than anoxic conditions.

The original demonstration of cytochromes (reversibly oxidizable and reducible components of the respiratory chain) was in several anemone species, including *Actinia equina* ($\equiv$ *A.mesembryanthemum*) and the compounds were termed 'actiniohaematin' by MacMunn (1885). Elmhirst and Sharpe (1923) noted a greater concentration of MacMunn's 'respiratory pigment' in intertidal than in deep-water specimens of *Urticina felina* ($\equiv$ *Tealia crassicornis*). Likewise, the activity of cytochrome *c* oxidase appears to be greater in high intertidal than in low intertidal individuals of *Anthopleura elegantissima* and is directly related to the mitochondrial content of the tissues (Table 3.1). Cytochrome spectra were measured in several additional anemone species and *Cerianthus membranaceus* by Roche (1932). The spectra, which almost certainly indicate the presence of cytochrome $a + a_3$ (cytochrome *c* oxidase), are more pronounced in species capable of prolonged,

Table 3.1   Concentrations of mitochondria and activities of cytochrome *c* oxidase in *Anthopleura elegantissima*. 'Low-shore' anemones were collected near mean low water, and 'high-shore' anemones approximately 1.3 m higher in the intertidal zone

	Number of mitochondrial/g wet weight *Entire anemones*	*Tentacles only*
Low shore	$0.31^a - 0.68^b \times 10^{10}$	$1.74^b \times 10^{10}$
High shore	$0.71^a - 1.04^b \times 10^{10}$	$1.81^b \times 10^{10}$

	Cytochrome c oxidase activity (Units/g wet weight; 15°C) *Entire anemones*
Low shore	$0.14^a - 0.55$
High shore	$0.23^a - 0.71$

Note: Superscripts indicate means of paired data in which both measurements were made on the same anemone (n = 5). Values designated by 'a' are mitochondrial concentrations and cytochrome *c* oxidase activities which were measured in the same individuals; 'b' denotes mitochondrial concentrations in entire individuals and in their tentacles.
Source: J.A. Dykens, unpublished.

forceful muscular contraction. An alternative suggestion by Roche was that the cytochrome content was richer in species from less well-oxygenated habitats (mud), presumably as a compensation for chronic hypoxia (see also section 3.8.5, page 159). Roche's (1936) later studies on *U.felina* indicate the presence of cytochromes *a*, *b* and *c*.

3.4 ANAEROBIC ENERGY METABOLISM

Metabolic pathways of anaerobiosis employed during environmental or physiological hypoxia have been little studied in sea anemones. This is perhaps because early observations suggested that sea anemones tend to occur in well-oxygenated habitats, and quantitative studies (Sassaman and Mangum, 1972, 1973) indicate that inshore species such as *D.leucolena*, *M.senile*, and *Haliplanella lineata* ($\equiv$ *H.luciae*) are not particularly tolerant of anoxia compared with more notably euryoxic metazoans such as some bivalve molluscs and annelids, and parasitic helminths, nor are they as strenuously active as some annelids, crustaceans, and molluscs. Also, the few available data indicate that most sea anemones store predominantly lipid rather than glycogen (section 2.5, page 80), a pattern inconsistent with a well-developed anaerobic capacity, as lipid cannot be used in energy metabolism under anoxia, whereas glycogen is the major energy reserve in euryoxic metazoans (de Zwaan, 1977; Hochachka, 1980; Hochachka and Somero, 1984).

More recently, the natural exposure of some anemones to anoxia, and their greater tolerance of it, have been appreciated. In a periodically hypoxic Danish fjord *Metridium senile* and *Sagartiogeton* sp. are the most resistant macrofauna (B.B. Jørgensen, 1980, and personal communication). Likewise, the median survival time of *M.senile* is 22 to 24 days, and maximum survival is 40 days under anoxia *in situ* in another fjord, while in the laboratory at 6–7°C the anoxic LT_{50} is 21 to 22 days (Wahl, 1984). The shorter survival time (four days at 22–24°C) in North American specimens of *M.senile* studied by Sassaman and Mangum (1972) almost certainly reflects higher temperatures and different conditions of exposure. Also, because the Scandinavian populations routinely experience prolonged anoxia in nature, a condition that rarely if ever occurs in the habitat of the North American populations, their different anoxic tolerances may be an example of genetically determined physiological races, consistent with the restricted gene flow between American and European populations of this species (Bucklin, 1985). It would be interesting to know whether glycogen content is greater in the Scandinavian anemones.

Storm-shifted sand may bury intertidal actiniids such as *A.elegantissima* for three months in winter (Taylor and Littler, 1982). Burial also occurs in

Bunodosoma cavernata and *Actinia equina*, and survival of anoxia in the laboratory is for 6 weeks at room temperature in the former (D.C. Mangum, 1980) and at least one month at 15°C in the latter (Shick, 1981). Unlike many anemones, *A.equina* appears to have relatively large glycogen reserves (Boury-Esnault and Doumenc, 1979; Ortega *et al.*, 1988; section 2.5, page 80), which may be related to its well-developed tolerance of anoxia. The rapid decline in cellular ATP levels and death of *B.cavernata* within hours of exposure to anoxia in the presence of iodoacetate (Ellington, 1981; D.C. Mangum, 1980, respectively) indicates that anaerobic glycolysis is necessary for maintenance of the anoxic cellular energy state and hence for survival. The very long anoxic survival time in this species in the absence of metabolic inhibitors suggests the use of fermentations that are more efficient than the classical lactate pathway.

In the lactate pathway the single end product, lactate, is formed in a terminal reaction catalysed by lactate dehydrogenase (LDH), which serves to reduce pyruvate and so maintain cytosolic redox balance by regenerating NAD^+ from NADH produced 'higher up' in the pathway:

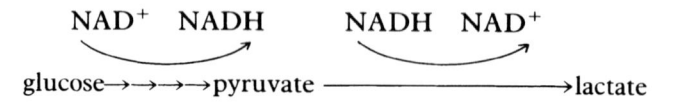

Although the biochemical efficiency (i.e. ATP yield per mol glucose or glycogen) is low, the *rate* of ATP provision can be very high owing to an increase in glycolytic flux. Thus the lactate pathway typically is found in muscles required to perform intense work for short periods during which ATP demand outstrips O_2 delivery (physiological hypoxia), and it seems ill-suited to allow prolonged survival of environmental anoxia (although in a few cases it is used for this). LDH is detectable in most sea anemones, but its activity is generally very low (Simpson and Awapara, 1966; Zammit and Newsholme, 1976; Ellington, 1979a, b; Livingstone *et al.*, 1983) and lactate does not accumulate during exposure to anoxia (Ellington, 1977, 1979a, 1980a, 1982). The report of much ^{14}C-lactate production from ^{14}C-glucose during anoxic exposure of *A.equina* (Navarro and Ortega, 1984) seems inconsistent with the very low LDH activity (Livingstone *et al.*, 1983) and prolonged anoxic survival in this species (see below) and bears further investigation. Even in the 'swimming' anemone *Stomphia coccinea* LDH activity is quite low and lactate does not accumulate during a bout of activity (W.R. Ellington, personal communication).

In many invertebrates, the lactate pathway is functionally substituted for by the 'opine' pathway in which the terminal reduction of pyruvate is replaced by its reductive condensation with one of several amino acids to form an imino dicarboxylic acid or 'opine':

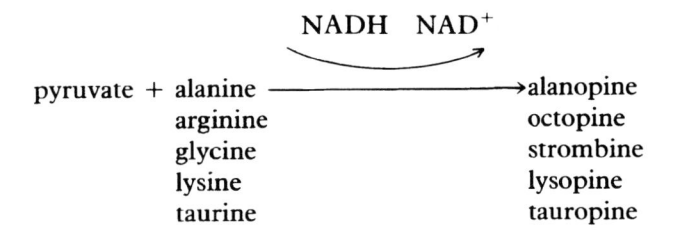

As in the lactate pathway, the enzyme is named on the basis of the reduction product, e.g. *octopine* dehydrogenase. In this case the source of arginine is frequently the hydrolysis of arginine phosphate during intense activity. This pathway has the same biochemical efficiency as the lactate pathway, although it may have a lower maximal rate of ATP generation (Livingstone, 1983).

Where it has been purified, the octopine dehydrogenase (ODH) of sea anemone species has shown a broad specificity for several amino and imino acids (Ellington, 1979b, 1980b; Walsh, 1981a) as well as keto acids in addition to pyruvate (Storey and Dando, 1982). A narrower specificity occurs in higher metazoans, leading Storey and Dando to suggest that the 'ODH' in sea anemones represents a primitive condition nearer to the ancestral enzyme from which more highly specific forms of the enzyme evolved. Thus the alanopine and strombine dehydrogenase activities reported in homogenates of sea anemones (Ellington, 1979b; Livingstone *et al.*, 1983) might actually represent a single broadly specific 'opine' dehydrogenase. No such enzyme was detected in *Ceriantheopsis americanus* (Ellington, 1979b), which apparently lacks the opine pathway and has a very low LDH activity as well. Despite its broad specificity, the opine dehydrogenase in *B.cavernata* appears to be a functional ODH, based on its much higher affinity (lower K_m, the substrate concentration at half-maximal reaction velocity) for arginine than for other amino acids (Ellington, 1980b).

When both LDH and opine dehydrogenase are present in an anemone, the activity of the latter enzyme is from 5 to 20 times that of the former (Zammit and Newsholme, 1976; Ellington, 1979b; Livingstone *et al.*, 1983) but still only one-tenth that in most annelids and molluscs (Livingstone *et al.*, 1983). In sea anemones, their sedentary habit and general reliance on low-speed muscular contraction apparently has not selected for highly active pyruvate oxidoreductases geared to maximizing power output.

Thus, although the substrate specificities and kinetics of the opine dehydrogenases in sea anemones are reasonably well understood, their physiological functions are not. ODH in molluscan muscles usually functions to sustain anaerobic glycolytic flux and maximize power output during burst activity. Such a situation is difficult to envisage in sea anemones. Muscular contractions during aerial exposure of *A.equina* have a peak power output of about -0.4 milliwatt (mW) per gram $_dW$ above the routine rate (from data in

Shick, 1981), far below the level of exercising molluscs and annelids. Even in the actively swimming *Stomphia coccinea* there is no detectable ODH activity, no accumulation of opines or lactate, and only a slight decline in cellular ATP levels during forced activity, suggesting that swimming is powered aerobically (W.R. Ellington, personal communication).

Likewise, there is no conversion of ^{14}C-glucose to ^{14}C-octopine in basilar muscle of *M.senile* during its KCl-induced contracture (Ellington, 1979a). Walsh (1981a) speculates that ODH might be invoked during crawling, but there has been no test of this idea. Although anoxia does occur beneath the basal disc, oxygen levels there are actually higher when the anemone is crawling than when stationary (Woolmington and Davenport, 1983), and the basilar muscles are also oxygenated via the coelenteron (section 3.7). Based on Ellington's results with *Stomphia* and *Metridium*, it seems that the activity of the basilar muscles could probably be sustained aerobically. This is consistent with the rather modest rate of locomotion in *M.senile* (McClendon, 1906; Parker, 1917; Robson, 1976; Robbins and Shick, personal communication in Walsh, 1981a) and hence low energy demand by this muscle. Moreover, ODH in *M.senile* and *B.cavernata* is highly subject to product inhibition (Ellington, 1979a, 1980b; Walsh, 1981a), thus limiting the amount of octopine that could be formed during prolonged locomotory activity. Finally, the rather low activity of arginine kinase in basilar muscle of *M.senile* indicates a low rate of hydrolysis of arginine phosphate (the principal phosphagen in sea anemones) there, which is in keeping with the low and apparently aerobically-supported energy demand of this tissue. It therefore seems that muscular contraction even in the most active sea anemones elicits neither an enhanced glycolysis ending in lactate or opine production, nor a wholesale hydrolysis of stored phosphagens characteristic of physiological hypoxia in more strenuously active invertebrates.

An additional role of the opine pathways postulated in bivalve adductor muscle has not previously been suggested in sea anemones. The involvement of anaerobic metabolism during aerobic recovery from environmental hypoxia, as evinced by the accumulation during recovery of strombine and octopine, has been suggested as a supplement to aerobic metabolism in restoring ATP stores in posterior adductor muscle of *Mytilus edulis* (de Zwaan, 1983). Subsequently this interpretation was questioned and opine accumulation seems more likely to reflect increased shell valve activity during recovery (Shick *et al.*, 1986). However, in sea anemones, anaerobic supplementation might be necessitated by their relatively small scope of aerobic respiration (sections 3.8.3, page 150, and 3.8.4, page 154). Such a role for the opine dehydrogenase pathway in sea anemones is admittedly speculative, but it might help to explain the existence of an otherwise enigmatic enzyme in these animals. Whether the small decline in arginine concentration during aerobic recovery from 96 h of anoxia in *B.cavernata*

(Ellington, 1982) reflects restoration of arginine phosphate or synthesis of octopine remains to be established. The decline in arginine concentration by $0.1 \, \mu mol \cdot g_w W^{-1}$ would yield $0.15 \, \mu mol \, ATP \cdot g_w W^{-1}$, assuming arginine was converted to octopine; the actual increase in ATP was $\approx 0.3 \, \mu mol \cdot g_w W^{-1}$ (Ellington, 1981).

Considering the long survival times of sea anemones under anoxia, the biochemical inefficiency of the opine pathway, and the product inhibition of ODH, it is not surprising that octopine does not accumulate during environmental anoxia (Ellington, 1980a). More efficient fermentations must be involved.

These additional pathways, including the sites of ATP production and mechanisms of maintaining redox balance, have been elucidated in a taxonomically wide array of euryoxic metazoans and have frequently been reviewed (Saz, 1981; de Zwaan, 1977, 1983; Hochachka and Somero, 1984; de Zwaan and Putzer, 1985). Although many variations exist, the pathways fall into two broad categories: those using glycogen or glucose as the substrate and producing succinate, propionate, and other volatile fatty acids (glucose–succinate pathway); and those using amino acids (and glucose) as substrates, producing mainly succinate and alanine (e.g. aspartate–succinate pathway). All of these pathways have a greater net yield of ATP per mole of substrate than the lactate and opine pathways (Gnaiger, 1977; de Zwaan, 1983). The evidence for the operation of these pathways in sea anemones is fragmentary and the full picture has not been assembled in any one species; what follows is a collage of data from various actinians.

Phosphoenolpyruvate (PEP) formed in glycolysis is a metabolic branch-point (Figure 3.1): through the action of pyruvate kinase (PK) it may be converted to pyruvate and thence to lactate or opines, or alternatively, converted to oxaloacetate (OAA) in a CO_2-fixing reaction catalysed by PEP carboxykinase (PEPCK). The latter represents diversion of PEP to the glucose–succinate pathway. Based on a relatively large ratio of PEPCK to PK activity, and various properties of PEPCK, it appears that *Metridium senile* has a well-developed glucose–succinate pathway (Zammit and Newsholme, 1978). Unfortunately, the end products formed during environmental anoxia have not been examined in this species. In the related mesomyarian, *Diadumene leucolena*, radioactivity from ^{14}C-glucose accumulates markedly in succinate during anoxia, suggesting the existence of this pathway (Ellington, 1977), which involves a reversal of part of the Krebs cycle (Figure 3.1). In another related species, *Haliplanella lineata*, succinate accumulates during the first two days of anoxia and subsequently declines; whether this reflects the activation of propionate synthesis from succinate is unknown (Ellington, 1980a).

Conversely, in the actiniid endomyarian *Bunodosoma cavernata* the ratio of PEPCK to PK is very low (Simpson and Awapara, 1966) and indeed this

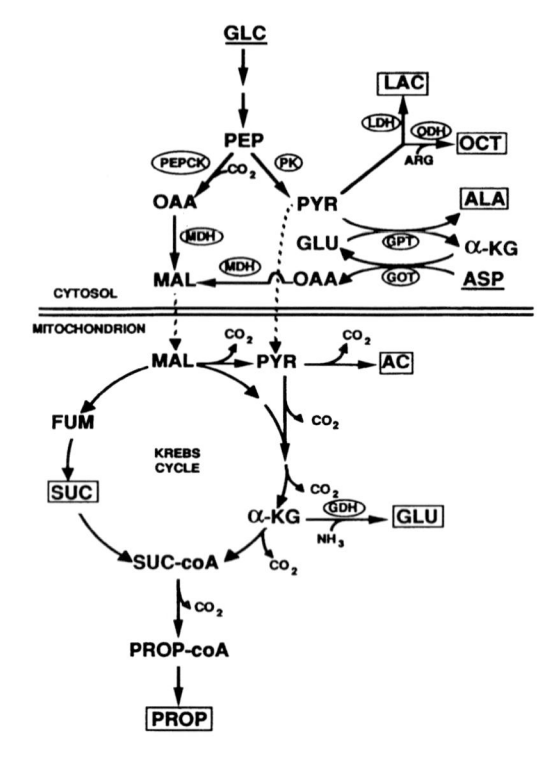

Figure 3.1 Pathways of anaerobic metabolism for which there is fragmentary evidence among several species of sea anemones. Underlined compounds are anaerobic substrates, and compounds in boxes are anaerobic end products. Enzymes catalysing key reactions are shown in ovals. Other than to illustrate the analogous roles of malate dehydrogenase and octopine dehydrogenase in maintaining cytosolic redox balance, sites of $NAD^+/NADH$ oxidoreduction are not shown, nor are sites and yields of ATP production. Extremely limited evidence suggests that mesomyarian anemones utilize the pathway to succinate initiated by PEPCK at the PEP branchpoint, whereas an actiniid endomyarian uses the pathway to propionate initiated by PK at that branchpoint. Unlike the analogous role of LDH in the vertebrates and some invertebrates, opine dehydrogenases (e.g. ODH) in anemones do not seem involved in providing high power output for intense activity, and their function remains unknown. See text for discussion. α-KG: α-ketoglutarate; AC: acetate; ALA: alanine, ARG: arginine; ASP: aspartate; FUM: fumarate; GDH: glutamate dehydrogenase; GLC: glycogen or glucose; GLU: glutamate; GOT: glutamate-oxaloacetate transaminase; GPT: glutamate-pyruvate transaminase; LAC: lactate; LDH: lactate dehydrogenase; MAL: malate; MDH: malate dehydrogenase; OAA: oxaloacetate; OCT: octopine; ODH: octopine dehydrogenase; PEP: phosphoenolpyruvate; PEPCK: phosphoenolpyruvate carboxykinase; PK: pyruvate kinase; PROP: propionate; PROP-coA: propionyl-coA; PYR: pyruvate; SUC: succinate; SUC-coA: succinyl-coA.

anemone does not accumulate succinate during four days under anoxia (Ellington, 1982). The seemingly paradoxical accumulation of propionate by *B.cavernata* might be explained by its formation from succinyl-coA (SUC-coA) via the forward ('clockwise') operation of the Krebs cycle (Ellington, 1982; Figure 3.1). The high energy yield associated with propionate formation is consistent with the marked anoxic tolerance of this species. Also, it appears that some of the pyruvate formed under anoxia is converted to acetate (AC; Figure 3.1), which yields additional ATP.

Quantitatively the most important end products of anaerobiosis in sea anemones are amino acids, especially alanine and glutamate (Ellington, 1977, 1980a, 1982; Navarro and Ortega, 1984). Thus, Livingstone (1983) proposes that 'amino acid pathways' are the most primitive fermentations in eumetazoans, and may have given rise to the aspartate–succinate pathway. In the latter, both glycolysis and aspartate degradation proceed simultaneously, and although succinate may be synthesized via OAA and malate, the OAA is produced not by carboxylation of PEP but via transamination of aspartate (ASP; Figure 3.1). The aspartate–succinate pathway typically operates in the early hours of anaerobiosis, and there is usually a 1 : 1 ratio between aspartate utilization and alanine accumulation, with glycogen-derived carbon appearing in alanine and aspartate carbon accumulating in succinate (de Zwaan, 1983; Figure 3.1). In sea anemones, these relationships do not strictly hold. While alanine and glutamate accumulate during six days of anoxia in *H.lineata*, there is no change in the aspartate concentration (Ellington, 1980a). Likewise in *B.cavernata*, a slight decrease in aspartate accounts for only 16% of the alanine accumulated during four days of anoxia (Ellington, 1982). In both species succinate accumulation is negligible. Moreover, the concentrations of other amino acids change only slightly during this time.

The foregoing observations suggest several interpretations. Although the transaminations producing OAA, glutamate, and alanine (Figure 3.1) are indicated by the positive correlation between the activities of glutamate-oxaloacetate (GOT) and glutamate-pyruvate (GPT) transaminases in sea anemones (Livingstone *et al.*, 1983), the substrates may be largely derived from general protein catabolism and additional transaminations during anoxia, not just from the aspartate pool. In *B.cavernata*, the low ratio of PEPCK : PK activities, and the elimination of alanine accumulation by aminooxyacetate (a general transaminase inhibitor) (W.R. Ellington, personal communication) suggest glycolytically-produced pyruvate as the carbon source for alanine. This would also account for the lack of a succinate pathway, and still be consistent with the anaerobic production of malate from OAA by malate dehydrogenase (MDH) (Livingstone *et al.*, 1983). Since propionate accumulates, entry of some pyruvate into the forward reactions of the Krebs cycle is indicated. The glutamate that also accumulates might thus be produced via condensation of the Krebs cycle intermediate α-ketoglutarate with ammonia (from general protein catabolism) by mitochondrial glutamate dehydrogenase (GDH; section 4.3, page 192) and so provide a means of detoxifying ammonia arising from catabolized amino acids not involved in transaminations where the amino group ultimately ends up in alanine. This would involve a reversal of the usual direction of the GDH reaction, however, and would only occur if ammonia levels were very high (see section 4.3), although the mitochondrial GDH in corals seems more poised toward ammonia fixation than does the cytosolic form of the enzyme (Dudler, Yellowlees and Miller, 1987).

The large PEPCK : PK ratio and very high MDH activity in *M.senile* (Livingstone *et al.*, 1983), and early accumulation of succinate in *D.leucolena* and *H.lineata*, suggest a more important role of the glucose−succinate pathway in these related mesomyarians than in the endomyarian *B.cavernata*. In the mesomyarians MDH acts analogously to LDH or ODH to regenerate NAD^+ and so maintain cytosolic redox balance. If some of the malate were also converted to pyruvate (de Zwaan, 1983), it would account for the production of alanine (via transaminations in Figure 3.1) and CO_2; if some of the malate entered the Krebs cycle operating in the forward direction, it could explain the accumulation of glutamate as well as the large anaerobic production of $^{14}CO_2$ from ^{14}C-glucose (Ellington, 1977).

A heavy reliance on amino acids in the anaerobic energy metabolism of sea anemones, perhaps necessitated by their modest glycogen reserves and accentuated by their carnivorous nature, is reminiscent of the situation in parasitic Platyhelminthes (Hochachka, 1980; Saz, 1981). Although the free amino acid pool of *B.cavernata* is not depleted by four days of anoxia, there is a marked transient decrease in the concentration of several amino acids (especially leucine, isoleucine, valine, and lysine) during the first 6 h of anoxia (Ellington, 1982). Their initial decline might represent the activation of anaerobiosis, and their gradual replenishment the initiation of protein catabolism. Because the utilization of the first three of these amino acids is a cardinal feature of anaerobic energy metabolism in parasitic helminths, might a similar situation apply in the Actiniaria? In view of the remarkable anoxic tolerance of some sea anemones, further investigation of their pathways of anaerobiosis seems worth the effort.

3.5 RATES OF ENERGY METABOLISM

Because of the central role of ATP as the cell's energy currency, metabolic rate is best expressed as the rate of ATP turnover, where consumption and generation of ATP are in balance under steady-state conditions (routine aerobic respiration or prolonged environmentally-induced anaerobiosis). In aerobic respiration the rate of oxygen consumption $(\dot{N}_{O_2})$ is often incorrectly called the metabolic rate; N_{O_2} can be converted to ATP equivalents using the stoichiometric coupling coefficient of ATP for O_2 (i.e. the $\sim P/O_2$ ratio: see Gnaiger, 1983b). The exact result will vary slightly according to the particular respiratory substrate (carbohydrate, lipid, protein) catabolized, which can be determined from measurements of O_2 uptake, CO_2 evolution and nitrogen excretion (section 3.6). Likewise, ATP generation in fermentations can be calculated from the molar amounts of the various end products formed and their respective ATP coupling coefficients, also given in Gnaiger (1983b) and de Zwaan (1983). Since there has not been a complete accounting of the products of anaerobiosis in any sea anemone, neither has the rate of anoxic ATP turnover been calculated.

Because of the much higher yield of ATP per mole of glucose catabolized in aerobic respiration than in any fermentation, it follows that the metabolic rate under environmental anoxia will be much lower than under oxygenated conditions unless there is an anoxic enhancement of glycolytic flux (Pasteur effect). This occurs to some extent during the initial 3 h of anoxia in *Actinia equina*, where utilization of ^{14}C-glucose is three times greater than in aerobic controls (Navarro and Ortega, 1984). Nevertheless, because the efficiency of anoxic ATP generation is at most one-sixth of that in aerobic respiration, metabolic rate is lower under anoxia despite the three-fold elevation of glucose utilization. As in other euryoxic animals (de Zwaan, 1983), glucose utilization subsequently declines during later stages of anoxia (Navarro and Ortega, 1984), perhaps through the activation of biochemically more efficient fermentations. Ellington (1977) did not detect a Pasteur effect in *Diadumene leucolena*.

The ability to survive prolonged anoxia involves not merely the utilization of biochemically efficient fermentations, but more importantly a reduction in total ATP demand. Such a reduction in energy demand in *B.cavernata* is indicated by the long-term anoxic stability of ATP, ADP, and AMP levels after an initial change at the onset of exposure (Ellington, 1981). This may stem from a reduction in ATP-consuming processes such as muscular activity and biosynthesis. In sea anemones the former includes a gradual relaxation and loss of tone of the musculature (e.g. Wahl, 1984). Enthalpy changes in catabolic reactions that are not conserved in mechanical work or biosynthesis are measurable as heat by direct calorimetry. This provides another means of estimating anaerobic and aerobic metabolic rates, through the use of the energetic equivalent of dissipative ATP turnover, $\Delta_k H_{\infty ATP}$ (Gnaiger, 1983b). This conversion is not straightforward, as $\Delta_k H_{\infty ATP}$ is not a constant, but varies according to the substrate (aerobic and anaerobic) and the particular anaerobic pathway, especially since much of the total enthalpy change is associated with the buffering of H^+ evolved with acidic end products. The value of $\Delta_k H_{\infty ATP}$ in units of $kJ \cdot (mol\,ATP)^{-1}$ is approximately -80 in aerobic respiration, and from approximately -40 to -70 in various fermentations (Gnaiger, 1983b). Thus, although the anoxic rate of heat dissipation, $_t\dot{q}$ ($-0.3 \, \mathrm{J \cdot g_d W^{-1} \cdot h^{-1}}$, or $-0.08 \, \mathrm{mW \cdot g_d W^{-1}}$), by *Actinia equina* is only 7% of the minimum aerobic $_t\dot{q}$ (Shick, 1981), it corresponds to a slightly higher ATP turnover of 11% of the aerobic rate, assuming an average anoxic $\Delta_k H_{\infty \mathrm{ATP}}$ of about $-50 \, \mathrm{kJ \cdot (mol\,ATP)^{-1}}$. Again, the exact value depends on the particular anaerobic end products, which have not been quantified; regardless, survival of prolonged anoxia by *A.equina* clearly involves lowering its demand for ATP by about an order of magnitude compared with the aerobic rate.

Finally, there is a real concern that the purely biochemical approach may significantly underestimate the anoxic rate of heat dissipation. Even in the mussel *Mytilus edulis*, certainly the most thoroughly investigated euryoxic marine animal, the heat flux calculated from the anoxic accumulation of end products of anaerobiosis, their stoichiometric coupling coefficients, and $\Delta_k H_{\infty \mathrm{ATP}}$ values is significantly less than total heat dissipation ($_tQ$) measured simultaneously (Shick, de Zwaan and de Bont, 1983; Shick, Widdows and Gnaiger, 1988). This biochemically unexplained 'anoxic excess heat' or 'exothermic gap' is seen in other organisms and remains enigmatic (Gnaiger, 1983b and references therein). Thus, although biochemical studies have done much to map the *routes* of anaerobic energy metabolism, they may be less suited to quantifying exact *rates* of heat (energy) dissipation associated with it.

3.6 RESPIRATORY SUBSTRATES AND ENERGETIC EQUIVALENTS OF O_2 CONSUMPTION

The foregoing consideration, and the increasing availability of calorimeters capable of measuring metabolic heat dissipation, argue for a direct calorimetric approach to measuring metabolic rate when complete or partial anaerobiosis is involved. Although the rate of ATP turnover is of interest in cellular energetics, energy (heat) flow is the common unit in ecophysiological studies, where the 'Respiration' component of the energy budget of fully aerobic individuals is most often measured by indirect calorimetry as O_2 consumption and converted to energetic units by use of standard oxycaloric or oxenthalpic equivalents (Gnaiger, 1983a; Gnaiger, Shick and Widdows, 1989). These vary according to the particular respiratory substrate, and in the case of the oxycaloric equivalent, the nature of the nitrogenous excretory product.

Although a generalized oxycaloric equivalent is often used for convenience since the proportions of different substrates oxidized are rarely known, the latter can be determined from molar ratios of CO_2 and N excreted to O_2

consumed, i.e. the respiratory quotient (RQ) and nitrogen quotient (NQ), respectively. Oxidation of carbohydrate has an RQ of 1.0, while lipids, which are more reduced, yield an RQ of 0.72. The RQ for protein oxidation depends on the form in which N is excreted; if it is combined with waste CO_2 to form urea, $RQ = 0.83$, whereas if ammonia is excreted, RQ ranges from 0.94 to 0.99 depending on the amino acid composition of the protein (Gnaiger, 1983a). Thus RQ and NQ can be used in stoichiometric equations to distinguish among the use of carbohydrate, lipid and protein as respiratory substrates. These equations and a useful nomogram can be found in Gnaiger (1983a).

Based on RQ values of near 1 for zooxanthellate specimens of *Anthopleura elegantissima* starved in the light, Fitt and Pardy (1981) concluded that the anemones relied on carbohydrate translocated from their zooxanthellae (section 2.6.6, page 103). The decline in RQ during the prolonged starvation of aposymbiotic anemones indicated lipid catabolism and agreed with the depletion of lipid stores in these anemones. However, the very high RQ of nearly 1 in well-fed aposymbiotic anemones was interpreted to reflect carbohydrate catabolism, which seems at variance with the very low carbohydrate content of their food (0.6% of $_dW$ of shrimp). This analysis did not consider nitrogen excretion, which if largely in the form of ammonia, together with the high RQ would indicate that protein oxidation predominated. Based on an RQ of 0.97 (Fitt and Pardy, 1981) and the measured rates of oxygen consumption and ammonia excretion (Table 4.1, page 177) by freshly-collected aposymbiotic anemones, protein indeed comprises more than half of the respiratory substrates used by *A.elegantissima*, with carbohydrate accounting for most of the rest (Table 3.2). Such a large reliance on protein as a fuel is perhaps expected in carnivores having a large percentage of protein in their diet, but the source of carbohydrate is unknown. It may be produced from amino acids via gluconeogenesis, or perhaps be in part derived from organic detritus in the diet (see section 2.2.4, page 51). A similar calculation for zooxanthellate individuals is not possible because of the re-

Table 3.2   Proportions of aerobic respiratory substrates oxidized by freshly-collected aposymbiotic specimens of *Anthopleura elegantissima*. Values were calculated using equations in Gnaiger (1983a), where $RQ = 0.97$ and $NQ = 0.156$

Carbohydrate	Lipid	Protein
0.44	0.02	0.54

Source: Zamer and Shick (1987)

cycling of ammonia between the host animal and its zooxanthellae (section 4.2, page 178).

Based on the proportions of respiratory substrates oxidized (Table 3.2), the oxycaloric equivalent ($\Delta_k H_{O_2}$) for aposymbiotic specimens of *A.elegantissima* is $-463\,kJ\cdot(mol\,O_2)^{-1}$. In routine practice, a generalized oxycaloric equivalent of $-455\,kJ\cdot(mol\,O_2)^{-1}$ may be applicable, especially if lipid having a $\Delta_k H_{O_2}$ of $-445\,kJ\cdot(mol\,O_2)^{-1}$ assumes increased importance as a fuel in anemones eating lipid-rich crustacean prey (sections 2.2.4 and 2.5), although when compiling a complete energy budget, a correction for nitrogen excretion must be applied. In the absence of data on the latter, the oxyenthalpic equivalent ($\Delta_c H_{O_2}$; Gnaiger, 1983a) that relates to the enthalpy of combustion of the catabolized organic mass can be used to calculate the energetic equivalent of $R + U$ (excretion), although this assumes some knowledge of the particular substrates catabolized. For *A.elegantissima* utilizing the mixture of respiratory substrates shown in Table 3.2, $\Delta_c H_{O_2}$ is $-502\,kJ\cdot(mol\,O_2)^{-1}$ (Zamer and Shick, 1987).

When oxygen consumption (N_{O_2}) and heat dissipation ($_tQ$) are measured simultaneously, an experimental calorespirometric ratio, $\Delta_t Q_{O_2}$, can be calculated as $_tQ/N_{O_2}$ (Gnaiger, Shick and Widdows, 1989). If this value exceeds the maximum theoretical $\Delta_k H_{O_2}$ of $-480\,kJ\cdot(mol\,O_2)^{-1}$, the excess is due to the contribution of anaerobiosis to $_tQ$. This is seen in *Actinia equina*: when subtidally-acclimatized anemones are acutely exposed to air, they become active and their $_t\dot{q}$ significantly exceeds heat dissipation calculated from $\dot{n}_{O_2}$, and $\Delta_t Q_{O_2} = -549\,kJ\cdot(mol\,O_2)^{-1}$, which means that 20–25% of $_t\dot{q}$ derives from anaerobiosis (Figure 3.2; see also section 3.8.5, page 158). Intertidally acclimatized individuals become quiescent upon exposure; both $\dot{n}_{O_2}$ and $_t\dot{q}$ decrease with time, and the calorespirometric ratio of $-19.37\,J\cdot(cm^3\,O_2)^{-1} = -434\,kJ\cdot(mol\,O_2)^{-1}$ does not differ significantly from the theoretical oxycaloric equivalents for fully aerobic metabolism. Likewise, intertidally-acclimatized specimens of *A.elegantissima* have an experimental calorespirometric ratio of $-438\,kJ\cdot(mol\,O_2)^{-1}$ during exposure to air, which indicates no anaerobic contribution to energy metabolism then (Shick and Dykens, 1984).

In absolute terms, the anaerobic component of $_t\dot{q}$ in active subtidal specimens of *A.equina* during aerial exposure is $-1.2\,J\cdot g_d W^{-1}\cdot h^{-1}$ ($= -0.33\,mW\cdot g_d W^{-1}$), whereas the $_t\dot{q}$ of quiescent conspecifics under imposed anoxia in water is $-0.3\,J\cdot g_d W^{-1}\cdot h^{-1}$ ($= -0.08\,mW\cdot g_d W^{-1}$). Thus *A.equina* has a four-fold anaerobic scope for activity; whether the extremes involve different pathways of anaerobiosis has not been determined. The partial anaerobiosis in subtidal anemones during acute exposure and its absence from the intertidal specimens is due both to the greater activity and the resultant loss of water from the coelenterons of the former, which leads to more hypoxic conditions in their tissues.

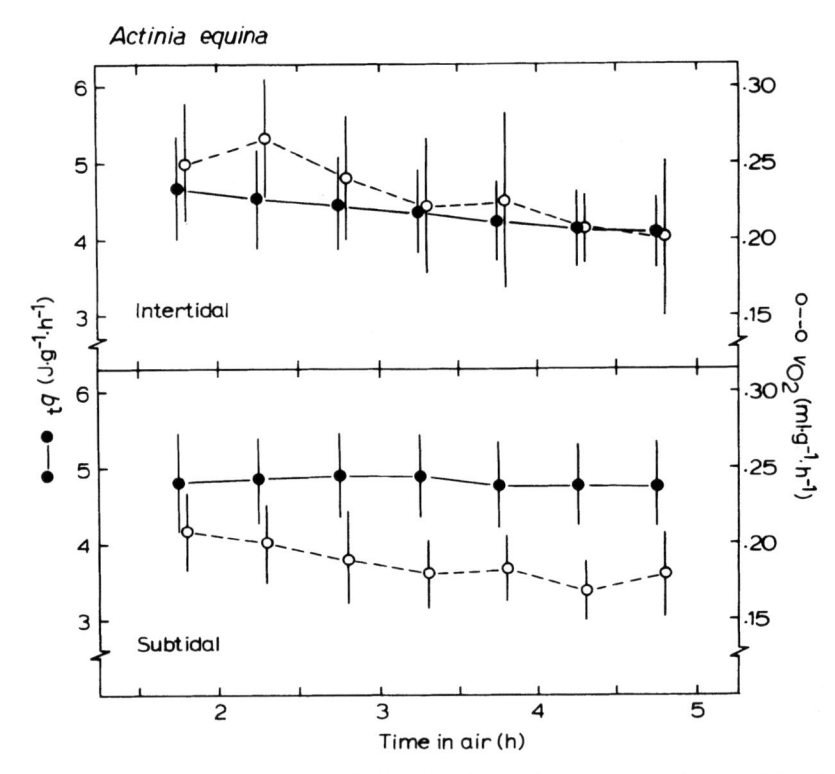

Actinia equina

Figure 3.2 Specific rates of heat dissipation ($_t\dot{q}$) and oxygen uptake ($\dot{v}_{O2}$) in air by specimens of *Actinia equina* acclimatized to intertidal (periodic emersion) and subtidal (continuous immersion) conditions in a tidal simulator. Measurements occurred during the normal 5-h emersion period in the intertidal anemones, and was acute in the subtidal specimens. Scales assume a generalized oxycaloric equivalent of -20.1 $J \cdot (cm^3 O_2)^{-1}$, or $-455 \, kJ \cdot (mol \, O_2)^{-1}$. Vertical bars represent 95% confidence limits. Measured heat dissipation significantly exceeds that calculated from $\dot{v}_{O2}$ during the last 2.5 h in air in the subtidal anemones, which indicates their partial reliance on anaerobic energy metabolism during acute exposure. Source: drawn from data in Shick (1981).

3.7 GAS EXCHANGE SURFACES, THEIR PERMEABILITY TO O_2 AND THEIR VENTILATION

Although sea anemones show no morphological features that serve purely to carry out gas exchange, their essentially laminar, epithelial body plan ensures that no cell is far removed from the surrounding medium, so that virtually all tissues are supplied with O_2 by direct diffusion. The O_2 flux at the exchange surface, $\mathscr{J}_{O_2}$ ($cm^3 \cdot min^{-1}$ at STP), can be calculated from Fick's first equation,

$$\mathcal{J}_{O_2} = K_{O_2} \cdot \Delta P_{O_2} \cdot (A/x),$$

where K_{O_2} is Krogh's diffusion constant, ΔP_{O_2} (atm) is the partial pressure gradient across the exchange surface, A (cm^2) is the area of the exchange surface, and x (cm) is the diffusion path length. K_{O_2} is the amount of O_2 (cm^3) that diffuses per min across 1 cm^2 of a given substance of 1 cm thickness down a P_{O_2} gradient of 1 atm. Units of K_{O_2}, which must be determined empirically for various biological materials, simplify to cm$^2 \cdot$atm$^{-1} \cdot$min^{-1}. $\mathcal{J}_{O_2}$ may be increased by increasing K_{O_2}, ΔP_{O_2}, and A, or by decreasing x; there is evidence for all of these compensations in sea anemones under various environmental circumstances (see below).

There is about a 20-fold range of K_{O_2} in various biological materials (summarized in Brafield and Chapman, 1983), and values for sea anemone tissues fall near its midpoint. K_{O_2} values for column wall (including ectoderm, mesoglea, and endoderm) of *Metridium senile* and *Anthopleura elegantissima* are 1.47×10^{-5} and 2.60×10^{-5} cm$^2 \cdot$atm$^{-1} \cdot$min^{-1}, respectively (incorrectly reported as ten times greater by Shick *et al.*, 1979a). The value for mesoglea alone in *Calliactis parasitica* is 0.95×10^{-5} (Brafield and Chapman, 1983). Because K_{O_2} appears to be directly related to the water content of a tissue, the lower value for *C. parasitica* mesoglea probably arises from its low water content of 70.4% of fresh weight, as well as the dense packing of the collagen fibres that O_2 must negotiate. Conversely, the mesoglea of *Anthopleura xanthogrammica* is 85.1% water (Koehl, 1977b); assuming a similar value in *A. elegantissima*, the high permeability of its body wall may derive in part from its proportionally large amount of more hydrated mesoglea (Shick *et al.*, 1979a). The apparently greater permeability of the column wall in *A. elegantissima* may also be partly owing to morphological features: the column is not uniformly smooth but contains many verrucae (see Figure 2.24), the walls of which are slightly thinner than that of the column in general, and so which locally reduce the diffusion distance (x). The measured x used in calculating K_{O_2} was the overall column thickness, and did not include local variations associated with verrucae.

Regardless, the greater permeability of the column wall in *A. elegantissima* than in *M. senile* (and probably *C. parasitica*) may reflect adaptation to intertidal exposure, a high diffusive permeability enhancing O_2 delivery to the endoderm during aerial exposure, when ventilation of the coelenteron is impaired (Shick *et al.*, 1979a). The greater tissue hydration of high-shore and intertidally-acclimatized anemones compared with low-shore and subtidally-acclimatized conspecifics (section 4.4, page 196) should likewise increase K_{O_2} and thus O_2 delivery to internal tissues of the former during aerial exposure (section 3.8.5). Both in air and in water delivery of O_2 to the ectoderm may be decreased slightly by the external layer of mucus, which has a lower K_{O_2} than seawater.

The K_{O_2} values in *A.elegantissima* and *M.senile* are for cyanide-poisoned tissues *in vitro*. *In vivo*, consumption of O_2 by the ectoderm would decrease the penetration of O_2 to deeper tissues, especially in *M.senile* with its relatively thick ectoderm. In *C.parasitica* the delivery of O_2 to the endoderm would be further impaired by its less permeable mesoglea. Both of these factors may necessitate ventilation of the coelenteron (see below).

Oxygen consumption by the ectoderm will diminish the P_{O_2} at the gas exchange surface, and hence decrease ΔP_{O_2}, unless O_2 is replenished by convective flow of the ambient medium. This is especially critical in seawater, where the diffusion coefficient of O_2 is about four orders of magnitude less than in air, and where the diffusional resistance presented by an unstirred layer (boundary layer) at the sea anemone–seawater interface may be large.

To a great extent, external convection must be accomplished by ambient water movements, as sea anemones themselves do not generate large-scale feeding or respiratory currents. Considering their speed of $<0.5\,\text{mm·s}^{-1}$ (Holley and Shelton, 1984), the ectodermal ciliary currents in sea anemones probably have a minimal effect on the boundary layer there. The thickness of the boundary layer, δ, around the cylindrical column of an anemone is proportional to

$$\sqrt{\frac{\text{column diameter}}{\text{current speed}}}$$

and will therefore decrease with decreasing body size or increasing current speed. The boundary layer associated with the complex tentacular crown of, e.g. *Metridium senile*, is more difficult to predict.

As shown by Patterson and Sebens (1989), the two-to-threefold increase in oxygen uptake by *M.senile* as ambient current speed increases from <4 to $\approx 9\,\text{cm·s}^{-1}$ is primarily owing to a reduction of the boundary layer thickness, which effectively reduces diffusional resistance and increases ΔP_{O_2}. A fraction of the increased oxygen consumption at higher current speeds may also arise from postural changes and muscular contraction necessary to maintain posture despite drag forces. Thus the current regime occupied by anemones in nature affects not only their intake of energy (by affecting the availability and catchability of prey: section 2.2.2, page 46) but also their energetic costs, the latter a consequence of changes in the boundary layer as well as of altered states of activity.

Haloclava producta, like other so-called 'athenarian' anemones, burrows in soft sediments. Its infaunal habit removes it from immediate contact with the ambient seawater ($P_{O_2} \approx 150\,\text{mm Hg}$), which is brought into the burrow by aborally-directed waves of peristalsis. In a $0.5\,\text{g}_w W$ individual, the ventilation volume is $21\,\text{cm}^3\,\text{H}_2\text{O·h}^{-1}$ (Sassaman and Mangum, 1972). The P_{O_2} in the burrow water is $128\,\text{mm Hg}$, which indicates that the anemone removes about 15% of the O_2 from the ventilation current. Delivery of O_2 to internal tissues (the simplicity and reduction in mass of which is a correlate of infaunality that is paralleled in other phyla: Sassaman and Mangum, 1972; Mangum and Van Winkle, 1973) is enhanced by the numerous thin-walled papillae on the already thin column, i.e. by an increase in A and a decrease in x in the Fick equation. It appears that infaunal ceriantharians do not ventilate their tubes (Sassaman and Mangum, 1974), from the unpredictable occurrence of peristalsis (Arai, 1972), the much lower P_{O_2} (27–53 mm Hg) in water in the tube, and the lack of mechanical detection of water movements.

More than half of the total body surface of a sea anemone (columnar, basal and tentacular endoderm, and all of the mesenteries) is not exposed directly to the ambient seawater but to the coelenteric fluid. Discontinuous measurements in this fluid indicate that O_2 levels there are 36% of that in the ambient, air-saturated seawater in *M.senile*, 41% in *H.producta* and 23% in *Ceriantheopsis americanus* (Sassaman and Mangum, 1972, 1974). Continuously-measured P_{O_2} in the coelenteric fluid of *C.parasitica* fluctuates rhythmically between 4% and 27% of air saturation (Brafield, 1980), suggesting a periodic ventilation of the coelenteron. Continuous recordings of O_2 levels in water near the oral surface in anemones also show periodic fluctuations in *Actinia equina*, *C.parasitica* and *M.senile* (Jones, Pickthall and Nesbitt, 1977; Brafield, 1980), particularly when the oxygen sensor is placed nearly in the mouth, indicating the expulsion of oxygen-depleted coelenteric fluid. The periodicity of these fluctuations matches that of overt muscular activity of the column and oral disc seen by Needler and Ross (1958), who postulated a role of such contractions in the circulation and exchange of the coelenteric fluid. Whether the periodic expulsion of deoxygenated fluid is under pacemaker control, or in response to increased hydrostatic pressure or decreased P_{O_2} is unknown.

Because they cannot forcefully extend, the muscles contracting to expel the coelenteric fluid cannot be used to inhale oxygenated seawater, which is taken in primarily via ciliary currents of the siphonoglyphs (Batham and Pantin, 1950a). Both peristalsis of the column and ciliation on the mesenteries may mix the coelenteric fluid. Considering the relatively large distances and volumes involved, peristalsis may serve more for mass transport of fluid while the ciliary currents maintain the separation of adjacent mesenteries (Sassaman and Mangum, 1972) and perhaps reduce the unstirred layer at the endodermal surface. This last possibility seems less likely on unfolded endodermal surfaces where the cilia-driven laminar flow and high shear rate (velocity gradient above the ciliated surface) would do little to reduce the boundary layer, but it would perhaps be more effective between adjacent mesenteries where the separation is not much greater than the distance spanned by the water capture zones (Sleigh, 1989) of cilia on opposing mesenteric faces.

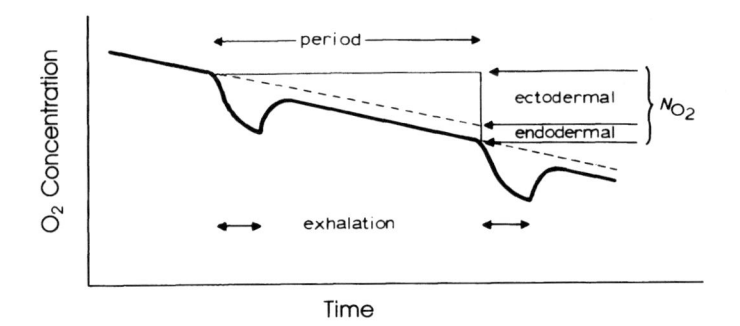

Figure 3.3 Idealized representation of the record of O_2 depletion from a closed chamber by an anemone as measured by an oxygen sensor near the anemone's mouth. The steadily declining curve represents O_2 uptake by the ectoderm, and the deflections indicate the periodic exhalation from the coelenteron of O_2-depleted water, which gradually equilibrates with the larger mass of water in the respirometry vessel. The vertical drop in O_2 concentration during one period indicates total O_2 consumption (N_{O2}) by the anemone, which can be divided as shown into its ectodermal and endodermal components. See text for discussion. Source: redrawn from Jones *et al.* (1977).

The extraction of O_2 from fluid isolated within the coelenteron is not detected immediately by an oxygen sensor placed in the ambient seawater, which supplies oxygen initially to the ectoderm. Periodic exhalation of O_2-depleted water from the coelenteron produces deflections in the recording made in the external medium before equilibration of the two liquids is achieved. By analysing these portions of the recording separately (Figure 3.3), the contributions of the ectoderm and endoderm to total N_{O_2} can be calculated. In *C.parasitica* the endoderm accounts for 18% of N_{O_2} (Brafield, 1980), while the value lies between 11% and 50% in *M.senile* (Jones *et al.*, 1977). Because serial cross-sections of entire anemones indicate a much greater bulk of endoderm than ectoderm (e.g. Figure 2.11B, page 70; Sassaman and Mangum, 1972; Bucklin, 1982; Sebens, 1983b), the generally small contribution of the endoderm to total N_{O_2} implies a low mass-specific n_{O_2} in those tissues. This probably results both from the effect of low P_{O_2} in the coelenteric fluid on the rate of oxygen uptake (see section 3.8.4), the low P_{O_2} itself being a consequence of limited exchange with the external medium, and the likelihood of unstirred layers over much of the endodermal surface.

The large ratio of surface area to body mass in sea anemones is accentuated by the numerous thin-walled tentacles, which account for 50% to 80% of the external surface area in various species (Table 3.3; see also section 2.2.1, page 37). The tentacles have sometimes been considered as analogous to gills, especially in the tubicolous cerianytharians, where based on the lack of ventilation of the massive tube and the pattern of endodermal ciliary

Table 3.3 Respiratory morphometry and parameters in the Fick equation for diffusive exchange of O_2 in sea anemones and ceriantharians. A represents the area of the ectodermal surface, x is the wall thickness, and ΔP_{O_2} is the difference between P_{O_2} in the ambient seawater and that in the coelenteric fluid. (Strictly speaking, ΔP_{O_2} and x should be the gradient and path length between environmental sources and mitochondrial sinks for O_2.) $_dW$ is dry weight, $_wW$ is wet weight, D is column diameter, L is body length, and T_b is thickness of the body wall (column).

Species	Size	K_{O_2} $(cm^2\ atm^{-1}\ min^{-1})$	ΔP_{O_2} (atm)	$A(cm^2)$	$x(cm)$	Source
Anthopleura	$0.05-1.75\,g\,_dW$					Shick *et al.* 1979a
elegantissima						
column		2.60×10^{-5}		$5.4-47.3$	$T_b = 0.053\,_dW^{0.306}$	
tentacles				$10.4-82.3$		
Calliactis	$1.31-2.70\,g\,_dW$					Brafield, 1980;
parasitica						Brafield and
column		0.95×10^{-5} (mesoglea only)	$0.153-0.201$			Chapman, 1983
Cerantheopsis	$2\,cm\,D,\ 20\,cm\,L$					Sassaman and
americanus						Mangum, 1974
column			0	125.6	0.145	
tentacles			0.155	95.0	0.020	
Haliplanella	$0.6-1.7\,mg\,_wW$					Zamer and
lineata						Mangum, 1979
column				$0.006-0.017\ (18°C)$		
				$0.004-0.009\ (28°C)$		
tentacles				$0.003-0.013\ (18°C)$		
				$0.012-0.032\ (28°C)$		

Species	Size					Reference
Haloclava producta	0.6 cm D					Sassaman and Mangum, 1972
column			0.082	18.8	0.014 (0.006, papillae)	
tentacles				3.1		
Metridium senile	0.05–4.00 g dW					Shick *et al.* 1979a;
column		1.47×10^{-5}	0.118	15.0–349.1	$T_b = 0.068\,dW^{0.307}$	Sassaman and
tentacles				63.9–920.7		Mangum, 1972
Pachycerianthus fimbriatus	2 cm D, 10 cm L					Sassaman and Mangum, 1974
column				62.8		
tentacles				109.9		
Pachycerianthus solitarius	0.5–0.7 cm D, 6.0–9.5 cm L					Sassaman and Mangum, 1974
column				9.8–19.8		
tentacles				25.8–38.6		

currents, the tentacles were assumed to be the major sites of uptake of O_2 that eventually reached the bulk of the endoderm (Sassaman and Mangum, 1974). This conclusion was strengthened by the agreement between measured oxygen consumption in *C.americanus*, and the $\mathcal{J}_{O_2}$ calculated from the surface area (A) and wall thickness (x) of its tentacles, ΔP_{O_2}, and K_{O_2} (Table 3.3). A tentacular site of O_2 uptake in infaunal ceriantharians is quite different from the adaptations to infaunality shown by the burrowing *Haloclava producta*, and highlights the flexibility of the relatively simple anthozoan body plan.

In epifaunal anemones, the tentacles may be major sites of oxygen consumption rather than important routes of O_2 entry to the rest of the animal, especially since these anemones ventilate their coelenterons directly. The concentration of mitochondria in the tentacles of *A.elegantissima* is twice as great as in the anemone as a whole (Table 3.1), and the volume density of mitochondria in tentacular endodermal cells of *Aiptasia pulchella* is about 3% of cell volume (J.P.S. Smith, personal communication). The mitochondrial concentration is also lower in the body wall of *M.senile* (1.56×10^{10} mitochondria/g $_wW$) than in the entire anemone (4.02×10^{10} mitochondria/g $_wW$), which implies a higher concentration of mitochondria in the tentacles (R.L. Blake, personal communication). This may mean that the tentacles have a correspondingly greater $\dot{n}_{O_2}$, which is the case in *Condylactis gigantea* (Herrera *et al.*, 1989). These relationships may be owing in part to the proportionally smaller mass of essentially acellular mesoglea in the tentacles than in the rest of the anemone, as indicated by a larger extracellular (inulin) space in the body wall than in the tentacles (Herrera *et al.*, 1989), as well as to a greater abundance of gland cells (which have relatively few mitochondria) in other than tentacular tissues. A higher concentration of mitochondria in the tentacles might also be associated with a high energy demand for synthesis there of cnidae used in prey capture, and for the continuous growth and cell movements that characterize the tentacles (see Robson, 1988).

3.8 FACTORS AFFECTING OXYGEN CONSUMPTION

3.8.1 Body Size

A central feature of the many comparative treatises on the relationship between body size and oxygen consumption in metazoans has been discussion of the ratio of the surface area for oxygen uptake to the mass of respiring tissue. Considering the essentially epithelial or laminar body plan of sea anemones, the surface area : mass ratio is maximal in these animals, which also grow very large, and so provide important subjects for examining the above relationships (Shick *et al.*, 1979a; Brafield, 1980). Ironically, 'coelenterates' were dismissed as aberrant by Hemmingsen (1960) in his monograph on this topic.

As in other metazoans, the rate of oxygen consumption by sea anemones increases exponentially with body mass (W), as described by the allometric equation $\dot{N}_{O_2} = aW^b$, where a is a constant and b is the mass exponent relating $\dot{N}_{O_2}$ to W. The logarithmic form of the equation is $\log \dot{N}_{O_2} = \log a + (b \cdot \log W)$, where a is the $\dot{N}_{O_2}$ when $W = 1$, and b is the slope of the logarithmic regression line. Values of b generally range from about 0.5 to slightly less than 1.0, indicating that $\dot{N}_{O_2}$ is less than directly proportional to body mass. This means that the mass-specific rate of oxygen consumption, $\dot{n}_{O_2}$ (i.e. $\dot{N}_{O_2}/W$), decreases with increasing body mass. Because rates of oxygen consumption are often given as $\dot{n}_{O_2}$, it is useful to consider the equation $\log \dot{n}_{O_2} = \log a + (b - 1) \cdot \log W$. Since b in the original equation has a value less than 1, $b - 1$ in the mass-specific equation is negative. The equation and covariance analysis can be used to adjust $\dot{n}_{O_2}$ in different individuals to a common body mass and thus eliminate the effect of this variable on measured $\dot{n}_{O_2}$.

The quest for a universal explanation of the value of b has ranged even beyond three dimensions, but a superficial analysis of the b values in sea anemones suggests that in this group an answer may be largely two-dimensional. Amid much variability, the b values (Table 3.4; also see Sebens, 1987a) often exceed that of 2/3 or 0.67 predicted from the surface area : mass relationship of a geometric solid, where surface area for O_2 uptake increases as the square of a linear measure and body mass increases as the cube of this measure. Moreover, b values for some anemones exceed the generalized slope of 0.75 for many metazoans having complex, vascularized respiratory surfaces (Hemmingsen, 1960). Slopes approaching 1 might result if body surface area and mass both increased as a similar function of a linear dimension, e.g. approximately its square. This would be expected in a laminar body where growth occurs more as increases in area than in thickness (section 5.6 and Figure 5.7, page 216). For example, in the particularly diaphanous anemones *Aiptasia pallida* and *A. tagetes*, the total mass of protein (W_P) in an individual scales as the 1.91 and 2.02 powers of oral disc diameter (Smith, 1984), and likewise in *A. pallida*, $_dW$ scales as the 1.45 power of that linear dimension (Clayton and Lasker, 1985).

The size of such an animal is limited by the mechanical strength of its tubular column, which must resist water currents without buckling if the anemone is to maintain its feeding posture (Koehl, 1977c). As an anemone grows larger, reinforcement of the column wall is provided by some increase in its thickness, which involves primarily a thickening of the mesoglea (which contains few cells) rather than of the cellular ectoderm (Figure 5.7), so that large individuals contain relatively more supportive but metabolically sluggish material. Also, the number of mesenteries increases ontogenetically

Table 3.4 Values of the mass exponent b in the allometric equation $\dot{N}_{O_2} = aW^b$ relating the rate of oxygen consumption ($\dot{N}_{O_2}$) to body mass (W) in sea anemones and a ceriantharian. In every case b was determined at the temperature to which the anemones were acclimated in the laboratory or acclimatized on the shore. $_dW$ = dry weight; $_wW$ = wet weight; $_{af}W$ = ash-free dry weight; $_rW$ = reduced or submerged weight; W_P = weight of protein

Species	Size Range	Temperature (°C)	b air	b water	Source
Actinia equina	?	20	0.37–0.71	0.28–0.46	Navarro et al., 1981
Aiptasia diaphana	4–30 mg W_P	24	–	0.51–1.03	Svoboda and Porrmann, 1980
Anemonia viridis	0.3–1.0 g $_{af}W$	10	–	' 0.97	Tytler and Davies, 1984
Anthopleura elegantissima	0.01–0.30 g $_rW$	20	–	0.54–0.57	Fitt et al., 1982
Anthopleura elegantissima	0.06–2.20 g $_dW$	22	0.38	0.83 (0.68, contracted)	Shick et al. 1979a
Calliactis parasitica	1.31–2.70 g $_dW$	10	–	0.92	Brafield, 1980
Ceriantheopsis americanus	1.6–9.6 g $_wW$	24	–	0.57	Sassaman and Mangum, 1974
Diadumene leucolena	0.01–0.29 g $_wW$ 0.01–0.26 g $_wW$	17.5 27.5	–	0.60 0.74	Sassaman and Mangum, 1972
Haliplanella lineata	0.023–0.265 g $_wW$	22.5	–	0.49	Sassaman and Mangum, 1972
Haliplanella lineata	0.7–3.7 mg $_wW$	18	–	0.57	Zamer and Mangum, 1979
Metridium senile	0.025–0.900 g $_dW$	15	–	0.89 (0.65, contracted)	Shumway, 1978
Metridium senile	0.05–3.1 g $_dW$	22	0.29	0.54	Shick et al., 1979a
Metridium senile	0.02–6.49 g $_dW$	15	–	0.89 (0.66, contracted)	Robbins and Shick, 1980
Metridium senile	0.88–7.65 g $_wW$ 0.48–8.51 g $_wW$	10 20	– –	0.74–0.86 0.41–0.77	Walsh and Somero, 1981

(Stephenson, 1928; section 1.1, page 6). Although themselves of laminar construction, the greater number of mesenteries in larger anemones increases the mass of tissue (especially in reproductively mature individuals having gametes in their mesenterial mesoglea) bathed in the coelenteric fluid, where oxygen levels are lower than in the ambient seawater. In large specimens proportionally more of the respiring biomass is therefore exposed to a lower P_{O_2} and so has a lower rate of oxygen consumption (sections 3.7 and 3.8.4), thus depressing $\dot{N}_{O_2}$ in larger individuals. This fact, and the impossibility of an infinitely thin column wall and mesenteries, which include a mass of scarcely-respiring mesoglea, probably combine to produce a *b* value for $\dot{N}_{O_2}$ slightly less than that of ≈ 1 predicted solely from a laminar construction of the oxygen-consuming epithelia.

The foregoing model must remain verbal in the absence of relevant morphometric data, few of which have been collected with respiratory design in mind. Although column wall thickness in *Anthopleura elegantissima* and *Metridium senile* increases as approximately the cube root of body mass, i.e. $W^{0.31}$ (Table 3.3), *W* includes the mesenteries which contribute disproportionally to the mass of large individuals, so that the mass of the column alone would indeed appear to increase in proportion to some power less than the cube of its thickness, as predicted from its two-dimensional construction.

The value of *b* may also depend on the relative thickness of the respiring layers of the column, principally the ectoderm and endoderm. Thus the generally higher value of *b* reported in *M. senile* than in *A. elegantissima* (Table 3.4) may be related to the greater proportion of respiring biomass (ectoderm) bathed directly in the well-oxygenated ambient seawater, as well as to the much smaller mass of mesoglea in the former (Shick *et al.*, 1979a). Assuming that the tentacles are especially important sites of oxygen consumption (as distinct from oxygen uptake), the greater contribution of the tentacles to total ectodermal surface area in *M. senile* than in *A. elegantissima* (Table 3.3) may also contribute to the larger *b* in the former species.

Finally, some of the variability in reported values of *b* (Table 3.4) no doubt arises from differences in the range of body sizes tested (e.g. *b* tends to be larger when a relatively narrow range of sizes is examined: Schmidt-Nielsen, 1984), and from different experimental conditions. There is no clear-cut thermal effect on *b*, although in several species *b* tends to decrease with increasing temperature (Sassaman and Mangum, 1970; Navarro, Ortega and Madariaga, 1981; Walsh and Somero, 1981).

Although most workers have taken care to avoid the effects of declining P_{O_2} on $\dot{N}_{O_2}$, the degree of mixing of the seawater and its flow characteristics in the respirometry vessels almost certainly varied widely among experiments, judging from the different stirring mechanisms employed and the varying ratios of anemone biomass to volume of seawater used. For example, relatively low values of *b* in *M. senile* (mean *b* = 0.67 reported by Sassaman and Mangum, 1970; $b = 0.54$ reported by Shick *et al.*, 1979a) were obtained in experiments using a YSI 5420 O_2 probe, which agitates the medium with a vibrating electromagnet. Higher values (mean $b = 0.73$) for this species were reported by Walsh and Somero (1981), who used a YSI 5720 probe, which has a rotating stirrer that produces faster currents and more rapid turbulent mixing of the water in the respirometry vessel. The highest slope ($b = 0.89$) was found in experiments using a continuous open-flow respirometer (Shumway, 1978), and also in a study using the YSI 5720 probe and large respirometry vessels having improved flow characteristics (Robbins and Shick, 1980).

As discussed by Robbins and Shick (1980), uniform flow moreover stimulates full expansion by *M.senile* (see also Patterson, 1985), which maximizes the surface area : mass ratio and hence should also maximize b. Thus, some of the intraspecific variability in b may result from postural differences among individuals. Sebens (1981a), for example, measured size-related catabolic costs in *A.elegantissima* and *M.senile* not as oxygen consumption but as weight loss during prolonged starvation. In both species b (0.77 and 0.80, respectively) was less than the maximum values of b measured in short-term respirometric experiments (Table 3.4), probably because the anemones did not remain fully expanded throughout two months of starvation.

3.8.2 Expansion and Contraction

Expansion and contraction of the column and oral disc, together with extension and retraction of the tentacles, is the most overt behaviour exhibited by sea anemones and has been studied extensively (sections 2.2.3 and 2.7.2). Both the area of the gas exchange surface (A) and the diffusion distance (x) are altered radically during such behaviour (Figure 3.4a), leading Sassaman and Mangum (1974) to the insight that an O_2 exchange system characterized by variable surface-area and diffusion-distance is an unavoidable correlate of the variable-volume hydrostatic skeleton.

Changes in expansion state thus would be expected to affect $\dot{N}_{O_2}$. In a fully expanded anemone, the ratio of surface area (A) to body mass is maximal and the thickness ($\propto x$) of the body wall is minimal. These relationships would predict a maximal $\dot{N}_{O_2}$, which in fact occurs (Shick *et al.*, 1979a). Retraction of the tentacles and of the column, and contraction of the oral disc, have the opposite effect on A and x, the former being reduced by at least half (see Table 3.3) and the latter increasing severalfold (Figure 3.4a); $\dot{N}_{O_2}$ is indeed always less under these conditions (Brafield and Chapman, 1965; Shick *et al.*, 1979a; Robbins and Shick, 1980; Shick and Dykens, 1984). Since $\dot{N}_{O_2}$ may vary continuously with slight changes in posture through effects on A and x, and since degree of expansion is an uncontrolled variable in most respirometric studies of sea anemones, much of the vari-

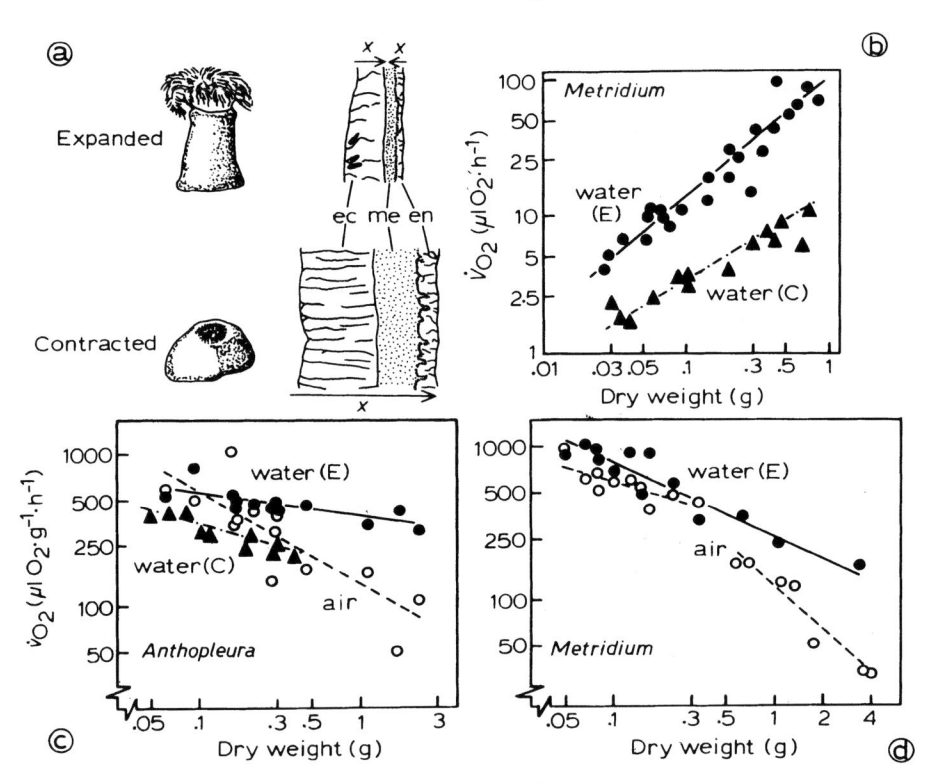

Figure 3.4 Effects of expansion and contraction behaviour on respiratory morphology and physiology in sea anemones. (a) Contraction in *Metridium senile* not only decreases the surface area for O_2 uptake, but also increases diffusion distance (x) as the mesoglea (**me**) thickens and the overlying cellular epithelia are deformed from cuboidal to columnar. Whereas the endoderm (**en**) may be ventilated directly in an expanded anemone, thus minimizing x, this does not occur in a contracted anemone, where O_2 uptake is entirely across the ectoderm (**ec**) and where the diffusion path is therefore unidirectional and much longer. (b) Relationship between oxygen uptake $(\dot{V}_{O_2})$ and body mass in *M.senile* when expanded (**E**) and contracted (**C**) in water. The shallower slope in contracted anemones (also see Table 3.4) arises from the morphological changes described in (a). (c) and (d) Specific rates of oxygen uptake $(\dot{v}_{O_2})$ in expanded specimens of *Anthopleura elegantissima* and *M.senile* in water, and in contracted anemones in air and water, emphasizing the greater mass-dependent reduction of $\dot{v}_{O_2}$ in contracted individuals. The higher $\dot{v}_{O_2}$ in *A.elegantissima* when contracted in air than in water may arise from loss of the buoyant support of water and concomitantly higher energetic cost of activity in air. See text for full discussion. Sources: (a) modified from Batham and Pantin (1951); (b) redrawn from Shumway (1978); (c) and (d) redrawn from Shick *et al.* (1979a).

ability in the data may have a behavioural basis. Maximal expansion in *A.elegantissima* and *D.leucolena*, for example, produces not only the highest $\dot{n}_{O_2}$, but also a significant reduction in the variability in the $\dot{n}_{O_2}$ data (Shick *et al.*, 1979a). Likewise, surgical prevention of variable extension of the pseudotentacles in *Lebrunia coralligens* reduces the variance in measured $\dot{n}_{O_2}$ (data in Lewis, 1984).

Contraction necessitates a cessation or reduction of ventilation of the coelenteron, which further increases x because O_2 reaching the endoderm must do so by diffusing across the entire thickened column wall (Figure 3.4a). Both of these factors reduce P_{O_2} in the coelenteron, which in turn contributes to the lower $\dot{N}_{O_2}$ in a contracted anemone. Retraction of the tentacles and contraction of the marginal sphincter over them not only reduces A but also exposes the tentacles to a lower P_{O_2}. Therefore the lower $\dot{N}_{O_2}$ in a contracted anemone is not merely owing to the loss of the tentacles as a site of O_2 *uptake* (i.e. loss of their 'branchial' function, as implied in some discussions), but especially to a hypoxia-induced reduction in their O_2 *consumption*.

This behavioural production of tissue hypoxia is a mechanism to reduce catabolic costs ($\dot{N}_{O_2}$) and so to save energy during periods of low food availability (section 2.2.3, page 49; Sebens and DeRiemer, 1977; Robbins and Shick, 1980; Sebens, 1987a). Although full expansion maximizes $\dot{N}_{O_2}$ in *M.senile*, sustained expansion is normally elicited only by external water currents together with high abundance of prey (Figure 2.3, page 48), so that maximal utilization of energy is generally restricted to periods of maximal availability of energy. As noted by Batham and Pantin (1950b), different phases of activity in *M.senile* that involve the same groups of effectors may conflict with each other. Since full expansion in response to only minimal prey availability might result in a net energy loss for the anemone, intermediate expansion states observed in nature may represent compromises between the need to expand to capture whatever prey is available and the need to conserve energy reserves by contracting (Robbins and Shick, 1980).

If, as suggested earlier, large anemones have a disproportionally larger mass of internal tissues than do small specimens, contraction-induced hypoxia should cause a correspondingly greater depression of oxygen consumption in larger individuals (i.e. decrease b or increase $b - 1$), which in fact occurs (Figure 3.4b–d). Other contributors to this relationship are the thinner column walls (smaller x) in very small anemones (which allows transport of O_2 to the endoderm), and a greater O_2 consumption by the especially thick ectoderm in contracted specimens (which will diminish O_2 delivery to the endoderm by reducing ΔP_{O_2}) and accentuate the reduction of b during contraction. The relatively smaller energy savings afforded to small anemones by contracting, together with their potentially lesser access to prey (section 2.2.2, page 47), may account for the greater time they spend expanded than do large sympatric conspecifics (Robbins and Shick, 1980).

3.8.3 Activity

Because muscular contraction may affect A and x, it is difficult to separate the effects of changing aerobic energy demand from those of altering variables in the Fick equation upon oxygen consumption in active sea anemones. Furthermore, the disequilibrium between coelenteric and ambient O_2 levels complicates analysis of the O_2 consumed by contracting myoepithelial cells and that consumed by the bulk of the endoderm, which is measured primarily upon contraction and expulsion of the coelenteric fluid (section 3.7). The 'respiratory rhythms' reported by Jones *et al.* (1977) and by Brafield (1980) were explicitly related to the periodic expulsion of oxygen-depleted coelenteric fluid and not to the energetic cost of this muscular activity. The continuous low-level nature of muscular contraction, the modest pressures generated (Batham and Pantin, 1950c), and the buoyant support of seawater probably mean that the increased energy demand and hence the increment of O_2 consumption during such activity (i.e. the aerobic scope for activity) is small. Accordingly, Sassaman and Mangum (1970, 1972) were unable to detect any distinct levels of $\dot{N}_{O_2}$ corresponding to 'active' or 'resting' metabolism. In view of the continuous and spontaneous nature of much of their activity, and in keeping with accepted physiological terminology, the rate of oxygen consumption by expanded sea anemones should be designated the 'routine' rate.

Aerobic scope for activity would be more readily measurable under conditions where either the frequency or the force (or both) of muscular contractions is greater than during routine activity. As discussed in section 3.4, swimming in *Stomphia coccinea* appears to be a purely aerobic activity, but the increment in $\dot{N}_{O_2}$ owing to such activity has not been measured. Increasing muscular activity to maintain posture as current speed increases may contribute to the current-induced increases in $\dot{N}_{O_2}$ in *M. senile*, but this effect is not clearly distinguishable from that of a thinner diffusional boundary layer at higher current speeds (Patterson, 1985).

The postural adjustments made by intertidal anemones during exposure to air (section 4.4, page 194) are energetically more expensive than similar movements in seawater, owing to loss of the buoyant support of the body by water during emersion and the concomitantly greater power required to effect movement. Thus Parker (1922) was able to discern distinctly greater rates of CO_2 evolution by specimens of *M. senile* when they were contracting actively in air than when they were hanging flaccidly (the latter condition no doubt being the inspiration for Linnaeus' original description of this anemone as *Priapus senilis*). On average, $\dot{n}_{CO_2}$ increased by 53% during aerial contractions. This agrees well with results on intertidal specimens of *Actinia equina*, which remain fully aerobic during emersion and in which contractions increase $_t\dot{q}$ by 50% above the routine level (see figure 3 in Shick, 1981). In absolute terms, the increment in $\dot{n}_{CO_2}$ during aerial contractions in *M.senile* is about $10\,\mu mol\,CO_2 \cdot g_d W^{-1} \cdot h^{-1}$ (calculated from data in Parker, 1922); assuming an RQ of 1 and a generalized $\Delta_k H_{O_2}$ of $-455\,kJ \cdot (mol\,O_2)^{-1}$, the aerobic heat flux increment (aerobic scope) of such activity is $-1.25\,mW \cdot g_d W^{-1}$. In *A.equina* the aerobic increment measured directly is $-0.43\,mW \cdot g_d W^{-1}$ at 15°C. These modest aerobic scopes for activity (less than one-half of the aerobic scope in various invertebrates summarized by Newell, 1979) reflect the relatively low speed and low force of muscular contractions in sea anemones.

3.8.4 Oxygen Availability

Despite the attention given to the metabolic and respiratory responses of sea anemones to declining P_{O_2} in seawater, there are remarkably few observations on the extent to which they actually experience such conditions in nature. Notable exceptions are the measurement of the P_{O_2} in the burrow and tube of the infaunal *Haloclava producta* and *Ceriantheopsis americanus* (Sassaman and Mangum, 1972, 1974), and the reports of periodic oxygen depletion in the habitat of *Metridium senile* living in fjords (Jørgensen, 1980; Wahl, 1984). Sea anemones might reasonably be expected to encounter hypoxia in stratified estuaries during summer, and during intertidal exposure in tidepools containing much oxygen-consuming biomass. Dense clones of *Anthopleura elegantissima* may also experience hypoxia if they restrict local water circulation (Fredericks, 1976).

In most other eumetazoan phyla, the occupation of variably-oxygenated environments has selected for the evolution of O_2-carrying respiratory pigments such as haemoglobin (Mangum, 1976; Weber, 1980). Owing to their lack of this molecular innovation, and their scant ability to effect convective flow in the surrounding medium, sea anemones must rely on morphological adjustments of parameters in Fick's first equation to compensate for declining environmental oxygen availability. Thus, distension of the body and extension of the tentacles that occur during hypoxia (Sassaman and Mangum, 1972, 1974; Shick *et al.*, 1979a) serve to increase the respiratory surface area (A) and to decrease the diffusion distance (x). This interpretation is supported by the observation that the usual response to total anoxia is contraction rather than expansion (Shick and Brown, 1977; Wahl, 1984). These short-term behavioural changes are paralleled evolutionarily in burrowing forms such as *H.producta*, which is notably elongate and has an especially thin column wall studded with even thinner-walled papillae (Sassaman and Mangum, 1972). Its vermiform shape and occupation of a burrow is associated with the peristaltic generation of a respiratory current, rare among anemones, but common among other elongate infauna (Clark, 1964; Mangum and Van Winkle, 1973; Mangum, 1976). The failure of hypoxia to elicit a compensatory increase in endodermal ciliary activity in *C.americanus* (Sassaman and Mangum, 1974) may reflect the relative unimportance of longitudinally-directed ciliary currents in the long-distance transport of O_2 (Clark, 1964; Mangum, 1976; Shick, 1983).

Cnidarians have often been viewed as 'oxyconformers' whose $\dot{N}_{O_2}$ declines more or less in proportion to declining environmental P_{O_2}. Sea anemones and ceriantharians typically show a monotonic decline in $\dot{N}_{O_2}$ in response to declining P_{O_2} (Figure 3.5). Attempts to describe such curves mathematically have a long history in physiology, and two models have been widely used: the hyperbolic model

$$\dot{N}_{O_2} = \frac{P_{O_2}}{B_1 + B_2 \cdot P_{O_2}}$$

and the quadratic model

$$\dot{N}_{O_2} = B_0 + B_1 P_{O_2} + B_2 (P_{O_2})^2.$$

The former has the advantage of ease of calculation (less of a factor now with the ubiquity of personal computers), whereas the latter can better describe curves that deviate from a rectangular hyperbola and those that indicate a cessation of $\dot{N}_{O_2}$ at $P_{O_2} > 0$. Because the quadratic term B_2 in the second model is an expression of the degree of curvilinearity in the response of $\dot{N}_{O_2}$ to P_{O_2} (the more negative the value of B_2, the less linear and hence more 'regulatory' the response), Mangum and Van Winkle (1973) have proposed its use as an index of oxyregulation, and the quadratic model has seen some use as a comparative tool.

Values of B_2 in various species of sea anemones are given in Table 3.5. These values span a range nearly as great as that shown for 31 species of marine invertebrates from eight phyla by Mangum and Van Winkle (1973), who viewed the respiratory response of anemones as 'pseudoregulatory'. As in that analysis, there is no clear ecological trend in the data for sea anemones and ceriantharians, i.e. infaunal species (*H.producta* and *C.americanus*) do not tend to be more regulatory than epifaunal forms, nor are zooxanthellate species (*Anemonia viridis* and *D.leucolena*) more or less regulatory than non-zooxanthellate species. As discussed by Mangum and Van Winkle, and by Shick (1983), the basis for oxyconformity versus oxyregulation may be the anatomical arrangement of the primary diffusion path, and the relevant morphometric measurements simply have not been made for sea anemones.

Laboratory measurements of oxygen consumption during progessive hypoxia in well-stirred seawater (the case in all of the studies reported in Table 3.5), however, may have limited relevance to the respiratory response in nature. Most situations of environmental hypoxia described earlier are re-

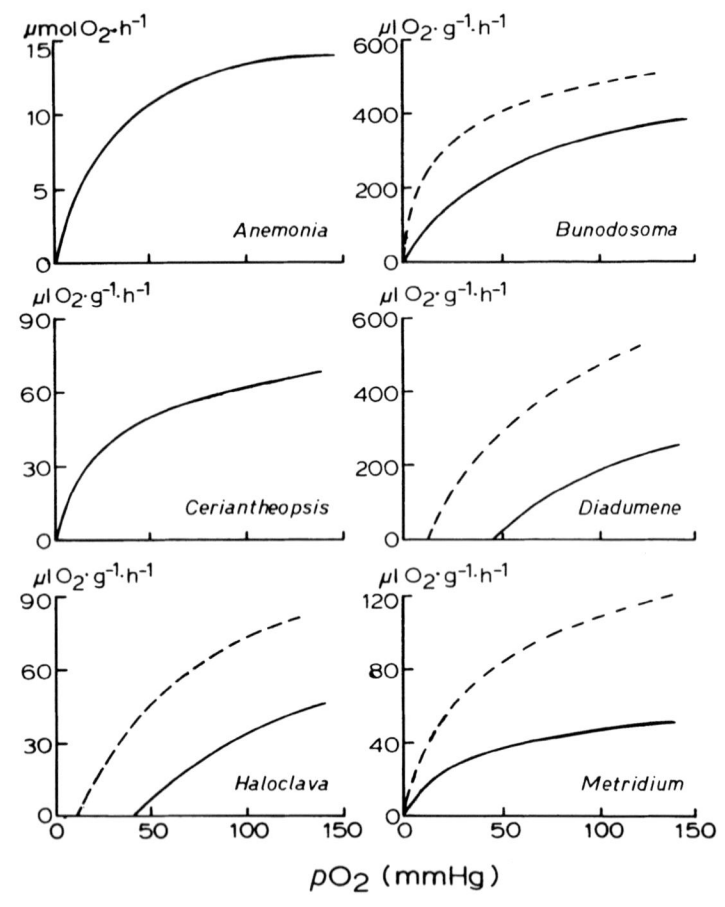

Figure 3.5 Effect of declining P_{O2} on the rate of oxygen uptake by several species of sea anemones and a cerianthid. Broken lines represent experiments in which specimens were reintroduced into air-saturated seawater after their oxygen uptake had ceased in initial O_2-depletion experiments. See text for discussion. Sources: redrawn from Tytler and Davies, 1984 (*Anemonia*); Ellington, 1982 (*Bunodosoma*); Sassaman and Mangum, 1974 (*Ceriantheopsis*); Sassaman and Mangum, 1973 (*Diadumene, Haloclava* and *Metridium*).

lated to decreases in mixing of the ambient medium, and since sea anemones themselves have only weak powers of external convection, the stirring of the respiratory medium necessary to continuous polarographic measurements of $\dot{N}_{O_2}$ at declining P_{O_2} is highly unnatural.

Furthermore, by combining a form of the hyperbolic model with the diffusion equation, Dromgoole (1978) has shown that not only does an in-

Table 3.5 Values of the quadratic coefficient B_2 in the equation $\dot{N}_{O_2} = B_0 + B_1 P_{O_2} + B_2(P_{O_2})^2$ relating oxygen consumption $(\dot{N}_{O_2})$ to partial pressure of oxygen (P_{O_2}) in sea anemones and a ceriantharian. Values calculated for normalized data, where $\dot{N}_{O_2}$ at air-saturation equals 1.0 and $\dot{N}_{O_2}$s at lower P_{O_2}s are fractions thereof (i.e. $\dot{N}_{O_2}/\dot{N}_{O_2,sat}$). The more negative the value of B_2, the less linear and thus more regulatory the response of $\dot{N}_{O_2}$ to declining P_{O_2}.

Species	$B_2 (\times 10^{-5})$	Source
Anemonia viridis	-10^*	Tytler and Davies, 1984
Bunodosoma cavernata	-6 (range -15 to $+1$)	Ellington, 1982
Ceriantheopsis americanus	-8	Sassaman and Mangum, 1974
Diadumene leucolena	-4	Mangum and Van Winkle, 1973
Haloclava producta	-2^*	Sassaman and Mangum, 1973
Metridium senile	-5^*	Sassaman and Mangum, 1982

Note: asterisk denotes value calculated from graphical data in source.

creasingly thick boundary layer (δ) decrease $\dot{N}_{O_2}$ at air-saturation as discussed earlier, but also that the effect is enhanced at low to intermediate P_{O_2} (Figure 3.6). Thus the amount of stirring of the medium by itself will variably affect δ and therefore the shape of the curve (i.e. B_2, or apparent oxyregulatory ability). Some of the variation in reported B_2 values may well be due to the variable extent of mixing in the respirometry vessels used by different investigators. Virtually no oxyregulatory ability was seen in early experiments with *Actinia equina*, *Anemonia viridis* (Henze, 1910) and *Calliactis parasitica* (Brafield and Chapman, 1965), where the water was stirred not at all or only at intervals. Assuming that environmental hypoxia and decreased water movement go hand in hand, $\dot{N}_{O_2}$ in sea anemones experiencing hypoxia in the field probably declines more precipitously than most recent laboratory studies would suggest. *Diadumene leucolena* may be an exception to this generalization, as it is found in periodically hypoxic benthic

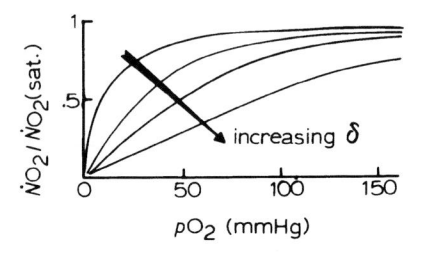

Figure 3.6 Simulated effect of an increasingly thick boundary layer (δ) on the rate of oxygen uptake over a range of P_{O_2}. See text for discussion. Source: modified from Dromgoole (1978).

habitats in the Chesapeake Bay estuarine system where bottom currents may nevertheless be substantial.

Although most sea anemones exhaust the available O_2 when placed in closed vessels, *D.leucolena* and *H.producta* cease aerobic respiration at P_{O_2} levels well above zero (Figure 3.5). This 'aerobic shutdown' occurs in other invertebrates and although it remains a mechanistically unexplained phenomenon, it may be a matter of cost accounting: for anemones regularly experiencing temporary aquatic hypoxia it may be cheaper energetically to rely briefly on efficient pathways of anaerobiosis than to spend energy increasing convection in order to extract all available oxygen. If *D.leucolena* and *H.producta* are returned to air-saturated seawater after aerobic shutdown has occurred, their $\dot{N}_{O_2}$ is greater than before the hypoxic excursion (Figure 3.5), that is, they develop an oxygen debt, payment of which probably reflects the reoxidation of anaerobic end products accumulated during hypoxia. Also, the residual P_{O_2} (P_{O_2} at which aerobic shutdown occurs) decreases under these conditions. *Metridium senile*, which in the northwestern Atlantic does not routinely encounter hypoxic conditions, does not show aerobic shutdown (Figure 3.5), and if returned to air-saturated seawater before $\dot{N}_{O_2}$ has ceased during progressive hypoxia, it does not show an oxygen debt (Sassaman and Mangum, 1973). However, this species, like most other anemones, shows an oxygen debt response after exposure to anoxia (Figure 3.5). When post-anoxic $\dot{N}_{O_2}$ is measured over a range of P_{O_2} (Figure 3.5), there is no clear-cut effect on the degree of oxyregulation, which may increase or decrease in the same species (Sassaman and Mangum, 1972; Ellington, 1982).

Other than measurement of maximum post-anoxic $\dot{N}_{O_2}$, there has been little quantitative analysis of the oxygen debt in sea anemones, in part because the response is at first glance so variable. Since the oxygen debt response in sea anemones is usually expressed as the mean increment of $\dot{N}_{O_2}$ above the pre-anoxic rate at air-saturation, much variation in the magnitude of the 'oxygen debt' is actually variability of pre-anoxic $\dot{N}_{O_2}$ (Shick *et al.*, 1979a). When the post-anoxic increase in O_2 consumption ($\Delta \dot{n}_{O_2}$) by individual anemones is plotted against their pre-anoxic $\dot{n}_{O_2}$, an inverse relationship emerges (Figure 3.7). Furthermore, post-anoxic $\dot{n}_{O_2}$ is significantly less variable than pre-anoxic $\dot{n}_{O_2}$, probably because while the degree of body expansion is variable before anoxia, it is maximal and strikingly uniform after anoxia (Shick *et al.*, 1979a). As discussed earlier, full expansion maximizes A and minimizes x in the Fick equation, thus maximizing O_2 delivery during this period of high metabolic oxygen demand. The good agreement between the sums of individual pre-anoxic $\dot{n}_{O_2}$ and post-anoxic $\dot{n}_{O_2}$ in several species (Figure 3.7) indicates that at air-saturated P_{O_2}, $\dot{n}_{O_2}$ varies continuously with the degree of expansion, and that both expansion and $\dot{n}_{O_2}$ are maximal during recovery from anoxia.

Although $\dot{n}_{O_2}$ after anoxia establishes the maximal capacity for O_2 de-

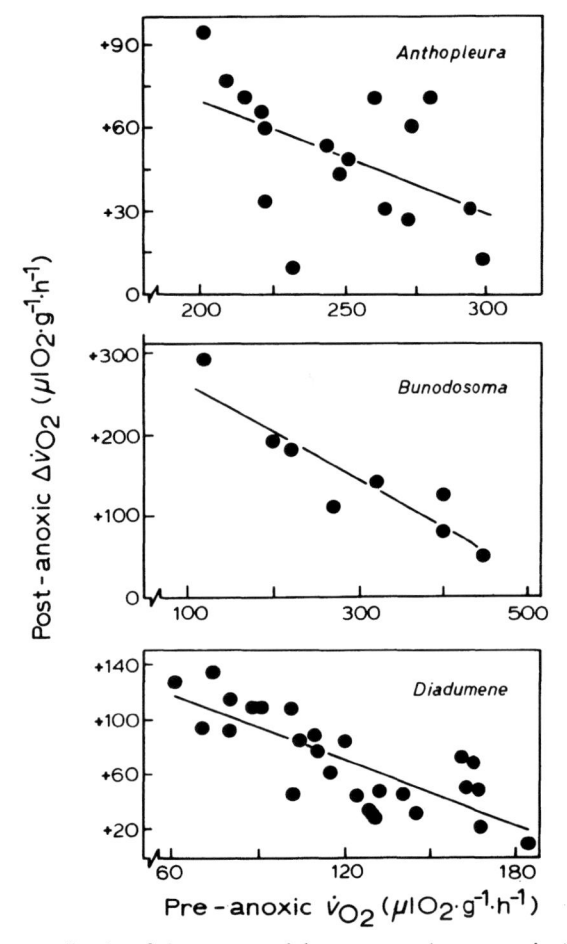

Figure 3.7 The amplitude of the oxygen debt response (post-anoxic $\Delta \dot{v}_{O_2}$) as related to pre-anoxic $\dot{v}_{O_2}$. See text for discussion. Sources: redrawn from Shick *et al.*, 1979a (*Anthopleura* and *Diadumene*); calculated and drawn from data in Ellington, 1982 (*Bunodosoma*).

livery, incorporating the time course of change in post-anoxic $\dot{n}_{O_2}$ (i.e. the oxygen debt integrated over time) is of greater metabolic relevance. Variability in pre-anoxic $\dot{n}_{O_2}$ makes it difficult to determine when post-anoxic $\dot{n}_{O_2}$ has returned to the routine level, so that although the size of the oxygen debt is positively related to the duration of anoxia, whether the two are directly proportional is uncertain (Ellington, 1982). It appears that the oxygen debt payment in *B.cavernata* is not fully explained by the oxidation of alanine (estimated from the decline in this amino acid and the increase in ammonia excretion during recovery; Table 4.1, page 177) and other identified anaerobic end products, and the metabolic basis of the oxygen debt is therefore unclear.

Various studies of the recovery of bivalve molluscs from anoxia indicate that this is a period of transiently increased aerobic energy demand due to the resumption of activity and the replenishment of the arginine phosphate pool. Also implicit in the relationship shown in Figure 3.7 is that an anemone showing near-maximal $\dot{n}_{O_2}$ prior to anoxia will have little remaining scope for increase during recovery. Might this necessitate an anaerobic contribution to recovery metabolism in such individuals, and perhaps provide a role for the otherwise enigmatic opine dehydrogenases in sea anemones (see section 3.4)?

A metabolic and thermodynamic analysis of the oxygen debt payment in the mussel *Mytilus edulis* also reveals an oxygen consumption in excess of that predicted by the oxidation of anaerobic end products, and further indicates the operation of conservative (endothermic), anabolic process (e.g. gluconeogenesis: E. Gnaiger, J.M. Shick and J. Widdows, unpublished). No such analysis is currently possible for any sea anemone, but considering their relatively small available rations, low levels of stored glycogen, and reliance on carbohydrate as 44% of their aerobic respiratory fuel (sections 2.2.6, 2.5, and 3.6), there would seem to be a premium placed on gluconeogenesis during recovery in sea anemones as well.

Gas exchange between symbiotic algae and host anemone was proposed very early (Geddes, 1882), as was a supplementary role of zooxanthella-produced O_2 during periods of environmental stagnation (Smith, 1939). The closer spacing in groups of zooxanthellate specimens of *A.elegantissima* than of aposymbiotic individuals suggests that O_2 availability may be limited in dense aggregations. This anemone is able to detect O_2 gradients resulting from the unequal illumination of its symbionts (Fredericks, 1976; Dykens and Shick, 1984). When zooxanthellate specimens of *A.elegantissima* are maintained under anoxia, they remain contracted in darkness but begin to expand as a direct response to illumination; full expansion of the oral disc and extension of the tentacles is a response to O_2 produced by the zooxanthellae, and it can be eliminated by chemical inhibition of photosynthesis by DCMU (Shick and Brown, 1977; Figure 2.24, page 112). A similar response is shown by *Anemonia viridis* (Dorsett, 1984). *A.elegantissima* develops an oxygen debt when maintained anoxically in the dark or when subjected to anoxia in the light but treated with DCMU, but not, however, when incubated under anoxia in the light in the absence of DCMU. This demonstrates that O_2 produced endogenously by the algal symbionts enables aerobic respiration to continue despite environmental anoxia.

Possession of intracellular photosynthetic symbionts is a two-edged sword, however, for in bright light the P_{O_2} in the animal tissues may exceed twice the normal atmospheric level (Figure 3.8). The fact that the animal tissues

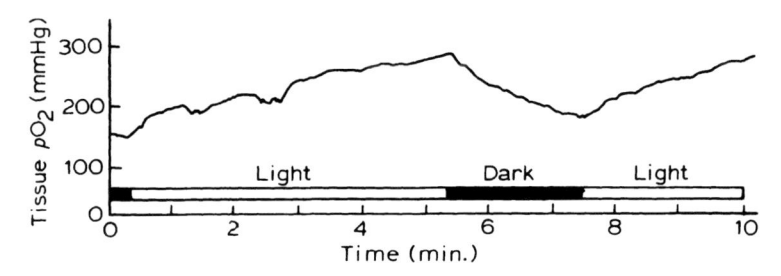

Figure 3.8 The effect of darkness and illumination on P_{O_2} in the tissues of a specimen of *Anthopleura elegantissima* containing zooxanthellae. Source: modified from Dykens and Shick (1982).

are chronically exposed to flux of O_2 well in excess of what they can consume is as important as the actual P_{O_2} achieved; this condition is toxic to metazoans because the production of reactive radicals such as superoxide (O_2^-) follows first-order kinetics with respect to C_{O_2}. As discussed in section 2.7.2, this necessitates enzymic defences (SOD, catalase, etc.) against toxic reduction products of O_2, so that SOD levels in zooxanthellate specimens of *A.elegantissima* are 50–100 times greater than in naturally aposymbiotic conspecifics (Dykens and Shick, 1982, 1984). Higher rates of photosynthesis (and exposure to UV: section 2.7.3, page 112) seem to necessitate higher SOD activity in the animal tissue and zooxanthellae of *Phyllodiscus semoni* (Shick *et al.*, 1990). Such an enzymic response is not universal, however, and the zooxanthellate species *Aiptasia pallida* appears to rely more on biochemical antioxidants such as uric acid (Tapley *et al.*, 1988).

Previous studies of the effect of P_{O_2} on oxygen consumption in sea anemones assumed that the rate reached an asymptote at air saturation, although the measurements did not extend above this P_{O_2}. Extrapolation of published curves (Figure 3.5; Henze, 1910; Brafield and Chapman, 1965) relating $\dot{n}_{O_2}$ to P_{O_2} suggests that various degrees of hyperoxic enhancement of respiration would occur. Because anemones symbiotic with zooxanthellae experience elevated oxygen levels (Figure 3.8), the possibility that oxygen consumption continues to increase with P_{O_2} above air saturation has implications in productivity studies, where respiration is assumed to be the same during the day (when the zooxanthellae are photosynthesizing) as at night.

Exposure of zooxanthellate *Aiptasia pallida* to hyperoxia (50% O_2) leads to a significant 10–11% increase in steady-state oxygen consumption and heat dissipation compared with the rates at air saturation (21% O_2). Still larger increases (26% and 43%) in respiration occur in *Heteractis crispa* and *Phyllodiscus semoni* under hyperoxia, even when the surrounding seawater is stirred (Shick, 1990). The greater increases in these species than in *A.pallida* seem related to their larger size and greater morphological complexity, both of which factors would increase the boundary layer at the body surface (see section 3.7). Therefore, zooxanthella-produced O_2 negates the effect of the boundary layer that develops even under well-stirred conditions, and measurements of oxygen flux in zooxanthellate anemones under air-saturated conditions in the dark will underestimate their daytime respiration under hyperoxia and so underestimate gross photosynthesis. Such a hyperoxic elevation of respiration during the day is irrespective of the effect of photosynthate translocated then, which would raise respiration further (section 3.8.6).

3.8.5 Intertidal Exposure

Despite the ready availability of oxygen in air, $\dot{N}_{O_2}$ generally declines in anemones during aerial exposure (Shick *et al.*, 1979a; Navarro *et al.*, 1981; Shick, 1981), probably because contraction during emersion (a behaviour that minimizes desiccation: section 4.4, page 193) decreases the surface area : mass ratio, increases diffusion distances and impairs irrigation of the coelenteron. Accordingly, the effect of emersion is pronounced in larger specimens while in small individuals aerial and aquatic values of $\dot{n}_{O_2}$ are scarcely distinguishable (Figure 3.4c, d; Griffiths, 1977a; Navarro *et al.*, 1981). As in water, contraction in air decreases the mass exponent b (increases $b - 1$), although this effect is not seen in small anemones over a narrow range of body mass (Figure 3.4d; Navarro *et al.*, 1981).

During muscular activity in air, $\dot{n}_{O_2}$ in small individuals may rise briefly above the routine aquatic rate (Griffiths, 1977a; Shick, 1981). Postural adjustments are transient in intertidally-acclimatized specimens of *A.equina* and *A.elegantissima*, which remain fully aerobic during aerial exposure (Figure 3.2; Shick and Dykens, 1984). Conversely, subtidally-acclimatized individuals upon acute exposure to air remain active and expel most of their coelenteric fluid, leading to internal hypoxia; both activity and hypoxia necessitate partial reliance on anaerobiosis in these anemones (Figure 3.2). Navarro, Ortega and Iglesias (1987) find also that high-shore specimens of *A.equina* maintain a higher level of aerobic respiration during aerial exposure than do subtidal conspecifics. Navarro and Ortega (1985) find further that radioactivity from ^{14}C-glucose accumulates preferentially in the amino acid fraction of ethanol-soluble molecules in *A.equina* during aerial exposure, particularly in the first 3 h of exposure. This may indicate reliance on anaerobiosis, especially as the amount of radioactive amino acids accumulated is correlated with the size of the post-aerial oxygen debt. During prolonged emersion the small intertidal anemone *Haliplanella lineata* does not accumulate end products of anaerobiosis (Ellington, 1980a); the increase in glutamate that it shows may represent a means of detoxifying ammonia derived from aerobic catabolism of amino acids and which cannot be excreted during aerial exposure.

In *A.elegantissima*, the degree of contraction in air depends on conditions of irradiance and relative humidity. Under moderate illumination and high humidity, this anemone relaxes its marginal sphincter and exposes the zooxanthellae in its oral disc to sunlight. Furthermore, slight muscular contractions of the column pump coelenteric fluid onto the oral disc; the fluid drains back into the coelenteron upon relaxation (Shick and Dykens, 1984). Both of these phenomena contribute to the maintenance of fully aerobic metabolism during aerial exposure.

Delivery of O_2 to the mitochondria in intertidal anemones might also be facilitated by cytological adaptations. Freshly collected high-shore anemones, and those acclimatized to periodic aerial exposure in tidal simulators in the laboratory, have a significantly greater tissue water content than do low-shore or subtidally acclimitized conspecifics (section 4.4, page 196). Because the intrinsic permeability of tissues to O_2 (K_{O_2}) appears directly related to their water content, K_{O_2} theoretically should be greater in high-shore anemones, although the actual difference would be slight and has not been tested. High-shore specimens of *A.elegantissima* also have higher concentrations of mitochondria in their tissues than do low-shore individuals (Table 3.1). This increased number of mitochondria may serve to reduce diffusion distances (x) for O_2 between its environmental source and its cellular sink and so help to maintain aerobic respiration under periodically hypoxic (emersed) conditions, similar to the role of mitochondrial proliferation seen during acclimatization of some mammals to high altitude and acclimation of fish to hypoxic water. Owing to the high solubility of O_2 in lipids, the rich lipid deposits in endodermal tissues theoretically have a large capacity to store O_2 and perhaps to help support aerobic metabolism despite diffusional limitations on O_2 delivery from the environment during intertidal exposure. A similar role has long been postulated for carotenoids (Karnaukhov, 1990), which are abundant in intertidal anemones (section 2.7.3, page 115).

Despite their greater numbers of mitochondria and higher *in vitro* activities of cytochrome *c* oxidase, freshly collected high-shore specimens of *A.elegantissima* have a lower aquatic and aerial $\dot{n}_{O_2}$ than low-shore individuals (Shick, 1981; Shick and Dykens, 1984), indicating that aerobic respiration in the high-shore anemones is operating at less than its maximum capacity. This probably is a result of the less well-nourished condition of high-shore individuals (Zamer, 1986) and hence the lower flow of carbon into oxidative pathways (see below).

The lower aerial and aquatic $\dot{n}_{O_2}$ in freshly collected high-shore specimens of *A.elegantissima* and *A.equina* as compared with low-shore individuals (Shick, 1981; Ortega, Iglesias and Navarro, 1984; Shick and Dykens, 1984; but see Navarro *et al.*, 1981; Navarro *et al.*, 1987) is probably a manifestation of the 'conservationist' response of high-shore anemones to their lesser availability of food (see Newell, 1979). This is supported by laboratory studies in which specimens of *A.equina* were acclimatized to intertidal and subtidal conditions of emersion, with an accompanying adjustment of available ration. Better-fed 'subtidal' specimens had a higher aquatic $\dot{n}_{O_2}$, and despite their lower aerial $\dot{n}_{O_2}$, their rate of heat dissipation in air $({}_r\dot{q})$ measured by direct calorimetry was greater (Shick, 1981).

Cross-acclimatization of clonemates of high- and low-shore specimens of *A.elegantissima* to the opposite tidal conditions in the laboratory indicate that intertidal differences in $\dot{n}_{O_2}$ depend primarily on food availability (section 3.8.6). The anemones are also closely entrained to the prevailing tidal cycle, and behavioural adaptations to emersion (e.g. quiescence during the normal period of exposure) further reduce aerial $\dot{n}_{O_2}$ in 'intertidal' individuals (Shick, 1981). The interpretation of different rates of oxygen consumption in high- and low-shore anemones in nature is complicated further by differences in the thermal regimes that they experience (section 3.8.7).

3.8.6 Feeding

As in other animals, oxygen consumption by sea anemones increases after feeding (Figure 3.9). The post-prandial peak in oxygen consumption is from 1.5 to 3 times the pre-prandial rate (Jones *et al.*, 1977; Svoboda and Porrmann, 1980; Fitt *et al.*, 1982; Tytler and Davies, 1984). The 'mechanical cost of feeding' (Newell, 1979) might be expected to be minimal in these sedentary feeders, an expectation borne out by experiment: feeding *Anemonia viridis* an indigestible meal had no detectable effect on $\dot{N}_{O_2}$ (Figure 3.9, centre). Peak rates of oxygen consumption occurred at 2–8 h after feeding in Mediterranean *Aiptasia diaphana* at 24°C, and at a mean of 9 h (but usually by 2 h) after ingestion in Scottish specimens of *A.viridis* at 10°C. This is in general agreement with the time-course of extracellular digestion and progress of intracellular digestion (section 2.3.2). Oxygen consumption returned to the pre-prandial rate within 12–24 h in *A.diaphana* and by 47 h in *A.viridis*; some of the interspecific difference is likely due to temperature differences, and some of the intraspecific variability no doubt arises from differences in the size of the meal ingested. Like the digestion of prey, catabolism of photosynthate translocated from the zooxanthellae also increases oxygen consumption in zooxanthellate anemones (Svoboda and Porrmann, 1980; Muller-Parker, 1984b; Tytler and Davies, 1984).

The post-prandial increase in oxygen consumption (or heat dissipation) has been called the 'specific dynamic effect' (SDE) of feeding, but despite a long history of investigation, there is no clear consensus regarding its biochemical basis. Concise reviews and discussions of the SDE are given by Bayne and Scullard (1977) and Brafield and Llewellyn (1982). Although lipid

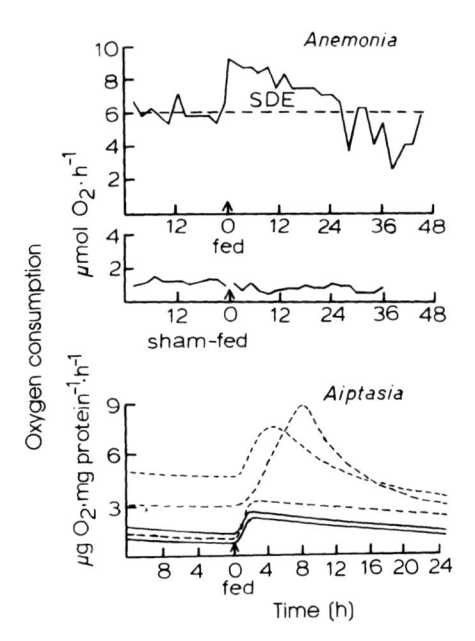

Figure 3.9 The effect of feeding on oxygen consumption in *Anemonia viridis* and *Aiptasia diaphana*. In *Anemonia*, the specific dynamic effect (SDE) of feeding is shown as the integral of oxygen consumed in excess of the mean pre-prandial rate (broken horizontal line in top graph). Ingestion of an indigestible meal at time 0 (sham-fed; centre graph) indicated no measurable mechanical cost of feeding. In *Aiptasia* (bottom graph), solid curves represent zooxanthellate anemones and broken curves represent aposymbiotic specimens of various sizes. Sources: modified from Tytler and Davies, 1984 (*Anemonia*), and Svoboda and Porrmann, 1980 (*Aiptasia*).

and carbohydrate may contribute to the SDE, protein metabolism (including both catabolism and anabolism) has the greatest effect.

By integrating the area beneath the curve shown in Figure 3.9 (top), Tytler and Davies (1984) calculated that the energetic equivalent of SDE in *A. viridis* amounted to 7% of the energy in the ingested ration (I) of squid mantle. This value is much lower than the 20–30% of I reported for the SDE in mammals and birds on high-protein diets, and supports the idea that much of the SDE in those groups represents a cost of synthesizing urea and uric acid, for sea anemones excrete primarily ammonia (section 4.2, page 175).

SDE has also been taken to include the energy lost in deaminating amino acids, and Bayne and Scullard (1977) found a good agreement between a post-prandial pulse of ammonia excretion and the increment in $\dot{N}_{O_2}$ in *Mytilus edulis*. Unfortunately, the effect of ammonia excretion has not been evaluated in sea anemones; moreover, all of those species in which post-prandial $\dot{N}_{O_2}$ has been quantified contain zooxanthellae, so that little ammonia excretion would be expected, owing to its internal recycling by the algae (section 4.2). Although oxidative deamination of amino acids might contribute significantly to post-prandial $\dot{N}_{O_2}$, the enthalpy change associated with these reactions would be small, so that the SDE calculated solely from $\dot{N}_{O_2}$ using a standard oxycaloric equivalent might overestimate the actual energetic SDE. However, the deamination of amino acids produces keto acids which may in turn enter the Krebs cycle and enhance aerobic energy metabolism and dissipative ATP turnover, so that post-prandial heat dissipation ($_t\dot{Q}$) would indeed increase. A thermodynamic interpretation of SDE would be complex, as SDE would further include endothermic, anabolic processes. Insight has recently been gained on *Mytilus edulis* by Widdows and Hawkins (1989).

Direct calorimetric measurements show that when *Metridium senile* is fed *ad libitum* on *Artemia* nauplii, $_t\dot{Q}$ increases by at least 1.7 times (Zamer, Robbins and Shick, 1988), and it declines with a time-course similar to those in Figure 3.9. These results qualitatively support the respirometric measurement of SDE. The existence of an SDE in *M. senile* fed *ad lib.* on particulate organic detritus (Zamer *et al.*, 1988) indicates the assimilation of some component of this material (section 2.2.4, page 51), since there is no detectable mechanical cost of feeding in anemones. Because the size of I was uncontrolled, it is not known whether the greater increase in $_t\dot{Q}$ shown by the anemones when fed *Artemia* than when fed detritus is due to a greater energetic content or to a higher proportion of protein in the former.

Like aerobic $_t\dot{Q}$, the rate of the heat dissipation under anoxia is greater in aposymbiotic specimens of *A. elegantissima* when recently fed ($_{t}\dot{q}$ = −0.62 mW·g$_d$W^{-1}) than when starved for 3 months ($_{t}\dot{q}$ = −0.37 mW·g$_d$W^{-1}). The former value (Shick, unpublished data) is for post-absorptive individuals (i.e. >36 h since feeding) and further demonstrates that anaerobic $_t\dot{Q}$ is not a fixed minimal rate of energy utilization but varies with nutritional status as well as with activity, as discussed earlier.

Feeding and starvation have no significant effect on the mass exponent b of $\dot{N}_{O_2}$ (Fitt *et al.*, 1982; Tytler and Davies, 1984). Since $\dot{N}_{O_2}$ includes the cost of growth, this finding is consistent with Parry's (1983) suggestion that the value of b is greater in long-lived ectotherms than in endotherms in part because large endotherms have much lower growth rates and hence a lower growth-related $\dot{N}_{O_2}$ than do small (young) endotherms (which would decrease the slope of the $\dot{N}_{O_2}$-size regression), whereas many ectotherms continue to have a metabolic cost of growth throughout their lives. Sea anemones showing indeterminate growth (i.e. having no genetically fixed upper limit to body size: section 5.7, page 217) fit Parry's model.

The greater rate of oxygen consumption (including SDE) by freshly collected low-shore specimens of *A. elegantissima* compared with high-shore conspecifics occurs despite a higher concentration of mitochondria and greater *in vitro* cytochrome *c* oxidase activity in the latter (Table 3.1). It is thus probably a result of greater carbon flow through the Krebs cycle in the better-nourished low-shore anemones. It may also be related to their greater protein content, which represents a slightly larger investment in metabolic machinery under better nutritional conditions (see Somero *et al.*, 1983). Maintenance in the laboratory on much larger rations than are likely to be obtained in the field increases both the mass-specific energetic content of tissues and $\dot{N}_{O_2}$ in both low- and high-shore anemones (section 5.3, page 202; Shick, 1981).

3.8.7 Geographical Distribution and Temperature

Temperature as a factor affecting rates of oxygen consumption has been extensively studied and exhaustively reviewed, both because of its obvious effect on survival and latitudinal limits to geographical distribution of marine invertebrates, as well as its ease of measurement and control in the laboratory. Zoogeographical limits agree well with lethal temperatures in those species of sea anemones that have been tested in this regard. The circumpolar, boreo-arctic *Metridium senile*, for example, survives temperatures of ≈0°C and its abundance is not affected by unusually cold winters (Allee, 1923; Crisp, 1964). It does not readily tolerate temperatures above about 27°C (Sassaman and Mangum, 1970), however, and on the Atlantic coast of North America it does not occur south of New Jersey (40°N latitude). On both Atlantic and Pacific coasts of North America it becomes increasingly sublittoral in distribution at lower latitudes (i.e. it exhibits equatorial submergence). Conversely, abundances of the temperate species *Actinia equina* (found from northern Europe to South Africa) and *Haliplanella lineata* (cosmopolitan in distribution) were reduced by exceptionally cold winters (Allee, 1923; Crisp, 1964). As expected in animals having such broad geographical distributions, local physiological races have developed in all of these species, in some cases associated with regional genotypic differentiation (see Chapter 6).

The Atlantic Coast of North America presents one of the steepest thermal gradients in the world. Formerly thought not to occur north of Massachusetts on this coast (Sassaman and Mangum, 1970), *H. lineata* has since been found in Maine (45°N latitude), where it experiences winter seawater temperatures of −1.8°C, and air temperatures as low as −29°C during intertidal exposure (Shick, 1976). The latter condition necessitates short-term resistance adaptation, i.e. tolerance of freezing of tissues during aerial exposure (Shick, unpublished data). In Virginia (37°N) the species shows a winter dormancy, encysting in mucus at water temperatures below 10°C, as does the related *Diadumene leucolena* (Sassaman and Mangum, 1970), whereas in Maine

H.lineata remains expanded and feeding at 0°C (Shick, 1976). The behavioural differences between anemones from different areas are accompanied by differences in the response of oxygen consumption to temperature (see below).

Ectotherms show a reduction in oxygen consumption when acutely exposed to lower temperature, but in many cases prolonged exposure to cold results in a higher $\dot{n}_{O_2}$ over a range of acute measurement temperatures when compared with warm-maintained individuals tested at the same temperatures (Figure 3.10). The latter phenomenon is called positive thermal acclimation when it occurs in response to laboratory manipulation of maintenance temperature alone, and (seasonal) thermal acclimatization when it occurs in nature. It is most pronounced in organisms that normally experience a wide range of environmental temperature, and represents a metabolic compensation that enables a continuation of biological activities (homeokinesis) despite the depressing effect of low temperature. Thermal acclima(tiza)tion of $\dot{n}_{O_2}$ has a varied biochemical basis, including an elevated concentration of oxidative enzymes at low temperatures (which may involve proliferation of mitochondria: Sidell, 1983), a higher affinity (lower K_m) of enzymes for their substrates as temperature declines, and the thermal induction of enzymes having different kinetic properties (Newell, 1979; Hochachka and Somero, 1984). When individuals are pre-exposed or acclimated for about 2 weeks to each temperature of measurement, this acclimated rate versus temperature (RT) curve typically is intermediate to the acutely-determined curves for warm- and cold-acclimated individuals (Figure 3.10).

The Maine population of *H.lineata*, which experiences a wide thermal range as well as temperatures below 10°C for most of the year, shows partial positive thermal acclimation of $\dot{n}_{O_2}$, i.e. $\dot{n}_{O_2}$ in cold-acclimated anemones is greater than that in warm-acclimated individuals at several temperatures (Figure 3.11). The Virginia population exhibits inverse thermal acclimation,

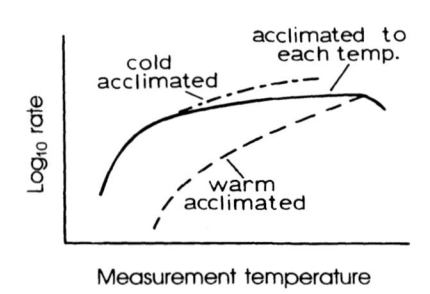

Figure 3.10 Hypothetical rate-temperature (RT) curves for individuals maintained either at a single low or high temperature and then tested acutely at a series of temperatures, and an acclimated RT curve for individuals acclimated to each experimental temperature. See text for discussion. Source: after Bullock (1955).

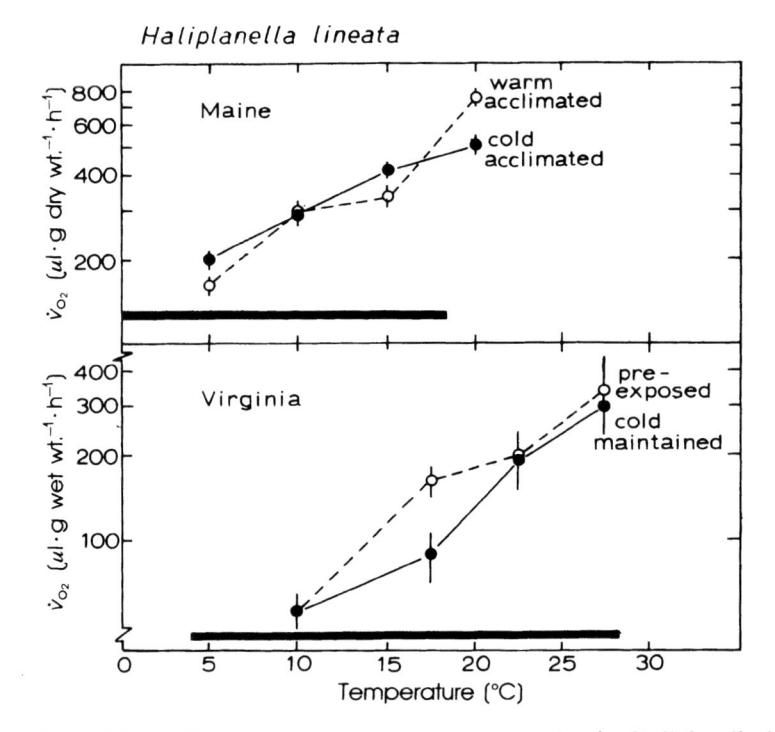

Figure 3.11 Effects of temperature on oxygen consumption in *Haliplanella lineata* from Maine and Virginia, USA. Vertical bars indicate ± 1 S.E.; Q_{10} values given for each temperature interval. Heavy horizontal lines indicate seasonal range of water temperature experienced by each population. Cold acclimated Maine anemones were maintained at 5°C, and warm acclimated individuals at 15°C. Cold acclimated Virginia specimens were maintained at 10°C, while the other group was pre-exposed to each experimental temperature. Source: redrawn from Sassaman and Mangum (1970) and Shick (1976).

typical of species showing hibernative behaviour, where cold-acclimation (10°C) depresses $\dot{n}_{O_2}$ below that of individuals pre-exposed to the measurement temperature. Although these different patterns of compensation versus avoidance seem in keeping with the rather different thermal regimes and seasonal availabilities of food experienced by the two populations, their actual determinants are unknown. Evolutionary adjustment to local thermal regimes in latitudinally separated populations may involve selection of enzymes appropriate to each locality (Hochachka and Somero, 1984). Because *H. lineata* apparently reproduces by asexual fission in most populations examined (section 6.5, page 268), local populations tend toward genotypic homogeneity (the large Maine population consisted of a single clone), and a biochemical genetic analysis of temperature acclimation is therefore precluded.

'Irreversible nongenetic adaptation' is occasionally invoked but rarely demonstrated as an explanation for physiological differences between populations that cannot be erased by acclimation to common conditions. Using monoclonal anemones from the Virginia population of *H.lineata* raised for three asexual generations at intermediate (18°C) and high (28°C) temperatures, Zamer and Mangum (1979) showed that the animals reared at 18°C always had higher $\dot{n}_{O_2}$ regardless of subsequent acclimation and measurement temperature (Figure 3.12). This relationship emerged only after data were adjusted to a common body size, since low developmental temperature resulted in larger anemones having relatively smaller tentacular surface areas, both of which factors would tend to decrease $\dot{n}_{O_2}$ (sections 3.7, page 142, and 3.8.1., page 143) and so mask the intrinsic metabolic effect of temperature. It is not known whether the persistent metabolic differences between the Maine and Virginia populations (separated by 7 degrees of latitude and >1 000 km) involve genotypic divergence or irreversible nongenetic adaptation.

Metridium senile also has the capacity for thermal acclimation of $\dot{n}_{O_2}$, as evinced by the upward translation of the RT curve for cold-acclimated individuals in the Barnstable (Massachusetts) and Santa Barbara (California) populations (Figure 3.13). The basis for the difference in acclimatory ability between the Santa Barbara and Bodega Bay (California) anemones is unclear. The two Californian populations experience similarly narrow thermal

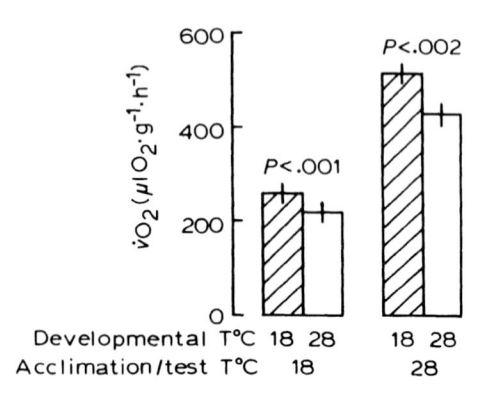

Figure 3.12 Irreversible non-genetic temperature adaptation of oxygen consumption in *Haliplanella lineata*. Groups of anemones were cultured for three asexual generations at developmental temperatures of 18° and 28°C, subsequently acclimated for 2–4 weeks to 18° or 28°C, and their rates of oxygen uptake measured at the acclimation temperature. Anemones cultured at 18°C had the higher rate of oxygen uptake at both acclimation/test temperatures. See text for discussion. Source: drawn from data in Zamer and Mangum (1979).

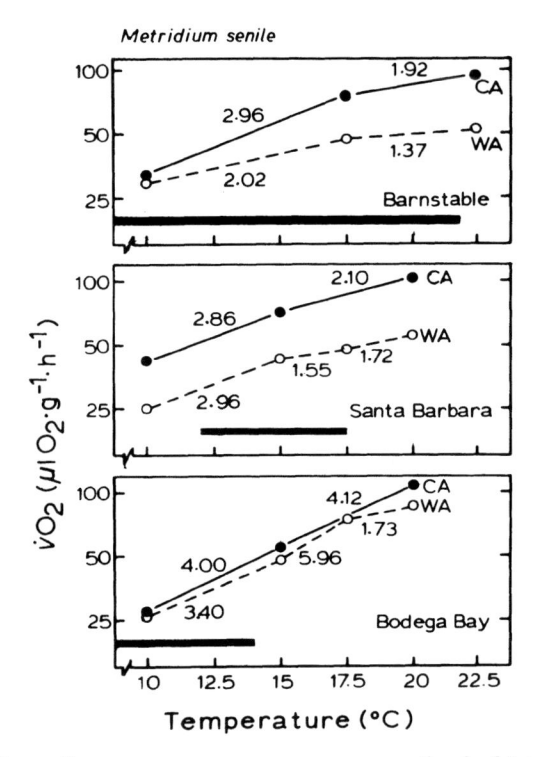

Figure 3.13 Effects of temperature on oxygen consumption in *Metridium senile* from Barnstable, Massachusetts, and Santa Barbara and Bodega Bay, California, USA. Q_{10} values shown for each temperature interval. Heavy horizontal bars indicate seasonal range of water temperature experienced by each population. CA and WA designate cold acclimated (10°C) and warm acclimated (20°C) anemones, respectively. See text for discussion. Source: modified from Sassaman and Mangum (1970) and Walsh and Somero (1981).

ranges, and show minimal genotypic divergence and no clear-cut differences in activities of various enzymes, which themselves show no systematic change with acclimation temperature (Walsh and Somero, 1981). Consistently greater enhancement of pyruvate kinase activity by cold acclimation in the Santa Barbara anemones as compared with the Bodega Bay population is consistent with the greater degree of cold-enhancement of acutely-measured $\dot{n}_{O_2}$ in the former.

For animals in thermally variable environments, minimizing the perturbing effects of acute temperature change is as important as seasonal acclimatization. Reduced sensitivity to temperature change is manifested as a low value of Q_{10}, the temperature coefficient, calculated as

$$Q_{10} = \left(\frac{k_2}{k_1}\right)^{\frac{10}{t_2 - t_1}}$$

where k_1 and k_2 are the rates at t_1 and t_2, respectively, t_2 being the higher temperature. Most biochemical and physiological processes have Q_{10} values that tend toward 2; Q_{10}s of ≈ 3 or greater indicate hypersensitivity to temperature, whereas Q_{10}s less than ≈ 1.6 indicate reduced temperature sensitivity, and $Q_{10} = 1.0$ indicates thermal insensitivity. When logarithms of rates are plotted, a change in slope of the RT curve is directly proportional to the change in Q_{10}.

Reduced thermal sensitivity of $\dot{N}_{O_2}$ represents a mechanism to save energy and is common among littoral invertebrates (Newell, 1979, for review). In *M. senile* it is most evident in the Barnstable (Massachusetts) population, which inhabits the most thermally variable habitat (Figure 3.13). In the two Californian populations, occupation of the warmer thermal regime apparently has selected for the ability of the Santa Barbara anemones to minimize thermal effects on $\dot{n}_{O_2}$ at the upper range of habitat temperatures, a phenomenon not seen in the cool-water Bodega Bay anemones (Figure 3.13).

Truly intertidal species such as *Actinia equina* encounter greater thermal variation because air temperatures fluctuate more dramatically than seawater temperatures, together with a reduced availability of food during exposure, and so they have a particular need to conserve energy. The thermal relationships of high- and low-shore individuals of this species have been studied intensively by Navarro, Ortega, and co-workers. Both low- and high-shore *A. equina* show seasonal acclimatizations of $\dot{n}_{O_2}$ (Figure 3.14), and the elevated rate in winter-acclimatized individuals may include the cost of gametogenesis (Ortega *et al.*, 1984). High-shore anemones tend to have lower rates than low-shore individuals, especially in summer at the prevailing habitat

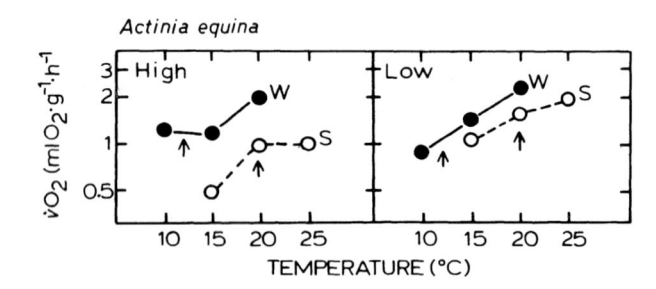

Figure 3.14 Seasonal acclimatization of oxygen consumption in high and low intertidal specimens of *Actinia equina*. W = winter specimens; S = summer specimens. Arrows indicate seasonal seawater temperatures when the anemones were collected and tested. Source: modified from Ortega *et al.* (1984).

temperature. The high-shore anemones in particular show thermal insensitivity of $\dot{n}_{O_2}$ at the seasonal habitat temperature both in winter ($Q_{10} = 0.91$, $10-15°C$) and in summer ($Q_{10} = 0.95$, $20-25°C$). Further, in both high- and low-shore individuals, Q_{10}s for aerial $\dot{n}_{O_2}$ tend to be lower than those for aquatic $\dot{n}_{O_2}$ (Navarro *et al.*, 1981).

Seasonal acclimatization of $\dot{n}_{O_2}$ is not apparent in subtropical and cool-temperate South African populations of *A.equina* over the annual range of seawater temperatures encountered in their respective habitats ($19-25°C$ in the former population; $10-16°C$ in the latter), once the data have been corrected for differences in body weight (Griffiths, 1977a). The lack of seasonal acclimatization may be related to the relatively narrow seasonal temperature range. Because the anemones were fed during maintenance in the laboratory at the prevailing field temperature, the effect of nutritional status on $\dot{n}_{O_2}$ is a confounding variable. The expected upward translation of the winter RT curve occurs, but only above $28°C$ in the subtropical population, an unnaturally high seawater temperature but a body temperature that may be achieved during intertidal exposure (Griffiths, 1977b). The suppression of $\dot{n}_{O_2}$ at high temperatures in summer anemones acclimated to these temperatures may be meaningful ecologically if it is irrelevant whether acclimatization in the field is in response to immersed or emersed body temperature, which itself will depend on shore height occupied. Both summer and winter specimens of the intertidal *A.equina* show lower Q_{10}s than do specimens of the locally sublittoral but otherwise sympatric *Anemonia natalensis*, probably reflecting adaptation of *Actinia* to a more variable thermal regime in its intertidal habitat (Griffiths, 1977b).

Molecular mechanisms of temperature adaptation have received far less attention in sea anemones than in other ectotherms. Although they have not been examined systematically with this in mind, the lipids of cold water species of sea anemones are more unsaturated than those in warm water forms, which may be a homeoviscous adaptation to maintain membrane fluidity at low temperature (section 2.5, page 87). Investigations of catalytic and thermodynamic parameters of enzymes have been extensive in other ectotherms, but little is known about them in sea anemones.

Various studies discussed by Hochachka and Somero (1984) show that species evolutionarily adapted to low temperature have enzymes with lower thermodynamic activation barriers to catalysis (i.e. free energy of activation, $\Delta G^{\ddagger}$; activation enthalpy, $\Delta H^{\ddagger}$; Arrhenius 'activation energy', E_a) than do warm-adapted species. This generalization applies to mitochondrial glutamate dehydrogenase (GDH) in sea anemones, where the lowest values of E_a and $\Delta H^{\ddagger}$ occur in the Antarctic species *Urticinopsis antarcticus*, intermediate values in cool-temperate populations of *M.senile*, and the highest values in *A.elegantissima*, which experiences the highest habitat temperatures (Table 3.6). Although the critical parameter $\Delta G^{\ddagger}$ has not been determined,

Table 3.6   Thermodynamic activation parameters for glutamate dehydrogenase (GDH) in sea anemones inhabiting different thermal regimes. Values are expressed in $cal \cdot mol^{-1}$, and $\Delta H^{\ddagger}$ values are calculated for the thermal midrange for each species

Species (population)	Habitat temperature (°C)	E_a	$\Delta H^{\ddagger}$
Urticinopsis antarcticus	-1.8	14,536	13,997
Metridium senile			
(Bodega Bay)	$8-13$	15,207	14,643
Metridium senile			
(Santa Barbara)	$12-17.5$	16,907	16,335
Anthopleura elegantissima	$15-35$ (air)	20,025	19,433

Source: Walsh, 1981b.

it would show the same pattern if the entropy of activation, $\Delta S^{\ddagger}$, were the same for GDH from the various species, since $E_a = \Delta H^{\ddagger} + RT$, and $\Delta G^{\ddagger} = \Delta H^{\ddagger} - T\Delta S^{\ddagger}$ (R being the gas constant and T the absolute temperature). The differences in E_a between the two Californian populations of *M. senile* (Table 3.6) described as physiological races by Walsh and Somero (1981) do not involve differences detectable by electrophoresis.

North American populations of *M. senile* on the Atlantic Coast exist along one of the steepest geographical thermal gradients in the world and show clinal variation in allele frequencies at several enzyme-coding loci, including a phosphoglucose isomerase (PGI) locus (Figure 3.15a, b). PGI catalyses the reversible conversion

$$\text{glucose-6-phosphate (G6P)} \rightleftharpoons \text{fructose-6-phosphate (F6P)},$$

and lies at the branchpoint of glycolysis and the pentose shunt. There are no differences in E_a between the two PGI allozymes (enzyme products of the two alternative alleles, designated as electrophoretically 'fast' and 'slow'), which show similar temperature sensitivity ($Q_{10} = 1.8-2.5$) of their glyco-lytic reation velocities at physiological substrate concentrations (Hoffmann, 1981, 1983). These Q_{10}s match those of aerobic respiration in the Barnstable (Massachusetts) population measured over the same temperature range (Figure 3.13). Both allozymes show a similar small decline in K_m with de-creasing temperature but a general conservation of K_m over the environ-mental temperature range (Figure 3.15c) as seen in other sea anemones (Walsh, 1981b) and in ectotherms in general (Hochachka and Somero, 1984). Hoffmann (1985) has suggested however that the cline is maintained by natural selection acting on functional differences between the allozymes, from the close correspondence of the clinal variation in allele frequencies with the latitudinal temperature gradient, differences in specific activities

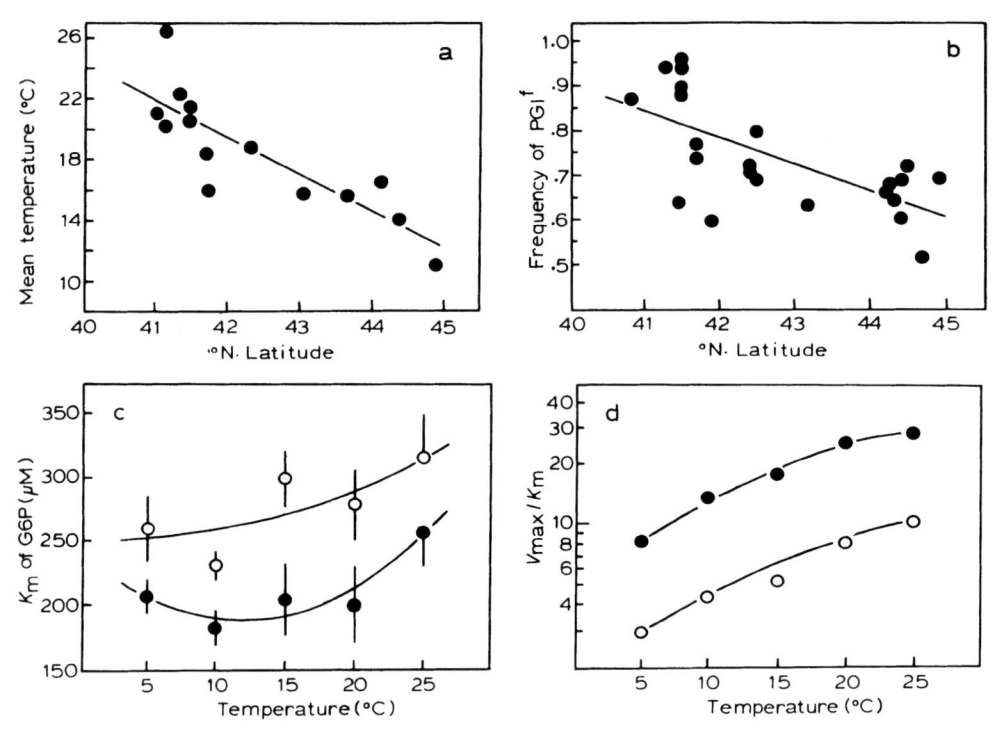

Figure 3.15 Thermal relationships of phosphoglucose isomerase (PGI) allozymes in *Metridium senile*. (**a**) Relationship between mean seawater temperature in the warmest month and latitude on the Atlantic coast of North America where the anemones were collected. (**b**) Relationship between latitude and the frequency of the electrophoretically fast PGI allozyme. (**c**) Relationship between K_m for glucose-6-phosphate and temperature for the fast (●) and slow (○) PGI allozymes. (**d**) Relationship between the ratio V_{max}/K_m of the fast (●) and slow (○) PGI allozymes measured in the glycolytic direction; the ordinate is logarithmic to emphasize the similar temperature sensitivity of this ratio in the two allozymes. See text for discussion. Source: redrawn from Hoffmann (1985).

and kinetic parameters between the allozymes, and the apparent superiority of PGI heterozygotes in a thermally variable habitat.

The PGI 'fast' allele is nearly fixed in some southern (warmest water) populations and it decreases in frequency to about 0.5 in the northern (cold water) populations (Figure 3.15b). It codes for an enzyme having higher specific activity and a consistently higher V_{max}/K_m ratio (an index of the flux of substrates at their physiological concentrations), and since the absolute difference between the fast and slow allozymes in the latter parameter increases with temperature over the environmental range (Figure 3.15d), it appears that the fast allozyme is selectively favoured in warm water: this is in agreement with its higher frequency there. Because the fast allozyme has a superior functional index at low temperature as well, however, the foregoing mechanistic explanation cannot account for the continued existence of the slow allozyme, even in cold environments. From allozymic differences in inhibition kinetics (section 3.3), Hoffmann (1983) suggested that functional superiority of the slow allozyme may lie not in its glycolytic function but in its enhancement of glucose flow into the pentose shunt, which assumes increased importance in metabolism at low temperature. Zamer and Hoffmann (1989) confirmed a greater flux of glucose through the pentose shunt in specimens of *M.senile* homozygous for the PGI 'slow' allele than in those homozygous for the 'fast' allele. This effect was pronounced at 5°C compared with 15°C, and thermal compensation of glucose flux was seen in fed but not in fasted anemones. These authors suggested that the Darwinian interpretation of differential modulation of pentose shunt activity by PGI allozymes is related to the generation by the shunt of NADPH used in lipid synthesis, since gonadal lipid production in northern populations must proceed at lower temperatures, where the frequency of the 'slow' allele increases.

3.8.8 Salinity

Because sea anemones typically contract in response to a change in salinity, the effect of osmotic concentration *per se* on their respiration is difficult to

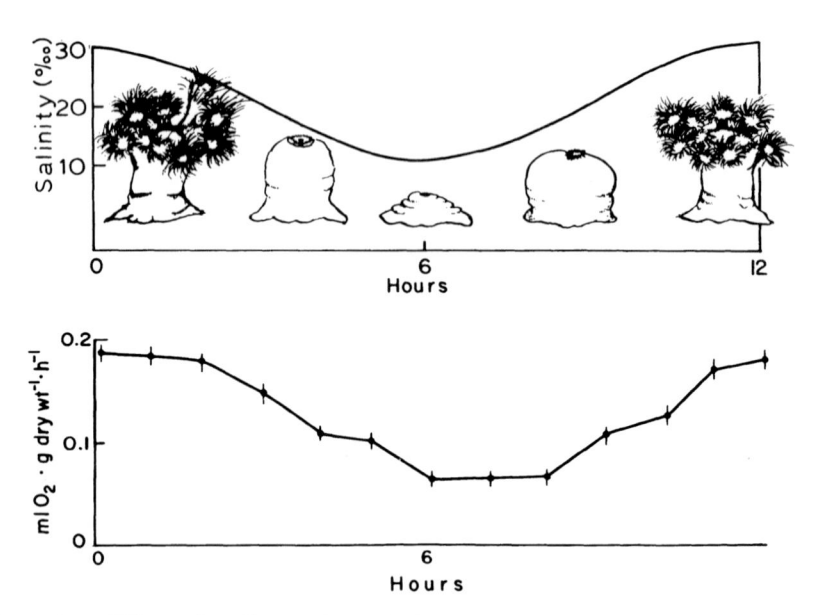

Figure 3.16 Effect of cyclic salinity variation on expansion state and oxygen uptake in *Metridium senile*. Source: modified from Shumway (1978).

assess. Shoup (1932) for example stated that the decrease in oxygen consumption by *M.senile* at salinities above 30 parts per thousand (30‰S) was due to retraction of the tentacles and column (section 3.8.2), and to secretion of mucus. It is not clear whether the reduction of $\dot{N}_{O_2}$ at low salinity had a similar cause, but it would appear to be so: when exposed to cyclic (tidal) fluctuations in salinity, *M.senile* contracts as salinity declines and reexpands when salinity increases, a behavioural response paralleled by a decrease and a subsequent increase in oxygen consumption (Figure 3.16). Further, the rates of oxygen consumption by contracted anemones at 32‰S are indistinguishable from those at 16‰S (Shumway, 1978), although in very small anemones, where oxygen and ionic diffusion limitations would be minimal, there is a tendency for $\dot{N}_{O_2}$ to be greater at the lower salinity. Likewise, oxygen consumption increases significantly in isolated tentacular and body wall tissues of *Condylactis gigantea* during incubation in hypo-osmotic seawater (Herrera *et al.*, 1989). An elevated oxygen consumption at low salinities is consistent with the oxidative degradation of intracellular organic osmolytes such as free amino acids, the concentrations of which decline during acclimation to hypo-osmotic media. These and other responses are discussed in the next chapter.

4 Nitrogen excretion and osmotic balance

4.1 SYNOPSIS

Sea anemones lack specialized excretory structures and, like most aquatic invertebrates, excrete as their principal nitrogenous waste ammonia (which in the pH range prevailing in seawater and body fluids occurs primarily as the ammonium ion, NH_4^+). Here, 'ammonia' is used generically, and 'NH_4^+' specifies the ionized form. Zooxanthellae are involved in the recycling of ammonia. Some zooxanthellate and azooxanthellate species retain uric acid (a product of nucleic acid catabolism) and perhaps other purines in their tissues. Like most other marine invertebrates, sea anemones tolerate a degree of dilution of the external medium, but they do not regulate the osmotic concentration of their coelenteric fluid. This necessitates regulation of cellular volume, in part involving active control of the concentration of intracellular free amino acids (FAA). Both ecological and taxonomic trends are apparent in the composition and concentration of the FAA pool, which accounts for 4% to 14% of the total osmotic concentration (and up to 25% of the intracellular osmotic concentration) of the tissues in various species that differ in their ability to regulate tissue water content. Occupation of the intertidal zone subjects sea anemones to desiccating conditions and requires morphological, physiological and behavioural mechanisms to conserve water. Juveniles are more susceptible to dehydration than adult anemones: this apparently sets the upper limit of intertidal distribution and probably selected for viviparous reproduction in littoral anemones of the genus *Actinia*.

4.2 NITROGEN EXCRETION

The heavy reliance by sea anemones on proteins as fuels in energy metabolism (see Table 3.2, page 133) implies a large production of nitrogenous wastes. Nitrogen metabolism has been little studied in sea anemones but, as in other metazoans, transamination reactions linked to the formation of glutamate are probably the major mechanism for removing the amino groups from a variety of amino acids. Glutamate may then be deaminated in a reaction catalysed by glutamate dehydrogenase (GDH), which in cnidarians alone among metazoans, utilises NADP(H) rather than NAD(H) (Bishop *et al.*, 1978; Male and Storey, 1983):

$$\text{L-glutamate} + \text{NADP}^+ + \text{H}_2\text{O} \rightleftharpoons$$
$$\text{NH}_4^+ + \alpha\text{-ketoglutarate} + \text{NADPH} + \text{H}^+.$$

In corals, a mitochondrial GDH using NAD(H) as a cofactor accounts for 15–25% of the total GDH activity (Dudler, Yellowlees and Miller, 1987; Rahav *et al.*, 1989). Additional ammonia may be produced during the turnover of nucleotides through the action of adenosine deaminase and guanase (Bishop, Barnes and Kirkpatrick, 1972; see below). Enzymes of oxidative deamination have not been studied.

There has been little study of the qualitative nature of nitrogenous excretory products in sea anemones since the early investigations by Pütter (1911), who found that ammonia comprised 77.6%, 94.1%, and 100% of the nitrogen excretion in *Calliactis parasitica* ($\equiv$ *Adamsia rondeletti*), *Actinia equina*, and *Anemonia viridis* ($\equiv$ *A.sulcata*), respectively. The balance was 'albuminoid N', which in well-fed *A.equina* consists largely of primary amines (Shick, unpublished). The concentration of ammonia in the tissues of zooxanthellate *Anthopleura xanthogrammica* is 1.13 mmol/kg H_2O (calculated from data in Male and Storey, 1983, assuming 80% water content of fresh tissue). It is unclear whether this very high value is an artifact of endogenous deamination reactions during the extraction procedure. Ammonia levels are much lower in zooxanthellate *Aiptasia pulchella* and *Aiptasia pallida*, tissue ammonia concentration being 40–50 μM in the former (Wilkerson and Muscatine, 1984) and cytosolic ammonia being estimated at 5 μM in the latter (D'Elia and Cook, 1988). Conversely, Robbins (1980) measured 181 μM ammonia in the coelenteric fluid of azooxanthellate *Metridium senile* (which implies higher levels intracellularly), and based on NH_4^+ infusion experiments, suggested that the need to void this toxic substance affected the anemone's expansion state and ventilation of the coelenteron.

Not all nitrogenous wastes are necessarily excreted by sea anemones, for purines (products of the catabolism of nucleic acids) are stored as membrane-bounded 'concretions' in the endodermal cells of the pharynx and of the reticular tract of the mesenteric filaments in many species (Mouchet, 1929, 1930; Van-Praët, 1977). From their solubility characteristics, Mouchet (1929) concluded that the concretions were xanthine, although Fox and Pantin (1941) questioned this and stated that in *M.senile* they were uric acid, based on the use of uricase in their analyses. Both xanthine oxidase (XOD, which univalently reduces O_2 as a cofactor and produces superoxide radical) and xanthine dehydrogenase (XDH, which uses NAD^+) are present in *Actinia equina* (Shick, unpublished, in Dykens and Shick, 1988), so the concretions in this species could contain uric acid derived from purine catabolism:

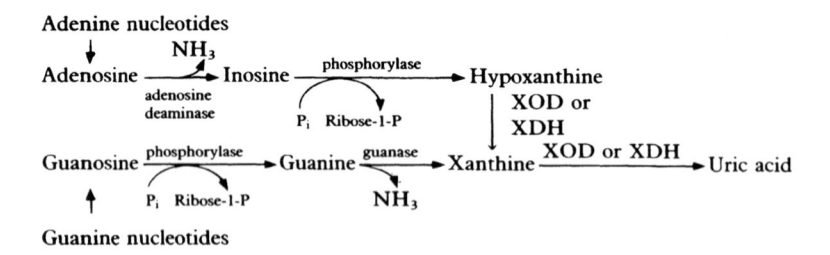

Uric acid has been reported in the related zooxanthellate actiniid *Anemonia viridis* (Nicol, 1967). Van-Praët (1977, 1985) did not observe exocytosis of the concretions in *A.equina* and was uncertain whether it occurred or whether the concretions were retained for the life of the individual cells. Fox and Pantin (1941) found uric acid in the mucus of *M.senile* and postulated that this was the route of its excretion. In *Aiptasia pallida*, uric acid in the endoderm of zooxanthellate individuals is an order of magnitude more concentrated (3–4 μmol/g $_wW_{anemone}$) than in aposymbiotic clonemates, and increases further during acclimation to bright sunlight, which suggests that it may function as an antioxidant defence against photochemically-generated forms of active oxygen (Tapley *et al.*, 1988; see also section 2.7.3, page 113).

Rates of ammonia excretion by several species of sea anemones are given in Table 4.1. These rates vary with the nutritional condition of the individual and particularly with the rate of protein catabolism. The highest rates are for aposymbiotic specimens of *Anthopleura elegantissima* freshly collected from the shore and for aposymbiotic *Aiptasia pulchella* fed brine shrimp nauplii. The lower values in azooxanthellate *Bunodosoma cavernata* are for individuals starved for one week, and the higher rate in this species during aerobic recovery from anoxia closely corresponds to the clearance of alanine, the major end product of anaerobiosis (section 3.4, page 129). The very low rates in aposymbiotic *Condylactis gigantea* likely reflect their reliance on lipid catabolism during 6–8 weeks of starvation. Fitt (1984) noted a high rate

Table 4.1 Rates of ammonium excretion ($\dot{n}_{NH4}^{+}$, µmol $NH_4^+ \cdot h^{-1} \cdot g^{-1}$ dry weight) by sea anemones. Negative values indicate net ammonium uptake.

Species	Temperature (°C)	Nutritional conditions	Illumination	$\dot{n}_{NH4}^{+}$	Source
Anthopleura elegantissima					Zamer and Shick, 1987
aposymbiotic	15	freshly collected	dark	2.142	
zooxanthellate	15	freshly collected	dark, following 8 h exposure to sunlight	0.245	
zooxanthellate	15	freshly collected	dark, following 8 h aerial exposure to sunlight	0.331	
Aiptasia pulchella[1]					Wilkerson and Muscatine, 1984
aposymbiotic	25	fed *Artemia* nauplii 3x weekly	$14-20\,\mu E \cdot m^{-2} \cdot s^{-1}$	2.6–5.2	
zooxanthellate	25–28	fed *Artemia* nauplii 3x weekly	$?1\,000\,\mu E \cdot m^{-2} \cdot s^{-1}$	-0.23 $[NH_4^+] = 10\,\mu M$	
Bunodosoma cavernata					Ellington, 1982
azooxanthellate	22.5	starved 1 week	–	0.173	
azooxanthellate	22.5	starved 1 week; $\dot{n}_{NH}^{+}$ measured 8–12 h after end of 4 days of exposure to anoxia	–	0.826	
Condylactis gigantea[2]					Cates and McLaughlin, 1976
aposymbiotic	25	starved 6–8 weeks	$\approx 32\,\mu E \cdot m^{-2} \cdot s^{-1}$	0.023	
aposymbiotic	25	starved 6–8 weeks	dark	0.090	
zooxanthellate	25	starved 6–8 weeks	$\approx 32\,\mu E \cdot m^{-2} \cdot s^{-1}$	-0.004	
zooxanthellate	25	starved 6–8 weeks	dark	0.001	

[1] Original data expressed per anemone or per µg chl *a*; mass-specific ammonium fluxes calculated by assuming average zooxanthellate individual contains 3.69 mg protein and 14 µg chl *a* (Muller-Parker, 1984b) and that protein is 50% of dry weight; from chl *a*: biomass ratio in zooxanthellate *A.pulchella*, aposymbiotic individuals were assumed to contain 3 mg protein and to have a dry weight of 6 mg.

[2] Rates calculated from wet weight assuming a tissue water content of 80%.

of ammonia excretion by *Aiptasia tagetes* several hours after feeding, and a sharp decline in excretion during the next several days. Likewise, Wilkerson and Muscatine (1984) found that the ammonia concentration in the tissues of *A.pulchella* was lower in starved than in fed individuals. Ammonia released by aposymbiotic individuals may be the chemical attractant used by motile zooxanthellae to locate potential hosts (Fitt, 1984; see also section 2.6.3, page 92).

As originally hypothesized by Geddes (1882), the algal endosymbionts affect the ammonia flux in zooxanthellate anemones. Whereas aposymbiotic anemones always excrete ammonia, the rate is much lower in zooxanthellate specimens and the flux may even be reversed, some zooxanthellate species showing a net uptake (Table 4.1). Pütter (1911) suggested that the algal symbionts of *Aiptasia diaphana* were responsible for an uptake of NH_4^+ from enriched seawater, an hypothesis verified in *A.pulchella* by Wilkerson and Muscatine (1984), who also showed the ability of this anemone to deplete natural seawater of NH_4^+. The rate of NH_4^+ uptake by zooxanthellate anemones and by isolated zooxanthellae increases linearly with NH_4^+ concentration and shows no sign of saturation up to $10\,\mu M$. Dark treatment for 19 h causes zooxanthellate anemones to excrete NH_4^+. Ammonium uptake in *Aiptasia pallida* seems to involve a 'depletion-diffusion' mechanism whereby active transport by the zooxanthellae depletes the host's cytoplasm of NH_4^+ and thus enhances its diffusion from the medium into the host's cells (D'Elia and Cook, 1988).

Unlike some corals, neither *A.pulchella* nor its freshly-isolated zooxanthellae take up dissolved nitrate, and the freshly-isolated zooxanthellae lack nitrate reductase activity (Wilkerson and Muscatine, 1984). These authors noted that prolonged starvation of *A.pulchella* lowers its tissue ammonia levels and results in a slight uptake of nitrate. Such an effect may account for the uptake of nitrate by starved *C.gigantea* (Cates and McLaughlin, 1979). Subsequently, Wilkerson and Trench (1985) showed that nitrate reductase appears to be inducible in cultured zooxanthellae from *A.pulchella*, but within the animal host, ammonia may repress this induction.

Pathways of ammonia assimilation in zooxanthellae remain a controversial topic. The GDH reaction, operating in the direction of glutamate synthesis, has a K_m of $4-5\,mM$ for NH_4^+ (Wilkerson and Muscatine, 1984), much higher than its tissue concentration in *A.pulchella*, and so this would be a mechanism of ammonia fixation only if the concentration were unusually high. Ammonia is incorporated into the algae via the amination of existing glutamate by glutamine synthetase (GS), which is very active in *A.pulchella* zooxanthellae, and its low K_m for glutamate and negative cooperativity with NH_4^+ suggest that it is operating at saturation (Wilkerson and Muscatine, 1984). These authors could not demonstrate glutamate synthase (glutamine : 2-oxoglutarate [$= \alpha$-ketoglutarate] aminotransferase, or GOGAT) activity in

A.pulchella zooxanthellae, and their assay conditions would also have detected any GDH activity using glutamine as an alternative substrate to NH_4^+; the latter reaction occurs in the animal tissue of *Anthopleura xanthogrammica* (Male and Storey, 1983). Based on its K_m of 33 μM for NH_4^+, GS has been suggested to be the primary ammonia-fixing enzyme in zooxanthellae freshly isolated from *Condylactis gigantea* (Anderson and Burris, 1987). These authors did not demonstrate the presence of GOGAT, however, which has yet to be clearly and directly demonstrated in zooxanthellae from anemones but which may be present in those from some corals (cf. Trench, 1987 and Rahav *et al.*, 1989). The importance of GOGAT lies in the observation that if GDH is not an ammonia-fixing mechanism in the zooxanthellae, and since the GS reaction is essentially irreversible, GOGAT would provide a mechanism for regenerating glutamate. Some of the glutamate would then be available for NH_4^+ trapping by GS, and some, by transamination with various α-keto acids, would be a source of other amino acids.

The recycling of the host's ammonia and the scavenging of exogenous inorganic nitrogen by zooxanthellae has received most attention in species inhabiting nutrient-poor tropical waters, where the algae may contribute substantially to the nitrogen budget of the symbiosis. Considering that the principal amino acid translocated from the zooxanthellae to the host animal is alanine, which is not an essential amino acid, the direct benefit of ammonia recycling appears to be to the algae and not to their host. Depletion of ammonia in starved specimens of *Aiptasia pallida* leads to a decrease in algal growth rates, whereas feeding the anemone or even supplementing the medium with ammonia alleviates this (Cook *et al.*, 1988; section 2.6.4, page 94). Based on experiments with zooxanthellate and aposymbiotic conspecifics, the zooxanthellae also appear to be responsible for the retention of excretory phosphate in *Anemonia viridis* (Smith, 1939), *C.gigantea* (Cates and McLaughlin, 1979) and *Aiptasia pallida* (Muller-Parker *et al.*, 1990).

4.3 OSMOCONFORMITY AND CELLULAR VOLUME REGULATION

There has been no large-scale, comparative study of the salinity tolerances of sea anemones. Based on numerous isolated accounts, the lower distributional limit for many species in nature is about 15–20‰S (i.e. a salinity of 15–20 parts per thousand, or 15–20 g salt per kg water). Cerianthids generally seem restricted to higher salinities. Although some species of actinians (e.g. *Diadumene* spp., *Haliplanella lineata*, *Edwardsia* spp. and *Nematostella* spp.) regularly inhabit brackish water, true estuarine species are rare (Braber and Borghouts, 1977), and only *D.leucolena* is reported to live below 10‰S in nature (Pierce and Minasian, 1974).

Haliplanella lineata (monoclonal)

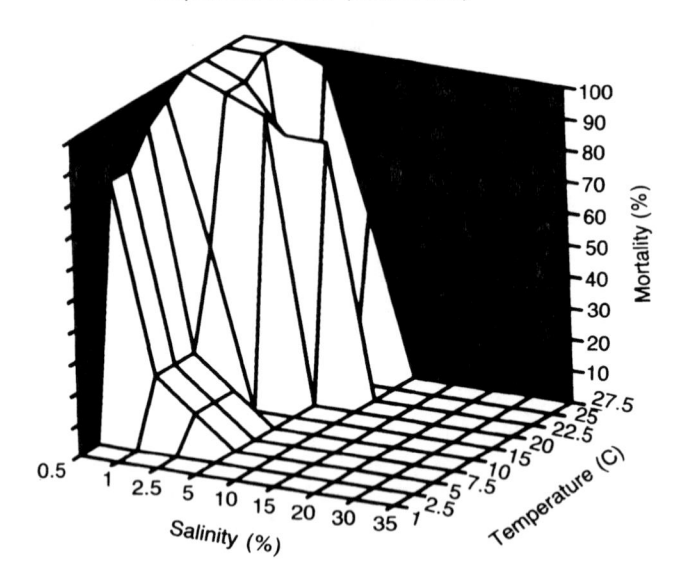

Diadumene leucolena (strictly sexual)

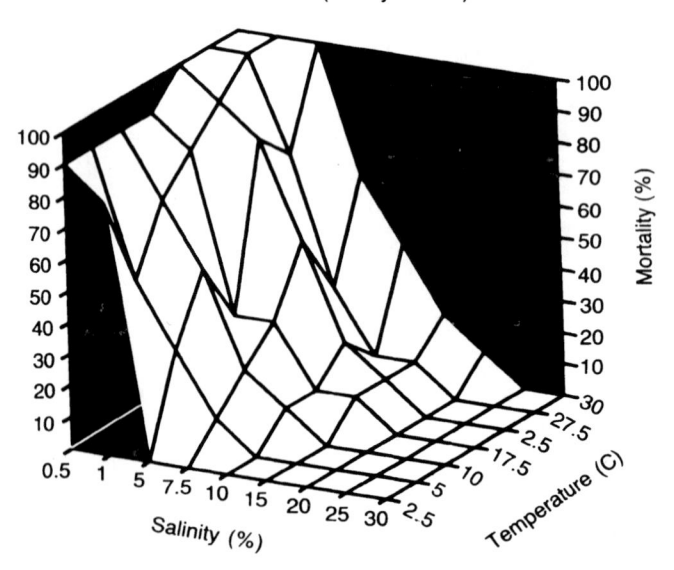

Figure 4.1 Effects of salinity and temperature on mortality in a monoclonal population of *Haliplanella lineata* and in a sexually reproducing population of *Diadumene leucolena* during two weeks of acclimation. Source: after Shick and Dowse (1985).

The results of salinity tolerance experiments on anemones in the laboratory are consistent with their distributions in nature (Miyawaki, 1951; Kiener, 1971; Pierce and Minasian, 1974; Shick, 1976; Bursey and Harmer, 1979; Benson-Rodenbough and Ellington, 1982; Kasschau *et al.*, 1984a; Deaton and Hoffmann, 1988), although the short-term survival at extremely low salinities (ca. 10‰S) by some species in the laboratory does not define their tolerance zone in the field. Short-term salinity tolerance is thermally sensitive, with lower temperatures enhancing survival at salinity extremes (Figure 4.1; Benson-Rodenbough and Ellington, 1982). This tolerance appears to have a genetic component, the temperature–salinity–mortality response surface being more complex in the outcrossing sexual species *D.leucolena* than in a genotypically homogeneous clonal population of *H. lineata* (Figure 4.1).

Because the coelenteron is ventilated and its contents periodically are replaced with fresh seawater (section 3.7, page 138), sea anemones are osmoconformers, their coelenteric fluid equilibrating with the ambient medium within 3 to 6 h after a change in salinity (Figure 4.2). The same pattern is seen for Na^+, K^+ and Cl^- (Benson-Rodenbough and Ellington, 1982). Dissolved macromolecules do not contribute to the osmotic concentration of the coelenteric fluid in *M.senile* (Mangum and Johansen, 1975), although its slight rise in concentration in *C.gigantea* after feeding (Bursey and Harmer, 1979) may be due to the products of digestion and excretion.

The usual response to hypo-osmotic stress is contraction and secretion of mucus (Shoup, 1932; Miyawaki, 1951; Shick, 1976; Shumway, 1978; Bursey and Harmer, 1979; Benson-Rodenbough and Ellington, 1982; Kasschau *et al.*, 1984a). The former action minimizes the surface area in contact with the external medium (especially since ventilation of the coelenteron ceases) and so reduces the osmotic influx of water and efflux of ions and organic solutes. It is often assumed that the layer of mucus presents a barrier to water and solute movements, but its diffusional permeability in sea anemones has not been studied. It certainly causes an unstirred layer to develop at the ectodermal surface, which will decrease the flux of solutes. Kirkpatrick and Bishop (1973) suggested that the phosphonic acid groups of the phosphonoglycoproteins abundant in sea anemone mucus (section 2.3.3, page 76) may act as ion exchangers, and cnidarian mucus indeed appears to sequester calcium ions (Goreau, 1959). In sea anemones, this may provide a mechanism to maintain Ca^{2+} available to bind to the external membranes when the ambient osmotic concentration is lowered, which reduces the efflux of free amino acids (see Pierce and Greenberg, 1973). Such a mechanism might allow anemones experiencing short-term (tidal) reductions in salinity to retain these organic solutes, especially since the trapped high-salinity coelenteric fluid and large extracellular space (see below) provide a reservoir against a transient decrease in environmental osmotic concentration.

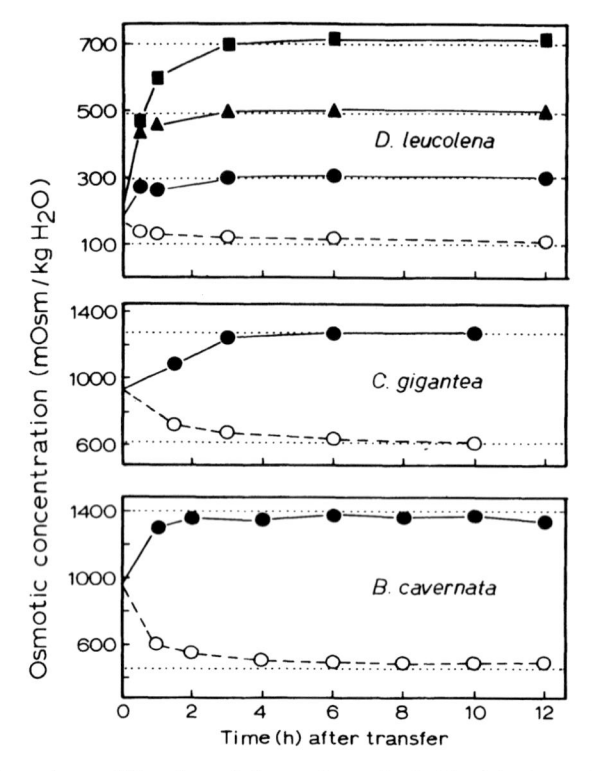

Figure 4.2 Osmotic equilibration of the coelenteric fluid with the ambient seawater in sea anemones transferred to media having higher (solid symbols) and lower (open circles) osmotic concentrations. Dotted horizontal lines indicate osmotic concentrations of the seawater to which the anemones were transferred. Source: redrawn from Pierce and Minasian (1974) for *Diadumene leucolena*; Bursey and Harmer (1979) for *Condylactis gigantea*; and Benson-Rodenbough and Ellington (1982) for *Bunodosoma cavernata*. Salinity (‰) = (mOsm × 36‰)/1054 mOsm.

Because sea anemones eventually re-expand in all but the lowest salinities (Shick, 1976; Kasschau *et al.*, 1984a; Deaton and Hoffmann, 1988) and reach osmotic equilibrium with the medium (Figure 4.2), individual cells must regulate their volume to avoid excessive swelling or shrinkage following a decrease or an increase in salinity. Figure 4.3 shows the tissue hydration of several species after 1–2 weeks of laboratory acclimation to a range of salinities. Since tissue hydration varies by only about 7% despite a three-fold variation in osmotic concentration over the normal ecological range (12–36‰S), cellular volume regulation clearly is occurring. There may be a genetic component to this regulation, for tissue hydration at most salinities is significantly more variable in the sexually outcrossing *D.leucolena* and in

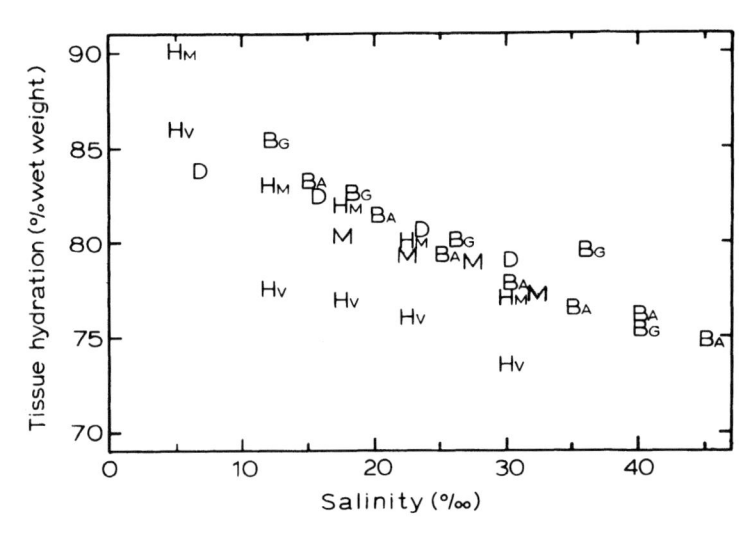

Figure 4.3 Effects of acclimation salinity on the tissue hydration (water content as percent of tissue wet weight) in populations of euryhaline sea anemones. BA = *Bunodosoma cavernata* from Port Aransas, Texas, USA (Benson-Rodenbough and Ellington, 1982); BG = *B.cavernata* from Galveston, Texas, USA (Kasschau *et al.*, 1984a); D = *Diadumene leucolena* from Maryland, USA (Pierce and Minasian, 1974); HM = *Haliplanella lineata* from Maine, USA (Shick, 1976); Hv = *H.lineata* from Virginia, USA (Shick, 1976); M = *Metridium senile* from Massachusetts, USA (Deaton and Hoffmann, 1988).

multiclonal *H.lineata* than in monoclonal *H.lineata* (Shick and Dowse, 1985).

Deaton and Hoffmann (1988) performed a mathematical analysis of the ability of several species of anemones to regulate their water content over a range of salinity. These authors calculated the tissue hydration of anemones following acclimation to progressively lower salinities as a function of the expected osmotic water gain that was not expelled (β). Theoretically, values of β can range from 1.0 (the anemone behaving as a simple osmometer and retaining all excess water at lowered salinity) to 0 (the anemone being a perfect regulator and retaining no excess water, maintaining the same water content irrespective of salinity). Thus one might expect more euryhaline species to have lower values of β (i.e. to be better regulators of water content and hence cell volume).

Values of β are remarkably similar over most of the non-lethal range of salinity in several species (Figure 4.4). *Diadumene leucolena* shows the best volume regulatory ability (lowest β value) at low salinity, in keeping with its truly estuarine distribution. At high salinity, *Bunodosoma cavernata* (which probably experiences fluctuating salinities at the upper end of the environmental range in its habitats on the Texas coast) is the best regulator. How-

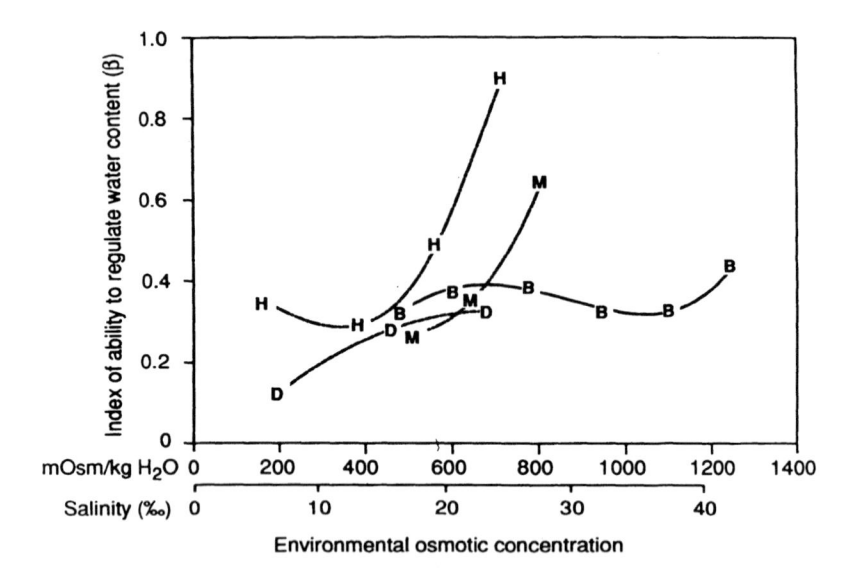

Figure 4.4 Ability of euryhaline sea anemones to regulate tissue water content over a range of environmental osmotic concentrations. Index of regulation (β, the proportion of maximum excess water retention, W_{2max}, retained following a transfer from higher to lower salinity) is calculated as $W_2 = (W_{2max} - W_1) \beta + W_1$, where W_1 and W_2 are tissue water contents at the higher and lower salinities, respectively. Decreasing values of β indicate increasing regulatory ability. B = *Bunodosoma cavernata* from Port Aransas, Texas; D = *Diadumene leucolena*; H = *Haliplanella lineata* from Maine; M = *Metridium senile*. For details of calculations, see Oglesby (1975) and Deaton and Hoffmann (1988).

ever, volume regulatory ability in *B.cavernata* does not change with salinity, whereas such ability increases with decreasing salinity in the more euryhaline *D.leucolena* and *H.lineata*, and in *M.senile* (Figure 4.4). It is unknown whether the increased ability to regulate tissue hydration at low salinity is due to a decrease in the anemones' 'apparent water permeability' (Deaton and Hoffmann, 1988). In *H.lineata*, acclimation to very low (and ultimately lethal) salinity is associated with a decrease in volume regulatory ability, whereas the estuarine *D.leucolena* increases its volume regulatory ability at the lowest salinity (Figure 4.4), which it survives indefinitely. The tolerance to reduced salinity and a strong ability to regulate tissue hydration are somewhat surprising in *M.senile*, which is not estuarine and does not usually experience drastically fluctuating salinities.

As in other marine invertebrates, cellular volume regulation in anemones is accomplished in part by controlling the intracellular free amino acid (FAA) pool, which increases in concentration with salinity (Figure 4.5). This increase is an active regulatory process, not a passive equilibrium, for in these species the change in FAA concentration predicted from changes in tissue hydration is less than 10 mmol/kg H_2O over the environmental range of salinity, whereas the actual FAA concentration change is 50–80 mmol/ kg H_2O (cf. Figures 4.3 and 4.5).

The volumes of intracellular and extracellular water (the latter measured as inulin space) have been determined only in *Condylactis gigantea* (Herrera

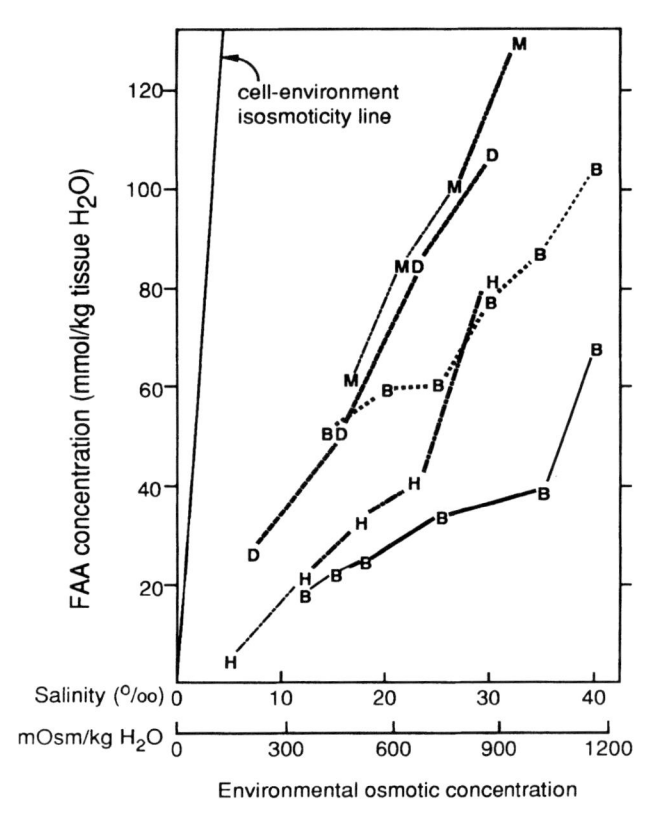

Figure 4.5 Effect of acclimation salinity on the concentration of free amino acids (FAA) in *Bunodosoma cavernata* from Port Aransas, Texas (**B**, dotted line) and from Galveston, Texas (**B**, solid line), *Diadumene leucolena* (**D**), *Haliplanella lineata* (**H**) and *Metridium senile* (**M**). Heavy portion of each line indicates the normal environmental range of salinity (osmotic concentration) for that species. Cell-environment isosmoticity line represents the calculated FAA concentration if FAA were the only intracellular solutes. See text for discussion. Source: compiled and recalculated from Pierce and Minasian (1974) for *D.leucolena*; Shick (1976) for *H.lineata*; Benson-Rodenbough and Ellington (1982) for *B.cavernata* (Port Aransas); Kasschau *et al.* (1984a) for *B.cavernata* (Galveston); Deaton and Hoffmann (1988) for *M.senile*.

et al., 1989). At 35‰S, extracellular water makes up 47% of total tissue water in the tentacles and 55% of the water in the column wall. This difference is probably owing to the proportionally greater amount of largely acellular mesoglea in the column. Such a large extracellular space (averaging ≈50% of total tissue water) potentially represents an osmotically inert buffer against cellular volume changes during salinity changes. FAA account for 13.4% of the osmotic concentration in total tissue water (25.3% of intracellular osmotic concentration) in the tentacles and 7.6% of tissue water osmotic concentration (16.2% of intracellular osmotic concentration) in the column wall; potassium, sodium and chloride comprise most of the balance of intracellular solutes.

Although the data are not corrected for the undetermined volume of extracellular water in the tissues of these species, the contribution of FAA to the change in the total osmotic concentration of tissue water over the environmental range of salinity is about 12–16% in *D.leucolena*, *H.lineata* and *M.senile*, and 3% (Kasschau *et al.*, 1984a) to 6% (Benson-Rodenbough and Ellington, 1982) in *B.cavernata*. All of these values are lower than in other marine invertebrates (e.g., 30–70% in molluscs), where the percentage contribution of FAA to tissue water osmolarity is directly related to the degree of euryhalinity and volume regulatory ability. Conversely, intracellular concentrations of Na^+, K^+ and Cl^- are greater in the anemone *Condylactis gigantea* than in marine molluscs (Herrera *et al.*, 1986), which reflects the lower FAA concentration in the anemone.

The greater volume regulatory ability at low salinity in *D.leucolena* and *M.senile* compared with that in *B.cavernata* seems due to the greater ability of the first two species to reduce their FAA concentrations under these conditions (evinced by their steeper slopes in the relationship shown in Figure 4.5). In *B.cavernata*, the concentration of taurine (the principal organic osmolyte) scarcely changes with salinity (Kasschau *et al.*, 1984a). In *M.senile* the ecological relevance of such strong volume regulatory ability is enigmatic. The population of *B.cavernata* from Port Aransas (Benson-Rodenbough and Ellington, 1982) relies more heavily on FAA as intracellular osmolytes than does that from Galveston at any given acclimation salinity (Figure 4.5), but it is unknown whether this reflects a physiological–racial difference related to the natural salinity regimes these populations experience, or the effects of the season at which the anemones were collected (see below).

Anthopleura xanthogrammica, *Condylactis gigantea* and *Metridium senile* typically occupy habitats experiencing full-strength seawater most of the time. *Actinia equina*, *Bunodosoma cavernata* and *Haliplanella lineata* are euryhaline but most often are found in relatively high-salinity water, whereas *Diadumene leucolena* commonly inhabits the upper reaches of estuaries. Despite the limited data available, ecological and possibly taxonomic trends are evident in the concentration and composition of FAA pools in these species (Table 4.2), as discussed in the following paragraphs.

Among the Mesomyaria, the sulfonic amino acid, taurine, is most concentrated in *Metridium senile* (see also Severin, Boldyrev and Lebedev, 1972), and is likewise a major constituent of the FAA pool in *Haliplanella lineata*. Both of these species routinely experience higher salinity than does the estuarine *Diadumene leucolena*, where there is far less reliance on taurine, with most of the FAA pool consisting of glycine and glutamate. Glycine is also a major constituent of the pool in *H.lineata*. Examination of the FAA pools in 'dwarf races' of *Metridium* from brackish water (Stephenson, 1935) might clarify the taxonomic and the environmentally induced aspects of these relationships. β-alanine is absent or present only in trace amounts in mesomyarian anemones.

In the Actiniidae, the stenohaline marine species *Anthopleura xanthogrammica* and *Condylactis gigantea* have exceptionally concentrated FAA pools, most of which is taurine. Taurine is less important in the more euryhaline *Bunodosoma cavernata*, and all but absent from *A.equina*. The exceptionally low FAA concentration reported in the euryhaline *Actinia equina*, which inhabits estuaries and also experiences drastic short-term reductions in salinity due to freshwater runoff in its intertidal habitat (Braber and Borghouts, 1977; Manuel, 1988), is almost certainly in error, as ten times the reported concentration seems more likely. The data for *A.equina* are for sphincter muscle only and may be peculiar to that tissue; tissue-specific differences in FAA composition have been reported in *B.cavernata* (i.e. a very high glycine concentration in the ripe gonads of males: Kasschau and McCommas, 1982). In actiniids β-alanine comprises about 10% of the FAA pool.

These trends may be interpreted as follows. Taurine is relatively inactive metabolically, and both its anabolism and catabolism are slow (Bishop, Ellis and Burcham, 1983). It would therefore seem most useful under stable high salinity conditions, especially because it is a 'compatible solute', being less perturbing to enzyme function than are inorganic salts and basic amino acids (Hochachka and Somero, 1984). The stable high salinities experienced by *A.xanthogrammica*, *C.gigantea* and *M.senile* populations may thus have selected for a very high concentration of organic osmolytes (predominantly taurine) to replace potentially perturbing inorganic salts. In species subjected to short-term fluctuations in salinity (*D.leucolena*, *H.lineata* and *A.equina*), there is a greater reliance on glycine and alanine (both compatible solutes) and on glutamate. Glycine is readily decarboxylated by cnidarians, with the remainder of the molecule going into the one-carbon pool for biosynthesis of osmotically inactive molecules (Shick, 1973). Alanine and glutamate are related by transamination and are readily catabolized or accumulated. β-alanine, another compatible solute, seems largely restricted to the actiniids,

Table 4.2 Free amino acid composition (percentage of total FAA concentration) in various species of sea anemones acclimated to similar salinities in the laboratory. Sources of data:
Actinia equina (sphincter muscle only) from Carlyle (1974);
Anthopleura xanthogrammica from Male and Storey (1983);
Bunodosoma cavernata from Kasschau *et al.* (1984a);
Condylactis gigantea from Herrera *et al.* (1989);
Diadumene leucolena from Pierce and Minasian (1974);
Haliplanella lineata from Shick (1976);
Metridium senile from Deaton and Hoffmann (1988).
Tr = trace; – = no data.

Amino acid	*A.equina* (≈30‰S)	*A.xanthogrammica* (33‰S)	*B.cavernata* (36‰S)	*C.gigantea* (35.5‰S) (tentacles)	*C.gigantea* (35.5‰S) (column wall)	*D.leucolena* (31‰S)	*H.lineata* (30‰S)	*M.senile* (33‰S)
Cysteic acid	1.1	–	–	–	–	–	–	–
Taurine	0.7	92.6	54.5	88.6	77.0	7	64.1	83.2
Aspartic acid	0.3	0.2	6.3	0.9	1.1	–	1.4	1.1
Hydroxyproline	0.5	0.3	–	–	–	–	–	–
Threonine	6.6	0.3	1.6	0.5	1.2	–	<0.1	–
Serine	5.2	0.3	3.5	0.8	1.6	–	0.9	0.5
Asparagine	2.1	–	–	–	–	–	–	–
Glutamic acid	22.2	0.7	7.4	2.1	3.6	Glu + Gln 26	4.2	3.7
Glutamine	0.2	<0.1	–	–	–		–	–
Proline	0.6	0.2	–	–	–	–	3.4	–
α-amino-butyric acid	0.8[a]	–	–	–	–	–	0.4	–

Glycine	5.3	1.4	7.1	0.9	1.3	61	20	5.2
Alanine	4.3	0.8	4.5	0.7	1.9	6	1.1	4
Citrulline	0.2	–	–	–	–	–	0.2	–
Valine	1.2	0.3	–	0.7	1.2	–	<0.1	1.2
Cysteine	0.5	0.2	–	–	–	–	0.8	–
Cystine	5.2	–	–	<0.1	0.2	–	–	–
Methionine	1.8	<0.1	–	0.3	0.3	–	0.1	–
Isoleucine	Tr	0.1	0.6	0.5	1.0	–	0.1	–
Leucine	1.4	<0.1	1.9	0.8	1.5	–	0.2	–
Tyrosine	2.4	0.2	2.6	0.6	1.5	–	0.7	–
Phenylalanine	2.1	0.1	0.9	0.3	0.9	–	0.2	–
β-alanine	10.1	–	9.1	–	–	Tr	–	–
Ornithine	1.2	<0.1	–	–	–	–	–	–
Lysine	3.8	0.2	–	1.1	2.6	–	1.7	–
Histidine	1.5	<0.1	–	0.4	0.8	–	0.4	–
Arginine	1.7	0.6	–	0.6	2.2	–	0.2	1.2
Total [FAA]								
μmol/g wet weight	7.2	108	31.5	114.3	65.3	85.7	63.6	101.2
μmol/g dry weight	37.9[b]	540[c]	154.4	632	376.4	410	276.5	444
% of total osmotic concentration								
of tissue water	1[b]	14[c]	3.8	13.4	7.6	12.2	9.4	13.8
% of total osmotic concentration								
of intracellular water	–	–	–	25.3	16.2	–	–	–

a: includes α-amino-isobutyric acid

b: assuming 81% tissue water content

c: assuming 80% tissue water content

where it is particularly important at high salinity, increasing from 1% to 22% of the FAA pool in *B.cavernata* over the range from 26‰ to 40‰S.

In such comparisons the range of intraspecific variation must be considered. In *B.cavernata* there is a large seasonal and sexual difference in the concentration of glycine, which reaches 207 µmol/g $_d$W in ripe testes and accounts for 56% of the total FAA pool there (39% of the pool in the whole anemone) (Kasschau and McCommas, 1982). Glycine concentration scarcely varies in females and unripe individuals of indeterminate sex, where it accounts for 6–7% of the FAA pool (Table 4.2). The role of such high concentrations of glycine in male gonads is unknown, but these authors suggest that it may serve as a feeding activator in females, causing ingestion of sperm and thus enhancing fertilization of eggs in their coelenterons (see Clark and Dewel, 1974). The role of other osmotically active nitrogenous compounds has not been studied. A quaternary ammonium base, homarine, is found in *A.equina, Anemonia viridis, Calliactis parasitica* and *M.senile*, and in the first of these reaches a concentration of 10 µ mol/g $_d$W (Mathias, Ross and Schachter, 1960), comparable to many free amino acids. It is unknown whether homarine serves these anemones as an antifoulant, as in some gorgonians (Targett *et al.*, 1983).

The time course of cellular volume regulation following a change in salinity has been studied in *H.lineata* and *B.cavernata*. In the former, tissue hydration initially increases upon transfer of the anemone from 30‰ to 12‰S, and stabilizes by 16 h after transfer, with an associated 40% reduction in FAA concentration (Figure 4.6, top). This time course parallels that for contraction, secretion of mucus and re-expansion (Shick, 1976). The long-term adjustment of cellular volume (by 344 h) involves a further reduction of the FAA concentration (Figure 4.6, top). Salinities below about 12‰S are ultimately lethal to *H.lineata* and produce a sharp increase in tissue hydration (Figure 4.3) and decrease in volume regulatory ability (Figure 4.4) associated with the loss of ability to regulate the FAA pool (Shick, 1976).

When *B.cavernata* is subjected to a decrease in salinity, tissue hydration shows a brief overshoot and then stabilizes by four days after transfer; the concentration of β-alanine decreases and stabilizes during the same period (Figure 4.6, centre and bottom). Conversely, after an increase in salinity cellular volume regulation takes longer and is associated with a slower accumulation of FAA. As in other marine invertebrates, the longer time required for cellular volume regulation following an increase in salinity compared with a decrease reflects the greater time necessary to synthesize or accumulate FAA, as opposed to that needed to oxidize or excrete them.

Mechanisms of reducing intracellular concentrations of FAA at low salinity include increasing the permeability of the cell membrane to them and so increasing their efflux, and increasing the rate of their oxidation. The latter apparently is stimulated early in *C.gigantea* during exposure to reduced

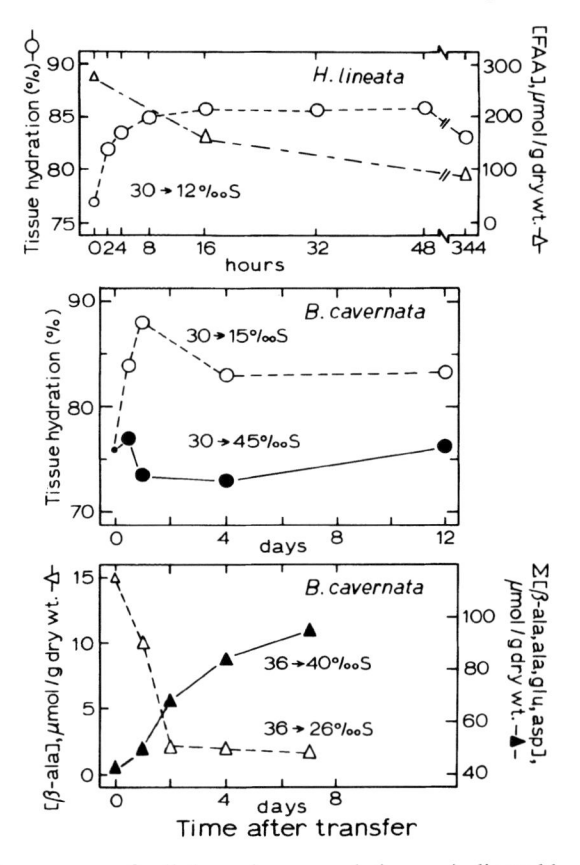

Figure 4.6 Time course of cellular volume regulation, as indicated by stabilization of tissue hydration and FAA concentration, following changes in salinity. Open symbols represent responses to decreased salinity; closed symbols represent responses to increased salinity. ○,●: tissue hydration. △,▲: FAA concentration. Source: modified from Shick (1976) for *Haliplanella lineata*; Benson-Rodenbough and Ellington (1982) for tissue hydration in *Bunodosoma cavernata*; Kasschau *et al.* (1984a) for FAA concentration in *B.cavernata*.

salinity, for the rate of oxygen consumption by tissues of this anemone increases during 6 h of hypo-osmotic stress (Herrera *et al.*, 1989).

Kasschau *et al.* (1984b) have studied the mechanism of β-alanine accumulation in *B.cavernata* at high salinity. Although salinity did not affect the rate of β-alanine synthesis via catabolism of uracil, there was a threefold increase in the rate of β-alanine production from the α-decarboxylation of aspartate. Accumulation of β-alanine at the expense of aspartate makes sense in light of the destabilizing effects of the latter on protein structure (Hochachka and Somero, 1984). The accumulation of β-alanine at high salinity was further enhanced by a threefold inhibition of its rate of catabolism.

In many metazoans the glutamate dehydrogenase reaction (section 4.2) may be the major site of ammonia incorporation into the *de novo* synthesis of amino acids. Male and Storey (1983) suggested that this enzyme, operating in the direction of glutamate synthesis, is important in the accumulation of FAA during hypersaline acclimation in *A. xanthogrammica*, especially because increasing concentrations of inorganic anions activate the reaction in this direction and inhibit the forward reaction (NH_4^+ formation). Although in osmoconforming bivalves a major role for GDH in FAA accumulation has been questioned because of the relatively low activity of this enzyme there, its activity is about ten times greater in *A. xanthogrammica* and its importance especially in euryhaline anemones bears investigation. Its suggested importance in *A. xanthogrammica* must be tempered by the fact that this anemone does not naturally experience such an elevated salinity as was used in the experiments (50‰S), and that even at this salinity, glutamate and alanine together account for <10%, while taurine still comprises 80%, of the total FAA concentration. Moreover, in *A. xanthogrammica* the affinity of GDH for ammonia is low, the half-saturation constant being 61 mM, or >50 times higher than the ammonia concentration in the tissues (section 4.2). In *B. cavernata* an elevation of tissue glutamate and alanine levels occurs also as a non-specific response to several organic and inorganic chemical stressors (Kasschau, Skaggs and Chen, 1980).

4.4 WATER BALANCE DURING AERIAL EXPOSURE

Perhaps because they are the preferred prey of subtidal predators such as sea stars and nudibranchs that are less tolerant of aerial exposure (section 7.4, page 308), actiniid sea anemones such as *Anthopleura elegantissima* in North America and *Actinia equina* in Europe are characteristically intertidal in distribution, reaching maximum densities at the mid-shore level. The sharp lower limit to the distribution of *A. elegantissima* is probably determined by predation (section 7.4), while the upper limit varies regionally and appears to be set by thermal and desiccative stresses (Dayton, 1971).

In Australia and New Zealand *Actinia tenebrosa* is likewise found in a definite zone at the mid-tide level. The distribution formed in a tidal tank corresponds to that in nature and involves vertical movements by the anemones, prolonged submergence initiating negative geotaxis and prolonged emersion eliciting positive geotaxis (Ottaway and Thomas, 1971). Downward movement likewise occurs in *Anthopleura* spp. under desiccating conditions (Sebens, 1982c). Clonal specimens of *A. elegantissima* living in aggregations (which decreases mortality during desiccative stress: Hart and Crowe, 1977;

Pineda and Escofet, 1989) are less likely to change locations than are non-aggregated clonal conspecifics (Pineda and Escofet, 1989). Selection of micro-habitat occurs in the smaller mesomyarian anemone, *Haliplanella lineata*, which tends to occupy the moist under surfaces of rocks in the high intertidal and the upper surfaces of rocks lower in the intertidal (Sassaman and Mangum, 1972).

Survival of adult *A.tenebrosa* in air ranges from 2.5 to 19.5 days, being related directly to relative humidity (*r.h.*) and inversely to temperature (Ottaway, 1973). Survival time in juveniles is much shorter and its relationship to temperature and *r.h.* is shown in Figure 4.7b. The saturation deficit or desiccation potential (the difference between the partial pressure of water vapour in air at saturation and the actual partial pressure of water vapour in a sample of air) increases with temperature at any relative humidity (Figure 4.7a). At temperatures below 25°C, the mean survival time contours are similar to those for saturation deficit, which indicates that desiccation is the major factor affecting survival. Above 25°C the survival contour is steep and nearly parallel to the *r.h.* axis, which suggests that thermal stress *per se*, rather than water loss, is the main cause of mortality at high temperature. This may be inferred also from the extent of dehydration reached at different temperatures and relative humidities. At temperatures below 25°C, juvenile *A.tenebrosa* have lost from about 25% to 70% (generally >40%) of their total

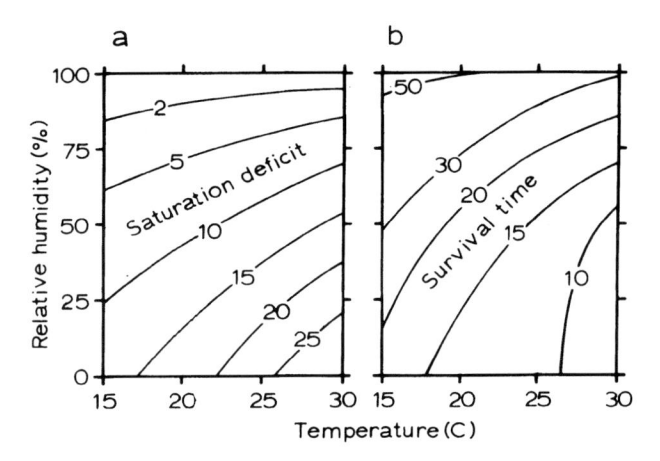

Figure 4.7 Contours showing the relationships to temperature and relative humidity of (a) water vapour saturation deficit in mmHg, and (b) survival time in hours of juvenile specimens of *Actinia tenebrosa*. The similarity of the profiles of saturation deficit and survival time at lower temperatures indicates that desiccation is the main factor limiting survival over that range, whereas the greater steepness of the survival time contour at high temperature indicates that thermal stress is the principal cause of mortality there. See text for discussion. Source: drawn from data in Ottaway (1973).

body water at the time of death (calculated from total water content of an average juvenile, absolute rates of water loss, and mean survival times given in Ottaway, 1973). At 25° and 30°C and *r.h.* >55%, only 5% to 11% of body water has been lost at the mean survival time, which suggests that death under these conditions is not due to dehydration. In the adults survival time at low temperature and high *r.h.* is very long, and death probably results from the accumulation of toxic wastes (Ottaway, 1973).

Because of the greater susceptibility of very small anemones to dehydration (largely owing to their very large surface area : mass ratio; see below), the intertidal distribution limits of *Actinia* spp. in nature may be set more by juvenile than by adult tolerance of desiccation (Ottaway, 1973; Griffiths, 1977b). The occupation of an intertidal refuge is probably selected for viviparous reproduction in *A.equina* and *A.tenebrosa*, where the young are brooded in the coelenteron up to the juvenile stage, which on release is capable of immediate attachment to the substrate and whose increased size reduces the rate of dehydration compared with that of a smaller embryo or planula.

An intertidal distribution requires mechanisms to conserve water. Actiniids and other intertidal anemones such as *Haliplanella lineata* respond to emersion at low *r.h.* by closing the mouth, thus trapping the coelenteric fluid; the tentacles are retracted and the marginal sphincter contracts so that the upper column closes over the oral disc and tentacles. The body assumes a squat cylindrical or hemispherical shape, presenting the minimum surface area for evaporation. Whereas intertidally-acclimatized specimens of *A. equina* become quiescent upon emersion, subtidally-acclimatized individuals become active and expel much of their coelenteric fluid when acutely exposed (Shick, 1981). This emphasizes that water conserving behaviour is an adaptive response to regular aerial exposure. At high *r.h.*, *A.equina* and *A.elegantissima* leave their oral discs expanded (Ottaway, 1973; Shick and Dykens, 1984), which facilitates aerobic respiration (and photosynthesis in *A.elegantissima*) when desiccation is not a threat.

The morphological correlates of water retention behaviour have been studied in two intertidal species (*Anthothoe chilensis* and *Phymactis clematis*) and one infralittoral species (*Antholoba achates*) by Stotz (1979). In the intertidal species the diameter of the oral disc approximates that of the column, which possesses a strong sphincter restricted to its upper portion. This allows for complete contraction of the upper portion of the column during aerial exposure, enabling water to be retained in the coelenteron. The parietobasilar and retractor muscles occur as compact bundles, thus providing better control of body shape during emersion. Similar musculature is present in *A.elegantissima* (Hand, 1955a). The highest-living species, *P.clematis*, has the thickest body wall. In the infralittoral species, however, the wide oral disc is scarcely covered by the column in contraction, and the musculature is more diffuse. During exposure this anemone either contracts totally, expelling most of the coelenteric fluid, or hangs flaccidly, losing water via the exposed oral disc. Similar findings were reported by Griffiths (1977b) for other littoral anemones.

In *A.tenebrosa*, *A.equina* and *P.clematis*, the coelenteric fluid reservoir is large, representing 50–83% of the anemones' live weight (Ottaway, 1973; Griffiths, 1977b; Stotz, 1979). Despite evaporation the ectodermal surface remains moist, water being replaced by exudation from the coelenteron through the body wall. The pathway of water movement (transcellular or paracellular) has not been determined. At temperatures of 23–25°C, a saturation deficit of 12.6 mmHg, and wind speed of $1 \, \text{m·s}^{-1}$, *A.equina* loses 3.2–4.0% of its initial weight per hour (Griffiths, 1977b). The rate of evaporation from the ectoderm of *A.tenebrosa* in still air increases with temperature at any *r.h.* <100% owing to an increase in the saturation deficit (see Figure 4.7a), but it is always less than $10 \, \text{mg} \, H_2O \cdot h^{-1} \cdot \text{cm}^{-2}$ (Ottaway, 1973). At 11°C and 80% *r.h.* in still air, adult specimens of *Anthopleura elegantissima* lost $14.7 \, \text{mg} \, H_2O \cdot h^{-1} \cdot \text{cm}^{-2}$ (Hart and Crowe, 1977). Although these data, unlike those of Ottaway, are not corrected for possible ejection of coelenteric fluid through the mouth, it appears that the column wall of *A.elegantissima* is more permeable to water than that of *A.tenebrosa* ($0.44–0.86 \, \text{mg} \, H_2O \cdot h^{-1} \cdot \text{cm}^{-2}$ at 15°C and 75–85% *r.h.*). The difference between the two species in their permeability to water may have a morphological basis, the verrucae on the column of *A.elegantissima* (see Figure 2.24, page 112). These thin-walled evaginations would offer less diffusional resistance than a uniformly thick column wall, and moreover, being filled with coelenteric fluid, would increase the volume of water in close proximity to the evaporative surface, effectively increasing the surface area : volume ratio. Also, cinclides perforating the column wall are absent from *Actinia* spp. but abundant in *Anthopleura elegantissima*, where they provide a direct route for water loss. Stotz (1979) speculates that the columnar vesicles of *P.clematis* (perhaps analogous with the verrucae) actually facilitate and regulate evaporative cooling.

In nature, however, verrucae do not always present a free surface for diffusion. At exposed sites, *A.elegantissima* attaches gravel and shell debris to its verrucae (Figure 2.24), which decreases the exposed ectodermal surface by 16% (Hart and Crowe, 1977). Furthermore, the gravel produces a boundary layer at the evaporative surface, which substantially reduces water loss below that calculated from a simple reduction in free surface area. This effect is pronounced at higher temperatures and wind speeds (Figure 4.8), conditions that promote evaporation by increasing the saturation deficit and reducing the thickness of the boundary layer in unprotected anemones. Hart and Crowe also demonstrated significantly enhanced survival in anemones with attached gravel compared with those lacking gravel during 6 h of aerial

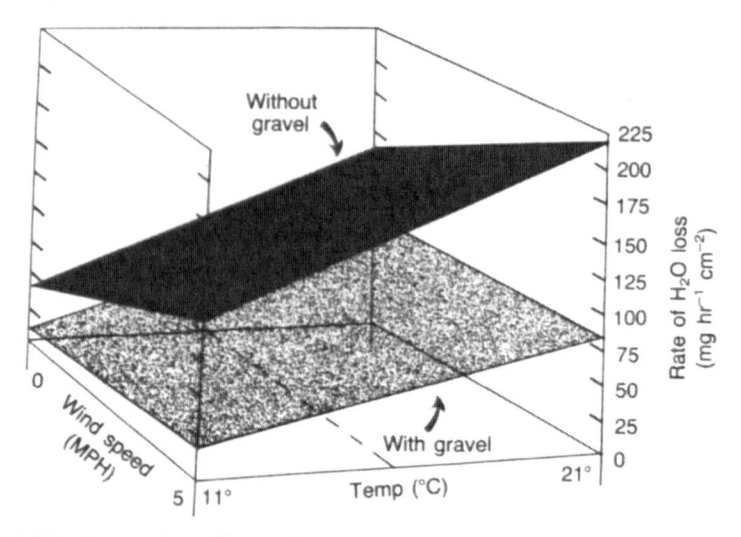

Figure 4.8 The interacting effects of temperature, wind speed and the attachment of gravel by anemones on the rate of evaporative water loss from *Anthopleura elegantissima*. Relative humidity in this laboratory experiment was held at 80%. Source: with permission from Hart and Crowe (1977).

exposure on the shore. When provided with gravel, high intertidal specimens of *A.elegantissima* attach more of it than low intertidal conspecifics that experience less desiccation stress (Dykens and Shick, 1984). As the body temperatures of dark green specimens of *A.elegantissima* may exceed that of ambient air, the attachment of reflective white gravel may also help maintain a lower body temperature without evaporative cooling and risk of potentially lethal dehydration (Dayton, 1971).

In the dense clones of *A.elegantissima*, aggregation presumably reduces both the free surface area and evaporation. Anemones living in aggregates show greater survival than solitary anemones following 6 h in air at the highest temperature and the highest wind speed (Hart and Crowe, 1977). A postulated role of mucus in resisting desiccation has not been tested. Fresh mucus presents little barrier to diffusion of water but it may produce a boundary layer as it dries and separates from the ectoderm (Griffiths, 1977b).

In high intertidal specimens of *A.elegantissima* the tissue water content (77.4% of $_wW$ ± 0.8 S.D.) is slightly greater than that in low intertidal individuals (76.9% ± 0.8 S.D.) (J.M. Shick and W.E. Zamer, unpublished data). Although this difference is small, it is consistent among field-fresh anemones in several collections over several years. A similar difference occurs in *Haliplanella lineata* acclimated to fluctuating immersion (76.7% tissue water) and constant immersion (75.6% tissue water) in the laboratory

(Johnson and Shick, 1977). The biological significance of this $\approx 1\%$ difference has not been demonstrated, but it would appear beneficial to anemones experiencing longer periods of exposure to increase their tissue water content as a hedge against desiccation.

In *A.elegantissima* the greater tissue water content in high shore individuals amounts to a difference of 167 mg H_2O in an average 1.75 g $_d W$ anemone compared with a low shore specimen of the same dry weight. Anemones of this size lose 450 mg $H_2O \cdot h^{-1}$ during aerial exposure under the least desiccating conditions (low temperature, still air, 80% *r.h.*, gravel attached: calculated from data in Hart and Crowe, 1977), so that a high shore individual would reach the same degree of tissue hydration as a low shore anemone in about 0.37 h. This is about 25% of the 1.5 h difference in aerial exposure experienced by these anemones at their respective shore heights (Zamer, 1986). Although the difference is slight, it may be relevant environmentally if repeated exposure to desiccating conditions has cumulative effects (Ottaway, 1973).

In *A.tenebrosa* the much greater tissue hydration of juvenile (91.6%) than adult (76.7%) anemones may likewise represent a buffer against dehydration in small individuals, which have greater relative rates of water loss. Higher water content may also have been selected for in intertidal populations of *H.lineata* (Maine), in which tissue hydration is approximately 5% greater than in a permanently sublittoral population (Virginia) at any acclimation salinity (Figure 4.3).

A last *caveat* is in order. The greater water content of *A.equina* at 18‰S in the field (85.8%) than in the laboratory (78.3%) (Ivleva, 1964) may be related to the better nutritional condition in the latter, perhaps reflecting a 'dilution' of the biomass in individuals receiving less food, similar to the situation in bathypelagic animals (Somero, Siebenaller and Hochachka, 1983). This reasoning might also apply to *A.elegantissima* high on the shore, but not to laboratory-maintained *H.lineata*, which received the same daily ration regardless of exposure conditions, and where differences in water content therefore arose from differences in aerial exposure (Johnson and Shick, 1977). The complications that such relationships pose for the measurement of growth will be discussed in the next chapter.

5 Growth

5.1 SYNOPSIS

Thus far eluding an exact and unqualified biological definition, 'growth' has nevertheless been extensively modelled by mathematicians and cyberneticists. Growth is best expressed as the change in an organism's energetic content with time, but in sea anemones this has been measured in only a few laboratory studies. Field studies have necessarily employed linear measurements, which can be converted to gravimetric and energetic units by using empirically derived allometric equations. Net growth efficiencies (K_2) in sea anemones in laboratory experiments may be very high, approximating the theoretical maximum based on costs of maintenance and work, which are very low in these sit-and-wait predators. In *Actinia equina*, K_2 is lower in newly released juveniles than in larger individuals, perhaps because of greater (unmeasured) production of cnidae or mucus in the former. In this species larger values of K_2 are associated with greater rates of growth. Growth rates in *A. equina* and *Anthopleura elegantissima* in the laboratory at $\approx 15°C$ are quite high, and when plotted against adult body weight, lie above those of most other ectotherms and on the regression line for mammals measured at 38°C. Maximization of growth rates in sea anemones has probably been selected for by size-dependent mortality, especially in intertidal species, where small individuals are far more susceptible to desiccation, predation and interference competition. In the field, *Actinia tenebrosa* and *Anthopleura xanthogrammica* require 5 to 10 years to reach maturity; this long delay in reproduction is counterbalanced by their very long lifespans (>50 years) and lack of reproductive senescence. Morphometric analyses suggest that in some sea anemones growth is allometric rather than isometric, probably in consequence of the laminar organization of these animals: body weight often scales as less than the third power of diameter for a geometric solid, and areal measurements frequently scale as a power of body weight greater than the 0.67 predicted from geometric similarity. Sea anemones are classic examples of organisms showing indeterminate growth, in which body size is not fixed genetically and is variable according to environmental factors that affect the balance of energy intake and maintenance costs. In *Metridium senile*, current is one such factor, and individual body size may be optimized to maximize prey capture in different flow regimes. Superimposed on the nutritional and biomechanical effects of current on body size is a possible genetic factor: among anemones in the same habitat with moderate water flow, more heterozygous individuals tend to be larger than less heterozygous individuals.

5.2 UNITS AND MEASUREMENT

Although growth of an organism involves a change in its size with time, the actual units of size employed have varied and have been largely a matter of convenience. Given the centrality of energy transformations in biology, a definition and mensuration which include the change in the energetic equivalent of body weight seem most generally useful. This is often impractical or impossible, however, as it necessitates both destroying the organism at the end of the growth period and making assumptions about the energetic equivalent of its body weight at the start of the growth period by comparison with a mean value for like-sized individuals. There is also a semantic problem that this energetic definition of growth includes 'storage', which is alternatively considered as 'a special form of growth' (Calow, 1981) or as the fate of absorbed materials 'for which there is no immediate metabolic demand, but which will be utilized later for metabolism, growth, defence or reproduction' (Pond, 1981).

5.2.1 Direct Measurements

The need to keep animals alive if they are to grow precludes direct determination of dry weights and energetic equivalents at the outset of growth measurements; by default some measurement of live weight is required. The accurate measurement of wet weight is difficult in sea anemones, which retain variable amounts of water in the coelenteron. Moreover, the degree of tissue hydration may change with time through ontogenetic and nutritional effects: Ivleva (1964) reported that juvenile specimens of *Actinia equina* newly released from their parents' coelenterons had a dry weight ($_dW$) of 21% of wet weight ($_wW$) but that the freshly collected adults had a $_dW$ of only 14% of $_wW$. Further, adults maintained on high rations during growth experiments increased their $_dW$ to 21% of $_wW$. It will be recalled that high shore anemones consistently have a higher tissue water content than low shore specimens (section 4.4, page 196). Wet weight thus seems a particularly inappropriate measurement in studies of growth in sea anemones.

Muscatine (1961) employed the useful 'reduced weight' technique of weighing anemones suspended in seawater, but the application of this to growth studies requires that there be no change in the specific gravity of the anemone tissues during the growth period. Testing this assumption involves weighing the anemone both in seawater and in distilled water, but very small changes in lipid content that demonstrably affect tissue energetic content and theoretically affect specific gravity are undetectable by this method (W.E. Zamer, unpublished data).

Linear measures (i.e. basal disc diameter, D) of growth have proved feasible in long-term field studies of *Actinia tenebrosa* (Ottaway, 1980) and *Anthopleura elegantissima* and *A.xanthogrammica* (Sebens, 1980, 1982a, b, 1983a) when measurements were taken frequently. Diameter may be less suitable for studies involving less frequent measurements of large individuals near their growth asymptote, where the mean increases in diameter of *A.xanthogrammica* are sometimes no greater than the range of repeated measurements of individuals over a period of days (Batchelder and Gonor, 1981), owing perhaps in part to seasonal negative growth (shrinkage) in this species.

5.2.2 Indirect Measurements

D is typically converted to $_dW$, ash free dry weight or organic weight $(_{af}W)$, or their energetic equivalents by using allometric equations relating D to the latter parameters, viz. $_dW = aD^b$. Such equations are determined empirically for individuals spanning a wide range of sizes. Although knowledge of these relationships can be very useful, it is risky to use a single equation to compare even conspecific anemones from different environmental or experimental circumstances. For example, Zamer (1986) has shown that $b = 1.91$ in freshly collected specimens of *A.elegantissima* from the high intertidal zone but that $b = 2.24$ in low shore conspecifics. Also, the value of a is greater in low shore anemones, so that for a given D, they have a greater $_dW$ than high shore anemones, which is probably related to the better nutritional conditions lower on the shore (see also section 2.2.1, page 37).

An indirect estimation of growth is the physiological 'scope for growth' (SFG), defined as the difference between the energetic value of ingested food and all uses and losses of it except for growth. It can be calculated from energetic values for ingestion, absorption, respiration, and excretion, all more easily measured than growth during short-term experiments. The error in the estimated SFG, however, will be compounded by the errors in each of the measured functions. SFG is limited to the particular experimental conditions imposed, and therefore it does not integrate the long-term effects of fluctuating prey availability, temperature, etc. that occur in nature. When SFG in *A.elegantissima* was estimated for a variety of environmentally relevant conditions of temperature and intertidal exposure, it showed reasonable agreement with growth measured directly under those conditions, allowing for realistic but unmeasured rates of mucus production (Zamer, 1986).

5.3 BIOCHEMICAL COMPOSITION AND ENERGETIC EQUIVALENTS OF BODY WEIGHT

The weight-specific energetic content of tissues can be determined directly as the enthalpy of their combustion in a bomb calorimeter, and indirectly from their proximate biochemical composition by applying specific enthalpy of combustion equivalents ($\Delta_c h$, $kJ \cdot g^{-1}$) for carbohydrate, lipid and protein. Proximate biochemical analysis has the advantage of providing additional qualitative information but is fraught with procedural difficulties, artifacts and inaccuracies, some understood, others not (see Hopkins *et al.*, 1984). These include the efficiency with which various components are extracted from the tissue, the inclusion of interfering substances and, especially in the case of protein, the particular analytical procedure chosen and the similarity of the protein composition of the sample to the pure protein standard (usually bovine serum albumin, BSA). Use of BSA as a standard in spectrophotometric analyses underestimates the protein content of anemone tissues because BSA has a higher weight-specific absorbance than does 'protein' extracted from anemones (Zamer, Shick and Tapley, 1989).

Thus it is not surprising that the few available data on the composition of sea anemones show large fractions of the total dry weight unaccounted for by protein, carbohydrate (or glycogen), lipid and ash (see data in Giese, 1966; Fitt and Pardy, 1981; Ortega *et al.*, 1988). Employing standard biochemical techniques (including use of protein extracted from anemones as the standard) and ashing analyses, Zamer *et al.* (1989) found the $_d W$ of laboratory maintained specimens of *A.elegantissima* to consist of the following: protein (66.6%), lipid (10.5%), carbohydrate (6.6%) and ash (7.7%), leaving 8.6% of $_d W$ unaccounted. A possible explanation is that glycoproteins, which are important components of mucus and also are bound to mesogleal collagen, which itself makes up 23% of the total protein in *Metridium senile* (Kirkpatrick and Bishop, 1973), comprise a large fraction of $_d W$ in sea anemones; depending on the extraction and analytical procedures used, these may not be cleaved into their protein and carbohydrate moieties and thus not accurately quantified, particularly as carbohydrate.

These and the foregoing uncertainties argue for more careful assessment and application of existing biochemical techniques (Hopkins *et al.*, 1984) or perhaps for an alternative approach. Elemental carbon, hydrogen and nitrogen (CHN) analysis, according to Gnaiger and Bitterlich (1984), is one alternative, and these authors have provided a stoichiometric method for calculating proximate biochemical composition from CHN content. Applying CHN analysis to the same individual anemones analysed by biochemical methods, Zamer *et al.* (1989) found a carbohydrate content of 15.6% of $_dW$ (16.9% of $_{af}W$), an increase from 6.6% that fully accounts for the 8.6% of $_dW$ unaccounted for by the biochemical method. Further, tissues of *A.elegantissima* from which lipid and carbohydrate nominally had been extracted to leave primarily protein contained only a trace of lipid (0.8%) and no carbohydrate when tested by biochemical methods; however, CHN analysis of this crude protein preparation revealed 83.5% protein and 13.6% carbohydrate fractions of its $_{af}W$ (residual water accounted for the remaining 2.9%). Again, this large amount of carbohydrate probably reflects the high glycoprotein content of sea anemones, especially *A.elegantissima* with its very thick collagenous mesoglea (see also section 1.2.2). Similarly, carbohydrate and protein each comprise 44.4% of $_{af}W$ of mucus from *Metridium senile* (Zamer *et al.*, 1989).

In tissues of *A.elegantissima*, protein appears to be highly conserved, showing smaller seasonal and experimental changes than lipid and carbohydrate (Fitt and Pardy, 1981; Zamer and Shick, 1989). Metabolic requirements for organic nitrogen are high in this species owing not only to dietary protein being a major respiratory substrate (Table 3.2, page 133), but also to its large mass fraction in mucus that is so copiously produced. In both high and low intertidal individuals a surplus of carbon is available for production, but in low intertidal anemones higher respiratory costs, and potentially greater mucus production associated with continuous feeding, result in severe nitrogen limitation (Zamer and Shick, 1989). During growth experiments, low shore anemones catabolized large amounts of carbohydrate reserves and stored less lipid than high intertidal specimens, conserving dietary and structural proteins when food was limiting. This in turn affected the energetic level of their tissues, and lowered their growth rate compared with high intertidal animals when food was plentiful (Zamer, 1986).

Considering the large numbers of marine invertebrates burnt on the altars of science, there are remarkably few data on the energetic content of sea anemones. Paine (in Sebens, 1982a) reports a bomb calorimetric value of $-22.7\,\mathrm{kJ\cdot(g_{af}}W)^{-1}$ for *A.xanthogrammica*, and Wacasey and Atkinson (1987) report a value of $-21.6\,\mathrm{kJ\cdot(g_{af}}W)^{-1}$ in *Halcampa arctica*. Applying $\Delta_c h$ values (Gnaiger and Bitterlich, 1984) to protein, lipid and carbohydrate levels determined by CHN analysis, Zamer and Shick (1989) found a mean tissue energy level of $-21.4\,\mathrm{kJ\cdot(g_{af}}W)^{-1}$ in *A.elegantissima* freshly collected from Bodega Harbor, California. In the better fed specimens from this population maintained in the laboratory and discussed above, the value was $-23.4\,kJ\cdot(g_{af}W)^{-1}$.

5.4 GROWTH EFFICIENCY

Growth efficiency is the efficiency with which ingested foodstuffs (I) are converted into consumer tissue (P), i.e. $(P/I) \times 100\%$. Because the efficiency of absorbing the ingested food is inversely related to ration (Figure 2.12, page 72), P/I (the gross growth efficiency, or K_1) will depend heavily on that relationship. A more restrictive quotient, P/A (K_2, the net growth efficiency), considers only the materials actually absorbed (A) and hence is more closely related to the inherent metabolic and thermodynamic efficiencies determining growth. Subsequent use of 'growth efficiency' in this chapter refers to K_2.

Calow (1977a) and Schroeder (1981) have calculated the maximum or best possible net growth efficiencies in heterotrophs by considering the efficiency of aerobic respiration (i.e. aerobic ATP generation), the ATP cost of synthesizing polymeric components of tissue from monomers absorbed and assimilated from food, and the cost of maintenance and work done by the consumer. These maximum values range from 80% (Calow, 1977a) to 88% (Schroeder, 1981), when expressed in energetic terms. The choice of units in which to express growth is more than just an exercise in the interconversion of matter and energy, for the particular units, gravimetric ($_dW$ or $_{af}W$) or energetic, may affect the perceived growth efficiency. This is because the major biochemical constituents of organisms do not have the same 'energetic density' (i.e. specific enthalpy of combustion, in $kJ\cdot g^{-1}$), and particularly because of the very high energetic density of lipid (see section 2.5). As noted by Schroeder (1981), the efficiency of lipid synthesis based on dry matter conversion from carbohydrate is only 31.5%, whereas in energetic terms the efficiency is 80%. This fact alone results in a lower net growth efficiency for lipid-enriched organisms when calculated in gravimetric rather than energetic units. Furthermore, if the energetic density of the predator is greater than that of the materials it absorbs from its prey, energy must be expended in chemical reduction, which lowers K_2. Conversely, when the energetic density of predator and prey are similar, K_2 (on both gravimetric and energetic bases) is higher.

Accordingly, K_2 in high shore specimens of *A. elegantissima* was 45.1% in gravimetric terms but 57.6% in energetic terms (Zamer, 1986). These anemones were fed adults of *Artemia salina*, which consisted of approximately 28% lipid per g_dW. It appears that the lipid fraction of the prey was used preferentially in growth or storage by the anemones, since their absorption efficiency for lipid was $>90\%$ and RQ and NQ measurements indicated that lipid accounted for only $\approx 2\%$ of their aerobic respiratory substrates (section 2.3.2, page 73, and Table 3.2, page 133). Consistent with this interpretation was the increase of the energetic density of these anemones from -21.2 to $-22.1\,kJ\cdot(g_{af}W)^{-1}$ during the 10-day growth period.

Attempts to explain the wide range of K_2 values in aquatic ectotherms have been numerous and the results conflicting. Conover (1978), following Welch (1968), discerned an inverse relationship between K_2 and absorption efficiency (A/I), where carnivores generally had high values of A/I and low values of K_2, while herbivores had low absorption efficiencies but high net growth efficiencies. This was interpreted to reflect the higher protein content (and hence high digestibility) of the food of carnivores, which supposedly expended a larger fraction of assimilated energy in activity to catch prey. Herbivores ate food that was less digestible but spent less energy in obtaining it. As sit-and-wait predators having very low costs of prey-capturing activity, sea anemones might deviate from this relationship and perhaps have both high absorption and high net growth efficiencies, an expectation that at first seems to be borne out. Unfortunately, the data used by Conover and by Welch were expressed in various gravimetric ($_dW$, W_C or W_N) and energetic units, which as we have seen can blur any relationship. Nevertheless, in Conover's plot of the data, a consumer having an absorption efficiency of 68% (the mean value for adult specimens of *Actinia equina*: Figure 2.12) would be expected to have a K_2 of $\approx 50\%$; the actual gravimetric K_2 for adult *A.equina* is 81% (Figure 5.1). Similarly, Conover's relationship between K_2 and A/I predicts a K_2 of $<10\%$ in a consumer having $A/I \approx 90\%$, the mean energetic absorption efficiency measured under field conditions in high intertidal specimens of *Anthopleura elegantissima* freshly collected from the shore; the actual energetic K_2 in these anemones is 38% (Zamer and Shick, 1989).

A more recent analysis by Schroeder (1981) using only energetic data shows no relationship between K_2 and A/I in aquatic ectotherms (including carnivores, herbivores, and detritivores). Since these data were chosen from studies employing energetic units exclusively, the variability probably arose from widely disparate laboratory protocols and treatments, including ration and food quality. For example, although the high locomotory costs of the predatory habit tend to 'push' K_2 down, might this be partially offset by the higher percentage of protein (including essential amino acids) and lipid in animal prey, which can be converted efficiently into predator biomass as new protein or lipid stores? (As argued earlier, a ration rich in protein carries with it an increased cost of the specific dynamic effect, but this has rarely been considered in intraspecific comparisons.) Conversely, although the generally lower activity cost of marine herbivores might push K_2 up as suggested, this could be offset by the lower quality of plant proteins absorbed, as well as by

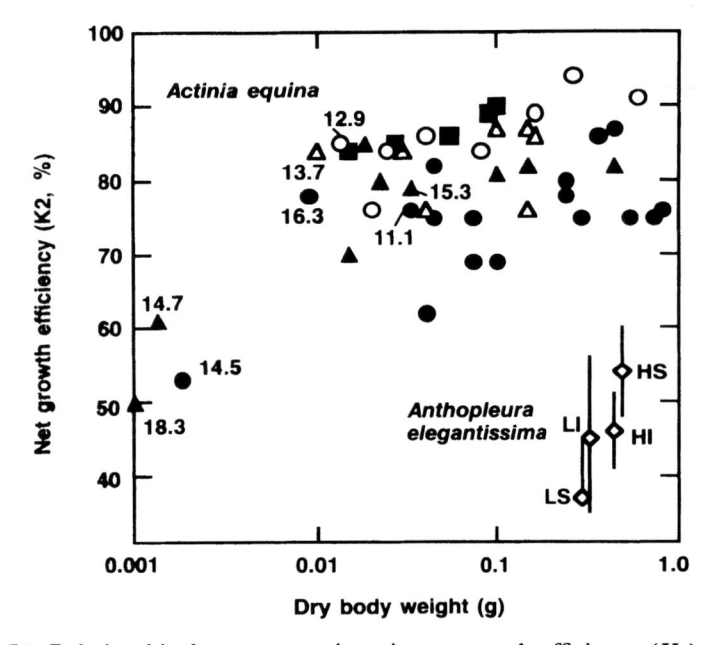

Figure 5.1 Relationship between gravimetric net growth efficiency (K_2) and body weight in *Actinia equina* from Sevastopol, USSR, and *Anthopleura elegantissima* from California, USA, under similar conditions of temperature and ration in laboratory experiments. For *A.equina*, mean daily ration was 5.2% of calculated anemone $_dW$ in individuals maintained at 13.8°C (■), 15.7°C (△), 18.7–19.9°C (○), 20–20.5°C (▲), and 21–22.7°C (●). Numbers associated with some data points represent daily rations >10% of $_dW$. In *A.elegantissima*, anemones from several clones of high shore and low shore origin were maintained under intertidal conditions (HI and LI, respectively) and received a daily ration of 4% of their estimated $_dW$, while high shore and low shore specimens from the same clones maintained at 15°C under subtidal conditions (HS and LS) received 5.6% of $_dW$. Vertical lines: ±95% confidence intervals. Source: drawn from data for *A.equina* in Ivleva (1964) and for *A.elegantissima* in Zamer (1986).

the relatively low level of lipid in the diet, which necessitates the added cost of reductive lipid synthesis from carbohydrate precursors. In short, such broad scale comparisons among trophic groups must contend with many factors other than the simple verbal dichotomy 'carnivore versus herbivore', and the lack of a clear relationship is not surprising.

Schroeder's analysis shows a large variability of K_2 even within each trophic group, which again may reflect differences in food quality, ration, etc., as well as genuine interspecific differences. With these caveats in mind, directly comparable gravimetric ($_dW$) data for K_2 in *Actinia equina* and *Anthopleura elegantissima* are shown in Figure 5.1. These experiments were conducted at similar temperatures (13.8–22.7°C in *A.equina*; 15°C in *A.elegantissima*), the anemones were of similar body size (mean weight $\approx 0.13\,\mathrm{g_d}W$ in *A.equina*; $0.3–0.5\,\mathrm{g_d}W$ in *A.elegantissima*), and both species received similar rations (mean value $\approx 5.2\%$ of body weight per day in adult *A.equina*; 4.0% and 5.6% of body weight per day, respectively, in 'intertidally' and 'subtidally' maintained specimens of *A.elegantissima*). Values of K_2 in *A.equina* approximate the theoretical maximum, probably owing both to the low cost of activity in the anemones and to their maintenance on a high quality, natural food (tissues of *Mytilus edulis*). The clearly higher values of K_2 in *A.equina* than in *A.elegantissima*, which occur despite the above similarities in their treatment, may arise from differences in prey quality, since *A.elegantissima* was fed adults of *Artemia salina*, hardly a natural prey item and one which may have less than an optimum protein composition for utilization by sea anemones.

With so few data available it is premature to speculate, but to the extent that the higher K_2 in *A.equina* is not due to more optimal diet, its higher conversion efficiency perhaps has been selected for as a result of poorer trophic conditions in its habitat. Calow (1977a) has noted that K_2 may increase with decreasing ration, inferring that it is due to a reduction in SDE; this has not been assessed in *A.equina*, in which respiration was measured only in starved individuals (Ivleva, 1964). It may also be relevant that unlike *A.elegantissima*, *A.equina* does not have algal endosymbionts to provide a nutritional supplement, which again would place a premium on a high efficiency of converting ingested food. (A possible contribution of the zooxanthellae to growth in *A.elegantissima* under experimental conditions was not measured but, if it occurred, would lower the stated K_2 values. The low irradiance used, $\approx 30\,\mu\mathrm{E\cdot m^{-2}\cdot s^{-1}}$, and the data in Figure 2.21c, suggest that any contribution would be slight.) A similar selection for high K_2 may also have occurred in high shore specimens of *A.elegantissima*, which experience poorer nutritional conditions and have higher conversion efficiencies than low intertidal specimens (Figure 5.1).

Unfortunately, neither Ivleva nor Zamer measured mucus production, which may be considerable in anemones and which if included would raise K_2. Assuming that the difference between measured growth and that calculated as scope for growth from the other terms in the balanced energy equation is an estimate of unmeasured mucus production, a $1\,\mathrm{g_d}W$ specimen of *A.elegantissima* produces $\approx 2\,\mathrm{mg_d}W$ of mucus per day (Zamer, 1986). Hunter (1984) estimated (by invoking the unaccounted energy in the balanced energy equation) that 50–80% of the energy assimilated by *Aiptasia pulchella* was used in mucus synthesis.

In *A.equina* there appears to be an ontogenetic or size effect on K_2, for the smallest juveniles have consistently lower net growth efficiencies than larger juveniles and adults spanning a range of $0.01–0.84\,\mathrm{g_d}W$ (Figure 5.1). This observation is potentially complicated by the inverse relationship between body size and ingested ration (Figure 2.5), which might necessitate a larger SDE and more mucus production (for use in digestion and egestion) as a percentage of the total energy budget in the smallest individuals and thus reduce their K_2. The limited data argue against such an interpretation, however: several individuals >0.01 g $_d W$ ingested disproportionally large rations for their size yet had K_2 values no different from similarly sized individuals ingesting much smaller rations (Figure 5.1). The lower K_2 (50–60%) in the smallest juveniles must therefore indicate some other cost. Juveniles of *Actinia* spp. freshly released from their parents are noticeably 'sticky', (Ottaway and Thomas, 1971), which perhaps enables their rapid and firm attachment to a suitable substrate when beginning their independent existence. This extra stickiness might reflect the utilization of more cnidae or production of greater amounts of mucus or other adhesive which was not taken into account in the growth study. Again, mucus and other secretions by marine invertebrates are rarely measured but they are frequently invoked as explanations for unbalanced energy budgets.

Finally, although temperature affects K_2 in *A.equina* (presumably by changing maintenance costs), there remains some unexplained variability in the data in Figure 5.1. The amount of variation in K_2 (which may arise from individual genetic differences in maintenance costs: Koehn and Shumway, 1982) that is due to genetic differences among individuals is unknown, and this is an active area of research (and speculation). In the data for *A.elegantissima* in Figure 5.1, some of the variability arises from different conditions of maintenance (intertidal versus subtidal), but there may be differences among clones of experimental anemones, although this possibility is complicated by differences in body size (cf. Zamer, 1986; and Zamer and Shick, 1989). Asexually reproducing sea anemones are valuable tools for assessing the effects of extrinsic factors on growth efficiencies without the complications of unknown genetic contributions: most of the variability reported in physiological and biochemical measures in sea anemones is due to differences among, rather than within, clones (Shick and Dowse, 1985).

5.5 GROWTH RATE

Growth rate is the product of the rate at which raw materials are supplied (itself the product of the rate of ingestion, I, times absorption efficiency) and the net conversion efficiency K_2. Since I, absorption efficiency and K_2 are not simultaneously maximized (Figure 2.12, page 72, and section 5.4 above), it follows that realized growth rates represent trade-offs among these variables, all of which appear to be matched so as to stabilize growth rate at the maximum over a range of conditions of food availability.

As pointed out by Calow and Townsend (1981), it is difficult to determine from experimental data whether growth rates are *maximized* or *optimized*. The maximization principle is generally invoked *a priori*, for it is reasonable to assume that reaching reproductive size as rapidly as possible maximizes fitness, and that rapid growth of offspring provides an 'escape in size' from predation and from physical environmental stresses. The extent to which sea anemones meet these expectations will be discussed below.

5.5.1 Laboratory Studies

The most extensive data on growth rates in sea anemones are those of Ivleva (1964) for *Actinia equina* (Figure 5.2). Although the individuals used covered a wide size range (Figure 5.1), ration was not controlled and the anemones were allowed to feed *ad lib*. Also, although a range of temperatures was used (Figure 5.1), the number of anemones at any given temperature was small, so all data have been pooled in Figure 5.2. Following Ivleva, data for newly-released juveniles are distinguished from those for larger individuals, for the reasons discussed in the previous section.

In both groups there is a tendency (highly significant in the case of the larger individuals) for growth rate to increase with K_2, i.e. higher growth

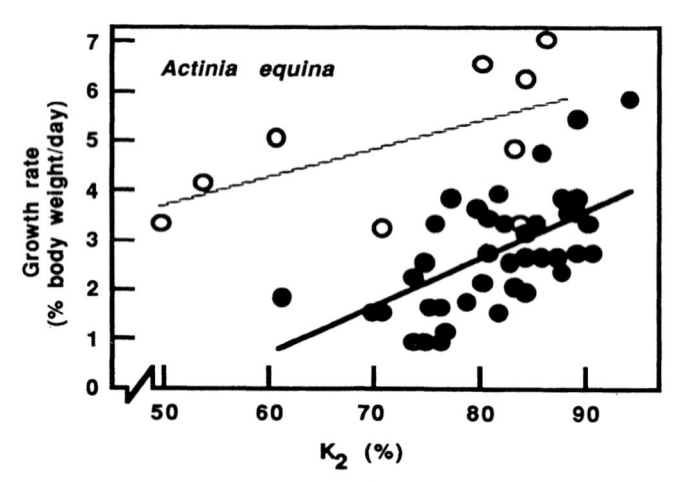

Figure 5.2 Relationship between gravimetric growth rate and net growth efficiency (K_2) in newly-released juveniles (○) and larger individuals (●) of *Actinia equina*. The relationship is not significant in the juveniles ($r = 0.550$, N = 9, $P > 0.10$) but is highly significant in the larger anemones ($r = 0.604$, N = 40, $P < 0.001$). Mean K_2 is significantly smaller in juvenile anemones (72.3% ± 4.7 S.E.) than in larger individuals (81.4% ± 1.1 S.E.) (Student's t for arcsin-transformed data = 2.671, df = 47, P = 0.01). Source: drawn and analysed from data in Ivleva (1964).

rates are associated with higher net conversion efficiencies. Overall, the juveniles show higher growth rates at any value of K_2, and have a lower mean K_2 (72%) than the larger anemones (81%). The achievement of faster growth rates despite lower net conversion efficiencies in the juveniles is due to their very large ingested rations (Figure 2.5, page 53), notwithstanding the lower absorption efficiencies that such large rations entail (Figure 2.12, page 72). Juvenile specimens of *A.equina* therefore seem to maximize growth rate by maximizing I. Larger individuals increase their growth rates to some extent by increasing K_2; in addition, much of the variability in growth rate at any given K_2 appears to arise from differences in I.

The mean and maximum growth rates (GR) of juvenile *A.equina* (3% and 7% of body weight per day) place them well above most invertebrates when the data are plotted as log GR $(g_wW.d^{-1})$ versus log adult body weight (g_wW) (Figure 5.3). The other invertebrate that achieves such a high growth rate (exceeding that of mammals at a temperature nearly 25°C higher) is an octopus, another sit-and-wait predator (at least when confined to an aquarium during growth experiments: in nature it is an active forager).

For juvenile *A.equina*, maximization of growth rate probably has been selected for by an extremely size-dependent mortality in the intertidal zone.

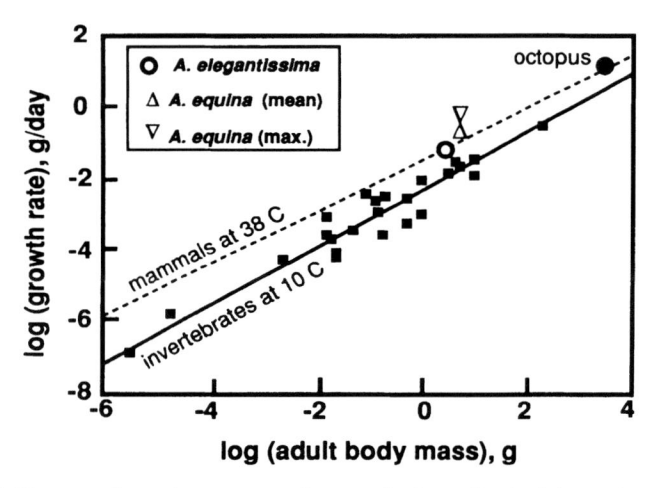

Figure 5.3 Mean and maximum growth rates in juvenile *Actinia equina*, and mean growth rates in *Anthopleura elegantissima*, as related to adult body $_wW$, compared with maximum growth rates in various consumers. With the exception of *A.elegantissima*, which received a daily ration of 1% of its $_wW$, all consumers received unrestricted rations. Temperature was ≈ 15°C in *A.equina* and *A.elegantissima*, but growth rates were adjusted to 10°C by assuming a Q_{10} of 2.0, as was done for the other invertebrates. See text for discussion. Source: anemone data from Ivleva (1964) and Zamer (1986); other data and figure modified after Calow and Townsend (1981).

Although there are no data for European *A. equina*, in the antipodal species *A. tenebrosa* up to a basal diameter of 15 mm there is a negative correlation between size and mortality (Ottaway, 1979b). Similarly, individuals of *Anthopleura* spp. have higher incidences of 'disappearance' when small than when large (Sebens, 1983a). Major causes of mortality in *A. tenebrosa* include desiccation during intertidal exposure (section 4.4, page 193), and interference (dislodgement) by grazing gastropods; predation by gastropods and intraspecific conflicts are lesser sources of mortality (Ottaway, 1979b). Whether susceptibility to predators is size-dependent in *Actinia* spp. is unknown, but the predatory nudibranch *Aeolidia papillosa* preys preferentially on small specimens of *Metridium senile* in the field (Harris, 1973) and is more attracted to small than to large individuals of this species in laboratory choice experiments (Stehouwer, 1952) (see also section 7.4.1, page 309). Thus rapid growth rate may also have been selected for to provide an escape in size from predation. In *Actinia* spp. rapid attainment of large size also may be favoured as a means to hold one's ground in intraspecific agonistic encounters, where larger individuals prevail (Brace and Pavey, 1978), and this is also the case in *Anthopleura xanthogrammica* (Sebens, 1984a). In addition, large specimens of *A. elegantissima* that occur low in the intertidal zone are less susceptible to burial by shifting sand than are smaller individuals (Pineda and Escofet, 1989).

For high shore specimens of *Anthopleura elegantissima* maintained under simulated intertidal conditions, including a daily ration of 1% of body weight (Zamer, 1986), plotting log GR versus log adult body weight likewise reveals a growth rate greater than for most invertebrates and on the regression line for mammals (Figure 5.3). As in *A. tenebrosa*, the intertidal habitat of *A. elegantissima* provides a refuge from predation by subtidal molluscs and sea stars (Mauzey, Birkeland and Dayton, 1968; Sebens, 1983a; section 7.4.2, page 314), so maximization of growth rate in the latter species may be more related to minimization of desiccation by rapidly achieving large size and small surface : volume ratio. Also, it may benefit an individual to grow quickly to avoid being screened from catching prey in dense aggregations.

Other laboratory studies have measured growth rates as increases in diameter of the basal disc or column. The actiniid *Urticina crassicornis* showed a prolonged period of exponential growth, with no sign of approaching a plateau even when well fed during 18 months in the laboratory (Figure 5.4). Individuals had not become reproductively mature at 4 cm diameter (Chia and Spaulding, 1972), so that in this long-lived subtidal species maximizing fitness seems to involve 'growing for longer' rather than growing faster (see Calow, 1977b), its maximum size being about 20 cm in diameter.

Although mean individual size varies among populations of *Metridium senile*, anemone growth rates (as increases in basal diameter) in the laboratory

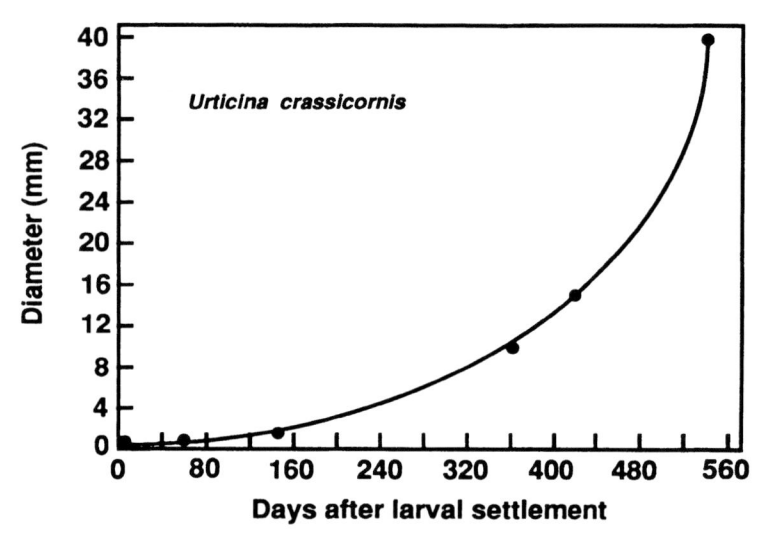

Figure 5.4 Growth of juvenile *Urticina crassicornis* in laboratory culture at ≈12°C. Source: drawn from data in Chia and Spaulding (1972).

are the same for the several populations, 0.05 to 0.08 cm·d^{-1} (Bucklin, 1985). Not surprisingly, then, size alone is a poor predictor of maximum growth rate, especially in this morphologically plastic species (see section 5.8). Growth rates in the laboratory are usually greater than those measured in the field, owing to the better nutritional conditions in the former (Bucklin, 1987a, b).

In sub-tropical and tropical forms such as *Aiptasia* spp. in laboratory culture, growth and sexual maturation occur much more rapidly than is the case with cool-temperate actiniids. Whether this difference is related to taxonomy (acontiate anemones versus actiniids) or biogeography (temperate versus tropical) is unknown. There appear to be no data on rates of growth or maturation of tropical species in their natural habitats.

5.5.2 Field Studies

Growth rates of anemones in the field are consistently lower than in the laboratory, a manifestation of a host of suboptimal factors (thermal variability, desiccative and osmotic stresses, variable availability of food, competition, etc.) occurring in nature, where growth is strongly habitat-dependent. The individual and interacting effects of these factors are considered in section 5.8.

The most extensive field data are those of Ottaway (1980) for *Actinia tenebrosa* and those of Sebens (1982c, 1983a) on *Anthopleura elegantissima* and

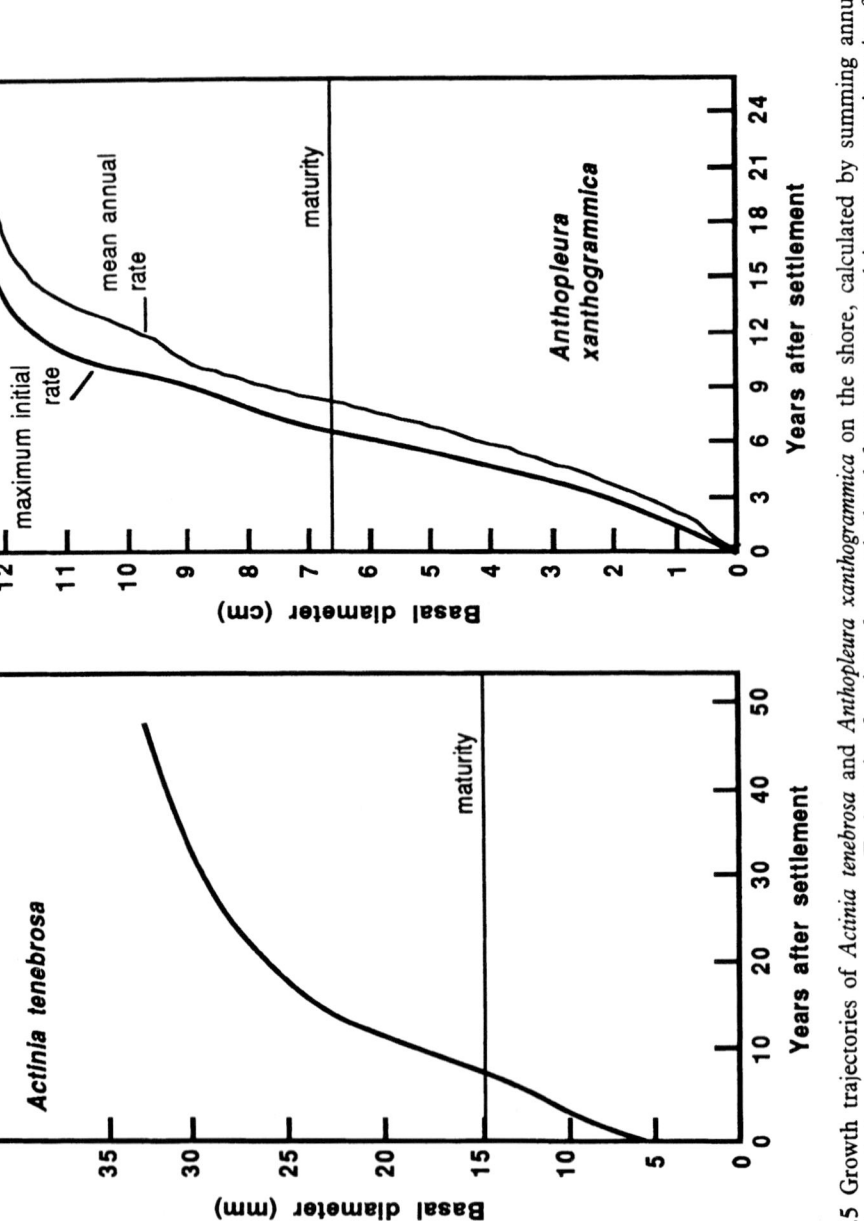

Figure 5.5 Growth trajectories of *Actinia tenebrosa* and *Anthopleura xanthogrammica* on the shore, calculated by summing annual measured growth increments over *n* years. Trajectories for *A.tenebrosa* calculated from mean annual increments; trajectories for *A.xanthogrammica* calculated both from mean annual increments of all individuals, and from maximum initial rate of juveniles and mean rate of adults > 6.5 cm diameter. Source: drawn from data on *A.tenebrosa* in Ottaway (1980); curves for *A.xanthogrammica* after Sebens

A.xanthogrammica. Absolute annual rates of growth (given as changes in basal diameter) are much greater in the larger *A.xanthogrammica* (maximum diameter >25 cm in ideal habitats) than in the smaller *A.tenebrosa* and *A.elegantissima* (maximum diameters of ≈4 and 5 cm, respectively), but relative growth rates are similar, ranging from approximately 100% per year in the smallest individuals of all species to ≈0% in the largest specimens. After following large numbers of individuals of a wide size range, Ottaway and Sebens used an iterative method to plot growth trajectories by summing mean growth increments for each size class over *n* years (Figure 5.5a, b). This method produces an accurate description of actual growth in each population but requires a large data set.

Sebens (1983a) also applied the Ford-Walford graphical method for fitting his data on *A.xanthogrammica* to the familiar von Bertalanffy growth model,

$$D_t = D_\infty(1 - e^{-kt}),$$

where D_t is diameter at time t and k is a constant. The method (see Sebens, 1983a, for its assumptions and limitations) involves plotting D_t against size one year later (D_{t+1}). The intersection of the regression line through all such points with the line of zero growth $(D_t = D_{t+1})$ estimates D_∞, the asymptotic or theoretical maximum size in a particular habitat. Since the slope of the regression estimates e^{-k}, the equation can be used to calculate the size at any time, or the length of time required to reach a given size, e.g. that of first sexual maturation.

Both the iterative (Figure 5.5b) and Ford–Walford methods predict that *A.xanthogrammica* at various sites reaches sexual maturity by ≈5 to 8 years after settlement (Sebens, 1983a). D_∞ varies according to local conditions, and the time required to achieve this size is ≥20 years. *A.tenebrosa* reaches sexual maturity $(D = 15$ mm) in 8.4 (Figure 5.5a; and Ottaway, 1980) to 10.8 years (calculated from the von Bertalanffy equation). D_∞ in the population studied as predicted from the Ford–Walford plot (Figure 5.6) is 35.3 mm; the largest individual observed in that population was ≈33 mm in diameter. Based on the average annual growth increments, *A.tenebrosa* requires 65.5 years to reach this size; individuals growing continuously at the maximum observed rate would reach it in 8.3 years (Ottaway, 1980), although it is unlikely that many, if any, individuals could sustain maximum rates indefinitely in nature. Also, using *mean* growth increments for *all* size classes may overestimate the time required to reach a fixed size, since mortality is so heavily concentrated in the smallest individuals (75% mortality within 4 months after release from the parents: Ottaway, 1980), in which there may therefore be selection for higher than average growth rates. That is, successful large anemones in the population probably are those that grew fastest as juveniles. Growth trajectories of *A.xanthogrammica* using the maximum

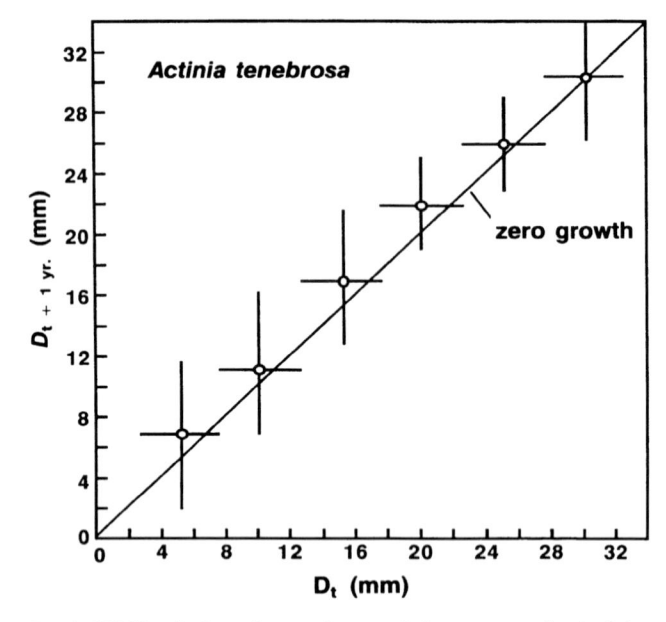

Figure 5.6 Ford–Walford plot of annual growth increments in *Actinia tenebrosa* (see text). Diagonal line is the zero-growth isocline. Data points represent the mean, and vertical and horizontal lines the ranges, of size classes (column diameter) and growth increments. Least-squares linear regression line for data intersects the zero-growth isocline at 35.3 mm diameter; maximum observed column diameter in this population was ≈33 mm. Source: drawn from data in Ottaway (1980).

growth rates of juveniles and mean rates of larger anemones are therefore slightly steeper than those using mean rates uniformly (Figure 5.5b).

How do these growth rates in the field compare with those in the laboratory? Unfortunately, laboratory measurements have not been made on *A.xanthogrammica* or *A.tenebrosa*. The closest available comparison is between Sebens' field data on *A.xanthogrammica* and those of Chia and Spaulding (1972) on *Urticina crassicornis* reared in culture. Both species have similarly large adult sizes. Whereas it required 18 months for the latter to reach $D = 4.0$ cm (Figure 5.4) in the laboratory, it would take at least 4 years for *A.xanthogrammica* to grow this large in nature. Much of the difference may be attributed to the regular feeding and constant temperature experienced by *U.crassicornis*, as opposed to the seasonality of prey availability and temperature in the field, which combine to halt growth of *Anthopleura* spp. during autumn and winter (section 5.8 and Figure 5.9).

Both *A.xanthogrammica* and *A.tenebrosa*, despite differences in their maximum sizes and modes of reproduction (the former produces planktotrophic larvae: Siebert, 1974; the latter broods its young for about one year: Ottaway, 1979a), require 5 to 10 years to reach sexual maturity (see Figure 5.5). The seemingly low fitness imposed by this long delay before reproduction is offset by the iteroparous reproduction of these anemones (section 6.3.5, page 244) which have estimated lifespans in nature of >50 (Ottaway, 1980) and >150 years (Sebens, 1983a) for individuals that survive to reach their growth asymptote. In very harsh habitats, mortality even among larger individuals of *A.tenebrosa* is size-dependent, being greater in specimens 10–15 mm D than in those >20 mm D, and minimum reproductive size is ≈20 mm (Ayre, 1984a). This suggests that maturation is delayed perhaps so that somatic growth can be maximized to enhance survivorship. The allocation of energy to reproduction will be considered in Chapter 6. In *A.xanthogrammica* the more rapid attainment of maximum size may be related to the inclusion of very large, energy rich items (mussels and echinoids) in its diet as it grows larger (Sebens, 1980), whereas *A.tenebrosa* remains predominantly plankti-vorous (Ayre, 1984b) in a nutritionally poorer, more physically stressful intertidal habitat.

5.6 DO SEA ANEMONES GROW ISOMETRICALLY OR ALLOMETRICALLY?

Data on the rates of growth in sea anemones tell us little about how they grow. The exponent b relating diameter to weight in the equation $_dW = aD^b$ may be used to infer whether growth is isometric (where all dimensions increase as in a geometric solid) or allometric (where some dimensions change disproportionally to others) (Figure 5.7). In an anemone growing isometrically b would be ≈3, for in a geometric solid, mass (or volume) increases as the cube of diameter. Although all metazoans show regional allometry, might this be pronounced in sea anemones due to their laminar architecture?

The data available indicate various degrees of allometric growth among different species of sea anemones. In *A.xanthogrammica* $b = 2.67$ and in *M.senile* $b = 2.78$ (Sebens, 1981a). The value of b in *A.elegantissima* ranges from 1.91 to 3.27 (Sebens, 1981a; Zamer, 1986). In *Aiptasia pallida* and *Aiptasia tagetes*, the total weight of protein is related to oral disc diameter to the powers 1.91 and 2.02, respectively (Smith, 1984). Clayton and Lasker (1985) found that in *A.pallida*, $_dW$ is proportional to oral disc diameter to the power of 1.45. As argued in section 3.8.1 (page 143), if growth occurs as increases in area with no increase in thickness, i.e. if surface area were directly proportional to volume or mass, b would be 2.0; individuals of *Aiptasia* spp. are particularly delicate and fit an allometric model. Values of b between 2 and 3 noted above for the other species indicate a less extreme

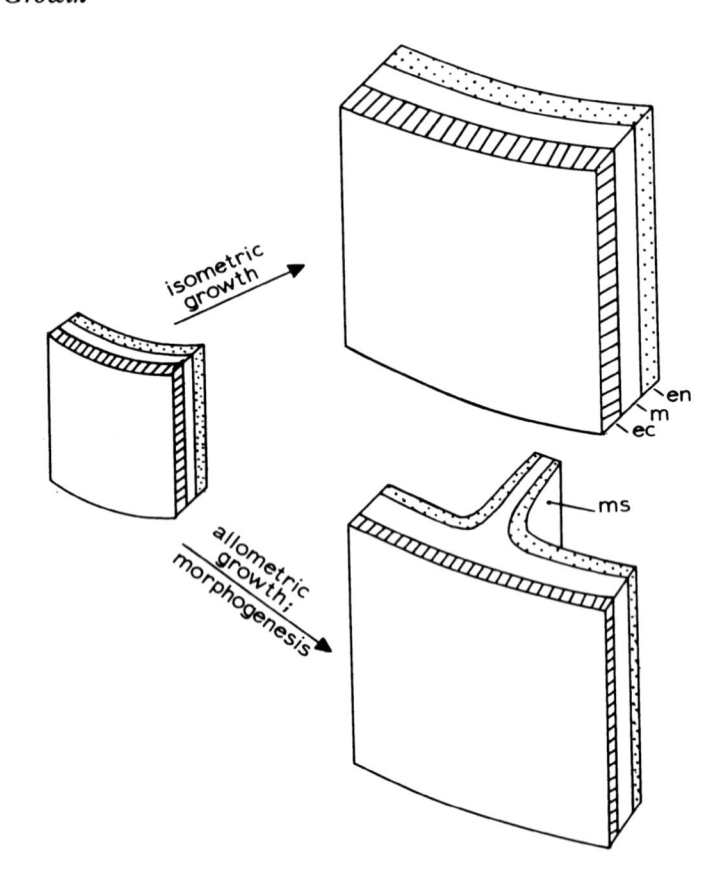

Figure 5.7 Models of growth in sea anemones pertaining to their laminar construction. In isometric growth, all linear dimensions increase at the same rate. In allometric growth, the diameter (and area) of the column increases more rapidly than its thickness. There appears to have been no explicit investigation of these relationships, although micrographs in sources cited by Shick *et al.* (1979a) and others suggest that column diameter increases more rapidly than does its wall thickness (i.e. growth is allometric), largely owing to a slower increase in the thickness of ectoderm (**ec**) and endoderm (**en**) relative to mesoglea (**m**). Rapid addition of mesoglea as column size increases may be necessary to provide reinforcement and resiliency to avoid kinking as the area of the body wall increases disproportionally to its thickness ($\propto$ mass). The morphogenetic addition of mesenteries (**ms**) as column area increases may act as battens and further reinforce the body wall. The linear and gravimetric relationships discussed in the text suggest a continuum of growth allometry in sea anemones: diaphanous forms such as *Aiptasia* spp., and *Haliplanella lineata*, tend toward allometric growth, *Metridium senile* is intermediate, and more massive forms such as *Anthopleura* spp. tend toward isometric growth. The consequences of these relationships in respiratory gas exchange are discussed in section 3.8.1.

condition of allometric growth in which thickness of the body wall increases less rapidly than column diameter.

Geometric similarity also predicts that surface area would scale as SA $\propto$ $_dW^{0.67}$, whereas if growth were purely two-dimensional, the exponent would be 1.0. Surface area of the tentacles, projected area of the tentacular crown, and total surface area of the oral disc and tentacles increase consistently to a power >0.67 (values range from 0.74 to 0.87) in *A.xanthogrammica*, *A.elegantissima* and *M.senile* (section 2.2.1, page 37). Similarly, tentacular surface area in *Haliplanella lineata* ($\equiv$ *H.luciae*) is proportional to $_wW^{1.1}$ (Zamer and Mangum, 1979). These values are consistently larger than 0.67 and support the idea of non-isometric (i.e. allometric) growth in these sea anemones. This bears on calculation of maximum and optimum sizes of anemones according to Sebens' energetic input–output model (section 5.7).

Depending on their environmental circumstances, sea anemones may be developmentally and morphologically plastic. While in high shore individuals of *A.elegantissima* prey capture surface area increases to a power of $_dW$ ($b = 0.82$) similar to low intertidal specimens ($b = 0.87$) (Zamer, 1986), for a given diameter high shore anemones weigh less (section 5.2.2). High shore anemones may be 'spreading themselves thin' to increase their apparent size, and especially their prey capture surface, in a habitat where less food is available per day.

5.7 INDETERMINATE GROWTH AND DETERMINANTS OF BODY SIZE: THE MODEL

The size attained by sea anemones varies according to conditions in the particular habitats that they occupy. Intrinsic causes of habitat-dependent size differences may include genetically determined differences among populations. These have long been suspected (Stephenson, 1935) and are now being investigated (Bucklin, 1985). Extrinsic (habitat) factors are numerous. Preferential predation on small individuals of *Metridium senile* by the nudibranch *Aeolidia papillosa*, for example, not only immediately affects the size and spatial structure of the anemone population (Harris, 1973, 1986) but among populations experiencing different predation pressures it may also select for differential rates of individual growth and asexual proliferation. In some fast current habitats, maximum size of individuals may be constrained by mechanical limitations of the anemone's body plan (Shick *et al.*, 1979b; Shick and Hoffmann, 1980; section 5.8 and Figure 5.10). Size-related differences in the availability and capture of prey, and in catabolic costs (Sebens, 1981a, 1982a, 1983a), which are affected by physical factors such as exposure and temperature, have been more thoroughly investigated.

The term 'indeterminate growth' refers to a capacity for pronounced size changes as environmental and nutritional conditions vary, and implies that maximum size is not genetically defined (Sebens, 1982a, 1987b). Whereas in many metazoans as size or age increases K_2 decreases, eventually reaching zero, (Calow, 1977a), no such relationship is seen in well-fed specimens of *Actinia equina* (Figure 5.1). Except during its initial growth, an anemone's size may therefore be independent of its age and more closely related to its nutritional history (Stephenson, 1928), especially in view of its potentially very long life span and apparent lack of senescence. Actual size, then, will represent the balance between energetic inputs and losses (rather than age) which, being sensitive to temperature, intertidal position, etc., will depend on habitat.

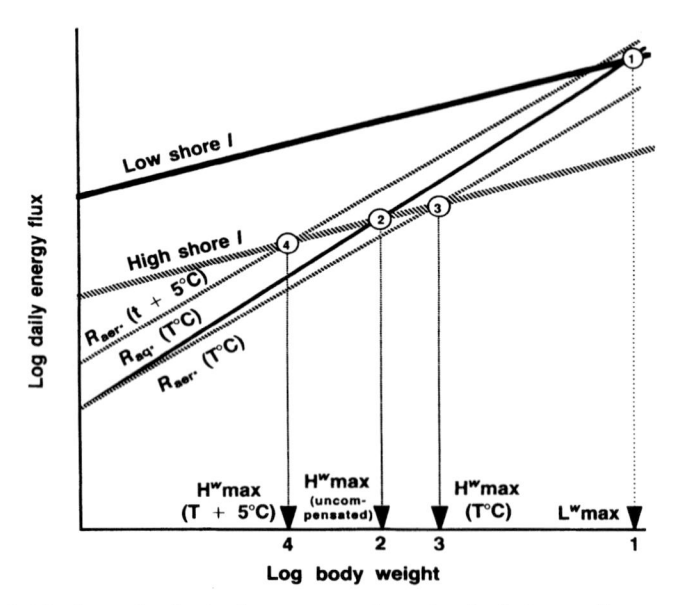

Figure 5.8 Maximum body size in anemones is set by the balance of energy intake (I) and respiratory cost (R). Owing to their longer time available for feeding, low shore anemones have a large maximum size, defined by the intersection of the lines for respiration in water (R_{aq}) and I (**1**). A lower I in high shore anemones accounts for their smaller maximum size (**2**), although this will be compensated somewhat by the shallower slope of the line for respiration in air (R_{aer}) at the same temperature (**3**). Conversely, if air temperature exceeds water temperature, R_{aer} but not I will increase and so decrease the maximum size of high shore anemones (**4**), although the low thermal sensitivity of routine metabolic rate will offset this to some extent. See text for discussion.

Historically, growth has been modelled as such a balance by Pütter, von Bertalanffy, Winberg and others. Most recently Sebens (1982a) has developed a model to analyse habitat-dependent body size in sea anemones. In several species of anemones food intake, I, is related to the area of their prey capture surfaces (section 2.2.1, page 38); this area in turn may or may not scale as the 0.67 power of body weight, depending on whether growth is isometric or allometric. Respiratory cost (routine metabolism, R) usually scales to a higher power of weight, 0.7 to 0.9 (Table 3.4), than does I. By plotting the lines for I and R (in energetic units) on a logarithmic scale it becomes obvious that body size can increase only up to some energetically determined maximum, W_{max}, beyond which R exceeds I (Figure 5.8). It is clear that factors affecting I or R will affect W_{max}.

Consider the case of a species having an extensive intertidal distribution. Individuals high on the shore are immersed for less time so their daily I is less than in low shore or sublittoral specimens. In the high intertidal anemones a reduction in daily I alone will reduce W_{max}. (This decrease may not be strictly proportional to emersion time, for Zamer, 1986, has shown that high shore individuals of *A.elegantissima* are more receptive to prey and capture more of it per hour of immersion than do low shore anemones, i.e. high shore anemones show some compensation for shore position in I.) There is also a compensation in energy expenditure, in that R is not constant but is lower during aerial exposure, being disproportionally reduced in larger anemones, so that the weight exponent of R decreases during exposure (Table 3.4, page 144, and Figure 3.4, page 147). Thus W_{max} of the high shore anemones is not reduced to the extent that it would be if the scaling of R were identical in air and seawater. Of course, the actual value of b for R is not that obtaining in air or in water, but an intermediate value that depends on the time spent in each medium. The intersections of the two R lines (R_{aq} and R_{aer}) with the I line define the extremes of W_{max} for intertidal anemones, and these values depend on the anemones' height on the shore.

The situation is complicated by thermal differences during immersion and aerial exposure. In a sit-and-wait predator, modest increases in temperature are more likely to affect R than I (although absorbed ration may be affected by a thermal effect on digestion or absorption, as in Table 2.2 (page 54), rather than on prey capture *per se*); the energetic savings afforded by a decrease in R due to aerial exposure and contraction of medium-to-large anemones (Figure 3.4c, page 147) will be partially offset by a temperature-dependent increase in R. In winter, a lower temperature during exposure might also accentuate the energetic disadvantage to intertidal anemones, if the thermal sensitivity of digestive enzymes is greater than that of R and especially if the digestive enzymes show inverse temperature acclimation, as seems to be the case in *M.senile* (Zamer *et al.*, 1987). Absorption efficiency may increase at low temperature (Table 2.2), but it is at the expense of a longer throughput time (perhaps associated with the lowered enzymic activities), and so daily absorbed ration may well decrease.

5.8 ENVIRONMENTAL EFFECTS ON GROWTH AND BODY SIZE: THE REALITY

How well do the body sizes of anemones on the shore fit this model, to what extent are they attributable to variations in energetic input and cost, and can intrinsic as well as extrinsic effects be discerned?

Regarding the first of these questions, in *A.xanthogrammica* the largest

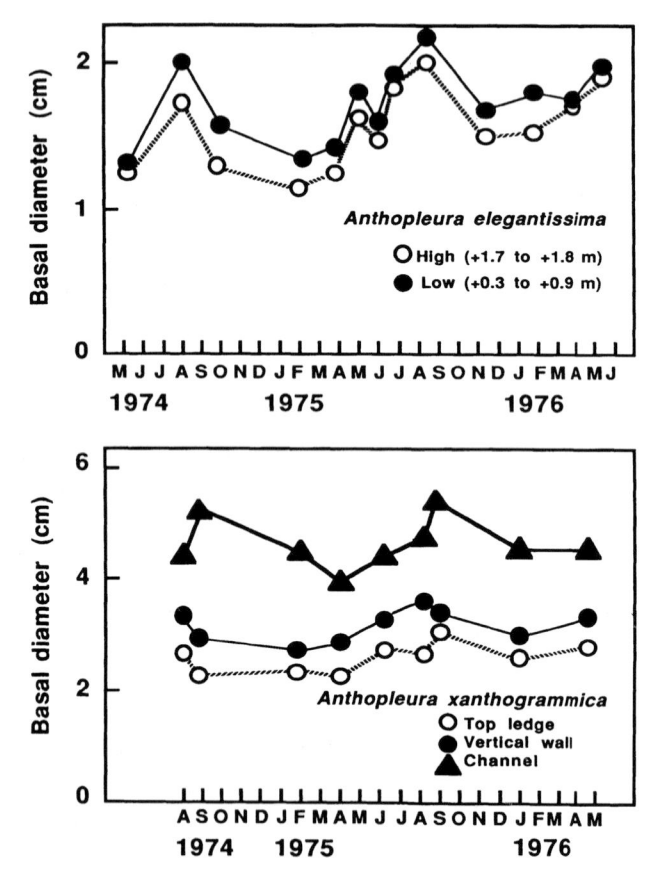

Figure 5.9 Effect of intertidal position on body size in *Anthopleura* spp. Source: after Sebens (1983a).

specimens are well below W_{max}. This is because, as predicted by Sebens' model, there is an *optimal* size W_{opt} below W_{max} at which the energetic surplus available for somatic and reproductive growth is maximal; that is, the anemone is optimizing rather than maximizing its final size so as to maximize reproductive output, an important component of its fitness. This aspect of the model will be treated in Chapter 6 (Figure 6.5, page 258). Still, for the same reasons as W_{max}, W_{opt} will vary among habitats.

The long-standing observation that the individual body sizes of sessile invertebrate species decrease with increasing shore height has been documented in *Anthopleura* spp. (Figure 5.9). There are no data on rates of prey capture or respiration in the various groups shown in this figure, so the relative contributions of these factors to final size are unknown. In the population of *A.elegantissima* on the breakwater at Bodega Harbor, California, individual size is often very large for this species, perhaps because the breakwater traps much debris which may provide a concentrated food source. At this site the intertidal size gradient is much less pronounced than in the populations studied by Sebens, and individuals collected at +1.3 to +1.5 m above mean lower low water are commonly as large as those living at 0 m (Zamer, 1986). This similarity in size probably involves compensation in prey capture by the high shore anemones, as mentioned in the preceding section, as well as a decrease in R during intertidal exposure in a habitat where air and seawater temperatures are similar for much of the year. Only small individuals are present very high (+1.8 m) on the shore, however, almost certainly owing to the great decrease in immersion and feeding time.

Relevant to the second question posed above, Sebens (1980) showed that body size decreased with increasing temperature, almost certainly because of thermal effects on R (section 3.8.7, page 168). This was done by examining individuals of *A.elegantissima* at a single intertidal height (so that immersion/ feeding time were the same), but in tidepools of different sizes (so that maximum water temperature at low tide varied among pools). His observations apply specifically to size, not to growth rate, and there are no field data pertaining exclusively to thermal effects on the latter.

In the laboratory, the optimum temperature for growth in *A.equina* appears to be 18.7–19.9°C, as growth rate declines above and below this range (Ivleva, 1964). As noted earlier, this seems to depend primarily on how much food the anemones will ingest when fed *ad lib.*, I also being maximum at 18.7–19.9°C (Table 2.2). In *Haliplanella lineata* (≡ *H.luciae*) maintained in laboratory culture, individual body size is inversely related to temperature (Johnson and Shick, 1977; Minasian, 1982). This relationship, however, is complicated by the fact that the frequency of asexual binary fission in this species is positively related to temperature, so that large body size results primarily from the inhibition of fission at lower temperatures. This caveat must also be applied to *A.elegantissima*, although Sebens (1983a) showed that the size at which division occurs is directly related to individual size at a particular site. In *H. lineata* individual body size is larger under fluctuating than constantly immersed conditions, although this again is due to an inhibition of fission by periodic exposure to air (Johnson and Shick, 1977; see also section 6.4.2, page 263). The environmental determinants and energetic consequences of asexual proliferation will be treated in Chapter 6.

In the field various physical and biotic factors vary with intertidal height, and discriminating among their effects on growth is complex. For example, at increasingly high shore levels, although decreased I (through less time for feeding) and increased R (an effect of higher temperature) will reduce the size of anemones, individual size may also be constrained mechanically by the damaging and deforming effects of waves and turbulence in the intertidal zone (Denny, Daniel and Koehl, 1985). Thus, irrespective of energetic limitations, intertidal anemones experience strong selective pressures to remain small, which has predisposed them to asexual fission, a form of growth that keeps individuals small but allows their aggregate biomass to be very large (section 6.4.2).

By studying mapped individuals on the shore for periods of several years, Ottaway (1980) and Sebens (1982b, 1983a) have shown that major size increases occur in spring and summer, and that decreases occur in late summer, autumn and winter in *Actinia tenebrosa*, *Anthopleura elegantissima* and *A. xanthogrammica*. Interpretation of these changes requires data on the seasonality of temperature, prey availability, sexual reproduction and (in *A. elegantissima*) asexual fission. In the spring the effects of increasing temperature are not distinguishable from those of increasing availability of planktonic prey, but considering the relatively small seawater temperature changes ($\approx 5°C$), thermal effects seem the less important. Superimposed on the effect of greater availability of prey is that of the sexual reproductive cycle. Some of the size increase in spring and summer may be due to the growth and maturation of gonads, which is consistent with the sharp decreases in size following spawning later in summer (Ottaway, 1979b, 1980; Sebens, 1981b), although emptying of the gonads would have relatively little effect on basal diameter. Continuing decrease in size in winter seems related to decrease in prey. In the planktivorous *A. elegantissima* this refers to the seasonal cycle of zooplankton abundance. In the macrophagous *A. xanthogrammica* the effect may be more indirect, for although its major prey, mussels, are continuously present, their availability to the anemones is dependent on their dislodgement by foraging sea stars, which are inactive in winter (Sebens, 1983a).

To the above factors must be added the complication of seasonal asexual fission in *A. elegantissima*, a process initiated by food deprivation (Sebens, 1980). Although some of the autumnal size decrease arises from individual anemones tearing themselves in half, size also declines in non-dividing specimens (Sebens, 1982b), associated not only with spawning but also with somatic shrinkage. As will be discussed in Chapter 6, asexual fission at a time when prey availability is decreasing is a mechanism to reduce individual body mass and hence energy requirement without falling below the size capable of capturing small prey (Sebens, 1979). These daughter individuals incur the cost of regenerative growth, which involves both internal reorganization (Sebens, 1983b) and cell proliferation (Singer, 1971). The timing of both asexual fission and sexual reproduction, however, produces regenerated and newly metamorphosed individuals of a size capable of taking advantage of the spring pulse of zooplankton and so of maximizing gonad production in the larger fission products and somatic growth in the juveniles.

Other factors affect the availability of prey to an individual. In *A.xanthogrammica*, for example, an anemone's chance of capturing dislodged mussels decreases with its distance from a mussel bed. The capture of mussels by some anemones makes them unavailable to others. This intraspecific competition is manifested in slower growth rates and smaller body sizes in more crowded habitats; removal experiments confirm that growth rate and body size increase when population density is lowered experimentally (Sebens, 1983a). If large individuals screen smaller anemones from falling mussels, selection may be operating to maximize growth rate and so to minimize time taken to reach a competitively successful size. Such conditions would also select against the development of asexual fission, which is not found in *A.xanthogrammica* nor in very large specimens of *A.elegantissima* low in the intertidal living under similar ecological circumstances (section 6.4.2).

Sessile sea anemones must rely on prey coming to them rather than vice-versa. Increases in water current speed therefore should increase the volume of seston-laden water cleared by an anemone and so increase I and W_{max} (but also R: section 3.7, page 137). This relationship has been elucidated in the planktivorous *Metridium senile* (Shick *et al.*, 1979b, and unpublished; Sebens, 1986), but it is more complex than originally thought. The former authors first noted an inverse rather than a direct relationship between current speed ($\propto$ prey availability: Robbins and Shick, 1980) and individual body size, but this was based on a simple division of the habitat into areas of low flow ($\leqslant 5\,cm \cdot s^{-1}$) and moderate flow (10 to $\approx 50\,cm \cdot s^{-1}$). A larger body size in the low flow area was interpreted as a means to provide vertical relief and so keep the feeding apparatus well above the substratum and out of the boundary layer (section 2.2.2, page 46), thus maximizing chances of encountering whatever prey was available. Although individual size was smaller in the moderate flow area (a seeming contradiction to the greater amount of prey impinging on the anemones per unit time there), there was significantly more asexual proliferation in that area. It appeared that individual body size was maximized in low-speed currents to provide the greatest individual height at the expense of vegetative reproduction, and that higher current speeds allowed smaller individual size with the greater food resources being put into clonal, not individual growth.

The interpretation of greater mean body size in the low-flow area is reasonable, but a finer resolution of current speeds and body sizes is desirable. Re-analysing the data for the moderate-flow area after subdividing it by $5\,\mathrm{cm\cdot s^{-1}}$ increments reveals that body size is not constant there, but increases in proportion to current speed up to $20\,\mathrm{cm\cdot s^{-1}}$, beyond which it declines (Figure 5.10). The net effect is a smaller (and highly variable) mean size in the moderate-flow anemones when considered as a whole than in the low-flow anemones. The increase in anemone size in currents from 10 to $20\,\mathrm{cm\cdot s^{-1}}$ almost certainly is due to the increasing encounters with and capture of prey. Reassuringly, over this range of current speeds the same relationship was seen in another population (Figure 5.10).

The decrease in size in currents above $20\,\mathrm{cm\cdot s^{-1}}$ may have multiple determinants, and it is not known whether it stems from adaptive growth, or from the reduction in I due to a biomechanically related decline in efficiency of prey capture by large anemones at high current speeds. The tentacular crown of *M.senile* deforms at high current speeds (Koehl, 1977b), which

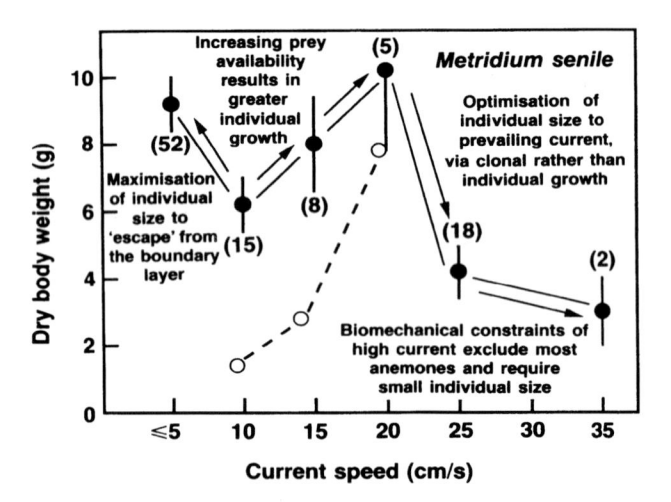

Figure 5.10 Interacting mechanical and nutritional effects of current speed on body size and clonal growth in *Metridium senile*. ●: *M.senile* at Blue Hill Falls, Maine. Numbers of anemones given in parentheses (large number of anemones at low current speeds $\leq 5\,\mathrm{cm\cdot s^{-1}}$ reflects larger area sampled, not asexual proliferation: see Shick *et al.*, 1979b). ○: *M.senile* at Nahant, Massachusetts; ash-free dry weights for these anemones were calculated from basal diameter using the relationship $_{af}W = 0.0073D^{2.78}$. Source: drawn from data in Shick *et al.* (1979b) for Maine population, and from data in Sebens (1984b, 1986) for Massachusetts population.

decreases its efficiency as a prey capture device. Also, although more encounters with prey will occur as current speed increases, captured prey may be dislodged before they can be ingested (section 2.2.2, page 46). The smaller body size above $20\,cm\cdot s^{-1}$ may therefore arise from a lower I despite a higher frequency of prey impacts. On the other hand, this smaller size may represent adaptive growth aimed at optimizing body size by matching it mechanically to the local current speed so as to maximize successful prey capture and I. If this is the case, energy surpluses could be put into gonad production, asexual propagules or both. The original finding of smaller mean size but greater asexual proliferation when all current speeds $\geqslant 10\,cm\cdot s^{-1}$ are considered supports the latter possibility.

At very high current speeds ($>50\,cm\cdot s^{-1}$) biomechanical constraints on individual size occur. Most specimens of *M. senile* (those $>1\,cm\,D$) cannot remain erect or maintain an expanded crown of tentacles in such flow. Yet *M. senile* occupies such flow regimes in nature, but only by being permanently small and avoiding the current mainstream by hiding among densely packed mussels (Shick and Hoffmann, 1980). Because this anemone can drastically alter its column height and hence potentially expose its tentacles to a range of very different current speeds (Figure 2.2, page 46), individual body size may be greater than predicted from its mechanical limitation by mainstream currents. That is, a moderately large individual may extend itself well into the mainstream when speeds are low to moderate, but retract nearer the substrate when speeds are high, perhaps maintaining the tentacles in the current speed that is optimal for interception and retention of prey. Indeed, H. Iken and L. Francis (personal communication) found that anemones fully extended their columns at current speeds up to $10\,cm\cdot s^{-1}$ in a flow tank, but shortened at speeds of 15 to $30\,cm\cdot s^{-1}$. Robbins (1980) showed a similar response by the tentacular crown of this species, a response that depended on the presence of planktonic prey: when none was available, the initial expansion was less and did not vary with current speed, suggesting that the degree of expansion was attuned more to prey capture than to current speed *per se*.

Regarding the final question (that of intrinsic effects on body size) posed at the beginning of this section, genetic differences may also contribute to differences in body size within a population, for more heterozygous individuals tend to be larger (Shick *et al.*, 1979b; Shick and Dowse, 1985). Although the data were originally analysed with regard only to a PGI locus, subsequent calculations based on heterozygosity at four polymorphic loci revealed a significant effect of heterozygosity on size, but only in the moderate current area. In the low-flow area all anemones tend to be large, but in the moderate-flow area only the most heterozygous individuals are large (Figure 5.11).

The mechanism by which greater heterozygosity manifests itself in larger body size is unknown, but it might involve either faster growth rates, higher

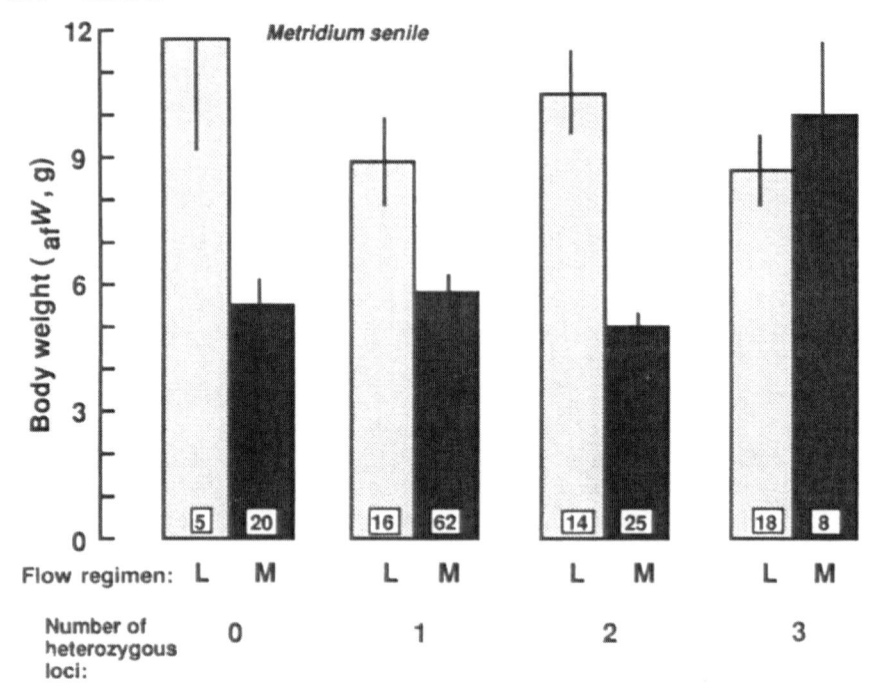

Figure 5.11 Interacting effects of current speed and genetic heterozygosity on body size in *Metridium senile* at Blue Hill Falls, Maine. Heterozygosity values are numbers of heterozygous loci per individual among four loci that were scored electrophoretically. Numbers of anemones are shown within each histogram. L = low current speed, $\leqslant 5\,\mathrm{cm\cdot s^{-1}}$; M = moderate current speed, $10\text{--}50\,\mathrm{cm\cdot s^{-1}}$. Source: Shick and Dowse (1985), from Shick *et al.* (1979b), and Hoffmann and Shick (unpublished).

net conversion efficiencies, or both over long periods of time. For oysters, Koehn and Shumway (1982) speculated that faster growth rates arise from higher growth efficiencies in more heterozygous individuals, which have lower routine rates of oxygen consumption (i.e. lower maintenance costs). In *M. senile* the ages of individuals are unknown, but considering the low rates of recruitment into the population (section 6.3.4, page 242) and potentially enormous individual longevity, it seems most likely that in more heterozygous anemones large size is associated with increased long-term net growth efficiencies, and perhaps also with greater asexual proliferation.

Evolutionary success or fitness is frequently measured in terms of individual body size, for larger size generally increases sexual reproductive output (Calow, 1977b; Sebens, 1981a). For anemones, which grow indeterminately, vegetative growth and clone formation provides not only a means to escape from mechanical and energetic constraints on individual size but also a way to increase a genotype's fitness by partitioning the phenotype into many independent units each of optimal size, the total mass of which may be immense and limited only by the extent of habitat available. For such animals, components of fitness include the sizes of both individuals and clones. Increases in the clonal 'soma' are viewed as a form of growth rather than as reproduction *per se*, as will be seen in the next chapter.

6 Reproduction and population structure

6.1 SYNOPSIS

Both taxonomic and ecological relationships are apparent in the patterns of sexual reproduction and development in sea anemones. The primitive Protantheae have the smallest eggs and planktotrophic larvae, as do most mesomyarian anemones regardless of their biogeographical distributions; the exceptions are polar species, which produce large eggs and brood their young, and members of the Hormathiidae (a large family undergoing rapid diversification), which have medium-sized, lecithotrophic eggs. The more advanced endomyarian anemones as a group are widely diverse in their sexual reproductive strategies, but within genera are fairly conservative in this respect. The few estimates of reproductive effort reveal mean allocations of about 10% of body mass to gonads. Within the same family, a planktotrophic species (*Anthopleura xanthogrammica*) allocates more to ovary production than does an equally large, sympatric, lecithotrophic species (*Urticina lofotensis*). Hermaphroditism is more frequent in anemones than in medusoid cnidarians. Hermaphroditism is often associated with small body size and brooding of young, and hermaphrodites tend to be larger than females in the same population. Hermaphroditism and asexual reproduction are mutually exclusive. All these suggest that hermaphroditism may compensate for low vagility in locating a mate, that it may be favoured by different optimal sizes for male and female functions, and that it maintains locally adapted genotypic associations.

In harsh environments reliance on asexual rather than sexual reproduction has been suggested to involve the supposedly lower energetic cost of the former, but there is evidence that asexual proliferation is not a cheaper way to reproduce. Whereas vegetative reproduction has less stringent environmental requirements, gametogenesis, vitellogenesis, spawning, fertilization, development, dispersal and metamorphosis each demand a narrow range of suitable conditions, and raise the problem of coordinating such activities spatially and temporally, so that the principal constraint may be more cybernetic than energetic. There is also the problem that vegetative proliferation may better be viewed as growth of the clonal soma than as reproduction of individuals. The particular mode of asexual reproduction is related both to taxonomy and to environment. Production of many asexual progeny by basal ($\equiv$ pedal) laceration is found predominantly in sublittoral anemones, which usually experience better growing conditions than intertidal anemones, which rely mostly on binary fission. Fission rather than laceration may be dictated by the need to remain large to avoid desiccation, and also by energetic constraints such as the balance of allometrically-scaled catabolic costs and the ability to capture prey. The population structures of clonal sea anemones are reminiscent of those seen in many plants, with individual clones often dominating large areas, sometimes by excluding competing clones agonistically, while dispersing sexual propagules beyond their local boundaries. Theories concerning the demography and adaptive potentials of such organisms have evolved independently, there having been until recently little intercourse between botanists and zoologists studying asexual reproduction.

6.2 INTRODUCTION

Reproduction has both energetic and genetic implications. In the former case, the production of gonads and gametes competes with somatic growth for absorbed resources, and a central feature of life history evolution is the timing and relative magnitudes of these allocations (e.g. Stearns, 1977). The genetic question relates to whether or not recombination occurs during the production of new individuals, and thus to aspects of population structure and genotypic variations in individual fitness.

Sexual reproduction involves the production of meiotically-reduced gametes in which recombination is possible. Asexual reproduction is usually non-recombinational, and it may be agametic, involving vegetative replication of the soma, or gametic, involving parthenogenetic development of individuals from unfertilized eggs. In sea anemones, all individuals (physically and physiologically discrete units or 'ramets' *sensu* Harper, 1977; Jackson, Buss and Cook, 1985; Hughes, 1989) bearing the same unrecombined genotype comprise a clone ($\equiv$ genet), whose members may be spatially separated or closely aggregated. Clone-forming (that is, clonal) anemones at times also engage in sexual reproduction, whereas aclonal anemones reproduce strictly sexually, each individual being a unique genet.

Asexual amplification of the genet increases its potential fitness and decreases its chances of extinction, in the former case by vastly increasing the combined size (mass) of clonal individuals (and their gonads) beyond that achievable by a single ramet, and in the latter by spreading the risk of mortality among many discrete units. Participation in sexual reproduction requires the meiotic production of gametes and thus breaks up coadapted genotypes proven to be successful under local conditions; this high 'cost of meiosis' must have a correspondingly large payoff if sex is to persist (G.C. Williams, 1975). Sexual reproduction will ultimately enhance fitness if it produces genetically diverse progeny able to disperse to and prosper in habitats distinct from that of the parental clone. Clonal sea anemones also reproduce sexually and are increasingly popular subjects in the testing of such predictions. Pearse, Pearse and Newberry (1989) reiterate the view that sex generates new genets in the gene pool and somehow enables continuation of the gene pool, but they forcefully advocate the distinction between sexual reproduction and asexual proliferation, the latter being seen as a mode of growth (see also Chapter 5).

6.3 SEXUAL REPRODUCTION

6.3.1 Gametogenesis

As in other Cnidaria, gametes in sea anemones probably arise from interstitial cells in the endoderm of the mesenteries. About the time that the oogonia cease mitosis and become oocytes, they migrate into the mesoglea, where they grow and undergo vitellogenesis. In many species, a funnel-shaped endodermal structure called the trophonema develops between the oocyte (usually adjacent to the germinal vesicle) and the border of the mesentery, penetrating the mesoglea (Figure 6.1). The trophonema has a nutritive function, transferring materials from the coelenteron to the growing oocyte (Larkman and Carter, 1982). Although mesoglea presents less of a barrier to the diffusion of small molecules than cell layers (Chapman and Pardy, 1972), the thickness of the endoderm is greatly reduced at the trophonema (Figure 6.1), cells of which appear to concentrate materials from the coelenteron more readily than do other endodermal cells (Larkman and Carter, 1982) and may thus be specialized in their transport kinetics. The region of the oocyte in contact with the trophonema has specialized cytospines that interdigitate with the trophonemal cells (Figure 6.1b) and presumably enhance nutrient transfer from the latter to the oocyte.

Ripening of the oocytes in a given female is frequently asynchronous, a

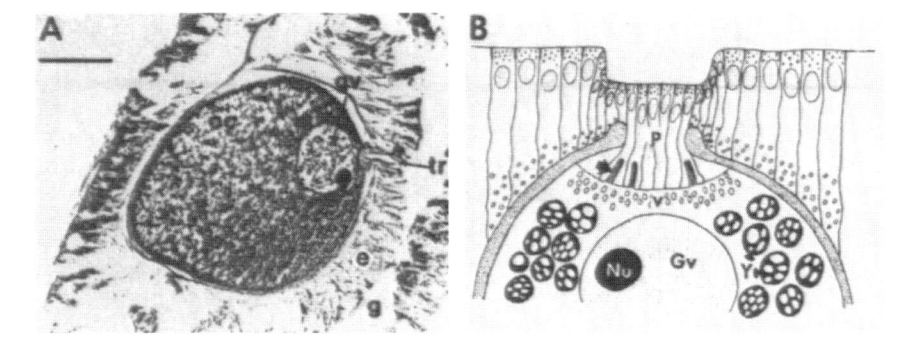

Figure 6.1 The trophonema connecting the oocyte to the coelenteron through a pore in the mesoglea. **A**. Section through an oocyte and its trophonema in *Urticina lofotensis*. Scale bar is 50 µm. **e** = endoderm; **g** = gastrovascular cavity (≡ coelenteron); **gv** = germinal vesicle; **oc** = oocyte; **tr** = trophonema. **B**. Diagram of trophonema based on electron micrographs of *Actinia fragacea*. Cytospines (arrow) from the oocyte surface interdigitate with the bases of trophonemal cells that extend through a pore (**P**) in the mesoglea. **Gv** = germinal vesicle, with nucleolus (**Nu**); **v** = ooplasmic vesicles; **Y** = heterogeneous yolk granules (with lipid inclusions). Notice that the endoderm is thinner at the trophonema, which typically abuts onto the oocyte adjacent to the germinal vesicle. Source: **A**. With permission from Wedi and Dunn (1983); **B**. With permission from Larkman and Carter (1982).

single anemone often containing oogonia, and pre- and post-vitellogenic oocytes. Spawning involves the passage of oocytes (via the trophonema) from the mesoglea through the endoderm and into the coelenteron, from which they may be ejected, or else fertilized *in situ*. Final maturation of the oocytes into eggs (indicated by the breakdown of the germinal vesicle) may occur prior to or after spawning. The function of the surface 'spines' (actually, twisted tufts of long microvilli: Schroeder, 1982) of actiniarian eggs is unknown. Absorptive and protective roles have been suggested (Schmidt and Schäfer, 1980; Schroeder, 1982).

Spermatogonia also arise in the mesenterial endoderm, and migrate singly or in groups into the mesoglea, where they are enclosed in cysts or vesicles. As the cysts enlarge, the maturation of sperm proceeds from the centre to the periphery. The cysts are occasionally surrounded by a layer of endodermal cells (often rich in lipid) that presumably have a nutritive function. A structure like a trophonema may be present (Larkman and Carter, 1982; Carter and Miles, 1989). When ripe, the cysts are virtually filled with sperm, and at spawning the cysts and surrounding endoderm rupture, releasing sperm into the coelenteron. Further details of gametogenesis, especially histological and ultrastructural aspects, can be found in many of the references in Table 6.1, and in Campbell (1974), Schmidt and Zissler (1979), Larkman

Table 6.1 Patterns of sexual reproduction in sea anemones (Actiniaria). Developmental schemes modified from Chia (1976). (?) = inferred

Species	Diameter of mature ovum (μm)	Spawning or maturation season	Pattern of development	Fecundity and reproductive effort	Distribution	Sexuality	Mode of asexual reproduction	Notes	Major source
SUBORDER PROTANTHEAE									
Gonactinia prolifera	70–80	July-Nov	Larviparous-planktonic-lecithotrophic		Temperate/cold-temperate	Dioecious	Transverse fission	Structurally simplest planula known	Gemmill, 1921; Chia, Lützen and Svane, 1989
Protanthea simplex	80	Sept-Oct	Oviparous-planktonic-planktotrophic		Cold-temperate/boreal	Dioecious	Regeneration of fragments(?)		Nyholm, 1959; Manuel, 1988
SUBORDER NYANTHEAE									
Tribe Boloceroidaria									
Alicia mirabilis	110	July-Oct	Oviparous-planktonic(?)-planktotrophic(?)		Temperate	Dioecious	None		Schmidt, 1972b
Tribe Mesomyaria									
Actinostola spetsbergensis	400–750	June-Sept	Viviparous	Fewer than 100 oocytes per female	Arctic	Dioecious	None		Riemann-Zürneck, 1976
Adamsia carciniopados (≡ A.palliata)	250	Spring-Autumn	Oviparous-planktonic-lecithotrophic		Temperate/cold-temperate	Dioecious	None	Iteroparous during same season	Gemmill, 1920
Aiptasia diaphana	125	Aug-Oct	Oviparous-planktonic(?)-planktotrophic(?)		Temperate	Dioecious	Basal laceration		Schmidt, 1972b
Bartholomea annulata	150–200	Oct-Apr	Oviparous-planktonic-planktotrophic		Subtropical/tropical	Imperfect gynodioecious hermaphrodite	Basal laceration	Rarely larviparous	Jennison, 1981
Cereus pedunculatus	110–151	June-Oct	Oviparous-planktonic-planktotrophic	3 000–30 000 ova per female	Temperate/cold-temperate	Dioecious, hermaphroditic, or parthenogenetic	Parthenogenesis	Viviparous, gynodioecious hermaphrodite in Atlantic populations	Schmidt, 1972b; Rossi, 1975; Shaw, 1989

Table 6.1 Continued

Species	Diameter of mature ovum (μm)	Spawning or maturation season	Pattern of development	Fecundity and reproductive effort	Distribution	Sexuality	Mode of asexual reproduction	Notes	Major source
Diadumene leucolena	98	Summer	Oviparous-planktonic-planktotrophic		Temperate	Dioecious	None	Eggs spawned by zooxanthellate females lacked zooxanthellae	Shick and Lamb, 1977
Halcampa duodecimcirrata	300	Oct-Nov	Oviparous-benthic-detritotrophic		Boreal	Dioecious	None	Male spawning triggers females	Nyholm, 1949
Metridium senile	100–145	June-Sept	Oviparous-planktonic-planktotrophic	Max. gonad index 35–50% of cross-sectional area at mid-column; index positively correlated with body size	Cold-temperate/boreal	Dioecious	Basal laceration		Bucklin, 1982, and references therein
Paracalliactis stephensoni	160	May-July	Oviparous-planktonic(?)-planktotrophic(?)		Bathyal (2 000–2 500 m)	Dioecious	None reported		Van-Praët and Duchateau, 1984
Paractina striata	420	June-Sept	Larviparous-planktonic-lecithotrophic		Temperate	Hermaphroditic	None		Schmidt, 1972b
Sagartia elegans	138	July-Aug	Oviparous-planktonic-lecithotrophic	400–20 000 ova per female	Cold-temperate	Dioecious	Basal laceration		Shaw, 1989
S. ornata	114	April	Larviparous	2 350 ova, 12 actinula larvae per female	Boreal/temperate	Parthenogenetic	Parthenogenesis only		Shaw, Beardmore and Ryland, 1987
S. troglodytes	80–119	Mar-May	Oviparous-planktonic-planktotrophic	2 450 ova per female	Boreal/temperate	Dioecious	None		Nyholm, 1943; Riemann-Zürneck, 1969; Shaw et al., 1987
Stomphia didemon	750–800	Spring	Oviparous-planktonic-lecithotrophic		Cold-temperate	Dioecious	None		Siebert, 1973
Tribe Endomyaria *Actinia equina*	≈150	Summer-early Autumn	Oviparous, larviparous, or viviparous	Broods contain up to 287 young	Cold-temperate	Dioecious (rarely hermaphroditic)	Parthenogenesis? Somatic embryogenesis?	Male, female, and non-sexual individuals all may brood young	Carter and Miles, 1989

Table 6.1   Continued

Species	Diameter of mature ovum (μm)	Spawning or maturation season	Pattern of development	Fecundity and reproductive effort	Distribution	Sexuality	Mode of asexual reproduction	Notes	Major source
Actinia equina mediterranea	≈200	June-Aug	Oviparous-planktonic(?)-planktotrophic(?)		Temperate	Dioecious	None	Reproductive modes extremely variable among nominal subspecies	Schmidt, 1972b
Anemonia viridis (≡ *A. sulcata*)	270–325	June-Aug	Oviparous-planktonic(?)-planktotrophic(?)		Temperate	Dioecious	Longitudinal fission	Ova contain zooxanthellae	Schmidt, 1972b
Anthopleura elegantissima	120–150	Late Summer-Autumn	Oviparous-planktonic-planktotrophic	Several thousand ova per spawning; ovary volume directly related to body volume, averaging 8.8% at peak season	Temperate/ cold-temperate	Dioecious	Longitudinal fission	Ova and planulae of zooxanthellate females lack zooxanthellae; male spawning triggers females	Siebert, 1974; Jennison, 1979; Sebens, 1981b
A. xanthogrammica	175–225	Summer-Autumn	Oviparous-planktonic-planktotrophic	Ovary volume directly related to body volume, averaging 12.4% at peak season	Temperate/ cold-temperate	Dioecious	None	Ova and planulae of zooxanthellate females lack zooxanthellae	Siebert, 1974; Sebens, 1981b
Aulactinia incubans	800–1 000		Viviparous		Cold-temperate	Imperfect gynodioecious(?) hermaphrodite	None		Dunn, Chia and Levine, 1980
Bolocera tuediae	1 100	Feb-March	Oviparous-planktonic-lecithotrophic		Boreal; abyssal	Dioecious	None		Gemmill, 1921

Table 6.1 Continued

Species	Diameter of mature ovum (µm)	Spawning or maturation season	Pattern of development	Fecundity and reproductive effort	Distribution	Sexuality	Mode of asexual reproduction	Notes	Major source
Bunodosoma cavernata	110		Oviparous-planktonic(?)-planktotrophic(?)		Temperate/sub-tropical/tropical	Dioecious	None	Ova may be fertilized within coelenteron	Clark and Dewel, 1974
Condylactis aurantiaca	290	Apr-June	Oviparous, larviparous, or viviparous		Temperate	Dioecious	None		Schmidt, 1972b
C. gigantea	500	Spring; continuous at low level throughout year	Oviparous-planktonic-lecithotrophic(?)	Relatively few ova	Tropical	Dioecious (rarely hermaphroditic)	None		Jennison, 1981
Cribrinopsis crassa	280	June-Aug	Oviparous-planktonic(?)-planktotrophic(?)		Temperate	Dioecious	None	Ova contain zooxanthellae	Schmidt, 1972b
C. fernaldi	700–750		Oviparous (larviparous)-planktonic-lecithotrophic		Cold-temperate	Dioecious	None	Facultatively larviparous	Siebert and Spaulding, 1976
Epiactis prolifera	400	Feb-Oct	Oviparous-brooding-lecithotrophic	350 ova, 35 young per individual	Temperate/cold-temperate	Gynodioecious hermaphrodite	None		Dunn, 1977a
Epicystis crucifer (≡ *Phymanthus crucifer*)	450	Feb-May; continuous?	Viviparous		Tropical	Dioecious	None	Larviparous in some populations	Jennison, 1981
Peachia quinquecapitata	120		Oviparous-planktonic-parasitic		Cold-temperate	Dioecious	None	Parasitic on medusae	Spaulding, 1974
Urticina crassicornis	500–700	Apr-June	Oviparous-planktonic-lecithotrophic		Temperate/cold-temperate	Dioecious	None	May be viviparous in some populations	Chia and Spaulding, 1972
U. lofotensis	700–800	'Prolonged' (Autumn-Winter)	Oviparous-planktonic-lecithotrophic	Ovary index positively related to body mass, averaging 9% at peak	Temperate/cold-temperate	Dioecious	None		Wedi and Dunn, 1983

1981), Schmidt and Höltken (1980), Schmidt and Schäfer (1980) and Doumenc and Van-Praët (1987).

6.3.2 Reproductive Cycles and Spawning

In temperate and cold-temperate zone anemones, oogonia and spermatogonia most commonly appear in late autumn and winter and take about one year to mature into gametes. Mature sperm frequently are present for much of the year, whereas the larger oocytes are usually restricted to a shorter period, typically late spring-autumn in temperate-zone species producing small eggs and having planktotrophic larvae (Table 6.1). Mature eggs may be present for much longer periods in tropical species, and in viviparous (Chia and Rostron, 1970; but see Carter and Miles, 1989) and externally brooding (Dunn, 1975a) anemones.

Lipogenesis in the oocytes of the deep sea species *Paracalliactis stephensoni* appears to be initiated by the arrival in the abyss of particles derived from the spring bloom of phytoplankton (Van-Praët and Duchateau, 1984), and coincides with an increase in amylase activity in this species (section 2.4, page 78). In littoral species where spawning is related to temperature more than to strong seasonality of prey, increases in food availability are manifested in the size of gonads more than in the maturity of their gametes (Jennison, 1979b; Sebens, 1981b; Wedi and Dunn, 1983). Whether variation in food availability affects egg quality (i.e. level of stored nutrients) is unknown. In *Actinia equina* glycogen increases in oocytes and other cells during gametogenesis (Boury-Esnault and Doumenc, 1979), but fluctuation in glycogen and lipid levels is not pronounced in this species (Ortega, Lopez de Pariza and Navarro, 1988), some populations of which do not show a strong seasonality of reproduction (Chia and Rostron, 1970; Schäfer, 1981; but see Carter and Miles, 1989). Conversely, marked reproductive seasonality in *Anthopleura elegantissima* and *Metridium senile* is accompanied by large annual fluctuations in their lipid stores (Jennison, 1979a; Hill-Manning and Blanquet, 1979). Males and females of *A.elegantissima* do not differ in their lipid levels, which may indicate that lipid is an energy reserve in sperm as well as eggs. The extremely high lipid content of *Bolocera tuediae* (Table 2.5, page 81) is due to the very large (Table 6.1), lipid-rich eggs in this boreal species.

Spawning in littoral species commonly occurs at the peak annual temperature (Schmidt, 1972b; Jennison, 1979b; Schäfer, 1981; Carter and Miles, 1989), which may explain earlier spawning in high shore compared with low shore individuals of *A.elegantissima* (Sebens, 1981b). *Sagartia troglodytes* in Britain, however, spawns synchronously in response to rising seawater temperature immediately after the winter minimum (Shaw, 1989). As in other marine invertebrates, interspecific differences among sea anemones in the season and duration of spawning (Table 6.1) seem related to nutrition of the larvae. Tropical species may have a poorly-defined spawning season, perhaps indicating a prolonged, gradual release of eggs (Jennison, 1981) to produce larvae in a biome where plankton production is less seasonal than at higher latitudes. Within the Actiniidae, *A.elegantissima* and *A.xanthogrammica* are strongly seasonal in their spawning, whereas the sympatric brooder *Epiactis prolifera* spawns over much of the year (Table 6.1). *Anthopleura* spp. produce planktotrophic larvae that are more dependent on seasonal plankton productivity than are the externally brooded larvae and juveniles of *E.prolifera*, which receive leftovers from the adult's meals (Dunn, 1975a). Similar considerations apply to the continuous presence of internally brooded actinula larvae in *Cereus pedunculatus* (Shaw, 1989) and juveniles in *Actinia equina* (Chia and Rostron, 1970; Carter and Miles, 1989), although such juveniles may be produced vegetatively in *A.equina* (see section 6.4.1, page 255) and so be uncoupled from egg production. In contrast *E.lisbethae* is a strongly seasonal brooder, and so brooding and aseasonal reproduction are not invariably linked; the difference may be related to the type of sexuality, for unlike *E.prolifera* (which is hermaphroditic and self-fertilizing) and *A.equina* (either vegetative or parthenogenetic), *E.lisbethae* is strictly dioecious (Fautin and Chia, 1986).

In several species, the release of sperm by males triggers spawning by nearby females (Nyholm, 1943, 1949; Clark and Dewel, 1974; Siebert, 1974). Nyholm (1949) described a behaviour in *Halcampa duodecimcirrata* in which females oriented toward spawning males, presumably increasing the chances of fertilization. He even observed a mating behaviour in *Sagartia troglodytes* in which females moved toward males, where once in contact, their joined basal discs formed a temporary brood chamber into which the eggs were released (see figure 26D in Nyholm, 1943). Also, spawned eggs of *Diadumene leucolena* remained attached by mucus to the base of the female, where fertilization by sperm from nearby males occurred (Shick and Lamb, 1977). The implications of such events for population structure could be profound, in that the spatial extent of panmixia may be much smaller than the reliance on (assumed) planktonically dispersed gametes would suggest (see section 6.5, page 275).

6.3.3 Patterns of Sexual Reproduction and Development

This topic was reviewed by Chia (1976), who discerned seven patterns of development, based on the site of fertilization (internal or external), larval habits, and larval nutrition. His scheme, used in compiling Table 6.1, is extended by including information on egg size, spawning season, geographic distribution and fecundity. The table is incomplete in that it does not include all isolated accounts falling into one or more of these categories, but it attempts to present as complete a picture as possible for species where information is available in several categories (also see Appendix for zoogeographical and habitat information).

As noted by Chia, oviparous — planktonic — planktotrophic development is the most primitive and widespread pattern taxonomically among sea anemones, and has the advantage of potentially wide dispersal albeit at the cost of high mortality in offspring. The suborder Protantheae includes the most primitive members of the Actiniaria, and their reproduction reflects this: they are dioecious, and produce the smallest eggs (<100 μm diameter) of any anemones, the larvae presumably being planktotrophic. In the suborder Nyantheae, the most primitive tribe is the Boloceroidaria. In *Alicia mirabilis* dioecy, small egg size and oviparity are consistent with its placement in this primitive group.

The tribe Mesomyaria also appears to be conservative in this respect, and there is a remarkable consistency of the pattern of sexual reproduction and development in this group. Small eggs (<200 μm diameter) and oviparous — planktonic — planktotrophic development are again the most common condition. This applies to boreal, temperate and tropical species, and surprisingly also to the deep-sea species *Paracalliactis stephensoni*, despite the occupation by these groups of a variety of biomes, habitats and substrates ranging from mudflats to coral reefs. From their primitive pattern of reproduction and the presence of tip-headed (as opposed to round-headed) sperm, the Mesomyaria, after the Protantheae and Boloceroidaria, are placed nearest the actiniarian ancestor that diverged from the order Madreporaria (Schmidt, 1974, and Appendix).

There are several exceptions to the rule of small eggs and planktotrophic larvae in the Mesomyaria, such as *Adamsia carciniopados* ($\equiv$ *A.palliata*) and *Paractinia striata*, which have medium-sized, yolky eggs and lecithotrophic larvae. Both of these species are members of the Hormathiidae, which is a large family by mesomyarian standards (T.A. Stephenson, in Carlgren, 1949), and includes several species that form symbiotic relationships with hermit crabs. It may be that the Hormathiidae is a rapidly evolving group, diversifying in its reproduction as well as in its behaviour.

It has recently been suggested that burrowing anemones lacking bases and basilar muscles (tribe 'Athenaria' in Carlgren's classification) such as *Edwardsia, Halcampa, Nematostella, Peachia*, etc. evolved from the 'Acontiaria' (Carlgren's classification: Hand, 1966), although they were traditionally considered as the stem of the Nyantheae. In Schmidt's (1974) scheme, they are placed in several families divided between the Mesomyaria and Endomyaria. Their morphological simplicity is possibly an adaptation to an infaunal existence (Hand, 1966; Sassaman and Mangum, 1972), rather than an indication of primitiveness. Their reproduction is consistent with this view: they show small to medium-sized eggs and oviparity, typical of mesomyarians, but have a highly specialized larval development, being benthic and detritotrophic, or planktonic and parasitic on medusae (Nyholm, 1949).

Further exceptions in the Mesomyaria to small eggs, oviparity and plank-totrophic development occur within the family Actinostolidae. These ane-mones have yolky eggs >400 μm in diameter, a fact that might be related to their cold-water distributions (see Thorson, 1936). Whereas the cold-tem-perate *Stomphia didemon* has large eggs but does not brood its young, its congener *S.selaginella* in the Antarctic does (Dunn, 1984). In the arctic species *Actinostola spetsbergensis*, large eggs and viviparity are associated with greatly reduced fecundity (Table 6.1), which is offset by parental protection of very large offspring (Riemann-Zürneck, 1976). Brooding is common in arctic anemones (Thorson, 1936), probably in consequence of poor condi-tions for planktotrophic development, and large eggs and internal brooding seem the rule in sub-antarctic and antarctic actinostolids as well (Dunn, 1983, 1984).

In contrast to the conservativeness of the Mesomyaria, the tribe Endo-myaria is sexually adventurous. Egg diameters range from 110 to 1 000 μm and four of Chia's seven reproductive schemes are present (Table 6.1). Such diversity is consistent with their position as the most advanced Actiniaria (see Schmidt, 1974). Several trends in egg size and larval development are apparent: cold-water species produce large eggs and may or may not brood young (the boreal *Bolocera tuediae* does not brood, but its congener *B.kergue-lensis* from the Antarctic does: Dunn, 1983); species from temperate waters have small to medium-sized eggs with planktotrophic development; and tropical species produce large eggs and may have planktonic, lecithotrophic larvae or else brood their young.

These observations on tropical endomyarian anemones are perhaps sur-prising, and seem related to life history constraints other than nutrition of the larvae. *Condylactis gigantea*, for example, is a large, solitary, macrophag-ous species that must compete for space with massive corals (Sebens, 1976) and for which suitable habitats may be patchy (Jennison, 1981). In restricted habitats the need to avoid intraspecific competition for large prey may have selected for planktonic dispersal, whereas interspecific spatial competition may have favoured large egg size and lecithotrophic development, assuming that this produces relatively large juveniles capable of agonistic behaviour soon after settlement. Conversely, *Epicystis* (≡ *Phymanthus*) *crucifer* is a non-agonistic, fugitive species that occupies relatively unstable sand pockets (Sebens, 1976). It shows viviparity, which would place its juveniles in a habitat proven suitable for adults and likely to be relatively free of inter-specific competitors.

Most of the endomyarian anemones in Table 6.1 belong to the family Actiniidae, the largest in the Actiniaria. In actiniids, other than the tendency already noted for cold-water species to have large eggs (and for polar representatives to brood young), there is no obvious ecological pattern to sexual reproduction and development.

Within genera of Actiniidae, the pattern of development seems a fairly conservative feature related more to evolutionary history than to ecological indices. In this family the capricious nature of development with regard to ecological correlates is highlighted on the west coast of North America by variability among sympatric species. *Anthopleura elegantissima* and *A. xanthogrammica* are oviparous and their small eggs develop into planktotrophic larvae. On the same shores, *Epiactis prolifera* (the only hermaphrodite in this comparison) produces somewhat larger eggs and broods its young externally. The predominantly subtidal *Urticina crassicornis* and *U. lofotensis* produce still larger eggs, are oviparous and have lecithotrophic larvae, characteristics shared by the closely related *Cribrinopsis fernaldi*, which may at times be larviparous. *Aulactinia incubans* produces the largest eggs and is viviparous. The most obvious correlation in the foregoing is taxonomic (although this begs the ecological question): *Anthopleura* spp., despite their great differences in body size and lifestyle, have a common reproductive pattern, which differs from that typical of the *Urticina* species, although like *A. xanthogrammica*, these are large, solitary anemones. The restriction of *Urticina* to colder waters and the extension of *Anthopleura* into more temperate and subtropical waters may account for differences between these genera. In *Aulactinia*, many species of which are polar, brooding is the norm. In the tropics it has brooding species as well (Dunn, Chia and Levine, 1980). Brooding is the rule in *Epiactis* spp. (Fautin and Chia, 1986).

To some extent, such conservativeness of reproductive patterns reflects the fact that congeners often experience similar ecological conditions. Intrageneric diversification in life history traits becomes evident when comparing species from widely different environmental circumstances. Some examples follow. The existence of viviparity in *Anthopleura handi*, exceptional for the genus, may be interpreted, in view of its lack of asexual reproduction (Dunn, 1978, 1982), as a mechanism to enhance local success where suitable habitat (isolated mangroves on vast mudflats) is patchy (see section 6.5). Conditions in the Antarctic require brooding in *Bolocera kerguelensis* (and in most other anemones there), whereas the boreal and abyssal species *B. tuediae* reproduces without brooding despite its very large eggs, which suggests that in the Antarctic factors other than low temperature (predation?) may select for brooding. *Condylactis aurantiaca* in the Mediterranean, unlike *C. gigantea* in the Caribbean, inhabits sandy substrates (Schmidt, 1972b). Judging from the smaller egg size in *C. aurantiaca*, there has been no pressure to have large (competitively superior?) larvae but it is unclear whether the facultative larviparity or viviparity in this species may have the same basis as in *Epicystis crucifer* from sand pockets, discussed previously. In *Cribrinopsis crassa* much smaller eggs compared with *C. fernaldi* may be related to the presence of zooxanthellae in the former, i.e. an energetic supplement provided to the larvae by the algae may obviate the need for lecithotrophic development. *C.crassa* previously has been placed in at least three other genera, however, and these reproductive differences may reflect still unresolved taxonomic differences. In *Urticina crassicornis* reports of viviparity and differences in larval anatomy in some populations may also indicate a taxonomic problem (cf., China and Spaulding, 1972 and Stricker, 1985).

6.3.4 Larval Settlement and Recruitment

Planula larvae of sea anemones are common enough in the plankton to provide material for morphological studies (Widersten, 1968), but there have been few studies of larval behaviour, especially regarding settlement, or of larval recruitment into benthic populations. The apical organ (sometimes including a tuft of cilia) of the planula appears not to function in feeding, a role suggested by Gemmill (1920) and Widersten (1968). Such a role was disproved in *A.elegantissima* by Siebert (1974), and it more probably serves in sensing and selecting substrata (Chia and Spaulding, 1972; Siebert, 1973; Chia and Koss, 1979). Contrary to early reports (Chia and Spaulding, 1972), in *Urticina crassicornis* the lecithotrophic larvae lack an apical organ, and larval discrimination among substrata may occur via a diffuse ectodermal sensory network (Stricker, 1985). Again, the difference may be due to unresolved taxonomic problems. The lack of a larval organ that functions to select settlement sites might also be explained if some specimens of '*Urticina crassicornis*' are viviparous.

Whereas the structure of the larval apical organ is fairly well known, the environmental factors to which it is sensitive are not. In planulae of *Sagartia troglodytes* metamorphosis occurs only if tubes of the polychaete *Sabellaria* are present (Riemann-Zürneck, 1969). Polychaete (*Phyllochaetopterus*) tubes facilitate settlement and metamorphosis of planulae in *Urticina crassicornis* (Chia and Spaulding, 1972) and *Cribrinopsis fernaldi* (Siebert and Spaulding, 1976) planulae. The chemical stimulus needs interpretation as these worms inhabit mudflats whereas the anemones occupy rocky substrata. Planulae of *Stomphia didemon* settle preferentially on sand and gravel compared with scallop shells or glass bowls, although the former substrates are effective only after the larvae begin to seek suitable sites (Siebert, 1973). In *A.elegantissima* the planktotrophic larvae continue swimming for at least two weeks and cannot be induced to settle on a variety of natural substrates (Siebert, 1974).

Recruitment of sexually produced planulae into natural populations of sea anemones seems rare. During a two-year study of *Anthopleura xanthogrammica* populations, larval settlement was never observed (Batchelder and Gonor, 1981). During a four-year study of *A.elegantissima*, a large larval settlement was seen only once, and settlement of *A.xanthogrammica* larvae was at least this infrequent (Sebens, 1982c). Sebens suggests that for planulae of these species mussel beds are the primary settlement site, with juveniles migrating into adjacent adult habitats as space becomes available. It is unknown whether the concentration of juveniles in the mussel beds is due to hydrodynamic forces that tend to collect larvae there, to preferential settlement there by larvae, or to higher larval mortality in more exposed settlement sites, and all three factors may be involved. In a population of *Metridium senile* the concentration of larvae by local hydrodynamic conditions has been inferred from current measurements and genotypic distributions (Shick *et al.*, 1979b; Shick and Hoffmann, 1980).

In predominantly sublittoral species such as *M.senile*, the recurrence of juvenile anemones on harbour floats and docks that are frequently cleared of fouling organisms suggests that successful larval settlement is fairly regular, at least when space is available. In this species some populations are genotypically diverse to the extent expected for sexually reproducing populations having free recombination, whereas other demes are typified by asexual proliferation of a few founder genotypes (Hoffmann, 1986; section 6.5). At one site analysis of juveniles revealed that they were genetically distinct from the local adult residents (Hoffmann, 1987), in consequence of planktonic dispersal of larvae. Recolonization of denuded substrates by larvae is infrequent in periodically anoxic fjords, because small individuals of *M.senile* are less resistant to anoxia than are large specimens (Wahl, 1985; see also section 3.4, page 123).

In *Actinia tenebrosa*, local populations are maintained primarily by ameiotic processes, although their genotypic diversity indicates that sexual recruitment must have occurred at some time and that it continues infrequently (Ayre, 1984b). Also, long-distance dispersal in this species seems to involve sexually produced planktonic larvae, as evinced by the conformity to Hardy-Weinberg expectations of pooled genotypic frequencies in 23 local populations distributed over 1400 km of shoreline. As indicated by genotypic diversity measures, sexual recruitment in *A.tenebrosa* although highly episodic, is more important on unstable shores, where existing populations may experience catastrophic mortality, than on stable shores, where asexual maintenance of fewer, longer-lived genotypes is the rule. The effects of sexual recruitment and asexual proliferation on local population structure is discussed more extensively in section 6.5.

6.3.5 Fecundity and Reproductive Effort

The few data available (Table 6.1) indicate that in sea anemones, as in other taxa, there is an inverse relationship between egg size and egg numbers (fecundity). As is often the case, large egg size and reduced fecundity are associated with brooding (larviparity, viviparity or external attachment) of the young. These phenomena are related most often to the scarcity or uncertain availability of food for developing young, and are the rule in polar species (Thorson, 1936). A large proportion of antarctic anemones have large eggs and are brooders (Dunn, 1983, 1984). Low fecundity may pose a diminished possibility for sexual recruitment, but this is presumably offset by the enhanced survivorship afforded by parental care; however, virtually no data are yet available on population dynamics and demography to support this assumption. In the temperate, externally brooding *Epiactis prolifera*, annual survivorship from egg to adult was calculated to be about 1%, from fecundity and numbers of juveniles brooded (Table 6.1) and from juvenile survivorship (Dunn, 1977a). The value may be even lower in more fecund species having planktotrophic larvae, as indirectly indicated by the very low incidence of larval recruitment.

In sea anemone species that have been examined in detail, great longevity of adults, low and sporadic larval recruitment, and high juvenile mortality are the norm. It is not surprising that these species are iteroparous, individuals reproducing many times during their lives. What is not so clear, because the critical measurements have not been made, is whether iteroparity necessitates a relatively low reproductive effort at any one time (one index of which is the percentage of net energy intake that is allocated to reproduction). Sea anemones certainly appear 'restrained' as opposed to 'reckless' in their sexual reproduction (see Calow, 1978). In certain species increased food availability results in larger gonads (Jennison, 1979b; Sebens, 1981b; Wedi and Dunn, 1983; section 6.3.2), which indicates that unlike reproductively reckless organisms, anemones do not maintain a constant reproductive effort irrespective of food intake. Such restraint is favoured when the adults have a higher probability of survival than their offspring (Calow, 1978).

Quantitative studies of reproductive effort in sea anemones are rare because of the nature of their gonads. The multiplicity of gamete-bearing tissues and their relative diffuseness involve chiefly histological investigation. Although there are accordingly many published studies of stages of gamete development, egg size, etc., there are fewer data on the overall size of the gonads or the volume they occupy, or on their total energetic content. Using linear measurements in *A. elegantissima*, Ford (1964) calculated that the ovary index (ratio of estimated ovary volume to weight of anemone, $\times$ 100%) was a maximum of 22%, with mean values ranging from 5 to 10% at the peak of the reproductive season. More refined techniques used by Sebens (1981b) in reproductively ripe females of this species yielded similar mean values (8.8%), but larger maximum values (up to 38%). In *A. xanthogrammica*, the mean ovary index for mature females of all sizes at peak season was 12.4% (Table 6.1). In *Urticina lofotensis* direct measurements of dissected gonads revealed a positive relationship between ovary index and body mass (Figure 6.2), mean ovary index in an average-sized individual at peak season being

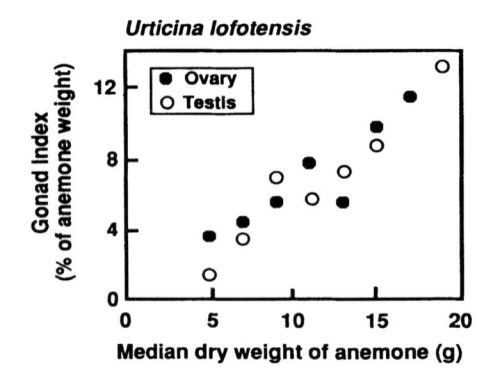

Figure 6.2 Gonad index (a measure of reproductive effort) as a function of body size in *Urticina lofotensis*. See text for discussion. Source: drawn from data in Wedi and Dunn (1983).

about 6.6% (Wedi and Dunn, 1983). Also using a gravimetric measure, Sauer (1989, and personal communication) found ovary index to range from about 2% to 11% in *Anemonia rustica*, and from 6% to 12% in *A.sulcata*; in both species ovary index was positively correlated with habitat suitability.

Sebens (1981b) reports that although anemone size varies among habitats, ovary volume as a function of body size does not, increasing directly with body mass (Figure 6.3) above a minimum size for sexual maturation (see also Figure 5.5, page 212). The mass of the ovaries in individuals of the same body size is extremely variable, however (possibly owing to differences in prey capture), and there is a discernable increase in relative ovary size in large individuals having more numerous ovaries. The increase in ovary index with body size in *U.lofotensis* (Figure 6.2) indicates an exponential increase in ovary mass with body size (Figure 6.3). In *M.senile* Bucklin (1982) also reports an increase in gonad index (areal measurements in histological sections) with increasing body size. Regardless of whether gonad mass increases directly or exponentially with anemone size, the continuous increase in reproductive output with size gives no suggestion of sexual senility in the species studied.

If gonad index is not a constant fraction of body size in individuals above the reproductive minimum, comparisons of their reproductive effort are complicated. Between the largest reproducing specimens of *A.elegantissima* and the smallest mature individuals of *A.xanthogrammica* there is little overlap (Figure 6.3), but in these species anemones of the same size have about the same the reproductive effort (ovary volume/$_d W_{anemone}$). As *A.xanthogrammica* has a much larger maximum unit size (and hence total reproductive output per individual) but has approximately the same egg size and mode of larval development as the sympatric species *A.elegantissima*, one

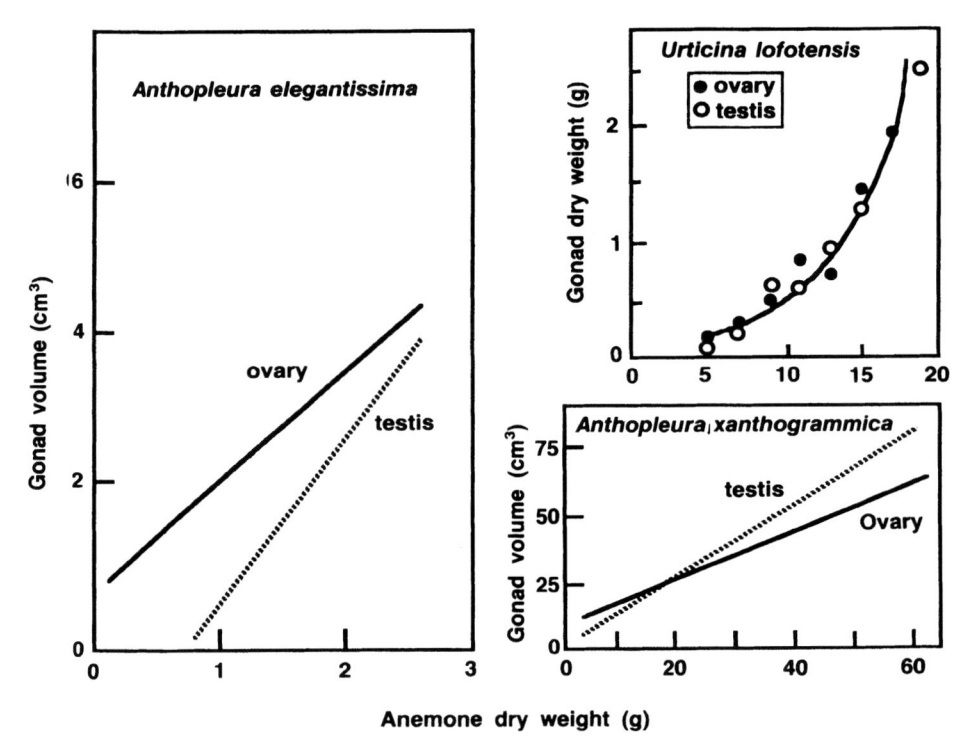

Figure 6.3 Relationship between gonad volume or weight and body weight in several actiniid species. See text for discussion and comparison of reproductive effort in *A.xanthogrammica* and *U.lofotensis* of similar size. Source: after Sebens (1981b) for *Anthopleura* spp; drawn from data in Wedi and Dunn (1983) for *Urticina lofotensis*.

might expect the former species to be numerically dominant. That the reverse is true illustrates the ability of asexual proliferation to affect population size, as discussed in section 6.5.

A.xanthogrammica and *U.lofotensis* afford an interesting comparison, as these sympatric actiniids are both large, aclonal macrocarnivores yet differ in egg size and mode of development (Table 6.1). As the gonads are largely emptied at spawning, (ovary mass/$_d W_{anemone}$) $\times$ 100% is a fair index of reproductive effort. An average-sized female *U.lofotensis* of $10\,g\,_d W$ has an ovary index of 6.6% (maximum 16.4%) (Wedi and Dunn, 1983), or $0.67-1.64\,g\,_d W_{ovary}$/individual. A specimen of *A.xanthogrammica* of this size has a mean ovary volume of $\approx 15\,cm^3$ (Figure 6.3) with a maximum of $25\,cm^3$ (Sebens, 1981b). Assuming that $1\,cm^3$ of fresh ovary weighs $\approx 1\,g$, and a tissue hydration of 80%, $_d W_{ovary}$ in this specimen would be $3.0-5.0\,g$, with an ovary index of 30–50%. Compared with lecithotrophic development of *U. lofotensis*, the planktotrophic development of *A. xanthogrammica*, which probably carries a high risk of larval mortality, is thus associated not only with greater fecundity (inferred from the smaller egg size and larger ovary mass), but also with greater reproductive effort. Why such differences in reproductive effort should be the case is not obvious, but they may be related to nutritional differences: in *A. xanthogrammica* perhaps the energy for maintenance metabolism provided by zooxanthellae (lacking in the azooxanthellate *U. lofotensis*) is manifested in a larger allocation of resources to reproduction. If so, it would be consistent with Chia's (1974, 1976) hypothesis that lecithotrophy and reduced reproductive effort are consequences of limited energy for gamete production.

The foregoing calculations assume the same energetic equivalent of $_dW_{ovary}$ in both species; if in the much larger eggs of *U. lofotensis* there is a preferential accumulation of lipid, the estimate of its energetic reproductive effort would be increased. There are, however, few quantitative data on the biochemical and energetic content of actiniarian eggs. 'Carbohydrate' and glycogen granules are present during the proliferative phase (Loseva, 1971; Boury-Esnault and Doumenc, 1979), while other histological studies indicate that in mature ova lipid is the major energy store (Larkman, 1980; Schmidt and Schäfer, 1980; Schäfer and Schmidt, 1980). This may be inferred from the much higher lipid levels in reproductively ripe individuals (Hill-Manning and Blanquet, 1979; Jennison, 1979a; Figure 2.14, page 85). Among individuals of *A. elegantissima*, variability in lipid levels (Jennison, 1979a) may be determined by the relative amount of gonad present, itself related to an individual's position within clonal aggregations: on the edge of an aggregation 'warrior' individuals in contact with a genotypically different clone invest energy in acrorhagial armaments (structures used in intraspecific agonistic behaviour: see section 7.2.1, page 282) at the expense of gonad production (Francis, 1976). This illustrates the idea expressed by many authors that reproductive and somatic growth 'compete' for resources (Calow, 1979) and that the latter takes precedence under stressful conditions.

Reserves in the egg also include several types of electron-dense yolk granules, chemically undefined but which appear to be synthesized by the Golgi apparatus. Primary yolk granules may fuse with lipid droplets to form more complex storage structures (Larkman, 1980; Schäfer and Schmidt, 1980). Larkman (1980) found a greater diversity of yolk granules in *Actinia fragacea*, which is oviparous, than in *A. equina*, and he suggested that the latter, being viviparous, needs to direct less of its resources into eggs. ·

The data on reproductive effort in *A. elegantissima*, *A. xanthogrammica* (Sebens, 1981b), and *U. lofotensis* (Figure 6.3) indicate no significant intraspecific sexual differences. In free-spawning species having external fertilization this may not be surprising, but it would be interesting to know whether in a self-fertilizing hermaphrodite such as *Epiactis prolifera* there is reduced individual allocation of energy to sperm production. On the populational level this is so, since all fertile individuals are female, but only some are male as well (Dunn, 1975a, b).

Ripe individuals do not show sexual differences in gonad size or total lipid content (Jennison, 1979a). Therefore, lipid is as important a fuel for motile sperm as it is a metabolic reserve for eggs. This makes sense in terms of its higher energy content per unit volume or mass in these cells having greatly reduced cytoplasms and a planktonic existence of uncertain duration. Schmidt and Höltken (1980) note that in *Aiptasia diaphana* developing testicular cysts are closely invested by endodermal cells rich in lipid. Lipid inclusions are common in mature sperm of all species examined, including *Bunodosoma cavernata* and *M.senile* (Clark and Dewel, 1974), *Urticina felina* (Schmidt and Höltken, 1980), and *Actinia equina* (Larkman, 1980), where they are often closely associated with mitochondria. Although glycogen-like inclusions may also be present in sperm (Clark and Dewel, 1974), lipid is far more abundant.

6.3.6 Sex Ratio and Hermaphroditism

There is no evidence for special sex chromosomes, but a genetic mechanism of sex determination is suggested by strict dioecy (gonochorism) in most sea anemone species (Table 6.1), unisexuality of individual clones (Francis, 1973b; Shick, 1976; Shick and Lamb, 1977; Sauer, Müller and Weber, 1986; Fujii, 1987; Ayre, 1988), and lack of observed sex change in individuals over time (Carter and Funnell, 1980; Ayre, 1988; Carter and Miles, 1989). However, in some species the normal occurrence of hermaphroditism, particularly of the sequential variety (see below), suggests also an environmental component of determination of sex. Theoretical considerations underlying the question of sex ratios have been summarized and extended most recently by Charnov (1982) and Herre, Leigh and Fischer (1987). As there is no evidence to the contrary, I assume that there is no advantage to a sea anemone of being one sex or the other, a supposition supported by the equal energetic cost of reproduction in males and females (Figure 6.3 and section 6.3.5). The 1:1 sex ratio commonly observed in dioecious anemones (*Adamsia carciniopados*: Gemmill, 1920; *Cereus pedunculatus*: Rossi, 1975; *Actinia fragacea*: Carter and Thorpe, 1981; *Condylactis gigantea* and *Epicystis crucifer*: Jennison, 1981; *Anthopleura xanthogrammica*: Sebens, 1981b; *Paracalliactis stephensoni*: Van-Praët and Duchateau, 1984; *Sagartia troglodytes*: Shaw, Beardmore and Ryland, 1987; *Oulactis muscosa*: Hunt and Ayre, 1989; but for exceptions, *Urticina lofotensis* and one population of *S.troglodytes*, see Wedi and Dunn, 1983, and Shaw, 1989, respectively) is in accord with the theory first elaborated over half a century ago by R.A. Fisher (1930). That is, even if individuals in a population were genetically constrained to produce an unbalanced sex ratio among their offspring, any mutant individual that produced more of the rarer sex would be favoured, as the rarer sex would have a greater probability of mating than would the more common sex. This would drive the sex ratio toward 1 : 1.

Marked deviations from a symmetrical ratio occur in brooders and in species relying to varying extents on hermaphroditism (see below) and on asexual reproduction. *Haliplanella lineata*, although dioecious, has rarely been observed to reproduce sexually, and many local populations consist of individuals of one gender (Shick and Lamb, 1977; Dunn, 1982), presumably asexual descendants of a few founder individuals. In an extreme case, a population estimated to contain over one million individuals consisted of a single male clone (Shick, 1976). In *Anthopleura elegantissima* the skewed sex ratio (sometimes toward males, other times females: Ford, 1964; Sebens, 1981b) probably results also from founder effects.

Sexuality is particularly complicated in species of the genus *Actinia*. In *A.equina*, some populations have approximately equal numbers of males and females, whereas others are entirely female or exclusively male (Schäfer, 1981). There exists a profusion of nominal subspecies of *A.equina*, based in part on differences in sexuality (Schmidt, 1971). In *A.tenebrosa*, sex ratio deviates significantly from 1 : 1 in some locations (Ottaway, 1979a), although it is unknown whether this reflects genetic, founder or environmental effects (Ayre, 1984c). Sexuality and asexuality in this genus are treated in detail in section 6.4.1.

As noted, the occurrence in sea anemones of hermaphroditism, particularly of the sequential variety, suggests environmental determinants of sex. Almost nothing is known of the epigenetic factors involved, but Tardent (1975) has hypothesized a role for variable numbers of interstitial cells in this phenomenon in hydras. Fautin (1990) reviews the literature on this topic in cnidarians. The widely documented association of hermaphroditism with small body size (Ghiselin, 1969) is seen among species in the genus *Epiactis*: the small *E.prolifera* and *E.fernaldi* are hermaphroditic, whereas the larger *E.lisbethae* and *E.* (≡ *Cnidopus*) *ritteri* are gonochoric (Fautin and Chia, 1986).

If simultaneous hermaphroditism compensates for limited mobility in finding a mate by allowing any individual to effect a fertilization with any other (an aspect of the 'low density model': Ghiselin, 1969), then hermaphroditic anthozoans, including anemones, would seem unexpectedly rare (Hand, 1959). Hermaphroditism has since been recognized to be more prevalent in sessile sea anemones than in vagile, medusoid hydrozoans and scyphozoans (Fautin, 1990). Adult, tubicolous ceriantharians seem even more sedentary than actiniarians, and all ceriantharians are hermaphroditic (Tiffon, 1987), as are many scleractinian corals.

Ghiselin (1969) proposed that sequential hermaphroditism may be favoured by different optimal sizes for male and female functions (size advantage model). It seems important, therefore, that in most hermaphroditic sea anemones, the condition is associated with viviparity or some form of brooding (Table 6.1; see also Stephenson, 1929; Ghiselin, 1969), and moreover, that (with a single known exception: *Bartholomea annulata*) hermaphroditic sea anemones (and ceriantharians) do not reproduce asexually. In these sea anemones advantages of hermaphroditism are also likely to be manifested in individual size-related functions, and in maintaining locally-adapted ecotypes. The latter hinges on the possibility of self-fertilization, which hinders the random association of alleles at different loci into gametes. Such 'gametic disequilibrium' reduces the opportunity for genetic recombination between loci by reducing the frequency of two-locus heterozygotes (Bucklin, Hedgecock and Hand, 1984).

The most thoroughly studied hermaphroditic sea anemone is *Epiactis prolifera*, which shows the phenomenon (rare among metazoans) of gynodioecy, in which reproductively mature individuals are either females or hermaphrodites; there are no males (Dunn, 1975a, b). From marked differences in the size distributions of females and hermaphrodites, Dunn inferred that individuals first mature as females and then grow and become hermaphrodites, although the developmental change of sexuality was not tested in individual anemones. Both females and hermaphrodites brood young externally, and the latter receive leftovers from parental meals (Dunn, 1975a). The number of brooded juveniles is positively correlated with parental size (Dunn, 1975a). Local populations of *E.prolifera* are highly homozygous, probably in consequence of self-fertilization. In brooded young of rare heterozygous parents, segregation ratios of enzyme phenotypes indicate that the hermaphrodites are indeed self-fertilizing (Bucklin *et al.*, 1984). As expected for self-fertilizing hermaphrodites (Maynard Smith, 1978), populations of *E.prolifera* appear to be highly adapted to local conditions (Dunn, 1977b), although in some populations there may be considerable turnover of genotypes (D. Hedgecock, in Bucklin *et al.*, 1984).

These facts support a resource allocation variant of the size advantage model, proposed by Maynard Smith (1978) and Charnov (1982), in addition to other aspects of Ghiselin's models: by brooding and so 'feeding' their young, hermaphroditic anemones can allocate a greater quantity of resources to reproduction over a longer period than can individual males or females (since spermatogenesis and maturation must preceed the period during which embryos and young develop). Although smaller, purely female individuals have a lower reproductive output than larger hermaphrodites, this is partially offset by their lack of allocation to male functions (again, it would be useful to know the relative sexual allocations in hermaphrodites). Since females must be fertilized by hermaphrodites, these small females provide at minimal energetic cost the outcrossing and genotypic diversity necessary for long-term evolutionary success. The greater number of juveniles produced by larger, self-fertilizing hermaphrodites reduces the genetic 'cost of meiosis' (see G.C. Williams, 1975) and thus enhances individual fitness and preserves locally adapted, highly homozygous genotypic associations. It also provides the potential for a single individual to colonize new habitats. In such cases, simultaneous hermaphroditism has taken the place of asexual reproduction, of which there is but one example in hermaphroditic anemones (i.e., *Bartholomea annulata*). In *Cereus pedunculatus*, both hermaphroditism and asexual reproduction (parthenogenesis) occur, but only in allopatric populations that represent different 'sexual races' (Rossi, 1975; Schäfer, 1981; Shaw, 1989).

Bartholomea annulata is a simultaneous hermaphrodite that also proliferates vegetatively (Table 6.1), and it would be interesting to know whether it is a self-fertilizer. If it is not (as is true for most hermaphroditic plants, and apparently in ceriantharians: Tiffon, 1987; but not for *Epiactis prolifera*), it may be that asexual reproduction provides a mechanism to attain local success in restricted habitats (section 6.5), while hermaphroditism compensates for a low population density of sexual individuals scattered among patches of suitable habitat.

6.4 ASEXUAL REPRODUCTION

6.4.1 Modes of Asexual Reproduction

Some form of asexual reproduction (here considered synonymous with ameiotic reproduction, including both agametic, vegetative proliferation and apomictic parthenogenesis, both of which processes produce offspring bearing the same genotype as the parent) occurs in all major groups of Actiniaria (Table 6.2), and in the related Zoantharia and Corallimorpharia, but apparently not in the Ceriantharia (although Tiffon, 1987, notes an isolated exception). The extreme rarity of anemones that have abandoned sexual recombination and rely exclusively on asexual proliferation is related to the fact that such a strategy would be an evolutionary dead end (see Shick and Lamb, 1977). The cosmopolitan, colonizing anemone *Haliplanella lineata* provides a poignant example: locally introduced populations are often unisexual and monoclonal, and although they may flourish transiently (Shick, 1976), most become extinct in the long run (including the male clone estimated by Shick to contain over one million anemones), presumably when local conditions exceed the tolerance limits dictated by the single genotype present. Although not yet observed in such founder populations, the greater diversity provided by sexual reproduction does occur in demes nearer geographic origin of this species (Fukui, 1986).

There appear to be no examples of sea anemones that reproduce exclu-

Table 6.2 Modes of asexual reproduction in sea anemones (Actiniaria)

SUBORDER PROTANTHEAE	
	Transverse fission
	Regeneration of fragments (?)
	Longitudinal fission
SUBORDER NYANTHEAE	
Tribe Boloceroidaria	Budding
	Tentacular autotomy and regeneration
	Basal laceration
Tribe Mesomyaria	Basal laceration (tearing or constrictive)
	Longitudinal fission
	Transverse fission (rare)
	Parthenogenesis
Tribe Endomyaria	Longitudinal fission
	Transverse fission (rare — one instance)
	Parthenogenesis
	Vegetative (Somatic) embryogenesis

sively by apomictic parthenogenesis, although examples do exist in other taxa (Hughes, 1989). Unlike the case in vegetative proliferation, a favourable mutation occurring in a parthenogenetic egg could subsequently be integrated into a multicellular animal, which might provide this asexual lineage with diversity on which natural selection could act (Buss, 1987; Pearse *et al.*, 1989).

Modes of agametic reproduction have been summarized by Chia (1976) and are illustrated in Figure 6.4. Some modes are restricted to particular groups, suggesting constraints to vegetative reproduction. Contrary to their expectations, Sibly and Calow (1982) noted the rarity of budding in solitary anthozoans, and suggested that it is incompatible with whole-body contraction, an important defence against predators in polyps large enough not to be eaten in a single bite (see section 7.4.1, page 311). The confinement of budding to the Boloceroidaria makes sense, as these anemones are good swimmers (Robson, 1966) and may escape predators by swimming rather than by contracting, which would be of little avail in these delicate anemones. The occurrence of budding seems related moreover to the ability of these anemones to autotomize tentacles in response to predators (see Lawn and Ross, 1982a). Also, autotomized tentacles when incidentally swallowed during feeding in *Bunodeopsis medusoides* may regenerate into offspring within the coelenteron (Cutress, 1979), although V.B. Pearse (personal communication) reports that the tentacles are routinely autotomized after insertion into the coelenteron during contraction. Such a mode of vegetative proliferation is not budding in the strict sense, as the developing offspring do not remain

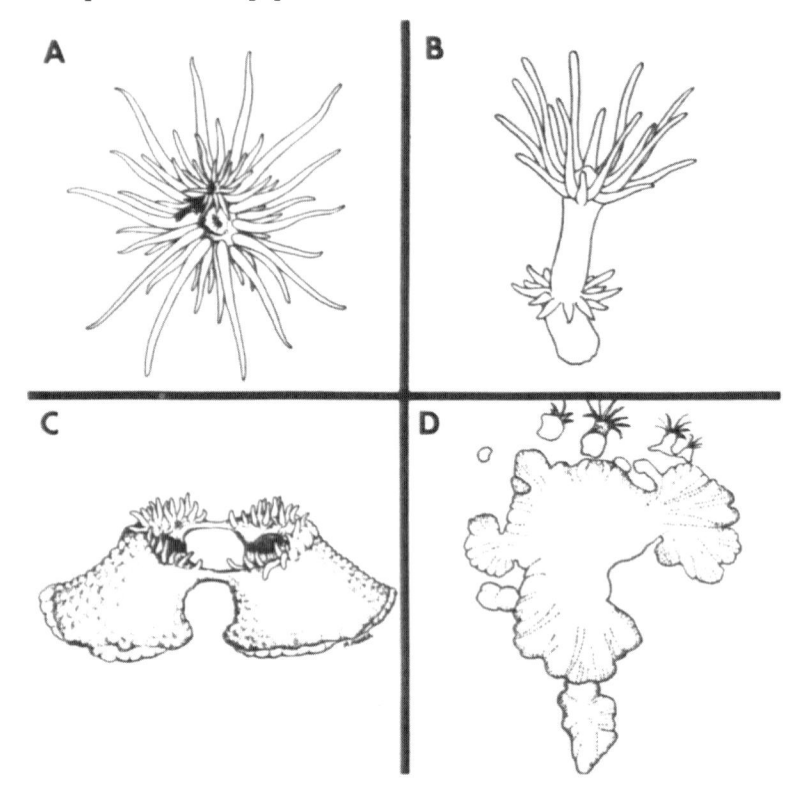

Figure 6.4 Modes of vegetative asexual reproduction in sea anemones. **A**. 'Budding', involving regeneration *in situ* of a small anemone (arrow) from a single tentacle of the adult specimen of *Boloceroides macmurrichi*. **B**. Transverse fission in *Gonactinia prolifera*. **C**. Longitudinal fission in *Anthopleura elegantissima*. **D**. Basal laceration in *Sagartiogeton laceratus* by constriction of fragments from the junction of the column and basal disc (view is from beneath a glass plate to which anemones are attached). Drawings not to same scale. Source: **A**. after Okada and Komori (1932); **B**. from Stephenson (1928); **C**. after Sebens (1983b); **D**. from Stephenson (1928).

anatomically connected to the parent during regeneration and growth.

Similar reasoning might explain the rarity of transverse fission: this process would hinder contraction, but it does occur in the primitive *Gonactinia prolifera* (suborder Protantheae), an active swimmer (Robson, 1966, 1971). Full retraction of its tentacles in response to disturbance does not occur in *Aiptasia mutabilis* (Manuel, 1988), apparently the only mesomyarian to rely normally on transverse fission. In *Anthopleura stellula* transverse fission is induced by abnormal salinities (Schmidt, 1970) but is not a mode of proliferation in nature.

Transverse fission requires more complex and unequal regeneration of structures than does longitudinal binary fission (see below), and may be constrained by differentiation of relatively large sea anemones along the oral–aboral axis. In small scyphozoan polyps and flatworms, internal reorganization may begin prior to the separation of transverse fission products. Perhaps informatively in this context, transverse fission is normally restricted to species of anemones having small body size and simplicity of organization, e.g. *G.prolifera*, *A.mutabilis*, *Fagesia lineata* (Crowell and Oates, 1980), and *Nematostella vectensis* (Manuel, 1988). Simplicity of internal organization is pronounced in the last two species, which are edwardsiid anemones (tribe Endomyaria), and which, being infaunal, are somewhat protected from predators without contracting. Parenthetically, transverse fission as the mode of asexual reproduction in morphologically simple, vermiform synaptid holothuroids seems another example of convergent evolution between these infaunal echinoderms and burrowing anemones (Sassaman and Mangum, 1972, and section 3.8.4).

Longitudinal fission is the most widespread form of vegetative proliferation among sea anemones (Table 6.2). In longitudinal fission each half retains the major structures, sometimes with internal reorganization prior to fission. It has been described in detail for *Anemonia viridis* ($\equiv$ *A.sulcata*), *Haliplanella lineata* and *Anthopleura elegantissima* by Louis (1960), Atoda (1976) and Sebens (1983b), respectively. Fission begins by a lateral stretching of the column along the directive axis, starting at the base. Tearing occurs perpendicular to the plane of stretching, starting with the column and ending with the oral disc and marginal sphincter (see Figure 6.4C). After separation of the two halves, two new directive mesenteries, one siphonoglyph and several pairs of mesenteries adjacent to the directives are regenerated. Sebens (1983b) describes a less common process seen in large individuals of *A.elegantissima*, in which the anemones first become tetraglyphic and the future fission products complete most of their internal reorganization before separation of the column. He speculates that this type of longitudinal fission may be important to larger individuals where rearrangement and reorganization would take longer, and where normal functions such as contraction and feeding would be impaired for longer. Very large, 'solitary' individuals of *A.elegantissima* in the low intertidal (proposed as a separate species by Francis, 1979, an hypothesis disproven by genetic analyses by Smith and Potts, 1987) do not undergo fission, however, perhaps because of mechanical constraints on separation and reorganization.

Basal (or pedal) laceration, a fourth type of agametic reproduction in anemones, is restricted to the tribes Boloceroidaria and Mesomyaria. It may occur by a tearing of fragments from the junction of the column and basal disc (as in *Metridium senile*), or by constriction and pinching-off of such fragments (as in *Sagartiogeton laceratus*; see Figure 6.4D). Basal laceration produces multiple daughter individuals far smaller than the parent, unlike binary fission, which yields approximately equal-sized products; lacerates undergo a pervasive regeneration of body parts, including the feeding apparatus. In either case, the asexual products are much larger than eggs and the probability of their survival is greater than for a sexually-produced larva, a reason suggested for the persistence of vegetative reproduction (G.C. Williams, 1975).

A generalization emerges from the data in Table 6.1: strictly sexual species tend to produce larger eggs than species capable of some form of vegetative reproduction. In 23 species of anemones lacking asexual reproduction, median egg diameter (300 μm) is significantly greater than that (145 μm) in seven species of vegetatively proliferating anemones (Mann-Whitney U test, $P<0.001$). Indeed, only one vegetatively reproducing anemone (*Anemonia viridis*) produces eggs that approach the median size of those in strictly sexual species. It seems relevant that in those additional species where asexual reproduction takes the derived form of parthenogenetic development from relatively small eggs, the progeny are brooded by the parent. These observations again suggest that the achievement of individual fitness involves maximizing the survivorship of offspring, be they asexual 'chips off the old block' (i.e. genetically identical fragments much larger than eggs, or even brooded parthenogenetic embryos), or genotypically diverse lecithotrophic larvae or brooded young developed from large fertilized eggs. The mutual exclusion of large eggs and asexual reproduction may be a case of avoiding redundancy in accomplishing the same end. The question concerns not the genetic aspects of sexual versus agametic reproduction, but rather the argument that larger propagules (ova or vegetative products) have greater chances of survival and shorter times required to reach reproductive maturity (Hughes, 1987; Calow and Sibly, 1987). It is also conceivable that the production of a few large eggs (which involves a relatively low reproductive effort: section 6.3.5) is related to chronically scarce food, with no energy being left over for vegetative proliferation. More data are required to substantiate either scenario.

Apomictic (i.e. non-recombinational), thelytokous parthenogenesis, whereby females develop from unfertilized eggs produced without meiotic reduction, occurs in *Sagartia ornata* ($\equiv$ *S. troglodytes* var. *ornata*: Shaw *et al.*, 1987), probably in *Cereus pedunculatus* (Rossi, 1975; Shaw, 1989) and in some specimens of *Actinia equina*. Reproductive, karyotypic and electrophoretic analyses of *Sagartia troglodytes* show that the two varieties are separate species, *S. troglodytes* being gonochoric and oviparous, and *S. ornata* being a (probably parthenogenetic) brooder (Shaw *et al.*, 1987). This perceptive study resolves earlier inconsistencies in the literature concerning the reproduction of '*Sagartia troglodytes*'. Histological examination of *S. ornata* during the time of maximal gonad development shows that all anemones are females, and electrophoretic screening of individual females and their broods reveals no evidence of segregation of alleles at heterozygous loci. Thus, reproduction is certainly asexual and probably parthenogenetic. This species has twice as many chromosomes (48) as *S.troglodytes*, and Shaw and coauthors discuss the basis for the association of such polyploidy with parthenogenesis (see also Hughes, 1989). Shaw *et al.* (1987) consider the tetraploid *S.ornata* to have originated from hybridization between *S.troglodytes* and a different species, or between genetically distinct populations of *S.troglodytes*.

In *Actinia equina*, females, rare hermaphrodites, males and individuals without gonads may all brood young internally, and the nature of their reproduction has been enigmatic. The young typically (but not invariably) have the same pigmentation (shades of red or green) as the adult. Dalyell's (1848, p. 206) early comment about this species still seems apt: 'there is no reason why a germ, — an organism should not be derived from the parent, which shall develope into complete form, more than that some organic part of the parent's body shall originate or be repaired from some analogous source, though the derivation of the elements of the offspring from a single individual should be through some physiological process yet unknown'. Subsequent suggestions for this unknown process have included self-fertilization (Cain, 1974), 'somatic embryogenesis' (i.e. vegetative reproduction), discrimination among genotypically diverse, vagile larvae by adoptive parents (Chia and Rostron, 1970), and apomictic parthenogenesis (Gashout and Ormond, 1979). The use of colour to infer genetic relationships was sometimes questionable, and the report by Lubbock and Allbut (1981) that adults may tolerate allogenic juveniles but alter their colour seemingly eliminated this character as a genetic marker for broods, although evidence to the contrary may exist (M.A. Carter, in Orr, Thorpe and Carter, 1982).

In adults of *A.tenebrosa* and their broods, the finding of identical genotypes at the catalase locus, including lack of segregation in heterozygotes, indicated the operation of vegetative reproduction or apomictic parthenogenesis (Ottaway and Kirby, 1975). These authors retained the less parsimonious interpretation, however, that adults may have rejected juveniles genetically dissimilar to themselves. Further electrophoretic studies of *A.tenebrosa* (Black and Johnson, 1979) and *A.equina* (Orr, Thorpe and Carter, 1982) confirm lack of recombination at several enzyme-coding loci in heterozygous adults and their broods, which together with the failure of pre- and post-metamorphic juveniles to enter the coelenterons of adults (Carter and Funnell, 1980), seriously weakens the hypothesis of selection of young by adoptive parents, and supports that of vegetative reproduction or apomictic parthenogenesis.

It appears that '*Actinia equina*' in Europe and Great Britain comprises several morphs and subspecies, distinguished in part by their modes of reproduction (Schmidt, 1971; Schäfer, 1981; Quicke, Donoghue and Brace, 1983; Haylor, Thorpe and Carter, 1984). The simplest case is presented by

A.equina atlantica II (Schmidt, 1971, for taxonomy), in which all individuals are females. Larvae removed from adults and reared in isolation through five successive generations gave rise only to females, which themselves produced larvae only after ripe oocytes had appeared. This strongly indicates that parthenogeneis is operating rather than fertilization by stored sperm or vegetative reproduction from somatic cells (Schäfer, 1981). The same results were obtained in some populations of *Cereus pedunculatus* (Rossi, 1971, 1975; Schäfer, 1981). Because no genetic analyses were performed, however, the apomictic nature of the parthenogenesis has not been established, i.e. automixis (meiotic parthenogenesis in which recombination is possible) has not been ruled out.

In studies of other *Actinia* populations (probably *A.equina equina* II of Schmidt, 1971), mature oocytes are purported to divide while still in the mesoglea of the mesenteries (Chia and Rostron, 1970; Gashout and Ormond, 1979), again suggesting parthenogenesis. At least in the latter case, however, the published photograph reveals closely appressed oocytes still bearing germinal vesicles and each oocyte apparently surrounded by mesoglea, which suggests that the oocytes have not divided. Therefore, these studies do not confirm the operation of parthenogenesis. In electrophoretic studies where the lack of recombination was confirmed (Orr, Thorpe and Carter, 1982), the sex of the parents was not reported, so while in these cases reproduction was non-recombinational, it was not parthenogenetic, if the parents were males. If some of the parents were females (which predominate in many British populations of *A.equina*), the observed maintenance of high heterozygosity in their offspring would argue against the operation of automictic (recombinational) and for apomictic parthenogenesis, but would not exclude vegetative (somatic) embryogenesis.

The possible role of males in producing sperm that stimulate eggs to develop parthenogenetically (i.e. pseudogamy or gynogenesis: Carter and Thorp, 1979; Brace and Quicke, 1986) has not been studied, but at least in *A.equina mediterranea* I, dioecy and oviparity are the norm (Schäfer, 1981). The continued presence of males that brood young in *Actinia* spp. complicates matters. Assuming that larval migration from females into adoptive males does not occur (see above), this leaves transient hermaphroditism and vegetative reproduction as the only possibilities for the origin of broods in males. The extreme rarity of hermaphrodites in *A.equina* (<0.2% of >1 000 individuals examined) (Chia and Rostron, 1970; Carter and Funnell, 1980; Carter and Miles, 1989) and their absence among >600 individuals of *A.tenebrosa* (Ottaway, 1979a; Ayre, 1988), plus the lack of evidence for sex change in individuals of these species (Carter and Funnell, 1980; Carter and Miles, 1989; Ayre, 1988), renders the possibility of hermaphroditism highly unlikely. 'Somatic embryogenesis' has been proposed as an asexual source of juveniles, especially in male *A.equina*, but morphological evidence for it is equivocal (Carter and Thorp, 1979; Gashout and Ormond, 1979). Its operation as a normal mode of vegetative reproduction would differ from the original suggestion by Polteva (1963) of a form of regeneration after injury. The frequent occurrence of brooding males, and the aforementioned constancy (i.e. genetic determination) of individual gender, nevertheless argue strongly for vegetative production by internal budding as the source of such broods.

Considering the regular genotypic identity between adults and their broods (Orr *et al.*, 1982), and the population structure characterized by multiple clones (Brace and Quicke, 1986), it seems likely that in *A.equina equina* II, most local population growth is asexual, with occasional outcrossing. Sexual reproduction may be more prevalent in some populations where genotypic diversity is very high (M.A. Carter, personal communication), and it seems to occur in summer or autumn (Carter and Miles, 1989). In *A.tenebrosa* conformity to Hardy–Weinberg expectations of allele frequencies across geographically widespread clones (Ayre, 1984b) suggests a similar pattern of reproduction. The relative contributions of sexual and asexual (vegetative and gametic) reproduction to the population structures of anemones, and their evolutionary implications, are considered in section 6.5.

6.4.2 Determinants of Asexual Reproduction and Clonal Growth

Chia (1976) generalizes that asexual reproduction is associated with stressful conditions, including poor nutrition, and suggests that such factors select against sexuality. The implication is that vegetative reproduction has a lower energetic cost (presumably the lack of need for proliferating and maintaining gametes), even if the costs of fission, basal laceration, etc. and regeneration are considered. At the same time, however, parthenogenesis, which necessarily involves gametes, is associated with harsh or marginal environments (Rossi, 1975; Shaw *et al.*, 1987), so that the issue may be more the likelihood of outright survival of the offspring (relatively large somatic bits derived from the adults, or brooded parthenogenetic young) than energy savings in the adult. Again, there is the problem of confusing growth of the clonal soma with expansion of the population by sexual reproduction (Pearse *et al.*, 1989).

Recent research indicates that vegetative proliferation may actually maximize the energy available for growth and sexual reproduction (Sebens, 1979). From this standpoint, early results on asexually reproducing sea anemones seem paradoxical, as they reveal an inverse relationship between feeding frequency and vegetative proliferation. Smith and Lenhoff (1976) first suggested that during periods of food limitation increased basal laceration by *Aiptasiogeton pellucidus* ($\equiv$ *A.comatus*) increases the number of mouths present to capture whatever food is available. Sebens (1979) developed a formal model to define the optimal size of anemones as that showing the maximum

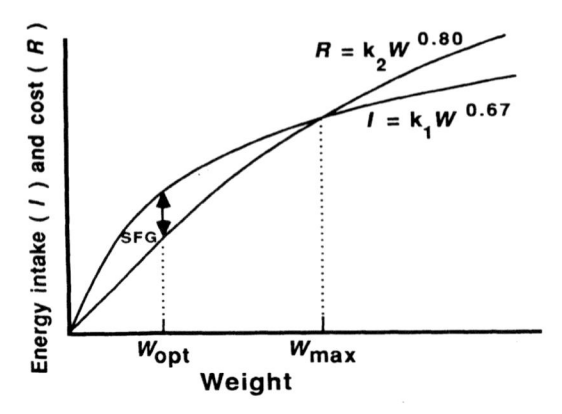

Figure 6.5 Graphical model relating body weight to the balance between energy intake (I) and cost (respiration, R). Optimal size (W_{opt}) is that at which the difference between I and R (i.e. scope for growth, **SFG**) is maximal. Maximal size (W_{max}) is defined by the intersection of the curves for I and R. See text for discussion. Source: after Sebens (1979).

difference between energy intake and 'metabolic cost' (i.e. maximum scope for growth; Figure 6.5), and to predict the occurrence of asexual reproduction in light of optimal polyp size and prey size.

The rationale for Sebens' model was to demonstrate that clonal biomass (including somatic and reproductive growth) is maximised by holding individual size at the optimum (W_{opt}) via asexual fission, a goal admirably achieved with respect to *Anthopleura elegantissima* (Sebens, 1980, 1982a). As a feeder on small plankton, there is no advantage to this anemone to be large to increase the size of prey taken, and its energy intake (I) scales as a surface area-related function, i.e. in proportion to $W^{0.67}$ (see section 2.2.1, page 39) whereas metabolic cost or respiration (R) scales as $W^{0.80}$ (see section 3.8.1, page 144). Actual values of intake depend on prey availability (k_1) and will vary among seasons and habitats, i.e. $I = k_1 W^{0.67}$, while cost will also vary with habitat, temperature, etc., so that $R = k_2 W^{0.80}$. Thus the difference between energy intake and cost increases to a maximum at W_{opt} and then declines to zero at W_{max} (Figure 6.5).

Laboratory experiments indicate that food deprivation in *A. elegantissima* stimulates longitudinal fission (Sebens, 1980). This corresponds with field observations that fission occurs annually after the period of maximal individual growth and when prey availability and body size are declining (Sebens, 1982b). Fission seems timed to allow non-feeding anemones to regenerate during a period of minimal food availability, and so prepare them to exploit abundant resources during the next growing season. Since gonad mass is positively related to individual anemone mass (Figure 6.3), and fission products have the same genotype, in this case vegetative reproduction can be likened to a form of growth in which fitness of the genetic entity (genet) is maximized by optimizing the size of its individual component units or ramets.

Unlike *A.elegantissima*, *Haliplanella lineata* is not restricted to a single annual division but it continuously reproduces vegetatively in laboratory culture (Johnson and Shick, 1977; Minasian, 1979, 1982; Minasian and Mariscal, 1979) and apparently on the shore (Minasian, 1979, 1982). Unlike *A.elegantissima*, it responds to starvation by decreasing the incidence of longitudinal fission. The basis for this difference is unknown, but it may be related to a less strongly seasonal availability of prey, as in nature this anemone feeds throughout the year (Shick, 1976). In a given feeding regime, increasing temperature increases fission in *H.lineata* in culture, as it does in *A.elegantissima*. At low temperature reduced fission activity is the major cause of large individual body size in *H.lineata* (Johnson and Shick, 1977; Minasian, 1982). Increased prey capture will increase individual size, but it will also increase fission, which in turn decreases individual size. Realized size in *H.lineata* thus depends heavily on whether the thermal regime permits fission (Minasian, 1982).

These effects have not been formally modelled in *H.lineata* to the extent

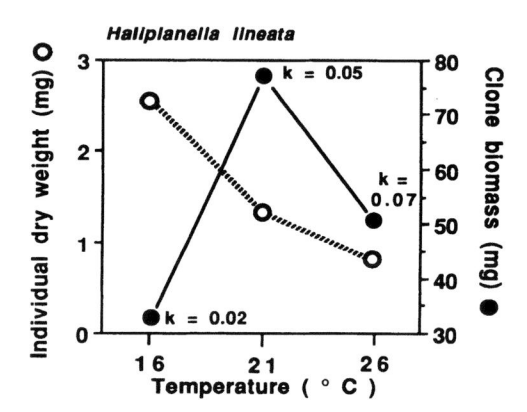

Figure 6.6 Interrelationships among weight of individual anemones, total biomass of clone, longitudinal fission activity and temperature in *Haliplanella lineata* in laboratory culture. Fission rate (k) was calculated from the equation $k = \ln(N_i/N_0)/t_i$, where N_i = number of individuals present on a given day of culture (t_i) and N_0 is the original number of anemones in the culture on day 0. Anemones were fed every second day. Total biomass of the clone is greatest at intermediate temperature and rate of fission, and declines with individual size as temperature and fission activity increase further. In anemones such as *H.lineata* which are capable of continuous fission, selection for maximum numbers rather than for optimal individual size or maximum clone biomass may be the case. See text for discussion. Source: drawn from data in Minasian (1982).

that they have in *A.elegantissima*, but some of Minasian's results suggest that a fundamental tenet of Sebens' model, that longitudinal fission is a means of maximizing energetic surplus as biomass, does not necessarily apply to *H.lineata*. Since maximal rates of vegetative proliferation in this species actually are an energetic liability (evinced by a decrease in clonal biomass when fission is maximal: Figure 6.6), the maximization of fission in *H.lineata* may have another basis.

Although maximization of surplus energy is a component of fitness, survival of the genet is the first requisite. Maximization of numbers may be one way to achieve this (even at the expense of individual size and clonal biomass), by decreasing the likelihood that all units of the genet will succumb to predators or random disturbances. Coates and Jackson (1985), like Chia (1976), noted the association in sea anemones of asexual reproduction with small body size, and showed in the British fauna that, on average, clonal species have smaller unit size (median diameter = 20 mm in 12 species) than do aclonal anemones (median diameter = 60 mm in 21 species). Rather than invoking poor nutritional conditions, the former authors note that genet size (the number of individual ramets) in clonal species can increase regardless of ramet size. Although large individual size enhances survival (sections 4.4, 7.2.1, 7.4.1, and 7.4.2) and gonad output (Figures 6.2 and 6.3), in clonal species there should be less selection for large unit size to enhance survivorship and sexual reproduction, 'at least so far as overall risk of [genet] mortality is concerned', since the risk is widely spread. Also, vegetative reproduction may enhance success of the genet in interspecific competition (Jackson, 1985).

Francis (1988) likewise notes the significantly larger size of aclonal anemones (which live low in the intertidal zone) compared with clonal anemones (usually mid-to-high intertidal in distribution). Following Denny, Daniel and Koehl (1985), she argues that large individual size is disadvantageous on the upper shore owing to the damaging and deforming forces of waves and turbulence, so that vegetative proliferation provides a mechanism for ramets to remain small while the genet increases in size. Lower on the shore and in the sublittoral, large size is not only feasible physically and energetically, but also necessary to enhance prey capture and to avoid predation (sections 5.8 and 7.4).

Haliplanella lineata exhibits classic attributes of a colonizing species (Shick, 1976). Considering the rarity of its sexual reproduction (Shick and Lamb, 1977, and references therein) and its eurytopic nature, asexual fission may represent a means of dispersal as well as of local proliferation. *Metridium exilis*, an intertidal species having very small determinate body size, reproduces continuously by fission, and in so doing, apparently keeps individual size below the threshold for sexual maturation (Bucklin, 1987a). In rapidly proliferating clones of *H.lineata*, sterility and small body size are quite common (Shick and Lamb, 1977; Minasian, 1982). It thus appears that in these species maximization of numbers at the expense of individual size and sexual reproduction has been selected for, their populations typically consisting of a few very large clones (Shick, 1976; Shick and Lamb, 1977; Bucklin and Hedgecock, 1982; Bucklin, 1987a).

Basal laceration may also be inversely related to feeding frequency (*Aiptasia pallida*: Clayton, 1985; Clayton and Lasker, 1985; *Aiptasiogeton pellucidus*: Smith and Lenhoff, 1976), although not invariably (*Aiptasia pulchella*: Hunter, 1984; *M.senile*: Bucklin, 1987b). Unlike longitudinal fission in *A.elegantissima*, but like that process in *H.lineata*, basal laceration is often continuous in cultures of anemones that exhibit it, even when food is scarce or absent. In this case, basal laceration appears to exemplify 'reproductive recklessness', which Calow (1978), referring to gametic reproduction, argues is selected when the progeny have an equal or greater chance than the adult of surviving food scarcity. Because the foregoing species use small prey, Sebens' argument that small size represents no disadvantage in capturing prey is relevant. Moreover, smaller body size involves a lower total maintenance cost, so that basal laceration by a large anemone may be a means to reduce this cost disproportionally compared with prey capture when prey is scarce. Not only do lacerates of *A.pallida* survive, but they increase clonal growth (biomass accretion) faster than individual growth, since clonal growth is significantly greater than that estimated from individual growth alone (Clayton and Lasker, 1985).

Aiptasia spp. contain zooxanthellae, which may or may not affect basal laceration, as will be seen. *Aiptasia pulchella* produced a greater mass of lacerates in the dark than in the light, despite the fact that in the light lacerates were larger (probably owing to the mass of the algae: see below). Hunter (1984) suggested that maintenance of a zooxanthellate anemone in darkness represents a form of starvation, and interpreted the higher rate of basal laceration in the dark accordingly, although he demonstrated no significant effect of feeding frequency on laceration in light or dark. In *A.pallida*, where there is an inverse relation between feeding and laceration frequency, at low feeding frequencies zooxanthellate anemones produced more lacerates than did aposymbiotic individuals, counter to expectations if starvation were cueing basal laceration (Clayton, 1985). The presence of zooxanthellae did not affect lacerate survivorship or rate of development into tentaculate juveniles as compared with aposymbiotic anemones, and the larger size of zooxanthellate lacerates was attributed entirely to the mass of the algae, which represented 60% of the total mass (Clayton, 1985). There was no significant difference in mass between lacerates and juveniles regenerating from them in either zooxanthellate or aposymbiotic individuals; since the juveniles cannot feed, this implies that algal photosynthate does not contribute to the maintenance of existing tissue, contrary to its effect in starving adults of several species (section 2.6.6 and Figure 2.21, page 102). In short, there is no clear-cut role of the zooxanthellae in the processes of basal laceration and juvenile regeneration in *Aiptasia* spp.

Longitudinal fission and basal laceration differ in the degree of tissue reorganization and regeneration necessary to reconstitute complete individuals, and so they probably differ in their energetics and environmental determinants as well. Sibly and Calow (1982) present a model that defines fitness as the rate of clonal growth, and which predicts that more and smaller offspring should be produced under conditions favourable for individual growth, whereas binary fission should be selected under poorer growing conditions. Insofar as growing conditions in intertidal habitats are generally poorer than in the sublittoral, an interspecific comparison of anemones supports that hypothesis, although taxonomic factors are also evident.

Within the acontiate Mesomyaria, for example, predominantly sublittoral species (see Appendix) such as *Acontiophorum niveum, Aiptasia* spp., *Aiptasiogeton pellucidus, Bartholomea annulata, Diadumene cincta, Metridium senile, Phellia gausapata, Sagartia elegans* and *Sagartiogeton laceratus* all proliferate asexually, and exclusively by basal laceration. (*M.senile* occurs intertidally in some benign habitats in California and Europe, but on a worldwide basis it is far more abundant sublittorally.) Species having predominantly intertidal distributions (*Aiptasiomorpha elongata, Anthothoe chilensis, Cereus herpetodes* and *Metridium exilis*) all show longitudinal fission. Basal laceration thus appears to be favoured in sublittoral species and binary fission in intertidal species. *Haliplanella lineata* is an outstanding exception. A generalist in the intertidal and sublittoral substrates it occupies, it is cosmopolitan and also belies Stephenson's (1929) generalization that a given species of sea anemone employs only one method of asexual reproduction. Both longitudinal fission and basal laceration occur regularly, even within a single clonal population (Johnson and Shick, 1977).

In *M.senile*, the amount of laceration increases with current speed and hence food availability (Shick *et al.*, 1979b; Shick and Hoffmann, 1980; Figure 5.8). Bucklin (1987a) confirms a positive relationship between feeding and laceration. For a relatively large anemone relying on currents to provide planktonic food, the advantage of laceration over fission may be that the former scarcely affects 'parental' body size and so does not hinder an adult's ability to feed effectively (section 2.2.2, page 47). At very low current speeds laceration is minimal, perhaps because of a very low likelihood of food capture by small lacerates in the boundary layer, rather than because of any direct cost to the parent. This is carried to its lower extreme in the very large *Metridium giganteum* which inhabits areas of extremely low current (Koehl, 1977a) and which is aclonal (Bucklin, 1987a).

In intertidal species the prevalence of fission may in addition be related to the danger of mortality through desiccation in very small ramets (section 4.4, page 194), that is, asexual products in the intertidal may need to be large to avoid drying out. Intertidal specimens of *H.lineata* (≡ *Diadumene luciae*) are larger and undergo fission less frequently than sublittoral conspecifics at the same site (Uchida, 1936). In *H.lineata* aerial exposure *per se* reduces fission activity and increases individual size (Johnson and Shick, 1977).

Basal laceration is lacking in actiniid anemones. Longitudinal fission is the norm in this family (Tables 6.1 and 6.2), particularly in intertidal species. The predominance of fission in intertidal species having broad vertical distributions (e.g. *A.elegantissima* and *Phymactis clematis*) agrees with the need to avoid desiccation and with Sibly and Calow's hypothesis (page 262). In characteristically brooding *Actinia* spp., the rare incidence of external vegetative reproduction also occurs as fission rather than laceration (Sebens and Paine, 1978; Schäfer, 1981; Cairns *et al.*, 1986). Predominantly sublittoral species and morphs (e.g. *A.xanthogrammica*, 'solitary' *A.elegantissima*, 'solitary' *P.clematis*, *Urticina* spp., etc.) normally do not reproduce vegetatively, apparently maximizing fitness by remaining large to capture large benthic prey (Sebens, 1982a; Sebens and Paine, 1978). In these sublittoral actiniids it is more evident that the absence of basal laceration under good growing conditions is determined taxonomically, and it may also suggest an intertidal origin of the Actiniidae.

Stephenson (1929) noted the mutual exclusion of 'asexual' (in his usage, synonymous with 'vegetative') reproduction and viviparity within species. This may reflect reliance on alternative mechanisms of achieving the same end — enhancing survival of progeny — although the genetic consequences will be different if brooded young are produced sexually rather than apomictically. Since the genetic consequences of vegetative reproduction and apomictic parthenogenesis are the same, the existence of species that brood apomictic, parthenogenetic young (see above) provides a special case that suggests that the mutual exclusion of vegetative reproduction and viviparity has more to do with avoiding redundancy in promoting the survival of offspring than with genetic systems and recombination. However, the brooding of vegetatively produced embryos in *Actinia* spp. and in *Bunodeopsis medusoides* contradicts Stephenson's (1929) generalization and my view of its significance. Viable size may be at the heart of the discrepancy. Vegetative embryos are smaller than either basal lacerates or binary fission products, and in *Actinia* spp. are incapable of an independent existence in the intertidal zone. Therefore, in intertidal *Actinia* spp. where vegetative embryogenesis rather than longitudinal fission evolved as the normal mode of asexual proliferation, brooding affords a protection from desiccation and it developed as a necessary coadaptation to an intertidal existence.

As in other marine invertebrates, in *Actinia* spp. there is an association between small body size and brooding: the larger, predominantly low-shore or sublittoral forms *A.fragacea* and *A.equina mediterranea* I are oviparous, for example, whereas the smaller, mid-to-upper shore *A.equina equina*, *A.prasina* and *A.tenebrosa* brood young internally. The basis for the association of small body size and brooding remains a subject of debate (Strathmann and Strathmann, 1982). In the case of *Actinia* species that brood *vegetative* offspring, the argument relating to different allometries of egg production and brood space does not apply. The suggestion that brooding is a mechanism for continuing to exploit locally favourable conditions for several generations (Strathmann and Strathmann, 1982) may be valid, but only secondarily, since vegetative proliferation alone would afford this advantage. In the case of *Actinia* spp., it seems most likely that brooding has been adopted as a means of protecting tiny asexual offspring from the rigours of an intertidal existence in anemones that do not normally rely on binary fission.

In *Actinia tenebrosa* adult body size, fertility, incidence of brooding and asexual fecundity are inversely related to adult population density (Ayre, 1984c; Figure 6.7). The last three measures are probably dependent on the first, adult body size being determined in turn by food availability. Thus, food limitation in dense populations apparently restricts the energetic allocation to 'reproduction', manifested in an asexual fecundity four-fold lower than in low-density populations.

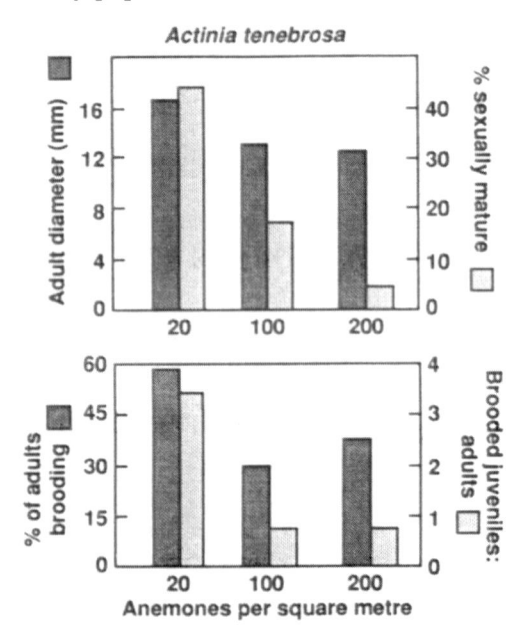

Figure 6.7 Demography and adult size in W. Australian populations of *Actinia tenebrosa* in which the local density of adults was manipulated experimentally. Duration of experiment was 14 months. See text for discussion. Source: drawn from data in Ayre (1984b).

6.4.3 Cost of Asexual Reproduction

A process as dynamic as tearing the body in half and regenerating the missing structures in each half surely entails a metabolic cost, but there has been no measurement of this. Singer and Palmer (1969) provided relevant data for *Aiptasia diaphana*, in which amputation of the oral disc and tentacles led to an increase in oxygen consumption in two stages. First, wound healing, which involved tissue reorganization but no cellular proliferation (Singer, 1971), was associated with a 30% increase in oxygen consumption compared with unamputated controls. Second, the development of tentacle buds involving cellular proliferation led to a further 50% increase in oxygen uptake, so that during regeneration the aerobic energy demand roughly doubled. In a species such as *H. lineata* in which fission and regeneration are frequent, the energetic cost of the processes may be high, and if such costs outstrip enhanced prey capture by clones (Minasian, 1982), they might explain the decrease in clonal biomass as fissions are maximized (Figure 6.6).

Compared with fission, metabolic costs of producing a single basal lacerate will be much lower, although the continuous production of multiple lacerates will increase the total cost. Clayton (1985) found no size difference between fresh lacerates and regenerating juveniles (i.e. no negative growth or shrinkage in the absence of feeding at a time of increased cost, even in aposymbiotic anemones), the cost presumably being supported by the uptake of dissolved organic matter; such an effect would be consistent with a supplementary nutritive role of DOM (section 2.2.8, page 57).

Asexual reproductive effort may be calculated analogously to the cost of sexual reproduction, and one expression of this is the ratio of the energy invested in reproduction to net ingested (in practice, absorbed or assimilated) energy, Rep/I_{net} ($\times$ 100%). Calow (1979) notes that this ratio does not reflect the true cost of reproduction to the individual because it does not necessarily quantify the extent to which energy needed in other functions is diverted to reproduction. Hunter (1984), however, recognizes that Rep/I_{net} (measured in adult *A. pulchella* starved in the dark as energy allocated to basal lacerates divided by the energetic equivalent of shrinkage) estimates just that quantity, because in starved individuals shrinkage presumably supports essential maintenance functions. Hunter concludes that a value for Rep/I_{net} of 4.4% in this species is very low compared with published values for sexual reproductive effort in various metazoans, and suggests that a low cost of asexual proliferation may contribute to the ecological success of anemones employing it.

Although a Rep/I_{net} of 4.4% is low when compared with a sexual reproductive cost of 17.5% to 49% in *semelparous* invertebrates (Calow, 1979), since basal laceration occurs continuously, it is more appropriately compared with the cost of *iteroparous* gametic reproduction, which is for example 2.3%,

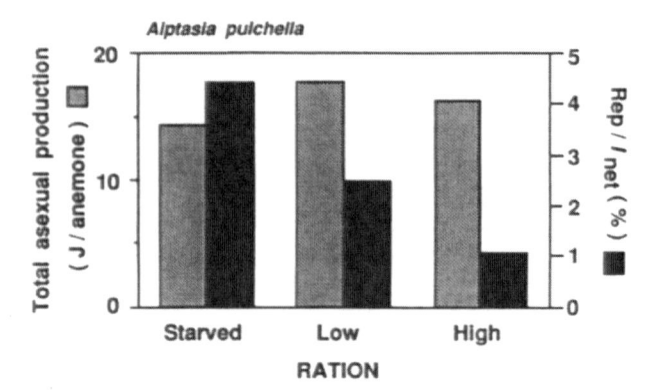

Figure 6.8 Evidence for 'asexual reproductive recklessness' in vegetatively proliferating cultures of *Aiptasia pulchella*. See text for discussion. Source: drawn from data in Hunter (1984).

5% and 16% in three gastropods (Calow, 1979), 20% in a triclad (Calow, 1979), and 0.4% in a scleractinian coral (Edmunds and Davies, 1986). On balance, there is no clear indication that vegetative proliferation is a particularly inexpensive way to reproduce. When the hidden costs of such reproduction (repair, reorganization, regeneration) are included, the total cost of vegetative reproduction may rise disproportionally more than sexual reproduction, as conversion efficiencies of food to somatic tissues are roughly an order of magnitude lower than those of food to gametes (Sibly and Calow, 1982).

The increasing asexual reproductive effort (as Rep/I_{net}) with decreasing ration in dark-maintained *A.pulchella* (Figure 6.8) is a manifestation of 'reproductive recklessness', as mentioned earlier. This is evinced by the fact that the total allocation to lacerates in individual starved anemones, anemones receiving 1.072 kJ of prey/8 weeks (low ration), and those fed 2.312 kJ/8 weeks (high ration) is remarkably similar, ranging from 14.4 to 18.1 J during this period (Figure 6.8). Such asexual recklessness contrasts with the sexual restraint exercised by planktotrophically and lecithotrophically developing anemones (section 6.3.5). Together with the arguments already given, this difference illustrates the idea that the enhancement of fitness of the genet via clonal growth may outweigh the energetic cost of doing so. That clonal growth in anemones is predominantly via vegetative processes rather than via apomictic parthenogenesis (which would have the same energetic cost as sexual reproduction and the same genetic outcome as vegetative proliferation) may involve the greater likelihood of survival of large somatic propagules compared with small parthenogenetic larvae.

6.5 POPULATION STRUCTURE

Interest in the roles of sexual and asexual reproduction in animals utilizing both has until recently been largely at the theoretical level (G.C. Williams, 1975; Maynard Smith, 1978; Bell, 1982). But Francis (1973a) described the profound effect of binary fission on spatial population structure in *Anthopleura elegantissima*, and Hoffmann (1976) and Shick *et al.* (1979b) added a temporal component to genetic studies of *Metridium senile* populations by using the abundance and distribution of clones to infer long-term differential success of sexually-derived, distinct genotypes. Since that time, Hoffmann's (1987) monitoring of *M.senile* populations has demonstrated the stability of established clones and the relative rarity of sexual recruitment (see below).

G.C. Williams noted the similarity between many plants and anthozoans, as sessile organisms that reproduce both by widely dispersed sexual propagules and by local vegetative proliferation. His 'strawberry-coral model', although under attack from some quarters as to its broad applicability to clonal organisms, has begun to be tested and is found to predict accurately several aspects of the population biology of sea anemones. The model holds that in organisms proliferating asexually and reproducing sexually, the former serves to preserve intact locally adapted multiple locus genotypes, whereas the persistence of sex, despite its reduction of fitness owing to the cost of meiosis (recombinational load), may ultimately enhance fitness by producing genotypically diverse progeny that are dispersed to novel or unpredictable habitats. The occurrence in an anemone of asexuality and sexuality thus optimizes its evolutionary potential, by allowing the ameiotic preservation and amplification of a proven successful genotype without abandoning the genotypic diversity afforded by recombination and outcrossing. Williams' model further predicts intense competition among genotypically distinct individuals, and an inverse relationship between the size of locally adapted clones and habitat heterogeneity.

There is some empirical evidence for all of the foregoing. The production and maintenance of large clones in nature via vegetative proliferation or parthenogenesis has been demonstrated repeatedly using enzyme electrophoresis and intergenotypic acrorhagial responses (see below) (Hoffmann, 1976, 1986, 1987; Shick, 1976; Shick and Lamb, 1977; Shick *et al.*, 1979b; Ayre, 1982, 1983, 1984b; Bucklin and Hedgecock, 1982; Sebens, 1982b; Shaw *et al.*, 1987). Rigorous proofs that such clones are highly adapted to local conditions, however, are rare. Preliminary evidence came from an unreplicated experiment in which monoclonal individuals of *Haliplanella lineata* from Rhode Island were transplanted to a site in Maine, where they showed lower survivorship than the local clone (Shick *et al.*, 1979b). A far more systematic study of *Actinia tenebrosa* by Ayre (1985) used multiple

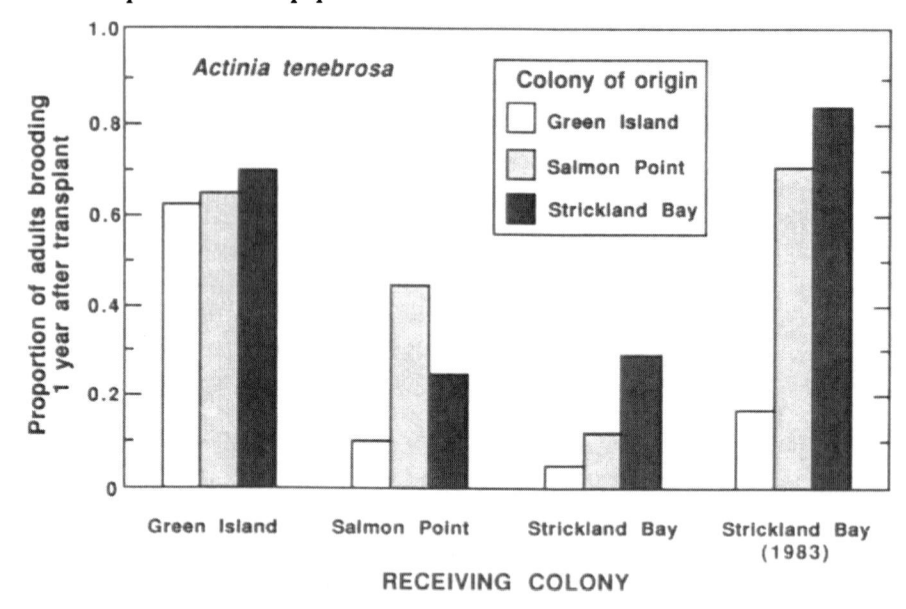

Figure 6.9 Localized adaptation of W. Australian clones of *Actinia tenebrosa*. Although survivorship was similar in all transplanted groups, asexual fecundity (another measure of fitness) was consistently greater in native anemones than in foreign specimens transplanted onto the same sites. Source: drawn from data in Ayre (1985).

reciprocal transplants of adults over distances of 2 km, and showed that indigenous anemones had significantly greater asexual fecundity (unrelated to body size) and proportion of individuals that brooded young than did transplants (Figure 6.9).

Although these studies demonstrate that clones introduced into non-native habitats are less well adapted to conditions there than are native clones, they do not indicate whether native clones are the only ones that may prosper in the area, or whether they are adapted only to that particular habitat. The predominance of one or a few clones of *H. lineata* at various sites may reflect the chance introduction and subsequent proliferation of a few broadly adapted, phenotypically plastic asexual colonists bearing 'general purpose genotypes' (Shick, 1976; Shick and Lamb, 1977). Similar founder effects in which relatively few clonal genotypes predominate in isolated locations are evident in populations of *Metridium senile* (Hoffmann, 1986) and *Sagartia ornata* (Shaw *et al.*, 1987). Fujii (1987) provides evidence that a single clone of *Anthopleura asiatica* has spread to several discrete habitats within 5 km of each other and monopolized them. Historical factors may also be involved: the largest clones at a site may be the oldest ones there, and their predominance may further involve the agonistic exclusion of potentially successful colonists, since in such conflicts established individuals tend to prevail (Ottaway, 1978; see below). Long-term monitoring of identified clones in particular habitats is clearly required but is fraught with difficulties.

The negative correlation of fitness for sexually-produced offspring in the parental habitat implied by Williams' model has not been tested, but the potential of such offspring for wide dispersal is a fact. In several clonal species sexual planulae remain planktonic for days to weeks or even months (Widersten, 1968; Siebert, 1974). Sexual recruitment of juveniles from a gene pool different from the local adult population has been observed in *M.senile* (Hoffmann, 1987). In *A.tenebrosa*, conformity of allozyme frequencies to Hardy–Weinberg expectations in populations collected over a 1 400 km range across southern Australia indicates extremely broad sexual dispersal and panmixia (Ayre, 1984b).

Intergenotypic competition for space in clonal anemones, manifested in agonistic behaviour involving acrorhagi, occurs in *Actinia equina* (Brace, Pavey and Quicke, 1979; Brace and Quicke, 1986), *Actinia tenebrosa* (Ottaway, 1978; Ayre, 1982, 1983), *Anemonia viridis* (Sauer, Müller and Weber, 1986), *Anthopleura elegantissima* (Francis, 1973b), *Anthopleura krebsi* (Bigger, 1980), and *Phymactis clematis* (Brace, 1981). The behaviour is not unique to clonal species, occurring also in aclonal *Anthopleura xanthogrammica* (Bigger, 1980; Sebens, 1984a) and *Bunodosoma cavernata* (Bigger, 1980). In *A.elegantissima*, an aggregating clonal species, the behaviour maintains the integrity of clonal boundaries, and the dominance of larger individuals (Francis, 1973b) suggests that acrorhagial conflict serves also to repel juveniles moving into an area (Sebens, 1982b). In non-aggregating but clonal *Actinia* spp., intergenotypic application of acrorhagi by adults onto juveniles may maintain suitable settlement sites for their own brooded offspring (Ayre, 1982, 1983), although it may also enhance adult survivorship in optimal microhabitats during harsh seasons (Brace and Quicke, 1986). In the zooxanthellate anemones *Anemonia rustica* and *A.sulcata*, interspecific conflicts allow clones of each species to dominate well-lighted areas at the species' respective depths of maximum abundance (measured as the number of clones); fitness (measured as gonad index and as number of anemones per clone) is directly related to clonal abundance in each species, which show opposite patterns of abundance with depth (Sauer, 1989 and personal communication).

An analogous agonistic behaviour involving catch tentacles in the clonal acontiate anemones *Metridium senile* and *Haliplanella lineata* is less thoroughly studied. In the former species, which may form clonal aggregates, it could help to maintain clonal boundaries, although it often does not do so (Purcell, 1977b; Purcell and Kitting, 1982). If it were directed specifically against genotypically distinct members of the same sex, it might also help to assure fertilization by increasing the probability that nearest neighbours would be of the opposite sex, as suggested by Kaplan (1983). In the non-aggregating species *H.lineata*, catch tentacles may maintain individual spacing in dense but genotypically depauperate founder populations (Shick and Lamb, 1977). Catch tentacles seem more common in populations where asexual reproduction is infrequent (Fukui, 1986), and they may thus be a form of communicating information about population density rather than of interference, as in the aclonal, acrorhagus-bearing *Anthopleura xanthogrammica* (Sebens, 1984a). Catch tentacles are not limited to clonal species (R.B. Williams, 1975). Intraspecific agonistic behaviour is discussed further in section 7.2.1 (page 280).

As predicted by the strawberry-coral model, in *Anthopleura elegantissima* (Sebens, 1982b) and *Actinia tenebrosa* (Ayre, 1984b) clone sizes (numbers of clonemates and area covered) are larger in stable, physically protected habitats than in unstable, exposed areas. In *A.equina*, noting their occupation of a temporally and spatially variable intertidal habitat, Quicke and Brace (1983) and Brace and Quicke (1985) report that only $\approx 10\%$ of the clones consist of more than ten individuals. Clonal (genotypic) diversity also seems positively related to environmental heterogeneity, although the data are few, assessment of heterogeneity is often subjective, and chance may contribute to observed patterns of diversity.

Genotypic diversity (G_o) may be quantified as

$$G_o = 1/\sum_{i=1}^{k} g_i^2$$

where g_i is the observed frequency of the ith of k multiple locus genotypes. G_o ranges between 1 and k, when each anemone is genotypically unique. Stoddart (1983) provided an expected value of diversity (G_e^*) to correct for a large number of genotypes of extremely low frequency. Black and Johnson (1979) and Ayre (1984b) used deviations of the ratio $G_o : G_e^*$ from unity as a qualitative index of the combined effects of departures from Hardy–Weinberg equilibria at single loci and multiple locus linkage disequilibria (i.e. those deviating from the expected frequency based on random assortment during recombination, due to the close proximity of groups of loci on a chromosome). Extensive asexual reproduction within genotypically variable (multiclonal) populations results in a low value of $G_o : G_e^*$. Values of the ratio approximating 1.0 are rare in most populations of *A.tenebrosa*, and values tend to be lower (asexual reproduction more common) on stable than on unstable shores (Ayre, 1984b). [Hoffmann (1986) showed that G_e^* overestimates the true expectation, so that the actual ratios are probably nearer to 1.0 than reported.] Genotypically diverse, highly heterozygous populations of *A.equina* occupy the 'temporally and spatially, highly variable' intertidal zone of eastern England, and they do not exhibit the clumping of like genotypes observed in more strongly clonal populations of *A.tenebrosa* (cf. Quicke and Brace, 1983, and Ayre, 1983, 1984b). The situation in *A.equina* is further complicated by the demonstration of distinct morphs (Quicke and Brace, 1984; Quicke *et al.*, 1985) or cryptic species (Haylor, Thorpe and Carter, 1984) adapted to different intertidal levels and microhabitats, and relying to different extents on asexual reproduction. In both *A.equina* and *A.tenebrosa*, recolonization of cleared space is by juvenile recruitment (clonal offspring of nearby adults, at least in the latter species: Ayre, 1983) rather than by immigration of adults from contiguous areas.

Apparent genotypic diversity may also be affected by sampling procedure.

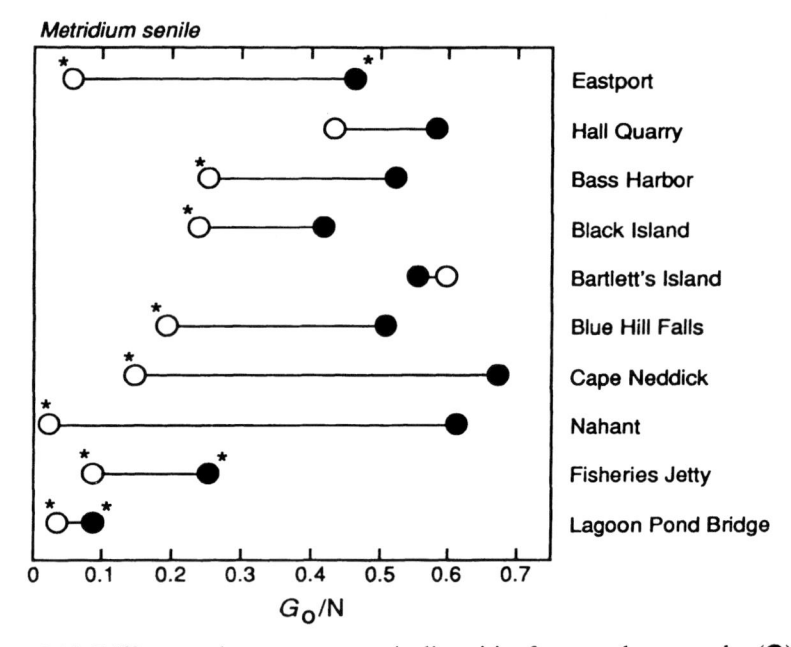

Figure 6.10 Differences between genotypic diversities from random samples (●) and transect samples (○) of populations of *Metridium senile* on the Atlantic Coast of the northeastern United States. Asterisks mark diversities that are significantly lower than expected for freely recombining, sexual populations, showing that cloning plays a significant role in determining genetic structure. Low values of G_o (genotypic diversity: see text) indicate the presence of only a few unique genotypes; values of G_o approach the sample size when each individual is unique. For transect samples, all anemones (up to $N = 50$) were removed from a transect through each population. In general, transect samples show that cloning is important, but, surprisingly, some transect samples show no significant effect of asexual reproduction. The differences between random and transect diversities from each population are quite variable, indicating that populations differ in the extent to which they grow by clonal proliferation. Source: data from R.J. Hoffmann and W.E. Zamer (unpublished).

R.J. Hoffmann and W.E. Zamer (personal communication) compared diversities for random samples of *Metridium senile* to those obtained when the same populations were cleared of all individuals along a transect. As expected, in nine of the ten populations genotypic diversities from transects were lower than those derived from random samples (Figure 6.10). Underlying this result, however, is surprising complexity. In two populations, diversities from transects were not significantly lower than expected for freely recombining, sexual populations, indicating that cloning plays a relatively minor role in determining genetic structure on a fine scale. In these populations, anemones occur in clusters, but those clusters are not the simple result of asexual reproduction. Genotypic diversity from random samples moreover is not a reliable predictor of the diversity from transects; differences between diversities from random and transect samples follow no particular pattern. In some populations with relatively high overall genotypic diversities, transect samples reveal extensive cloning on a very local level, whereas in others asexual proliferation is a less important contributor to population growth. The contrast between these two ways of measuring clone structure emphasizes that the interplay between sexual recruitment and asexual proliferation may be quite variable, even within the same species.

Departures from Hardy–Weinberg expectations (heterozygote excesses and deficiencies) are common in local populations of clonal anemones (Black and Johnson, 1979; Bucklin and Hedgecock, 1982; Ayre, 1983; Quicke and Brace, 1983; Haylor *et al.*, 1984; Bucklin, 1985; Hoffmann, 1986; Shaw *et al.*, 1987; Smith and Potts, 1987) and are best explained by random asexual reproduction of genotypes, which would lower genotypic diversity without systematically affecting heterozygosity (Hoffmann, 1986). In *A.tenebrosa*, when each unique multiple locus genotype is considered as a single clonal entity (genet), the departures from Hardy–Weinberg equilibria disappear, suggesting not only that these are due to asexual amplification of some genotypes, but that genotypic diversity in this clonal anemone arises from sexual recombination rather than from isolated mutations (Black and Johnson, 1979; Ayre, 1983). In *Urticina eques* and *U.felina* the absence of multiple individuals having the same 14-locus genotype, and the conformity of both populations to Hardy–Weinberg expectations, indicate that these species do not reproduce asexually (Solé-Cava, Thorpe and Kaye, 1985). Similar genetic results were obtained for the strictly sexual species *Oulactis muscosa* (Hunt and Ayre, 1989).

Estimates of genetic variation (e.g. proportion of loci that are polymorphic, and mean individual heterozygosity: Table 6.3) in sea anemones span the range for other marine invertebrate taxa (Valentine, 1976) and show no predictable relationship to habitat (intertidal vs. sublittoral), reproductive mode (clonal vs. aclonal), body size, biome or taxonomy (Actiniidae vs. Metriidae). *Epiactis prolifera* may be an exception to this unpredictability, as its very low observed heterozygosity differs significantly from expected, together with predicted phenotypic segregation ratios in adults and brooded young, is attributable to self-fertilization and infrequent outcrossing (Bucklin, Hedgecock and Hand, 1984). Again, the high heterozygosity in the polyploid *Sagartia ornata* may arise from its suggested hybrid origin (Shaw *et al.*, 1987). Smith and Potts (1987) propose that greater heterozygosity in clonal *Anthopleura artemisia* and *A.elegantissima* than in aclonal *A.xanthogrammica* (Table 6.3) may result from the asexual amplification and potential immortality of many genets, large stores of genetic diversity being maintained by great longevity and iteroparous sexual reproduction of large, old clones. Their hypothesis lacks general applicability, however, as the pattern of heterozygosity in *Metridium* spp. is the opposite: aclonal *Metridium giganteum* is genetically more variable than sympatric populations of clonal *M.exilis* and *M.senile* (Table 6.3).

Heterozygote deficiencies, seen at individual loci and in the mean condition (Table 6.3), characterize many benthic invertebrates, clonal and aclonal. In some cases, this may result from the mixing of genetically distinct populations, leading to an overestimate of overall expected heterozygosity (Wahlund effect). Hoffmann (1986) argues convincingly that this cannot explain observed genotypic diversities in local populations of *M.senile*, in which heterozygote excesses and deficiencies are equally common. Using computer simulations to generate an expected distribution for statistically testing deviations of local genotypic diversity, Hoffmann demonstrated significant negative departures of such diversity from that expected in sexually breeding demes with free recombination and no linkage disequilibrium, in six of 23 populations. He interpreted this to indicate a founder effect in areas of the North American Atlantic coast where suitable substrate is patchily distributed and sexual recruitment is rare, so that local populations comprise a few clones derived from founder individuals. This population structure prevails in British locations as well (Bucklin, 1985).

Cloning cannot explain the heterozygote deficiencies in aclonal *A.xanthogrammica* (Smith and Potts, 1987) and *Oulactis muscosa* (Hunt and Ayre, 1989), or in clonal *A.artemisia* and *A.elegantissima*, where sampling procedure successfully avoided collecting clonemates (Smith and Potts, 1987). Since there was a clear lack of differentiation of local populations in all of these species, a geographic Wahlund effect is unlikely to cause the heterozygote deficiencies, nor are they explained by the presence of null (silent) alleles. Smith and Potts (1987), like earlier workers on sessile bivalves, invoke an interesting explanation: a highly localized fertilization of eggs before larval dispersal, such that higher probabilities of mating with close neighbours would result in the effective panmictic gamete pool being a small, non-random sample of the larger population. A gene present at locally higher frequencies than the population mean will produce an excess of homozy-

Table 6.3 Estimates of biochemical genetic variation in natural populations of sea anemones (Actiniaria) and a ceriantharian.
P: proportion of surveyed enzyme-coding loci that are polymorphic, where $P > 0.05$;
$\bar{H}_{obs}$: mean observed proportion of heterozygous individuals averaged over all loci;
$\bar{H}_{exp}$: proportion of heterozygous individuals expected from Hardy-Weinberg equilibrium

Species	Number of loci	P	Average number of alleles per locus*	$\bar{H}_{obs}$	$\bar{H}_{exp}$	Source
Actinia equina (Isle of Man)	17	0.176	1.24	0.047	0.057	Haylor, Thorpe and Carter, 1984
A.equina (Isle of Man)	18	0.833	2.11	0.245	0.261	Solé-Cava and Thorpe, 1987
A.equina (South Africa)	13	0.385	1.46	0.149	0.155	Ayre, 1984a
A.prasina	17	0.118	1.18	0.068	0.059	Haylor, Thorpe and Carter, 1984
A.prasina (Isle of Man)	18	0.722	1.78	0.276	0.250	Solé-Cava and Thorpe, 1987
A.tenebrosa	13	0.308	1.31	0.093	0.097	Ayre, 1984a
Anthopleura artemisia	17	0.941	3.29	0.151	0.375	Smith and Potts, 1987
A.elegantissima	18	0.889	3.44	0.154	0.328	"
A.orientalis	40	0.381	1.80	0.150	0.144	Manchenko and Balakirev, 1984
A.xanthogrammica	18	0.944	2.61	0.063	0.122	Smith and Potts, 1987
Bunodosoma cavernata	12	0.583	1.75	–	0.20	McCommas and Lester, 1980
B.granulifera	12	0.500	1.83	–	0.16	"

Ceriantheopsis americanus	8	0.500	2.75	0.232	0.251	R.J. Hoffmann and J.M. Shick, unpublished
Epiactis (≡ *Cnidopus*) *japonica*	17	0.394	–	0.169	0.157	Manchenko, 1985
E.prolifera	14	0.214	1.43	0.004	0.098	Bucklin, Hedgecock and Hand, 1984
Metridium exilis	16	0.250	1.31	0.110	0.086	Bucklin and Hedgecock, 1982
M.giganteum (California)	15	0.750	2.47	0.217	0.268	"
M.giganteum (Puget Sound)	16	0.750	2.44	0.203	0.264	"
M.senile (California)	16	0.625	2.00	0.145	0.164	"
M.senile (Puget Sound)	16	0.688	2.31	0.132	0.161	"
M.senile (Maine)	16	0.438	1.44	0.101	0.124	"
M.senile (Sea of Japan)	31	0.290	1.68	0.130	0.120	Manchenko and Shed'ko, 1987
Sagartia ornata	14	0.619	2.0	0.47	0.32	Shaw, Beardmore and Ryland, 1987
S.troglodytes	14	0.607	3.1	0.27	0.29	"
Urticina eques	14	0.857	2.93	0.424	0.436	Solé-Cava, Thorpe and Kaye, 1985
U.felina	14	0.929	2.93	0.348	0.410	"

*when not given in source, effective number of alleles/locus calculated from expected heterozygosity at individual loci as $1/1 - \bar{H}_{exp}$
– not given.

gotes, and the chances of such localized departures are enhanced by asexual proliferation of a few genotypes. Although the explanation is speculative, it seems feasible in view of highly localized fertilization, surprising mating behaviours and intergenotypic, intrasexual aggression described in section 6.3.2 and earlier in the present section. The situation probably is common in other taxa of sessile invertebrates having aggregated population structures. In clonal species, local vegetative spread of a few successful founders, and mating with nearest neighbours, may structure the sexually dispersed phase of the life cycle in ways unsuspected from the occurrence of freely broadcast, planktonic gametes. The matter again relates to the genotypic diversity in clonal populations.

Sebens and Thorne (1985) performed computer simulations of clonal diversity or duration of multiclonal coexistence for aggregated and dispersed clones differing in their growth rates and competitive abilities, under varying levels of habitat disturbance. The results for aggregated clones after 100 simulated generations generally agreed with predictions of similar models for species diversity: clones that differed inversely in growth rate and competitive ability had the highest diversity at intermediate levels of disturbance, whereas the best competitor took over at low levels of disturbance, and the fastest grower dominated under high disturbance. Disturbance also affected diversity in dispersed clones, although differential competitive abilities and growth (asexual recruitment) rates had less of an effect, apparently owing to density dependence of asexual recruitment: a large, widespread clone had little additional space to gain, but a recruit from a small clone with any competitive ability stood to gain substantially. The simulations also supported the intuitive expectation that under high levels of disturbance, recruits from external sexual populations contributed substantially to local clonal diversity.

Owing to the difficulty of identifying clonal genotypes and following them through time, there are few data from natural populations to compare with computer simulations. An outstanding exception is the work of Hoffmann (1987), who sampled clonal populations of *M. senile* in duplicate over one to six year intervals, and assessed the temporal stability of multiple locus, probably clonal genotypes. In his analysis, the number of genotypes found in the first collection but missing from the second was recorded, as was the number of genotypes found only in the second sample. Total apparent turnover was calculated as the sum of missing and new genotypes. Computer simulations derived from those used to assess clonal diversity in *M. senile* (see above) generated expectations for repeated samplings of populations having free recombination and no linkage disequilibrium. Most of the 14 populations studied remained genotypically stable over several years, implying equilibrium conditions of clonal coexistence during this interval. Only four populations had a total turnover significantly different than expected, in all cases genotypic turnover being less than predicted for freely recombining gene pools: this is undoubtedly an effect of local asexual proliferation, perhaps with a further lack of sexual recruitment. In three of the four populations, there were fewer new genotypes than expected. The rarity of sexual recruitment was likewise suggested by the occurrence in only one population of recruits possibly from outside that population.

The potential for outside sexual recruitment into unoccupied habitat space exists, however, as evinced by the settlement in one site of larvae different in allelic frequencies from local adults (Hoffmann, 1987). In that case, the larvae settled on artificial surfaces cleared annually of epifauna, in keeping with the prediction that sexual recruitment contributes to clonal diversity especially in highly disturbed areas. That such recruits may not often persist in established populations may not so much reflect strong genotype-specific selection against them as size-selective predation by the nudibranch *Aeolidia papillosa* (Harris, 1973, 1986), which prevents new clonal aggregations from becoming established (Sebens, 1986) (see also section 7.4.1, page 313).

Asexual proliferation has increasingly evident advantages not only for anemones making use of it, but also for the experimenter. The replication of physiological and biochemical measurements on multiple yet genetically identical clonemates significantly reduces experimental variance (Shick and Dowse, 1985). This can be a benefit when investigating the effect of an experimental variable on physiological performance, although it risks overlooking genetically determined differences in physiological responses, unless many clones are tested. It may prove useful to those studying the adaptedness of particular genetic combinations (Zamer and Hoffmann, 1989) or the levels of individual heterozygosity under different environmental conditions.

7 Biotic interactions

7.1 SYNOPSIS

In sea anemones, intraspecific competition for space involving specialized catch tentacles and acrorhagi occurs between members of different clonal aggregations in the intertidal zone and in other restricted habitats where space is limiting. In aclonal actiniids (which tend to be large, solitary and sublittoral in distribution), acrorhagial conflict is rare, and it seems to provide information about availability of space rather than be an agonistic competition for that resource. The complete acrorhagial response typically requires physical contact between allogeneic individuals (i.e. conspecifics bearing different genotypes) and involves different (chemo)receptors on the tentacles and acrorhagi. Most allogeneic individuals discharge acrorhagial nematocysts (predominantly holotrichs) when brought into contact, but that not all will do so may indicate the existence of special histocompatibility or allorecognition loci; allogeneic individuals may occasionally bear the same recognition markers (allotypes) and not recognize each other as non-self. The (1) evocation of agonistic behaviour involving catch tentacles and acrorhagi and (2) specificity of induced morphogenesis of catch tentacles meet at least two of the three criteria for an immunological response. An instance of 'inducible memory' (the third criterion) has not been proved to be immunological in nature. Interspecific competition is less well documented in sea anemones, but it occurs between species of anemones, between anemones and other anthozoans, and between anemones and other aggregating organisms, particularly in the sublittoral.

Ectosymbioses between sea anemones and decapod crustaceans and pomacentrid fishes may be commensal or mutualistic in nature. In some cases, host and symbiont demonstrably protect each other from predators, and some anemones are fed by their mutualistic partners. Some crabs have exploited the tendency of hormathiid anemones to attach to organic substrates and they actively transfer anemones to their carapaces or to the gastropod shells that they inhabit. The mucous coat of symbiotic shrimps, crabs and fishes protects them from being stung by their anemone partners, but the basis for the protection remains uncertain. Alternative hypotheses both supported by experimental evidence are acquisition of 'chemical camouflage' from the host anemone's mucus, and autoproduction of inert mucus that does not stimulate nematocysts. In pomacentrid anemonefishes, protection appears to require a period of 'acclimation' to the anemone, at least in adult fishes that are introduced to a new host. The duration of 'acclimation' necessary changes ontogenetically and is shortest (or perhaps non-existent) in newly-metamorphosed juveniles.

The presence of predators such as the sea star *Dermasterias imbricata* limits the vertical distribution of anemone prey, and size-selective predation by sea stars and aeolid nudibranchs accounts for observed population structures of some anemones. As often happens, careful study of a special case can shed light on the general. The surprising acrobatics of shell-climbing hormathiid anemones during their interactions with hermit crab hosts and of swimming actinostolid and boloceroidid anemones set off by asteroid and nudibranch predators have provoked anatomical, behavioural and electrophysiolgical investigations to which we owe much of our knowledge of the actiniarian neuromuscular system.

7.2 COMPETITION

It is axiomatic that space is the primary limiting physical resource for sedentary organisms in the intertidal zone. Despite their seeming vulnerability, sea anemones (especially actiniids) often dominate large expanses of the upper-middle and high intertidal, from which most other organisms are excluded by harsh physical conditions. This prevalence is brought about by a suite of behavioural, morphological, physiological and reproductive characteristics (sections 4.4, page 194, and 6.4.2, page 263), including dense packing of clonemates produced by longitudinal fission. Since few species exist there, but those that do have the asexual potential to monopolize space, most competition is intraspecific, and between members of allogeneic clones.

Lower in the intertidal, species diversity is greater and interspecific competition for space accordingly more frequent, and although sea anemones may dominate locally there, too, there is little information on the nature of their competitive interactions, other than with other anthozoans. Incidences of dislodgement of juvenile anemones by foraging gastropods and chitons (e.g. Ottaway, 1978, 1979b) seem to be isolated cases of random blundering rather than of ongoing interference. Some nudibranchs, however, are important predators on anemones (section 7.4.1, page 308).

7.2.1 Intraspecific Competition

In addition to typical feeding tentacles, some mesomyarian anemones possess so-called catch tentacles ('Fangtentakeln': Carlgren, 1929). The cnidome (complement of nematocysts) of catch tentacles consists primarily of atrichous and holotrichous isorhizas (atrichs may actually also be holotrichs, but not necessarily: cf. Bigger, 1976; Fukui, 1986; see also section 1.5.1, page 26), which are absent from feeding tentacles. These contain mostly spirocysts and b-mastigophore nematocysts (Hand, 1955b; R.B. Williams, 1975; Purcell, 1977b; Watson and Mariscal, 1983a, b; Fukui, 1986). Scanning electron micrographs of catch tentacles of *Haliplanella lineata* ($\equiv$ *H.luciae*) reveal numerous ciliary cones, putative mechanoreceptors and perhaps contact chemoreceptors (Bigger, 1982) that are seen also in feeding tentacles (Mariscal, 1974a, b; Mariscal *et al.*, 1978; section 2.2.10, page 65).

Catch tentacles are employed solely in fighting with conspecifics and other anthozoans, as first documented by R.B. Williams (1975). The tip of the catch tentacle breaks off and remains attached to the 'victim'. Almost as surprising as the agonistic behaviour involving catch tentacles is the fact that they can be induced to form from feeding tentacles. Noting that catch tentacles regressed during prolonged isolation of individuals bearing them (see Hand, 1955b), and that catch tentacles were conspicuously abundant in specimens of *Metridium senile* at borders between individual clones, Purcell went on to show that maintaining non-clonemates in close contact led to the conversion of feeding tentacles into catch tentacles, including an increase in tentacle size and a major change in their cnidome (loss of spirocysts and a large increase in holotrichs and atrichs). This transformation was also seen in *H.lineata* by Watson and Mariscal (1983a). Catch tentacles are absent from monoclonal natural populations of *H.lineata* but abundant in multiclonal populations (R.B. Williams, 1975; Shick and Lamb, 1977; Fukui, 1986; Figure 7.1F).

The apparent function of agonistic behaviour involving catch tentacles is to maintain individual spacing in genotypically diverse populations of clonal anemones, as following an encounter even the 'aggressor' may move away (Fukui, 1986). Conflicts are rarely fatal, and may serve to communicate information about local density, inducing individuals to move if space is available. In crowded populations of *M.senile* where essentially all space is occupied (>95% cover is common: Purcell and Kitting, 1982), the behaviour and possibly the catch tentacles themselves may be lost in a form of 'habitu-

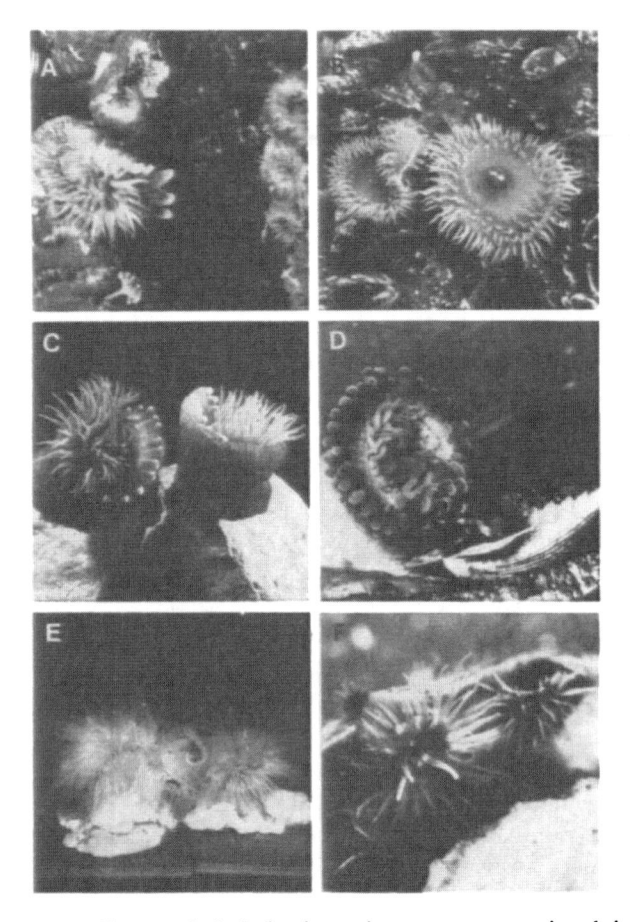

Figure 7.1 Intraspecific agonistic behaviours in sea anemones involving acrorhagi and catch tentacles. **A.** The large specimen of *Anthopleura elegantissima* has expanded its blunt, conical acrorhagi in response to tentacular contact with an adjacent non-clonemate. Note the anemone-free zone maintained between the combative individual and the allogeneic clone of smaller specimens on the right. **B.** The specimen of the aclonal *Anthopleura xanthogrammica* on the left is applying its expanded acrorhagi to a conspecific on the right. **C.** The specimen of *Actinia tenebrosa* on the right applied its acrorhagi to the allogeneic individual on the left and then pulled away; the individual on the left in turn showed an acrorhagial response. **D.** A specimen of the aclonal *Bunodosoma cavernata* has applied its acrorhagi to a contracted conspecific located in the scallop shell. The dark patches on the acrorhagi are areas from which the ecto-dermal 'peels' have been removed (remaining on the target anemone). In **C** and **D**, notice that the tentacles adjacent to expanded acrorhadi have been withdrawn toward the centre of the oral disc. **E.** A specimen of *Metridium senile* has inflated an opaque catch tentacle and applied it to an adjacent non-clonemate. **F.** Opaque catch tentacles are evident in a specimen of *Haliplanella lineata* surrounded by non-clonemates (see Shick and Lamb, 1977, p. 612). Source: **A.** Courtesy of L. Francis (unpublished); **B.** With permission from Bigger (1980); **C.** With permission from Ottaway (1978); **D.** With permission from Bigger (1980); **E.** With permission from Purcell (1977b); **F.** J.M. Shick (unpublished).

ation' or 'induced tolerance' to long-term neighbours. This avoids wasting energy and materials in conflicts in which no combatant is likely to prevail. Nothing is known of the mechanism of habituation, except that the ability to respond using catch tentacles is retained, since habituated anemones employ them when exposed to novel non-clonemates (Purcell and Kitting, 1982). Such a specificity may be important from an immunological perspective (see below).

Insights concerning catch tentacles came from earlier realization of the agonistic function of the acrorhagi (hollow extensions of the column at the base of the tentacles: Figure 1.2, page 4, and Figure 7.1A–D) of actiniids such as *Actinia equina* (Abel, 1954; Bonnin, 1964). Like catch tentacles, acrorhagi have a distinctive cnidome comprised predominantly of holotrichs. There have been numerous descriptions of behaviour involving acrorhagi (Bigger, 1980, and Sebens, 1984a for reviews). The general sequence is: (1) excitation and tentacular withdrawal, in which feeding tentacles of one individual contact another and then contract or bend away from that area; (2) swelling and elongation of the acrorhagi adjacent to the tentacles making allogeneic (non-clonemate conspecific) contact (Figure 7.1B–D); (3) bending of the 'aggressor' toward the 'victim' or 'target' (Figure 7.1C) and application of its acrorhagi to the latter; (4) massive discharge of nematocysts and peeling of the acrorhagial ectoderm away from the mesoglea (Figure 7.1D), with the 'peel' remaining attached to the target, where it may cause local necrosis within minutes. The behaviour may be repeated before return to the non-combative state, and the victim may respond in kind, contract or move away.

Details of the foregoing behaviours have been elucidated in several studies. There is still debate over whether or not the chemical recognition stimulus eliciting agonistic behaviour is bound to the cell surface. Using a porous barrier, Bigger (1976) showed that actual contact between the tentacles of *Anthopleura krebsi* and a foreign anemone was required for the acrorhagial response to occur. Freshly-secreted mucus from *A.krebsi* fails to elicit an acrorhagial reponse in non-clonemates (Bigger, 1976), and mucus from *A.elegantissima* fails to evoke discharge of acrorhagial nematocytes in non-clonemates that responded to direct contact (Lubbock, 1980a), suggesting that the effective stimulus is bound to the cell surface, or at least not free in the mucus. Conversely, specimens of *Anemonia viridis* ($\equiv$ *A.sulcata*) separated only by a membrane filter (0.45 µm pore size) or dialysis tubing (>15 kDa retention) showed an acrorhagial response, which would imply that a stimulus not bound to the cell surface is involved (Sauer, Müller and Weber, 1986). These workers isolated a glycoprotein having a molecular weight of 12–14 kDa that causes tentacular deflation and acrorhagial inflation and claimed that this compound in the mucus elicits the agonistic behaviour without contact between the anemones. To yield the glycoprotein, however, tentacles were frozen along with the mucus, and so the active component could originally have been bound to the cell surface. In short, it has not been shown unequivocally that mucus is capable of initiating agonistic behaviour in anemones of different genotype.

The initial receptors involved in triggering acrorhagial fighting are presumably the microvilli or ciliary cones of sensory cells and cnidocytes on the tentacles (Bigger, 1982). These ultrastructurally distinct, putative mechano- and chemoreceptors may be the morphological correlate of those independent factors evoking the acrorhagial response (against only allogeneic conspecifics and anthozoans, with a single exception — polyps of the scyphozoan *Cassiopeia*: Bigger, 1976, 1982) and those causing discharge of tentacular nematocytes (against allogeneic conspecifics and all xenogeneic individuals of different species and taxa) (see Lubbock, 1980a). Many taxonomically diverse organisms cause discharge of tentacular nematocysts without inducing agonistic behaviour (Francis, 1973b; Lubbock, 1980a).

Where it has been studied explicitly, expansion of the acrorhagi has been found necessary for the 'acrorhagial peel' to occur (*Actinia equina*: Bonnin, 1964; *Anthopleura krebsi* and *Bunodosoma cavernata*: Bigger, 1982). The latter author postulated that expansion of the acrorhagus increases the exposure of sensory microvilli in ciliary pits associated with holotrich nematocysts (Figure 2.10, page 67). This seems crucial because the factor eliciting discharge of acrorhagial nematocysts and the associated peel is not diffusable, so that direct contact of foreign tissue with the acrorhagial receptors is necessary (Bigger, 1976; Lubbock, 1980a).

Lubbock and Shelton (1981) recorded electrophysiological correlates of recognition of allogeneic tissue and discharge of acrorhagial nematocysts. They showed that although touching inanimate objects or syngeneic tissue (i.e. bearing the same genotype) to an expanded acrorhagus of *Anthopleura elegantissima* evoked no electrical activity, contact by an allogeneic tentacle produced numerous brief discharges of low amplitude, but no immediate discharge of nematocysts. They presumed that the small electrical potentials (which were distinct from SS1, SS2 and TCNN activity) were produced by chemoreceptors (specifically, ciliary cones) on the acrorhagus. Such potentials then summated to produce massive discharge of nematocysts, which was associated with a more prolonged electrical spike of higher amplitude. It was unclear to Lubbock and Shelton whether the spike caused the discharge of nematocysts or resulted from it, although it is now known that a change in the membrane potential of a cnidocyte does not cause its cnida to discharge (McKay and Anderson, 1988a, b).

The responsiveness of some tentacular receptors to free chemical markers (as opposed to those bound to the cell surface) suggests a simple concentration effect in the differential reponsiveness of tentacles and acrorhagi, the former having a lower threshold. However, it is also possible that tentacular receptors and acrorhagial inflation are stimulated by one substance, and acrorhagial peeling by another (Bigger, 1980; Lubbock and Shelton, 1981; Sauer *et al.*, 1986).

Together with the information presented in section 2.2.10 (page 65), the present observations indicate a hierarchy of responsiveness to various stimuli. Discharge of tentacular spirocysts and nematocysts is effected by both mechanical and non-specific chemical stimuli, whereas acrorhagial behaviour is evoked by a narrower range of chemical stimulation of the tentacles and acrorhagi. The acrorhagial peel reaction is even more specific, requiring physical contact with precise surface markers. The highly specific nature of the acrorhagial peel reaction, and its failure to be elicited by purely mechanical stimuli (Lubbock and Shelton, 1981), may avoid unnecessary discharge of nematocysts and loss of the ectoderm and so save the cost of regenerating ectoderm and secreting nematocysts. The foregoing may ultimately reflect the fact that foreign materials are more likely to be food than potential competitors. It is interesting that *Pseudactinia melanaster* (≡ *Anemonia sargassensis*) shows both feeding and acrorhagial responses to different individuals of other species of actinians, although the behaviours are mutually exclusive; that is, *P. melanaster* may recognize other anemones as prey or competitors, but not simultaneously, and uses the appropriate structures on these different occasions (tentacles in the former case, acrorhagi in the latter) (Bigger, 1980).

The principal role of catch tentacles and acrorhagi is to maintain individual spacing among genotypically distinct individuals, but in the recognition of self and non-self the evolutionary basis and advantages are less generally agreed. Francis (1988) argues that fighting in anemones arose primarily in intraspecific competition among clones but she does not consider the origin of the recognition system. As pointed out by Buss, McFadden and Keene (1984), it is unlikely that specialized agonistic structures and behaviours would have evolved unless systems to identify potential antagonists already existed. Sauer *et al.* (1986) agree with Francis that recognition of self and non-self is particularly advantageous in asexually reproducing organisms, and they seem to suggest that agonistic interactions underlie the ability to discriminate among genotypes.

Crozier (1986), however, considers that clonal recognition abilities must be maintained by selection for something else. Taking as his (unelaborated) fundamental premise that 'the fitness of a genotype is proportional to the fraction of the population with which it can interact peaceably', he goes on to show by a frequency-dependent selection model that among several possibilities at a recognition locus some allele will ultimately become fixed. He states that selection may favour anemones able to distinguish clonemates from allogeneic individuals and to respond antagonistically to the latter, but he argues that such selection will result in the loss of the polymorphism necessary for recognition. This is because costs of such agonistic behaviour outweigh the benefits, especially if an individual bears a rare allele for a recognition marker ('allotype': Grosberg and Quinn, 1989) and so faces nearly universal antagonism from other allotypic individuals; the result is that rare recognition alleles will be lost and that novel ones will not arise. Crozier suggests that variation at the recognition locus therefore is maintained by host–parasite relationships, an idea that harks back to J.B.S. Haldane. As it happens, incidences of parasitism are rare in cnidarians (Bigger and Hildemann, 1982).

It is not clear, however, that the premise on which selection coefficients in Crozier's model are based holds in crowded multiclonal populations where competition for space and prey may be intense. A genotype is then potentially of greater fitness if it can recognize and exclude agonistically any and all others, rather than coexisting and sharing limited resources with them. Crozier's selection coefficients incorporate only the costs of recognition and exclusion of non-clonemates and none of the benefits (or else include them as reduced costs), so that in his model fixation of one allele is inevitable. Most importantly, the model relates to individual selection and does not allow for a reduction in *per capita* costs among multiple clonal ramets, in which non-agonistic ramets may benefit from agonistic behaviour by their clonemates directed against non-clonemates, without themselves bearing any of the cost (Francis, 1988; Grosberg and Quinn, 1989). Francis in particular advocates considering such a case as kin selection at the level of the clone. The partitioning of the clonal soma into multiple ramets having varying degrees of interdependence poses a particular difficulty for such theoretical models of agonistic behaviour. Dicquemare's (1773) question still seems apropos: 'Are there animals among which an *individual* is not a *simple* being?'

Buss *et al.* (1984), based on their work with hydroids, offered the 'somatic cell parasitism hypothesis' to explain the origin of allorecognition. In cnidarians, fusion of allogeneic colonies would allow totipotent cells (e.g. those competent to produce gametes) to pass from one genet into another. If the totipotent cells of one genet are more successful in elaborating gametes than are those of the other genet, the former genet has effectively parasitized the other. Fitness of the chimera is potentially compromised by competition between its component genets for resources for gamete growth, thus providing the basis of selection for self/non-self recognition ability. Parenthetically, these authors suggested that the existence of multipotent cell lines in cnidarians allowed the development of structures specialized for agonistic behaviour, which is manifested in non-genetic polymorphism among clonemates, e.g. the induced morphogenesis of catch tentacles (including receptors and nematocysts lacking in feeding tentacles), and the higher frequency of acrorhagi in anemones at interclonal borders (see below). But the somatic cell parasitism hypothesis has seemingly little relevance to sea anemones, which do not naturally fuse and which apparently never have been colonial (section 1.6, page 31, and Buss, 1987).

Although Francis (1988) considers the primary function of catch tentacles and acrorhagi to be in intraspecific conflict, they are in fact used against other anemone species and against other anthozoans such as octocorals (Sebens, 1986). That they are not used against members of other phyla, nor generally against other classes of cnidarians, suggests an evolutionary constraint relevant to consideration of the recognition system. The general restriction of specialized agonistic behaviours and acrorhagial discharge in response to anemones and other anthozoans but not to other cnidarians (Lubbock, 1980a; but for the single exception, see Bigger, 1980) is reminiscent of the cell-mediated immune response in vertebrates: both have a stronger reaction to allogeneic than to xenogeneic cells (i.e. those belonging to a different species) (Bigger and Hildemann, 1982). Still, it is not clear in anemones whether this has as its ultimate basis competition or avoidance of somatic cell parasitism, although the former seems favoured because of the absence of fusion in anemones. Also, (spatial) competition is more likely between anemones and other anthozoans than between anemones and non-anthozoan cnidarians such as hydroids, in part owing to the very different growth forms in the latter (Jackson, 1977; Sebens, 1986).

Although fusion between allogeneic anemones seems unlikely, such is not the case for their relatives among the corals (see Stoddart *et al.*, 1985, for consideration of fusion in corals). Thus, cellular recognition of non-self in unitary, competitive anemones might have been a 'preadaptation' retained in their colonial descendants where allogeneic fusion was a real possibility. The matter also relates to the uncertain evolutionary relationship between the corals and the actiniarians (section 1.6). If, as Hand (1966) argues, anemones are descended from (colonial) corals, then cellular recognition of non-self might be a carryover from an ancestral state where allogeneic fusion was a real possibility.

As far as recognition of self and non-self is concerned, despite the high specificity of acrorhagial behaviour, individual anemones are not necessarily unique. From her experiments involving 75 different allogeneic pairings, Francis (1973b) concluded that a given specimen of *Anthopleura elegantissima* will employ acrorhagi against any and all non-clonemates, but not against any clonemate. In 162 pairings of *Anemonia viridis*, Sauer *et al.* (1986) demonstrated 324 mutual histoincompatibility responses. Lubbock (1980a), however, found one case among 102 allogeneic combinations of *A. elegantissima* in which the acrorhagial peel reaction did not occur, and Brace (1981) reported three instances where agonistic behaviour did not occur among 82 allogeneic pairings of *Phymactis clematis*. In 21 assumed allogeneic pairings of *Anthopleura krebsi*, Bigger (1980) found ten instances in which no response occurred, and Ayre (1982) reported similar results on *Actinia tenebrosa* (see below). Bigger (1980) postulated that rather than each genetic individual recognizing all others as foreign, the situation is more that related individuals share alleles at a locus or loci coding for molecules involved in recognition (allotypes). An anemone would not recognize another as a target for agonistic behaviour if they shared identical alleles among the multiple possibilities at these allorecognition loci, although they might differ at non-recognition loci. Lubbock's (1980a) single case of lack of acrorhagial peeling in a definitely allogeneic pairing (the individuals were of distinctly different colour morphs) is telling. Although the individuals did not provoke acrorhagial peeling, they did discharge their tentacular nematocysts against each other, which clone-mates do not. This supports the idea that receptors associated with tentacular nematocysts respond to molecules different from those concerned with clonal recognition. If, therefore, genotypically distinct clones sometimes bear the same allotypes, they may not recognize each other as allogeneic.

Acrorhagial responses meet the first two of three criteria proposed by Hildemann, Bigger and Johnston (1979) for an immunological response: (1) the existence of antagonistic responses; (2) specificity of these responses; and (3) an induced memory component, in which the response is altered selectively on subsequent contact. Lubbock (1980a) was unable to show inducible memory in the discharge of acrorhagial nematocysts, since repeated aggression against one clone of *A.elegantissima* did not enhance the discharge of nematocysts against that clone. Acrorhagial nematocyst discharge and peeling is the final act in a hierarchy of specific recognition responses, however, so that a memory component might exist elsewhere in the sequence. But, since acrorhagial discharge will occur against allogeneic and xenogeneic individuals in addition to the one causing acrorhagial expansion initially (Lubbock, 1980a), acrorhagial peeling would seem a poor candidate in support of specific memory.

Sauer *et al.* (1986) have confirmed the operation of inducible memory in acrorhagial expansion behaviour in *Anemonia viridis* ($\equiv$ *A.sulcata*). Following initial allogeneic contact, the time required to initiate an acrorhagial response in subsequent contacts was signficantly reduced. This 'alloimmune memory' persisted reliably for five days, but was absent after eight days without further contact. Unfortunately, Sauer and his colleagues tested for 'second-set' responses only the allogeneic pairings that caused the primary response, so the specificity of the memory component is not definitively established, and 'third-party' combinations (i.e. exposure to novel allotypes) are necessary to confirm or deny the existence of 'specific sensitization'. As emphasized by Bigger (1980), Bigger and Hildemann (1982) and Buss *et al.* (1984), nothing is known of the cell types involved in these phenomena, including primary sensitization and subsequent alloimmune memory. Certainly the duration of the latter (5–8 days) is somewhat less than in sponges and corals, owing perhaps to a very rapid cell turnover in anemones (Bigger and Hildemann, 1982), and is far shorter than for vertebrate immune systems. Whether any or all of these systems share a common ancestral genetic basis is of intense interest but unknown. The possibility remains that the memory demonstrated by Sauer *et al.* (1986) is not immunological in nature but a form of behavioural facilitation, which would be more in keeping with its relatively short duration. Further investigations on this fascinating topic clearly are warranted.

Inference of immune specificity assumes that the criteria used to select genotypically different clones for testing were reliable. These criteria were usually morphological (based on different colour and stripe patterns of the oral disc and tentacles) and topographic (individuals collected from different aggregations, especially if quite distant from each other, were assumed to be non-clonemates). A more powerful tool for distinguishing clones is electrophoresis of allozymes at multiple polymorphic enzyme-coding loci. Using this technique, Ayre (1982) found instances in which adults of *Actinia tenebrosa* that were different electrophoretically (and therefore allogeneic) failed to recognize each other as foreign, as well as cases of individuals engaging in combat despite their sharing identical allozymes at five polymorphic loci. The former indicates a recognition scheme involving special allorecognition loci as described above, while the latter means that five polymorphic loci may not be sufficient to distinguish among all clones. Hoffmann (1986) has shown that this number is insufficient to recognize all clones in populations of *Metridium senile*, as indicated by the failure of curves of genotypic diversity (section 6.5, page 270) versus number of loci to reach an asymptote at five loci. When adults of *A.tenebrosa* were tested against their own asexual progeny, they reassuringly failed to show aggression (Ayre, 1982). That adults did not attack juveniles from broods of some other adults may indicate their genotypic identity at allorecognition loci.

Such results call into question the practice of using acrorhagial responses to assess clonal population structure in the field, an area of active discussion among workers on sponges and cnidarians (Grosberg, Rice and Palumbi, 1985; Neigel and Avise, 1985; Stoddart *et al.*, 1985). Given Francis' (1973b) and Lubbock's (1980a) results, the method probably has an error rate in *A.elegantissima* on the order of 1%. Bigger (1980) collected specimens of *A.krebsi* from seven discrete aggregations separated by 0.6 to 250 m. No morphological criteria were stated other than overall colour. It seems important that all failures of 'allogeneic' recognition occurred in five 'groups' (rather than 'clones' in Bigger's more carefully qualified terminology) that did not distinguish among one another but showed acrorhagial responses to the two remaining groups. This would indicate either an allorecognition system involving fewer alleles or loci than in *A.elegantissima*, or a lower genotypic diversity of the sampled population of *A.krebsi* with duplicated sampling of a single, widespread clone. Fujii (1987) used the monosexual nature of discrete groups of *Anthopleura asiatica* and acrorhagial responses among them to infer similarly low local genotypic diversity in this species, as well as the apparent presence of a single clone at six locations distributed over a distance of 5 km (section 6.5, page 268).

On the Pacific coast of North America, anemones in the upper intertidal show low species diversity and high species density. Acrorhagi and catch tentacles are more prevalent in intertidal, clonal anemones (as opposed to predominantly sublittoral, aclonal species), and Francis (1988) contends that agonistic behaviour involving these structures arose in interference with conspecific non-clonemates.

Francis' (1973a, b) studies of *Anthopleura elegantissima* first suggested the monoclonal nature of individual aggregations, and showed that the conspicuous anemone-free zones between aggregations were maintained by acrorhagial conflicts (Figure 7.1A), with the likelihood that agonistic behaviour occurs only against members of allogeneic clones. She showed that anemones living on interclonal borders had more and larger acrorhagi than clonemates further removed from the combat zone (Francis, 1976). Heavier investment in 'armaments' by such 'warrior' individuals was at the expense of their growth and reproduction, as they were smaller than clonemates elsewhere in the aggregation (not an effect of a different fission rate) and lacked gonads. These observations imply a cost in maintaining the fighting structures, which importantly takes precedence even over individual growth. (Regression of the catch tentacles in *Metridium senile* likewise implies a cost in their maintenance.) Holding space for the genet, then, is at the expense of some of its component ramets, which Francis (1976) views as a simple form of social organization, and which she argues (1988) represents kin selection at the level of the clone.

Spatial effects of acrorhagial fighting are less dramatic in clonal but solitary anemones of the genus *Actinia*. In the New Zealand population of *A. tenebrosa* studied by Ottaway (1978), small random movements were seen, but larger movements resulted from physical disturbances. During a two-year study, 44% of the adults were involved in conflicts, which invariably altered the direction and rate of locomotion of the anemone that was wounded. The anemone losing the conflict was usually the one moving into contact with an established resident or defender. Most conflicts did not cause fatalities (although one juvenile victim died), and while space did not appear limiting, suitable sites for attachment of juveniles were scarce (Ottaway, 1973). Although the species does not form aggregates, there is a fine-scale clumping of adults and juveniles of identical (five-locus) genotypes in a natural population, and disproportionally more close pairings of anemones are clonemates than are genotypically different (Ayre, 1983). Adult conflicts are interpreted as a mechanism to retain recruitment space. When multiclonal adults were transplanted into foreign rock pools, similar patterns of clumping were seen after 11 months, which suggests that association of like genotypes was the result of interclonal aggression and subsequent differential movements of non-clonemates (Ayre, 1987). Ayre also discerned a much higher incidence of mortality or disappearance of transplanted individuals following an acrorhagial encounter (75%) than the average (7%) for all adults as a group.

No fine-scale clumping of genotypes was detected in populations of *Actinia equina* in Great Britain, where individuals were dispersed at random or significantly overdispersed (Brace and Quicke, 1985). These authors could find no evidence that allogeneic conflicts led to overdispersion, and suggested that it resulted from interference between basal discs alone. The differences in spatial population structure between *A. equina* and *A. tenebrosa* may reflect local topographic conditions, the populations studied by Ayre being confined more to rock pools where dispersal may be restricted (Brace and Quicke, 1985). The difference may also be a consequence of the lower population density at the British sites (Ayre, 1987). The role of local topography is highlighted by Ayre's (1987) results at a site where the anemones (*A. tenebrosa*) were not deposited in rock pools but on an open, smooth shore and there was no genotypic clumping, probably because anemones were confined to individual small depressions and showed little locomotion.

Species of *Actinia* differ in the predictability of the outcome of agonistic encounters based on the sizes of the combatants. Brace and Pavey (1978) and Brace, Pavey and Quicke (1979) demonstrated that in a red-brown morph of *A. equina*, larger anemones generally attacked sooner than smaller individuals when brought into mutual contact, and subsequently won the encounters. They also discerned branching and sometimes overlapping dominance hierarchies. These situations do not occur in *A. tenebrosa*, where individual weight does not affect the outcome of conflicts, although conflicts develop more often when opponents differ both in genotype and weight (Ayre, 1982). Ayre's results might indicate also that genotype is a good predictor of weight in the population studied. If so, this would affect the interpretation of their results by Brace and colleagues on the basis of size alone, especially as large individuals did not invariably prevail in their studies, and since they found a (genotypic) difference in responsiveness between red-brown and green morphs of *A. equina* (Brace and Reynolds, 1989). The latter morph has distinguishing ecological and genotypic differences, and it has been proposed as a separate species, *A. prasina* (Haylor *et al.*, 1984).

As pointed out by Brace (1981), selection for a lower threshold of agonistic behaviour regardless of size raises the possibility that small individuals initiating conflicts with larger ones might be more severely damaged during retaliation by the latter, which could offset any advantage from having attacked first. Were the threshold higher in the small individual, the larger anemone would prevail, so selection would favour lower thresholds in larger individuals. Interacting genotypic effects on size and proclivity for agonistic behaviour, then, might help explain the mixed outcomes seen by Ayre in *A.tenebrosa* and by Brace (1981) in *Phymactis clematis*. It would be interesting to see whether the size reduction after fission (and when regeneration is complete) in adult *P.clematis* affects the outcome in previously predictable pairings. Such experiments might also shed light on the currently enigmatic neurophysiological mechanism underlying size-specific antagonism.

In indeterminately-growing organisms size is a poor predictor of age, and except in juvenile anemones that lack acrorhagi it is hard to envisage a purely ontogenetic cause underlying size-dependent aggressiveness. Allogeneic recognition among juveniles of *A.elegantissima* does occur, but not all components of agonistic behaviour are manifested (Francis, 1973b). Reproductive state appears not to affect agonistic behaviour, as Ayre (1982) found that individuals of *A.tenebrosa* whether brooding, non-brooding, or without gonads all showed acrorhagial behaviour. In the aclonal *Anthopleura xanthogrammica*, juveniles (individuals <6.5 cm in diameter that lack gonads but possess acrorhagi) were involved in fewer conflicts than were adults, but in larger individuals of adult size those that lacked gonads were observed in agonistic encounters as often as sexual adults (Sebens, 1984a).

In *A.xanthogrammica*, the likelihood of conflict did not depend on the sex of the individuals involved, and specifically, pairs of like sex were no more likely to fight than were pairs of the opposite sex (Sebens, 1984a). Based on the spatial distribution (which itself reflects interclonal conflicts), genotype, and sex of adults, Ayre (1987) came to the same conclusion for *Actinia tenebrosa*. Only in *Metridium senile* has an individual's sex been shown to be a factor in fighting behaviour. Kaplan (1983) found that allogeneic conflicts involving catch tentacles in this species occurred only between individuals of the same sex, and speculated that this helped to ensure that nearest neighbours of unlike genotype were potential mates.

In *M.senile* the extent of interclonal fighting and its effect on spatial population structure are unclear. Unlike *A.elegantissima*, aggregations of this anemone are not necessarily monoclonal, as individuals of several distinct phenotypes are often intermingled (Hoffmann, 1976; Shick *et al.*, 1979b; Purcell and Kitting, 1982). The existence of dense monoclonal stands of this species, separated from other clones by fighting at the borders, probably results from the initial colonization and subsequent asexual occupation of abundant space by different founding clones. Mixed clones might be accounted for by settlement of genotypically diverse larvae into more restricted space. In such groups, inflation of the catch tentacles (i.e. actual fighting) was less frequent than the numerical presence of catch tentacles would have suggested. Laboratory studies revealed that allogeneic individuals habituated to each other (i.e. ceased fighting) during 5–6 days of enforced intermingling. Purcell and Kitting therefore suggested that such habituation would occur in dense multiclonal populations in nature and reduce competition for space, so that a single clone would be unlikely to eliminate all others (death from conflicts involving catch tentacles being rare). In less densely populated sites, the conflict presumably causes the retreat of non-clonemates into whatever space is available. These authors conclude by speculating that the existence of mixed aggregations in *M.senile* but their absence in *A.elegantissima* indicates that competition for space is more important in the latter. This is consistent with the major occurrence of clonal *A.elegantissima* in the space-limited intertidal, whereas *M.senile* (including the population studied by Purcell and Kitting) extends well into the sublittoral, where space may be less limiting.

The seeming rarity of acrorhagial fighting in aclonal *Anthopleura xanthogrammica* (Francis, 1973b; Bigger, 1980) may be in consequence of observing this species only in calm tidepools and in the laboratory. Sebens (1984a) found the behaviour to be more frequent among individuals inhabiting low intertidal surge channels, where water movement produced more frequent tentacular contacts between allogeneic individuals. Although solitary, this anemone tends to occur in high densities in surge channels where it specializes on large prey dislodged by wave action (section 2.2.2, page 39). Despite its aclonal nature and occurrence lower on the shore than much of the sympatric population of *A.elegantissima*, intraspecific competition for limited favourable sites in restricted surge channels may be intense, so there probably has been selection for agonistic behaviour. Other large, sublittoral actiniids tend to be solitary and non-agonistic, and to lack acrorhagi (Francis, 1988).

Like *M.senile*, *A.xanthogrammica* shows habituation to long-term conspecific neighbours but expands acrorhagi in response to transplanted non-neighbours (Sebens, 1984a). Continuously crowded individuals show little movement other than 'jockeying for position', but when space is provided, they increase their movement and individual spacing. Large adults are more likely to show acrorhagial fighting than juveniles, as already noted. As in *M.senile*, combat results in little damage, and an attacked individual rarely retaliates, rather, it may remain contracted or move away. These observations suggest that acrorhagial interactions serve less a purely combative function than an informational role: an anemone initiating a conflict is likely to be large (again, the physiological basis for this is enigmatic), and the smaller victim is better off not retaliating. If space is available, it is advantageous to move and avoid overcrowding that may interfere with prey capture, but in continuously crowded populations, it pays to get along with one's neighbours.

In *A.xanthogrammica*, an agonistic encounter occurs, on average, every one to three days (Sebens, 1984a). The existence of (alloimmune) memory has not been tested in this species, but its duration ($\approx$ 5 days) in *Anemonia viridis* (Sauer *et al.*, 1986) seems in accord with the observed frequency of allogeneic contacts. If within other populations and species of anemones (especially clonal species) allogeneic contact also occurs with a frequency on the order of days, the existence of memory of similar duration would effect responses to long-term neighbours.

Crowded individuals of *A.xanthogrammica* have more acrorhagi than isolates, but the former have fewer acrorhagi than those adjacent to clones of *A.elegantissima* (Francis, 1988). Apparently the clonal species is more of a threat to monopolize space than other individuals of the aclonal *A. xanthogrammica*.

7.2.2 Interspecific Competition

Taylor and Littler (1982) found that intertidal areas experimentally cleared of *Anthopleura elegantissima* were colonized by opportunistic species of macroalgae, although the basis of the latter's previous exclusion is not known. Monopolization of suitable hard substrate by densely-packed anemones is one possibility. The sublittoral tropical anemone *Condylactis gigantea* releases allelopathic substances that hinder algal growth (Bak and Borsboom, 1984). In *A.elegantissima* nothing is known of this phenomenon, although the anemone releases macromolecules into its local environment (Martin, 1968).

Removal of high intertidal aggregations of *A.elegantissima* affects sympatric coralline algae negatively, presumably by eliminating the degree of shading and moisture afforded by the anemones (Taylor and Littler, 1982). These authors also observe that under more benign conditions, the colonial polychaete *Phragmatopoma californica* excludes *A.elegantissima* (by monopolizing space with its sand tubes, which are unsuitable for attachment by anemones). Periodic physical disturbance removes *P.californica* and allows *A.elegantissima* to become established.

Lower in the intertidal zone, and especially sublittorally, the corallimorpharian *Corynactis californica* occupies large areas of sublittoral and extreme low-intertidal rock substrates by means of longitudinal fission (Chadwick, 1987). Although superficially similar to sea anemones, these anthozoans are more closely related to scleractinian corals (Carlgren, 1949; Hand, 1966; Schmidt, 1974), which helps to explain some of the following observations. Like corals, *C.californica* employs its mesenteric filaments both in digesting large prey externally and in fighting against other cnidarians, especially anthozoans. Different extrusion behaviours and lengths of filaments extruded are associated with these two functions.

Corynactis extruded its filaments in response to every contact with *Anthopleura elegantissima*, *Metridium senile* and *Epiactis prolifera* in laboratory trials, killing 75–100% of the individuals of the former two species during three weeks of enforced contact (Chadwick, 1987). When the sea anemones responded initially with acrorhagi or catch tentacles, they were ineffective against *Corynactis*, although the acontia of *M.senile* did kill some of the corallimorpharians. The anemones frequently leaned or crawled away from the corallimorpharian, or detached their basal discs and rolled or floated away. *C.californica* never reacted to conspecifics, either clonemate or non-clonemate. The nature of its agonistic behaviour is decidedly unlike that of actiniarians but is similar to that of scleractinian corals, which generally show interspecific but not intraspecific aggression.

The ecological significance of the agonistic behaviour shown by *Corynactis* is unknown, as the frequency of its occurrence in the field has not been studied, nor has the spatial overlap of this corallimorpharian with actiniarians been quantified. Chadwick cites unpublished studies noting that corridors occur between adjacent clones of *C.californica* and those of *A.elegantissima* and *M.senile* inhabiting wharf pilings, and hypothesizes that the open zones are maintained by avoidance behaviour or death of sea anemones that have been attacked by the corallimorpharian.

Sebens (1976) discerns a gradient of substratum stability and along it a trend in interspecific combativeness in coral reef anemones. Living massive corals afford the most stable substrate, and anemones (*C.gigantea*) inhabiting these compete with the corals by overgrowing or killing them outright with their feeding tentacles (see also Albrecht, 1977). Anemones living on less stable dead coral are actively agonistic against sympatric anemones with which they must compete for attachment sites. Fugitive species of anemones that inhabit the least stable habitats are not agonistic but rely instead on clonal proliferation to occupy substrate as it becomes available.

Physical disturbance is a minor factor in temperate sublittoral, hard-bottom communities, where interspecific competition may be intense. The distributions of two nominal species of the zooxanthellate anemone *Anemonia* (*A.rustica* and *A.sulcata*) completely overlap to a depth of 10–12 m in the Mediterranean Sea (Sauer, 1989, and personal communication). These species show a reciprocal relationship in their depths of maximum abundance (measured as number of clones), and maxima in gonad index and in number of individuals per clone (i.e. two measures of fitness: section 6.4.2, page 258) for each species occur in the zone of its maximum abundance, where acrorhagial conflicts allow clones of each species to dominate well-lighted sites. Such site-specific variation in fitness apparently has selected for differences in the time required to initiate an acrorhagial response, so that the distribution pattern is maintained by inverse competitive superiority: *A.rustica* shows a quicker acrorhagial response and wins encounters in its habitat in deeper water, whereas *A.sulcata* prevails in shallow water.

On sublittoral rock walls in the Gulf of Maine, *Metridium senile* dominates a complex assemblage of encrusting ascidians, bryozoans, sponges, coralline algae and other anthozoans (Sebens, 1986). Mechanisms of the anemone's competitive success are direct overgrowth of algal crusts, large size and dense packing of individuals that exclude even colonial ascidians, and direct attacks using catch tentacles against the potentially dominant octocoral, *Alcyonium siderium*. The octocoral may persist adjacent to clones of *Metridium* by occupying suboptimal habitats having less water movement. Total domination by *Metridium* is avoided only through seasonal cropping by the predatory nudibranch, *Aeolidia papillosa* (sections 6.5, page 277, and 7.4.1).

Gastropod shells inhabited by hermit crabs provide a rare hard substrate in otherwise soft-bottom communities, and competition occurs for this limited resource (see references in Brooks and Mariscal, 1986a). Mutual exclusion of the anemone *Calliactis tricolor* and various hydroids from these shells suggests such competition. The competitive mechanisms may be biological (nematocyst discharge) as well as physico-chemical (evinced by the failure of anemones to attach to shells bearing only non-living hydroid perisarc) (Brooks and Mariscal, 1986a). The response appears to be one of mutual avoidance rather than of antagonism.

7.3 ECTOSYMBIOSIS

Associations of sea anemones with mobile macrofauna such as decapod crustaceans and fishes comprise some of the most familiar marine symbioses (Figure 7.2). Although such symbioses have been known for over a century, understanding of their nature is comparatively recent, and natural products chemistry is now beginning to provide knowledge of the proximal causes of symbiotic behaviour.

7.3.1 Symbiosis with Crustaceans

Caridean shrimps of the families Alphaeidae and Palaemonidae (especially members of the genus *Periclimenes*) form symbiotic associations with several species of actinians; most of these associations occur in the tropics. The symbioses are sometimes species-specific, and in several cases, the relationship appears to be obligate for the shrimp, which are not found separate from the anemones (Ross, 1983, and references therein). *Periclimenes pedersoni* uses *Bartholomea annulata* as a station from which it cleans a diverse assemblage of reef fishes (Limbaugh, Pederson and Chace, 1961). Shrimp-actinian symbioses are usually viewed as commensalisms, the shrimps deriving benefits (food scraps and protection) from their hosts but having no obvious effect on them. Removal of the snapping shrimp, *Alpheus armatus*, from *B.annulata*, however, resulted in predation on the anemone, apparently by stomatopods (Limbaugh *et al.*, 1961).

Another alpheid, *A.immaculata*, is an obligate symbiont of *B.annulata*, and despite the potential of its larvae for long distance dispersal, shows

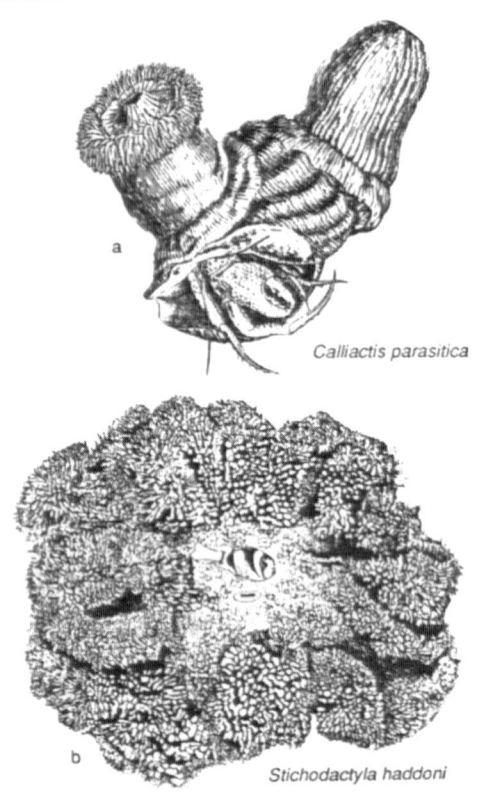

Figure 7.2 Macrofaunal symbionts with sea anemones. **a.** *Calliactis parasitica* (oral disc diameter approximately 30 mm) attached to the shell of a whelk inhabited by a hermit crab. Source: Johnston (1847). **b.** Clownfish (*Amphiprion* sp.) living among tentacles of *Stichodactyla haddoni* (oral disc diameter approximately 350 mm) Source: with permission from Doumenc and Van-Praët (1987).

enhanced recruitment into anemones within several metres of the parents (Knowlton and Keller, 1986). Larvae of this shrimp are usually killed when they contact the anemone's tentacles, and the mechanism whereby the juveniles become protected from the host's nematocysts is unknown.

The shrimp's exoskeleton does not afford the necessary protection in itself. Experiments by Levine and Blanchard (1980) in which *Periclimenes* spp. were isolated from their hosts for 24 h showed that a 1–5 h period of reacclimation, during which the shrimp picked at the anemones' tentacles, was necessary before the shrimp could walk on the oral disc and tentacles without being stung. Reciprocal experiments involving acclimated and unacclimated shrimp, and anemones with and without commensal shrimp, indicated that 'acclimation' of the shrimp to the anemones involves a change in the former. By analogy with Schlichter's (1972, 1976) interpretation of the mechanism of protection of anemonefish (section 7.3.2), Levine and Blanchard speculated that transfer of mucus from anemone to shrimp is responsible for the latter's protection.

A similar commensalism exists between the majid (spider) crab *Inachus phalangium* and *Anemonia viridis* (≡ *A.sulcata*), this anemone being preferred to *Urticina* (≡ *Tealia*) *felina* and *Aiptasia diaphana* in choice experiments (Hartnoll, 1970; Weinbauer, Nussbaumer and Patzner, 1982). Although the crab is normally able to move with impunity among the tentacles of *A.viridis*, treating the crab's surface with acetone removes its protection and results in a feeding response by the anemone (Weinbauer *et al.*, 1982). Protection can be regained only if the crab first repeatedly contacts the anemone's tentacles. Larger majid, calappid, and xanthid crabs acquire actinians actively and carry them on their carapaces or chelipeds (Ross, 1967, 1983, for reviews). In some cases the anemone, notably *Calliactis tricolor*, assists its host in the transfer.

Anemones in the family Hormathiidae have a tendency to attach to organic substrates (Manuel, 1988), and this is carried to an extreme by members of the genera *Calliactis*, *Paracalliactis* and *Adamsia* in their association with pagurid hermit crabs (Figure 7.2a). These are by far the best known and most thoroughly studied symbioses between actinians and crustaceans (for reviews, see Ross, 1967; 1974a, b; 1983). The number of anemone species is small compared with that of host decapods, and a symbiotic anemone is rarely restricted to a single host.

The prevalence of actinian–hermit crab symbioses in which the latter inhabits the empty shells of gastropods probably stems from the response of the anemone (e.g. *Calliactis parasitica*) to an organic factor in the shell of the gastropod (e.g. *Buccinum undatum*), rather than from an affinity for the crab, as demonstrated by Ross and Sutton (1961). Ross (1983) considers paguran–actinian symbioses to have originated when certain actinians attached themselves to the shells of living gastropods and thereby gained a means of transport. This behaviour persists in the symbiosis between *Pagurus bernhardus* and *C.parasitica*, in which the anemone usually transfers itself unaided to the shell inhabited by the hermit (Ross, 1960c; but see Ross, 1979a). Ross considers that it would be only a small step for the pagurids to acquire their anemones actively if there were a selective advantage for them to do so. Also, since the living gastropod is a passive carrier of the anemone, the balance would swing heavily in favour of pagurid–anemone associations once the crab became active in obtaining its symbionts. Such an explanation is supported by the high incidence of *Calliactis* living on gastropods only in areas without crabs that actively transfer anemones (Ross, 1974b).

Shell-climbing behaviour in *Calliactis parasitica* has several distinct stages (Ross and Sutton, 1961): (1) tentacles attach to the shell; (2) basal disc detaches; (3) column extends and bends, and basal disc moves to the shell; (4)

basal disc attaches to the shell; (5) tentacles release from the shell and the anemone resumes its normal posture. McFarlane (1982) summarizes the neuromuscular events occurring during these behaviours, and emphasizes that the SS1 and SS2 conducting systems are active during behaviours (1) to (4), being evoked initially by ectodermal contact chemoreceptors.

McFarlane and Shelton (1975) hypothesize that the ectodermal SS1 is involved in lowering the threshold for discharge of spirocysts in the tentacles (the principal means of their attachment to the shell), although the hypothesis remains untested. During shell-climbing behaviour release of the basal disc also appears to be mediated by the SS1, perhaps by causing fibres inside ectodermal cells of the disc to contract and pull their microvilli away from the cement layer on the shell (Robson, 1976). Such contraction might also cause release of a (proteolytic) enzyme that destroys the adhesive (McFarlane, 1982; Shelton, 1982). During extension of the column, SS2 activity presumably inhibits inherent activity of endodermal muscles and allows the SS1 to control the sequence of muscular contractions (via transmesogleal connections to multipolar nerve cells in the endoderm: Lawn, 1980) (McFarlane, 1982). Column extension may by reflexes excite the parietal muscles, which cause shortening or bending of the column, and which in turn may trigger the observed pulses in the through-conducting nerve net (TCNN). In shell-climbing behaviour the TCNN seems to be involved only with the swelling of the basal disc (enabled by TCNN inhibition of circular muscles) during re-attachment to the shell (McFarlane, 1982).

In cases where the hermit crab actively transfers an anemone to the shell that it inhabits, the mechanism is one whereby mechanical stimulation of the anemone's column by the crab's walking legs causes detachment of the basal disc (Ross and Sutton, 1968). This is presumably mediated by the SS1 as just described, since both mechanical and low-frequency electrical stimulation of the column of *Calliactis parasitica* evoke SS1 activity and detachment (McFarlane, 1969).

The advantage to the crab of acquiring a symbiotic actinian is in obtaining protection from predators, i.e. octopus and oxystomatid crabs. In laboratory experiments, specimens of *Dardanus* spp. with *Calliactis parasitica* on their shells were completely protected from *Octopus vulgaris* that in similar trials had consistently eaten anemone-free *Dardanus* (Ross, 1971). Hermits bearing multiple anemones survived longer in the presence of octopus than those having none or only one anemone, as did those bearing an anemone near the shell aperture (Brooks, 1988). The predatory crab *Calappa flammea* rejected specimens of *Pagurus pollicaris* having symbiotic *C.tricolour* in 67% of the trials, whereas anemone-free hermits were never rejected (McLean and Mariscal, 1973). In the presence of octopus, hermits preferentially place anemones near the shell aperture, presumably to afford greatest protection from the predator (Brooks, 1989a). The symbiosis is mutualistic, as the locomotion by the hermit crab removes the anemone from predation by the sea star *Echinaster spinosus* (Brooks, 1989b).

The role of predators in motivating hermits to obtain actinians was emphasized by Balasch and Mengual (1974), who observed that when specimens of *Dardanus arrosor* were isolated from octopus for 4–5 months, the crabs failed to transfer anemones to their shells. Reintroduction of octopus into the aquaria renewed the crabs' transferral behaviour. Similar results were obtained by Ross and Boletzky (1979), who showed moreover that chemical, not visual, cues from the octopus were involved.

The operation of such phenomena in nature is strongly suggested by the experiments of Bach and Herrnkind (1980) and Brooks and Mariscal (1986b). The former authors demonstrated a significant positive relationship between the intensity of predation in the field (incidence of hermit shells freshly damaged by *Calappa*) and the percentage of hermits (*P.pollicaris*) bearing *C.tricolor*. The latter workers showed that specimens of *P.pollicaris* from an area lacking octopus transferred fewer anemones than hermits from an area rich in octopus. In both populations the tendency to transfer anemones declined when the hermits were isolated but increased in the chemical presence of octopus. The mutualism in such cases is facultative, depending on the intensity of predation on the hermits.

Pagurus prideauxi and the cloak anemone *Adamsia carciniopados* ($\equiv$ *A.palliata*) form an obligate and intimate association. Although the anemone benefits by being fed by its host (Fox, 1965), the anemone appears not to participate actively in a transferral process, detached individuals showing no response to shells (Ross, 1974b). The crab must actively acquire its actinian, but the advantages of doing so are not obvious, since the anemone provides little protection from predatory octopus (Ross, 1971). The partners show several unique adaptations nevertheless. The basal disc of the anemone is unusually broad and asymmetrical, so that it envelops the part of the crab's abdomen that is not covered by the proportionally small (gastropod) shell, actually extending the shell's lip by depositing a cuticle. Growth of the anemone is so synchronized with that of the hermit that 'it provides the hermit crab with a means of avoiding that critical and sometimes fatal necessity of replacing the shell as it grows' (Ross, 1974b). An extreme case is provided by the actiniid *Stylobates aeneus*, which itself secretes a shell consisting of protein and chitin remarkably resembling a gastropod shell, and that is inhabited by *Parapagurus dofleini* (Dunn, Devaney and Roth, 1980; Dunn and Liberman, 1983).

As noted by Ross (1983), in transferral behaviour no formula is apparent for the partitioning of the behavioural contributions of the pagurid and the actinian. Presumably neither partner would develop transferral behaviour unless it were advantageous for it to do so. No one who has seen Don Ross' motion pictures of pagurid–actinian interactions can fail to be impressed with the purposive nature of the behaviours of the partners. An underlying assumption (rarely tested) is that the anemone gains additional food and access to 'better' habitats when transported by a host, so that it should always benefit an anemone to participate actively in transferral (indeed, to be the sole active participant when the host is a living gastropod), or at least not to hinder transfer. This seems to be the case. The protection of anemone-bearing hermit crabs from predators should strongly select for their developing transferral behaviour, and crabs compete with and 'steal' from subordinate individuals when anemones are scarce (Ross, 1979b).

7.3.2 Symbiosis with Fishes

One of the most surprising and striking animal symbioses is that between sea anemones (especially Indo-Pacific members of the family Stichodactylidae) and various fishes, especially damselfishes or clownfishes (family Pomacentridae) (Figure 7.2b). Thorough reviews of the earlier literature, including zoogeography, are by Mariscal (1966, 1972) and Dunn (1981). Since its first description in 1868 as 'quasi-parasitic', this symbiotic relationship has variously been called a friendship, a partnership, a commensalism and a mutualism. Although many accounts are anecdotal and inferred advantages of observed behaviours are never quantified, both partners demonstrably benefit from their symbiosis and the available evidence favours the mutualistic definition (Mariscal, 1970a).

The fundamental advantage to the partners is their protection of each other from predatory fishes. Field and laboratory observations show that clownfishes, particularly *Amphiprion ocularis* ($\equiv$ *A.percula*), in association with anemones are unharmed by larger predatory fishes, but they are quickly eaten when separated from their hosts (Mariscal, 1970c). The clownfish is strongly territorial (Mariscal, 1972) and defends its host anemone against potential predators. *Amphiprion bicinctus* preferentially attacks anemone predators such as chaetodontid fishes (Fricke, 1975). The importance to *Entacmaea quadricolor* of such protection by its resident *Amphiprion melanopus*, *A.akindynos*, and *Premnas biaculeatus* was strikingly demonstrated in field experiments by Fautin (1986): when the clownfish were removed from clones of *Entacmaea*, other reef fishes swarmed over the area and all of the unprotected anemones disappeared (presumably eaten) within a day.

Adults of *Amphiprion* (25 species) and *Premnas biaculeatus* occur in symbiosis only with one or more of ten species of actiniarians (one thalassianthid, two actiniids, and seven stichodactylids), but many of these species of anemone may be found without resident anemonefishes. The symbiosis is obligate for all of the fishes (except during a week-long planktonic larval period: Verwey, 1930) and facultative for most of the anemones (Mariscal, 1972; Dunn, 1981; Fautin, 1986). Other pomacentrids (*Dascyllus* spp.) are often (but not necessarily) resident with anemones as juveniles but not when adult, and thus they are considered facultative symbionts (Mariscal, 1972; Dunn, 1981). In the Caribbean Sea of the approximately 30 species of fishes in several families associated with anemones, most are facultative symbionts, and only a few appear to be obligate (Hanlon and Kaufman, 1976; R.N. Mariscal, personal communication). Other facultatively symbiotic fishes include the Mediterranean *Gobius bucchichii*, which may inhabit *Anemonia viridis* ($\equiv$ *A.sulcata*) (Abel, 1960).

In the Pacific, the most highly 'desirable' host appears to be *Entacmaea quadricolor* (Fautin, 1986), serving as host to the largest number (11) of clownfish species, including at least three that occur in no other anemone (Dunn, 1981). Although the cause of the fishes' attraction to this or other anemone species is unknown, evolutionary theory and empirical data suggest that the host has evolved specific mechanisms to attract symbionts because the latter substantially increase its survival. This seems to be the case especially for *E.quadricolor* and its symbionts (see above) and in most of the documented cases of clownfishes defending their host anemone from predatory fishes, the anemone in question is the particularly vulnerable *E.quadricolour* (Fautin, 1986). *Amphiprion akallopisos* was also very aggressive toward intruders, however, and frequently attacked Mariscal (1970b) when he approached its host *Heteractis magnifica* ($\equiv$ *Radianthus ritteri*).

The association of relatively short-lived anemonefishes with longer-lived anemones, and their demonstrably mutualistic interaction, prompted Roughgarden (1975) to examine the evolution of mutualism. A key feature is that the host must have moderate survivorship, for if it is too low, the symbiont would do better not to spend time and energy searching for a short-lived host. Conversely, host survivorship must not be too high, since the symbiont would receive little benefit from enhancing it, i.e. the symbiosis would not be mutualistic. The population sizes of symbiotic fishes appear to be limited by the availability of potentially long-lived host anemones (Allen, 1975; Fricke, 1979), emphasizing the obligate nature of the symbiosis for the fish.

The specificity of clownfish–anemone symbioses has been much studied, since the fishes in nature inhabit only certain sympatric potential hosts (Verwey, 1930; Mariscal, 1966, 1971, 1972; Dunn, 1981; Miyagawa, 1989). *A.clarkii*, geographically the most widespread and complex species of the *Amphiprion*, is also the least discriminating, occurring in nine of the ten species of host anemones, in two of these as the only symbiont (Dunn, 1981). Fautin (1986, and 1981, writing as Dunn) summarizes the data for other symbioses, but no clear pattern of specificity emerges, with the possible exception that members of the *A.clarkii* species complex may be the 'generalists' among clownfishes. As such, Miyagawa (1989) suggests that *A.clarkii* represents an early stage in the evolution of symbiosis with sea anemones, some of which are scarcely suitable as hosts. Fautin suggests that patterns among the symbioses are determined largely by the adult fishes, which are the shorter-lived and more mobile partners. Accounting for the patterns observed in nature, however, is difficult. Covering all eventualities, Fautin (1986) suggests that the determinants include: (1) innate or learned preferences (Eibl-Eibesfeldt, 1960, showed in choice experiments that fishes preferred the species of host with which they usually associate); (2) territoriality, agonistic behaviour, and competition among anemonefishes for hosts (Fautin reported spatial partitioning of a large clone of *E.quadricolour* by clownfishes on an interspecific and age-related basis; also, when ousted from an 'attractive' host, individuals of *A.akindynos* sought refuge in less 'desirable' anemones — 'attractiveness' and 'desirability' being operationally defined as attributes of a host inhabited by more than one, potentially competing, sympatric symbiont); and (3) stochastic processes, which encompass otherwise inexplicable situations.

Given that the fishes govern the pattern of symbioses observed in nature, and that in aquaria they may associate with some unnatural hosts that they would never encounter in the field (e.g. *Anthopleura xanthogrammica* and *Condylactis gigantea*), how do they recognize potential host anemones? Foster (unpublished thesis cited by Losey, 1978) showed that both visual and olfactory stimuli are involved in attracting a fish (*Dascyllus albisella*) to an anemone (*Heteractis malu* ≡ *Radianthus papillosa*), and that the most attractive case involves chemical and visual stimuli from a specimen of this anemone already harbouring a symbiotic fish. From his own work and a critical review of the literature, Mariscal (1970b, 1972) reports that visual cues appear to be the primary basis for recognition of anemones and their surroundings, at least by adult anemonefishes. It may be that a fish locates a host initially using both visual and chemical cues, but once established in a particular anemone, it relies primarily on vision to recognize it when returning from brief forays away from the anemone.

The extent to which adult anemonefishes may switch hosts is poorly known, but clearly they have the behavioural plasticity to do so. Might this ability, and the nature of the key stimuli, change ontogenetically? Miyagawa and Hidaka (1980) and Miyagawa (1989) did controlled experiments to demonstrate that juvenile *A.clarkii* (reared in isolation from their parents and from anemones) were attracted by chemical dues from potential host anemones but were indifferent to or avoided potentially dangerous non-symbiotic actinians in similar tests (Figure 7.3). The juvenile fish did not recognize symbiotic anemones when only visual information was provided, and moreover, would preferentially orient to chemical stimuli emanating from an anemone while simultaneously ignoring visual input from the same individual, when the stimuli were spatially separated. The ability to recognize chemical cues may not develop until the fishes are ready to assume a benthic existence, since pelagic larvae of *A.clarkii* were indifferent to *E.quadricolor*

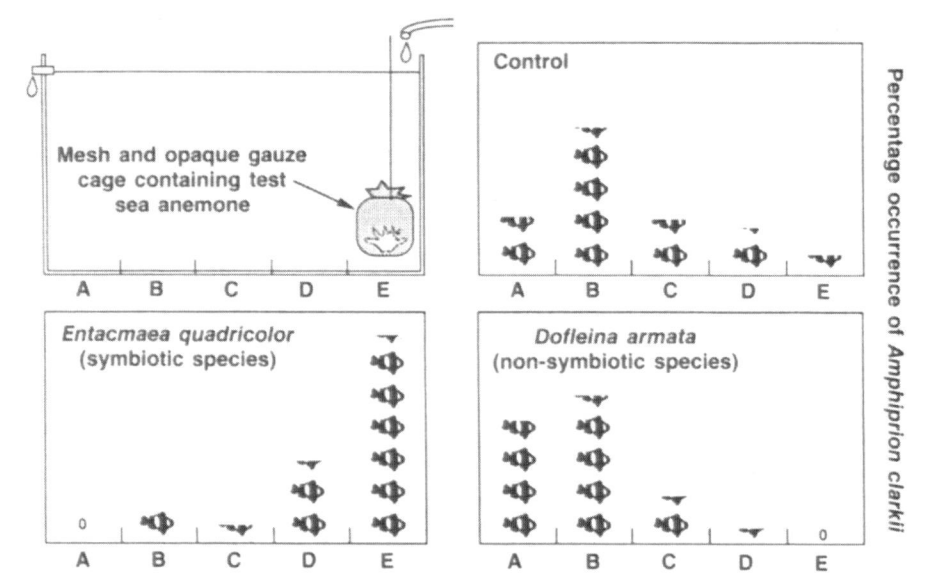

Figure 7.3 Responses of naïve juvenile anemonefish *Amphiprion clarkii* to only chemical stimuli from symbiotic and non-symbiotic species of sea anemones. Anemones (invisible to the fish in an opaque gauze cage located in section E of a 400-litre aquarium divided longitudinally into five equal sections) were tested independently. Five juvenile fish (60 to 90 days old) were tested in each trial (total of three or five trials for each anemone species; new fish in each trial), during which the position of the fish was noted every 1.5 min for 1 h. Each fish represents a 10% occurrence of juveniles in that section for pooled data. See text for discussion. Source: drawn from data in Miyagawa and Hidaka (1980).

($\equiv$ *Parasicyonis actinostoloides*) but became symbiotic with the same anemone as postlarval juveniles (Tanase and Araga, 1975, cited in Miyagawa and Hidaka, 1980). Considering their planktonic habitat and the relatively great distances involved, a chemical rather than a visual cue would seem more effective in location of a host by juvenile fish.

Subsequent investigations (on different symbioses) showed that juvenile fishes (*A.perideraion*) collected from nature and maintained with host anemones (*Heteractis crispa*) in the laboratory were attracted to crude mucus extract from the host (Murata et al., 1986). Even 'naïve' individuals of *A.ocellaris* were attracted to the mucus of their normal host, *Stichodactyla gigantea*. 'Attracted swimming' by *A.perideraion* was also evoked by the compound amphikuemin, a quaternary amine purified from the mucus of *H.crispa*. *Amphiprion clarkii*, however, which is also symbiotic with *H.crispa*, did not respond to amphikuemin, which indicates species-specificity in the chemical recognition process (although since neither the age nor the symbiotic status of the *A.clarkii* tested was stated, ontogenetic or acclimatization effects could be involved). The result does not, as the authors claim, prove that different species of anemonefishes recognize the same host by different chemicals, but only that *A.clarkii* did not recognize a chemical that attracts *A.perideraion*. An attractant for *A.clarkii* has yet to be identified. Tyramine purified from *S.gigantea* mucus evoked attracted swimming behaviour in *A.ocellaris*, and tryptamine acted synergistically with unidentified compounds from the mucus to evoke active searching behaviour by the fish. Tyramine was also found in *H.crispa* but had no effect on *A.perideraion* or *A.clarkii*, which further indicates a specificity of attractants in different symbioses. Although preliminary, these data provide a fascinating glimpse of the role of marine natural products chemistry in elucidating the proximal causes of animal behaviours and associations.

It is also chemistry at the anemonefish-sea anemone interface that allows the former to wallow unharmed in its host's tentacles. The distinctive 'acclimation' behaviour by the fish (reviewed by Mariscal, 1971, 1972), which is necessary for an adult fish eventually to be protected from an anemone's nematocysts, was thought by some investigators to result in the anemone's habituation to tactile or other stimuli from the fish, particularly in cases where the acclimation was complete within minutes. It is the mucous coating of an acclimated clownfish, however, and not simply a change in its host's behaviour, that is responsible for protecting it, as first suggested by Davenport and Norris (1958). Similar protection of *Gobius bucchichii* against *Anemonia viridis* by the goby's mucus was shown by Abel (1960). Lubbock (1980b) observed that the mucous layer of symbiotic fishes was significantly thicker than that of related non-symbiotic species. Reciprocal experiments in which acclimated and unacclimated fish were exposed to anemones with and without resident fish show unequivocally that it is the fish, not the anemone, that changes during acclimation (Mariscal, 1969).

Once a protective role for the fish's mucous layer was established, research centred on the mechanism and on the nature of the protection, i.e. was it innate, induced, or even acquired from the host? Because acclimated fish lose their protection within a variable length of time after removal from their host anemone, and must then undergo a period of reacclimation before being able to re-enter the host unharmed, most workers agree that the protection of adult fish is not innate. Miyagawa and Hidaka (1980) suggest the opposite for juveniles, however, finding that juveniles of *A.clarkii* reared in isolation from their parents and from anemones are not killed when acutely placed for 3 min among the tentacles of *E.quadricolor*, their natural host (although the fish were killed in similar experiments with non-symbiotic species of anemones). Adult *A.clarkii* acclimate to one host, *Stichodactyla haddoni*, however, within 1–2 min of exposure to it (Lubbock, 1980b), and it is not clear from Miyagawa and Hidaka's account how frequently the juveniles actually contacted the anemone's tentacles, or whether some stinging may have occurred within the first minute or so, after which the fish might have been acclimated.

Eggs of *Amphiprion ocellaris* (≡ *A.percula*) collected from near the base of *Stichodactyla gigantea* (≡ *Stoichactis kenti*) were not stung by the anemone when placed in contact with its tentacles (Davenport and Norris, 1958). Likewise, eggs of *A.ocellaris* were not taken as food by the parents' host *Stichodactyla gigantea* (≡ *Stoichactis kenti*) nor were those of *A.sandaracinos* stung by the host *Stichodactyla mertensii* (≡ *Stoichactis giganteum*) (Miyagawa, 1989). Freshly hatched postlarvae of these species of *Amphiprion* were killed by the host anemones, however. Planktonic postlarvae of *A.frenatus* which hatched in the presence of *E.quadricolor* were killed by the anemone when forced to contact it, but after metamorphosis their siblings were not stung (Miyagawa and Hidaka, 1980).

These results clearly indicate an ontogenetic effect on the capacity of fishes to form symbiosis with anemones. The ability of postembryonic fish to associate with an anemone without being stung develops after a planktonic stage during which the fish do not encounter anemones and are killed when forced into contact with them. The basis for the protection of eggs is unknown, but might involve transfer of anemone-specific chemicals by the acclimated male parent during his care of the eggs (Miyagawa, 1989). Whether developing embryos require a 'chemical imprinting' for the subsequent expression of protective mechanisms at the appropriate time is not known. If it exists, it is apparently not species-specific, however, for juvenile *A.ocellaris* that hatched in proximity to *Stichodactyla gigantea* were protected also from four other species (Miyagawa, 1989).

Until recently, the accepted view was that adult anemonefishes were acquiring mucus from their hosts and using it as a 'chemical camouflage' or 'macromolecular mimicry' to avoid being recognized as potential prey (Schlichter, 1968, 1972, 1975b, 1976). The basis for this hypothesis was that fishes maintained in close proximity to, or in actual contact with, host anemones became protected, and that specific components of the anemone's mucus were shown by radiochemical and electrophoretic assays to become associated with the fishes' surface. Central to Schlichter's hypothesis was that anemone mucus contains an inhibiting substance that prevents self-stimulation and discharge of an individual's nematocysts, and that it is such a substance, if not bulk mucus, that the fish adopts for its own protection.

In testing Schlichter's hypothesis, Lubbock (1980b) found that the mucus from *A.clarkii* kept isolated from anemones for 8 months did not elicit nematocyst discharge, and Lubbock considered it unlikely that anemone-derived, nematocyst-inhibiting substances would have remained on the fish for so long. Mariscal (1970c), however, reported that *A.clarkii* lost its protection from anemones in less than 24 h. Further experiments by Lubbock showed that the mucus of *A.clarkii* is chemically different (containing predominantly neutral polysaccharide) from the mucus of non-symbiotic pomacentrids (containing acidic residues), and that the latter always elicited nematocyst discharge. Severe denaturation of *A.clarkii* mucus did not change the anemone's lack of response to it, and *A.clarkii* mucus did not prevent non-symbiotic fish mucus from exciting nematocysts. Lubbock concluded that rather than containing inhibiting or masking substances, the mucus of *A.clarkii* was inert and lacked excitatory substances that were present in the mucus of non-symbiotic fishes.

A specimen of *A.clarkii* acclimated to *Stichodactyla haddoni*, however, could not enter a specimen of *Entacmaea quadricolor* ($\equiv$ *Gyrostoma hertwigi*) without first undergoing a 4-day acclimation period (Lubbock, 1981). This confirmed earlier observations (Mariscal, 1970c, 1971) that protection from one host is not universally effective against other hosts, perhaps because of interspecific differences among anemones in their response to chemical stimuli (Lubbock, 1979). Miyagawa (1989) found similarly that specimens of *A.perideraion* removed from *Heteractis crispa* ($\equiv$ *Radianthus keukenthali*) were stung and killed when placed on *Stichodactyla gigantea*, although naïve juveniles were not. Lubbock (1981) concluded that since the mucus on unacclimated *A.clarkii* was as thick as that on acclimated conspecifics (albeit both were variable and possibly damaged during measurement), the acclimation process involves not a quantitative change (i.e. an increase in the thickness of a protective barrier against nematocysts), rather, a qualitative change (i.e. a decrease in the synthesis of substances that excite nematocyst discharge) in the mucus.

In an inspired and provocative experiment, Brooks and Mariscal (1984) showed that association of *A.clarkii* with a surrogate 'anemone' (rubber bands imbedded in silicone) decreased by eight-fold the time required for the fish to acclimate to a real *Macrodactyla doreenensis*. This result indicates that the fish was not protecting itself by transferring mucus from the anemone to itself, since the artificial surrogate obviously had no mucus. It supports the idea that the fish was altering its own mucus in response to association with the surrogate anemone. Since the fish still required a brief period of acclimation to a real anemone to become fully protected, a more complete set of stimuli associated with a living host seems to be required in order to complete acclimation. This might involve either some component of the anemone's mucus that the fish complexes with its own to complete a chemical disguise (as *per* Schlichter), or a chemical cue that causes the anemonefish to change its own mucus qualitatively or quantitatively, obtained via olfactory sensors, nematocyst venom injection, or actual ingestion of anemone tissue (a common behaviour in anemonefishes: Mariscal, 1972).

Although a period of acclimation is required for an adult anemonefish to associate with a host anemone without being stung, it is uncertain whether such protection in juveniles is innate or requires brief acclimation. Miyagawa, who has extensive experience with juvenile anemonefishes, is a strong advocate of the hypothesis of innate protection (Miyagawa and Hidaka, 1980; Miyagawa, 1989). There is a striking difference in the response of anemones to naïve postlarvae, which are quickly stung and killed, and to juveniles, which are not. Miyagawa concludes that naïve juveniles are never actually stung when first in contact with a potential host anemone, from the lack of adhesion of the anemone's tentacles to them and their failure to withdraw or jerk back from the tentacles. Microscopical examination of the skin of postlarvae revealed large numbers of discharged cnidae, whereas in juveniles cnidae were 'almost absent' from the skin after an initial encounter with a prospective host. However, the presence of even a few discharged nematocysts on juveniles calls into question the hypothesis of their absolute innate protection. It may be that an ontogenetic change in its mucous coat renders the fish less stimulating to anemones when it assumes its demersal existence than when it is a planktonic postlarva only 12–24 h younger, but a brief acclimation to the anemone is required for complete protection of the juvenile. This may involve slight stinging or other host-specific stimuli that elicit the distinctive behaviour in which juveniles rub against the tentacles.

In summary, the capacity for an anemonefish to be protected from stinging develops ontogenetically. The relative ease with which juveniles become acclimated to anemones suggests that there is a critical period in the establishment of most associations, which last ideally for the lifetime of the fish. Adults may lose this protection if removed from their host. They may regain their protection despite some difficulty, due perhaps to age-related changes in their metabolism or mucus chemistry. The taxonomic confusion regarding both the fishes and their actiniarian hosts has been resolved (Allen, 1975; Dunn, 1981), and with the advent of techniques for rearing the fishes under controlled conditions, we can anticipate 'global' experiments investigating animal behaviour, nematocyst specificity, mucus chemistry, and ontogenetic changes in these factors.

7.3.3 Symbiosis with Molluscs

The marked tendency for anemones to settle on mollusc shells (Ross, 1965) may provide them with a hard substrate for attachment in otherwise soft-bottom habitats. This is the case for some populations of *Metridium senile* living on *Mytilus edulis*, where the anemone provides protection to the mussel, significantly reducing predation by the sea star *Asterias forbesi* (Kaplan, 1984). As already mentioned (section 7.3.1), *Calliactis parasitica* is associated with living gastropods only in areas lacking hermit crabs that actively transfer anemones. By attaching itself to a gastropod, *C. parasitica* gains a means of transport, which may provide better feeding opportunities (Ross, 1983).

The neogastropod *Neptunea pribiloffensis* preferentially deposits its egg masses near the large anemone *Urticina* (≡ *Tealia*) *crassicornis*, where more egg capsules and significantly more juvenile snails survive the year-long developmental period than when deposition occurs >10 cm away from the anemone (Shimek, 1981). Field observations and laboratory experiments suggest that the principal predator on the egg masses is the sea urchin *Strongylocentrotus droebachiensis*, and that the anemone protects the snail's egg masses by eating approaching sea urchins.

7.4 PREDATION ON SEA ANEMONES

The taxonomically diverse array of predators on sea anemones was catalogued by Ottaway (1977a) and there is little to add to this, other than the occasional report involving a different species. In a review of predation on anemones by fishes, however, Ates (1989) concludes that such predation is not necessarily incidental as has often been reported, but that some fishes (including certain Chimaeridae, Triakidae, Pleuronectidae, Notacanthidae, Cottidae, Haemulidae, Sparidae, Chaetodontidae, Ostraciidae and Tetraodontidae) actually prefer or specialize on sea anemones or cerianthids. Although fishes comprise most of the vertebrates reported to prey on anemones, a novel instance of avian predation was noted by Donoghue, Quicke and Brace (1986). In this case, turnstones were feeding on the coelenteron contents (arthropods, molluscs and annelids) of specimens of *Actinia equina* exposed at low tide, although the anemones involved were so badly damaged that they likely would not have survived. Most studies of invertebrate predation on anemones have centred on aeolid nudibranchs and sea stars, and emphasis has been on the predators' preference for particular prey species, alarm and escape responses by the prey, and effects of predation on the distribution of anemones.

7.4.1 Predation by Aeolid Nudibranchs

The most intensively studied aspect of predation on anemones concerns aeolid nudibranchs and their utilization of different prey species. *Aeolidia papillosa* is circum-arctic in distribution and it co-occurs with a variety of anemone species, often (but not invariably) preferring one species among several available to it at a given locality (Harris, 1973, 1987; Waters, 1973; Hall, Todd and Gordon, 1982). Criteria for establishing 'preference' in laboratory studies have included chemotactic orientation (the usual method by which aeolids locate prey) to anemone effluents in multiple choice olfactometers, and the actual biting or eating of test anemones offered singly or in mixed-species groups to nudibranchs. By these criteria, the preferred anemone prey of *A.papillosa* are *Anthopleura elegantissima*, *A.xanthogrammica* and *Epiactis prolifera* (central California: Waters, 1973; Puget Sound, USA: Hall, Todd and Gordon, 1984); *Actinia equina* (continental Europe and British Isles: Braams and Geelen, 1953; Edmunds *et al.*, 1974); *Metridium senile* (continental Europe: Stehouwer, 1952; New England, USA: Harris and Duffy, 1980); and *Stomphia coccinea* (Danish Sound: K.W. Ockelmann, in Robson, 1961a).

As pointed out by Hall *et al.* (1982), in some of the foregoing studies the particular prey with which the anemones were associated in the field is uncertain, especially just prior to the experiments. The role of previous dietary experience, and especially the operation of 'ingestive conditioning' in which a nudibranch eating a particular anemone species may form an 'olfactory search image' of it and orient to it preferentially in subsequent tests, were tentatively suggested by Harris (1973) and Waters (1973). Hall *et al.* (1982) then showed that *A.papillosa* known to feed on *Sagartia troglodytes* in the field preferred that species over five others in laboratory multiple choice trials in an olfactometer. Another acontiate species, *Metridium senile*, ranked above any actiniid in the preference hierarchy. When the maintenance diet in the laboratory was changed to *Actinia equina*, the nudibranchs subsequently preferred this species. *A.papillosa* could distinguish, furthermore, between the red and green 'morphs' of *A.equina*, something only recently accomplished by taxonomists, who now relegate the latter to a separate species, *A.prasina*.

In *A.papillosa* feeding on sea anemones, the presumed advantages of ingestive conditioning related to optimal foraging have not been tested. In conditioned predators there was no disproportional change in the tendency to select a prey species relative to its fractional representation to total prey available, and 'switching' behaviour could not be demonstrated (Hall *et al.*, 1984). These authors noted that although ingestion of a prey species predisposed *A.papillosa* to select it in subsequent trials, preference was not absolute, and conditioned nudibranchs often took other species. They suggested that such plasticity of response may allow monitoring of the abundance of prey species, which may show dramatic local fluctuations (see Shick and Lamb, 1977, and references therein).

Stehouwer (1952) noted early that small specimens of *Metridium senile* were more attractive to *A.papillosa* than large individuals, but little attention has been paid to this. Harris (1987) suggested that in most studies where *M.senile* was not a preferred prey the effects of anemone size on aeolid preference underlie conflicting results. *A.papillosa* preferred small individuals of *M.senile* to large ones in olfactometer trials (Harris and Duffy, 1980), even when maintained on a diet of *Anthopleura elegantissima*, but when offered large rather than small *M.senile* they switched to *A.elegantissima* (Harris, 1986). Avoidance of large *M.senile* under laboratory conditions appears due to effective defence involving extrusion of acontia (Harris, 1986, and below). Whether small specimens of *M.senile* release effluents that are inherently more attractive to *A.papillosa*, or whether large anemones exude a repellent, is unknown.

It still is not clear that the preference of *Aeolidia papillosa* for small specimens of *Metridium senile* is strictly due to a more effective acontial defence in large anemones. Harris (1986) observed that acontia are most effective in the laboratory where there is little water movement and nothing to hinder their application to attacking nudibranchs, but that in the field the acontia of large anemones under attack may be carried off by surge or hung up on sea urchin spines, algae or hydroid colonies. Sebens (1986) likewise noted in an area of heavy surge that even the largest specimens of *Metridium* may be attacked. It could be that attacks on large anemones reflect hunger in the predator, since a starved nudibranch will attack even nonpreferred prey species. The tendency to attack smaller specimens of *M.senile* may have a simple mechanical basis, such specimens likely being easier to handle yet providing an ample meal. If so, the olfactory preference of *A.papillosa* for small *M.senile* might be interpretable in terms of energy maximization in optimal foraging behaviour (see Townsend and Hughes, 1981; Hall *et al.*, 1984).

Aeolid nudibranchs may use anemones not only as food, but also as a source of nematocysts, which the nudibranchs store undischarged in special cnidosacs in their dorsal cerata (Edmunds, 1966; Conklin and Mariscal, 1977; Day and Harris, 1978; Greenwood and Mariscal, 1984a, b, c). It is of particular interest that nudibranchs retain relatively few types of nematocyst (usually the largest and most penetrating) among the broader array available in the prey's cnidome. Day and Harris (1978) suggest that the mechanism for this selectivity involves digestion of the 'nonpreferred' types. How nematocysts are transported undischarged from the prey anemone into the cells of the cnidosacs of the nudibranch has been a major unanswered question. Greenwood and Mariscal (1984a, b, c) have shown that *Spurilla neapolitana* feeding on *Condylactis gigantea* and *Haliplanella lineata* incorporates immature nematocysts that are incapable of discharge into its cnidosacs. The nematocysts complete their development and become functional within the 'host' nudibranch's cells, apparently with the utilization of the host's ATP (Greenwood *et al.*, 1989).

Since the nematocysts stored by aeolids are fully functional and capable of being discharged when expelled from the cerata, a defensive function against predators is indicated (Edmunds, 1966; Conklin and Mariscal, 1977). Wrasses prefer small individuals of *A.papillosa* and learn to avoid large specimens (Harris, 1986), but whether size-related differences in the numbers of anemone-derived nematocysts are involved has not been studied. Stored nematocysts may also be used offensively: Tardy (1964) reports that *Eolidiella alderi* applies its cerata to the column of *Sagartia* sp. and stings it with the nematocysts of conspecific anemones, and then feeds on the damaged area.

The aeolid *Berghia major* retains in its cerata not only nematocysts but also viable zooxanthellae obtained when feeding on *Aiptasia pulchella* (Muller-Parker, 1984a). Zooxanthellae survive passage through the gut both of this nudibranch, and of puffers and butterfly fishes that prey on *A.pulchella*. The predators are a means of dispersal of the algae and their faeces may represent a source of zooxanthellae for planulae or newly-settled juvenile anemones lacking endosymbionts (section 2.6.3, page 92).

How the nudibranch avoids being stung by its anemone prey is a question that remains unanswered. Various workers have suggested that the copious mucus produced by feeding nudibranchs protects them physically or chemically from nematocysts (reviews by Harris, 1973; and Conklin and Mariscal, 1977). The latter authors suggest that the nudibranch may become acclimated to its prey in a manner similar to that of anemonefish, since after an initial 1–3 min of being stung, *Spurilla neapolitana* can crawl unharmed among the tentacles of *Pseudactinia melanaster* ($\equiv$ *Anemonia sargassensis*), *Anthopleura krebsi* and *Lebrunia danae*.

The striking resemblance in morphology and colour of certain aeolids to their prey has been noted often (Lawn and Ross, 1982a; Sebens, 1983a; Hall *et al.*, 1984; Harris, 1986, 1987). It may afford a degree of crypsis for nudibranchs while feeding on anemones; *A.papillosa* in the Gulf of Maine, for example, rarely moves away from its prey (Harris, 1986).

Sea anemones have various defences against predatory nudibranchs. The preferred sites of attack by nudibranchs (and by a pleurobranch gastropod) are the tentacles and oral disc (Conklin and Mariscal, 1977; Ottaway, 1977b; Howe and Harris, 1978; Harris and Howe, 1979; Lawn and Ross, 1982a; Muller Parker, 1984a; but see Waters, 1973), and it is not surprising that the initial response of most anemones to the predator is to retract the tentacles (Edmunds *et al.*, 1976). Bulging or inflation of the column appears to protect the anemone from further bites (Edmunds *et al.*, 1976), especially on the tentacles (Harris and Howe, 1979). Other defensive responses include creeping away from the attack (Harris, 1973; Edmunds *et al.*, 1976; Conklin and Mariscal, 1977; Harris and Howe, 1979), or releasing the basal disc from the substrate (Rosin, 1969; Harris, 1973; Edmunds *et al.*, 1976; Shick *et al.*, 1979b), thus allowing an anemone to drift away in the current. Active swimming affords a similar escape in *Stomphia coccinea* (Robson, 1961c, 1966) and *Boloceroides mcmurrichi* (Lawn and Ross, 1982a). Among actiniids and actinostolids, defensive behaviours (inflation of the column, detachment, swimming) are elicited by contact with the mucus of *Aeolidia papillosa*, and the receptors involved appear to be concentrated on the column (Robson, 1961a; Harris and Howe, 1979), usually the site of initial contact.

Ejection of acontia in anemones containing these structures is a universal response to aeolid predation (Harris, 1973, 1986; Edmunds *et al.*, 1976).

Acontia in particular discharge numerous detachable darts (formed from microbasic p-mastigophore nematocysts: section 1.5.1, page 26), which Conklin, Bigger and Mariscal (1977) suggest are an important defence against predatory nudibranchs because they do not anchor the prey to the predator. Corallimorpharians rank low in several prey preference hierarchies, and *Corynactis* spp. seem to be protected by the particularly large nematocysts in their tentacles, which cause *A.papillosa* to break off an attack (Edmunds *et al.*, 1976). *Lebrunia danae* autotomizes pseudotentacles that are under attack by *S.neapolitana* (Conklin and Mariscal, 1977), and *B.mcmurrichi* autotomizes tentacles seized by *Berghia major* and then swims away (Lawn and Ross, 1982a).

Unlike swimming in actinostolid anemones which involves a whip-like action of the column (described in section 7.4.2), swimming in *Boloceroides mcmurrichi* is driven by synchronous flexions of the very numerous tentacles (the latter comprising >90% of the anemone's wet weight). The logarithmic regression of the maximum force developed against tentacular crown diameter has a slope of about 2 (Josephson and March, 1966). This relationship is in accord with maximum force being a function of the musculature available, which being laminar, will increase approximately as the square of a linear dimension such as crown diameter (sections 3.8.1, page 143, and 5.6, page 215). In keeping with the unusual morphological and mechanical nature of swimming in this anemone, electrophysiological studies failed to detect activity of the usual conduction systems (TCNN, SS1, and SS2) that operate during escape responses in more advanced actiniarians (Lawn and Ross, 1982a; and section 7.4.2). The authors inferred a high degree of local autonomy of regional conduction systems in *B.mcmurrichi*, perhaps in association with a swimming pacemaker (see also Josephson and March, 1966). A similar mode of tentacle-powered swimming is seen in members of the primitive Protantheae, where it may be generated by an ectodermal nerve net (Robson, 1966, 1971). The predators of these anemones are unknown, although some nudibranchs will elicit their swimming behaviour (Robson, 1971).

The alarm pheromone anthopleurine (a quaternary ammonium compound) is present in various tissues of *Anthopleura elegantissima* at concentrations up to $120 \mu mol/g_w W$. When released from damaged anemones to yield subnanomolar concentrations in seawater, it excites receptors located primarily on the tentacles. In nearby conspecifics the tentacles flex rapidly and are withdrawn by the mesenteric retractor muscles, and the marginal sphincter contracts (Howe and Sheikh, 1975; Howe, 1976b). This sterotyped alarm response covers the tentacles and oral disc (the preferred sites of attack by *A.papillosa*) and leaves exposed columnar tissues which have the highest concentrations of the pheromone (Howe and Harris, 1978). Five days after a laboratory meal of *A.elegantissima*, some specimens of *A.papillosa* contained sufficiently high levels of anthopleurine to evoke an alarm response in other anemones without contacting them. This transfer phenomenon is probably active in the field, since some nudibranchs freshly collected near groups of *A.elegantissima* could evoke the alarm reaction. The response can be competitively inhibited by proline, a potent feeding activator in *A.elegantissima* (section 2.2.9 and Table 2.3, page 61). In these anemones, to remain expanded and able to feed during brief periods of immersion has proved more important than 'overreacting' to a distant threat of predation (Howe, 1976a).

An anemone that may benefit from the warning provided by anthopleurine released from a neighbour during predatory attack is likely to be a clonemate; if the entire genet is viewed as an individual, no appeal to altruism is necessary in considering the origin of this system. Non-clonemates and *A.xanthogrammica* however also respond to anthopleurine purified from *A.elegantissima* (Howe, 1976b), although *A.artemisia* (which is genetically closer to *A.elegantissima* than is *A.xanthogrammica*, based on allozyme frequency analyses: Smith and Potts, 1987) does not, and unlike its congeners it is not preferred as prey by *A.papillosa* (Waters, 1973). These seeming incongruities may be related to the infaunal nature of *A.artemisia* (Hand, 1955a), which is not as exposed to predatory nudibranchs. The concordance of physiological, chemical-ecological and allozymic measures of species relatedness is an interesting evolutionary question.

The intertidal distribution of *Anthopleura elegantissima* affords some relief from predation by *A.papillosa*, which is less tolerant of desiccation than is the anemone (Harris and Howe, 1979). Occupation of the intertidal zone by *Actinia tenebrosa* as a refuge from a predatory pleurobranch gastropod in the sublittoral has also been suggested (Ottaway, 1977b). None of *A.elegantissima*'s observed defensive behaviours will prevent it from being eaten by an adult *A.papillosa*, but some behaviours may be more effective against smaller predators. Harris and Howe (1979) suggest that the anemone's primary defence lies in minimizing damage to clone members (whose close packing protects individuals away from the periphery) until the growing nudibranchs are removed by wave action or desication. Perhaps as a result, in the same localities, *A.papillosa* is more often associated with a less preferred prey, the sublittoral *Metridium senile*.

Harris' long-term field observations have discerned size-related interaction among *A.papillosa*, *M.senile* and *Tautogolabrus adspersus* (a predatory wrasse) in New England (Harris, 1986, 1987). In areas where wrasses are common, the nudibranch appears later in the year and is less abundant, and *M.senile* occurs as relatively small individuals in large clones. In more open areas lacking wrasses, *A.papillosa* appears earlier in the year and is more common, and specimens of *M.senile* tend to be large and solitary. The negative effect of wrasses on recruitment in the nudibranch apparently allows the development of large clones of small anemones in areas where the fishes are abundant. The observed preference of *A.papillosa* for small individuals of *M.senile* (Harris and Duffy, 1980; Harris, 1986), and the seasonal cropping especially of juvenile anemones and recent basal lacerates (Shick *et al.*, 1979b) by increasingly abundant nudibranchs after the wrasses have moved offshore for the winter (Harris, 1986) seem responsible for the observed size structures of some *M.senile* populations. The population of *Haliplanella lineata* ($\equiv$ *H.luciae*) studied by Shick and Lamb (1977) in the same area was restricted to the intertidal by strictly sublittoral *A.papillosa*, which quickly removed *H.lineata* transplanted into the sublittoral (Shick *et al.*, 1979b).

7.4.2 Predation by Sea Stars

Dermasterias imbricata is a major predator of anemones on the open Pacific coast of Washington State, USA. Actiniids figure prominently in its diet, which may vary locally according to the relative abundance of individual species (e.g. *Epiactis prolifera* and *Anthopleura* spp.: Mauzey, Birkeland and Dayton, 1968; Sebens, 1983a). The general restriction of *Dermasterias* to the sublittoral (Figure 7.4) and the dearth of anemones at some sublittoral sites led Mauzey *et al.* (1968) to suggest that predation by the sea star restricted the vertical distribution of anemones; similar observations were made in California by Annett and Pierotti (1984). Transplantation and caging experiments by Sebens (cited in his 1983a monograph) show that *Dermasterias* removes. *A.elegantissima* and small specimens of *A.xanthogrammica* in sublittoral areas, but that large *A.xanthogrammica* achieve an 'escape in size' from predation. These facts, and observations of *Dermasterias* feeding on *Anthopleura* spp. in the lowest reaches of the intertidal (R.T. Paine, in Mauzey *et al.*, 1968; Sebens, 1983a), indicate that the intertidal is a refuge from this sea star both for *A.elegantissima* and for small individuals of *A.xanthogrammica*, which migrate into the sublittoral as they grow larger (Sebens, 1983a). For large *A.elegantissima* low in the intertidal, Harris and Howe (1979) similarly suggest an escape in size from predation by *Aeolidia papillosa*. The intertidal restriction of this anemone seems due to sublittoral predation by *Dermasterias* (Sebens, 1983a), which can take even the largest *A.elegantissima* (Annett and Pierotti, 1984).

The discovery that some actinostolid anemones (*Stomphia* spp.) detach and swim in response to contact with certain asterozoan sea stars puzzled early investigators (Yentsch and Pierce, 1955; Sund, 1958; Robson, 1961a, 1966; Ward, 1965a) because the sea stars were not known to prey on the anemones. But if swimming does provide an effective escape from such predators, one would expect observations of predation in the field to be rare (Mauzey *et al.*, 1968, who also noted that the reluctance of sea stars to feed in the laboratory complicates assessment of their diets).

With this in mind, Mauzey *et al.* (1968) provide a wonderfully detailed account of the natural diets of sea stars, some of which specialize on anemones and other anthozoans, and some of which were previously assumed not to eat anemones (see above) but were observed by these authors to do so in nature. All of the following asteroids have been reported to evoke swimming responses in *Stomphia coccinea* and *S.didemon* (the latter formerly referred to as *Actinostola* sp.: Ross, 1979c; Siebert, 1973), and all have been observed to eat sea anemones (those reported by Mauzey *et al.*, 1968, or personal communicants to them, to eat *Stomphia* are marked with an asterisk): *Crossaster papposus**, *Dermasterias imbricata**, *Gephyreaster swifti** and *Hippasteria spinosa* (which specializes on the anthozoan sea pen, *Pennatula*). Elicitation of the swimming response in *S.didemon* by asteroids that are not its predators is consistent with their phylogenetic relatedness and presumed biochemical similarity to *Dermasterias imbricata* (Dalby, Elliott and Ross, 1988; Elliott *et al.*, 1989). In addition, *S.coccinea* itself elicits a swimming response in *S.didemon* ($\equiv$ *Actinostola* sp.) (Ross and Sutton, 1967; Mauzey *et al.*, 1968).

Initiation of escape behaviour in *Stomphia* occurs after contact with a sea star, in the case of *D.imbricata* with its aboral surface, which contains a chemical that apparently triggers swimming (Ward, 1965b). Originally thought to be an aminopolysaccharide (Ward, 1965b), the active chemical has since been identified as imbricatine, a member of a class of alkaloids formerly known only from plants (Pathirana and Andersen, 1986; Elliott *et al.*, 1989). A solution of imbricatine is most effective in causing detachment and swimming in *S.coccinea* but less so in *S.didemon*, and does not cause detachment in *Epiactis lisbethae* and *Urticina piscivora* (Elliott *et al.*, 1989). The last two species require physical contact with the sea star to elicit detachment, and it is not known whether the effective stimulus involves different chemicals or a combination of mechanical and chemical stimulation. Chemical stimulants from asteroids and *Aeolidia papillosa* seem to be different, because sensory adaptation to prolonged stimulation by *Aeolidia* can be bypassed by contact with *Hippasteria* (Robson, 1961b).

Rapid detachment of the anemone's basal disc probably is effected as in the response to nudibranchs (section 7.4.1). Swimming, which may carry the anemone as much as 1.5 m (Sund, 1958), is effected by alternating contractions of the parieto-basilar muscles of the endoderm causing a whip-like motion of the column, already elongated by the endodermal circular muscle sheet (Sund, 1958; Robson, 1961b). Lawn (1976) detected only SS1 pulses and no TCNN or SS2 activity during *Dermasterias*-evoked swimming in *S.coccinea*. The SS1 pulses (ectodermal) are associated with the ectodermal sensory response to the stimulant from the sea star (Lawn, 1976); stimulation of the endodermal musculature probably occurs via a transmesogleal system (TMS) demonstrated electrophysiologically by Lawn (1980), which may have as its anatomical basis endodermal multipolar neurons that send

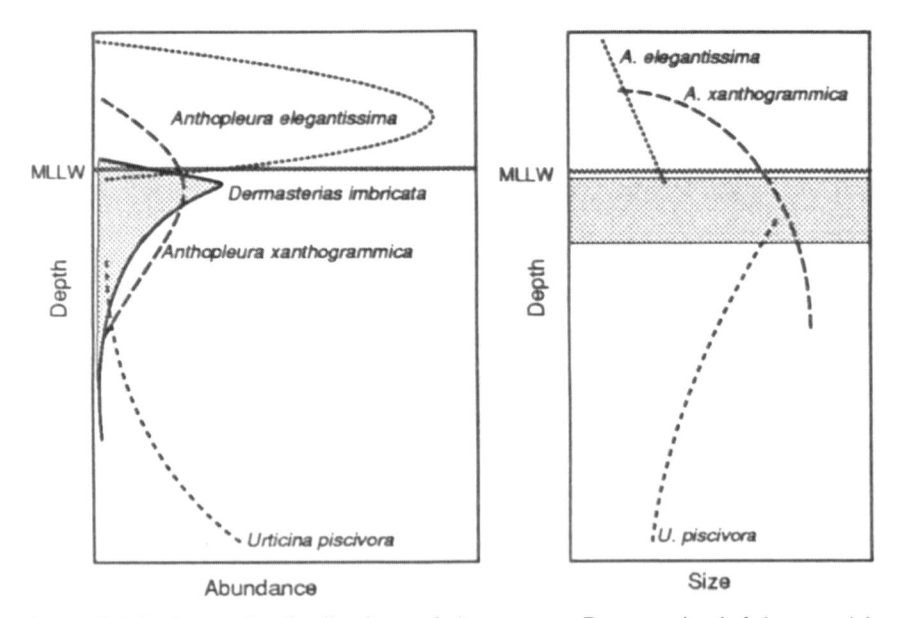

Abundance   Size

Figure 7.4 Bathymetric distributions of the sea star *Dermasterias imbricata* and its anemone prey, showing abundance and size. Where predator and prey overlap (left figure), *Anthopleura xanthogrammica* and *Urticina piscivora* achieve an 'escape in size' (right figure) from the sea star (for which no size data are available). MLLW = mean lower low water. See text for discussion. Source: drawn from data in Elliott *et al.* (1985), and observations in Sebens (1983a).

processes into the mesoglea and toward the ectoderm (Robson, 1963; see also section 1.3, page 15).

The bathymetric distribution of *Urticina piscivora*, another prey of *Dermasterias*, is the mirror image of that of *Anthopleura elegantissima* and the sea star. *U.piscivora* is more abundant at depths exceeding 12 m and *D.imbricata* reaches its maximum abundance at depths shallower than 3 m (Elliott *et al.*, 1985; Figure 7.4). Individuals of *U.piscivora* tend to be larger at shallower depths where they overlap with *Dermasterias*. Their experiments led Elliott *et al.* (1985) to suggest several explanations for the distribution of *U.piscivora*. Small anemones unfailingly and rapidly detach their basal disc when contacted by the sea star, whereas large specimens never do. (Detachment presumably is mediated by the SS1: Lawn and Ross, 1982b.) This behaviour results in the escape of many small anemones, which are taken if their detachment is prevented. The predominance of small anemones at greater depths might result from their sinking there after detaching, although it might just as likely result from the settlement of planulae in deep water and the subsequent migration of anemones into the shallows as they grow (the inverse of the pattern shown by *Anthopleura xanthogrammica*). Large individuals achieve an escape in size and coexist with the sea star (Figure 7.4). Large specimens of *U.piscivora*, which are not attacked by the sea star, show a feeding reponse to it, expanding the oral disc, bending toward the asteroid, and stinging its aboral surface when incidentally or experimentally brought into contact with it. A similar response by a large *A.elegantissima* caused *Dermasterias* to move away from the anemone (Annett and Pierotti, 1984).

The bathymetric disjunction between *Dermasterias imbricata* and *Stomphia didemon* does seem due to the escape response of the anemone, a behaviour that is not size-dependent and results in the movement of the anemones to deeper water following an interaction with the sea star (Dalby *et al.*, 1988). In sublittoral habitats in California, *Dermasterias imbricata* was found by Annett and Pierotti (1984) to be primarily associated with the corallimorpharian *Corynactis californica*, which constituted most of the sea star's diet, yet which the sea star avoided in laboratory choice experiments involving *C.californica*, *A.elegantissima* and *A.xanthogrammica*, even when previously fed on *C.californica*. This seeming paradox is resolved by the observation that despite its abundance intertidally, *A.elegantissima* was virtually absent from adjacent sublittoral sites, where only *Corynactis* and large *A.xanthogrammica* were present. Since large *A.xanthogrammica* escaped predation, the only possible prey was *Corynactis*, although it was avoided when other prey were available. Avoidance of the corallimorpharian by the sea star seems due to its particularly large tentacular nematocysts, a sufficiently effective defence that, when coupled with frequent asexual reproduction, enables the corallimorpharian to persist despite predation. This evidence supports the important *caveat* that in the field apparent prey preference and specialization may reflect the absence or local extinction of preferred prey, and the predator's subsequent exploitation of a less preferred but abundant food item.

7.5 CONCLUSION

Studies of sea anemones and their interactions with their ectosymbionts and predators have ranged from the community to the biochemical levels of organization, although a single study rarely involves more than one or two such levels. The adaptive values of isolated anatomical and physiological traits sometimes remain puzzling until relevant natural historical and quantitative ecological observations are forthcoming. Conversely, the causes and mechanisms of sometimes enigmatic ecological and behavioural relationships have been elucidated by biochemical, physiological and ultrastructural studies.

CODA

The proposition of this book has been to present sea anemones as integrated, resource-using systems that are the evolutionary result of identifiable selective forces in their natural environment. The rigorous restriction to a single taxon has had as a benefit the sometimes detailed treatment of morphological constraints and functional responses that have shaped the evolution of this group, but perhaps at the cost of failing to convey the taxonomic variability and broader relevance of the processes and principles involved.

Keeping strictly to sea anemones has meant presenting less than the full details of pertinent biological phenomena that have been studied elsewhere in the Cnidaria: allorecognition has been probed extensively among other Anthozoa such as scleractinian corals and octocorals, and in the Hydrozoa; coloniality, absent from the Actiniaria, has been a major feature in the evolution of most other Cnidaria, and the calcified scleractinians in particular have left a detailed fossil record of this; insight concerning calcification mechanisms has been gained in scleractinians and octocorals; many additional details of the functioning of algal endosymbionts have come from the study of scleractinians, Scyphozoa and Hydrozoa; the developmental roles of interstitial cells (multipotent stem cells) have been discerned largely in the Hydrozoa, where details of cnidogenesis are well known; allelochemical interactions just beginning to be appreciated in sea anemones are extensive in the octocorals, which have been especially rich sources for natural products chemists and ecologists; much knowledge of cnidarian toxins has been forthcoming in studies of, especially, Scyphozoa and Cubozoa. Still, the Actiniaria offer sufficient diversity so that their functional biology can be studied by applying the principle first expounded by Claude Bernard and later by August Krogh: there exist particular species that are anatomically or otherwise suited for the investigation of particular phenomena.

Owing to the relative simplicity of the actiniarian body plan and its plasticity of form, behavioural responses to one environmental variable may have physiological consequences not directly related to that variable. This has been discussed with reference to the extension of the column and tentacles to capture prey (energy intake), a behaviour that also increases the exposed surface area of the anemone and decreases diffusion distances for oxygen, and so increases the rate of oxygen consumption (energy expenditure). Also, the complex shell-climbing behaviours in some sea anemones are enabled by their relatively thick, dense mesogleas; these morphological and anatomical features increase diffusion distances and decrease the inherent permeability of the column to oxygen, and may necessitate ventilation of the coelenteron, manifested as a 'respiratory rhythm'. The rhythmic behaviours seen in many anemones thus may reflect ongoing compromises necessitated by conflicting physiological and energetic demands and the morphological constraints of the simple body plan.

The balanced energy equation is a cornerstone of functional biology, and this book relies heavily on energetic units and concepts. Despite the utility of the notion of the 'energetic organism', it has practical limitations in sea anemones and other slimy animals where as much as one-third of the energy budget may be unaccounted; the physiological scope for growth may therefore be misleading, unless energy lost in copious mucus and other secretions (e.g. cnidae and digestive enzymes), usually unmeasured, can be quantified.

The fascination that feeding in sea anemones has held for generations of biologists is an outgrowth of the early discovery of the animal nature of these 'zoophytes'. Anemones have been viewed in turn as voracious predators, gardeners of symbiotic algae, osmotrophs relying heavily on dissolved organic matter, and polytrophic opportunists. Phylogenetically the first extant Metazoa to develop extracellular digestion, cnidarians thereby overcame the energetic constraint of purely microphagous feeding; enzymic constraints on what foods they can use is a topic requiring further study. Chemical stimuli that elicit various feeding behaviours have been especially well studied; which particular free amino acids are effective stimuli may not be divorced from the anemones' own endogenous pools of these compounds used in cellular volume regulation. By harbouring primary producers within their own bodies, zooxanthellate sea anemones become experimentally tractable microcosms of coral reef ecosystems in which organic productivity and structural diversity are maintained by internal recycling of scarce nutrients, with much of the required energy coming from sunlight.

The laminar organization of actiniarians provides a means whereby surface area may increase more nearly in proportion to mass than in geometrically more corpulent metazoans. Accordingly, their oxygen consumption scales as a greater power of body mass than in most metazoans. As sit-and-wait predators having low energy costs for activity and capture of protein-rich food, some sea anemones show relatively high growth efficiencies compared with more active animals, including medusae.

By incorporating vegetative proliferation into their sexual life cycle, many sea anemones have optimized their evolutionary potential, where the soma bearing a locally-adapted genotype may flourish and expand asexually, and still export recombined, potentially successful genotypes to novel habitats. Vegetative (clonal) growth allows maximization of biomass of the clonal soma by partitioning it into many independent units each of optimal size for maximizing the scope for growth and reproduction, at the same time minimizing risk of mortality of the genotype by spreading the risk among these units. The sizes both of individuals and clones thus are components of fitness. Individual size in indeterminately-growing anemones may vary locally according to physical (e.g. intertidal exposure) and biological (e.g. presence of predators) factors; particular habitats may have predisposed various groups of anemones toward particular modes of asexual proliferation.

Competitive interactions among sea anemones have led to insight concerning the evolution of allorecognition (i.e. immunological) processes. Interactions of sea anemones with their ectosymbionts such as crustaceans and fishes, and predators such as nudibranchs and sea stars, have prompted studies that yielded much of our knowledge of the actiniarian neuromuscular system. Future investigations of sea anemones will be progressively comparative and integrative, and this will necessitate the multidisciplinary, collaborative approach that increasingly characterizes the field of physiological ecology.

References

This database is available as a Pro-Cite® file (Macintosh™ or IBM-compatible format; Personal Bibliographic Software, Inc.) or as an alphabetized ASCII text file. Send a formatted floppy disk (specify which type of file is required) and a self-addressed return envelope to the author at the Department of Zoology, University of Maine, Orono, ME 04469-0146 U.S.A.

Abel, E.F. (1954) Ein Beitrag zur Giftwirkung der Aktinien und Funktion der Randsäckchen. *Zool. Anz.*, **153**, 259–68.

Abel, E.F. (1960) Liaison facultative d'un poisson (*Gobius bucchichii* Steindachner) et d'une anémone (*Anemonia sulcata* Penn.) en Méditerranée. *Vie et Milieu*, **11**, 517–31.

Abeloos-Parize, M. and Abeloos-Parize, R. (1926) Sur l'origine alimentaire du pigment carotinoide d'*Actinia equina*. *C.R. Soc. Biol., Paris*, **94**, 560–2.

Albrecht, H. (1977) Einige Beobachtungen an Anemonefischen in der karibischen See. *Bijdr. Dierkunde*, **47**, 109–19.

Allee, W.C. (1923) Studies in marine ecology: IV. The effect of temperature in limiting the geographical range of invertebrates of the Woods Hole littoral. *Ecology*, **4**, 341–54.

Allen, G. R. (1975) *The Anemonefishes. Their Classification and Biology*, 2nd ed., T.F.H. Publications, Neptune City, New Jersey, 352 pp.

Amerongen, H.M. and Peteya, D.J. (1976) The ultrastructure of the muscle system of *Stomphia coccinea*. In G.O. Mackie (ed.), *Coelenterate Ecology and Behavior*, Plenum Publishing Corporation, New York, pp. 541–7.

Anderson, P.A.V. (1980) Epithelial conduction: its properties and functions. *Prog. Neurobiol.*, **15**, 161–203.

Anderson, P.A.V. and Schwab, W.E. (1982) Recent advances and model systems in coelenterate neurobiology. *Prog. Neurobiol.*, **19**, 591–600.

Anderson, S.L. and Burris, J.E. (1987) Role of glutamine synthetase in ammonia assimilation by symbiotic marine dinoflagellates (zooxanthellae). *Mar. Biol.*, **94**, 451–8.

Annett, C. and Pierotti, R. (1984) Foraging behavior and prey selection of the leather seastar *Dermasterias imbricata*. *Mar. Ecol. Prog. Ser.*, **14**, 197–206.

Ansell, A.D. and Trueman, E.R. (1968) The mechanism of burrowing in the anemone, *Peachia hastata* Gosse. *J. Exp. Mar. Biol. Ecol.*, **2**, 124–34.

Arai, M.N. (1972) The muscular system of *Pachycerianthus fimbriatus*. *Can. J. Zool.*, **50**, 311–17.

Arai, M.N. and Walder, G.L. (1973) The feeding response of *Pachycerianthus fimbriatus* (Ceriantharia). *Comp. Biochem. Physiol.*, **44A**, 1085–92.

Asada, K. and Takahashi, M. (1987) Production and scavenging of active oxygen in photosynthesis. In D.J. Kyle, C.B. Osmond and C.J. Arntzen (eds.), *Photoinhibition*, Elsevier Science Publishers, Amsterdam, pp. 227–87.

Ates, R.M.L. (1989) Fishes that eat sea anemones, a review. *J. Nat. Hist.*, **23**, 71–9.

Atoda, K. (1954) Postlarval development of the sea anemone, *Anthopleura* sp. *Sci. Rept. Tôhoku Univ.*, *4th Ser.*, *Biology*, **20**, 274–86 + 2 plates.

Atoda, K. (1976) Development of the sea anemone, *Haliplanella luciae*. V. Longitudinal fission and the origin of mono-, di- and tri-glyphic individuals. *Bull. Mar. Biol. Sta. Asamushi*, **15**, 133–46.

Ayre, D.J. (1982) Inter-genotype aggression in the solitary sea anemone *Actinia tenebrosa*. *Mar. Biol.*, **68**, 199–205.

Ayre, D.J. (1983) The effects of asexual reproduction and inter-genotypic aggression on the genotypic structure of populations of the sea anemone *Actinia tenebrosa*. *Oecologia*, **57**, 158–65.

Ayre, D.J. (1984a) The sea anemone *Actinia tenebrosa*: an opportunistic insectivore. *Ophelia*, **23**, 149–53.

Ayre, D.J. (1984b) The effects of sexual and asexual reproduction on geographic variation in the sea anemone *Actinia tenebrosa*. *Oecologia*, **62**, 222–9.

Ayre, D.J. (1984c) Effects of environment and population density on the sea anemone *Actinia tenebrosa*. *Aust. J. Mar. Freshw. Res.*, **35**, 735–46.

Ayre, D.J. (1985) Localized adaptation of clones of the sea anemone *Actinia tenebrosa*. *Evolution*, **39**, 1250–60.

Ayre, D.J. (1987) The formation of clonal territories in experimental populations of the sea anemone *Actinia tenebrosa*. *Biol. Bull.*, **172**, 178–86.

Ayre, D.J. (1988) Evidence for genetic determination of sex in *Actinia tenebrosa*. *J. Exp. Mar. Biol. Ecol.*, **116**, 23–34.

Bach, C.E. and Herrnkind, W.F. (1980) Effects of predation pressure on the mutualistic interaction between the hermit crab, *Pagurus pollicaris* Say, 1817, and the sea anemone, *Calliactis tricolor* (Lesueur, 1817). *Crustaceana*, **38**, 104–8.

Bak, R.P.M. and Borsboom, J.L.A. (1984) Allelopathic interaction between a reef coelenterate and benthic algae. *Oecologia*, **63**, 194–8.

Balasch, J. and Mengual, V. (1974) The behaviour of *Dardanaus arrosor* in association with *Calliactis parasitica* in artificial habitat. *Mar. Behav. Physiol.*, **2**, 251–60.

Batchelder, H.P. and Gonor, J.J. (1981) Population characteristics of the intertidal green sea anemone, *Anthopleura xanthogrammica*, on the Oregon coast. *Est., Coast. Shelf Sci.*, **13**, 235–45.

Batham, E.J. (1965) The neural architecture of the sea anemone *Mimetridium cryptum*.

Amer. Zool., 5, 395–402.

Batham, E.J. and Pantin, C.F.A. (1950a) Inherent activity in the sea-anemone, *Metridium senile* (L.). *J. Exp. Biol.*, 27, 290–301.

Batham, E.J. and Pantin, C.F.A. (1950b) Phases of activity in the sea-anemone, *Metridium senile* (L.), and their relation to external stimuli. *J. Exp. Biol.*, 27, 377–99.

Batham, E.J. and Pantin, C.F.A. (1950c) Muscular and hydrostatic action in the sea-anemone *Metridium senile* (L.). *J. Exp. Biol.*, 27, 264–89.

Batham, E.J. and Pantin, C.F.A. (1951) The organization of the muscular system of *Metridium senile. Quart. J. Microsc. Sci.*, 92, 27–54 + 2 plates.

Batham, E.J. and Pantin, C.F.A. (1954) Slow contraction and its relation to spontaneous activity in the sea-anemone *Metridium senile* (L.). *J. Exp. Biol.*, 31, 84–103.

Batham, E.J., Pantin, C.F.A. and Robson, E.A. (1960) The nerve-net of the sea anemone, *Metridium senile* (L.): the mesenteries and the column. *Quart. J. Microsc. Sci.*, 101, 487–510.

Battey, J.F. and Patton, J.S. (1984) A reevaluation of the role of glycerol in carbon translocation in zooxanthellae-coelenterate symbiosis. *Mar. Biol.*, 79, 27–38.

Battey, J.F. and Patton, J.S. (1987) Glycerol translocation in *Condylactis gigantea. Mar. Biol.*, 95, 37–46.

Bayne, B.L. and Scullard, C. (1977) An apparent specific dynamic action in *Mytilus edulis L. J. Mar. Biol. Ass. UK*, 57, 371–8.

Beattie, C.W. (1971) Respiratory adjustments of an estuarine coelenterate to abnormal levels of environmental phosphate and oxygen. *Comp. Biochem. Physiol.*, 40B, 907–16.

Bell, G. (1982) *The Masterpiece of Nature: The Evolution and Genetics of Sexuality*, University of California Press, Berkeley, 600 pp.

Bennett, L.W. and Stroud, E. (1981) Occurrence and possible functions of γ-glutamyl transpeptidase in external epithelia of *Metridium senile. Trans. Amer. Microsc. Soc.*, 100, 316–21.

Benson-Rodenbough, B. and Ellington, W.R. (1982) Responses of the euryhaline sea anemone *Bunodosoma cavernata* (Bosc) (Anthozoa, Actiniaria, Actiniidae) to osmotic stress. *Comp. Biochem. Physiol.*, 72A, 731–5.

Béress, L. (1982) Biologically active compounds from coelenterates. *Pure Appl. Chem.*, 54, 1981–94.

Béress, L., Béress, R. and Wunderer, G. (1975) Isolation and characterisation of three polypeptides with neurotoxic activity from *Anemonia sulcata. FEBS Lett.*, 50, 311–14.

Bergmann, W., Creighton, S.M. and Stokes, W.M. (1956) Contributions to the study of marine products. XL. Waxes and triglycerides of sea anemones. *J. Org. Chem.*, 21, 721–8.

Bernheimer, A.W. and Avigad, L.S. (1976) Properties of a toxin from the sea anemone *Stoichactis helianthus*, including specific binding to sphingomyelin. *Proc. Nat. Acad. Sci. USA*, 73, 467–71.

Bigger, C.H. (1976) The acrorhagial response in *Anthopleura krebsi*: intraspecific and interspecific recognition. In G.O. Mackie (ed.), *Coelenterate Ecology and Behavior*, Plenum, New York, pp. 127–36.

Bigger, C.H. (1980) Interspecific and intraspecific acrorhagial aggressive behavior among sea anemones: a recognition of self and not-self. *Biol. Bull.*, **159**, 117–34.

Bigger, C.H. (1982) The cellular basis of the aggressive acrorhagial response of sea anemones. *J. Morphol.*, **173**, 259–78.

Bigger, C.H. and Hildemann, W.H. (1982) Cellular defense systems of the Coelenterata. In N. Cohen and M.M. Sigel (eds.), *The Reticuloendothelial System, Vol. 3*, Plenum, New York, pp. 59–87.

Bikfalvi, A., Binder, A., Béress, L. and Wassermann, O. (1988) Isolation and blood coagulation inhibition of a new proteinase inhibitor from the sea anemone *Anemonia sulcata. Comp. Biochem. Physiol.*, **89B**, 305–8.

Bishop, S.H., Barnes, L.B. and Kirkpatrick, D.S. (1972) Adenosine deaminase from *Metridium senile* (L.), a sea anemone. *Comp. Biochem. Physiol.*, **43B**, 949–63.

Bishop, S.H., Ellis, L.L. and Burcham, J.M. (1983) Amino acid metabolism in molluscs. In P.W. Hochachka (ed.), *The Mollusca. Vol. 1. Metabolic Biochemistry and Molecular Biomechanics*, Academic Press, New York, pp. 243–327.

Bishop, S.H., Klotz, A., Drolet, L.L., Smullin, D.H. and Hoffmann, R.J. (1978) NADP-specific glutamate dehydrogenase in *Metridium senile* (L.). *Comp. Biochem. Physiol.*, **61B**, 185–7.

Black, R. and Johnson, M.S. (1979) Asexual viviparity and population genetics of *Actinia tenebrosa. Mar. Biol.*, **53**, 27–31.

Blank, R.J. and Trench, R.K. (1985) Speciation and symbiotic dinoflagellates. *Science*, **229**, 656–8.

Blank, R.J. and Trench, R.K. (1986) Nomenclature of endosymbiotic dinoflagellates. *Taxon*, **35**, 286–94.

Blanquet, R. (1970) Ionic effects on discharge of the isolated and *in situ* nematocysts of the sea anemone, *Aiptasia pallida*: a possible role of calcium. *Comp. Biochem. Physiol.*, **35**, 451–61.

Blanquet, R.S., Emanuel, D. and Murphy, T.A. (1988) Suppression of exogenous alanine uptake in isolated zooxanthellae by cnidarian host homogenate fractions: species and symbiosis specificity. *J. Exp. Mar. Biol. Ecol.*, **117**, 1–8.

Blanquet, R.S., Nevenzel, J.C. and Benson, A.A. (1979) Acetate incorporation into the lipids of the anemone *Anthopleura elegantissima* and its associated zooxanthellae. *Mar. Biol.*, **54**, 185–94.

Bodansky, M. (1923) Comparative studies of digestion III. Further observations on digestion in coelenterates. *Amer. J. Physiol.*, **67**, 547–50.

Bohn, G. (1906a) Sur les courbures dues à la lumière. *C.R. Soc. Biol., Paris*, **61**, 420–1.

Bohn, G. (1906b) La persistance du rhythme des mareés chez l'*Actinia equina. C.R. Soc. Biol., Paris*, **61**, 661–3.

Bohn, G. (1908) L'épanouissement des actinies dans les milieux asphyxiques. *C.R. Soc. Biol., Paris*, **65**, 317–20.

Bonnin, J.-P. (1964) Recherches sur la 'réaction d'agression' et sur le functionnement des acrorrhages d'*Actinia equina* L. *Bull. Biol. Fr. Belg.*, **98**, 225–50.

Boothby, K.M. and McFarlane, I.D. (1986) Chemoreception in sea anemones: betaine stimulates the pre-feeding response in *Urticina eques* and *U.felina. J. Exp. Biol.*, **125**, 385–9.

Boschma, H. (1925) The nature of the association between Anthozoa and zooxanthellae. *Proc. Nat. Acad. Sci. USA*, **11**, 65–7.

Boury-Esnault, N. and Doumenc, D.A. (1979) Glycogen storage and transfer in primitive invertebrates: Demospongea and Actiniaria. In C. Levi and N. Boury-Esnault (eds.), *Biologie des Spongiaires*, Colloques Internationaux du CNRS No. 291, Centre National de la Recherche Scientifique, Paris, pp. 181–92.

Braams, W.G. and Geelen, H.F.M. (1953) The preference of some nudibranchs for certain coelenterates. *Arch. Neerland. de Zoologie*, **10**, 241–64.

Braber, L. and Borghouts, C.H. (1977) Distribution and ecology of Anthozoa in the estuarine region of the rivers Rhine, Meuse and Scheldt. *Hydrobiologia*, **52**, 15–21.

Brace, R.C. (1981) Intraspecific aggression in the colour morphs of the anemone *Phymactis clematis* from Chile. *Mar. Biol.*, **64**, 85–93.

Brace, R.C. and Pavey, J. (1978) Size-dependent dominance hierarchy in the anemone *Actinia equina. Nature*, **273**, 752–3.

Brace, R.C., Pavey, J. and Quicke, D.L.J. (1979) Intraspecific aggression in the colour morphs of the anemone *Actinia equina*: the 'convention' governing dominance ranking. *Anim. Behav.*, **27**, 553–61.

Brace, R.C. and Quicke, D.L.J. (1985) Further analysis of individual spacing within aggregations of the anemone, *Actinia equina. J. Mar. Biol. Ass. UK*, **65**, 35–53.

Brace, R.C. and Quicke, D.L.J. (1986) Dynamics of colonization by the beadlet anemone, *Actinia equina. J. Mar. Biol. Ass. UK*, **66**, 21–47.

Brace, R.C. and Reynolds, H.A. (1989) Relative intraspecific aggressiveness of pedal disc colour phenotypes of the beadlet anemone, *Actinia equina. J. Mar. Biol. Ass. UK*, **69**, 273–8.

Brafield, A.E. (1980) Oxygen consumption by the sea anemone *Calliactis parasitica* (Couch). *J. Exp. Biol.*, **88**, 367–74.

Brafield, A.E. and Chapman, G. (1965) The oxygen consumption of *Pennatula rubra* Ellis and some other anthozoans. *Z. vergl. Physiol.*, **50**, 363–70.

Brafield, A.E. and Chapman, G. (1983) Diffusion of oxygen through the mesogloea of the sea anemone *Calliactis parasitica. J. Exp. Biol.*, **107**, 181–7.

Brafield, A.E. and Llewellyn, M.J. (1982) *Animal Energetics*, Blackie & Son, Glasgow and London, 168 pp.

Brasier, M.D. (1979) The Cambrian radiation event. In M.R. House (ed.), *The Origin of Major Invertebrate Groups*. Systematics Association Special Vol. No. 12, Academic Press, London, pp. 103–59.

Brooks, W.R. (1988) The influence of the location and abundance of the sea anemone *Calliactis tricolor* (Le Sueur) in protecting hermit crabs from octopus predators. *J. Exp. Mar. Biol. Ecol.*, **116**, 15–21.

Brooks, W.R. (1989a) Hermit crabs alter sea anemone placement patterns for shell balance and reduced predation. *J. Exp. Mar. Biol. Ecol.*, **132**, 109–22.

Brooks, W.R. (1989b) Hermit crabs protect their symbiotic cnidarians — true cases of mutualism. *Amer. Zool.*, **29**, 36A (abstract).

Brooks, W.R. and Mariscal, R.N. (1984) The acclimation of anemone fishes to sea anemones: protection by changes in the fish's mucous coat. *J. Exp. Mar. Biol. Ecol.*, **81**, 277–85.

Brooks, W.R. and Mariscal, R.N. (1986a) Interspecific competition for space by hydroids and a sea anemone living on gastropod shells inhabited by hermit crabs. *Mar. Ecol. Prog. Ser.*, **28**, 241–4.

Brooks, W.R. and Mariscal, R.N. (1986b) Population variation and behavioral changes in two pagurids in association with the sea anemone *Calliactis tricolor* (Leseur). *J. Exp. Mar. Biol. Ecol.*, **103**, 275–89.

Buck, M. and Schlichter, D. (1987) Driving forces for the uphill transport of amino acids into epidermal brush border membrane vesicles of the sea anemone, *Anemonia sulcata* (Cnidaria, Anthozoa). *Comp. Biochem. Physiol.*, **88A**, 273–9.

Bucklin, A. (1982) The annual cycle of sexual reproduction in the sea anemone *Metridium senile*. *Can. J. Zool.*, **60**, 3241–8.

Bucklin, A. (1985) Biochemical genetic variation, growth and regeneration of the sea anemone, *Metridium*, of British shores. *J. Mar. Biol. Ass. U.K.*, **65**, 141–57.

Bucklin, A. (1987a) Growth and asexual reproduction of the sea anemone *Metridium*: Comparative laboratory studies of three species. *J. Exp. Mar. Biol. Ecol.*, **110**, 41–52.

Bucklin, A. (1987b) Adaptive advantages of patterns of growth and asexual reproduction of the sea anemone *Metridium senile* (L.) in intertidal and submerged populations. *J. Exp. Mar. Biol. Ecol.*, **110**, 225–43.

Bucklin, A. and Hedgecock, D. (1982) Biochemical genetic evidence for a third species of *Metridium* (Coelenterata, Actiniaria). *Mar. Biol.*, **66**, 1–7.

Bucklin, A., Hedgecock, D. and Hand, C. (1984) Genetic evidence of self- fertilization in the sea anemone *Epiactis prolifera*. *Mar. Biol.*, **84**, 175–82.

Bullock, T.H. (1955) Compensation for temperature in the metabolism and activity of poikilotherms. *Biol. Rev.*, **30**, 311–42.

Bullock, T.H. and Horridge, G.A. (1965) Coelenterata and Ctenophora. In T.H. Bullock and G.A. Horridge, *Structure and Function in the Nervous Systems of Invertebrates, Vol. I*, W.H. Freeman, San Francisco, pp. 459–534.

Bunde, T.A., Dearlove, G.E. and Bishop, S.H. (1978) Aminoethylphosphonic acid-containing glycoproteins: the acid mucopolysaccharide-like components in mucus from *Metridium senile* (L.). *J. Exp. Zool.*, **206**, 215–22.

Bursey, C.R. and Guanciale, J.M. (1977) Feeding behavior of the sea anemone *Condylactis gigantea*. *Comp. Biochem. Physiol.*, **57A**, 115–17.

Bursey, C.R. and Harmer, J.A. (1979) Induced changes in the osmotic concentration of the coelenteron fluid of the sea anemone *Condylactis gigantea*. *Comp. Biochem. Physiol.*, **64A**, 73–6.

Burton, R.S. and Feldman, M.W. (1982) Changes in free amino acid concentrations during osmotic response in the intertidal copepod *Tigriopus californicus*. *Comp. Biochem. Physiol.*, **73A**, 441–5.

Buss, L.W. (1987) *The Evolution of Individuality*, Princeton University Press, Princeton, New Jersey, 202 pp.

Buss, L.W., McFadden, C.S. and Keene, D.R. (1984) Biology of hydractiniid hydroids. 2. Histocompatibility effector system/competitive mechanism mediated by nematocyst discharge. *Biol. Bull.*, **167**, 139–58.

Cain, A.J. (1974) Breeding system of a sessile animal. *Nature*, **247**, 289–90.

Cairns, S., Hartog, J.D. den and Arneson, C. (1986) Class Anthozoa (Corals, anemones). In W. Sterrer (ed.), *Marine Fauna and Flora of Bermuda. A Systematic Guide to the Identification of Marine Organisms*, John Wiley & Sons, New York, pp. 159–94.

Calow, P. (1977a) Conversion efficiencies in heterotrophic organisms. *Biol. Rev.*, 52, 385–409.

Calow, P. (1977b) Ecology, evolution and energetics: a study in metabolic adaptation. In A. Macfayden (ed.), *Advances in Ecological Research, Vol. 10*, Academic Press, New York, pp. 1–62.

Calow, P. (1978) *Life Cycles: An Evolutionary Approach to the Physiology of Reproduction, Development and Ageing*, Chapman and Hall, London, 164 pp.

Calow, P. (1979) The cost of reproduction — a physiological approach. *Biol. Rev.*, 54, 23–40.

Calow, P. (1981) Growth in lower invertebrates. In M. Rechcigl (ed.), *Physiology of Growth and Nutrition*, S. Karger, Basel, pp. 53–76.

Calow, P. and Sibly, R.M. (1987) Conflicting predictions concerning clonal reproduction? *Functional Ecol.*, 1, 161–3.

Calow, P. and Townsend, C.R. (1981) Resource utilization in growth. In C.R. Townsend and P. Calow (eds.), *Physiological Ecology. An Evolutionary Approach to Resource Use*, Sinauer Associates, Sunderland, Massachusetts, pp. 220–44.

Campbell, R.D. (1974) Development. In L. Muscatine and H. M. Lenhoff (eds.), *Coelenterate Biology: Reviews and New Perspectives*, Academic Press, New York, pp. 179–210.

Carlgren, O. (1905) Über die Bedeutung der Flimmerbewegung für den Nahrungstransport bei den Actiniarien und Madreporarien. *Biol. Zentralbl.*, 25, 308–22.

Carlgren, O. (1929) Über eine Actiniariengattung mit besondern Fangtentakeln. *Zool. Anz.*, 81, 109–13.

Carlgren, O. (1949) A survey of the Ptychodactiaria, Corallimorpharia and Actiniaria. *Kungl. Sven. Vetenskapsakad. Handlingar, Fjärde Ser.*, 1, 1–121 + 4 plates.

Carlyle, R.F. (1969a) The occurrence of catecholamines in the sea anemone *Actinia equina*. *Brit. J. Pharm.*, 36, 182P.

Carlyle, R.F. (1969b) The occurrence of pharmacologically active substances in, and the actions of drugs on, preparations of the sea anemone *Actinia equina*. *Brit. J. Pharm.*, 37, 532P.

Carlyle, R.F. (1974) The occurrence in and actions of amino acids on isolated supra oral sphincter preparations of the sea anemone *Actinia equina*. *J. Physiol.*, 236, 635–52.

Carter, M.A. and Funnell, M. (1980) Reproduction and brooding in *Actinia*. In P. Tardent and R. Tardent (eds.), *Developmental and Cellular Biology of Coelenterates*, North-Holland Biomedical Press, Amsterdam, pp. 17–22.

Carter, M.A. and Miles, J. (1989) Gametogenic cycles and reproduction in the beadlet sea anemone *Actinia equina* (Cnidaria: Anthozoa). *Biol. J. Linn. Soc.*, 36, 129–55.

Carter, M.A. and Thorp, C.H. (1979) The reproduction of *Actinia equina* L. var. *mesembryanthemum*. *J. Mar. Biol. Ass. UK*, 59, 989–1001.

Carter, M.A. and Thorpe, J.P. (1981) Reproductive, genetic and ecological evidence that *Actinia equina* var. *mesembryanthemum* and var. *fragacea* are not conspecific. *J. Mar. Biol. Ass. UK*, 61, 71–93.

Cates, N. and McLaughlin, J.J.A. (1976) Differences of ammonia metabolism in symbiotic and aposymbiotic *Condylactus* and *Cassiopea* spp. *J. Exp. Mar. Biol. Ecol.*, 21, 1–5.

Cates, N. and McLaughlin, J.J.A. (1979) Nutrient availability for zooxanthellae derived from physiological activities of *Condylactus* spp. *J. Exp. Mar. Biol. Ecol.*, 37, 31–41.

Chadwick, N.E. (1987) Interspecific aggressive behavior of the corallimorpharian *Corynactis californica* (Cnidaria: Anthozoa): effects on sympatric corals and sea anemones. *Biol. Bull.*, 173, 110–25.

Chang, S.S., Prézelin, B.B. and Trench, R.K. (1983) Mechanisms of photoadaptation in three strains of the symbiotic dinoflagellate *Symbiodinium microadriaticum*. *Mar. Biol.*, 76, 219–29.

Chapman, D.M. (1974) Cnidarian histology. In L. Muscatine and H.M. Lenhoff (eds.), *Coelenterate Biology. Reviews and New Perspectives*, Academic Press, New York, pp. 1–92.

Chapman, G. (1949) The mechanism of opening and closing of *Calliactis parasitica*. *J. Mar. Biol. Ass. UK*, 28, 641–9.

Chapman, G. (1953) Studies of the mesogloea of coelenterates. II. Physical properties. *J. Exp. Biol.*, 30, 440–51.

Chapman, G. and Pardy, R.L. (1972) The movement of glucose and glycine through the tissues of *Corymorpha palma* Torrey (Coelenterata, Hydrozoa). *J. Exp. Biol.*, 56, 639–45.

Charnov, E.L. (1982) *The Theory of Sex Allocation*, Princeton University Press, Princeton, New Jersey, 355 pp.

Chia, F.-S. (1972) Note on the assimilation of glucose and glycine from seawater by the embryos of a sea anemone, *Actinia equina*. *Can. J. Zool.*, 50, 1333–4.

Chia, F.-S. (1974) Classification and adaptive significance of developmental patterns in marine invertebrates. *Thalassia Jugosl.*, 10, 121–30.

Chia, F.-S. (1976) Sea anemone reproduction: patterns and adaptive radiations. In G.O. Mackie (ed.), *Coelenterate Ecology and Behavior*, Plenum, New York, pp. 261–70.

Chia, F.-S. and Koss, R. (1979) Fine structural studies on the nervous system and the apical organ in the planula larva of the sea anemone *Anthopleura elegantissima*. *J. Morph.*, 160, 275–98.

Chia, F.-S., Lützen, J. and Svane, I. (1989) Sexual reproduction and larval morphology of the primitive anthozoan *Gonactinia prolifera* M. Sars. *J. Exp. Mar. Biol. Ecol.*, 127, 13–24.

Chia, F.-S. and Rostron, M.A. (1970) Some aspects of the reproductive biology of *Actinia equina* (Cnidaria: Anthozoa). *J. Mar. Biol. Ass. UK*, 50, 253–64.

Chia, F.-S. and Spaulding, J.G. (1972) Development and juvenile growth of the sea anemone, *Tealia crassicornis*. *Biol. Bull.*, 142, 206–18.

Clark, E.D. and Kimeldorf, D.J. (1971) Behavioral reactions of the sea anemone, *Anthopleura xanthogrammica*, to ultraviolet and visible radiations. *Rad. Res.*, 45, 166–75.

Clark, K.B. and Jensen, K.R. (1982) Effects of temperature on carbon fixation and carbon budget partitioning in the zooxanthellal symbiosis of *Aiptasia pallida* (Verrill). *J. Exp. Mar. Biol. Ecol.*, 64, 215–30.

Clark, R.B. (1964) *Dynamics in Metazoan Evolution. The Origin of the Coelom and Segments*, Clarendon Press, Oxford, UK, 313 pp.

Clark, W.H., Jr. and Dewel, W.C. (1974) The structure of the gonads, gametogenesis, and sperm-egg interactions in the Anthozoa. *Amer. Zool.*, **14**, 495–510.

Clarke, A. (1983) Life in cold water: the physiological ecology of polar marine ecto-therms. *Oceanogr. Mar. Biol. Ann. Rev.*, **21**, 341–453.

Clayton, R.K. (1977) *Light and Living Matter. Vol. 2, The Biological Part*, Robert E. Krieger, Huntington, New York, 243 pp.

Clayton, W.S., Jr. (1985) Pedal laceration by the anemone *Aiptasia pallida*. *Mar. Ecol. Prog. Ser.*, **21**, 75–80.

Clayton, W.S., Jr. and Lasker, H.R. (1984) Host feeding regime and zooxanthellal photosynthesis in the anemone, *Aiptasia pallida* (Verrill). *Biol. Bull.*, **167**, 590–600.

Clayton, W.S., Jr. and Lasker, H.R. (1985) Individual and population growth in the asexually reproducing anemone *Aiptasia pallida* Verrill. *J. Exp. Mar. Biol. Ecol.*, **90**, 249–58.

Coates, A.G. and Jackson, J.B.C. (1985) Morphological themes in the evolution of clonal and aclonal marine invertebrates. In J.B.C. Jackson, L.W. Buss and R.E. Cook (eds.), *Population Biology and Evolution of Clonal Organisms*, Yale University Press, New Haven, pp. 67–106.

Conklin, E.J., Bigger, C.H. and Mariscal, R.N. (1977) The formation and taxonomic status of the microbasic q-mastigophore nematocyst of sea anemones. *Biol. Bull.*, **152**, 159–68.

Conklin, E.J. and Mariscal, R.N. (1976) Increase in nematocyst and spirocyst dis-charge in a sea anemone in response to mechanical stimulation. In G.O. Mackie (ed.), *Coelenterate Ecology and Behavior*, Plenum, New York, pp. 549–58.

Conklin, E.J. and Mariscal, R.N. (1977) Feeding behavior, ceras structure, and nematocyst storage in the aeolid nudibranch, *Spurilla neapolitana* (Mollusca). *Bull. Mar. Sci.*, **27**, 658–67.

Conover, R.J. (1978) Transformation of organic matter. In O. Kinne (ed.), *Marine Ecology, Vol. 4, Dynamics*, John Wiley & Sons, New York, pp. 221–499.

Cook, C.B. (1971) Transfer of ^{35}S-labeled material from food ingested by *Aiptasia* sp. to its endosymbiotic zooxanthellae. In H.M. Lenhoff, L. Muscatine and L.V. Davis (eds.), *Experimental Coelenterate Biology*, University of Hawaii Press, Honolulu, pp. 218–24.

Cook, C.B. (1983) Metabolic interchange in algae — invertebrate symbiosis. *Int. Rev. Cytol.*, Suppl. **14**, 177–210.

Cook, C.B., D'Elia, C.F. and Muller-Parker, G. (1988) Host feeding and nutrient sufficiency for zooxanthellae in the sea anemone *Aiptasia pallida*. *Mar. Biol.*, **98**, 253–62.

Cook, C.B. and Kelty, M.O. (1982) Glycogen, protein, and lipid content of green, aposymbiotic, and nonsymbiotic hydra during starvation. *J. Exp. Zool.*, **222**, 1–9.

Cook, P.A., Gabbott, P.A. and Youngson, A. (1972) Seasonal changes in the free amino acid composition of the adult barnacle, *Balanus balanoides*. *Comp. Bio-chem. Physiol.*, **42B**, 409–21.

Corner, E.D.S., Leon, Y.A. and Bulbrook, R.D. (1960) Steroid sulphatase, aryl-sulphatase and β-glucuronidase in marine invertebrates. *J. Mar. Biol. Ass. UK*, **39**, 51–61.

Crisp, D.J. (ed.) (1964) The effects of the severe winter of 1962–63 on marine life in

Britain. *J. Anim. Ecol.*, **33**, 165–210.

Crowell, S. and Oates, S. (1980) Metamorphosis and reproduction by transverse fission in an edwardsiid anemone. In P. Tardent and R. Tardent (eds.), *Developmental and Cellular Biology of Coelenterates*, Elsevier/North-Holland Biomedical Press, Amsterdam, pp. 139–42.

Crozier, R.H. (1986) Genetic clonal recognition abilities in marine invertebrates must be maintained by selection for something else. *Evolution*, **40**, 1100–1.

Cutress, C.E. (1979) *Bunodeopsis medusoides* Fowler and *Actinodiscus neglectus* Fowler, two Tahitian sea anemones: redescription and biological notes. *Bull. Mar. Sci.*, **29**, 96–109.

Dahl, E., Falck, B., von Mecklenburg, C. and Myhrberg, H. (1963) An adrenergic nervous system in sea anemones. *Quart. J. Microsc. Sci.*, **104**, 531–4.

Dalby, J.E., Jr., Elliott, J.K. and Ross, D.M. (1988) The swim response of the actinian *Stomphia didemon* to certain asteroids: distributional and phylogenetic implications. *Can. J. Zool.*, **66**, 2484–91.

Dalyell, J.G. (1848) *Rare and Remarkable Animals of Scotland, Represented from Living Subjects: with Practical Observations on Their Nature*, Vol.2, Van Voorst, London, 322 pp. + 56 colour plates.

Davenport, D. and Norris, K.S. (1958) Observations on the symbiosis of the sea anemone *Stoichactis* and the pomacentrid fish, *Amphiprion percula*. *Biol. Bull.*, **115**, 397–410.

Davenport, D., Ross, D.M. and Sutton, L. (1961) The remote control of nematocyst-discharge in the attachment of *Calliactis parasitica* to shells of hermit crabs. *Vie et Milieu*, **12**, 197–209.

Day, R.M. and Harris, L.G. (1978) Selection and turnover of coelenterate nematocysts in some aeolid nudibranchs. *The Veliger*, **21**, 104–9.

Dayton, P.K. (1971) Competition and community organization: the provision and subsequent utilization of space in a rocky intertidal community. *Ecol. Monogr.*, **41**, 351–89.

Dayton, P.K. (1973) Two cases of resource partitioning in an intertidal community: making the right prediction for the wrong reason. *Amer. Nat.*, **107**, 662–70.

Dayton, P.K., Robilliard, G.A., Paine, R.T. and Dayton, L.B. (1974) Biological accommodation in the benthic community at McMurdo Sound, Antarctica. *Ecol. Monogr.*, **44**, 105–28.

Deaton, L.E. and Hoffmann, R.J. (1988) Hypoosmotic volume regulation in the sea anemone *Metridium senile*. *Comp. Biochem. Physiol.*, **91C**, 187–91.

D'Elia, C.F. and Cook, C.B. (1988) Methylamine uptake by zooxanthellae/invertebrate symbioses: insights into host ammonium environment and nutrition. *Limnol. Oceanogr.*, **33**, 1153–65.

Denny, M.W., Daniel, T.L. and Koehl, M.A.R. (1985) Mechanical limits to size in wave-swept organisms. *Ecol. Monogr.*, **55**, 69–102.

Dicquemare, L'Abbé (1773) An essay, towards elucidating the history of the sea-anemonies. *Phil. Trans. R. Soc. Lond.*, **63**, 361–403.

Donoghue, A.M., Quicke, D.L.J. and Brace, R.C. (1986) Turnstones apparently preying on sea anemones. *Brit. Birds*, **79**, 91.

Dorsett, D.A. (1984) Oxygen production in the intertidal anemone *Anemonia sulcata*. *Comp. Biochem. Physiol.*, **78A**, 225–8.

Doumenc, D.A. (1979) Structure et origine des systèmes squelettiques et neuro-musculaires au cours de l'organogenèse des stades postlarvaires de l'actinie *Cereus pedunculatus*. *Arch. Zool. Exp. Gén.*, **120**, 431–76.

Doumenc, D.A. and Van-Praët, M. (1987) Ordre des actiniaires. Ordre des ptycho-dactiniaires. Ordre des corallimorphaires. In P.-P. Grassé (ed.), *Traité de Zoologie. Anatomie, Systématique, Biologie. Tome III. Cnidaires Anthozoaires*, Masson, Paris, pp. 257–401.

Doumenc, D. and Foubert, A. (1984) Microinformatique et taxonomie des actinies: clé mondiale des genres. *Ann. Inst. Océanogr., Paris*, **60**, 43–86.

Dromgoole, F.I. (1978) The effects of oxygen on dark respiration and apparent photosynthesis of marine macro-algae. *Aq. Bot.*, **4**, 281–97.

Dudler, N., Yellowlees, D. and Miller, D.J. (1987) Localization of two L-glutamate dehydrogenases in the coral *Acropora latistella*. *Arch. Biochem. Biophys.*, **254**, 368–71.

Dunlap, W.C. and Chalker, B.E. (1986) Identification and quantitation of near-UV absorbing compounds (S-320) in a hermatypic scleractinian. *Coral Reefs*, **5**, 155–9.

Dunlap, W.C., Chalker, B.E. and Oliver, J.K. (1986) Bathymetric adaptations of reef-building corals at Davies Reef, Great Barrier Reef, Australia. III. UV-B absorbing compounds. *J. Exp. Mar. Biol. Ecol.*, **104**, 239–48.

Dunn, D.F. (1975a) Reproduction of the externally brooding sea anemone *Epiactis prolifera* Verrill, 1869. *Biol. Bull.*, **148**, 199–218.

Dunn, D.F. (1975b) Gynodioecy in an animal. *Nature*, **253**, 528–9.

Dunn, D.F. (1977a) Dynamics of external brooding in the sea anemone *Epiactis prolifera*. *Mar. Biol.*, **39**, 41–9.

Dunn, D.F. (1977b) Variability of *Epiactis prolifera* (Coelenterata: Actiniaria) in the intertidal zone near Bodega Bay, California. *J. Nat. Hist.*, **11**, 457–63.

Dunn, D.F. (1978) *Anthopleura handi* n. sp. (Coelenterata, Actiniaria), an internally brooding, intertidal sea anemone from Malaysia. *Wasmann J. Biol.*, **35**, 54–64.

Dunn, D.F. (1981) The clownfish sea anemones: Stichodactylidae (Coelenterata: Actiniaria) and other sea anemones symbiotic with pomacentrid fishes. *Trans. Amer. Phil. Soc.*, **71**, 1–115.

Dunn, D.F. (1982) Sexual reproduction of two intertidal sea anemones (Coelenterata: Actiniaria) in Malaysia. *Biotropica*, **14**, 262–71.

Dunn, D.F. (1983) Some Antarctic and sub-Antarctic sea anemones (Coelenterata: Ptychodactiaria and Actiniaria). In L.S. Kornicker (ed.), *Biology of the Antarctic Seas XIV, Antarctic Research Series Volume 39*, Amer. Geophysical Union, Washington, D.C., pp. 1–67.

Dunn, D.F. (1984) More Antarctic and Subantarctic sea anemones (Coelenterata: Corallimorpharia and Actiniaria). In L.S. Kornicker (ed.), *Biology of the Antarctic Seas XVI, Antarctic Research Series Volume 41*, Amer. Geophysical Union, Washington, D.C., pp. 1–42.

Dunn, D.F., Chia, F.-S. and Levine, R. (1980) Nomenclature of *Aulactinia* (= *Bunodactis*), with description of *Aulactinia incubans* n.sp. (Coelenterata: Actiniaria), an internally brooding sea anemone from Puget Sound. *Can. J. Zool.*, **58**, 2071–80.

Dunn, D.F., Devaney, D.M. and Roth, B. (1980) *Stylobates*: a shell-forming sea anemone (Coelenterata, Anthozoa, Actiniidae). *Pacific Sci.*, **34**, 379–88.

Dunn, D.F. and Hamner, W.M. (1980) *Amplexidiscus fenestrafer* n. gen, n. sp. (Coelenterata: Anthozoa), a tropical Indo-Pacific corallimorpharian. *Micronesica*, **16**, 29–36.

Dunn, D.F. and Liberman, M.H. (1983) Chitin in sea anemone shells. *Science*, **221**, 157–9.

Dykens, J.A. (1984) Enzymic defenses against oxygen toxicity in marine cnidarians containing endosymbiotic algae. *Mar. Biol. Lett.*, **5**, 291–301.

Dykens, J.A. and Shick, J.M. (1982) Oxygen production by endosymbiotic algae controls superoxide dismutase activity in their animal host. *Nature*, **297**, 579–80.

Dykens, J.A. and Shick, J.M. (1984) Photobiology of the symbiotic sea anemone, *Anthopleura elegantissima*: defenses against photodynamic effects, and seasonal photoacclimatization. *Biol. Bull.*, **167**, 683–97.

Dykens, J.A. and Shick, J.M. (1988) Relevance of purine catabolism to hypoxia and recovery in euryoxic and stenoxic marine invertebrates, particularly bivalve molluscs. *Comp. Biochem. Physiol.*, **91C**, 35–41.

Edmunds, M. (1966) Protective mechanisms in the Eolidacea (Mollusca Nudibranchia). *J. Linn. Soc. (Zool.)*, **46**, 27–71.

Edmunds, M., Potts, G.W., Swinfen, R.C. and Waters, V.L. (1974) The feeding preferences of *Aeolidia papillosa* (L.) (Mollusca, Nudibranchia). *J. Mar. Biol. Ass. UK*, **54**, 939–47.

Edmunds, M., Potts, G.W., Swinfen, R.C. and Waters, V.L. (1976) Defensive behaviour of sea anemones in response to predation by the opisthobranch mollusc *Aeolidia papillosa* (L.). *J. Mar. Biol. Ass. UK*, **56**, 65–83.

Edmunds, P.J. and Davies, P.S. (1986) An energy budget for *Porites porites* (Scleractinia). *Mar. Biol.*, **92**, 339–47.

Eibl-Eibesfeldt, I. (1960) Beobachtungen und Versuche an Anemonenfischen (*Amphiprion*) des Malediven und der Nicobaren. *Z. Tierpsychol.*, **17**, 1–10.

El Ayeb, M., Bahraoui, E.M., Granier, C., Béress, L. and Rochat, H. (1986) Immunochemistry of sea anemone toxins: structure-antigenicity relationships and toxin-receptor interactions probed by antibodies specific for one antigenic region. *Biochemistry*, **25**, 6755–61.

Ellington, W.R. (1977) Aerobic and anaerobic degradation of glucose by the estuarine sea anemone, *Diadumene leucolena*. *Comp. Biochem. Physiol.*, **58B**, 173–5.

Ellington, W.R. (1979a) Octopine dehydrogenase in the basilar muscle of the sea anemone, *Metridium senile*. *Comp. Biochem. Physiol.*, **63B**, 349–54.

Ellington, W.R. (1979b) Evidence for a broadly-specific, amino acid requiring dehydrogenase at the pyruvate branchpoint in sea anemones. *J. Exp. Zool.*, **209**, 151–9.

Ellington, W.R. (1980a) Some aspects of the metabolism of the sea anemone *Haliplanella luciae* (Verrill) during air exposure and hypoxia. *Mar. Biol. Lett.*, **1**, 255–62.

Ellington, W.R. (1980b) Partial purification and characterization of a broadly-specific octopine dehydrogenase from the tissues of the sea anemone, *Bunodosoma cavernata* (Bosc). *Comp. Biochem. Physiol.*, **67B**, 625–31.

Ellington, W.R. (1981) Effect of anoxia on the adenylates and the energy charge in the sea anemone, *Bunodosoma cavernata* (Bosc). *Physiol. Zool.*, **54**, 415–22.

Ellington, W.R. (1982) Metabolic responses of the sea anemone *Bunodosoma cavernata* (Bosc) to declining oxygen tensions and anoxia. *Physiol. Zool.*, 55, 240–9.

Elliott, J. and Cook, C.B. (1989) Diel variation in prey capture behavior by the corallimorpharian *Discosoma sanctithomae*: mechanical and chemical activation of feeding. *Biol. Bull.*, 176, 218–28.

Elliott, J., Dalby, J. Jr., Cohen, R. and Ross, D.M. (1985) Behavioral interactions between the actinian *Tealia piscivora* (Anthozoa: Actiniaria) and the asteroid *Dermasterias imbricata*. *Can. J. Zool.*, 63, 1921–9.

Elliott, J.K., Ross, D.M., Pathirana, C., Miao, S., Andersen, R.J., Singer, P., Kokke, W.C.M.C. and Ayer, W.A. (1989) Induction of swimming in *Stomphia* (Anthozoa: Actiniaria) by imbricatine, a metabolite of the asteroid *Dermasterias imbricata*. *Biol. Bull.*, 176, 73–8.

Ellis, V.L., Ross, D.M. and Sutton, L. (1969) The pedal disk of the swimming sea anemone *Stomphia coccinea* during detachment, swimming and resettlement. *Can. J. Zool.*, 47, 333–42.

Elmhirst, R. and Sharpe, J.S. (1920) On the colours of two sea anemones, *Actinia equina* and *Anemonia sulcata*. Part I. Environmental. Part II. Chemical. *Biochem. J.*, 14, 48–57.

Elmhirst, R. and Sharpe, J.S. (1923) On the colours of the sea anemone, *Tealia crassicornis*. *Ann. Mag. Nat. Hist.*, 11, 615–21.

Elyakova, L.A. (1972) Distribution of cellulases and chitinases in marine invertebrates. *Comp. Biochem. Physiol.*, 43B, 67–70.

Elyakova, L.A., Shevchenko, N.M. and Avaeva, S.M. (1981) A comparative study of carbohydrase activities in marine invertebrates. *Comp. Biochem. Physiol.*, 69B, 905–8.

Ewer, D.W. (1960) Inhibition and rhythmic activity of the circular muscles of *Calliactis parasitica* (Couch). *J. Exp. Biol.*, 37, 812–31.

Fautin, D.G. (1986) Why do anemonefishes inhabit only some host actinians? *Envir. Biol. Fishes*, 15, 171–80.

Fautin, D.G. (1987) Effects of symbionts on anthozoan body form. *Amer. Zool.*, 27, 14A (abstract).

Fautin, D.G. (1988) Importance of nematocysts to actinian taxonomy. In D.A. Hessinger and H.M. Lenhoff (eds.), *The Biology of Nematocysts*, Academic Press, San Diego, California, pp. 487–500.

Fautin, D.G. (1990) Sexual differentiation and behaviour in Phylum Cnidaria. In K.G. Adiyodi and R.G. Adiyodi (eds.), *Reproductive Biology of Invertebrates*, Vol. V, Oxford and IBH Publishing Co., New Delhi (in press).

Fautin, D.G., Bucklin, A. and Hand, C. (1990) Systematics of sea anemones belonging to genus *Metridium* (Coelenterata: Actiniaria), with a description of *M.giganteum* new species. *Wasmann J. Biol.*, 47, 77–85.

Fautin, D.G. and Chia, F.-S. (1986) Revision of the sea anemone genus *Epiactis* (Coelenterata: Actiniaria) on the Pacific coast of North America, with descriptions of two new brooding species. *Can. J. Zool.*, 64, 1665–74.

Fautin, D.G. and Mariscal, R.N. (1990) Cnidaria (Coelenterata), Anthozoa. In F.W. Harrison and J.A. Westfall (eds.), *Microscopic Anatomy of Invertebrates*, 2, 267–358.

Fautin, D.G., Spaulding, J.G. and Chia, F.-S. (1989) Cnidaria. In K.G. Adiyodi and

R.G. Adiyodi (eds.), *Reproductive Biology of Invertebrates, Vol. IV, Fertilization, Development, and Parental Care*, Oxford and IBH Publishing Co., New Delhi, pp. 43–62.

Féral, J.P., Fusey, P., Gaill, F., López, E., Martelly, E., Oudot, J. and Van-Praët, M. (1979) Évolution des teneurs en hydrocarbures chez quelques organismes marins du Nord Finisterre, depuis l'échouage de L'Amoco Cadiz et comparaison des méthodes de dosage en infrarouge et spectrofluorimetrie. *C.R. Acad. Sci. Paris*, **288**, 713–16.

Fisher, R.A. (1930) *The Genetical Theory of Natural Selection*, Oxford University Press, London, 272 pp.

Fitt, W.K. (1984) The role of chemosensory behavior of *Symbiodinium microadriaticum*, intermediate hosts, and host behavior in the infection of coelenterates and molluscs with zooxanthellae. *Mar. Biol.*, **81**, 9–17.

Fitt, W.K. and Pardy, R.L. (1981) Effects of starvation, and light and dark on the energy metabolism of symbiotic and aposymbiotic sea anemones, *Anthopleura elegantissima. Mar. Biol.*, **61**, 199–205.

Fitt, W.K., Pardy, R.L. and Littler, M.M. (1982) Photosynthesis, respiration, and contribution to community productivity of the symbiotic sea anemone *Anthopleura elegantissima* (Brandt, 1835). *J. Exp. Mar. Biol. Ecol.*, **61**, 213–32.

Fleure, H.J. and Walton, C.L. (1907) Notes on the habits of some Sea Anemones. *Zool. Anz.*, **31**, 212–20.

Ford, C.E., Jr. (1964) Reproduction in the aggregating sea anemone, *Anthopleura elegantissima. Pacific Sci.*, **18**, 138–45.

Ford, T.D. (1979) Precambrian fossils and the origin of the Phanerozoic phyla. In M.R. House (ed.), *The Origin of Major Invertebrate Groups*. Systematics Association Special Vol. No. 12, Academic Press, London, pp. 7–21.

Fox, D.L. (1953) *Animal Biochromes and Structural Colours*, Cambridge University Press, Cambridge, UK, 379 pp.

Fox, D.L. and Pantin, C.F.A. (1941) The colours of the plumose anemone *Metridium senile* (L.). *Phil. Trans. R. Soc. London, B*, **230**, 415–50.

Fox, D.L., Wilkie, D.W. and Haxo, F.T. (1978) Carotenoid fractionation in the plumose anemone *Metridium*-II. Search for dietary sources of ovarian astaxanthin. *Comp. Biochem Physiol.*, **59B**, 289–94.

Fox, H.M. (1965) Confirmation of old observations on the behaviour of a hermit crab and its commensal sea anemone. *Ann. Mag. Nat. Hist., 13th Ser.*, **8**, 173–5.

Francis, L. (1973a) Clone specific segregation in the sea anemone *Anthopleura elegantissima. Biol. Bull.*, **144**, 64–72.

Francis, L. (1973b) Intraspecific aggression and its effect on the distribution of *Anthopleura elegantissima* and some related sea anemones. *Biol. Bull.*, **144**, 73–92.

Francis, L. (1976) Social organization within clones of the sea anemone *Anthopleura elegantissima. Biol. Bull.*, **150**, 361–76.

Francis, L. (1979) Contrast between solitary and clonal lifestyles in the sea anemone *Anthopleura elegantissima. Amer. Zool.*, **19**, 669–81.

Francis, L. (1988) Cloning and aggression among sea anemones (Coelenterata: Actiniaria) of the rocky shore. *Biol. Bull.*, **174**, 241–53.

Frank, P.G. and Bleakney, J.S. (1978) Asexual reproduction, diet, and anomalies of the anemone *Nematostella vectensis* in Nova Scotia. *Can. Field-Nat.*, **92**, 259–63.

Fredericks, C.A. (1976) Oxygen as a limiting factor in phototaxis and in intraclonal spacing of the sea anemone *Anthopleura elegantissima*. *Mar. Biol.*, **38**, 25–8.

Frelin, C., Vigne, P., Schweitz, H. and Lazdunski, M. (1984) The interaction of sea anemone and scorpion neurotoxins with tetrodotoxin-resistant Na^+ channels in rat myoblasts. A comparison with Na^+ channels in other excitable and non-excitable cells. *Mol. Pharm.*, **26**, 70–4.

Fricke, H.W. (1975) Selektives Feinderkennen bei dem Anemonenfisch *Amphiprion bicinctus* (Rüppell). *J. Exp. Mar. Biol. Ecol.*, **19**, 1–7.

Fricke, H.W. (1979) Mating system, resource defence and sex change in the anemone-fish *Amphiprion akallopisos*. *Z. Tierpsychol.*, **50**, 313–26.

Friese, U.E. (1972) *Sea Anemones*, T.F.H. Publications, Neptune City, New Jersey, 128 pp.

Fujii, H. (1987) The predominance of clones in populations of the sea anemone *Anthopleura asiatica* (Uchida). *Biol. Bull.*, **172**, 202–11.

Fukui, Y. (1986) Catch tentacles in the sea anemone *Haliplanella luciae*. Role as organs of social behavior. *Mar. Biol.*, **91**, 245–52.

Gashout, S.E. and Ormond, R.F.G. (1979) Evidence for parthenogenetic reproduction in the sea anemone *Actinia equina* L. *J. Mar. Biol. Ass. UK*, **59**, 975–87.

Geddes, P. (1882) On the nature and functions of the 'yellow cells' of radiolarians and coelenterates. *Proc. R. Soc. Edinburgh*, **11**, 377–96.

Gemmill, J.F. (1920) The development of the sea-anemones *Metridium dianthus* (Ellis) and *Adamsia palliata* (Bohad). *Phil. Trans. R. Soc. Lond.*, *B*, **209**, 351–75.

Gemmill, J.F. (1921) The development of the sea anemone *Bolocera tuediae* (Johnst.). *Quart. J. Microsc. Sci.*, **65**, 577–81 + 1 plate.

George, R.Y. (1981) Functional adaptations of deep-sea organisms. In F.J. Vernberg and W.B. Vernberg (eds.), *Functional Adaptations of Marine Organisms*, Academic Press, New York, pp. 279–332.

Ghiselin, M. (1969) The evolution of hermaphroditism among animals. *Q. Rev. Biol.*, **44**, 189–208.

Gibson, D. and Dixon, G.H. (1969) Chymotrypsin-like proteases from the sea anemone, *Metridium senile*. *Nature*, **222**, 753–6.

Giese, A.C. (1966) Lipids in the economy of marine invertebrates. *Physiol. Rev.*, **46**, 244–98.

Gilles, R. (1975) Mechanisms of ion and osmoregulation. In O. Kinne (ed.), *Marine Ecology, Vol. II, Physiological Mechanisms, Part 1*, John Wiley and Sons, London, pp. 259–347.

Gladfelter, W.B. (1975) Sea anemone with zooxanthellae: simultaneous contraction and expansion in response to changing light intensity. *Science*, **189**, 570–1.

Glaessner, M. (1984) *The Dawn of Animal Life. A Biohistorical Study*, Cambridge University Press, Cambridge, UK, 241 pp.

Glider, W.V., Phipps, D.W., Jr. and Pardy, R.L. (1980) Localization of symbiotic dinoflagellate cells within tentacle tissue of *Aiptasia pallida* (Coelenterata, Anthozoa). *Trans. Amer. Microsc. Soc.*, **99**, 426–38.

Gnaiger, E. (1977) Thermodynamic considerations of invertebrate anoxibiosis. In I. Lamprecht and B. Schaarschmidt (eds.), *Applications of Calorimetry in Life Sciences*, W. de Gruyter, Berlin, pp. 281–303.

Gnaiger, E. (1983a) Calculation of energetic and biochemical equivalents of respiratory oxygen consumption. In E. Gnaiger and H. Forstner (eds.), *Polarographic Oxygen Sensors: Aquatic and Physiological Applications*, Springer-Verlag, Berlin and Heidelberg, pp. 337–45.

Gnaiger, E. (1983b) Heat dissipation and energetic efficiency in animal anoxibiosis: economy contra power. *J. Exp. Zool.*, **228**, 471–90.

Gnaiger, E. and Bitterlich, G. (1984) Proximate biochemical composition and caloric content calculated from elemental CHN analysis: a stoichiometric concept. *Oecologia*, **62**, 289–98.

Gnaiger, E., Shick, J.M. and Widdows, J. (1989) Metabolic microcalorimetry and respirometry of aquatic animals. In C.R. Bridges and P.J. Butler (eds.), *Techniques in Comparative Respiratory Physiology. An Experimental Approach*, Cambridge University Press, Cambridge, UK, pp. 113–35.

Godknecht, A. and Tardent, P. (1988) Discharge and mode of action of the tentacular nematocysts of *Anemonia sulcata* (Anthozoa: Cnidaria). *Mar. Biol.*, **100**, 83–92.

Gomme, J. (1982) Epidermal nutrient absorption in marine invertebrates: a comparative analysis. *Amer. Zool.*, **22**, 691–708.

Gooley, P.R. and Norton, R.S. (1986) Secondary structure in sea anemone polypeptides: a proton nuclear magnetic resonance study. *Biochemistry*, **25**, 2349–56.

Goreau, T.F. (1959) The physiology of skeleton formation in corals: I. A method for measuring the rate of calcium deposition by corals under different conditions. *Biol. Bull.*, **116**, 59–75.

Gosline, J.M. (1971) Connective tissue mechanics of *Metridium senile* I. Structural and compositional aspects. *J. Exp. Biol.*, **55**, 763–74.

Gosline, J.M. and Lenhoff, H.M. (1968) Kinetics of incorporation of C^{14} proline into mesogleal protocollagen and collagen of the sea anemone *Aiptasia*. *Comp. Biochem. Physiol.*, **26**, 1031–9.

Gosse, P.H. (1860) *Actinologia Britannica: A History of the British Sea-Anemones and Corals*, Van Voorst, London, 362 pp. + 11 plates.

Graff, D. and Grimmelikhuijzen, C.J.P. (1988) Isolation of <Glu-Ser-Leu-Arg-Trp-NH_2, a novel neuropeptide from sea anemones. *Brain Res.*, **442**, 354–8.

Grasshoff, M. (1981) Polypen und Kolonien der Blumentiere (Anthozoa) III: Die Hexacorallia. *Natur und Museum*, **111**, 134–50.

Grasshoff, M. (1984) Cnidarian phylogeny — a biomechanical approach. In *Recent Advances in the Paleobiology and Geology of the Cnidaria, Palontographica Americana*, No. 54, Paleontological Research Institution, Ithaca, New York, pp. 127–35.

Grebel'nyi, S.D. (1981) Symmetry of the Actiniaria and the significance of symmetry features for the classification of the Anthozoa. *Dokl. Acad. Sci. USSR, Biol. Sci.*, **253**, 430–2.

Greenwood, P.G., Johnson, L.A. and Mariscal, R.N. (1989) Depletion of ATP in suspensions of isolated cnidae: a possible role of ATP in the maturation and maintenance of anthozoan cnidae. *Comp. Biochem. Physiol.*, **93A**, 761–5.

Greenwood, P.G. and Mariscal, R.N. (1984a) Immature nematocyst incorporation by the aeolid nudibranch *Spurilla neapolitana*. *Mar. Biol.*, **80**, 35–8.

Greenwood, P.G. and Mariscal, R.N. (1984b) The utilization of cnidarian nematocysts by aeolid nudibranchs: nematocyst maintenance and release in *Spurilla*. *Tissue & Cell*, **16**, 719–30.

Greenwood, P.G. and Mariscal, R.N. (1984c) Nematocyst maturation *in vitro*: the effects of ATP on isolated nematocysts. *Amer. Zool.*, **24**, 31A (abstract).

Griffiths, D. (1975) Prey availability and the food of predators. *Ecology*, **56**, 1209–14.

Griffiths, R.J. (1977a) Thermal stress and the biology of *Actinia equina* L. (Anthozoa). *J. Exp. Mar. Biol. Ecol.*, **27**, 141–54.

Griffiths, R.J. (1977b) Temperature acclimation in *Actinia equina* L. (Anthozoa). *J. Exp. Mar. Biol. Ecol.*, **28**, 285–92.

Grimmelikhuijzen, C.J.P., Graff, D. and McFarlane, I.D. (1989) Neurones and neuropeptides in coelenterates. *Arch. Histol. Cytol.*, Suppl., **52**, 265–76.

Grosberg, R.K., Rice, W.R. and Palumbi, S.R. (1985) Graft compatibility and clonal identity in invertebrates. *Science*, **229**, 487–8.

Grosberg, R.K. and Quinn, J.F. (1989) The evolution of selective aggression conditioned on allorecognition specificity. *Evolution*, **43**, 504–15.

Hall, S.J., Todd, C.D. and Gordon, A.D. (1982) The influence of ingestive conditioning on the prey species selection in *Aeolidia papillosa* (Mollusca: Nudibranchia). *J. Anim. Ecol.*, **51**, 907–21.

Hall, S.J., Todd, C.D. and Gordon, A.D. (1984) Prey-species selection by the anemone predator *Aeolidia papillosa* (L.): the influence of ingestive conditioning and previous dietary history, and a test for switching behaviour. *J. Exp. Mar. Biol. Ecol.*, **82**, 11–33.

Halliwell, B. and Gutteridge, J.M.C. (1985) *Free Radicals in Biology and Medicine*, Oxford University Press, Oxford, UK, 346 pp.

Hamner, W.M. and Dunn, D.F. (1980) Tropical Corallimorpharia (Coelenterata: Anthozoa) feeding by envelopment. *Micronesica*, **16**, 37–41.

Hand, C. (1955a) The sea anemones of central California Part II. The endomyarian and mesomyarian anemones. *Wasmann J. Biol.*, **13**, 37–99.

Hand, C. (1955b) The sea anemones of central California Part III. The acontiarian anemones. *Wasmann J. Biol.*, **13**, 189–251.

Hand, C. (1959) On the origin and phylogeny of the coelenterates. *Syst. Zool.*, **8**, 191–202.

Hand, C. (1966) On the evolution of the Actiniaria. In W.J. Rees (ed.), *The Cnidaria and Their Evolution*, Academic Press, London, pp. 135–46.

Hanlon, R.T. and Kaufman, L. (1976) Associations of seven West Indian reef fishes with sea anemones. *Bull. Mar. Sci.*, **26**, 225–32.

Harper, J.L. (1977) *Population Biology of Plants*, Academic Press, New York, 892 pp.

Harris, L.G. (1973) Nudibranch associations. In T.C. Cheng (ed.), *Current Topics in Comparative Pathobiology*, Vol. 2, Academic Press, New York, pp. 213–315.

Harris, L.G. (1986) Size-selective predation in a sea anemone, nudibranch, and fish food chain. *The Veliger*, **29**, 38–47.

Harris, L.G. (1987) Aeolid nudibranchs as predators and prey. *Amer. Malacol. Bull.*, **5**, 287–92.

Harris, L.G. and Duffy, S.J. (1980) The influence of prey size on the preference hierarchy of the nudibranch *Aeolidia papillosa* (L.). *Amer. Zool.*, **20**, 923 (abstract).

Harris, L.G. and Howe, N.R. (1979) An analysis of the defensive mechanisms observed in the anemone *Anthopleura elegantissima* in response to its nudibranch predator *Aeolidia papillosa*. *Biol. Bull.*, **157**, 138–52.

Hart, C.E. and Crowe, J.H. (1977) The effect of attached gravel on survival of intertidal anemones. *Trans. Amer. Microsc. Soc.*, **96**, 28–41.

Hartnoll, R.G. (1970) The relationship of an amphipod and a spider crab with the snakelocks anemone. *Ann. Rep. Mar. Biol. Sta. Port Erin*, **83**, 37–42.

Haylor, G.S., Thorpe, J.P. and Carter, M.A. (1984) Genetic and ecological differentiation between sympatric colour morphs of the common intertidal sea anemone *Actinia equina*. *Mar. Ecol. Prog. Ser.*, **16**, 281–9.

Hemmingsen, A.M. (1960) Energy metabolism as related to body size and respiratory surfaces, and its evolution. *Rep. Steno. Mem. Hosp. (Copenhagen)*, **9**, 1–110.

Henze, M. (1910) Über den Einfluss des Sauerstoffdrucks auf den Gaswechsel einiger Meerestiere. *Biochem. Z.*, **26**, 255–78.

Herndl, G.J. and Velimirov, B. (1985) Bacteria in the coelenteron of Anthozoa: control of coelenteric bacterial density by the coelenteric fluid. *J. Exp. Mar. Biol. Ecol.*, **93**, 115–30.

Herndl, G.J., Velimirov, B. and Krauss, R.E. (1985) Heterotrophic nutrition and control of bacterial density in the coelenteron of the giant sea anemone *Stoichactis giganteum*. *Mar. Ecol. Prog. Ser.*, **22**, 101–5.

Herre, E.A., Leigh, E.G., Jr. and Fischer, E.A. (1987) Sex allocation in animals. In S.C. Stearns (ed.), *The Evolution of Sex and Its Consequences*, Birkhäuser, Boston, pp. 219–61.

Herrera, F.C., López, I., Egea, R. and Zanders, I.P. (1989) Short-term osmotic responses of cells and tissues of the sea anemone, *Condylactis gigantea*. *Comp. Biochem. Physiol.*, **92A**, 377–84.

Herrera, F.C., Rodríguez, A., López, I. and Weitzmann, H. (1986) Characterization of cell ion exchange in the sea anemone *Condylactis gigantea*. *J. Comp. Physiol.*, B, **156**, 591–7.

Hertwig, O. and Hertwig, R. (1879–80) Die Actinien anatomisch und histologisch mit besonderer Berücksichtigung des Nervenmuskelsystems untersucht. *Jena Z. Naturw.*, **13, 14**, 457–640; 39–89.

Hertzberg, S., Liaaen-Jensen, S., Enzell, C.R. and Francis, G.W. (1969) Animal carotenoids 3. The carotenoids of *Actinia equina* — structure determination of actinioerythrin and violerythrin. *Acta Chem. Scand.*, **23**, 3290–312.

Hessinger, D.A. and Lenhoff, H.M. (1976) Mechanism of hemolysis induced by nematocyst venom: roles of phospholipase A and direct lytic factor. *Arch. Biochem. Biophys.*, **173**, 603–13.

Hessinger, D.A. and Lenhoff, H.M. (eds.) (1988) *The Biology of Nematocysts*, Academic Press, San Diego, California, 600 pp.

Hessinger, D.A., Lenhoff, H.M. and Kahan, L.B. (1973) Haemolytic, phospholipase A and nerve-affecting activities of sea anemone nematocyst venom. *Nature New Biol.*, **241**, 125–7.

Hidaka, M. and Mariscal, R.N. (1988) Effects of ions on nematocysts isolated from acontia of the sea anemone *Calliactis tricolor* by different methods. *J. Exp. Biol.*, **136**, 23–34.

Hildemann, W.H., Bigger, C.H. and Johnston, I.S. (1979) Histoincompatibility reactions and allogeneic polymorphism among invertebrates. *Transplant. Proc.*, **11**, 1136–41.

Hill, D. (1956) Rugosa. In R.C. Moore (ed.), *Treatise on Invertebrate Paleontology. Part F, Coelenterata*, University of Kansas, Lawrence, pp. F233–F324.

Hill-Manning, D.N. and Blanquet, R.S. (1979) Seasonal changes in the lipids of the sea anemone, *Metridium senile* (L.). *J. Exp. Mar. Biol. Ecol.*, **36**, 249–57.

Hochachka, P.W. (1980) *Living without Oxygen: Closed and Open Systems in Hypoxia Tolerance*, Harvard University Press, Cambridge, Massachusetts, 181 pp.

Hochachka, P.W. and Somero, G.N. (1984) *Biochemical Adaptation*, Princeton University Press, Princeton, New Jersey, 537 pp.

Hoffmann, R.J. (1976) Genetics and asexual reproduction of the sea anemone *Metridium senile*. *Biol. Bull.*, **151**, 478–88.

Hoffmann, R.J. (1981) Evolutionary genetics of *Metridium senile*. I. Kinetic differences in phosphoglucose isomerase allozymes. *Biochem. Genet.*, **19**, 129–44.

Hoffmann, R.J. (1983) Temperature modulation of the kinetics of phosphoglucose isomerase genetic variants from the sea anemone *Metridium senile*. *J. Exp. Zool.*, **227**, 361–70.

Hoffmann, R.J. (1985) Thermal adaptation and the properties of phosphoglucose isomerase allozymes from a sea anemone. In P.E. Gibbs (ed.), *Proceedings of the Nineteenth European Marine Biology Symposium*, Cambridge University Press, Cambridge, UK, pp. 505–14.

Hoffmann, R.J. (1986) Variation in contributions of asexual reproduction to the genetic structure of populations of the sea anemone *Metridium senile*. *Evolution*, **40**, 357–65.

Hoffmann, R.J. (1987) Short-term stability of genetic structure in populations of the sea anemone *Metridium senile*. *Mar. Biol.*, **93**, 499–507.

Holley, M.C. (1984) The ciliary basal apparatus is adapted to the structure and mechanics of the epithelium. *Tissue & Cell*, **16**, 287–310.

Holley, M.C. (1985) Adaptation of a ciliary basal apparatus to cell shape changes in a contractile epithelium. *Tissue & Cell*, **17**, 321–34.

Holley, M.C. and Shelton, G.A.B. (1984) Reversal of the direction of mucus-flow on the ciliated pharynx of a sea anemone. *J. Exp. Biol.*, **108**, 151–61.

Hooper, S.N. and Ackman, R.G. (1971) *Trans*-6-hexadecenoic acid and the corresponding alcohol in lipids of the sea anemone *Metridium dianthus*. *Lipids*, **6**, 341–6.

Hopkins, C.C.E., Seiring, J.V., Nyholmen, O. and Hermannsen, A. (1984) Ecological energetics from total lipid and total protein: fact and artifact using a gravimetric method for lipid and a biuret method for protein. *Oceanogr. Mar. Biol. Ann. Rev.*, **22**, 211–61.

Horridge, G.A. (1957) The co-ordination of the protective retraction of coral polyps. *Phil. Trans. Royal Soc. Lond.*, B, **240**, 495–528.

Hovland, M. and Thomsen, E. (1989) Hydrocarbon-based communities in the North Sea? *Sarsia*, **74**, 29–42.

Howe, N.R. (1976a) Proline inhibition of a sea anemone alarm pheromone response. *J. Exp. Biol.*, **65**, 147–56.

Howe, N.R. (1976b) Behavior of sea anemones evoked by the alarm pheromone anthopleurine. *J. Comp. Physiol.*, **107**, 67–76.

Howe, N.R. and Harris, L.G. (1978) Transfer of the sea anemone pheromone, anthopleurine, by the nudibranch *Aeolidia papillosa*. *J. Chem. Ecol.*, **5**, 551–61.

Howe, N.R. and Sheikh, Y.M. (1975) Anthopleurine: a sea anemone alarm pheromone. *Science*, **189**, 386–8.

Hughes, R.N. (1987) The functional ecology of clonal animals. *Functional Ecol.*, **1**, 63–9.

Hughes, R.N. (1989) *A Functional Biology of Clonal Animals*, Chapman and Hall, London, 331 pp.

Hunt, A. and Ayre, D.J. (1989) Population structure in the sexually reproducing sea anemone *Oulactis muscosa. Mar. Biol.*, **102**, 537–44.

Hunter, T. (1984) The energetics of asexual reproduction: pedal laceration in the symbiotic sea anemone *Aiptasia pulchella* (Carlgren, 1943). *J. Exp. Mar. Biol. Ecol.*, **83**, 127–47.

Hyman, L.H. (1940) Chapter VII. Metazoa of the tissue grade of construction — the radiate phyla — Phylum Cnidaria. In *The Invertebrates: Protozoa through Ctenophora*, McGraw-Hill, New York, pp. 365–661.

Isay, S.V. and Busarova, N.G. (1984) Study on fatty acid composition of marine organisms — I. Unsaturated fatty acids of Japan Sea invertebrates. *Comp. Biochem. Physiol.*, **77B**, 803–10.

Ishida, J. (1936) Digestive enzymes of *Actinia mesembryanthemum. Annot. Zool. Japon.*, **15**, 285–305.

Ivleva, I.V. (1964) Elements of energetic balance in sea anemones. *Trans. Sevastopol Biol. Sta., Acad. Sci. USSR*, **25**, 410–28 (in Russian).

Jackson, J.B.C. (1977) Competition on marine hard substrata: the adaptive significance of solitary and colonial strategies. *Amer. Nat.*, **111**, 743–67.

Jackson, J.B.C. (1979) Morphological strategies of sessile animals. In G. Larwood and B.R. Rosen (eds.), *Biology and Systematics of Colonial Organisms*. Systematics Association Special Vol. No. 11, Academic Press, London, pp. 499–555.

Jackson, J.B.C. (1985) Distribution and ecology of clonal and aclonal benthic invertebrates. In J.B.C. Jackson, L.W. Buss and R.E. Cook (eds.), *Population Biology and Evolution of Clonal Organisms*, Yale University Press, New Haven, pp. 297–355.

Jackson, J.B.C., Buss, L.W. and Cook, R.E. (eds.) (1985) *Population Biology and Evolution of Clonal Organisms*, Yale University Press, New Haven, 530 pp.

Janssen, H.H. and Möller, H. (1981) Effects of various feeding conditions on *Anemonia sulcata. Zool. Anz.*, **206**, 161–70.

Jennison, B.L. (1979a) Annual fluctuations of lipid levels in the sea anemone *Anthopleura elegantissima* (Brandt, 1835). *J. Exp. Mar. Biol. Ecol.*, **39**, 211–21.

Jennison, B.L. (1979b) Gametogenesis and reproductive cycles in the sea anemone *Anthopleura elegantissima* (Brandt, 1835). *Can. J. Zool.*, **57**, 403–11.

Jennison, B.L. (1981) Reproduction in three species of sea anemones from Key West, Florida. *Can. J. Zool.*, **59**, 1708–19.

Jeuniaux, C. (1962) Digestion de la chitine chez les actiniaires (Coelentérés Anthozoaires). *Cah. Biol. Mar.*, **3**, 391–400.

Johnson, L.L. and Shick, J.M. (1977) Effects of fluctuating temperature and immersion on asexual reproduction in the intertidal sea anemone *Haliplanella luciae* (Verrill) in laboratory culture. *J. Exp. Mar. Biol. Ecol.*, **28**, 141–9.

Johnston, G. (1847) *A History of the British Zoophytes, Vol. II*, 2nd ed., Van Voorst, London, 74 plates.

Jones, W.C., Pickthall, V.J. and Nesbitt, S.P. (1977) A respiratory rhythm in sea anemones. *J. Exp. Biol.*, **68**, 187–98.

Jørgensen, B.B. (1980) Seasonal oxygen depletion in the bottom waters of a Danish fjord and its effect on the benthic community. *Oikos*, **34**, 68–76.

Josephson, R.K. (1966) Neuromuscular transmission in a sea anemone. *J. Exp. Biol.*, **45**, 305–19.

Josephson, R.K. and March, S.C. (1966) The swimming performance of the sea-anemone *Boloceroides*. *J. Exp. Biol.*, **44**, 493–506.

Kaplan, S.W. (1983) Intrasexual aggression in *Metridium senile*. *Biol. Bull.*, **165**, 416–18.

Kaplan, S.W. (1984) The association between the sea anemone *Metridium senile* (L.) and the mussel *Mytilus edulis* (L.) reduces predation by the starfish *Asterias forbesi* (Desor). *J. Exp. Mar. Biol. Ecol.*, **79**, 155–7.

Karnaukhov, V.N. (1990) Carotenoids: recent progress, problems and prospects. *Comp. Biochem. Physiol.*, **95B**, 1–20.

Kasschau, M.R. and McCommas, S.A. (1982) Glycine concentration as a biochemical indicator of sex and maturation in the sea anemone *Bunodosoma cavernata*. *Comp. Biochem. Physiol.*, **72A**, 595–7.

Kasschau, M.R., Ragland, J.B., Pinkerton, S.O. and Chen, E.C.M. (1984a) Time related changes in the free amino acid pool of the sea anemone, *Bunodosoma cavernata*, during salinity stress. *Comp. Biochem. Physiol.*, **79A**, 155–9.

Kasschau, M.R., Skaggs, M.M. and Chen, E.C.M. (1980) Accumulation of glutamate in sea anemones exposed to heavy metals and organic amines. *Bull. Envir. Contam. Toxicol.*, **25**, 873–8.

Kasschau, M.R., Skisak, C.M., Cook, J.P. and Mills, W.R. (1984b) β-alanine metabolism and high salinity stress in the sea anemone, *Bunodosoma cavernata*. *J. Comp. Physiol.*, *B*, **154**, 181–6.

Kellogg, R.B. and Patton, J.S. (1983) Lipid droplets, medium of energy exchange in the symbiotic anemone *Condylactis gigantea*: a model coral polyp. *Mar. Biol.*, **75**, 137–49.

Kem, W.R. (1988a) Peptide chain toxins of marine animals. In D.G. Fautin (ed.), *Biomedical Importance of Marine Organisms*. Memoirs of the California Academy of Sciences, No. 13, California Academy of Sciences, San Francisco, pp. 69–83.

Kem, W.R. (1988b) Sea anemone toxins: structure and action. In D.A. Hessinger and H.M. Lenhoff (eds.), *The Biology of Nematocysts*, Academic Press, San Diego, California, pp. 375–406.

Kiener, A. (1971) Contribution à l'écologie, la physiologie et l'éthologie de l'actinie *Diadumene luciae* (Verrill). *Bull. Soc. Zool. Fr.*, **séance du 14 Décembre 1971**, 581–603.

Kinzie, R.A., III (1974) Experimental infection of aposymbiotic gorgonian polyps with zooxanthellae. *J. Exp. Mar. Biol. Ecol.*, **15**, 335–45.

Kinzie, R.A., III and Chee, G.S. (1979) The effect of different zooxanthellae on the growth of experimentally reinfected hosts. *Biol. Bull.*, **156**, 315–27.

Kirkpatrick, D.S. and Bishop, S.H. (1973) Phosphonoprotein. Characterization of aminophosphonic acid-rich glycoproteins from sea anemones. *Biochemistry*, **12**, 2829–40.

Kittredge, J.S. and Roberts, E. (1969) A carbon-phosphorus bond in nature. *Science*, **164**, 37–42.

Kleiber, M. (1961) *The Fire of Life. An Introduction to Animal Energetics*, John Wiley and Sons, New York, 454 pp.

Knowlton, N. and Keller, B.D. (1986) Larvae which fall far short of their potential: highly localized recruitment in an alpheid shrimp with extended larval development. *Bull. Mar. Sci.*, **39**, 213–23.

Koehl, M.A.R. (1977a) Effects of sea anemones on the flow forces they encounter. *J. Exp. Biol.*, **69**, 87–105.

Koehl, M.A.R. (1977b) Mechanical diversity of connective tissue of the body wall of sea anemones. *J. Exp. Biol.*, **69**, 107–25.

Koehl, M.A.R. (1977c) Mechanical organization of cantilever-like organisms: sea anemones. *J. Exp. Biol.*, **69**, 127–42.

Koehl, M.A.R. (1977d) Water flow and the morphology of zoanthid colonies. In D.L. Taylor (ed.), *Proceedings of the Third International Coral Reef Symposium*, Vol. 1, *Biology*, Rosenstiel School of Marine and Atmospheric Science, University of Miami, Miami, Florida, pp. 438–44.

Koehn, R.K. and Shumway, S.E. (1982) A genetic/physiological explanation for differential growth rate among individuals of the American oyster, *Crassostrea virginica* (Gmelin). *Mar. Biol. Lett.*, **3**, 35–42.

Krijgsman, B.J. and Talbot, F.H. (1953) Experiments on digestion in sea-anemones. *Arch. Int. Physiol.*, **61**, 277–91.

Krinsky, N.I. (1978) Non-photosynthetic functions of carotenoids. *Phil. Trans. R. Soc. Lond.*, B, **284**, 581–90.

Krinsky, N.I. (1982) Photobiology of carotenoid protection. In J.D. Regan and J.A. Parrish (eds.), *The Science of Photomedicine*, Plenum, New York, pp. 397–407.

Krukenberg, C.F.W. (1880) Über den Verdauungsmodus der Aktinien. *Vergl. physiol. Studien an den Küste der Adria*, **1**, 33–56.

Larkman, A.U. (1980) Ultrastructural aspects of gametogenesis in *Actinia equina* L. In P. Tardent and R. Tardent (eds.), *Developmental and Cellular Biology of Coelenterates*, Elsevier/North-Holland Biomedical Press, Amsterdam, pp. 61–6.

Larkman, A.U. (1981) An ultrastructural investigation of the early stages of oocyte differentiation in *Actinia fragacea* (Cnidaria; Anthozoa). *Int. J. Invert. Reprod.*, **4**, 147–67.

Larkman, A.U. and Carter, M.A. (1982) Preliminary ultrastructural and autoradiographic evidence that the trophonema of the sea anemone *Actinia fragacea* has a nutritive function. *Int. J. Invert. Reprod.*, **4**, 375–9.

Lawn, I.D. (1975) An electrophysiological analysis of chemoreception in the sea anemone *Tealia felina*. *J. Exp. Biol.*, **63**, 525–36.

Lawn, I.D. (1976) Swimming in the sea anemone *Stomphia coccinea* triggered by a slow conduction system. *Nature*, **262**, 708–9.

Lawn, I D. (1980) A transmesogloeal conduction system in the swimming sea anemone *Stomphia*. *J. Exp. Biol.*, **83**, 45–52.

Lawn, I.D. and Ross, D.M. (1982a) The behavioural physiology of the swimming sea anemone *Boloceroides mcmurrichi*. *Proc. R. Soc. Lond.*, B, **216**, 315–34.

Lawn, I.D. and Ross, D.M. (1982b) The release of the pedal disk in an undescribed species of *Tealia* (Anthozoa: Actiniaria). *Biol. Bull.*, **163**, 188–96.

Lawrence, J.M. (1987) *A Functional Biology of Echinoderms*, Croom Helm, London, 340 pp.

LeBoeuf, R.D., McCommas, S.A., Howe, N.R. and Tauber, J.D. (1981) The role of carotenoids in the color polymorphism of the sea anemone, *Bunodosoma granulifera* (Anthozoa: Actiniaria). *Comp. Biochem. Physiol.*, **68B**, 25–9.

Lee, R.F., Hirota, J. and Barnett, A.M. (1971) Distribution and importance of wax esters in marine copepods and other zooplankton. *Deep-Sea Res.*, **18**, 1147–65.

Leghissa, S. (1965) Nervous organization and the problem of the synapse in *Actinia equina*. *Amer. Zool.*, **5**, 411–24.

Lehninger, A.L. (1973) *Bioenergetics*, 2nd ed., W.A. Benjamin, Menlo Park, California, 245 pp.

Lenhoff, H.M., Heagy, W. and Danner, J. (1976) A view of the evolution of chemoreceptors based on research with cnidarians. In G.O. Mackie (ed.), *Coelenterate Ecology and Behavior*, Plenum, New York, pp. 571–9.

Lesser, M.P. (1989) Photobiology of natural populations of zooxanthellae from the sea anemone *Aiptasia pallida*: assessment of the host's role in protection against ultraviolet radiation. *Cytometry*, **10**, 653–8.

Lesser, M.P. and Shick, J.M. (1989a) Effects of irradiance and ultraviolet radiation on photoadaptation in the zooxanthellae of *Aiptasia pallida*: primary production, photoinhibition, and enzymic defenses against oxygen toxicity. *Mar. Biol.*, **102**, 243–55.

Lesser, M.P. and Shick, J.M. (1989b) Photoadaptation and defenses against oxygen toxicity in zooxanthellae from natural populations of symbiotic cnidarians. *J. Exp. Mar. Biol. Ecol.*, **134**, 129–41.

Lesser, M.P., Stochaj, W.R., Tapley, D.W. and Shick, J.M. (1990) Physiological mechanisms of bleaching in coral reef anthozoans: effects of irradiance, ultraviolet radiation, and temperature on the activities of protective enzymes against active oxygen. *Coral Reefs*, **8**, 225–32.

Levine, D.M. and Blanchard, O.J., Jr. (1980) Acclimation of two shrimps of the genus *Periclimenes* to sea anemones. *Bull. Mar. Sci.*, **30**, 460–6.

Lewis, J.B. (1984) Photosynthetic production by the coral reef anemone, *Lebrunea coralligens* Wilson, and behavioral correlates of two nutritional strategies. *Biol. Bull.*, **167**, 601–12.

Limbaugh, C., Pederson, H. and Chace, F.A., Jr. (1961) Shrimps that clean fishes. *Bull. Mar. Sci.*, **11**, 237–57.

Lindstedt, K.J. (1971a) Biphasic feeding response in a sea anemone: control by asparagine and glutathione. *Science*, **173**, 333–4.

Lindstedt, K.J. (1971b) Chemical control of feeding behavior. *Comp. Biochem. Physiol.*, **39A**, 553–81.

Lindstedt, K.J., Muscatine, L. and Lenhoff, H.M. (1968) Valine activation of feeding in the sea anemone *Boloceroides*. *Comp. Biochem. Physiol.*, **26**, 567–72.

Livingstone, D.R. (1983) Invertebrate and vertebrate pathways of anaerobic metabolism: evolutionary considerations. *J. Geol. Soc. London*, **140**, 27–37.

Livingstone, D.R., Zwaan, A. de, Leopold, M. and Marteijn, E. (1983) Studies on the phylogenetic distribution of pyruvate oxidoreductases. *Biochem. Syst. Ecol.*, **11**, 415–25.

Logan, C.A. (1975) Topographic changes in responding during habituation to waterstream stimulation in sea anemones (*Anthopleura elegantissima*). *J. Comp. Physiol. Psychol.*, **89**, 105–17.

Logan, C.A. and Beck, H.P. (1978) Long-term retention of habituation in the sea anemone (*Anthopleura elegantissima*). *J. Comp. Physiol. Psychol.*, **92**, 928–36.

Loseva, L.M. (1971) Observations on oogenesis of actinians. II. Oogenesis in *Tealia crassicornis* (Muell), *Metridium senile* (L.) and *Protanthea simplex* (Carlg.). *Vestn. Leningr. Univ. Biol.*, **9**, 22–9 (in Russian).

Losey, G.S., Jr. (1978) The symbiotic behavior of fishes. In D.I. Mostofsky (ed.), *The Behavior of Fish and Other Aquatic Animals*, Academic Press, New York, pp. 1–31.

Louis, C. (1960) Modalités et déterminisme expérimental de la scissiparité chez l'Actinie *Anemonia sulcata* Pennant. *C.R. Acad. Sci. Paris*, **251**, 134–6.

Lubbock, R. (1979) Chemical recognition and nematocyte excitation in a sea anemone. *J. Exp. Biol.*, **83**, 283–92.

Lubbock, R. (1980a) Clone-specific cellular recognition in a sea anemone. *Proc. Nat. Acad. Sci. USA*, **77**, 6667–9.

Lubbock, R. (1980b) Why are clownfishes not stung by sea anemones? *Proc. R. Soc. Lond.*, *B*, **207**, 35–61.

Lubbock, R. (1981) The clownfish/anemone symbiosis: a problem of cellular recognition. *Parasitology*, **82**, 159–73.

Lubbock, R. and Allbut, C. (1981) The sea anemone *Actinia equina* tolerates allogeneic juveniles but alters their phenotype. *Nature*, **293**, 474–5.

Lubbock, R., Gupta, B.L. and Hall, T.A. (1981) Novel role of calcium in exocytosis: mechanism of nematocyst discharge as shown by X-ray microanalysis. *Proc. Nat. Acad. Sci. USA*, **78**, 3624–8.

Lubbock, R. and Shelton, G.A.B. (1981) Electrical activity following cellular recognition of self and non-self in a sea anemone. *Nature*, **289**, 59–60.

Mackie, G.O., Anderson, P.A.V. and Singla, C.L. (1984) Apparent absence of gap junctions in two classes of Cnidaria. *Biol. Bull.*, **167**, 120–3.

MacMunn, C.A. (1885) Observations on the chromatology of Actiniæ. *Phil. Trans. Royal Soc. London, Ser. II*, **176**, 641–63.

Male, K.B. and Storey, K.B. (1983) Kinetic characterization of NADP-specific glutamate dehydrogenase from the sea anemone, *Anthopleura xanthogrammica*: control of amino acid biosynthesis during osmotic stress. *Comp. Biochem. Physiol.*, **76B**, 823–9.

Manchenko, G.P. (1985) New data on high level of allozymic variation in marine invertebrates. *Genetika*, **21**, 936–44 (in Russian).

Manchenko, G.P. and Balakirev, E.S. (1984) Allozymic variation in actinia *Anthopleura orientalis* from Peter the Great Bay of the Sea of Japan. *Genetika*, **20**, 2072–4 (in Russian).

Manchenko, G.P. and Shed'ko, S.V. (1987) Comparative genetic study of red and white actinians *Metridium senile fimbriatum* from Peter the Great Bay, Sea of Japan. *Soviet J. Mar. Biol.*, **13**, 99–104.

Mangum, C.P. (1976) Primitive respiratory adaptations. In R.C. Newell (ed.), *Adaptation to Environment: Essays on the Physiology of Marine Animals*, Butterworth's, London, pp. 191–278.

Mangum, C.P. and Johansen, K. (1975) The colloid osmotic pressures of invertebrate body fluids. *J. Exp. Biol.*, **63**, 661–71.

Mangum, C. and Van Winkle, W. (1973) Responses of aquatic invertebrates to declining oxygen conditions. *Amer. Zool.*, **13**, 529–41.

Mangum, D.C. (1980) Sea anemone neuromuscular responses in anaerobic conditions. *Science*, **208**, 1177–8.

Manuel, R.L. (1988) *British Anthozoa*. Synopses of the British Fauna No. 18 (revised), E.J. Brill, Leiden, 241 pp.

Mariscal, R.N. (1966) The symbiosis between tropical sea anemones and fishes: a review. In R.I. Bowman (ed.), *The Galápagos. Proceedings of the Symposia of the Galápagos International Scientific Project*, University of California Press, Berkeley, pp. 157–71.

Mariscal, R.N. (1969) The protection of the anemone fish, *Amphiprion xanthurus*, from the sea anemone, *Stoichactis kenti*. *Experientia*, **25**, 1114.

Mariscal, R.N. (1970a) The nature of the symbiosis between Indo-Pacific anemone fishes and sea anemones. *Mar. Biol.*, **6**, 58–65.

Mariscal, R.N. (1970b) A field and laboratory study of the symbiotic behavior of fishes and sea anemones from the tropical Indo-Pacific. *Univ. of California Publ. in Zoology*, **91**, 1–33 + 4 plates.

Mariscal, R.N. (1970c) An experimental analysis of the protection of *Amphiprion xanthurus* Cuvier & Valenciennes and some other anemone fishes from sea anemones. *J. Exp. Mar. Biol. Ecol.*, **4**, 134–49.

Mariscal, R.N. (1971) Experimental studies on the protection of anemone fishes from sea anemones. In T.C. Cheng (ed.), *Aspects of the Biology of Symbiosis*, University Park Press, Baltimore, Maryland, pp. 283–315.

Mariscal, R.N. (1972) Behavior of symbiotic fishes and sea anemones. In H.E. Winn and B.L. Olla (eds.), *Behavior of Marine Animals, Vol. 2*, Plenum Publishing Corp., New York, pp. 327–60.

Mariscal, R.N. (1973) The control of nematocyst discharge during feeding by sea anemones. *Publ. Seto Mar. Biol. Lab. (Proc.Second Int. Symp. on Cnidaria)*, **20**, 695–702.

Mariscal, R.N. (1974a) Scanning electron microscopy of the sensory epithelia and nematocysts of corals and a corallimorpharian sea anemone. In *Proceedings of the Second International Coral Reef Symposium, Vol. 1*, Great Barrier Reef Committee, Brisbane, pp. 519–32.

Mariscal, R.N. (1974b) Scanning electron microscopy of the sensory surface of the tentacles of sea anemones and corals. *Z. Zellforsch.*, **147**, 149–56.

Mariscal, R.N. (1974c) Nematocysts. In L. Muscatine and H.M. Lenhoff (eds.), *Coelenterate Biology: Reviews and New Perspectives*, Academic Press, New York, pp. 129–78.

Mariscal, R.N. (1984) Cnidaria: cnidae. In J. Bereiter-Hahn, A. G. Matoltsy and K. S. Richards (eds.), *Biology of the Integument. Vol. 1. Invertebrates*, Springer-Verlag, Berlin, pp. 57–8.

Mariscal, R.N. (1988) X-ray microanalysis and perspectives on the role of calcium and other elements in cnidae. In D.A. Hessinger and H.M. Lenhoff (eds.), *The Biology of Nematocysts*, Academic Press, San Diego, California, pp. 95–114.

Mariscal, R.N., Bigger, C.H. and McLean, R.B. (1976) The form and function of cnidarian spirocysts 1. Ultrastructure of the capsule exterior and relationship to the tentacle sensory surface. *Cell Tiss. Res.*, **168**, 465–74.

Mariscal, R.N., Conklin, E.J. and Bigger, C.H. (1977) The ptychocyst, a major new category of cnida used in tube construction by a cerianthid anemone. *Biol. Bull.*, **152**, 392–405.

Mariscal, R.N., Conklin, E.J. and Bigger, C.H. (1978) The putative sensory receptors associated with the cnidae of cnidarians. In *Scanning Electron Microscopy, Vol. II*, SEM, Inc., O'Hare, Illinois, pp. 959–66.

Marks, P.S. (1976) Nervous control of light responses in the sea anemone, *Calamactis praelongus. J. Exp. Biol.*, **65**, 85–96.

Martin, E.J. (1968) Specific antigens released into sea water by contracting anemones (Coelenterata). *Comp. Biochem. Physiol.*, **25**, 169–76.

Mason, W.T. (1972) Isolation and characterization of the lipids of the sea anemone *Metridium senile. Biochim. Biophys. Acta*, **280**, 538–44.

Mathias, A.P., Ross, D.M. and Schachter, M. (1960) The distribution of 5-hydroxytryptamine, tetramethylammonium, homarine, and other substances in sea anemones. *J. Physiol.*, **151**, 296–311.

Mauzey, K.P., Birkeland, C. and Dayton, P.K. (1968) Feeding behavior of asteroids and escape responses of their prey in the Puget Sound region. *Ecology*, **49**, 603–19.

Maynard Smith, J. (1978) *The Evolution of Sex*, Cambridge University Press, Cambridge, UK, 222 pp.

McClendon, J.F. (1906) On the locomotion of a sea anemone (*Metridium marginatum*). *Biol. Bull.*, **10**, 66–7.

McClendon, J.F. (1911) On adaptations in structure and habits of some marine animals of Tortugas, Florida. *Pap. Tortugas Lab., Carnegie Inst. Washington*, **3**, 57–62 + 2 plates.

McCloskey, L.R., Wethey, D.S. and Porter, J.W. (1978) Measurement and interpretation of photosynthesis and respiration in reef corals. *Monogr. Oceanogr. Methodol. (UNESCO)*, **5**, 379–96.

McCommas, S.A. and LeBoeuf, R.D. (1981) Reduced color polymorphism in a population of *Bunodosoma granulifera. Biochem. Syst. Ecol.*, **9**, 329–32.

McCommas, S.A. and Lester, L.J. (1980) Electrophoretic evaluation of the taxonomic status of two species of sea anemone. *Biochem. Syst. Ecol.*, **8**, 289–92.

McFarlane, I.D. (1969) Co-ordination of pedal-disc detachment in the sea anemone *Calliactis parasitica. J. Exp. Biol.*, **51**, 387–96.

McFarlane, I.D. (1970) Control of preparatory feeding behaviour in the sea anemone *Tealia felina. J. Exp. Biol.*, **53**, 211–20.

McFarlane, I.D. (1973) Spontaneous contractions and nerve net activity in the sea anemone *Calliactis parasitica. Mar. Behav. Physiol.*, **2**, 97–113.

McFarlane, I.D. (1974) Excitatory and inhibitory control of inherent contractions in the sea anemone *Calliactis parasitica. J. Exp. Biol.*, **60**: 397–422.

McFarlane, I.D. (1975) Control of mouth opening and pharynx protrusion during feeding in the sea anemone *Calliactis parasitica. J. Exp. Biol.*, **63**, 615–26.

McFarlane, I.D. (1976) Two slow conduction systems coordinate shell-climbing behaviour in the sea anemone *Calliactis parasitica. J. Exp. Biol.*, **64**, 431–46.

McFarlane, I.D. (1982) *Calliactis parasitica.* In G.A.B. Shelton (ed.), *Electrical Conduction and Behaviour in 'Simple' Invertebrates*, Oxford University Press, New York, pp. 243–65.

McFarlane, I.D. (1983) Nerve net pacemakers and phases of behaviour in the sea anemone *Calliactis parasitica*. *J. Exp. Biol.*, **104**, 231–46.

McFarlane, I.D. (1984a) Nerve nets and conducting systems in sea anemones: two pathways excite tentacle contractions in *Calliactis parasitica*. *J. Exp. Biol.*, **108**, 137–49.

McFarlane, I.D. (1984b) Nerve nets and conducting systems in sea anemones: co-ordination of ipsilateral and contralateral contractions in *Protanthea simplex*. *Mar. Behav. Physiol.*, **11**, 219–28.

McFarlane, I.D., Graff, D. and Grimmelikhuijzen, C.J.P. (1987) Excitatory actions of Antho-RFamide, an anthozoan neuropeptide, on muscles and conducting systems in the sea anemone *Calliactis parasitica*. *J. Exp. Biol.*, **133**, 157–68.

McFarlane, I.D. and Lawn, I.D. (1972) Expansion and contraction of the oral disc in the sea anemone *Tealia felina*. *J. Exp. Biol.*, **57**, 633–49.

McFarlane, I.D. and Lawn, I.D. (1990) The senses of sea anemones: responses of the SS1 nerve net to chemical and mechanical stimuli. *Hydrobiologia/Developments in Hydrobiology*, (in press).

McFarlane, I.D. and Shelton, G.A.B. (1975) The nature of adhesion of tentacles to shells during shell-climbing behaviour in the sea anemone *Calliactis parasitica* (Couch). *J. Exp. Mar. Biol. Ecol.*, **19**, 177–86.

McKay, M.C. and Anderson, P.A.V. (1988a) Preparation and properties of cnido-cytes from the sea anemone *Anthopleura elegantissima*. *Biol. Bull.*, **174**, 47–53.

McKay, M.C. and Anderson, P.A.V. (1988b) On the preparation and properties of isolated cnidocytes and cnidae. In H.M. Lenhoff and D.A. Hessinger (eds.), *The Biology of Nematocysts*, Academic Press, San Diego, California, pp. 273–94.

McLean, R.B. and Mariscal, R.N. (1973) Protection of a hermit crab by its symbiotic sea anemone *Calliactis tricolor*. *Experientia*, **29**, 128–30.

Mesnil, F. (1901) Recherches sur la digestion intracellulaire et les diastases des actinies. *Ann. Inst. Pasteur*, **15**, 352–97.

Metschnikoff, E. (1880) Über die intracelluläre Verdauung bei Coelenteraten. *Zool. Anz.*, **3**, 261–3.

Minasian, L.L., Jr. (1979) The effect of exogenous factors on morphology and asexual reproduction in laboratory cultures of the intertidal sea anemone, *Haliplanella luciae* (Verrill) (Anthozoa: Actiniaria) from Delaware. *J. Exp. Mar. Biol. Ecol.*, **40**, 235–46.

Minasian, L.L., Jr. (1982) The relationship of size and biomass to fission rate in a clone of the sea anemone, *Haliplanella luciae* (Verrill). *J. Exp. Mar. Biol. Ecol.*, **58**, 151–62.

Minasian, L.L., Jr. and Mariscal, R.N. (1979) Characteristics and regulation of fission activity in clonal cultures of the cosmopolitan sea anemone, *Haliplanella luciae* (Verrill). *Biol. Bull.*, **157**, 478–93.

Miyagawa, K. (1989) Experimental analysis of the symbiosis between anemonefish and sea anemones. *Ethology*, **80**, 19–46.

Miyagawa, K. and Hidaka, T. (1980) *Amphiprion clarkii* juvenile: innate protection against and chemical attraction by symbiotic sea anemones. *Proc. Japan Acad.*, *B*, **56**, 356–61.

Miyawaki, M. (1951) Notes on the effect of low salinity on an actinian, *Diadumene luciae*. *J. Fac. Sci. Hokkaido Univ., Ser. VI, Zool.*, **10**, 123–6.

Möller, H. (1978) Nahrungsökologische Untersuchungen an *Anemonia sulcata* Investigations of the feeding ecology of *Anemonia sulcata*. *Zool. Anz.*, **200**, 369–73.

Molodtsov, N.V. and Vafina, M.G. (1972) The distribution of β-N-acetylglucos-aminidase in marine invertebrates. *Comp. Biochem. Physiol.*, **41B**, 113–20.

Moore, R.E. and Scheuer, P.J. (1971) Palytoxin: a new marine toxin from a coelen-terate. *Science*, **172**, 495–8.

Mouchet, S. (1929) Présence de xanthine chez les actinies. *Soc. Zool. Fr. Bull.*, **54**, 345–50.

Mouchet, S. (1930) L'excrétion chez les actinies. *Sta. Oceanogr. Salammbô Notes*, **15**, 1–14.

Muller-Parker, G. (1984a) Dispersal of zooxanthellae on coral reefs by predators on cnidarians. *Biol. Bull.*, **167**, 159–67.

Muller-Parker, G. (1984b) Photosynthesis-irradiance responses and photosynthetic periodicity in the sea anemone *Aiptasia pulchella* and its zooxanthellae. *Mar. Biol.*, **82**, 225–32.

Muller-Parker, G. (1985) Effect of feeding regime and irradiance on the photophysio-logy of the symbiotic sea anemone *Aiptasia pulchella*. *Mar. Biol.*, **90**, 65–74.

Muller-Parker, G. (1987) Seasonal variation in light-shade adaptation of natural populations of the symbiotic sea anemone *Aiptasia pulchella* (Carlgren, 1943) in Hawaii. *J. Exp. Mar. Biol. Ecol.*, **112**, 165–83.

Muller-Parker, G., Cook, C.B. and D'Elia, C.F. (1990) Feeding affects phosphate fluxes in the symbiotic sea anemone *Aiptasia pallida*. *Mar. Ecol. Prog. Ser.*, **60**, 283–90.

Muller-Parker, G., D'Elia, C.F. and Cook, C.B. (1988) Nutrient limitation of zoo-xanthellae: effects of host feeding history on nutrient uptake by isolated algae. In J.H. Choat *et al.* (eds.), *Proceedings of the 6th International Coral Reef Sym-posium, Townsville, Australia, Vol. 3*, pp. 15–19.

Murata, M., Miyagawa-Kohshima, K., Nakanishi, K. and Naya, Y. (1986) Charac-terization of compounds that induce symbiosis between sea anemone and anemone fish. *Science*, **234**: 585–7.

Muscatine, L. (1961) Symbiosis in marine and freshwater coelenterates. In H. Len-hoff and W.F. Loomis (eds.), *The Biology of Hydra*, University of Miami Press, Miami, Florida, pp. 255–68.

Muscatine, L. (1971) Experiments on green algae coexistent with zooxanthellae in sea anemones. *Pacific Sci.*, **25**, 13–21.

Muscatine, L., Falkowski, P.G. and Dubinsky, Z. (1983) Carbon budgets in symbio-tic associations. In E.A. Schenk and W. Schwemmler (eds.), *Endocytobiology*, *Vol. 2*, Walter de Gruyter, Berlin, pp. 649–58.

Muscatine, L. and Hand, C. (1958) Direct evidence for the transfer of materials from symbiotic algae to the tissues of a coelenterate. *Proc. Nat. Acad. Sci. USA*, **44**, 1259–63.

Muscatine, L. and Lenhoff, H.M. (eds.) (1974) *Coelenterate Biology. Reviews and New Perspectives*, Academic Press, New York, 501 pp.

Muscatine, L., McCloskey, L.R. and Marian, R.E. (1981) Estimating the daily con-tribution of carbon from zooxanthellae to coral animal respiration. *Limnol. Oceanogr.*, **26**, 601–11.

Muscatine, L. and Porter, J.W. (1977) Reef corals: mutualistic symbioses adapted to nutrient-poor environments. *BioScience*, **27**, 454–60.

Muscatine, L., Weissman, D. and Doino, J. (1989) By what mechanism does low temperature shock evoke exocytosis of symbiotic algae in the sea anemone *Aiptasia pulchella?* In R.B. Williams (ed.), *5th International Conference on Coelenterate Biology. Programme and Abstracts*, University of Southampton, Southampton, UK, p. 69.

Nagai, Y. and Nagai, S. (1973) Feeding factors for the sea anemone *Anthopleura midorii*. *Mar. Biol.*, **18**, 55–60.

Navarro, E. and Ortega, M.M. (1984) Amino acid accumulation from glucose during air exposure and anoxia in the sea anemone *Actinia equina* (L.). *Comp. Biochem. Physiol.*, **78B**, 199–202.

Navarro, E. and Ortega, M.M. (1985) Efectos metabólicos de la exposición al aire y repuesta postaérea en el antozoo intermareal *Actinia equina* L. *Rev. Españ. Fisiol.*, **41**, 471–8.

Navarro, E., Ortega, M.M. and Iglesias, J.I.P. (1987) An analysis of variables affecting oxygen consumption in *Actinia equina* L. (Anthozoa) from two shore positions. *Comp. Biochem. Physiol.*, **86A**, 233–40.

Navarro, E., Ortega, M.M. and Madariaga, J.M. (1981) Effect of body size, temperature and shore level on aquatic and aerial respiration of *Actinia equina* (L.) (Anthozoa). *J. Exp. Mar. Biol. Ecol.*, **53**, 153–62.

Needler, M. and Ross, D.M. (1958) Neuromuscular activity in the sea anemone *Calliactis parasitica* (Couch). *J. Mar. Biol. Ass. UK*, **37**, 789–805.

Neigel, J.E. and Avise, J.C. (1985) The precision of histocompatibility response in clonal recognition in tropical marine sponges. *Evolution*, **39**, 724–32.

Newell, R.C. (1979) *Biology of Intertidal Animals*, Marine Ecological Surveys, Ltd., Faversham, Kent, UK, 781 pp.

Nicol, J.A.C. (1959) Digestion in sea anemones. *J. Mar. Biol. Ass. UK*, **38**, 469–76.

Nicol, J.A.C. (1967) *The Biology of Marine Animals*, 2nd ed., John Wiley and Sons, New York, 699 pp.

North, W.J. (1957) Sensitivity to light in the sea anemone *Metridium senile* (L.) II. Studies of reaction time variability and the effects of changes in light intensity and temperature. *J. Gen Physiol.*, **40**, 715–33.

North, W.J. and Pantin, C.F.A. (1958) Sensitivity to light in the sea-anemone *Metridium senile* (L.): adaptation and action spectra. *Proc. R. Soc. London B.*, **148**, 385–96.

Nyholm, K.-G. (1943) Zur Entwicklung und Entwicklungsbiologie der Ceriantharien und Aktinien. *Zool. Bidr. Uppsala*, **22**, 87–248.

Nyholm, K.-G. (1949) On the development and dispersal of Athenaria actinia with special reference to *Halcampa duodecimcirrata*, M. Sars. *Zool. Bidr. Uppsala*, **27**, 466–505.

Nyholm, K.-G. (1959) On the development of the primitive actinian *Protanthea simplex*, Carlgren. *Zool. Bidr. Uppsala*, **33**, 69–78.

O'Brien, T.L. (1978) An ultrastructural study of zoochlorellae in a marine coelenterate. *Trans. Amer. Microsc. Soc.*, **97**, 320–29.

O'Brien, T.L. (1980) The symbiotic association between intracellular zoochlorellae (Chlorophyceae) and the coelenterate *Anthopleura xanthogrammica*. *J. Exp. Zool.*, **211**, 343–55.

O'Brien, T.L. and Wyttenbach, C.R. (1980) Some effects of temperature on the symbiotic association between zoochlorellae (Chlorophyceae) and the sea anemone *Anthopleura xanthogrammica*. *Trans. Amer. Microsc. Soc.*, **99**, 221–5.

Oglesby, L.C. (1975) An analysis of water-content regulation in selected worms. In F.J. Vernberg (ed.), *Physiological Ecology of Estuarine Organisms*, University of South Carolina Press, Columbia, pp. 181–204.

Okada, Y.K. and Komori, S. (1932) Reproduction asexuelle d'une actinie (*Boloceroides*) et sa régénération aux dépens d'un tentacule. *Bull. Biol. Fr. Belg.*, **66**, 164–99.

Oliver, W.A., Jr. (1980) The relationship of the scleractinian corals to the rugose corals. *Paleobiology*, **6**, 146–60.

Orlando Munoz, M., Atkinson, B. and Idler, D.R. (1976) Sterol and lipid composition of *Phymactis clematis* (Drayton). *Comp. Biochem. Physiol.*, **54B**, 231–2.

Orr, J., Thorpe, J.P. and Carter, M.A. (1982) Biochemical genetic confirmation of the asexual reproduction of brooded offspring in the sea anemone *Actinia equina*. *Mar. Ecol. Prog. Ser.*, **7**, 227–9.

Ortega, M.M., Iglesias, J.I.P. and Navarro, E. (1984) Acclimation to temperature in *Actinia equina* L.: effects of season and shore level on aquatic oxygen consumption. *J. Exp. Mar. Biol. Ecol.*, **76**, 79–87.

Ortega, M.M., Lopez de Pariza, J.M. and Navarro, E. (1988) Seasonal changes in the biochemical composition and oxygen consumption of the sea anemone *Actinia equina* (L.) as related to body size and shore level. *Mar. Biol.*, **97**, 137–43.

Ortega, M.M. and Navarro, E. (1988) Seasonal changes of the major lipid classes in *Actinia equina* L. (Anthozoa) in relation to body size and tidal position. *Comp. Biochem. Physiol.*, **89A**, 699–704.

Ottaway, J.R. (1973) Some effects of temperature, desiccation, and light on the intertidal anemone *Actinia tenebrosa* Farquhar (Cnidaria: Anthozoa). *Aust. J. Mar. Freshw. Res.*, **24**, 103–26.

Ottaway, J.R. (1974) Resistance of juvenile *Actinia tenebrosa* (Cnidaria: Anthozoa) to digestive enzymes. *Mauri Ora*, **2**, 73–83.

Ottaway, J.R. (1977a) Predators of sea anemones. *Tuatara*, **22**, 213–21.

Ottaway, J.R. (1977b) *Pleurobranchaea novazelandiae* preying on *Actinia tenebrosa*. *N. Z. J. Mar. Freshw. Res.*, **11**, 125–30.

Ottaway, J.R. (1978) Population ecology of the intertidal anemone *Actinia tenebrosa* I. Pedal locomotion and intraspecific aggression. *Aust. J. Mar. Freshw. Res.*, **29**, 787–802.

Ottaway, J.R. (1979a) Population ecology of the intertidal anemone *Actinia tenebrosa* II. Geographical distribution, synonymy, reproductive cycle and fecundity. *Aust. J. Zool.*, **27**, 273–90.

Ottaway, J.R. (1979b) Population ecology of the intertidal anemone *Actinia tenebrosa* III. Dynamics and environmental factors. *Aust. J. Mar. Freshw. Res.*, **30**, 41–62.

Ottaway, J.R. (1980) Population ecology of the intertidal anemone *Actinia tenebrosa* IV. Growth rates and longevities. *Aust. J. Mar. Freshw. Res.*, **31**, 385–95.

Ottaway, J.R. and Kirby, G.C. (1975) Genetic relationships between brooding and brooded *Actinia tenebrosa*. *Nature*, **255**, 221–3.

Ottaway, J.R. and Thomas, I.M. (1971) Movement and zonation of the intertidal anemone *Actinia tenebrosa* Farqu. (Cnidaria: Anthozoa) under experimental conditions. *Aust. J. Mar. Freshw. Res.*, 22, 63–78.

Paffenhöfer, G.-A. (1968) Nahrungsaufnahme, Stoffumsatz und Energiehaushalt des marinen Hydroidenpolypen *Clava multicornis*. *Helgoländer wiss. Meeresunters.*, 18, 1–44.

Palincsar, E.E., Jones, W.R., Palincsar, J.S., Glogowski, M.A. and Mastro, J.L. (1989) Bacterial aggregates within the epidermis of the sea anemone *Aiptasia pallida*. *Biol. Bull.*, 177, 130–40.

Palincsar, J.S., Jones, W.R. and Palincsar, E.E. (1988) Effects of isolation of the endosymbiont *Symbiodinium microadriaticum* (Dinophyceae) from its host *Aiptasia pallida* (Anthozoa) on cell wall ultrastructure and mitotic rate. *Trans. Amer. Microsc. Soc.*, 107, 53–66.

Pantin, C.F.A. (1935a) The nerve net of the Actinozoa I. Facilitation. *J. Exp. Biol.*, 12, 119–38.

Pantin, C.F.A. (1935b) The nerve net of the Actinozoa II. Plan of the nerve net. *J. Exp. Biol.*, 12, 139–55.

Pantin, C.F.A. (1942) The excitation of nematocysts. *J. Exp. Biol.*, 19, 294–310.

Pantin, C.F.A. (1952) The elementary nervous system. *Proc. R. Soc. Lond.*, B, 140, 147–68.

Pantin, C.F.A. (1960) Diploblastic animals. *Proc. Linn. Soc. Lond.*, 171, 1–14 + 4 plates.

Pantin, C.F.A. (1965) Capabilities of the coelenterate behavior machine. *Amer. Zool.*, 5, 581–9.

Pantin, C.F.A. and Pantin, A.M.P. (1943) The stimulus to feeding in *Anemonia sulcata*. *J. Exp. Biol.*, 20, 6–13.

Parker, G.H. (1905) The reversal of ciliary movements in metazoans. *Amer. J. Physiol.*, 13, 1–16.

Parker, G.H. (1916) The effector systems of actinians. *J. Exp. Zool.*, 21, 461–84.

Parker, G.H. (1917) Pedal locomotion in actinians. *J. Exp. Zool.*, 22, 111–24.

Parker, G.H. (1919) *The Elementary Nervous System*, Lippincott, Philadelphia, 229 pp.

Parker, G.H. (1922) The excretion of carbon dioxide by relaxed and contracted sea anemones. *J. Gen. Physiol.*, 5, 45–64.

Parry, G.D. (1983) The influence of the cost of growth on ectotherm metabolism. *J. Theor. Biol.*, 101, 453–77.

Passano, L.M. and Pantin, C.F.A. (1955) Mechanical stimulation in the sea-anemone *Calliactis parasitica*. *Proc. R. Soc. Lond.*, B, 143, 226–38.

Pathirana, C. and Andersen, R.J. (1986) Imbricatine, an unusual benzyltetrahydroisoquinoline alkaloid isolated from the starfish *Dermasterias imbricata*. *J. Amer. Chem. Soc.*, 108, 8288–9.

Patronelli, D.L., Zamponi, M., Bustos, A. and Vega, F.V. (1987) Morphological and physiological adaptations in the marginal sphincter of anemone *Phymactis clematis*, Dana 1849 from different environments. *Comp. Biochem. Physiol.*, 88A, 337–40.

Patterson, M.R. (1984) Patterns of whole colony prey capture in the octocoral, *Alcyonium siderium*. *Biol. Bull.*, 167, 613–29.

Patterson, M.R. (1985) The Effects of Flow on the Biology of Passive Suspension Feeders: Prey Capture, Feeding Rate, and Gas Exchange in Selected Cnidarians.

Ph.D. dissertation, Harvard University, Cambridge, Massachusetts, 342 pp.

Patterson, M.R. and Sebens, K.P. (1989) Forced convection modulates gas exchange in cnidarians. *Proc. Nat. Acad. Sci. USA*, **86**, 8833–6.

Pearse, J.S., Pearse, V.B. and Newberry, A.T. (1989) Telling sex from growth: dissolving Maynard Smith's paradox. *Bull. Mar. Sci.*, **45**, 433–46.

Pearse, V.B. (1974a) Modification of sea anemone behavior by symbiotic zooxanthellae: phototaxis. *Biol. Bull.*, **147**, 630–40.

Pearse, V.B. (1974b) Modification of sea anemone behavior by symbiotic zooxanthellae: expansion and contraction. *Biol. Bull.*, **147**, 641–51.

Penry, D.L. and Jumars, P.A. (1987) Modeling animal guts as chemical reactors. *Amer. Nat.*, **129**, 69–96.

Percival, E. (1968) Marine algal carbohydrates. *Oceanogr. Mar. Biol. Ann. Rev.*, **6**, 137–61.

Percival, E. and McDowell, R.H. (1967) *Chemistry and Enzymology of Marine Algal Polysaccharides*, Academic Press, New York, 219 pp.

Peterson, C.H. and Black, R. (1986) Abundance patterns of infaunal sea anemones and their potential benthic prey in and outside seagrass patches on a Western Australian sand shelf. *Bull. Mar. Sci.*, **38**, 498–511.

Peteya, D.J. (1973) A possible proprioreceptor in *Ceriantheopsis americanus* (Cnidaria, Ceriantharia). *Z. Zellforsch.*, **144**, 1–10.

Peteya, D.J. (1975) The ciliary-cone sensory cell of anemones and cerianthids. *Tissue & Cell*, **7**, 243–52.

Piavaux, A. (1977) Distribution and localization of the digestive laminarinases in animals. *Biochem. Syst. Ecol.*, **5**, 231–9.

Picken, L.E.R. and Skaer, R.J. (1966) A review of researches on nematocysts. *In* W.J. Rees (ed.), *The Cnidaria and Their Evolution*, Academic Press, London, pp. 19–50.

Pierce, S.K., Jr. and Minasian, L.L., Jr. (1974) Water balance of a euryhaline sea anemone, *Diadumene leucolena*. *Comp. Biochem. Physiol.*, **49A**, 159–67.

Pierce, S.K. and Greenberg, M.J. (1973) The initiation and control of free amino acid regulation of cell volume in salinity stressed marine bivalves. *J. Exp. Biol.*, **59**, 435–46.

Pineda, J. and Escofet, A. (1989) Selective effects of disturbance on populations of sea anemones from northern Baja California, Mexico. *Mar. Ecol. Prog. Ser.*, **55**, 55–62.

Pollero, R.J. (1983) Lipid and fatty acid characterization and metabolism in the sea anemone *Phymactis clematis* (Dana). *Lipids*, **18**, 12–17.

Polteva, D.G. (1963) Regeneration and somatic embryogenesis of *Actinia equina* in different stages of ontogenetic development. *Acta Biol. Hung.*, **14**, 199–208.

Pond, C.M. (1981) Storage. In C.R. Townsend and P. Calow (eds.), *Physiological Ecology. An Evolutionary Approach to Resource Use*, Sinauer Associates, Sunderland, Massachusetts, pp. 190–219.

Powers, D.A., Lenhoff, H.M. and Leone, C.A. (1968) Glucose-6-phosphate dehydrogenase and 6-phosphogluconate dehydrogenase activities in coelenterates. *Comp. Biochem. Physiol.*, **27**, 139–44.

Prézelin, B.B. (1987) Photosynthetic physiology of dinoflagellates. In F.J.R. Taylor (ed.), *The Biology of Dinoflagellates*, Botanical Monographs, No. 21, Blackwell

Scientific Publications, Oxford, UK, pp. 174–223.

Purcell, J.E. (1977a) The diet of large and small individuals of the sea anemone *Metridium senile. Bull. S. Cal. Acad. Sci.*, **76**, 168–72.

Purcell, J.E. (1977b) Aggressive function and induced development of catch tentacles in the sea anemone *Metridium senile* (Coelenterata, Actiniaria). *Biol. Bull.*, **153**, 355–68.

Purcell, J.E. and Kitting, C.L. (1982) Intraspecific aggression and population distributions of the sea anemone *Metridium senile. Biol. Bull.*, **162**, 345–59.

Pütter, A. (1911) Der Stoffwechsel der Aktinien. *Z. allg. Physiol.*, **12**, 297–322.

Quaglia, A. and Grasso, M. (1986) Ultrastructural evidence for a peptidergic-like neurosecretory cell in a sea anemone. *Oebalia*, **13** (n.s.), 147–56.

Quicke, D.L.J. and Brace, R.C. (1983) Phenotypic and genotypic spacing within an aggregation of the anemone, *Actinia equina. J. Mar. Biol. Ass. UK*, **63**, 493–515.

Quicke, D.L.J. and Brace, R.C. (1984) Evidence for the existence of a third, ecologically distinct morph of the anemone, *Actinia equina. J. Mar. Biol. Ass. UK*, **64**, 531–4.

Quicke, D.L.J., Donoghue, A.M. and Brace, R.C. (1983) Biochemical-genetic and ecological evidence that red/brown individuals of the anemone *Actinia equina* comprise two morphs in Britain. *Mar. Biol.*, **77**, 29–37.

Quicke, D.L.J., Donoghue, A.M., Keeling, T.F. and Brace, R.C. (1985) Littoral distributions and evidence for differential post-settlement selection on the morphs of *Actinia equina. J. Mar. Biol. Ass. UK*, **65**, 1–20.

Quin, L.D. (1965) The presence of compounds with a carbon-phosphorus bond in some marine invertebrates. *Biochemistry*, **4**, 324–30.

Rahav, O., Dubinsky, Z., Achituv, Y. and Falkowski, P.G. (1989) Ammonium metabolism in the zooxanthellate coral, *Stylophora pistillata. Proc. R. Soc. Lond., B*, **236**, 325–37.

Rajagopal, M.V. and Sohonie, K. (1957) Studies on the sea anemone *Gyrostoma* sp. Lipids of *Gyrostoma* sp. *Biochem. J.*, **65**, 34–6.

Reimer, A.A. (1973) Feeding behavior in the sea anemone *Calliactis polypus* (Forskål, 1775). *Comp. Biochem. Physiol.*, **44A**, 1289–1301.

Richardson, K., Beardall, J. and Raven, J.A. (1983) Adaptation of unicellular algae to irradiance: an analysis of strategies. *New Phytol.*, **93**, 157–191.

Riemann-Zürneck, K. (1969) *Sagartia troglodytes* (Anthozoa). Biologie und Morphologie einer schlickbewohnenden Aktinie. *Veröff. Inst. Meeresforsch. Bremerhaven*, **12**, 169–230.

Riemann-Zürneck, K. (1976) Reproductive biology, oogenesis and early development in the brood-caring sea anemone *Actinostola spetsbergensis* (Anthozoa: Actiniaria). *Helgoländer wiss. Meeresunters.*, **28**, 239–49.

Robbins, R.E. (1980) The Importance of Water Flow in the Biology of the Sea Anemone *Metridium senile* (L.). M. Sc. thesis, University of Maine, Orono, Maine, 54 pp.

Robbins, R.E. and Shick, J.M. (1980) Expansion-contraction behavior in the sea anemone *Metridium senile*: environmental cues and energetic consequences. In D.C. Smith and Y. Tiffon (eds.), *Nutrition in the Lower Metazoa*, Pergamon Press, Oxford, UK, pp. 101–16.

Robson, E.A. (1957) The structure and hydromechanics of the musculo-epithelium in *Metridium. Quart. J. Microsc. Sci.*, **98**, 265–78.

Robson, E.A. (1961a) A comparison of the nervous systems of two sea-anemones, *Calliactis parasitica* and *Metridium senile. Quart. J. Microsc. Sci.*, **102**, 319–26.

Robson, E.A. (1961b) The swimming response and its pacemaker system in the anemone *Stomphia coccinea. J. Exp. Zool.*, **38**, 685–94.

Robson, E.A. (1961c) Some observations on the swimming behaviour of the anemone *Stomphia coccinea. J. Exp. Biol.*, **38**, 343–63.

Robson, E.A. (1963) The nerve-net of a swimming anemone, *Stomphia coccinea. Quart. J. Microsc. Sci.*, **104**, 535–49.

Robson, E.A. (1965) Some aspects of the structure of the nervous system in the anemone *Calliactis. Amer. Zool.*, **5**, 403–10.

Robson, E.A. (1966) Swimming in Actiniaria. In W.J. Rees (ed.), *The Cnidaria and Their Evolution*, Academic Press, London, pp. 333–60.

Robson, E.A. (1971) The behaviour and neuromuscular system of *Gonactinia prolifera*, a swimming sea-anemone. *J. Exp. Biol.*, **55**, 611–40.

Robson, E.A. (1976) Locomotion in sea anemones: the pedal disk. In G.O. Mackie (ed.), *Coelenterate Ecology and Behavior*, Plenum, New York, pp. 479–90.

Robson, E.A. (1985) Speculations on coelenterates. In S.C. Morris, J.D. George, R. Gibson and H.M. Platt (eds.), *The Origins and Relationships of Lower Invertebrates*, Systematics Association Special Vol. No. 28, Clarendon Press, Oxford, UK, pp. 60–77.

Robson, E.A. (1988) Problems of supply and demand for cnidae in Anthozoa. In D.A. Hessinger and H.M. Lenhoff (eds.), *The Biology of Nematocysts*, Academic Press, San Diego, California, pp. 179–207.

Roche, J. (1932) Actiniohématine et cytochrome. *C.R. Hebd. Soc. Biol.*, **111**, 904–6.

Roche, J. (1936) Les pigments hématiniques des actinies (actiniohématine) et le cytochrome b. *C. R. Hebd. Soc. Biol.*, **121**, 69–71.

Romey, G., Abita, J.P., Schweitz, H., Wunderer, G. and Lazdunski, M. (1976) Sea anemone toxin: a tool to study molecular mechanisms of nerve conduction and excitation-secretion coupling. *Proc. Nat. Acad. Sci. USA*, **73**, 4055–9.

Rosin, R. (1969) Escape response of the sea-anemone *Anthopleura nigrescens* (Verrill) to its predatory eolid nudibranch *Herviella* Baba spec. nov. *The Veliger*, **12**, 74–7.

Ross, D.M. (1960a) The effects of ions and drugs on neuromuscular preparations of sea anemones. I. On preparations of the column of *Calliactis and Metridium. J. Exp. Biol.*, **37**, 732–52.

Ross, D.M. (1960b) The effects of ions and drugs on neuromuscular preparations of sea anemones. II. On sphincter preparations of *Calliactis and Metridium. J. Exp. Biol.*, **37**, 753–73.

Ross, D.M. (1960c) The association between the hermit crab *Eupagurus bernhardus* (L.) and the sea anemone *Calliactis parasitica* (Couch). *Proc. Zool. Soc. Lond.*, **134**, 43–57.

Ross, D.M. (1965) Some problems of neuromuscular activity and behaviour in the 'elementary nervous system'. In J.W.S. Pringle (ed.), *Essays on Physiological Evolution*, Pergamon Press, New York, pp. 253–61.

Ross, D.M. (1967) Behavioural and ecological relationships between sea anemones and other invertebrates. *Oceanogr. Mar. Biol. Ann. Rev.*, **5**, 291–316.

Ross, D.M. (1971) Protection of hermit crabs (*Dardanus* spp.) from octopus by commensal sea anemones (*Calliactis* spp.). *Nature*, **230**, 401–2.

Ross, D.M. (1974a) Behavior patterns in associations and interactions with other animals. In L. Muscatine and H. Lenhoff (eds.), *Coelenterate Biology: Reviews and New Perspectives*, Academic Press, New York, pp. 281–312.

Ross, D.M. (1974b) Evolutionary aspects of associations between crabs and sea anemones. In W.B. Vernberg (ed.), *Symbiosis in the Sea*, University of South Carolina Press, Columbia, pp. 111–25.

Ross, D.M. (1979a) A behaviour pattern in *Pagurus bernhardus* L. towards its symbiotic actinian *Calliactis parasitica* (Couch). *J. Mar. Biol. Ass. UK*, **59**, 623–30.

Ross, D.M. (1979b) 'Stealing' of the symbiotic anemone, *Calliactis parasitica*, in intraspecific and interspecific encounters of three species of Mediterranean pagurids. *Can. J. Zool.*, **57**, 1181–9.

Ross, D.M. (1979c) A third species of swimming actinostolid (Anthozoa: Actiniaria) on the Pacific Coast of North America. *Can. J. Zool.*, **57**, 943–5.

Ross, D.M. (1983) Symbiotic relations. In F.J. Vernberg and W.B. Vernberg (eds.), *The Biology of Crustacea, Vol. 7, Behavior and Ecology*, Academic Press, New York, pp. 163–212.

Ross, D.M. and Boletzky, S. von (1979) The association between the pagurid *Dardanus arrosor* and the actinian *Calliactis parasitica*. Recovery of activity in 'inactive' *D. arrosor* in the presence of cephalopods. *Mar. Behav. Physiol.*, **6**, 175–84.

Ross, D.M. and Sutton, L. (1961) The response of the sea anemone *Calliactis parasitica* to shells of the hermit crab *Pagurus bernhardus*. *Proc. R. Soc. Lond., B*, **155**, 266–81.

Ross, D.M. and Sutton, L. (1967) Swimming sea anemones of Puget Sound: swimming of *Actinostola* new species in response to *Stomphia coccinea*. *Science*, **155**, 1419–21.

Ross, D.M. and Sutton, L. (1968) Detachment of sea anemones by commensal hermit crabs and by mechanical and electrical stimuli. *Nature*, **217**, 380–1.

Rossi, L. (1971) Thelytochous parthenogenesis in *Cereus pedunculatus* (Actiniaria). *Experientia*, **27**, 349–51.

Rossi, L. (1975) Sexual races in *Cereus pedunculatus* (Boad.). *Pubbl. Staz. Zool. Napoli (Suppl., VIII Eur. Mar. Biol. Symp.)*, **39**, 462–70.

Roughgarden, J. (1975) Evolution of marine symbiosis — a simple cost-benefit model. *Ecology*, **56**, 1201–8.

Rubenstein, D.I. and Koehl, M.A.R. (1977) The mechanisms of filter feeding: some theoretical considerations. *Amer. Nat.*, **111**, 981–94.

Runnegar, B. (1982) Oxygen requirements, biology and phylogenetic significance of the late Precambrian worm *Dickinsonia*, and the evolution of the burrowing habit. *Alcheringa*, **6**, 223–39.

Salleo, A., La Spada, G. and Denaro, M.G. (1988) Release of free Ca^{2+} from the nematocysts of *Aiptasia mutabilis* during discharge. *Physiol. Zool.*, **61**, 272–9.

Sammarco, P.W. (1982) Polyp bail-out: an escape response to environmental stress and a new means of reproduction in corals. *Mar. Ecol. Prog. Ser.*, **10**, 57–65.

Sandberg, D.M. (1972) The influence of feeding on behavior and nematocyst discharge of the sea anemone *Calliactis tricolor*. *Mar. Behav. Physiol.*, **1**, 219–38.

Sargent, J.R. (1976) The structure, metabolism and function of lipids in marine organisms. In D.C. Malins and J.R. Sargent (eds.), *Biochemical and Biophysical Perspectives in Marine Biology, Vol. 3*, Academic Press, London, pp. 149–212.

Sargent, J.R. (1978) Marine wax esters. *Sci. Prog.*, **65**, 437–58.

Sargent, J.R. and McIntosh, R. (1974) Studies on the mechanism of biosynthesis of wax esters in *Euchaeta norvegica. Mar. Biol.*, **25**, 271–7.

Sassaman, C. and Mangum, C.P. (1970) Patterns of temperature adaptation in North American Atlantic coastal actinians. *Mar. Biol.*, **7**, 123–30.

Sassaman, C. and Mangum, C.P. (1972) Adaptations to environmental oxygen levels in infaunal and epifaunal sea anemones. *Biol. Bull.*, **143**, 657–78.

Sassaman, C. and Mangum, C.P. (1973) Relationship between aerobic and anaerobic metabolism in estuarine anemones. *Comp. Biochem. Physiol.*, **44A**, 1313–19.

Sassaman, C. and Mangum, C.P. (1974) Gas exchange in a cerianthid. *J. Exp. Zool.*, **188**, 297–306.

Sauer, K.P. (1989) Aggression and competition for space in sea-anemones. In R.B. Williams (ed.), *5th International Conference on Coelenterate Biology, Programme and Abstracts*, University of Southampton, Southampton, UK, pp. 82–83.

Sauer, K.P., Müller, M. and Weber, M. (1986) Alloimmune memory for glycoproteid recognition molecules in sea anemones competing for space. *Mar. Biol.*, **92**, 73–79.

Saville-Kent, W. (1893) *The Great Barrier Reef of Australia; Its Products and Potentialities*, Allen, London, 387 pp. + 16 colour plates.

Saz, H.J. (1981) Energy metabolism of parasitic helminths. *Ann. Rev. Physiol.*, **43**, 323–41.

Scelfo, G.M. (1986) Relationship between solar radiation and pigmentation of the coral *Montipora verrucosa* and its zooxanthellae. In P.L. Jokiel, R.H. Richmond and R.A. Rogers (eds.), *Coral Reef Population Biology*, Hawaii Inst. Mar. Biol. Tech. Rept. No. 37, pp. 440–51.

Scelfo, G.M. (1988) Ultraviolet-B absorbing compounds in *Anthopleura elegantissima. Amer. Zool.*, **28**, 105A (abstract).

Schäfer, W. (1981) Fortpflanzung und Sexualität von *Cereus pedunculatus* und *Actinia equina* (Anthozoa, Actiniaria). *Helgoländer Meeresunters.*, **34**, 451–61.

Schäfer, W.G. and Schmidt, H. (1980) The anthozoan egg: differentiation of internal oocyte structure. In P. Tardent and R. Tardent (eds.), *Developmental and Cellular Biology of Coelenterates*, Elsevier/North-Holland Biomedical Press, Amsterdam, pp. 47–52.

Schlichter, D. (1968) Das Zusammenleben von Riffanemonen und Anemonefischen. *Z. Tierpsychol.*, **25**, 933–54.

Schlichter, D. (1972) Chemische Tarnung. Die stoffliche Grundlage der Anpassung von Anemonefischen an Riffanemonen. *Mar. Biol.*, **12**, 137–50.

Schlichter, D. (1973) Ernährungsphysiologische und ökologische Aspekte der Aufnahme in Meerwasser gelöster Aminosäuren durch *Anemonia sulcata* (Coelenterata, Anthozoa). *Oecologia*, **11**, 315–50.

Schlichter, D. (1974) Der Einfluss physikalischer und chemischer Faktoren auf die Aufnahme in Meerwasser gelöster Aminosäuren durch Aktinien. *Mar. Biol.*, **25**, 279–90.

Schlichter, D. (1975a) Die Bedeutung in Meerwasser gelöster Glucose für die Ernährung von *Anemonia sulcata* (Coelenterata: Anthozoa). *Mar. Biol.*, **29**, 283–93.

Schlichter, D. (1975b) Produktion oder Übernahame von Schutzstoffen als Ursache des Nesselschutzes von Anemonefischen? *J. Exp. Mar. Biol. Ecol.*, **20**, 49–61.

Schlichter, D. (1976) Macromolecular mimicry: substances released by sea anemones and their role in the protection of anemone fishes. In G.O. Mackie (ed.), *Coelenterate Ecology and Behavior*, Plenum, New York, pp. 433–41.

Schlichter, D. (1978a) On the ability of *Anemonia sulcata* (Coelenterata: Anthozoa) to absorb charged and neutral amino acids simultaneously. *Mar. Biol.*, **45**, 97–104.

Schlichter, D. (1978b) The extraction of specific proteins for the simultaneous ectodermal absorption of charged and neutral amino acids by *Anemonia sulcata* (Coelenterata: Anthozoa). In D.S. McLusky and A.J. Berry (eds.), *Physiology and Behavior of Marine Organisms. Proc. 12th Eur. Symp. Mar. Biol.*, Pergamon Press, Oxford, UK, pp. 155–63.

Schlichter, D. (1980) Adaptations of cnidarians for integumentary absorption of dissolved organic matter. *Rev. Can. Biol.*, **39**, 259–82.

Schlichter, D., Bajorat, K.H., Buck, M., Eckes, P., Gutknecht, D., Kraus, P., Krisch, H., and Schmitz, B. (1987) Epidermal nutrition of sea anemones by absorption of organic compounds dissolved in the oceans. *Zool. Beitr. N.F.*, **30**, 29–47.

Schmidt, G.H. (1982) Replacement of discharged cnidae in the tentacles of *Anemonia sulcata*. *J. Mar. Biol. Ass. UK*, **62**, 685–91.

Schmidt, H. (1969) Die Nesselkapseln der Aktinien und ihre differentialdiagnostische Bedeutung. *Helgoländer wiss. Meeresunters.*, **19**, 284–317.

Schmidt, H. (1970) *Anthopleura stellula* (Actiniaria, Actiniidae) and its reproduction by transverse fission. *Mar. Biol.*, **5**, 245–55.

Schmidt, H. (1971) Taxonomie, Verbreitung und Variabilität von *Actinia equina* Linné 1766 (Actiniaria; Anthozoa). *Z. f. zool. Syst. Evolutionsforsch.*, **9**, 161–9.

Schmidt, H. (1972a) Die Nesselkapseln der Anthozoen und ihre Bedeutung für die phylogenetische Systematik. *Helgoländer wiss. Meeresunters.*, **23**, 422–58.

Schmidt, H. (1972b) Prodromus zu einer Monographie der mediterranen Aktinien. *Zoologica*, **42**: 1–120 + 37 figures.

Schmidt, H. (1974) On evolution in the Anthozoa. In *Proceedings of the Second International Coral Reef Symposium, Vol. 1*, Great Barrier Reef Committee, Brisbane, pp. 533–60.

Schmidt, H. and Béress, L. (1971) Phylogenetische Betrachtungen zur Toxizität und Nesselwirkung einiger Actiniaria (Anthozoa) im Vergleich zur Morphologie ihrer Nesselkapseln. *Kieler Meeresforsch.*, **27**, 166–70.

Schmidt, H. and Höltken, B. (1980) Peculiarities of spermatogenesis and sperm in Anthozoa. In P. Tardent and R. Tardent (eds.), *Developmental and Cellular Biology of Coelenterates*, Elsevier/North-Holland Biomedical Press, Amsterdam, pp. 53–9.

Schmidt, H. and Schäfer, W.G. (1980) The anthozoan egg: trophic mechanisms and oocyte surfaces. In P. Tardent and R. Tardent (eds.), *Developmental and Cellular Biology of Coelenterates*, Elsevier/North-Holland Biomedical Press, Amsterdam, pp. 41–6.

Schmidt, H. and Zissler, D. (1979) Die Spermien der Anthozoen und ihre phylogenetische Bedeutung. *Zoologica*, **44**, 1–46 + 25 plates.

Schmidt-Nielsen, K. (1984) *Scaling: Why Is Animal Size So Important?*, Cambridge

University Press, Cambridge, UK, 241 pp.

Schoenberg, D.A. and Trench, R.K. (1980a) Genetic variation in *Symbiodinium* (= *Gymnodinium*) *microadriaticum* Freudenthal, and specificity in its symbiosis with marine invertebrates. I. Isoenzyme and soluble protein patterns of axenic cultures of *Symbiodinium microadriaticum*. *Proc. R. Soc. Lond., B*, **207**, 405–27.

Schoenberg, D.A. and Trench, R.K. (1980b) Genetic variation in *Symbiodinium* (= *Gymnodinium*) *microadriaticum* Freudenthal, and specificity in its symbiosis with marine invertebrates. II. Morphological variation in *Symbiodinium microadriaticum*. *Proc. R. Soc. Lond., B*, **207**, 429–44.

Schoenberg, D.A. and Trench, R.K. (1980c) Genetic variation in *Symbiodinium* (= *Gymnodinium*) *microadriaticum* Freudenthal, and specificity in its symbiosis with marine invertebrates. III. Specificity and infectivity of *Symbiodinium microadriaticum*. *Proc. R. Soc. Lond., B*, **207**, 445–60.

Schroeder, L.A. (1981) Consumer growth efficiencies: their limits and relationships to ecological energetics. *J. Theor. Biol.*, **93**, 805–28.

Schroeder, T.E. (1982) Novel surface specialization on a sea anemone egg: 'spires' of actin-filled microvilli. *J. Morphol.*, **174**, 207–16.

Schweitz, H., Bidard, J.-N., Frelin, C., Pauron, D., Vijverberg, H.P.M., Mahasneh, D.M. and Lazdunski, M. (1985) Purification, sequence, and pharmacological properties of sea anemone toxins from *Radianthus paumotensis*. A new class of sea anemone toxins acting on the sodium channel. *Biochemistry*, **24**, 3554–61.

Schweitz, H., Vincent, J.-P., Barhanin, J., Frelin, C., Linden, G., Hugues, M. and Lazdunski, M. (1981) Purification and pharmacological properties of eight sea anemone toxins from *Anemonia sulcata, Anthopleura xanthogrammica, Stoichactis giganteus*, and *Actinodendron plumosum*. *Biochemistry*, **20**, 5245–52.

Scrutton, C.T. (1979) Early fossil cnidarians. In M.R. House (ed.), *The Origin of Major Invertebrate Groups*. Systematics Association Special Vol. No. 12, Academic Press, London, pp. 161–207.

Sebens, K.P. (in press) Anthozoa: Actiniaria, Zoanthidea, Corallimorpharia and Ceriantharia. *Marine Flora and Fauna of the Northeastern United States. NOAA Tech. Rept.*

Sebens, K.P. (1976) The ecology of Caribbean sea anemones in Panama: utilization of space on a coral reef. In G.O. Mackie (ed.), *Coelenterate Ecology and Behavior*, Plenum, New York, pp. 67–77.

Sebens, K.P. (1979) The energetics of asexual reproduction and colony formation in benthic marine invertebrates. *Amer. Zool.*, **19**, 683–97.

Sebens, K.P. (1980) The regulation of asexual reproduction and indeterminate body size in the sea anemone *Anthopleura elegantissima* (Brandt). *Biol. Bull.*, **158**, 370–82.

Sebens, K.P. (1981a) The allometry of feeding, energetics, and body size in three sea anemone species. *Biol. Bull.*, **161**, 152–71.

Sebens, K.P. (1981b) Reproductive ecology of the intertidal sea anemones *Anthopleura xanthogrammica* (Brandt) and *A.elegantissima* (Brandt): body size, habitat, and sexual reproduction. *J. Exp. Mar. Biol. Ecol.*, **54**, 225–50.

Sebens, K.P. (1982a) The limits to indeterminate growth: an optimal size model applied to passive suspension feeders. *Ecology*, **63**, 209–22.

Sebens, K.P. (1982b) Asexual reproduction in *Anthopleura elegantissima* (Anthozoa:

Actiniaria): seasonality and spatial extent of clones. *Ecology*, **63**, 434–44.

Sebens, K.P. (1982c) Recruitment and habitat selection in the intertidal sea anemones, *Anthopleura elegantissima* (Brandt) and *A.xanthogrammica* (Brandt). *J. Exp. Mar. Biol. Ecol.*, **59**, 103–24.

Sebens, K.P. (1983a) Population dynamics and habitat suitability of the intertidal sea anemones *Anthopleura elegantissima* and *A.xanthogrammica*. *Ecol. Monogr.*, **53**, 405–33.

Sebens, K.P. (1983b) Morphological variability during longitudinal fission of the intertidal sea anemone, *Anthopleura elegantissima* (Brandt). *Pacific Sci.*, **37**, 121–32.

Sebens, K.P. (1984a) Agonistic behavior in the intertidal sea anemone *Anthopleura xanthogrammica*. *Biol. Bull.*, **166**, 457–72.

Sebens, K.P. (1984b) Water flow and coral colony size: interhabitat comparisons of the octocoral *Alcyonium siderium*. *Proc. Nat. Acad. Sci. USA*, **81**, 5473–7.

Sebens, K.P. (1986) Community ecology of vertical rock walls in the Gulf of Maine, USA: small-scale processes and alternative community states. In P.G. Moore and R. Seed (eds.), *The Ecology of Rocky Coasts: Essays Presented to J.R. Lewis*, Columbia University Press, New York, pp. 346–71.

Sebens, K.P. (1987a) Coelenterata. In T.J. Pandian and F.J. Vernberg (eds.), *Animal Energetics, Vol. 1, Protozoa through Insecta*, Academic Press, New York, pp. 55–120.

Sebens, K.P. (1987b) The ecology of indeterminate growth in animals. *Ann. Rev. Ecol. Syst.*, **18**, 371–407.

Sebens, K.P. and DeRiemer, K. (1977) Diel cycles of expansion and contraction in coral reef anthozoans. *Mar. Biol.*, **43**, 247–56.

Sebens, K.P. and Koehl, M.A.R. (1984) Predation on zooplankton by two benthic anthozoans, *Alcyonium siderium* (Alcyonacea) and *Metridium senile* (Actiniaria), in the New England subtidal. *Mar. Biol.*, **81**, 255–71.

Sebens, K.P. and Laakso, G. (1978) The genus *Tealia* (Anthozoa: Actiniaria) in the waters of the San Juan Archipelago and the Olympic Peninsula. *Wasmann J. Biol.*, **35**, 152–68.

Sebens, K.P. and Paine, R.T. (1978) Biogeography of anthozoans along the west coast of South America: habitat, disturbance, and prey availability. In *Proceedings of the International Symposium on Marine Biogeography and Evolution in the Southern Hemisphere*, Auckland, New Zealand, N.Z. DSIR Inf. Ser. 137, Vol. 1, pp. 219–37.

Sebens, K.P. and Thorne, B.L. (1985) Coexistence of clones, clonal diversity, and the effects of disturbance. In J.B.C. Jackson, L.W. Buss and R.E. Cook (eds.), *Population Biology and Evolution of Clonal Organisms*, Yale University Press, New Haven, pp. 357–98.

Seilacher, A. (1983) Paleozoic sandstones in southern Jordan: trace fossils, depositional environments and biogeography. In A.M. Abed and H.M. Khaled (eds.), *Geology of Jordan. Proc. First Jordanian Geol. Conf.*, Jordan Geologists Association, Amman, pp. 209–22.

Seilacher, A. (1989) Vendozoa: organismic construction in the Proterozoic biosphere. *Lethaia*, **22**, 229–39.

Severin, S.E., Boldyrev, A.A. and Lebedev, A.V. (1972) Nitrogenous extractive compounds of muscle tissue of invertebrates. *Comp. Biochem. Physiol.*, **43B**, 369–81.

Shaw, P.W. (1989) Seasonal patterns and possible long-term effectiveness of sexual reproduction in three species of sagartiid sea anemones. In J.S. Ryland and P.A. Tyler (eds.), *Reproduction, Genetics and Distributions of Marine Organisms*, Olsen & Olsen, Fredensborg, Denmark, pp. 189–99.

Shaw, P.W., Beardmore, J.A. and Ryland, J.S. (1987) *Sagartia troglodytes* (Anthozoa: Actiniaria) consists of two species. *Mar. Ecol. Prog. Ser.*, **41**, 21–8.

Shelton, G.A.B. (1982) Anthozoa. In G.A.B. Shelton (ed.), *Electrical Conduction and Behaviour in 'Simple' Invertebrates*, Oxford University Press, New York, pp. 203–42.

Shelton, G.A.B. and Holley, M.C. (1984) The role of a 'local electrical conduction system' during feeding in the Devonshire cup coral *Caryophyllia smithii* Stokes and Broderip. *Proc. R. Soc. Lond.*, *B*, **220**, 489–500.

Shick, J.M. (1973) Effects of salinity and starvation on the uptake and utilization of dissolved glycine by *Aurelia aurita* polyps. *Biol. Bull.*, **144**, 172–9.

Shick, J.M. (1975) Uptake and utilization of dissolved glycine by *Aurelia aurita* scyphistomae: Temperature effects on the uptake process; nutritional role of dissolved amino acids. *Biol. Bull.*, **148**, 117–40.

Shick, J.M. (1976) Ecological physiology and genetics of the colonizing actinian *Haliplanella luciae*. In G.O. Mackie (ed.), *Coelenterate Ecology and Behavior*, Plenum, New York, pp. 137–46.

Shick, J.M. (1981) Heat production and oxygen uptake in intertidal sea anemones from different shore heights during exposure to air. *Mar. Biol. Lett.*, **2**, 225–36.

Shick, J.M. (1983) Respiratory gas exchange in echinoderms. In M. Jangoux and J.M. Lawrence (eds.), *Echinoderm Studies, Vol. 1*, Balkema Publishers, Rotterdam, pp. 67–110.

Shick, J.M. (1990) Diffusion limitation and hyperoxic enhancement of oxygen consumption in zooxanthellate sea anemones, zoanthids, and corals. *Biol. Bull.*, **179**, 148–58.

Shick, J.M. and Brown, W.I. (1977) Zooxanthellae-produced O_2 promotes sea anemone expansion and eliminates oxygen debt under environmental hypoxia. *J. Exp. Zool.*, **201**, 149–55.

Shick, J.M., Brown, W.I., Dolliver, E.G. and Kayar, S.R. (1979a) Oxygen uptake in sea anemones: effects of expansion, contraction, and exposure to air, and the limitations of diffusion. *Physiol. Zool.*, **52**, 50–62.

Shick, J.M. and Dowse, H.B. (1985) Genetic basis of physiological variation in natural populations of sea anemones: intra- and interclonal analyses of variance. In P.E. Gibbs (ed.), *Proceedings of the Nineteenth European Marine Biology Symposium*, Cambridge University Press, Cambridge, UK, pp. 465–79.

Shick, J.M. and Dykens, J.A. (1984) Photobiology of the symbiotic sea anemone, *Anthopleura elegantissima*: photosynthesis, respiration, and behavior under intertidal conditions. *Biol. Bull.*, **166**, 608–19.

Shick, J.M., Gnaiger, E., Widdows, J., Bayne, B.L. and Zwaan, A. de (1986) Activity and metabolism in the mussel *Mytilus edulis* L. during intertidal hypoxia and aerobic recovery. *Physiol. Zool.*, **59**, 627–42.

Shick, J.M. and Hoffmann, R.J. (1980) Effects of the trophic and physical environments on asexual reproduction and body size in the sea anemone *Metridium senile*. In P. Tardent and R. Tardent (ed.), *Developmental and Cellular Biology of Coelenterates*, Elsevier/North Holland Biomedical Press, Amsterdam, pp. 211–16.

Shick, J.M., Hoffmann, R.J. and Lamb, A.N. (1979b) Asexual reproduction, population structure, and genotype–environment interactions in sea anemones. *Amer. Zool.*, **19**, 699–713.

Shick, J.M. and Lamb, A.N. (1977) Asexual reproduction and genetic population structure in the colonizing sea anemone *Haliplanella luciae*. *Biol. Bull.*, **153**, 604–17.

Shick, J.M., Lesser, M.P. and Stochaj, W.R. (1990) Ultraviolet radiation and photooxidative stress in zooxanthellate Anthozoa: the sea anemone *Phyllodiscus semoni* and the octocoral *Clavularia* sp. *Symbiosis*, **10**, (in press).

Shick, J.M., Widdows, J. and Gnaiger, E. (1988) Calorimetric studies of behavior, metabolism and energetics of sessile intertidal animals. *Amer. Zool.*, **28**, 161–81.

Shick, J.M., Zwaan, A. de and Bont, A.M.T. de (1983) Anoxic metabolic rate in the mussel *Mytilus edulis* L. estimated by simultaneous direct calorimetry and biochemical analysis. *Physiol. Zool.*, **56**, 56–63.

Shimek, R.L. (1981) *Neptunea pribiloffensis* (Dall, 1919) and *Tealia crassicornis* (Müller, 1776): on a snail's use of babysitters. *The Veliger*, **24**, 62–6.

Shoup, C.S. (1932) Salinity of the medium and its effect on respiration in the seaanemone. *Ecology*, **13**, 81–5.

Shumway, S.E. (1978) Activity and respiration in the anemone, *Metridium senile* (L.) exposed to salinity fluctuations. *J. Exp. Mar. Biol. Ecol.*, **33**, 85–92.

Sibly, R. and Calow, P. (1982) Asexual reproduction in Protozoa and invertebrates. *J. Theor. Biol.*, **96**, 401–24.

Sidell, B.D. (1983) Cellular acclimatisation to environmental change by quantitative alterations in enzymes and organelles. In A.R. Cossins and P. Sheterline (eds.), *Cellular Acclimatization to Environmental Change*. Society for Experimental Biology Seminar Series No. 17, Cambridge University Press, Cambridge, UK, pp. 103–20.

Siebert, A.E., Jr. (1973) A description of the sea anemone *Stomphia didemon* sp. nov. and its development. *Pacific Sci.*, **27**, 363–76.

Siebert, A.E., Jr. (1974) A description of the embryology, larval development, and feeding of the sea anemones *Anthopleura elegantissima* and *A. xanthogrammica*. *Can. J. Zool.*, **52**, 1383–8.

Siebert, A.E. and Spaulding, J.G. (1976) The taxonomy, development and brooding behavior of the anemone, *Cribrinopsis fernaldi* sp. nov. *Biol. Bull.*, **150**, 128–38.

Simon, G. and Rouser, G. (1967) Phospholipids of the sea anemone: quantitative distribution; absence of carbon-phosphorus linkages in glycerol phospholipids; structural elucidation of ceramide aminoethylphosphonate. *Lipids*, **2**, 55–9.

Simpson, J.W. and Awapara, J. (1966) The pathway of glucose degradation in some invertebrates. *Comp. Biochem. Physiol.*, **18**, 537–48.

Singer, I.I. (1971) Tentacular and oral-disc regeneration in the sea anemone, *Aiptasia diaphana*. III. Autoradiographic analysis of patterns of tritiated thymidine uptake. *J. Embryol. Exp. Morph.*, **26**, 253–70.

Singer, I.I. and Palmer, J.D. (1969) Tentacular and oral-disc regeneration in the sea anemone *Aiptasia diaphana*. II. Oxidative metabolism during wound healing and tentacular differentation. *Naturwissenschaften*, **56**, 574–5.

Sleigh, M.A. (1989) Adaptations of ciliary systems for the propulsion of water and mucus. *Comp. Biochem. Physiol.*, **94A**, 359–64.

Smith B.L. and Potts, D.C. (1987) Clonal and solitary anemones (*Anthopleura*) of western North America: population genetics and systematics. *Mar. Biol.*, **94**, 537–46.

Smith, G.J. (1984) Ontogenetic variation in the symbiotic associations between zooxanthellae (*Symbiodinium microadriaticum* Freudenthal) and sea anemone (Anthozoa: Actiniaria) hosts. Ph.D. dissertation, University of Georgia, Athens, 225 pp.

Smith, G.J. (1986) Ontogenetic influences on carbon flux in *Aulactinia stelloides* polyps (Anthozoa: Actiniaria) and their endosymbiotic algae. *Mar. Biol.*, **92**, 361–9.

Smith, H.G. (1939) The significance of the relationship between actinians and zooxanthellae. *J. Exp. Biol.*, **16**, 334–45.

Smith, N., III and Lenhoff, H.M. (1976) Regulation of frequency of pedal laceration in a sea anemone. In G.O. Mackie (ed.), *Coelenterate Ecology and Behavior*, Plenum, New York, pp. 117–25.

Solé-Cava, A.M. and Thorpe, J.P. (1987) Further genetic evidence for the reproductive isolation of green sea anemone *Actinia prasina* Gosse from common intertidal beadlet anemone *Actinia equina* (L.) *Mar. Ecol. Prog. Ser.*, **38**, 225–9.

Solé-Cava, A.M., Thorpe, J.P. and Kaye, J.G. (1985) Reproductive isolation with little genetic divergence between *Urticina* (= *Tealia*) *felina* and *U.eques* (Anthozoa: Actiniaria). *Mar. Biol.*, **85**, 279–84.

Somero, G.N., Siebenaller, J.F. and Hochachka, P.W. (1983) Biochemical and physiological adaptations of deep-sea animals. In G.T. Rowe (ed.), *The Sea, Vol. 8, Deep-Sea Biology*, Wiley-Interscience, New York, pp. 261–330.

Spaulding, J.G. (1974) Embryonic and larval development in sea anemones (Anthozoa: Actiniaria). *Amer. Zool.*, **14**, 511–20.

Stambler, N. and Dubinsky, Z. (1987) Energy relationships between *Anemonia sulcata* and its endosymbiotic zooxanthellae. *Symbiosis*, **3**, 233–48.

Stearns, S.C. (1977) The evolution of life history traits: a critique of the theory and a review of the data. *Ann. Rev. Ecol. Syst.*, **8**, 145–71.

Steele, R.D. (1976) Light intensity as a factor in the regulation of the density of symbiotic zooxanthellae in *Aiptasia tagetes* (Coelenterata, Anthozoa). *J. Zool., Lond.*, **179**, 387–405.

Steele, R.D. (1977) The significance of zooxanthella-containing pellets extruded by sea anemones. *Bull. Mar. Sci.*, **27**, 591–4.

Steele, R.D. and Goreau, N.I. (1977) The breakdown of symbiotic zooxanthellae in the sea anemone *Phyllactis* (= *Oulactis*) *flosculifera* (Actiniaria). *J. Zool., London*, **181**, 421–37.

Steen, R.G. (1986) Evidence for heterotrophy by zooxanthellae in symbiosis with *Aiptasia pulchella*. *Biol. Bull.*, **170**, 267–78.

Steen, R.G. (1987) Evidence for facultative heterotrophy in cultured zooxanthellae. *Mar. Biol.*, **95**, 15–23.

Steen, R.G. (1988) The bioenergetics of symbiotic sea anemones (Anthozoa: Actiniaria). *Symbiosis*, 5, 103–42.

Steen, R.G. and Muscatine, L. (1987) Low temperature evokes rapid exocytosis of symbiotic algae by a sea anemone. *Biol. Bull.*, **172**, 246–63.

Stehouwer, H. (1952) The preference of the slug *Aeolidia papillosa* (L.) for the sea anemone *Metridium senile* (L.). *Arch. Neerland. de Zoologie*, **10**, 161–70.

Steiner, G. (1957) Über die chemische Nahrungswahl von *Actinia equina* L. *Naturwissenschaften*, **44**, 70–1.

Stephenson, T.A. (1928) *The British Sea Anemones, Vol. I*, The Ray Society, London, 148 pp. + 14 plates.

Stephenson, T.A. (1929) On methods of reproduction as specific characters. *J. Mar. Biol. Ass. UK*, **16**, 131–72.

Stephenson, T.A. (1935) *The British Sea Anemones, Vol. II*, The Ray Society, London, 426 pp. + 19 plates.

Stevenson, K.J., Gibson, D. and Dixon, G.H. (1974) Amino acid analyses of chymotrypsin-like proteases from the sea anemone (*Metridium senile*). *Can. J. Biochem.*, **52**, 93–100.

Stiven, A.E. (1965) The relationship between size, budding rate, and growth efficiency in three species of hydra. *Res. Pop. Ecol.*, **7**, 1–15.

Stochaj, W.R. (1988) The effects of ultraviolet and visible radiation on UV absorbing compounds in cnidarians. *Amer. Zool.*, **28**, 192A (abstract).

Stochaj, W.R. (1989) Photoprotective Mechanisms in Cnidarians: UV-Absorbing Compounds and Behavior. M. Sc. thesis, University of Maine, Orono, Maine. 67 pp.

Stoddart, J.A. (1983) A genotypic diversity measure. *J. Hered.*, **74**, 489.

Stoddart, J.A., Ayre, D.J., Willis, B. and Heyward, A.J. (1985) Self-recognition in sponges and corals? *Evolution*, **39**, 461–3.

Storer, T.I., Usinger, R.L., Stebbins, R.C. and Nybakken, J.W. (1979) *General Zoology*, 6th ed., McGraw-Hill, New York, 902 pp.

Storey, K.B. and Dando, P.R. (1982) Substrate specificities of octopine dehydrogenases from marine invertebrates. *Comp. Biochem. Physiol.*, **73B**, 521–8.

Stotz, W.B. (1979) Functional morphology and zonation of three species of sea anemones from rocky shores in southern Chile. *Mar. Biol.*, **50**, 181–8.

Strathmann, R.R. and Strathmann, M.F. (1982) The relationship between adult size and brooding in marine invertebrates. *Amer. Nat.*, **119**, 91–101.

Stricker, S.A. (1985) An ultrastructural study of larval settlement in the sea anemone *Urticina crassicornis* (Cnidaria, Actiniaria). *J. Morphol.*, **186**, 237–53.

Sund, P.N. (1958) A study of the muscular anatomy and swimming behaviour of the sea anemone, *Stomphia coccinea*. *Quart. J. Microsc. Sci.*, **99**, 401–20.

Svoboda, A. and Porrmann, T. (1980) Oxygen production and uptake by symbiotic *Aiptasia diaphana* (Rapp), (Anthozoa, Coelenterata) adapted to different light intensities. In D.C. Smith and Y. Tiffon (eds.), *Nutrition in the Lower Metazoa*, Pergamon, Oxford, UK, pp. 87–99.

Szmant-Froelich, A. (1981) Coral nutrition: comparison of the fate of ^{14}C from ingested labelled brine shrimp and from the uptake of $NaH^{14}CO_3$ by its zooxanthellae. *J. Exp. Mar. Biol. Ecol.*, **55**, 133–44.

Tapley, D.W. (1989) Photoinactivation of catalase but not superoxide dismutase in the symbiotic sea anemone *Aiptasia pallida*. *Amer. Zool.*, **29**, 53A (abstract).

Tapley, D.W., Shick, J.M. and Smith, J.P.S., III (1988) Defenses against oxidative stress in the sea anemones *Aiptasia pallida* and *Aiptasia pulchella. Amer. Zool.*, **28**, 105A (abstract).

Tardent, P. (1975) Sex and sex determination in coelenterates. In R. Reinboth (ed.), *Intersexuality in the Animal Kingdom*, Springer-Verlag, Berlin, Heidelberg, New York, pp. 1–13.

Tardy, J. (1964) Comportement prédateur de *Eolidiella alderi* (Mollusque, Nudibranche). *C. R. Acad. Sci. Paris*, **258**, 2190–2.

Targett, N.M., Bishop, S.S., McConnell, O.J. and Yoder, J.A. (1983) Antifouling agents against the benthic marine diatom *Navicula salinicola*: homarine from the gorgonian *Leptogorgia virgulata* and *L.setacea* and analogs. *J. Chem. Ecol.*, **9**, 817–29.

Taylor, D.L. (1969a) On the regulation and maintenance of algal numbers in zooxanthellae-coelenterate symbiosis, with a note on the nutritional relationship in *Anemonia sulcata. J. Mar. Biol. Ass. UK*, **49**, 1057–65.

Taylor, D.L. (1969b) The nutritional relationship of *Anemonia sulcata* (Pennant) and its dinoflagellate symbiont. *J. Cell Sci.*, **4**, 751–62.

Taylor, P.R. and Littler, M.M. (1982) The roles of compensatory mortality, physical disturbance, and substrate retention in the development and organization of a sand-influenced, rocky-intertidal community. *Ecology*, **63**, 135–46.

Thorington, G.U. and Hessinger, D.A. (1988) Control of cnida discharge: I. Evidence for two classes of chemoreceptor. *Biol. Bull.*, **174**, 163–71.

Thorson, G. (1936) The larval development, growth, and metabolism of arctic marine bottom invertebrates compared with those of other seas. *Meddelelser om Grønland*, **100**, 1–155.

Tiffon, Y. (1973) Latency and sedimentability of acid hydrolases in sterile septa homogenates of *Cerianthus lloydi* G. *Comp. Biochem. Physiol.*, **45B**, 731–40.

Tiffon, Y. (1975) Hydrolases dans l'ectoderme de *Cerianthus lloydi* Gosse, *Cerianthus membranaceus* Spallanzani et *Metridium senile* (L.): mise en évidence d'une digestion extracellulaire et extracorporelle. *J. Exp. Mar. Biol. Ecol.*, **18**, 243–54.

Tiffon, Y. (1987) Ordre des cérianthaires (Ceriantharia Perrier, 1883). In P.-P. Grassé (ed.), *Traité de Zoologie. Anatomie, Systématique, Biologie. Tome III. Cnidaires Anthozoaires*, Masson, Paris, pp. 211–56.

Tiffon, Y. and Bouillon, J. (1975) Digestion extracellulaire dans la cavité gastrique de *Cerianthus lloydi* Gosse. Structure du gastroderme, localisation et propriétés des enzymes protéolytiques. *J. Exp. Mar. Biol. Ecol.*, **18**, 255–69.

Tiffon, Y. and Daireaux, M. (1974) Phagocytose et pinocytose par l'ectoderme et l'endoderme de *Cerianthus lloydi* Gosse. *J. Exp. Mar. Biol. Ecol.*, **16**, 155–65.

Tiffon, Y. and Franc, S. (1982) Crystal-bearing vesicles and 3 β-hydroxysterols in non calcifying Anthozoa. *J. Submicrosc. Cytol.*, **14**, 141–8.

Tiffon, Y. and Hugon, J.S. (1977) Localisation ultrastructurale de la phosphatase acide et de la phosphatase alcaline dans les cloisons septales stériles de l'anthozoaire *Pachycerianthus fimbriatus*. *Histochemistry*, **54**, 289–97.

Tiffon, Y., Rasmont, R., Vos, L. de and Bouillon, J. (1973) Digestion in lower Metazoa. In J.T. Dingle (ed.), *Lysosomes in Biology and Pathology, Vol. 3*, North-Holland/American Elsevier, New York, pp. 49–68.

Townsend, C.R. and Hughes, R.N. (1981) Maximizing net energy returns from foraging. In C.R. Townsend and P. Calow (eds.), *Physiological Ecology. An Evolutionary Approach to Resource Use*, Sinauer Associates, Sunderland, Massachusetts, pp. 86–108.

Trench, R.K. (1971a) The physiology and biochemistry of zooxanthellae symbiotic with marine coelenterates I. The assimilation of photosynthetic products of zooxanthellae by two marine coelenterates. *Proc. R. Soc. Lond., B*, 177, 225–35.

Trench, R.K. (1971b) The physiology and biochemistry of zooxanthellae symbiotic with marine coelenterates II. Liberation of fixed 14C by zooxanthellae *in vitro*. *Proc. R. Soc. Lond., B*, 177, 237–50.

Trench, R.K. (1971c) The physiology and biochemistry of zooxanthellae symbiotic with marine coelenterates III. The effect of homogenates of host tissues on the excretion of photosynthetic products *in vitro* by zooxanthellae from two marine coelenterates. *Proc. R. Soc. Lond., B*, 177, 251–64.

Trench, R.K. (1979) The cell biology of plant–animal symbiosis. *Ann. Rev. Plant Physiol.*, 30, 485–531.

Trench, R.K. (1987) Dinoflagellates in non-parasitic symbioses. In F.J.R. Taylor (ed.), *The Biology of Dinoflagellates*. Botanical Monographs, No. 21, Blackwell Scientific Publications, Oxford, UK, pp. 530–70.

Trench, R.K. and Blank, R.J. (1987) *Symbiodinium microadriaticum* Freudenthal, *S.goreauii* sp. nov., *S.kawagutii* sp. nov. and *S.pilosum* sp. nov.: gymnodinioid dinoflagellate symbionts of marine invertebrates. *J. Phycol.*, 23, 469–81.

Turner, J.R. (1989) Host reproduction and algal symbiont acquisition in temperate Anthozoa. In R.B. Williams (ed.), *5th International Conference on Coelenterate Biology. Programme and Abstracts* (unpaginated supplement), University of Southampton, Southampton, UK.

Tytler, E.M. and Davies, P.S. (1984) Photosynthetic production and respiratory energy expenditure in the anemone *Anemonia sulcata* (Pennant). *J. Exp. Mar. Biol. Ecol.*, 81, 73–86.

Tytler, E.M. and Davies, P.S. (1986) The budget of photosynthetically derived energy in the *Anemonia sulcata* (Pennant) symbiosis. *J. Exp. Mar. Biol. Ecol.*, 99, 257–69.

Tytler, E.M. and Trench, R.K. (1986) Activities of enzymes in β-carboxylation reactions and of catalase in cell-free preparations from the symbiotic dinoflagellates *Symbiodinium* spp. from a coral, a clam, a zoanthid and two sea anemones. *Proc. R. Soc. Lond., B*, 228, 483–92.

Tytler, E.M. and Trench, R.K. (1988) Catalase activity in cell-free preparations of some symbiotic and nonsymbiotic marine invertebrates. *Symbiosis*, 5, 247–54.

Uchida, T. (1936) Influence of the currents upon the distribution of races and frequency of asexual reproduction in the actinian, *Diadumene luciae. Zool. Mag., Tokyo*, 48, 895–906 (in Japanese, with English summary).

Valentine, J.W. (1976) Genetic strategies of adaptation. In F.J. Ayala (ed.), *Molecular Evolution*, Sinauer Associates, Sunderland, Massachusetts, pp. 78–94.

Van Marle, J. (1977) Contribution to the knowledge of the nervous system in the tentacles of some coelenterates. *Bijdr. Dierkunde*, 46, 220–60.

Van-Praët, M. (1976) Les activités phosphatasiques acides chez *Actinia equina* L. et *Cereus pedunculatus* P. *Bull. Soc. Zool. France*, 101, 367–76.

Van-Praët, M. (1977) Les cellules à concrétions d'*Actinia equina* L. *C. R. Acad. Sci.*

Paris, **285**, 45–8.

Van-Praët, M. (1978) Étude histochimique et ultrastructurale des zones digestives d'*Actinia equina* L. (Cnidaria, Actiniaria). *Cah. Biol. Mar.*, **19**, 415–32.

Van-Praët, M. (1980) Absorption des substances dissoutes dans le milieu, des particules et des produits de la digestion extracellulaire chez *Actinia equina* (Cnidaria, Actiniaria). *Reprod. Nutr. Dével.*, **20**, 1393–9.

Van-Praët, M. (1981) Comparaison des taux d'activité amylasique, trypsique et chymotrypsique, ainsi que des types cellulaires intervenant dans la digestion chez les Actinies littorales et abyssales. *Oceanis*, **7**, 687–703.

Van-Praët, M. (1982a) Absorption et Digestion chez *Actinia equina* L., Nutrition des Actiniaires. Thèse de Doctorat d'État ès Sciences Naturelles, Muséum National d'Histoire Naturelle et Université Pierre et Marie Curie, Paris, 218 pp.

Van-Praët, M. (1982b) Amylase and trypsin- and chymotrypsin-like proteases from Actinia equina L.; their role in the nutrition of this sea anemone. *Comp. Biochem. Physiol.*, **72A**, 523–8.

Van-Praët, M. (1983a) Régime alimentaire des Actinies. *Bull. Soc. Zool. France*, **108**, 403–7.

Van-Praët, M. (1983b) Fluctuations d'activités enzymatiques digestives chez les actinies abyssales: indices d'une nutrition particulière. *Oceanol. Acta*, **1983**, 197–200.

Van-Praët, M. (1985) Nutrition of sea anemones. *Adv. Mar. Biol.*, **22**, 65–99.

Van-Praët, M. and Duchateau, G. (1984) Mise en évidence chez une Actinie abyssale (*Paracalliactis stephensoni*) d'un cycle saisonnier de reproduction. *C. R. Acad. Sci. Paris*, **299**, 687–90.

Verwey, J. (1930) Coral reef studies. I. The symbiosis between damselfishes and sea anemones in Batavia Bay. *Treubia*, **12**, 305–66.

Voogt, P.A., Ruit, J.M. van de and Rheenen, J.W.A. van (1974) On the biosynthesis and composition of sterols and sterolesters in some sea anemones (Anthozoa). *Comp. Biochem. Physiol.*, **48B**, 47–57.

Wacasey, J.W. and Atkinson, E.G. (1987) Energy values of marine benthic invertebrates from the Canadian Arctic. *Mar. Ecol. Prog. Ser.*, **39**, 243–50.

Wahl, M. (1984) The fluffy sea anemone *Metridium senile* in periodically oxygen depleted surroundings. *Mar. Biol.*, **81**, 81–6.

Wahl, M. (1985) The recolonization potential of *Metridium senile* in an area previously depopulated by oxygen deficiency. *Oecologia*, **67**, 255–9.

Walsh, P.J. (1981a) Purification and characterization of two allozymic forms of octopine dehydrogenase from California populations of *Metridium senile*. The role of octopine dehydrogenase in the anaerobic metabolism of sea anemones. *J. Comp. Physiol.*, *B*, **143**, 213–22.

Walsh, P.J. (1981b) Purification and characterization of glutamate dehydrogenases from three species of sea anemones: adaptation to temperature within and among species from different thermal environments. *Mar. Biol. Lett.*, **2**, 289–99.

Walsh, P.J. and Somero, G.N. (1981) Temperature adaptation in sea anemones: physiological and biochemical variability in geographically separate populations of *Metridium senile*. *Mar. Biol.*, **62**, 25–34.

Ward, J.A. (1965a) An investigation on the swimming reaction of the anemone *Stomphia coccinea*. II. Histological location of a reacting substance in the asteroid

Dermasterias imbricata. J. Exp. Zool., **158**, 365–72.

Ward, J.A. (1965b) An investigation on the swimming reaction of the anemone *Stomphia coccinea*. I. Partial isolation of a reacting substance from the asteroid *Dermasterias imbricata. J. Exp. Zool.*, **158**, 357–64.

Waters, V.L. (1973) Food-preference of the nudibranch *Aeolidia papillosa*, and the effect of the defenses of the prey on predation. *The Veliger*, **15**, 174–92.

Watson, G.M. and Hessinger, D.A. (1987) Receptor-mediated endocytosis of a chemoreceptor involved in triggering the discharge of cnidae in a sea anemone tentacle. *Tissue and Cell*, **19**, 747–55.

Watson, G.M. and Hessinger, D.A. (1988) Localization of a purported chemoreceptor involved in triggering cnida discharge in sea anemones. In D.A. Hessinger and H.M. Lenhoff (eds.), *The Biology of Nematocysts*, Academic Press, San Diego, California, pp. 255–74.

Watson, G.M. and Hessinger, D.A. (1989) Cnidocyte mechanoreceptors are tuned to the movements of swimming prey by chemoreceptors. *Science*, **243**, 1589–91.

Watson, G.M. and Mariscal, R.N. (1983a) Comparative ultrastructure of catch tentacles and feeding tentacles in the sea anemone *Haliplanella. Tissue and Cell*, **15**, 939–53.

Watson, G.M. and Mariscal, R.N. (1983b) The development of a sea anemone tentacle specialized for aggression: morphogenesis and regression of the catch tentacle of *Haliplanella luciae* (Cnidaria, Anthozoa). *Biol. Bull.*, **164**, 506–17.

Watson, G.M. and Mariscal, R.N. (1984a) Calcium cytochemistry of nematocyst development in catch tentacles of the sea anemone *Haliplanella luciae* (Cnidaria: Anthozoa) and the molecular basis for tube inversion into the capsule. *J. Ultrastruct. Res.*, **86**, 202–14.

Watson, G.M. and Mariscal, R.N. (1984b) Ultrastructure and sulphur cytochemistry of nematocyst development in catch tentacles of the sea anemone *Haliplanella luciae* (Cnidaria: Anthozoa). *J. Ultrastruct. Res.*, **87**, 159–71.

Weber, R.E. (1980) Functions of invertebrate hemoglobins with special reference to adaptations to environmental hypoxia. *Amer. Zool.*, **20**, 79–101.

Wedi, S.E. and Dunn, D.F. (1983) Gametogenesis and reproductive periodicity of the subtidal sea anemone *Urticina lofotensis* (Coelenterata: Actiniaria) in California. *Biol. Bull.*, **165**, 458–72.

Weill, R. (1934) Contribution à l'étude des cnidaires et de leurs nématocystes. *Trav. Sta. Zool. Wimereux*, **10–11**, 1–701.

Weinbauer, G., Nussbaumer, V. and Patzner, R.A. (1982) Studies on the relationship between *Inachus phalangium* Fabricius (Maiidae) and *Anemonia sulcata* Pennant in their natural environment. *P.S.Z.N.I.: Mar. Ecol.*, **3**, 143–50.

Weis, V.M. (1989) Induction of carbonic anhydrase activity in symbiotic cnidarians. In R.B. Williams (ed.), *5th International Conference on Coelenterate Biology. Programme and Abstracts*, University of Southampton, Southampton, UK, p. 97.

Weis, V.M., Smith, G.J. and Muscatine, L. (1989) A 'CO$_2$ supply' mechanism in zooxanthellate cnidarians: role of carbonic anhydrase. *Mar. Biol.*, **100**, 195–202.

Welch, H.E. (1968) Relationships between assimilation efficiencies and growth efficiencies for aquatic consumers. *Ecology*, **49**, 755–9.

Wells, J.W. (1956) Scleractinia. In R.C. Moore (ed.), *Treatise on Invertebrate Paleontology. Part F, Coelenterata*, University of Kansas, Lawrence, pp. F328–F444.

Werner, B. (1973) New investigations on systematics and evolution of the class Scyphozoa and the phylum Cnidaria. *Publ. Seto Mar. Biol. Lab.*, **20**, 35–61.

Westfall, J.A. (1970) Synapses in a sea anemone, *Metridium* (Anthozoa). *Proc. 7th Int. Congr. Electron Microscopy; Soc. Fr. Microsc. Elect.*, **3**, 717–18.

Widersten, B. (1968) On the morphology and development in some cnidarian larvae. *Zool. Bidr. Uppsala*, **37**, 139–79 + 3 plates.

Widdows, J. and Hawkins, A.J.S. (1989) Partitioning of rate of heat dissipation by *Mytilus edulis* into maintenance, feeding, and growth components. *Physiol. Zool.*, **62**, 764–84.

Wilkerson, F.P., Muller-Parker, G. and Muscatine, L. (1983) Temporal patterns of cell division in natural populations of endosymbiotic algae. *Limnol. Oceanogr.*, **28**, 1009–14.

Wilkerson, F.P. and Muscatine, L. (1984) Uptake and assimilation of dissolved inorganic nitrogen by a symbiotic sea anemone. *Proc. R. Soc. Lond.*, B, **221**, 71–86.

Wilkerson, F.P. and Trench, R.K. (1985) Nitrate assimilation by zooxanthellae maintained in laboratory culture. *Mar. Chem.*, **16**, 385–93.

Williams, G.C. (1975) *Sex and Evolution*, Princeton University Press, Princeton, New Jersey, 200 pp.

Williams, R.B. (1968) Control of the discharge of cnidae in *Diadumene luciae* (Verrill). *Nature*, **219**, 959.

Williams, R.B. (1972a) Chemical control of feeding behaviour in the sea anemone *Diadumene luciae* (Verrill). *Comp. Biochem. Physiol.*, **41A**, 361–71.

Williams, R.B. (1972b) Notes on the history and invertebrate fauna of a poikilohaline lagoon in Norfolk. *J. Mar. Biol. Ass. UK*, **52**, 945–63.

Williams, R.B. (1973) Are there physiological races of the sea anemone *Diadumene luciae*? *Mar. Biol.*, **21**, 327–30.

Williams, R.B. (1975) Catch-tentacles in sea anemones: occurrence in *Haliplanella luciae* (Verrill) and a review of current knowledge. *J. Nat. Hist.*, **9**, 241–8.

Wilson, D.M. (1959) Long-term facilitation in a swimming sea anemone. *J. Exp. Biol.*, **36**, 526–32.

Windt-Preuss, H. (1959) Beobachtungen über die Nahrungsaufnahme und das Verhalten der Seenelke *Metridium senile* L. *Kieler Meeresforsch.*, **15**, 84–8.

Woolmington, A.D. and Davenport, J. (1983) pH and P_{O2} levels beneath marine macro-fouling organisms. *J. Exp. Mar. Biol. Ecol.*, **66**, 113–24.

Yentsch, C.S. and Pierce, D.C. (1955) 'Swimming' anemone from Puget Sound. *Science*, **122**, 1231–3.

Yonge, C.M. (1930) *A Year on the Great Barrier Reef*, Putnam, London, 246 pp.

Zahl, P.A. and McLaughlin, J.J.A. (1959) Studies in marine biology. IV. On the role of algal cells in the tissues of marine invertebrates. *J. Protozool.*, **6**, 344–52.

Zamer, W.E. (1986) Physiological energetics of the intertidal sea anemone *Anthopleura elegantissima* I. Prey capture, absorption efficiency and growth. *Mar. Biol.*, **92**, 299–314.

Zamer, W.E. and Hoffmann, R.J. (1989) Allozymes of glucose-6-phosphate isomerase differentially modulate pentose-shunt metabolism in the sea anemone *Metridium senile*. *Proc. Nat. Acad. Sci. USA*, **86**, 2737–41.

Zamer, W.E. and Mangum, C.P. (1979) Irreversible nongenetic temperature adaptation of oxygen uptake in clones of the sea anemone *Haliplanella luciae* (Verrill). *Biol. Bull.*, **157**, 536–47.

Zamer, W.E., Robbins, R.E. and Shick, J.M. (1987) β-glucuronidase activity and detritus utilization in the sea anemones *Metridium senile* and *Anthopleura elegantissima. Comp. Biochem. Physiol.*, **87B**, 303–8.

Zamer, W.E. and Shick, J.M. (1987) Physiological energetics of the intertidal sea anemone *Anthopleura elegantissima* II. Energy balance. *Mar. Biol.*, **93**, 481–91.

Zamer, W.E. and Shick, J.M. (1989) Physiological energetics of the intertidal sea anemone *Anthopleura elegantissima* III. Biochemical composition of body tissues, substrate-specific absorption, and carbon and nitrogen budgets. *Oecologia*, **79**, 117–27.

Zamer, W.E., Shick, J.M. and Tapley, D.W. (1989) Protein measurement and energetic considerations: Comparisons of biochemical and stoichiometric methods using bovine serum albumin and protein isolated from sea anemones. *Limnol. Oceanogr.*, **34**, 256–63.

Zammit, V.A. and Newsholme, E.A. (1976) The maximum activities of hexokinase, phosphorylase, phosphofructokinase, glycerol phosphate dehydrogenases, lactate dehydrogenase, octopine dehydrogenase, phosphoenolpyruvate carboxykinase, nucleoside diphosphatekinase, glutamate-oxaloacetate transaminase and arginine kinase in relation to carbohydrate utilization in muscles from marine invertebrates. *Biochem. J.*, **160**, 447–62.

Zammit, V.A. and Newsholme, E.A. (1978) Properties of pyruvate kinase and phosphoenolpyruvate carboxykinase in relation to the direction and regulation of phosphoenolpyruvate metabolism in muscles of the frog and marine invertebrates. *Biochem. J.*, **174**, 979–87.

Zamponi, M.O. (1981) Estructuras anatomicas adaptativas en anemonas (Coelenterata Actiniaria). *Neotropica*, **27**, 165–9.

Zwaan, A. de (1977) Anaerobic energy metabolism in bivalve molluscs. *Oceanogr. Mar. Biol. Ann. Rev.*, **15**, 103–87.

Zwaan, A. de (1983) Carbohydrate catabolism in bivalves. In P.W. Hochachka (ed.), *The Mollusca. Vol. 1. Metabolic Biochemistry and Molecular Biomechanics*, Academic Press, New York, pp. 137–75.

Zwaan, A. de and Putzer, V. (1985) Metabolic adaptations of intertidal invertebrates to environmental hypoxia (a comparison of environmental anoxia to exercise anoxia). In M.S. Laverack (ed.), *Physiological Adaptations of Marine Animals*, Cambridge University Press, Cambridge, UK, pp. 33–62.

Appendix: Classification of extant anthozoans, particularly sea anemones (Actiniaria)

Modified after Carlgren (1949), Schmidt (1974), and Dunn (1981). In this appendix, only families and species of sea anemones mentioned in the text or figures are given, with notes on their distribution, habits, and habitats.

Phylum Cnidaria, Class Anthozoa
Subclass Octocorallia
Subclass Hexacorallia
  Order Ceriantharia
  Order Madreporaria
    Suborder Scleractinia
    Suborder Corallimorpharia
  Order Zoantharia
  Order Antipatharia
  Order Ptychodactiaria
  Order Actiniaria
    Suborder Protantheae
      Family Gonactiniidae
        Gonactinia prolifera — N.E. Atlantic and Mediterranean; sublittoral; swimmer

        Protanthea simplex — N.E. Atlantic; sublittoral-bathyal
      Suborder Endocoelantheae
      Suborder Nyantheae
        Tribe Boloceroidaria
          Family Boloceroididae

Boloceroides mcmurrichi	Pan-tropical; shallow sublittoral; swimmer
Bunodeopsis medusoides	Tropical Pacific; shallow sublittoral; swimmer
Family Aliciidae	
Alicia mirabilis	Subtropical E. Atlantic, Mediterranean; sublittoral
Lebrunia coralligens	Caribbean; coral reefs
Lebrunia danae	Caribbean; coral reefs
Phyllodiscus semoni	W. Pacific; coral reefs
Tribe Mesomyaria	
Family Diadumenidae	
Diadumene cincta	Temperate N.E. Atlantic and E. Pacific; intertidal pools-sublittoral
Diadumene leucolena	Temperate N. America; low intertidal-shallow sublittoral; estuarine
Haliplanella lineata	Cosmopolitan; intertidal
Family Aiptasiidae	
Aiptasia diaphana	Mediterranean; shallow sublittoral
Aiptasia mutabilis	Temperate N.E. Atlantic, Mediterranean; shallow sublittoral
Aiptasia pallida	Carolinian, Caribbean; shallow sublittoral
Aiptasia pulchella	Pan-central Pacific, Japan to C. America; intertidal-sublittoral
Aiptasia pallida	Carribean; shallow sublittoral
Aiptasiogeton pellucidus	Temperate N.E. Atlantic, Mediterrannean; low intertidal-sublittoral
Bartholomea annulata	Caribbean; shallow sublittoral
Capnea lucida	Caribbean; shallow sublittoral
Family Aiptasiomorphidae	
Aiptasiomorpha elongata	Gulf of California
Family Hormathiidae	
Actinauge sp.	Atlantic; bathyal-abyssal
Adamsia carciniopados	N.E. Atlantic, Mediterranean; sublittoral; symbiotic with hermit crab
Amphianthus radiatus	N. Atlantic; abyssal; congeners epifaunal on hydroids, octocorals
Calliactis parasitica	Temperate N.E. Atlantic, sublittoral; symbiotic with hermit crab
Calliactis polypus	Red Sea, E. Africa; sublittoral; symbiotic with hermit crab
Calliactis tricolor	Caribbean, Gulf of Mexico; shallow sublittoral; symbiotic with hermit crab
Paracallactis stephensoni	N. Atlantic; bathyal-abyssal; symbiotic with hermit crab

Paractinia striata	Mediterranean; sublittoral; epifaunal on seagrass
Phelliactis robusta	N. Atlantic; abyssal
Family Metridiidae	
Metridium exilis	C. California; rocky intertidal
Metridium giganteum	Temperate N.E. Pacific; sublittoral; hard substrates
Metridium senile	Circumboreal; low intertidal-sublittoral; hard substrates
Family Acontiophoridae	
Acontiophorum niveum	Mission Bay, California; sublittoral
Mimetridium cryptum	New Zealand; sublittoral; burrower
Family Sagartiidae	
Anthothoe chilensis	S.E. Pacific; rocky intertidal
Cereus herpetodes	S.E. Pacific; rocky intertidal
Cereus pedunculatus	Temperate N.E. Atlantic, Mediterranean; intertidal-shallow sublittoral; often infaunal
Phellia gausapata	N.E. Atlantic; low intertidal-sublittoral
Sagartia elegans	N.E. Atlantic and Mediterranean; intertidal-shallow sublittoral; hard substrates
Sagartia ornata	N.E. Atlantic and Mediterranean; intertidal; hard substrates
Sagartia troglodytes	N.E. Atlantic and Meditterranean; intertidal-shallow sublittoral; often infaunal
Sagartiogeton laceratus	N.E. Atlantic; sublittoral
Family Actinostolidae	
Actinostola callosa	Arctic; sublittoral
Actinostola spetsbergensis	Circumarctic; sublittoral
Antholoba achates	S.E. Pacific; shallow sublittoral; rocky coast
Stomphia coccinea	Boreo-Arctic, circumpolar; sublittoral; swimmer
Stomphia didemon	N.E. Pacific; sublittoral; swimmer
Stomphia selaginella	S.W. Atlantic and Antarctic; bathyal
Family Halcampidae	
Halcampa arctica	Circumarctic; sublittoral; burrower
Halcampa duodecimcirrata	Circumboreal; sublittoral; burrower
Family Halcampoididae	
Calamactis praelongus	Gulf of California; burrower
Tribe Endomyaria	
Family Edwardsiidae	
Edwardsia claparedii	Temperate N.E. Atlantic; sublittoral; burrower

Fagesia lineata	Temperate N.W. Atlantic; sublittoral; rock crevices
Nematostella vectensis	Temperate N. Hemisphere; intertidal-shallow sublittoral; burrower
Family Haloclavidae	
Haloclava producta	Temperate E. Coast N. America; low intertidal; burrower
Peachia hastata	Temperate N.E. Atlantic; sublittoral; burrower (larvae parasitic on medusae)
Peachia quinquecapitata	N.E. Pacific; sublittoral; burrower (larvae parasitic on medusae)
Family Actiniidae	
Actinia equina	N.E. Atlantic and Mediterranean; intertidal-shallow sublittoral; hard substrates
Actinia fragacea	British Isles and W. Europe; low intertidal
Actinia prasina	British Isles; low intertidal
Actinia tenebrosa	Temperate Australia and New Zealand; rocky intertidal
Anemonia natalensis	S. Africa; intertidal-shallow sublittoral
Anemonia viridis	Temperate N.E. Atlantic and Mediterranean; intertidal-shallow sublittoral
Anthopleura artemisia	Alaska-S. California; low intertidal; often buried in sand
Anthopleura asiatica	E. Asia and Japan; rocky intertidal
Anthopleura ballii	British Isles and W. Europe; intertidal-sublittoral
Anthopleura elegantissima	Alaska-Mexico; rocky intertidal
Anthopleura handi	S.E. Asia; intertidal hard substrates
Anthopleura krebsi	Gulf of Mexico
Anthopleura midorii	Japan; intertidal
Anthopleura orientalis	Sea of Japan
Anthopleura rubripunctata	Mediterranean; sublittoral
Anthopleura stellula	Red Sea
Anthopleura xanthogrammica	Alaska-S. California; low intertidal-shallow sublittoral
Aulactinia incubans	N.E. Pacific (Puget Sound); intertidal
Aulactinia stelloides	Caribbean
Bolocera kerguelensis	S.W. Atlantic and Antarctic; sublittoral-bathyal
Bolocera tuediae	Boreal Atlantic; sublittoral-bathyal
Bunodosoma cavernata	Carolinian, Gulf of Mexico, Caribbean; intertidal
Bunodosoma granulifera	Caribbean; intertidal

Condylactis aurantiaca	Mediterranean; sublittoral
Condylactis gigantea	Caribbean; often on coral reefs
Cribrinopsis crassa	Mediterranean; sublittoral
Cribrinopsis fernaldi	N.E. Pacific (Puget Sound); sublittoral rock walls
Dofleinia armata	Japan; sublittoral
Entacmaea quadricolor	Indo-Pacific and Red Sea; coral reefs; symbiotic with clownfishes
Epiactis japonica	Sea of Japan; low intertidal
Epiactis lisbethae	British Columbia-Oregon; intertidal-shallow sublittoral
Epiactis prolifera	Puget Sound-C. California; intertidal-shallow sublittoral
Epiactis ritteri	Alaska-C. California; intertidal-shallow sublittoral
Gyrostoma sp.	Indo-Pacific
Macrodactyla doreenensis	W. Pacific (Japan to Queensland); shallow sublittoral; symbiotic with clownfishes
Oulactis muscosa	S. Australia-New Zealand; mid- to low intertidal
Phymactis clematis	S.E. Pacific; rocky intertidal
Pseudactinia flagellifera	S. Africa; intertidal
Pseudactinia melanaster	Carolinian, Caribbean; shallow sublittoral; often on *Sargassum*
Stylobates aeneus	C. Pacific; bathyal; symbiotic with hermit crab
Urticina crassicornis	Alaska-California; low intertidal-shallow sublittoral rocky coast (possibly ≡ *U.felina*)
Urticina eques	North Sea; sublittoral-bathyal; hard substrates
Urticina felina	Circumboreal; low intertidal-sublittoral; exposed rocky coasts
Urticina lofotensis	Alaska-California; shallow sublittoral; exposed rocky coasts (possibly ≡ *U.eques*)
Urticina piscivora	Alaska-California; shallow sublittoral; rocky coasts
Urticinopsis antarcticus	Antarctic; sublittoral
Family Phymanthidae	
Epicystis crucifer	Caribbean; shallow sublittoral and coral reefs
Family Stichodactylidae	
Heteractis crispa	Indo-Pacific; coral reefs; symbiotic with clownfishes
Heteractis magnifica	Indo-Pacific; coral reefs; symbiotic with clownfishes

Heteractis malu	Indo-Pacific; coral reefs; symbiotic with clownfishes
Stichodactyla gigantea	Indo-Pacific and Red Sea; shallow lagoons; symbiotic with clownfishes
Stichodactyla haddoni	Indo-Pacific and Red Sea; sublittoral; symbiotic with clownfishes
Stichodactyla helianthus	Caribbean; shallow sublittoral; sand
Stichodactyla mertensii	Indo-Pacific; coral reefs; symbiotic with clownfishes

Family Actinodendridae
  Actinodendron plumosum   N. Australia; shallow sublittoral

Index

Page numbers in **bold** type refer to definitions;
page numbers in *italics* refer to illustrations

MIX
Papier aus verantwortungsvollen Quellen
Paper from responsible sources
FSC® C105338

FSC
www.fsc.org

Printed by Books on Demand, Germany